THE GROUP OF 77 AT THE UNITED NATIONS

Third Series

The Collected Documents of the Group of 77

VOLUME VII

Global Environmental Governance: Climate Change

Edited by

MOURAD AHMIA

OXFORD
UNIVERSITY PRESS

OXFORD
UNIVERSITY PRESS

Oxford University Press is a department of the University of Oxford. It furthers the University's objective of excellence in research, scholarship, and education by publishing worldwide. Oxford is a registered trade mark of Oxford University Press in the UK and certain other countries.

Published in the United States of America by Oxford University Press
198 Madison Avenue, New York, NY 10016, United States of America.

Library of Congress Control Number: 2005936604

ISBN 978-0-19-062300-5

Printed in Canada by Marquis Book Printing

Note to Readers

This publication is designed to provide accurate and authoritative information in regard to the subject matter covered. It is based upon sources believed to be accurate and reliable and is intended to be current as of the time it was written. It is sold with the understanding that the publisher is not engaged in rendering legal, accounting, or other professional services. If legal advice or other expert assistance is required, the services of a competent professional person should be sought. Also, to confirm that the information has not been affected or changed by recent developments, traditional legal research techniques should be used, including checking primary sources where appropriate.

(Based on the Declaration of Principles jointly adopted by a Committee of the American Bar Association and a Committee of Publishers and Associations.)

In Memory of my beloved parents:
Houria Sekki (1936–2014)
Salah Ahmia (1926–2019)

Contents

Detailed Contents

Foreword

REPÚBLICA DE CUBA
EL PRESIDENTE
Climate Change and its impacts represent the most daunting global concerns of our time. It threatens not only the development prospects and objectives of developing countries but it also threatens their legitimate aspirations of achieving sustainable development. The existence and survival of many islands, countries, communities, and ecosystems of the world, particularly in the South, is seriously affected by climate change.

Developing countries, that are the least responsible for climate change, suffer the most from its adverse impacts but are the least able and equipped to cope with them. The international community is aware that the response to the challenges presented by this phenomenon must be global. Developed countries are called to take the lead in accordance with their historic responsibilities of climate degradation by making more ambitious commitments, both in terms of mitigation and the provision of means of implementation to developing countries for their climate actions.

In our world today, where relations and economic interest among all countries are interdependent and interconnected, a global approach to resolving the consequences of climate change has to be adopted so that a setback to the efforts exerted by the international community may be avoided.

Climate change already has serious impacts in developing countries. Many of them now experience unsustainable rising sea levels, while others experience the devastating effects of extreme weather phenomena, such as heavy floods, greater frequency and intensity of cyclones, severe droughts, and water and food insecurity. These impacts are also steadily eroding the development gains of developing countries.

Consequently, many developing countries are already taking the most ambitious measures they can to prevent further harm and to adapt to inevitable changes. However, the South's efforts will not be enough, and the cooperation of all countries, particularly developed countries, is needed to make a difference in the fight against climate change.

In this regard, developing countries, gathered in the G-77, have been resolutely calling for their partners to fulfill their commitments in finance, technology transfer, and capacity building. Particularly, they have constantly urged developed nations to comply with the provision of the USD 100 billion per year to developing countries and to engage seriously in the negotiation process towards the definition of the New Collective Quantified Goal before 2025, on the basis of the needs and priorities of developing world.

Similarly, G-77 has claimed for doubling the funding for adaptation and managed to defend and reach, through a strong unity, the adoption of a decision establishing a fund for loss and damage resulting from climate change, which is still pending being built.

The UN Framework Convention on Climate Change constitutes the international and intergovernmental forum for formulating the global response to climate change.

Since the inception of this Treaty, during the early years of the 1990s, the Group of 77 has advocated, on behalf of the global South, that the UN Framework Convention on Climate Change is, and must remain, the primary comprehensive framework for addressing climate change.

Developing countries believe that the developed countries have an obligation to support them to achieve growth and the environmentally friendly sustainable development by providing additional and substantial financial and technological assistance.

Clearly, the challenge of sustaining economic development and achieving social development and ensuring environmental protection is too overwhelming and beyond the capacity of developing countries to address on their own. It can only be effectively addressed through international cooperation as well as a partnership with the developed countries, premised on the principle of common but differentiated responsibilities.

The South has consistently called for addressing climate change in a manner that enhances and ensures the sustainable development and sustained economic growth of the developing countries and the elimination of poverty, hunger, and diseases. To this end, developing countries have always stressed the importance of addressing all three pillars of sustainable development, i.e., economic development, social development, and environmental protection, in an integrated, coordinated, and balanced manner.

Since the beginning, Cuba participated in the negotiation process of the Climate Change Convention prior to the UN Conference on Environment and Development, held in Rio de Janeiro in 1992, and since then Cuba has helped to unite developing countries around cardinal principles that still have a central place in multilateral environmental agreements today.

Cuba played a leading role in the negotiations held during the 21st Conference of the Parties of the UNFCCC that took place in Paris, France, from 30 November to 11 December 2015, which led to the adoption of the Paris Agreement, and most recently, as part of the G-77 and China at the 26th Conference of the Parties of the UN Framework Convention on Climate Change, held in Sharm el-Sheikh, Egypt, from 6 to 18 November 2022.

The Paris Agreement was an ambitious step forward in our efforts to address climate change.

It is the collective achievement of all parties, and seeks to enhance the implementation of the Convention, in accordance with its objectives, principles, and provisions, in the particular equity and common but differentiated responsibilities and respective capabilities, in the light of different national circumstances, needs, and priorities and the right to development, in the context of sustainable development and efforts to eradicate poverty and leave no one behind.

It is also essential to maintain focus on the implementation of commitments by developed countries in the pre-2020 period, including the Doha Amendment to the Kyoto Protocol, which entered into force on 31 December 2020. Therefore, the global effort to fight climate change is an irreversible process that should not be overlooked, undermined, weakened, or postponed.

It is vital, therefore, that all the countries concerned pledge themselves to fully and faithfully implement the commitments they have undertaken under the UN Framework Convention on Climate Change. These should allow us to successfully address climate change within the context of North-South as well as South-South cooperation. This vision was stressed by the First South Summit convened in Havana, Cuba, from 10 to 14 April 2000.

This publication is particularly timely and valuable since it coincides also with the preparations of the Summit on Science, Technology and Innovation to be held in Havana, Cuba, in September 2023, which will be followed by the Third South Summit scheduled to take place in Kampala, Uganda in January 2024.

This volume, exclusively devoted to climate change, translates the unique experience of the Group of 77 and its great contribution to this lengthy process and provides a new vision and better understanding of the way developing countries are addressing this global issue.

Miguel Díaz-Canel Bermúdez
President of the Republic of Cuba
President of the Group of 77 for 2023

Prólogo

Las preocupaciones globales más desalentadoras de nuestro tiempo están relacionadas con el Cambio Climático y sus impactos, que amenazan las perspectivas y objetivos de los países en desarrollo, para alcanzar sus aspiraciones de modo sostenible. La existencia y supervivencia de muchas islas, países, comunidades y ecosistemas del mundo, especialmente en el Sur, están gravemente afectadas ya por el cambio climático.

Los menos responsables de ese dramático resultado son los que más sufren sus efectos y, al mismo tiempo, son los menos capacitados y equipados para lidiar con ellos. La comunidad internacional es consciente de que la respuesta a los retos que plantea este fenómeno debe ser global y que los países desarrollados están llamados a tomar la iniciativa, en correspondencia con sus responsabilidades históricas en la degradación climática. Les corresponde asumir compromisos más ambiciosos, tanto en términos de mitigación como de provisión de medios de implementación a los países en desarrollo para sus acciones climáticas.

En el mundo actual, donde las relaciones y los intereses económicos de todos los países son interdependientes y están interconectados, sólo un enfoque global permitiría amortiguar las consecuencias del problema, de modo que pueda evitarse un retroceso en los esfuerzos realizados hasta hoy.

El cambio climático ya tiene serios impactos en los países en desarrollo, muchos de los cuales experimentan una elevación insostenible del nivel del mar, mientras que otros sufren los efectos devastadores de fenómenos meteorológicos extremos, como fuertes inundaciones, mayor frecuencia e intensidad de los ciclones, severas sequías e inseguridad hídrica y alimentaria. En consecuencia, esos impactos también están erosionando de forma constante sus avances en materia de desarrolo.

Para hacer frente al problema, muchos países en desarrollo están adoptando las medidas más ambiciosas posibles para evitar daños mayores y adaptarse a los cambios inevitables. Sin embargo, los esfuerzos del Sur no serán suficientes. Se necesita la cooperación de todas las naciones, en particular las desarrolladas, para marcar la diferencia en la lucha contra el cambio climático.

Es en ese sentido que los países reunidos en el G77, han estado demandando de manera decidida a sus contrapartes para que cumplan sus compromisos en materia de financiación, transferencia de tecnología y desarrollo de capacidades. En particular, se ha instado constantemente a las naciones con mayor disponibilidad de recursos, a cumplir con la provisión de 100.000 millones de dólares anuales a los países en desarrollo, y a comprometerse seriamente con el proceso de negociación para la definición de una Nueva Meta Colectiva Cuantificada sobre financiamiento climático antes de 2025, sobre la base de las necesidades y prioridades de las economías menos favorecidas.

Del mismo modo, el G77 ha reclamado que se duplique la financiación para la adaptación y ha conseguido defender y alcanzar, a través de una fuerte unidad, la adopción de una decisión por la que se establece un fondo para pérdidas y daños resultantes del cambio climático, que aún está pendiente de implementarse.

La Convención Marco de las Naciones Unidas sobre el Cambio Climático constituye el foro internacional e intergubernamental para formular la respuesta global al cambio climático.

Desde el nacimiento de este Tratado, a inicios de la década del noventa de siglo pasado, el Grupo de los 77 ha defendido, en nombre del Sur global, que la Convención Marco de las Naciones Unidas sobre el Cambio Climático es, y debe seguir siendo, el principal marco global para abordar el cambio climático.

Los países en desarrollo consideran que los países desarrollados tienen la obligación de apoyarles para lograr el crecimiento y un desarrollo sostenible respetuoso del medio ambiente, proporcionándoles una ayuda financiera y tecnológica adicional y sustancial.

Obviamente, el reto de sostener la economía y lograr el desarrollo social, garantizando la protección del medio ambiente, resulta abrumador para los países en desarrollo, en tanto supera sus capacidades para enfrentarlo de manera aislada. Sólo puede abordarse eficazmente a través de la cooperación internacional, así como de una asociación con los países desarrollados, basada en el principio de responsabilidades comunes pero diferenciadas.

El Sur ha demandado constantemente que el enfrentamiento al cambio climático potencie y garantice el desarrollo sostenible y un crecimiento económico estable, así como la eliminación de la pobreza, el hambre y las enfermedades. Para ello, los países en desarrollo siempre han insistido en la importancia de abordar los tres pilares del desarrollo sostenible: económico, social y con protección del medio ambiente, de manera integrada, coordinada y equilibrada.

Cuba participó desde el comienzo en el proceso de negociación de la Convención de Cambio Climático previo a la Conferencia de las Naciones Unidas sobre Medio Ambiente y Desarrollo, celebrada en Río de Janeiro en 1992, y desde entonces contribuye a nuclear a los países en desarrollo en torno a principios cardinales que todavía hoy tienen un lugar central en los acuerdos multilaterales ambientales.

Cuba desempeño un papel protagónico durante las negociaciones celebradas en la 21 Conferencia de las Partes de la CMNUCC que se realizó en París, Francia, del 30 de noviembre al 11 de diciembre de 2015, que condujo a la adopción del Acuerdo de París, y más recientemente como parte del G77 más China en la 27 Conferencia de las Partes de la Convención Marco de las Naciones Unidas sobre el Cambio Climático, celebrada en Sharm el-Sheikh, Egipto, del 6 al 18 de noviembre de 2022.

El Acuerdo de París supuso un ambicioso paso adelante en nuestros esfuerzos por hacer frente al cambio climático. Es el logro colectivo de todas las Partes, y pretende mejorar la aplicación de la Convención, de conformidad con sus objetivos, principios y disposiciones, en particular la equidad y las responsabilidades comunes pero diferenciadas y las capacidades respectivas, a la luz de las diferentes circunstancias, necesidades y prioridades nacionales y del derecho al desarrollo, en el contexto del desarrollo sostenible y de los esfuerzos por erradicar la pobreza y no dejar a nadie atrás.

También es esencial centrar la atención en la aplicación de los compromisos de los países desarrollados en el periodo anterior a 2020, incluida la Enmienda de Doha al Protocolo de Kyoto, que ha entrado en vigor el 31 de diciembre de ese propio año. El esfuerzo mundial para luchar contra el cambio climático es un proceso irreversible que no debe pasarse por alto, socavarse, debilitarse ni posponerse.

Es vital que todos los países implicados se comprometan a aplicar plena y fielmente los compromisos asumidos en el marco de la Convención Marco de las Naciones sobre el Cambio Climático. Ello debe permitirnos abordar con éxito el cambio climático en el contexto de la cooperación Norte-Sur, así como de la Sur-Sur, visión subrayada por la Primera Cumbre Sur convocada en La Habana, Cuba, del 10 al 14 de abril de 2000.

Esta publicación es especialmente oportuna y valiosa, además, por coincidir los preparativos de la Cumbre sobre Ciencia, Tecnología e Innovación que celebraremos en La Habana, Cuba, en septiembre de 2023, a la que seguirá la Tercera Cumbre Sur prevista en Kampala, Uganda, en enero de 2024.

Dedicarlo exclusivamente al cambio climático, en tanto traduce la experiencia única del Grupo de los 77 y su gran contribución a este largo proceso, aporta una nueva visión y una mejor comprensión sobre la manera en que los países en desarrollo abordamos este crucial tema de alcance mundial.

Miguel Díaz-Canel Bermúdez
Presidente de la República de Cuba
Presidente del Grupo de los 77 para 2023

Preface by the Editor

The present publication is the seventh volume of a continuing series entitled *The Group of 77 at the United Nations*, which aims to carry forward the process of documenting the actions of the developing countries at the United Nations. The other six previously published volumes are, respectively, *The Collected Documents of the Group of 77: Special Anniversary Edition; South-South Cooperation; North-South Dialogue; Environment and Sustainable Development; The Perez-Guerrero Trust for South-South Cooperation (PGTF); and Fiftieth Anniversary Edition.*

The materials in this volume are the result of a compilation effort that comprises a selection of major documents and statements by the Group of 77 on global climate governance, presenting in chronological order, a record of the Group's coordination and its joint positions in the climate arena and its participation in multilateral discussions and negotiations at the United Nations and the UN Framework Convention on Climate Change.

Documents on other thematic issues relevant to multilateral environmental negotiations will be published in future thematic volumes in the series. However, the interested readers wishing to trace the origins of the G-77's role in climate governance, its negotiating positions over time and the historic role that developing countries have played in its evolution should find in this volume a valuable reference on the subject.

This volume is divided into three chapters which contain selected documents related to the role of the Group of 77 in the Global Environmental Governance with special focus on Climate Change:

- **Chapter I** brings together documents in which the G-77 addressed the emerging issue of climate change at the United Nations since its beginnings in the early 1990s;
- **Chapter II** provides statements, position documents, and other texts that the G-77 formulated in the context of the Intergovernmental Negotiating Committee that culminated in the UN Framework Convention on Climate Change;
- **Chapter III** consists of statements, document submission, and other relevant materials under the UN Framework Convention on Climate Change and related bodies.

Also included in this compendium are two Annexes: a list of Acronyms and the Member States of the Group of 77 contained respectively in Annex I and Annex II.

In compiling this volume, reasonable efforts were made to retrieve all the relevant documents. Because of space requirements, however, the volume was not able to include the documents related to the various Ad-hoc Working Groups under the UNFCCC and others which will be made available online through the website of the Group of 77 (www.g77.org) in the near future, together with the latest documents issued by the Group of 77 on climate change. In addition, several documents dating from the early period chronicled in this volume could not be retrieved due to their non-availability. Last but not least, a few minor edits were made in some documents to correct punctuation and typographical errors and to ensure spelling consistency without changing the actual text of the documents.

In compiling this documentary record, I am most indebted to the staff members of the Executive Secretariat of the Group of 77 at the United Nations Headquarters in New York for their invaluable contributions and continued support in the publication of the series. Finally, I wish to record a particular debt of gratitude to the memory of staff member Rafiqul Alam Khan for his dedicated work and the remarkable efficiency in undertaking a most time-consuming and painstaking chore of typing and proofreading the entire manuscript (much of it more than once) and who devoted much time and skill to the editing of the material shaping it into a coherent whole just before he sadly passed away, as an early victim of health complications derived from the COVID-19 pandemic. We will miss him, but we will have the lasting memory of his contributions to this series.

Finally, the views expressed in this series do not necessarily reflect the views of the United Nations.

Mourad Ahmia

I

ENVIRONMENT AND SUSTAINABLE DEVELOPMENT: PROTECTION OF GLOBAL CLIMATE FOR PRESENT AND FUTURE GENERATIONS OF MANKIND

(a) Statements made on behalf of the Group of 77 and China on the Environment and Sustainable Development: Protection of Global Climate for Present and Future Generations of Mankind

Statements in the United Nations General Assembly

Remarks by H.E. Ambassador Hassan Adamu, Minister of Environment of the Federal Republic of Nigeria, on behalf of the Group of 77 and China, at the Informal High-Level Consultative Meeting on Climate Change (New York, 28 April 2000)

Mr. President,

I wish to express, on behalf of the Group of 77 and China, our profound appreciation to you for convening this informal high-level consultative meeting. It came at a crucial time when we are bound to focus on issues that must be addressed and resolved on climate change and sustainable development to achieve substantive progress in COP-6.

It is pertinent, therefore, to recall the objectives of the Convention on Climate Change vis-à-vis the Kyoto Protocol in order to get clear picture of the enormous tasks before us. The Convention was envisaged to build a process that would limit greenhouse gases emission with a view of controlling global warming. The Kyoto Protocol was established to advance the implementation of the Convention as well as address the issue of sustainable development, which is one of the twin components of climate change.

Mr. President,

The Group notes that, to date, significant progress has been made on the issue of climate change at the expense of sustainable development. In fact, the Group of 77 and China has participated actively to advance progress on the issue of climate change which obviously has been detrimental to the underlying concerns on sustainable development. The time has come, therefore, to address the issues of concern to the developing countries.

These issues, among others, are capacity-building, provision of adequate financial resources, and transfer of technology. What the Group is thereby calling for is simply a matter of fairness, equity, justice, and transparency. We have had enough of platitudes and rhetoric. We are asking for concrete commitment within specific timeframe and operational modalities for their implementation. To achieve substantial progress in COP-6, Annex I parties have to fulfil their commitments on these issues of serious concern to developing countries. Having gone through COP-5 without still resolving all those key issues to mitigate the devastating impact of climate change on developing countries, most of whom are burdened, *inter alia*, with crushing poverty, unsustainable debt, distressed economies, and various debilitating environmental problems, it demands that the focus now should be on modalities for implementation of the commitments.

Mr. President,

It is obvious that the success of the forthcoming COP-6 will depend on the extent to which these issues on mechanisms, policies and measures, compliance and commitment are being handled. It will be futile to encourage the high expectation for success being built towards COP-6 if there is no political will to commit ourselves to implement already agreed commitments and recommendations, particularly as it concerns Annex II parties.

There is, therefore, dire need to balance the diverse interests of the parties. We in the Group of 77 and China will facilitate the process, in so far as our interests are taken care of adequately, and in line with the principles and content of the Convention. The Group is favourable to further dialogue and consultations by the Ministers to seek for concrete strategies to address these problems.

Statement on behalf of the Group of 77 and China by H.E. Mukhdoom Faisal Saleh Hayat, Minister for Environment of the Islamic Republic of Pakistan during the

Informal Thematic Debate on "Climate Change as a Global Challenge" convened by the President of the General Assembly (New York, 1 August 2007)

Madam President,

1. It is my honour and privilege to speak on behalf of the Group of 77 and China at this important thematic debate on "Climate Change as a Global Challenge."

2. I also take this opportunity to commend you, Madam President, for your initiative and leadership in convening a series of thematic debates on a number of important issues including on MDGs and Gender.
3. The Group of 77 and China welcomes today's thematic debate on "climate change as a global challenge."

Madam President,

4. As we are all aware, Climate Change poses serious risks and challenges particularly to developing countries and, therefore, demands urgent global action and response. We are concerned about the fact that adverse effects of climate change and the associated phenomena including sea level rise and the increase in frequency and intensity of hurricanes, cyclones, floods, and other weather patterns as well as de-glaciation, drought and desertification threaten the sustainable development, livelihoods and the very existence of many developing countries and in particular countries in Africa, the LDCs, the LLDCs, and disaster-prone developing countries.
5. The Group of 77 and China, therefore, views these discussions as an integral part of the wider sustainable development debate.

Madam President,

6. The entry into force of the Kyoto Protocol provided renewed optimism for effectively tackling this problem at the multilateral level. We, once again, take this opportunity to renew our call upon all member states that have yet not done so to ratify and implement the UNFCCC and the Kyoto Protocol.
7. We would also like to reaffirm the Rio principles on environment and development, in particular Principle 7 of Common but Differentiated Responsibilities. We would like to highlight that without effective mitigation, all efforts to address climate change will remain fruitless. Developed countries have a specific responsibility in instituting deeper cuts in Greenhouse Gas emissions in accordance with the commitments made under the UNFCCC and its Kyoto Protocol.
8. In this regard, the G-77 and China has consistently called for efforts to address climate change in a manner that enhances the sustainable development and sustained economic growth of the developing countries and the universal elimination of poverty hunger and disease. To this end, all three pillars of sustainable development—economic development, social development, and environmental protection—we strongly believe, should be addressed in an integrated, coordinated, and balanced manner.
9. This challenge is beyond the capacity of the developing countries to address on their own. In fact, the challenge can only be effectively addressed through a partnership with the developed countries premised on the principle of common but differentiated responsibilities.

10. It is the view of G-77 and China that the decisions on Climate Change should, therefore, fulfil the commitments, undertaken at the Rio and Johannesburg Conferences, including Agenda 21 and the Rio Principles, specially taking into account the principle of common but differentiated responsibilities.

Madam President,

11. Looking back at what the international community has achieved in the past, we notice that the world showed tremendous stewardship in outlining a comprehensive global development agenda through the agreements reached and commitments made in major UN Summits and Conferences. Unfortunately, these commitments have not been translated into action on the ground. Implementation remains the Achilles' heel of the global development agenda and the biggest challenge for sustainable development. So far, the implementation of the development agenda remains the biggest challenge for sustainable development.
12. Perhaps the most formidable challenges before us in addressing climate change and its adverse effects include: lack of fulfilment of commitments in the Kyoto Protocol; inadequacy of financial resources for adaptation efforts; lack of progress to secure access to and transfer of adaptation technologies; degradation of natural resources leading to people's vulnerability; lack of capacity to predict the timing, frequency, scale of adverse impacts of climate change; inadequate integration of climate change policy and adaptation measures in national development strategies; weak or sometimes absence of climate observation systems and networks; insufficient national institutional capacity for participation in CDMs; lack of adequate arrangements for joint activities at regional and sub-regional levels; huge gaps in knowledge relating to climate change; inadequate insurance markets and arrangements to deal with extreme weather patterns associated with climate change; lack of action to address needs and concerns arising from the implementation of response measures.
13. The G-77 and China also emphasizes the urgent need for building the resilience of communities and nations to natural disasters including those related to climate change and establishing early warning systems in order to prevent and reduce the adverse impact of such events.
14. In order to enable the developing countries to pursue sustainable development and to address the challenges posed by climate change, the developed countries should:
    (a) Provide adequate, new and additional financing for adaptation;
    (b) Support and assist developing countries efforts to adapt to climate change and the response measures designed to address climate change;
    (c) Transfer technology to the developing countries, including through improved financial instruments and mechanisms;

(d) Ensure access to and transfer of technologies required for this purpose at affordable, preferential, and concessional terms;
(e) Support and assist the developing countries in their efforts to enhance capacity building to pursue their efforts of mitigation and adaptation within the framework of UNFCCC;
(f) Implement their commitments made in the UN summits and conferences relating to economic and social development and environmental sustainability, specially the Millennium Development Goals and the Internationally Agreed Development Goals and the promotion of equitable structures of international trade and finance;
(g) Call for strengthening of North-South, South-South, and triangular cooperation in research, development, and demonstration (RD&D) initiatives towards mitigation and adaptation to climate change and its adverse impacts.

15. Besides the above measures, let me also suggest, in my national capacity, the following, which may also be taken into account:
Firstly, to augment the efforts of combating climate efforts, the Adaptation Fund and LDC Fund may be made operational at the earliest. The CDM seems to be developing in favour of large commercial type of projects, which generate substantial amount of Carbon Credits and could have lesser impacts on sustainable development in the host country. Ways need to be explored to increase the number of small-scale community-based projects in order to increase the sustainable development benefits in developing countries.
Secondly, there is need to integrate adaptation into future planning and investment and Poverty Reduction Strategies. The Global Environment Facility (GEF) resources may be availed for adaptation projects for supporting the interventions that increase resilience to the adverse impacts of climate change.

Madam President,

16. The Group of 77 and China also welcomes the Secretary-General's proposal to convene an "Informal High-Level Event on Climate Change" on September 24, 2007, on the margins of the 62nd Session of the UN General Assembly. The special event together with the thematic debate today, we believe, should sensitize the international community on the challenges we face in the important area of climate change and is, therefore, a most timely initiative.
17. The United Nations has always been at the centre of the Sustainable Development debate, including on its environmental pillar. This must be maintained and climate change should be pursued within the framework of the United Nations. It is important to emphasize that any special events or initiatives, whether individual, national, regional, or multilateral should complement ongoing negotiations under the UNFCCC, which serve as the

multilateral agreed structure within which the international community agreed to address the challenges of climate change. Such initiatives, in our view, should in fact provide impetus and political support to the ongoing processes by promoting global consensus on climate change and contribute to a successful conclusion of the forthcoming 13th Conference of Parties (COP-13) of UNFCCC/Third Meeting of Parties of the Kyoto Protocol, to be held in Bali, Indonesia, in December 2007. A successful conclusion is one that takes fully into account the needs and concerns of all developing countries.

Madam President,

18. Pakistan, if I may add in my national capacity, strongly believes and urges that the international community must reach an agreement on post-2012 Kyoto regime during the Bali Conference. With the clock continuing to click, we need to move fast and act before climate change turns into a climate crisis. A comprehensive and clear timeframe evolved in Bali will be an adequate and visible measure of the success of our deliberations.

Statement by H.E. Mukhdoom Syed Faisal Saleh Hayat, Minister for Environment and Special Envoy of the President of Pakistan, on behalf of the Group of 77 and China, at the High-Level Event on Climate Change Entitled: The Future in Our Hands: Addressing the Leadership Challenge of Climate Change (New York, 24 September 2007)

Honourable Co-Chairs,

1. It is my honour and privilege to present the views of the Group of 77 and China at this important high-level event on climate change, which has been entitled: "The future in our hands: addressing the leadership challenge of climate change."

Honourable Co-Chairs,

2. Climate change poses serious risks and challenges particularly to developing countries and, therefore, demands urgent global action and response.
3. We are concerned about the fact that the adverse effects of climate change and the associated phenomena threaten the sustainable development, livelihoods and the very existence of many developing countries and in particular Africa, the LDCs, the LLDCs, SIDS, and disaster-prone developing countries.
4. The most important question facing us here today is: Can we muster the political will to agree on a strategy to respond to this challenge? More importantly, can we display the political will to implement the commitments and policies to which we commit ourselves?
5. The Group of 77 and China has consistently called for efforts to address climate change in a manner that enhances and ensures the sustainable development

and sustained economic growth of the developing countries and the universal elimination of poverty, hunger, and disease. To this end, all three pillars of sustainable development, i.e., economic development, social development, and environmental protection, should be addressed in an integrated, coordinated, and balanced manner.

6. It is vital, therefore, that all concerned should pledge themselves to fully and faithfully implement the commitments they have undertaken under the Internationally Agreed Development Goals, including the Millennium Development Goals. These commitments must constitute an integral component of the commitments and obligations which all of us undertake in the context of addressing climate change.
7. The entry into force of the Kyoto Protocol provided renewed optimism for effectively tackling this problem at the multilateral level. Once again we take this opportunity to renew our call upon all Member States that have yet not done so to ratify and implement the UNFCCC and the Kyoto Protocol. The UNFCCC, and its Kyoto Protocol, remains the central multilateral framework for cooperative actions to address climate change.

Honourable Co-Chairs,

8. In elaborating a global strategy to address climate change, we must continue to adhere to the Rio principles and in particular the Principle of Common but Differentiated Responsibility. This central principle must be given tangible content. We would like to highlight that effective mitigation efforts are essential to address the challenges posed by climate change. Developed countries must continue to take the lead, as they have committed to, in combating climate change and the adverse effects thereof including through significantly reducing GHG emissions.
9. The developed countries also have an obligation to support the developing countries to adapt an environment-friendly path to development and growth by providing additional and substantial financial and technological assistance. Clearly, the challenge of sustaining economic development and achieving social development and ensuring environmental protection is too overwhelming and beyond the capacity of the developing countries to address on their own. It can only be effectively addressed through international cooperation as well as a partnership with the developed countries, premised on the principle of common but differentiated responsibilities. It is the view of the G-77 and China that the decisions on climate change should, therefore, fulfil the commitments, undertaken at the Rio and Johannesburg Conferences, including Agenda 21 and the Rio Principles.
10. Developed countries should support and assist the efforts of developing countries to adapt to climate change and the response measures designed to address climate change.

11. We strongly believe that no adaptation plan or strategy would be effective without enhanced financing and greater technological support and access for developing countries.
12. Enabling the developing countries to respond to climate change will require substantial additional official assistance, over and above the long-standing 0.7 ODA target as well as the 0.15–0.20 ODA target for LDCs. In this context, the recent negative trend in ODA levels is highly regrettable.
13. Similarly, technology is essential to address the climate change challenge. The present restraint on access to advanced technologies, imposed particularly by the IPR regime, need to be lifted, at least for technologies that can assist in meeting climate change challenge. The developing countries must also be helped, on affordable preferential and concessional terms, through technology transfer, directed R&D, and other assistance, to acquire and build capacity for the application of technologies to meet sustainable development targets and goals.
14. The Group of 77 and China would also like to emphasize the urgent need for building the resilience of communities and nations to natural disasters, including those related to climate change, and establishing early warning systems in order to prevent and reduce the adverse impacts of such events.

Honourable Co-Chairs,

15. The Group of 77 and China further advocates that the developed countries assist developing countries in integrating adaptation into future planning and investment and Poverty Reduction Strategies.
16. We also call for an evaluation and the streamlining of the GEF funding mechanisms in the Resource Allocation Framework (RAF) in order to ease the developing countries, including LDCs, LLDCs, and SIDS access to GEF financial resources.
17. Equally important is to work towards strengthening North-South, South-South, and triangular cooperation in research, development, and demonstration (RD&D) and to undertake initiatives towards mitigation and adaptation to climate change and its adverse impacts.
18. The United Nations has always been at the centre of the Sustainable Development debate, including on its environmental protection pillar. This must be maintained. Climate change should be pursued within the framework of the United Nations. It is important to emphasize that any special events or initiatives, whether individual, national, regional, or multilateral should complement ongoing negotiations under the UNFCCC, which serve as the multilateral agreed structure within which the international community agreed to address the challenges of climate change. Such initiatives, in our view, should in fact provide impetus and political support to the ongoing processes by promoting global consensus on climate change and contribute to a successful conclusion of the forthcoming 13th Conference of Parties (COP-13) of UNFCCC/Third Meeting of Parties of the Kyoto Protocol, to be held in Bali, Indonesia, in December 2007.

Distinguished Co-Chairs,

19. Let me say a few words about my own country. Although Pakistan is a large country, with the fifth largest population, it is a low Greenhouse Gas (GHG) emitter. Our total annual emissions are only 0.43% of world's total, i.e., 135th among all countries. However, the low emission status of the country provides no safety from the adverse effects of changing climate. Dry lands cover about 80% of Pakistan's land area.
20. Climate change is causing irrevocable damage to Pakistan, with tremendous social, environment, and economic impacts. Agricultural productivity in Pakistan is being affected due to changes in land and water regimes. Dry land areas, in arid and semi-arid regions, are the most vulnerable. This is negatively affecting agricultural productivity by altering bio-physical relationships such as changing growing periods of the crops, altering scheduling of cropping seasons, changing irrigation water requirements, and increasing the risk of pests and diseases. Thus, climate change has put our food security at a great risk.
21. Climate change also has adverse impacts on forest resources and natural ecosystems of the country. Even the glaciers in Himalayas are receding faster than any other part of the world. There are fears that many may disappear by 2050.
22. I take this opportunity to state that Pakistan is deeply committed to the global efforts to mitigate climate change impacts and has taken the following measures for improvement and protection of the environment:
    (i) A Prime Minister's Committee on Climate Change has been constituted as policy and review forum.
    (ii) A Global Change Impact Studies Centre (GCISC) has been established for undertaking research on climate change and suggesting appropriate adaptation measures.
    (iii) A Clean Development Mechanism (CDM) Cell has been established under the Climate Change Wing of the Ministry of Environment, to facilitate approval of CDM projects in the country.
    (iv) Despite resource constraints, a mega forestry project worth US$240 million is being launched by Government of Pakistan for carbon sequestration without financial assistance from international donors.
    (v) Other interventions which also contribute to climate change adaptation include the Mountain Areas Conservancy Programme, Pakistan Wetlands Programme, and Sustainable Land Management Project.
23. As a developing country, Pakistan needs to undertake the following:
    (i) Development of efficient water management systems, so that adverse impacts of climate change may be reduced on our ecosystems and agriculture. In this connection, the increase in glacier melting in the Karakoram, Hindukush, and Himalaya ranges in Pakistan need to be arrested by rehabilitation of damaged areas, largely through afforestation and mountain conservancy programmes.

(ii) Mass awareness campaign sensitizing the general masses to adapt the changed lifestyle, change in cropping pattern, and change in weather cycles due to climate change.
(iii) Development of a Satellite-linked Early Warning System and satellite e-mapping system to comprehensively deal with natural disasters emanating from climate change.

24. These measures, however, need additional financial resources to be obtained through international and regional cooperation. As earlier stated, the worst hit countries, like Pakistan, should be allocated a major share of the Adaptation Fund, the GEF, and other resources to meet these challenges. I would also urge the developed countries to fulfil their commitments made in UN Conferences.
25. Let me also take this opportunity to highlight the increasing energy needs of Pakistan in the backdrop of our sound economic performance and high growth rates. We will have to rely on both traditional and non-traditional sources of energy including renewables to sustain the existing high growth rates and to take them to the next higher level. Use of hydel and nuclear energy would, therefore, be a natural option for Pakistan. We urge the international community, including the private sector, to support Pakistan's endeavours in this regard.
26. To combat climate change, the international community should:
    (i) First, extend the First Commitment Period of Kyoto Protocol beyond 2012. All Annex I countries should accede to the Protocol and fully implement their commitments made under the Protocol and the UNFCCC.
    (ii) Two, the Adaptation Fund and Least Developed Countries Fund should be made operational and augmented as soon as possible to support the efforts for combating climate change.
27. Pakistan will work closely to ensure that international community reaches an understanding on this vital issue during the 13th Session of Conference of Parties (COP-13) to be held in Bali in December 2007.

Statement on Behalf of the Group of 77 and China by Ambassador John Ashe, Permanent Representative of Antigua and Barbuda to the United Nations, at the Thematic Debate of the General Assembly on "Addressing Climate Change: The United Nations and the World at Work" (New York, 12 February 2008)
Introduction

Mr. President,

1. The Group of 77 and China thanks you for convening this debate in the General Assembly on the theme "Addressing Climate Change: The United Nations and the World at Work." It provides the Assembly with an additional opportunity to exchange views among member States and with other partners on one of the important issues on the development agenda of the UN.

2. At the outset, the Group of 77 and China reiterates that the UN Framework Convention on Climate Change is, and should remain, the primary comprehensive framework for addressing climate change. Therefore, this thematic debate should be recognized as an opportunity for member States to dialogue on ways of increasing support for the Framework and on meeting the urgent need for immediate action to fully implement commitments under the Convention and its Kyoto Protocol; supporting the Bali Action Plan and other mechanisms of the Convention.

Mr. President,

3. The Group of 77 and China is of the view that there should not be a parallel process of debates that would detract from the negotiation process under the Convention. The Group of 77 and China believes that multilateral action to address climate change should remain firmly rooted in the UNFCCC and the Kyoto Protocol.
4. Furthermore, this thematic debate, as well as the Secretary-General's report on the overview of UN activities in relation to climate change, should not attempt to influence any other processes such as the system-wide coherence debate or the discussions on international environmental governance.

Climate Change as a Sustainable Development Challenge

Mr. President,

5. The Group of 77 and China is of the view that discussions on climate change should be placed within the proper context of sustainable development. It is imperative that our discussion reinforces the promotion of sustainable development, highlighting the three pillars—economic development, social development, and environmental protection—and the need to promote all three in an integrated, coordinated, and balanced manner.
6. We must not lose sight of the fact that climate change is a sustainable development challenge. As such we should adhere steadfastly to the Rio principles, in particular the principle of common but differentiated responsibilities. We must take fully into account that poverty eradication and economic and social development are the paramount priorities of developing countries. Hence, we must ensure that the discussion on climate change is placed in its proper context so that it does not undermine the overall discourse on sustainable development.

Mr. President,

7. Urgent action is needed now to fully implement the commitments under the Convention and the Kyoto Protocol, especially commitments on financing for adaptation, technology transfer, and capacity-building, if we are to make progress towards the achievement of the sustainable development goals of

developing countries, in particular the Internationally Agreed Development Goals (IADGs) including the MDGs.

8. Urgent action is particularly needed on commitments, as climate change threatens the livelihoods of the very poor and vulnerable developing countries, in particular Africa, the LDCs, LLDCs, SIDS, and disaster-prone developing countries. The G-77 and China is of the view that while addressing the challenge of climate, the most affected countries and most vulnerable countries should be given adequate attention and support.
9. Developed countries parties must take the lead in addressing the implementation gap, since the extent to which developing countries parties can effectively respond to the challenge depends on the effective implementation by developed country parties of their commitments relating to financing and technology transfer.

Scaling-up Financing, Technology Transfer and Capacity-Building Support

10. While the UN can support the efforts of developing countries in formulating policies for attracting climate change related investment flows, adaptation and nationally appropriate mitigation actions will have to be enabled by technology, financing, and capacity-building that are commensurate with the magnitude of the tasks ahead of us, that is, in a measurable, reportable, and verifiable manner, as agreed in the Bali Action Plan. The provision of financial resources is a binding commitment of developed country parties. Clear guidance should be given to facilitate access to financial resources and investments without conditionalities. It is essential that such financial resources not be considered as official development assistance (ODA), but additional, and in compliance with existing binding commitments under the Convention. Further, financing for adaptation to climate change and the impact of response measures should not be a reallocation or realignment of existing development financing.
11. Developing countries should be provided with greater access to cost-effective, efficient, and affordable advanced clean technologies. The Group of 77 and China has repeatedly led calls for developing countries to have greater access to climate-friendly technologies. Efforts in this regard need to be scaled up. Furthermore, the UN can play an important role through the promotion of an intellectual property rights (IPR) regime that facilitates the transfer of such technologies.
12. The Group of 77 and China reiterates its call for increased support for capacity-building in developing countries to enhance national efforts to promote an integrated approach to climate change response measures and sustainable development planning.

Greater Support by the UN System for Developing Countries to Address the Climate Change Challenge

13. The UN's efforts in supporting national adaptation activities must be strengthened, so that developing countries can achieve their sustainable development goals while responding to the challenges of climate change. The role of the UN in supporting the overall development efforts is vital. However, the G-77 and China finds that technology transfer and financing have not been addressed adequately in the background documents made available in preparation for today's debate.
14. On the issue of partnerships, Mr. President, the G-77 and China is of the view that multi-stake holder partnerships have an important role to play in addressing climate change. The UN system should assist in fostering and promoting partnerships in support of national efforts. However, partnerships should not replace ODA or international cooperation.
15. Additionally, South-South cooperation is useful in the area of adaptation efforts, and greater support for South-South cooperation can also help developing countries better respond to the challenges of climate change. However, South-South cooperation should not be considered within the context of multi-stakeholder partnerships. Further, South-South cooperation on climate change should complement North-South cooperation.

Report on the Overview of UN Activities in Relation to Climate Change

Mr. President,

16. In General Assembly resolution 62/8 member States requested a comprehensive report providing an overview of the activities of the UN system in relation to climate change. Based on this mandate, the G-77 and China anticipated a factual report that takes stock of current UN system activities in this regard. As such there is no mandate with regard to "an indication of the way forward" and "coordination of the UN system action on climate change." This remains the purview of the member States to decide on. Work on coordination mechanisms, and structures or frameworks, including clusters of activity or lead agencies, must be subject of intergovernmental consideration and decision prior to implementation.
17. In general, the UN system entities should assist in the effective implementation of the provisions, commitments, and action plans of the UNFCCC. Coordination of UN system activities to enhance its role in meeting the challenge of climate change requires intergovernmental consideration, agreement, and oversight by member States.
18. The G-77 and China recognizes the primacy of the UN in directing and supporting global efforts to meet the global challenge of climate change, and in supporting its

Framework Convention on Climate Change (UNFCCC). The General Assembly, given its universality, should unequivocally urge parties to undertake urgent action now to meet their commitments under the Convention, provide clear policy direction in this regard, and support to the Bali Plan of Action.

Mr. President,

19. The G-77 and China believes that the road to Copenhagen, where the concluding talks on the current process on the Bali Roadmap will be held in 2009, will be a difficult one, particularly for developing countries and the poorest and most vulnerable. Leadership will, therefore, be critical if our response is to reflect the scale of the challenge. We need effective and comprehensive global response, within the principle of common but differentiated responsibilities, to cover adaptation, technology transfer, and financing, as well as mitigation. Without rapid and tangible efforts by developed countries in this regard, climate change will lead to increased poverty and will negate our efforts at achieving sustainable development.

Statement on Behalf of the Group of 77 and China by Ms. Nadia M. Osman, Minister Plenipotentiary, Permanent Mission of the Republic of the Sudan to the United Nations, at the Briefing on the September 22 Summit on Climate Change convened by the Secretary-General (New York, 6 August 2009)

Mr. Secretary-General,

I have the honour to speak on behalf of the G-77 and China.

Let me convey our sincere appreciation for the opportunity to hear from you your expectations for the Climate Change Summit and also to discuss the organization of that meeting.

The Group of 77 and China welcomes the initiative of convening the September 22 Summit. This Summit is of utmost importance in the run-up to the Copenhagen Conference, where we will decide on the quantified emission reduction targets for developed countries in the subsequent commitment periods of the Kyoto Protocol and the enhanced implementation of the Convention in order to achieve its ultimate objective.

While fully respecting the prerogative of the Secretary-General in preparing this Summit, for the Summit to be a success, we must ensure that the full membership of the United Nations is able to participate at the highest possible level. The roundtables should thus be inclusive and open to the active participation of all UN member States in the discussions, including to delegations that are unable to participate at the Head of State level and regardless of the level in which they will participate. We are confident that an appropriate format can be secured to ensure the universal participation of all delegations in all aspects of the event.

Mr. Secretary-General,

In preparing for this Summit, we must bear in mind that negotiations are ongoing under the UNFCCC in the Ad-Hoc Working Group on the Kyoto Protocol and the Ad-Hoc Working Group on the Long-Term Cooperative Action.

The Group is of the view that the Summit should, in no way, attempt to prejudge the outcome of these critical negotiations. In this regard, the proposed concept paper should aim at galvanizing political will from all countries to participate in the negotiations under the UNFCCC in a manner that will address meaningfully the challenges of climate change. We are confident that this paper issued by the Secretary-General will be made available in a timely manner and in the six official languages.

The Group also trusts that the Chair's Summary of the Summit will reflect the discussions and views expressed during the meeting, including during the roundtables and the pre-recorded national statements, and that the summary also will in no way prejudge the negotiations in Copenhagen.

Your leadership, Mr. Secretary-General, in climate change is crucial to galvanize the political will necessary to address this global challenge. Rest assured of the Group's cooperation and support.

Statement by His Excellency Mr. Ahmad Babiker Nahar, Minister of Environment and Urban Development of the Republic of the Sudan, at the Closing Plenary Session of the Summit on Climate Change convened by the Secretary-General (New York, 22 September 2009)

Excellencies Heads of State and Government,
Mr. Secretary-General, Distinguished Delegates,

It is indeed a great honour for us to speak at the conclusion of this Summit on the global challenge of climate change, which is taking place at a very critical time of the ongoing intergovernmental negotiations under the UNFCCC.

We would like to express our sincere appreciation to His Excellency the Secretary-General for his initiative of convening this Summit, his personal commitment and leadership in galvanizing the necessary impetus and the political support to address this global challenge facing humanity and threatening our planet.

We reiterate the need to ensure that all countries, large and small, rich and poor, are included in such initiatives, in a manner that is transparent and inclusive, if we are to move forward and build on the momentum created at this Summit, and send a strong collective message of political support to guide the negotiations leading up to the Fifteenth Session of the Conference of the Parties in December of the UN Framework Convention on Climate Change (UNFCCC), and the Fifth Session of the Meeting of the Parties to the Kyoto Protocol (CMP-5).

We re-affirm that the sole forum for negotiations on climate change in preparation for the Copenhagen Conference is the UNFCCC, and that the Summit should in no way pre-empt negotiations taking place under the UNFCCC.

It is our conviction that the global nature of climate change calls for the widest possible cooperation by all countries and their participation in an effective and appropriate international response, in accordance with their common but differentiated responsibilities and respective capabilities, and national circumstances.

In this regard, we reiterate that UNFCCC and its Kyoto Protocol remains the central multilateral framework for cooperative action to address climate change.

Excellencies Heads of State and Government,
Mr. Secretary-General, Distinguished Delegates,

Developing countries that are the least responsible for climate change, suffer the most from its adverse impacts, but are the least able and equipped to cope with them. We are therefore the most concerned about success in Copenhagen, and believe that success must be measured mainly in three ways:

> Firstly, by the extent to which all parties to the UNFCCC in this almost universally agreed, science-based, legally binding agreement will fulfil their commitments in accordance with the principles and obligations we have all agreed upon.
>
> Secondly, success will be measured by the willingness of all developed countries to undertake ambitious targets, in the second and subsequent commitment periods, given their historical responsibilities.
>
> Thirdly, by the level of assistance given by the international community to developing countries to address the consequences of climate change, particularly through new, additional and predictable financial resources, capacity-building, and access to development and transfer of technology.

The Group of 77 reaffirms that responses to climate change should be coordinated with social and economic development, the first and overriding priorities of developing countries, in an integrated manner, with a view to avoiding adverse impact on the latter, taking into account the legitimate priority needs of developing countries for the achievement of sustained economic growth and the eradication of poverty, in accordance with the principle of common but differentiated responsibilities and respective capabilities.

The Group urges Annex I countries to undertake serious steps to show their willingness in addressing the root causes of climate change. They must particularly change their unsustainable patterns of production and consumption, and meet the cost of adaptation of the developing countries, particularly the urgent and medium-term needs to adapt to the unavoidable level of climate change described in the Intergovernmental Panel on Climate Change (IPCC) fourth assessment report.

The Group of 77 is seriously concerned by the slow progress in deciding the second and subsequent commitment periods under the Kyoto Protocol and the delay shown by Annex I countries in pledging their individual and aggregated GHG reduction targets. We are concerned by the fact that the current targets proposed by

Annex I countries are far below the level of ambition required to adequately address the unequivocal climate change and its devastating impacts on developing countries. What we have seen so far from developed countries does not bode well for Copenhagen, a situation that must be rectified, if a successful conclusion is to ever be reached.

Developed countries should step up to their responsibilities and adopt more ambitious commitments to reduce greenhouse gases emissions, and provide the necessary financial and technological support for developing countries.

We sincerely hope that today's events will help in generating the sort of political will from Annex I countries that is required for agreement to be reached in Copenhagen.

We are committed to the Convention and the Bali Action Plan, and will further undertake nationally appropriate mitigation actions in the context of sustainable development, supported and enabled by technology, financing and capacity-building from developed countries, in a measurable, reportable, and verifiable manner, as stipulated in the Bali Action Plan.

The Group strongly urge the Annex I parties under the UNFCCC to fulfil their clearly stated commitments and obligations. From our side, we are committed to making all necessary efforts to ensure that a comprehensive and equitable outcome that is consistent with the Convention and its principles is reached in COP-15 of the UNFCCC and CMP-5 of the Kyoto Protocol, to ensure the full, effective and sustained implementation of the Convention, now up to and beyond 2012.

Statement by His Excellency Ambassador Abdalmahmood Abdalhaleem Mohamad, Permanent Representative of the Republic of the Sudan to the United Nations and Chairman of the Group of 77, at the Informal Meeting of the Plenary of the General Assembly to Hear a Briefing by the UN Secretary-General on the Outcome of the UN Climate Change Conference (New York, 21 December 2009)

Mr. Secretary-General,
Excellencies, Distinguished Delegates,

The Group of 77 and China thanks the Secretary-General for convening this meeting so soon after Copenhagen. The truth is that those of us who went are still recovering not just physically but also psychologically.

The Conference was supposed to be one of the most important meetings even held by the UN or by mankind in history. Its topic is a most serious one: how to save the world and humankind from climate change.

Unfortunately, the results were far below what we expected. The developing countries are not responsible for most of the emissions accumulated in the atmosphere but we will be most affected by climate change, so we have the most to lose. We thus took Copenhagen and its preparations very seriously. We worked very hard in the two working groups on long-term cooperation and on Kyoto Protocol. These two groups were the main venues where most of the work went on in Copenhagen, and our delegates worked sometimes till 5.00 a.m. to try to draft compromise texts.

From the beginning of the Conference, the G-77 and China and our individual countries sought an assurance that there would not be any surprises in the form of a text dropped from the Presidency or worked out by a small group of parties, as this would be untransparent and undemocratic, and against the principles and practices of the UN. At the opening session itself on 8 December, we stated that no parallel tracks of negotiations should be created.

We were given this assurance. Even when the second week began we were assured by the Presidency of the Conference that the real work was being done in the two working groups and their subsidiary drafting groups. Unfortunately, some of the key issues being negotiated were then removed from some of the key drafting groups, for example on shared vision. The issues were transferred to somewhere else but we did not know to where.

Then in the early hours of 19 December, after the Conference was supposed to have ended on 18 December, the Conference of Parties was finally convened and we were informed for the first time by the Presidency that a small representative group of leaders had come up with the Copenhagen Accord, and that the COP was invited to look at it and adopt it.

This way of running a UN conference is unhealthy, to say the least, what more a meeting of a treaty-based organization like the UNFCCC, which is charged with preventing the most dangerous threat the world has known.

It was said that the 26 countries were a representative set of countries. But who is representative of who has to be decided by the whole body. It is not the prerogative of the host country to select who it thinks can represent the world.

Before the vast majority of delegations were informed even about the small meeting, some leaders of powerful countries were already informing the media that an agreement had been reached.

It was only hours later than a Copenhagen Accord was shown to the COP members with a request we study it and join the consensus.

There was an easy assumption that the COP of 192 nations would simply rubber-stamp a document hastily put together by 26 countries. We are disappointed that this way of conducting business was done. It disrespects the hard work put in by thousands of delegates in the open-ended working groups that were discussing these issues in a transparent and democratic way. It is disrespectful of the United Nations and its member states.

Of course, having the participation of all parties consumes time. But this is what works in the end. On such a crucial issue like climate change on which the lives of the people in each country depends, the decision-making process must be democratic and participatory. If indeed a smaller group is negotiate on behalf of all, then this decision has to be taken by all, the mandate and terms of reference must be agreed to by all, and the choice of countries must be made by all.

This is the most important lesson to draw from Copenhagen. We now know what happened when the Copenhagen Accord was given over to the COP. Because of the inappropriate process and the lack of time to seriously consider the contents, it was not possible to adopt the Accord. The parties decided to "take note" of the Copenhagen Accord. The meaning of the term "takes note" may not be well known to the media or the public but in the UN context it is known to us. It is a neutral term that means the document is not adopted, nor is it viewed either positively or negatively. Each member can have its own opinion on it.

Although the Copenhagen Accord is not a document agreed to by consensus, I am sure that each of us will study it thoroughly now that we have more time, and each of the members can draw lessons from it and key points from it and they have the opportunity to feed these points into the negotiations next year in the two working groups. The points in the Accord can thus provide contributions and inputs into the negotiations.

It should not be misunderstood that the G-77 and China or our members have over-prioritizing process over substance. In this case, our concern about process is also primarily a concern on substance. We do not want texts of substance that we have worked on together with our partners in Annex I countries in the working groups to be superseded or deleted by texts of substance coming from a select group.

It must be recorded that the Copenhagen Conference was not only or mainly about the 26-country meeting or the Accord. It mainly consisted of the work in the AWG-LCA and the AWG-KP. We are glad to note that there was some progress in various issues in the AWG-LCA, with the text advancing in several areas. Of course, there are still many options and square brackets in the various texts. This is to be expected since it was known that Copenhagen would not reach a full agreement.

We are much more disappointed that the work on the Kyoto Protocol was much slower and that up to now we do not have the numbers for emission reduction commitments for Annex I parties in aggregate or as individual countries. This is the biggest substantive failure in Copenhagen, that these most vital figures of all are still missing. They are missing in the report of the AWG-KP. They are also missing in the Copenhagen Accord. Thus, the developed countries did not take the lead as they promised in Copenhagen. We believe that obtaining adequate numbers in line with what science demands is still our most important task.

Mr. Secretary General,
Excellencies, Distinguished Delegates,

We are most disappointed that the comprehensive deal was not sealed in Copenhagen. But we must also remember that in the last two years we have made good progress in defining the issues, in defining our different positions, and in clarifying the methodologies and narrowing the options. There is a good foundation to base our work for the future. The G-77 and China believes that there is no substitute for all of us, big or small countries, to work hard through the participatory and open-ended channels of the AWG-LCA and the AWG-KP to advance our work, in line with the mandates of the working groups and in accordance with the principles and provisions of the Convention and the Kyoto Protocol.

We know that we now have a new deadline to complete the work by December 2010 in time for or at the COP-16.

We, therefore, propose the following:

- The work should progress along the two tracks as mandated in Bali.
- There should be an assurance as soon as possible from Annex I parties in the Kyoto Protocol that they intend to remain in the Protocol and undertake a second commitment period beginning in 2013.
- Top priority must be given to agreeing on the figures for Annex I emission reduction in the second commitment period.
- The figures must be credible. Many developing countries have proposed that the aggregate figure is more than a 40% cut by 2020 compared to 1990.
- Annex I members that are not a party in the Kyoto Protocol should undertake a comparable effort inside the Convention through the AWG-LCA track.
- Developing countries will undertake nationally appropriate mitigation actions, which are supported and enabled by finance and technology and a method of measuring, reporting, and verifying is to be worked out for the supported NAMAs and the financing and technology transfer.
- The new and more effective structures for finance and technology transfer, both of which should be under the authority of the COP, should be established. The quantum and sources and uses of funds and the critical issues in technology are to be worked out.
- In adaptation, a strengthened mechanism to give this issue the highest status it deserves, and the provision of adequate financing, must also be worked out.

These are some of the key issues that we have to and we can succeed in finalizing in the next 12 months.

Indeed, we should give ourselves a stricter deadline. We should finish in a comfortable period before December 2010, so that we can have a much more predictable and smooth Conference in Mexico, with the decisions already agreed to before the Conference itself, and thus we can avoid the problems and tensions that we had in Copenhagen.

Mr. Secretary-General,
Excellencies, Distinguished Delegates,

The G-77 and China is very committed to the multilateral process and especially to the UNFCCC, which we consider the only legitimate body in which the international decisions can be taken on climate change policies. We understand that it may take a little bit more time and effort to forge a consensus among so many members of the Convention and the Kyoto Protocol, and often the differences of views make it more complicated for the issues to be resolved.

Nevertheless, we believe it is vital to invest in this truly bottom-up and democratic process because the issues are so important and affect all countries, and moreover the best guarantee of an enduring and sustainable implementation of what is agreed is that we all have ownership of the decision-making process and of the decisions.

Like all our partners, the G-77 and China is disappointed that we did not achieve more in Copenhagen. However, we believe we did make significant progress in Copenhagen and we are committed to working even harder in the next year to come to final conclusions on both the Convention track and the Kyoto Protocol track.

Climate change and its effects continue to threaten us and we must all make the utmost effort to close the remaining gaps between us and to conclude a comprehensive deal that is both environmentally ambitious and that is just and fair and balanced.

Statement on behalf of the Group of 77 and China by H.E. Mr. Peter Thomson, Ambassador, Permanent Representative of Fiji to the United Nations, Chairman of the Group of 77, at the General Assembly Thematic Debate on Sustainable Development and Climate Change: Practical Solutions in the Energy-Water Nexus (New York, 16 May 2013)

Mr. President,

I have the honour to deliver this statement on behalf of the Group of 77 and China.

We thank you, Mr. President, for convening this thematic debate. The Group of 77 and China strongly advocates the achievement of sustainable development and eradication of poverty, which are our first and overriding priorities. We highlighted at the UN Conference on Sustainable Development last year the urgent need for practical and effective solutions to sustainable development. Our development aspirations face real threats from the pressure being put on natural resources and the threat of climate change. Addressing unsustainable consumption patterns and lifestyles in developed countries is a fundamental response in this regard.

The Group of 77 and China is of the view that it is vital for all member States to promote sustainable development in accordance with the Rio Principles, in particular, the principle of common but differentiated responsibilities. It is equally important that we fully implement Agenda 21 and the Outcomes of other relevant UN Conferences in the economic, environmental, and social fields, including the Millennium Development Goals Declaration. The principle of sovereignty of States over their natural resources should also be at the core of our discussions.

We further emphasize the critical role of the international community in the provision of adequate, predictable, new, and additional financial resources, transfer of technology, and capacity-building to developing countries.

With regard to climate change, we reiterate our view that the UNFCCC is the primary international, intergovernmental forum for negotiating the global response to climate change.

Mr. President,

Developing countries are facing significant risks from the adverse impacts of climate change, and already experiencing increased impacts, including persistent drought and extreme weather events, sea-level rise, coastal erosion, and ocean acidification. These climate impacts further threaten our food security, efforts to eradicate poverty, and achieve sustainable development. For small island developing states, for instance, climate change and sea-level rise represent the gravest of threats to their survival and viability, including for some the loss of territory. It is important that we proceed with a sense of urgency in the climate change negotiations in accordance with the principles and provisions of the climate change Convention.

In this regard, we reiterate our call for the fulfilment of climate-related and environmental commitments by developed countries, in particular those under the UNFCCC and the Kyoto Protocol. Moreover, we call for the full and effective implementation of the commitments made under the various sustainable development frameworks applicable to developing countries, including the MDGs.

Access to clean water and sanitation is of vital importance in meeting food security and the eradication of poverty. Water is also essential to promote socio-economic development and for the protection of the environment. Issues of access to potable water, water quality, underground water, management, and planning as well as water being an energy source are essential to the future of our populations.

We need to clearly identify and utilize the link between policy, decision-making, science, and practice in order to transcend the rhetoric between the reality and our desired goals in both the energy and water sectors. It requires unifying a variety of know-how and experience to attain sustainable development and address the climate change and environmental objectives in a meaningful manner.

There is a need to share technologies, experiences, and best practices on the effective use of water, not only as a basic necessity but also as an energy source. In view of the importance of water and energy to promoting socio-economic growth, support should be provided to developing countries in their efforts to improve the development and deployment of clean technologies, management, conservation, and sustainable use of water and water-related energy resources.

As with water, energy access remains critical to the development aspirations of our people. With more than 1.3 billion people in developing countries outside the pale of energy access and 2.6 billion still dependent on firewood for domestic needs, the urgency to act cannot be overemphasized.

We recognize that technologies are now available for making water potable, for saving and redistributing its supplies, for reducing the demand for water and securing new sources of water, as well as maximizing energy efficiency, energy conservation, and increasing use of water-related renewable energy resources.

The United Nations system plays an important role in addressing the issues of water and energy by providing support to the efforts of countries and institutions to accelerate progress in water and energy resources management.

There is a need to explore new ways and avenues to tackle basic needs in terms of water and energy resources. There is an equally urgent need for meaningful international cooperation in sharing cutting-edge technologies, best practices, and capacity-building to assist developing countries in providing universal access to energy and water to their peoples. We must be active both in the management and development of the relevant resource infrastructures in order to increase access to and effective use of safe water and reliable energy supply for all.

Statement on behalf of the Group of 77 and China by H.E. Ambassador Sacha Llorentty Soliz, Permanent Representative of the Plurinational State of Bolivia to the United Nations and Chair of the Group of 77, on the Seventh Session of the General Assembly's Open Working Group on Sustainable Development Goals on "Climate Change and Disaster Risk Reduction" (New York, 9 January 2014)

CoChair,

1. I have the honour, as the new Chair of the Group of 77 and China, to deliver this statement on behalf of the Group.
2. I would like to take this opportunity to wish everyone a fruitful 2014. The Group acknowledges the issue brief prepared by the Technical Support Team and thanks Mr. Andrew Steer, President and CEO of the World Resources Institute, for his keynote address on "climate change and disaster risk reduction" and also the one made by Professor Jiahua Pan.

CoChair,

3. Climate change and disaster risk are serious threats to poverty eradication and sustainable development. Developing countries are facing significant risks from the adverse impacts of climate change, and are already experiencing increased impacts, including persistent drought and extreme weather events, massive flooding, sea-level rise, coastal erosion, glacial retreat, land and forest degradation, loss of biodiversity, desertification, and ocean acidification. For many developing countries, climate change and disaster risk represent one of the biggest threats to food security in the twenty-first century. Their impacts are already causing disruptions in the livelihoods in many parts of the world, particularly for those that are dependent on predicable weather and arable land. For small island developing states, for instance, climate change and sea-level rise represent the gravest of threats to their survival and viability, including for some the loss of territory.
4. We are deeply concerned that more than 226 million people globally are affected on average by disaster associated with natural hazards every year. While hazards are natural, disasters are preventable. We have been informed

by the scientific community that the current drivers of risk are linked to poor policies and practices in land use planning, governance, urbanisation, natural resource management, ecosystem management, as well as increasing poverty levels. We recognize, therefore, that the current model of development needs to be realigned to the changing world in order to address climate change and disaster risk reduction. It must be a model that is inclusive, equitable, risk sensitive, adaptive, and disaster resilient.

CoChair,

5. With regard to climate change, the Group reiterates its view that the United Nations Framework Convention on Climate Change (UNFCCC) is the primary international, intergovernmental forum for negotiating the global response to climate change. We stress that the international community, particularly the developed countries, given their historical responsibility, need to take the lead in addressing the climate change challenge within the UNFCCC and its principles and provisions, particularly, the principles of equity and common but differentiated responsibilities and respective capabilities, and provide financial and technology support to developing countries.
6. To mitigate damage from climate change and to reduce disaster risk, we call for the fulfilment of climate-related and environmental commitments by developed countries, in particular those under the UNFCCC, the Kyoto Protocol, as well as all commitments made under the various sustainable development frameworks applicable to developing countries, including the MDGs. Moreover, we urge our development partners to honour their commitments made through the Cancun Agreement at the 16th Conference of the Parties of the UNFCCC. These include a work programme on Loss and Damage; a Technology Mechanism; and the establishment of the Green Climate Fund which developed countries have expressed broad agreement to mobilise 100 billion US dollars per year both for adaptation and mitigation by 2020.
7. It is important that we proceed with a sense of urgency in the climate change negotiations in accordance with the principles and provisions of the climate change Convention. It is important to ensure coherence between climate negotiations and other intergovernmental agreements such as a successor to the Hyogo Framework for Action. In the context of the SDGs, we should give due consideration for a global goal and targets to address disaster risk and resilience in the context of sustainable development.

CoChair,

8. The Group underscores the importance of global efforts to strengthen action on climate change and disaster risk reduction as part of the international sustainable development agenda. The climate change challenges are multidimensional while disaster risk reduction is cross cutting, both of which are intricately linked to different elements of the three dimensions of sustainable

development. To address climate change and build resilience to disaster and climate impacts, the international community should embrace a multi-stakeholder, multisector approach within the global development agenda. This requires coordinated policies and actions across all sectors and at all levels of decision-making with all aspects of sustainable development.

9. Lastly, the Group recognises the interrelationship between climate change, loss of biodiversity and desertification and the need to intensify efforts to combat desertification and promote sustainable land management, and stress the need for enhanced cooperation and coordination among the Secretariats of the United Nations Convention to Combat Desertification, UNFCCC, and the Convention on Biological Diversity, while respecting their individual mandates. We reiterate our call on all parties to fully support the implementation of these Conventions in all their aspects, including the promotion the exchange of knowledge on best practices and lessons learned from global and regional cooperation.

Statement On Behalf of the Group of 77 and China by H.E. Mr. Rene Orellana, Ambassador on Environment and Development Issues of the Plurinational State of Bolivia, at the 11th Session of the Open Working Group on Sustainable Development Goals (SDGs) on "Sustainable Consumption and Production and Climate Change" (New York, 8 May 2014)

Distinguished CoChairs,

1. I have the honour to deliver this statement on behalf of the Group of 77 and China.
2. The Group underscores that achieving sustainable patterns of consumption and production is fundamental to the sustainable development agenda. This view is consistent with the call made by our political leaders more than twenty years ago at the 1992 Earth Summit.

Chapter 4 of Agenda 21 recognized that "the major cause of the continued deterioration of the global environment is unsustainable patterns of consumption and production, particularly in industrialized countries" and Principle 8 of the Rio Declaration urges states to reduce and eliminate unsustainable patterns of consumption and production.

This call was subsequently reaffirmed in the Johannesburg Plan of Implementation, the 2002 World Summit on Sustainable Development, and the Rio+20 Summit, which led to the adoption of the Ten-Year Framework of Programmes on Sustainable Consumption and Production Patterns (the "10 YFP") in 2012 at Rio.

3. As previously stated by the Group in early January of this year, there is an urgent need to change current consumption and production patterns, including the prevention of high rates of food loss and waste.

We express deep concern on the serious imbalanced and inequitable nature of global consumption and call for timebound effective implementation of the 10Year Framework of Programmes on Sustainable Consumption and Production Patterns, which is a concrete and operational outcome of the Rio+20 Conference.

Furthermore, based on the principle of common but differentiated responsibilities, developed countries need to take the lead.

4. As previously stated, the Group reiterates that enabling conditions must be created for new and innovative solutions by using a mix of regulatory and economic instruments, existing and new technologies, empowerment of stakeholders, and a governance structure that entails decision-making founded upon inclusive and participatory approaches.

International cooperation on financing, innovation, and technology transfer is essential to assist developing countries to progress towards sustainable development goals. Furthermore, the means of implementation should ensure that impediments to achieving sustainable consumption and production are reduced or even removed, particularly in international agreements and trade rules.

5. In the context of the SDGs, the Group holds the view that the 10Year Framework of Programmes on Sustainable Consumption and Production Patterns should serve as a global cooperative framework to help accelerate the shift towards sustainable patterns of consumption and production, including sound chemical and waste management.

Making this global shift requires strong leadership from developed countries, as recognised in a number of international declarations. With developed countries taking the lead and developing countries following a similar pattern, we are convinced that our collective efforts could mitigate or even reverse the damage to the global environment, thereby preserving a sustainable future for our children.

On Climate Change

6. As the Group of 77 and China highlighted in the last session on the OWG, we call once again for your attention since the alarming average of 226 million people in the world who are affected by disaster or natural hazards; and it has been shown that this is linked to poor policies and practices in land use planning, governance, urbanization, natural resource management, ecosystem management, and poverty levels. With this in mind, we would like to underscore the importance of modifying our current model of development to one that is inclusive, equitable, risk sensitive, adaptive and disaster risk reducing, in harmony with nature, so as to successfully address the impacts of climate change we are facing. Disasters are preventable; therefore, it is crucial that we act while we can.

7. We understand and recall that the international community, in particular the developed countries, need to take the lead in addressing the climate change challenge within the UNFCCC and its principles and provisions, particularly, the principles of equity and common but differentiated responsibilities and respective capabilities, and provide financial and technology support to developing countries.
8. Furthermore, we urgently call for the fulfilment of the commitments made by developed countries in the context of the second commitment period of the Kyoto Protocol and urge the developed countries that are not part of the second commitment period to make comparable quantified commitments of mitigation. Developed countries have to take the lead in the solution of the climate change crisis. Developing countries should enhance mitigation actions in the context of Common but Differentiated Responsibilities with the respective support of means of implementation as it is stated in the Climate Change Framework Convention.
9. There is an urgent need also to advance supporting adaptation plans and actions and a Loss and Damage programme, a Technology Mechanism, and the establishment of the Green Climate Fund in which developed countries have expressed their commitment to reinforce and the International Mechanism on Loss and damage recently created in the Warsaw Decision at COP-19. There is also a need to have a clear commitment about the commitment of development countries to mobilize 100 billion US dollars per year both for adaptation and mitigation by 2020. We also urge developed countries to transfer technologies to developing countries, so that developing countries will have affordable and appropriate technologies to combat climate change.
10. These elements have to be part of our approach to the issue of climate change. And it has to be clear that it is in the context of the UNFCCC that the decisions are going to be taken.
11. To address climate change and build resilience to disaster and climate impacts, the international community should embrace a multistakeholder, multisector approach within the global development agenda. This requires coordinated policies and actions across all sectors and at all levels of decision-making with all aspects of sustainable development.
12. We would like to highlight that in order to address further discussions on this issue, the Group recognizes the interrelationship between climate change, loss of biodiversity and desertification and the need to intensify efforts to combat desertification and promote sustainable land management, and stress the need for enhanced cooperation and coordination among the Secretariats of the United Nations Convention to Combat Desertification, UNFCCC and the Convention on Biological Diversity, while respecting their individual mandates.

Statement by H.E. Mr. Evo Morales Ayma, President of the Plurinational State of Bolivia and Chair of the Group of 77, at the Climate Summit (New York, 23 September 2014)

Mr. Secretary-General,

1. Climate change is one of the most serious global challenges of our times. We underscore the fact that developing countries continue to suffer the most from the adverse impacts of climate change, the increasing frequency and intensity of extreme weather events, and the impact of response measures, even though they are historically the least responsible for climate change. Accordingly, we call for developed countries to take the lead in responding to climate change. Climate change threatens not only the development prospects of developing countries and their achievement of sustainable development but also the very existence and survival of countries, societies, and the ecosystems of our Mother Earth.
2. We affirm that the United Nations Framework Convention on Climate Change (UNFCCC) is the primary international, intergovernmental forum for negotiating the global response to climate change. In this regard, we stress that the international response to climate change must fully respect the principles, provisions, and ultimate objective of the Convention, in particular the principles of equity and of common but differentiated responsibilities.
3. Fulfilling the ultimate objective of the United Nations Framework Convention on Climate Change will require strengthening the multilateral, rules-based regime under the Convention and we, therefore, further reaffirm the importance of continuing the negotiations on climate change under the Convention. We, therefore, further reaffirm the importance of the negotiations on climate change under the Convention in accordance with its principles and provisions and of adopting, in 2015, a protocol, another legal instrument or an agreed outcome with legal force under the Convention applicable to all parties. The new agreement must address all elements of the Convention including adaptation in a balanced manner and be ambitious, equitable, and firmly based on science.

Mr. Secretary-General,

4. Developed countries, given their historical responsibility, need to take the lead in addressing this challenge in accordance with the principles and provisions of the United Nations Framework Convention on Climate Change.
5. There is an urgent need to close the ambition gap. We express concern about the lack of fulfilment of commitments by developed countries. In addressing this gap, the focus must not be limited to mitigation only but also address gaps relating to finance, technology, and support for capacity-building, balanced with a focus on adaptation to climate change. We emphasize that developed

countries must take robust and ambitious mitigation commitments, with ambitious quantitative targets for limiting and reducing emissions.

6. The Kyoto Protocol remains an important instrument to contribute to close the ambition gap and to addressing the climate crisis. In Doha (Qatar) we took a fundamental step to further enhance the international climate change regime, through the historic adoption of a fully ratifiable amendment to the Kyoto Protocol for its second commitment period. We have reached concrete provisions for ensuring the environmental integrity of the Kyoto Protocol.

Mr. Secretary-General,

7. The Group of 77 and China urges Annex I parties to fully implement the decisions achieved in Doha on the second commitment period. This will be essential for allowing the Kyoto Protocol to continue to serve as a cornerstone of the multilaterally agreed rules based system under the Convention and a full reflection of its principles, in particular the principles of equity and common but differentiated responsibilities and respective capabilities.
8. Increasing pre-2020 ambition must be primarily achieved through the implementation of the second commitment period of the Kyoto Protocol and the outcome of the Bali Action Plan in accordance with principles and provisions of the Convention, with developed country parties taking the lead. The pre-2020 mitigation gap would not even have existed if the developed countries had committed to an emission reduction of 40% below their 1990 levels by 2020.
9. We emphasize our extreme disappointment and concern over those developed country parties that are not parties to the Kyoto Protocol, have withdrawn from the KP, or that have not yet ratified the second commitment period of the Kyoto Protocol. We believe that the failure of any developed country party to ratify a legally binding, quantified commitment under the Kyoto Protocol for the post-2020 period raises serious concerns about its credibility and sincerity in combating climate change. We urge all parties to the Kyoto Protocol to revisit and increase the ambition of their second commitment period targets and ratify these enhanced commitments. We further urge all developed country parties, whether they are parties to the Kyoto Protocol or not, to revisit and increase the level of their mitigation ambition for the pre-2020 period under the Convention, without conditionality.
10. The full ratification of the Doha amendment by Annex I parties will be crucial to build trust. Ratification of the second commitment period is an important steppingstone towards the new 2015 Agreement and its entry into force and implementation from 2020.
11. The extent to which developing countries will effectively implement their commitments under the United Nations Framework Convention on Climate Change will depend on the effective implementation by developed countries of their commitments under the Convention related to financial resources

and transfer of technology and will take fully into account that economic and social development and poverty eradication are the first and overriding priorities of developing countries.

Mr. Secretary-General,

12. There is an urgent need to have a clear commitment of Developed country Parties to provide at least USD70 billion per year by 2016 rising to USD100 billion per year by 2020 as a floor for accounting, and leading to further increased commitments on the provision of financial support for the post-2020 period.
13. The efforts of developing countries for contributing with mitigation actions should be undertaken through the provision of finance, development, and transfer of technology and capacity-building, taking into account the imperatives of equitable access to sustainable development, the right to development, the survival of countries, and protecting the integrity of Mother Earth;

Mr. Secretary-General,

14. The adverse impacts of climate change are devastating societies in the developing world, threatening the right to development and survival of peoples and nations. Developing countries are suffering the permanent hits of extreme events, eroding drastically our advances in the process of poverty eradication and sustainable development. We need structural solutions to the climate crisis as well as immediate measures in order to address the impacts of extreme events. The Group welcomes the outcome of the COP-19 decision of the Warsaw international mechanism for loss and damage associated with climate change impacts, and the need to make this mechanism functional is paramount. This mechanism must address the needs of developing countries emerging from extreme and slow-onset events, and the urgency for this mechanism has only increased. We call for the operationalization of the mechanism established by this decision, taking into account the principles of the Convention and the national development processes. Carrying out such actions requires the provision of adequate support and creating the appropriate arrangements and for meaningful activities.

Mr. Secretary-General,

15. The objective of the Convention, as set out in article 2, is to achieve the stabilization of GHG concentrations in the atmosphere. It further provides for the parameters of the timeframe, in which this ultimate objective should be achieved, to allow ecosystems to adapt naturally to climate change, to ensure that food production is not threatened and to enable economic development to proceed in a sustainable manner.

16. We all have to contribute to the solutions to climate change, it is true, but in accordance with the principle of common but differentiated responsibilities and respective capabilities. We underscore that Intended Nationally Determined Contributions (INDCs) need to be seen in a balanced and comprehensive context of the 2015 agreement, and therefore have to include and equally address mitigation, adaptation, finance, technology, transfer, capacity-building, and transparency of action and support. Developing countries will also require provision of support for their domestic preparations for their INDCs.

Mr. Secretary-General,

17. The twenty-first century is the time for the countries and the peoples from the South to develop their economies and societies in order to fulfil human needs sustainably, in harmony with nature and respect for Mother Earth and its ecosystems.
18. The Earth and its ecosystems are our home, and we are convinced that, in order to achieve a just balance among the economic, social, and environmental needs of present and future generations, it is necessary to promote harmony with nature and the Earth
19. We consider that mitigation of and adaptation to climate change are contingent upon different sociocultural contexts, taking particular account of indigenous peoples and local communities and their traditional knowledge systems and practices, including their holistic view of community and environment, as a major means of adapting to climate change.
20. Sustainable development involves a change in the order of priorities from the generation of material wealth to the satisfaction of human needs in harmony with nature. The excessive orientation towards profit neither respects Mother Earth nor takes into account human needs. The continuation of this unequal system will lead to further inequality.

Statement on Behalf of the Group of 77 and China by H.E. Mr. Virachai Plasai, Ambassador and Permanent Representative of the Kingdom of Thailand, at the Special Event on Promoting South-South and Triangular Cooperation on Climate Change and Launch of the Southern Climate Partnership Incubator to Support the SDGs (New York, 21 April 2016)

Mr. Moderator,

1. I have the honour to deliver this statement on behalf of the Group 77 and China to share our views and experience on this important and cross-cutting issue of climate change and South-South and triangular cooperation which stands at the heart of the Group.
2. At the outset, allow me to express appreciation to the Executive Office of the Secretary-General (EOSG) and the UN Office for South-South Cooperation

(UNOSSC) for the invitation to speak on behalf of the Group at this special event on the eve of the signing ceremony of the Paris Agreement of the UNFCCC COP-21. The Group also takes note with great interest of the launch of the Southern Climate Partnership Incubator (SCPI). Today's event clearly demonstrates the high-level of importance the United Nations attaches to the inter-linkage between South-South and triangular cooperation and climate change challenges. As South-South and triangular cooperation are dear to the heart of the Group, we wish to see the momentum created by this initiative to promote South-South and triangular cooperation be carried forward in other important areas apart from climate change.

Mr. Moderator,

3. The 2030 Agenda calls for a revitalized global partnership for sustainable development. The Group of 77 and China is of the view that this new initiative will be crucial for mobilizing multi-stakeholder partnerships on the cross-cutting environmental dimension, in particular the issue of climate change through the traditional North-South cooperation and complementary South-South and triangular cooperation towards that end to ensure sustainability of the economic and social dimensions.
4. The launch of the Southern Climate Partnership Incubator (SCPI) could support developing countries in their efforts to implement the 2030 Agenda and, once it comes into force, the Paris Agreement. The Group reiterates the open and inclusive nature of this initiative while attaching importance to relevant flexibility for national space in accordance with national priority and policy. In addition to the four key areas of interest specified, namely, renewable energy, climate resilience, smart cities, and big data, the Group is of the view that further consultation with larger membership would be beneficial in identifying other key areas of interest under this initiative.
5. Furthermore, we stress the need for more clarity on the mechanism, both financial and logistical aspects, to support and sustain the implementation of partnerships under this new initiative as well as the role and mandates of EOSG and UNOSSC including the UN development system in this regard. This would provide great benefits for the membership of the Group in pursuing and taking active part in this initiative.
6. The Group of 77 and China would like to reaffirm its position that South-South cooperation is a manifestation of solidarity among peoples and countries of the South that contributes to their national well-being, national and collective self-reliance and the attainment of the internationally agreed development goals. Such cooperation should also be guided by the principles of respect for national sovereignty, national ownership and independence, equality, non-conditionality, non-interference in domestic affairs, and mutual benefit. At the same time, we reiterate that South-South and triangular

cooperation are not a substitute for, but rather a complement to, North-South cooperation.

Mr. Moderator,

7. The Group would also like to reaffirm that as we try to promote and strengthen South-South and triangular cooperation in the field of climate change, focus should be on supporting developing countries in their efforts towards adaptation. Financing for adaptation is critical and securing the continued role of the Adaptation Fund beyond 2020 is welcomed.
8. On mitigation, developing countries are still in a great need for capacity building to take effective climate change action. Apart from undertaking economy-wide absolute emission reduction targets for Nationally Determined Contributions (NDCs) by developed countries, it is also equally important to enhance support for developing countries to allow higher ambition in the NDCs. The Group is of a firm belief that capacity-building should be based on and responsive to national needs and to fostering country ownership. The process of capacity-building must be participatory, country-driven, and cross-cutting.
9. In closing, the Group is of the view that in addressing climate change to yield sustainable future for all, genuine, open and inclusive partnership is crucial to make that difference. Towards this end, we wish you great success in this endeavour and stand ready to engage in and contribute actively and constructively to the implementation of this initiative.

Statement on behalf of the Group of 77 and China by H.E. General Surasak Karnjanarat, Minister of Natural Resources and Environment of the Kingdom of Thailand, at the High-Level Signature Ceremony for the Paris Agreement (New York, 22 April 2016)

Mr. Chairman,

1. I have the honour to deliver this statement on behalf of the Group of 77 and China.
2. At the outset, allow me to express appreciation to the Secretary-General for convening this high-level signature ceremony for the Paris Agreement.
3. The Agreement is a result of the collective and tireless efforts of all parties working constructively in a spirit of compromise and represents a step forward in our efforts on climate change.
4. While we are signing the Paris Agreement today, we must not forget the urgent need to enhance pre-2020 ambition, including the ratification of the Doha amendment to the Kyoto Protocol, which will provide a strong basis for post-2020 efforts under the Paris Agreement. We also need to address the significant gap between the aggregate effect of parties' mitigation pledges in terms of global annual emissions of greenhouse gases by 2020 and aggregate

emission pathways consistent with holding the increase in the global average temperature to well below 2°C above pre-industrial levels and pursuing efforts to limit the temperature increase to 1.5°C.

5. In our view, the focus now should both be on the entry into force of the Paris Agreement and on delivering major tasks to enhance pre-2020 implementation. This includes action on adaptation, which is an urgent priority for developing countries. Financing for adaptation is critical and securing the continued role of the Adaptation Fund pre-2020 and beyond 2020 is welcomed and should be enhanced.
6. On mitigation, developed countries should continue taking the lead by undertaking and increasing economy-wide absolute emission reduction targets for their pledges and nationally determined contributions (NDCs). For developing countries, capacity-building support for climate action is critical and should be based on and responsive to national needs and foster country ownership. The process of capacity-building must be participatory, country-driven, and cross-cutting. Enhanced financial and technological support from developed countries will allow for effective implementation and enhanced ambition of developing countries.

Mr. Chairman,

7. While the Group of 77 and China remains committed in implementation, our Group has been the most affected by the adverse impacts of climate change which are steadily eroding the development gains and the 2030 Agenda on Sustainable Development that we seek to achieve.
8. We are already taking ambitious measures to prevent further harm and to adapt to inevitable changes in line with our capacities. For our endeavours to be achieved, it is critical that developed countries enhance the ambition of their actions and ensure that actions of developing countries are adequately supported.

Mr. Chairman,

9. Transformation of our economies to low carbon development pathways requires adequate, predictable, and sustainable climate financing. Means of implementation is a key pillar for the implementation of the Agreement. We welcome the approval of the first projects by the Green Climate Fund. We envision that a substantive discussions and decision on increasing climate finance will be an important outcome of COP-22 in Morocco.

Mr. Chairman,

10. In this fight against climate change, we need genuine cooperation. We, the Group of 77 and China, are willing and ready, as always, to play our constructive part in this cooperation, which underscores our commitments to our generation and the future generations to come.

Statements in the United Nations Security Council

Statement on Behalf of the Group of 77 and China by Mr. Farukh Amil, Deputy Permanent Representative of the Islamic Republic of Pakistan to the United Nations, in the Security Council Open Debate on "Energy, Security and Climate" (New York, 17 April 2007)

Madam President,
Excellencies,
Ladies and gentlemen,

I have the honour to make this contribution on behalf of the Group of 77 and China on the decision by the Security Council to hold a debate on "Energy, Security and Climate."

The Group is of the view that Security Council's primary responsibility is for the maintenance of international peace and security as set out in the UN Charter. On the other hand, other issues, including those relating to economic and social development, are assigned by the Charter to the Economic and Social Council and the General Assembly. The ever-increasing encroachment by the Security Council on the roles and responsibilities of other principal organs of the UN represents a distortion of the principles and purposes of the UN Charter, also infringes on their authority and compromises the rights of the general membership of the United Nations.

The issues of energy and climate change are vital for sustainable development. Responsibilities in the field of sustainable development belong to the General Assembly, ECOSOC, and their relevant subsidiary bodies including the CSD and the UNEP. Climate change has a binding multilateral agreement the UN Framework Convention on Climate Change (UNFCCC) and a supportive protocol the Kyoto Protocol. No role was envisaged for the Security Council.

Madam President,

We are of the view that it is vital for all member States to promote sustainable development adhering to the Rio principles—especially the principle of "common but differentiated responsibility"—and fully implement Agenda 21 and other commitments related to provision of financial resources, transfer of technology, and capacity-building of developing countries, undertaken at the Rio and Johannesburg and other relevant UN Conferences in the economic and social fields.

The Group has consistently maintained that the UNFCCC is the appropriate forum to consider risks associated with climate change and actions needed to address climate change in accordance with the principles enshrined in the Convention. Developed countries should take urgent action to fulfil their commitments to reduce Green House Gas (GHG) emissions in accordance with the Kyoto Protocol. Those countries that have not yet done so, should accede to the Kyoto Protocol.

The Group also feels it inappropriate to consider the issue of energy in the Security Council. We reaffirm the key role of energy in achieving the goals of sustainable development, poverty eradication, and achieving the MDGs. Therefore, we emphasize the critical role of international community for provision of adequate, predictable, new, and additional financial resources, technology transfer, and enhancing capacity-building of the developing countries as agreed in Agenda 21, Johannesburg Plan of Implementation (JPOI), and decisions of Commission on Sustainable Development (CSD). Also, there is need for political will and commitment to explore innovative ways of applying energy efficient, environmentally sound, cost-effective, and socially acceptable technologies and systems.

Madam President,

The Group of 77 and China will continue to pursue the realization of the goals of sustainable development, as well as the fulfilment of commitments by developed countries in all relevant bodies, especially in the forthcoming 15th Session of the Commission on Sustainable Development (CSD-15) and we urge others to do likewise.

We hope that the decision by the Council to hold this debate does not create a precedent or undermine the authority or mandate of the relevant bodies, processes, and instruments, which are already addressing these issues.

Statements in the Second Committee

Statement by the Representative of Ghana On Behalf of the Group of 77 in the Second Committee on Agenda Items 78 and 79: UNCED and Protection of Global Climate for Present and Future Generations of Mankind (New York, 18 November 1991)

Mr. Chairman,

On behalf of the Group of 77, I wish to thank the Secretary-General of UNCED for his statement on the work of the third session of the Prepcom.

At the third session, the Group of 77 was able to put the development dimension back on the agenda of UNCED pursuant to the mandate of the General Assembly in its resolution 44/228. We were pleased that agreement was reached to incorporate the development issues in all Agenda 21 programme documents as follows:

(a) poverty, economic growth, and environment;
(b) international trade and environment;
(c) structural adjustment and environment;
(d) commodities and environment;
(e) external indebtedness, resource flows, and environment;
(f) large industrial enterprises, including transnational corporations, business practices, and environment.

Means of implementation of the programmes are also to be specified. In particular, ways and means to provide new and additional financial resources are to be clearly identified and action-oriented proposals for effective modalities for favourable access to and transfer of environmentally sound technology, in particular to developing countries including on concessional and preferential terms as well as for the development of the endogenous capacities of developing are also to be incorporated in agenda 21. The respective responsibilities of developed and developing countries are to be clearly stated.

The developed countries bear the main responsibility for cleaning the environmental problems that confront the world today because they are the principal source of pollution of the planet. Resolution 44/228 makes this point quite clearly.

The Group of 77 also made specific and detailed proposals relating to new and additional resources and the transfer of environmentally sound technology to developing countries. Unfortunately, the developed countries were not prepared to engage in substantive discussions of these proposals. This attitude contrasted with the willingness of developing countries to discuss such issues as forests, biodiversity, protection of the atmosphere, protection of the oceans and freshwater resources which enabled the Prepcom to make good progress in these areas. In effect, the developed countries came prepared to discuss issues in which they were seeking environmental concessions from the South, but were unprepared to discuss issues on which they must also make concessions to the South. In future sessions, we will make sure that parallel progress is made on all issues to ensure a balanced outcome.

Mr. Chairman, although negotiations must be reserved for the fourth session of the Prepcom, it is important to restate certain basic principles. Environmental protection cannot be undertaken at the expense of the development objectives of developing countries. The South has a right to adequate "environmental space" for its present and future development needs. As the South Centre rightly points out, " 'sustainable development' does not mean only that the needs of the present have to be met without prejudice to the satisfaction of future needs. It means also that the needs of the North should be met in ways that do not compromise the satisfaction of the present and future needs of the South." This is a basic non-negotiable requirement. All resources within our territorial domain are our national heritage and cannot in any way be transmitted through any device, legal or otherwise, as "global commons."

In the negotiations relating to the protection of the atmosphere, developed countries must make firm commitments to reduce and stabilize their present excessive levels of emissions. Since they are responsible for over 80% of all greenhouse gas emissions they must bear the main responsibility for their reduction. Discretionary arrangement that allows the developed countries to do as they please with regard to the level of their emissions are unacceptable. It would be wrong and counterproductive for poor forest dwellers to be removed from their habitat in the interest of forest conservation so that unsustainable consumption patterns in the developed countries may be maintained. That is why it is important that the developed countries live up to their responsibilities and not seek to shift the burden of environmental protection on to the South. We are prepared to cooperate, based on our own free will, for the protection of the environment of our planet, but only on the basis of equitable burden-sharing. Why is it that we are negotiating a biodiversity convention and there is no corresponding convention on biotechnology?

Institutions to be established after UNCED must be based on democratic principles in which all have equal opportunity to participate in the decision-making process.

Mr. Chairman, some of these issues would have to be raised and addressed during the next session of the Prepcom. It is our hope that the developed countries would come to the fourth session fully prepared and equipped to discuss and negotiate all issues within the mandate of the Prepcom.

Statement by Mr. Mourad Ahmia, from the Permanent Mission of Algeria to the United Nations, on Behalf of the Group of 77 and China, on Agenda Item 89 Entitled: "Environment and Sustainable Development: (a) Implementation of the Decisions and Recommendations of UNCED; (b) Protection of Global Climate for Present and Future Generations of Mankind" (New York, 19 October 1994)

Mr. Chairman,

I have the honour of speaking on behalf of the Group of 77 and China under the following two sub-agenda items:

a) Implementation of decisions and recommendations of the United Nations Conference on Environment and Development.
b) Protection of global climate for present and future generations of mankind.

The Algerian delegations will also speak later on behalf of the Group of 77 and China in the Plenary of the General Assembly on the other two sub-items relating to the Conference on Small Island Developing States and the International Convention to combat desertification, in particular in Africa.

Mr. Chairman,

More than two years have gone by since the United Nations Conference on Environment and Development, which was held in June 1992 in Rio. At the time of the assessment of the implementation of the decisions and recommendations of the Earth Summit, the overall results have not met the expectations of the developing countries, despite the few modest actions undertaken by the Commission on Sustainable Development. Hence, the enthusiasm that had characterized the preparatory process for UNCED has diminished and the solemn commitments freely agreed to risk being questioned and compromised.

The work of the Commission on Sustainable Development, the World Conference on Small Island Developing States, and the negotiating process on an International

Convention to combat desertification, in particular in Africa, all have confirmed this state of affairs and the principle of common but differentiated responsibility, accepted by everyone in Rio, still has not taken tangible form.

The principle of providing new and additional financial resources to the developing countries to allow them to meet their commitments under Agenda 21 did not materialize at the time of the replenishment of the resources of the International Development Association (IDA) and the Global Environment Facility (GEF). The initial commitments for mobilizing financial resources, which Agenda 21 called for at the forty-seventh session of the General Assembly, did not take place at that session nor at any other forum.

Similarly, the transfer of environmentally sound technology for the benefit of the developing countries on concessional and preferential terms in accordance with the provisions of Chapter 34 of Agenda 21 remains far from meeting the commitments agreed to by the developed countries in this area.

The Group of 77 and China, on many occasions, had to express their disappointment over the insufficient progress achieved since the Earth Summit and today, on their behalf, I wish to reaffirm this frank and direct message.

The developing countries still feel themselves bound by the commitments which they signed in Rio and remain confident of the relevance of the analyses and the foundations contained in Agenda 21, including that of the concept of a global partnership for sustainable development and the notion of common but differentiated responsibility.

This renewal of our confidence reflects, once again, the highly political interest which the Group of 77 and China attaches to the comprehensive and effective implementation of the decisions and recommendations of the Conference at Rio.

In this spirit, the matter of new and additional resources, the matter of the transfer of environmentally sound technologies as well as the matter of consumption and production patterns must remain priorities on the agenda of the Commission on Sustainable Development and under the High-level Council on Sustainable Development and they should be studied in depth by the Secretariat.

Mr. Chairman,

The Group of 77 and China is happy that the framework convention on climate change has entered into force and they welcome the action taken by the secretariat of the negotiating committee to prepare for the first session of the Conference of Contracting Parties, scheduled to take place in Berlin at the beginning of next year.

On this occasion, they wish to reaffirm their commitment to the integrity of the mandate given to the Intergovernmental Negotiating Committee by the General Assembly in provisions of its resolution 45/212.

In this context, the Group of 77 and China cannot remain silent over their concern regarding the turn taken at the deliberations of the tenth session of the Intergovernmental Negotiating Committee, which was held in Geneva last August, during which we found a strong commitment by certain developed countries to involve the committee in a path that was outside its mandate. This state of affairs does not strengthen the climate of confidence among the different partners involved in implementing this Convention.

The wish to amend the framework convention under the pretext of developments in the situation and the inadequacy of commitments made with regard to the goals being pursued runs the risk, in our view, of compromising the precarious balance and the fragile context against which the Convention was very carefully drafted.

The Group of 77 and China feels that any attempt to question such a consensus on the pretext that there are some innovative procedures under way, such as the concept of the joint implementation of commitments made, may have damaging consequences and may question the cardinal principle on which the Convention is based, namely, the principle of common but differentiated responsibility of the parties.

In this respect, it is important to emphasize that among all the international agreements in force on environmental matters, only the framework convention on climate change was conceived on the basis of distinct categories of parties enjoying differentiated obligations which were developed on the basis of a degree of responsibility and the amount of damage caused by them.

Hence, the concept of joint implementation can only be conceived between parties having similar responsibilities, that is to say the parties contained in Annex I of the Convention. This concept in no case can be applied between parties having differentiated responsibilities and obligations, that is to say between industrialized countries and developing countries.

Any other approach runs the risk of harming the basic principle of differentiated responsibility of States by unjustly and illegally transferring the heaviest part of the burden to the weakest links in the chain of nations.

With regard to the historical responsibility of the industrialized countries in this area, the Group of 77 and China remains convinced that the concept of joint implementation should be strictly limited to parties contained in Annex I in conformity with the relevant provisions of that Convention.

Mr. Chairman,

In conclusion, let me say that the implementation of the decisions and recommendations of the Rio Conference for the developing countries have a highly political meaning. The results of the Earth Summit, including the adoption of binding legal instruments, were based on the cardinal principles at the original convening of UNCED. Holding this very conference was made possible by the principle of compromise and to the concessions agreed to by the developing countries. This is to say that today there is an overriding necessity to insure that their interests are not ignored in any event during the course of future developments in the process which was born at the Earth Summit.

Statement of the Delegation of the Philippines on Behalf of the Group of 77 and China at the Fiftieth Session of the UN General Assembly Second Committee on Agenda Items 96: Environment and Sustainable Development 96(d): Protection of Global Climate for Present and Future Generation of Mankind and 96(e): Implementation of the Outcome of the Global Conference on the Sustainable Development of Small Island Developing States (New York, 15 November 1995)

Mr. Chairman,

I have the honour to make this statement on behalf of the Group of 77 and China.

At the outset, I wish to thank the Secretary-General for the documents which were submitted on the two sub-items under consideration.

The protection of global climate is an issue which is very important to all of us. What used to be a topic discussed only by experts and scientists has now become a concern of everybody. Indeed, protection of the global climate is synonymous to ensuring the safety of future generations of mankind.

It is, therefore, satisfying to note that the United Nations Framework Convention on Climate Change has been ratified by 142 States and one regional economic integration organization. It is hoped that it will soon receive global ratification.

The Group of 77 and China is also pleased to note that the First Session of the Conference of Parties was held early this year in Germany and that the COP's subsidiary bodies were established in that meeting, and in fact, have started their work. The Group looks forward to a fruitful conclusion of the Berlin mandate process which is aimed at strengthening the Convention.

Mr. Chairman,

The Group of 77 recognizes the crucial importance of the implementation of the Convention on Climate Change. We remain fully committed to the objective of the Convention, and the fulfilment of our obligations. The urgency of addressing the adverse effects of climate change has been underscored by the recent findings of the Intergovernmental Panel on Climate Change which confirmed continued global warming and its disastrous effects, particularly on the developing countries. Action must be taken now on the basis of the principle of common but differentiated responsibilities.

The Group of 77 and China urges our partners from the developed world to remain firmly committed to the full implementation of the Convention. We urge them to fulfil their obligations under the Convention, particularly, the provision of new and additional resources and the transfer of environmentally sound technologies on preferential and concessional basis.

Mr. Chairman,

At their 19th Annual Meeting in September, the Ministers for Foreign Affairs of the member States of the Group of 77 and China called on the international community and the United Nations system to give special priority to the implementation of the Programme of Action for the Sustainable Development of Small Island Developing States.

The implementation of the Programme of Action needs the provision of adequate resources, facilitating the transfer of technologies, and promoting fair, equitable and non-discriminatory trading arrangements, capacity-building, and human resource development. In particular, the GEF should constitute an important channel of assistance to Small Island Developing States in responding to their special needs and vulnerabilities, in particular with regard to the potential effects of climate change and the preservation of the important biodiversity and marine assets that they contribute to the global environment.

Statement on Behalf of the Group of 77 and China by Mr. Katinda E. Kamando, Representative of the United Republic of Tanzania, in the Second Committee of the UN General Assembly on Agenda Item 98: (c) Protection of the Global Climate for the Present and Future Generations of Mankind; (e) Convention on Biological Diversity; (f) Implementation of the Outcome of the Global Conference, Sustainable Development of Small Islands Developing States (New York, 6 November 1997)

Mr. Chairman,

At the outset, on behalf of the Group of 77 and China, I would like to thank the Secretary-General for making available to the Committee documents A/52/413, A/52/441, and A/52/319.

I would also like to thank Mr. Michael Zemmit Cutjar for the introductory statement made yesterday, and Mr. Calistus Juma for the introductory statement made today.

Mr. Chairman,

As we are preparing for the Third Conference of Parties on the United Nations Framework Convention on Climate Change to be held in Kyoto, Japan, from 1 to 10 December 1997, most of the developing countries continue to be the most vulnerable to the adverse effects of climate change as a result of increased emissions of carbon dioxide, methane, and nitrous oxide gasses into the atmosphere.

The concentration of these greenhouse gasses into the atmosphere is a result of the activities of industrialized countries which continue to pursue their industrialization strategies in wanton disregard for the environment, leading to global warming of the planet causing extreme weather events, sea-level rise, increase in number and intensity of typhoons, and drought.

Mr. Chairman,

While there is no agreement on emissions reduction by countries in the North, it is unfair and, indeed, unacceptable that the developing countries which are struggling to attain decent standards of living should be asked to curtail their industrial activity and share in the efforts to reduce emissions so that the industrialized countries can continue with their unsustainable production and consumption patterns. In this context, the Group of 77 and China strongly maintains that in accordance with principles of common but differentiated responsibilities, developed countries must take the lead and not merely reduce emissions, but according to the Climate Change Convention, to modify longer-term trends in anthropogenic emissions, their production and consumption lifestyles.

Furthermore, the Group of 77 and China's proposal presented at the just-ended meeting of the Ad Hoc Group on the Berlin Mandate, that developed countries reduce emissions below 1990 levels of 7.5% by the year 2005, 15% by 2010, and 35% by the year 2020, is a realistic proposal and should be seriously considered if we are to preserve our globe for future generations.

Mr. Chairman,

The proposal by the Group of 77 and China is not a new invention. Under the Climate Change Convention, developed countries have agreed to take measures aimed at returning their greenhouse gas emissions to 1990 levels by the year 2000. This commitment was reiterated again at the First Session of the Conference of the Parties in 1995 whereby the international community recognized that stronger measures were needed to minimize the risk of climate change. In this regard, the Group of 77 and China maintains its call for meeting the targets for the reduction of greenhouse gasses by developed countries.

Mr. Chairman,

The Group of 77 and China attaches greater importance to the Convention on Biological Diversity and we are pleased to note that there is progress in the implementation of Agenda 21 through its focus on marine and coastal biodiversity, agricultural biological diversity, forest biological diversity, and inland waters. In this regard, the CBD is therefore an important instrument for translating international commitments into national action. For this to happen, there is a need to increase resources so that the needs of the developing countries can be addressed more adequately.

The Group of 77 and China is pleased to learn that negotiations for a protocol on biosafety have reached an advanced stage and are expected to be finalized in 1998. However, there is a need for the parties to the Convention to redouble their efforts so that negotiations are completed by next year.

Mr. Chairman,

The fourth meeting of the Conference of the Parties (COP-4) will be held in Bratislava, Slovakia, in May 1998. At the last COP, we requested parties to submit their national reports on the implementation of the Convention by 31 December 1997. Since national reports constitute an important element in the evaluation of the activities of the Convention, it is our hope, that parties will heed this appeal in order to have a fruitful fourth COP.

Mr. Chairman,

Scientific research plays a key role in the implementation of the CBD, especially in the work of the Subsidiary Body for Scientific, Technical and Technological Advice (SBSTTA) of the Convention. The Group of 77 and China is pleased to note that SBSTTA is exploring ways of enhancing its ability to mobilize the best available scientific knowledge for the implementation of the Convention's objectives. In this context, it is important that the COP strengthens its role in mobilizing scientific knowledge related to biological diversity and to make it available to the rest of the United Nations system.

Mr. Chairman,

For the Convention to succeed, it is important that adequate financial resources are provided to parties in a timely manner. In this context, we would like to urge donors to make adequate financial resources available to parties through the GEF and through other sources including from bilateral sources.

Mr. Chairman,

The report of the Secretary-General on the implementation of the outcome of the Global Conference on Sustainable Development of Small Island Developing States contained in document A/52/319 is illuminating on the progress made so far and the future programme of work. Indeed, we note with appreciation the positive developments attained in some of the priority areas of concern to these countries, in particular actions by the United Nations of supporting the system-wide implementation of the Programme of Action for the Sustainable Development of Small Island Developing States.

We welcome the outcome of the fifth session of the Commission on Sustainable Development and UNGASS on the recommendations to propel the implementation of the Programme of Action, especially undertaking a review of the outstanding chapters of the POA in 1998, scheduling a comprehensive review of the POA in 1999 and holding a special session of the General Assembly immediately preceding its fifty-fourth session.

We underscore the fact that considerable and strenuous efforts have been and are being made by these island states at the national and regional levels and these endeavours are not complemented and supplemented adequately by the international community consistent with the commitments undertaken in the outcome of the global conference to operationalize and implement the POA. It is, therefore, imperative for the bilateral and multilateral donor community to mobilize and provide adequate financial resources and technical assistance which enable the Small Island Developing States to address their special socio-economic development constraints more effectively.

Statement by Ambassador Bagher Asadi, Chairman of the Group of 77 (Islamic Republic of Iran), before the Second Committee of the General Assembly on Agenda Item 98(f): Protection of Global Climate for Present and Future Generations of Mankind (New York, 28 November 2001)

Mr. Chairman,

Speaking on behalf of the Group of 77 and China, let me express, first and foremost, our deep appreciation and gratitude to Mr. Michael Zammit Cutajar, distinguished Executive Secretary of the United Nations Framework Convention on Climate Change, for an excellent introductory statement, particularly with regard to the Marrakech Accords as well as the institutional linkages between the UNFCCC Secretariat and the United Nations and the status of the global climate change process. I should as well thank the Secretary-General for a good concise report.

Mr. Chairman,

This is a rather short statement. Having started with the question of institutional linkages between the UNFCCC and the United Nations let me add that these linkages have been functioning well and should continue as in the past. I am sure colleagues here concur with me on the importance of the institutional linkage and simultaneously appreciate the independent functioning of the Secretariat. Therefore, we support the continuation of the current institutional linkage and related administrative arrangements for a further five-year period, as proposed in the report and also contained in the draft resolution we intend to submit to the Committee.

Our meeting here today at the Second Committee takes place in the backdrop of a very important development in the global climate change process. This 10-year-old process has entered a new phase after the successful meeting in Bonn back in July and the COP-7 held just two weeks ago in Marrakech. With the historic achievements and agreements reached first in Bonn and then completed and sealed in Marrakech, the international community rose to the challenge of making the embattled Kyoto Protocol ratifiable before the Johannesburg Summit. This is indeed the best substantive—and if I may add, symbolic—contribution that the Kyoto Protocol process could have made to the Johannesburg Summit. What is expected now is to witness the expeditious ratification of the Kyoto Protocol by Annex I parties so that we would all go to Johannesburg with the Kyoto Protocol in force. In the wake of this historic development, it could be said now, with a sense of certitude and satisfaction, that the climate change process has got new blood in its veins. The Climate Change Convention in general and the Buenos Aires Plan of Action in particular now stand a real chance of effective implementation. Let us undertake, all of us, collectively, to make that a reality.

Mr. Chairman,

This is not the proper occasion for me to engage in an in-depth analysis of the substance of the agreements and decisions in Bonn and Marrakech. Instead, I merely suffice to assert that the Marrakech Accords, to some of which Michael referred, represent an overall balance, where concerns and interests of different quarters have been accommodated in a general sense. Equally important is that every effort was made to preserve the environmental integrity of this multilateral environmental agreement. Of course, one could always speculate on the contours of a perfect, ideal agreement that may exist on paper only and rarely, if ever, as the practical, tangible outcome of a multilateral negotiating process.

Apart from substance and speculation on what might or could have been, the long, tortuous process ending with the Marrakech Accords carries a very important lesson and message: multilateralism and international cooperation work. I believe recent negotiations on the Kyoto Protocol have renewed hope and optimism in the value of dialogue, understanding, engagement, and cooperation in addressing such global issues and problems as climate change and resolving seemingly intractable difficulties. And on a related note, as is generally acknowledged, the Bonn and Marrakech agreements could have hardly been achieved without the positive, constructive approach and contribution of the Group of 77 and China. Let me seize the opportunity right here to register my deep personal gratitude to the Group in its entirety for the trust, confidence, and support that made it possible for myself and my colleagues in the Chair's team to represent the Group and negotiate on its behalf. I should go on to add that the developing countries, who are the most vulnerable to the adverse effects of climate change, will continue their active and proactive engagement in the ongoing multilateral process in this field with the very clear objective of safeguarding and further promoting our genuine, long-term collective interests. All our negotiating partners can be assured of our commitment and engagement.

Mr. Chairman,

Let me conclude the statement on a note of special tribute to Michael Zammit Cutajar, for his invaluable service for a whole decade to the climate change process, the Convention, the Protocol, and the Secretariat. I find myself short of words to do justice to such an excellent record of dedication, experience, discretion, and selfless service. Let me thank him, on behalf of the whole Group, for all he has done and also for the fine legacy he leaves behind. Michael, let me wish you health, prosperity, success, and good luck.

Statement by Minister Counselor Marisol Black, Director for International Economic Affairs, Ministry of External Relations, on Behalf of the Group of 77 and China, on Agenda Item 87(c): Environment and Sustainable Development: Protection of Global Climate for Future Generations of Mankind (New York, 14 November 2002)

Mr. Chairman,

It is an honour to address the Committee on behalf of the Group of 77 and China on this important issue, as climate change is a common concern of humankind, as set out in the preamble to the United Nations Framework Convention on Climate Change. It represents a key factor to achieving the goal of sustainable development in developing countries, due to its linkage to economic, social, and environmental problems such as poverty, land degradation, access to water and food, as well as to human health, amongst others.

Ten years from the signing of the Convention at the Conference on Environment and Development, meeting the goals of stabilizing greenhouse gasses in the atmosphere and for developed countries to fulfil 1990 emissions by 5% in the period of 2008–2012, respectively, adopted in the Convention and in the subsequent Protocol adopted in Kyoto in 1997, continues to be a challenge. Meanwhile, atmospheric concentrations of CO_2 originating in developed countries have increased, whilst developing countries continue to be most affected by the adverse effects of climate change, particularly due to the economic and social consequences which we most face. The Group of 77 and China expresses its firm opposition to the discussion of new commitments for developing countries in the COP and reiterates its call to move ahead on adaptation measures, through the increase in financial and technical assistance for developing countries, particularly vulnerable to adverse effects of climate change.

In this regard, the Marrakech Accords, which made important inputs to the World Summit on Sustainable Development, recognize, amongst other things, that developing countries are the most vulnerable to climate change and underline the need for capacity creation, technical innovation in key sectors of development such as energy and cooperation, as well as for the establishment of synergies with other Conventions, such as the ones on Biodiversity and Desertification.

Recently, the Eighth Conference of Parties to the Convention on Climate Change, held at New Delhi, India, which country demonstrated unequalled hospitality that we would like to gratefully acknowledge, adopted the New Delhi Declaration on Climate Change and Sustainable Development, which reiterates the call for the fulfilment of all commitments and obligations derived from the Convention and its Protocol, amongst other aspects. The Group of 77 and China calls for the full consideration of this Declaration and for the fulfilment of all the common but differentiated responsibilities under the Convention and its Protocol, as set out in the Convention itself when it recognizes that developed countries must take the lead in the fight against climate change and its adverse effects.

The Group of 77 and China would also reiterate the call made by the Conference of Parties to the Global Environmental Facility, for the strengthening of the Facility in order to allow the three Funds created to help developing countries, i.e., The Special Fund for Climate Change, the Least Developed Countries' Fund, and the Adaptation Fund. These funds were created, *inter alia*, to support programmes and measures in the fields of adaptation, transfer of technology and energy management, to assist in the diversification of economies heavily dependent on the production, processing, and export of fossil fuels.

Finally, we call upon the Secretary-General to guarantee, within the UN budget, the Secretarial services for the meetings of the Conference of Parties.

(b) Draft Resolutions Initiated by the Group of 77 in the Second Committee of the United Nations General Assembly entitled "Environment and Sustainable Development: Protection of Global Climate for Present and Future Generations of Mankind"

Revised Draft Resolution A/C.2/47/L.38/Rev.1 of 18 November 1992 entitled: "Protection of Global Climate for Present and Future Generations of Mankind"

Pakistan*: revised draft resolution

Protection of global climate for present and future generations of mankind

The General Assembly,

Recalling its resolutions 43/53 of 6 December 1988 and 44/207 of 22 December 1989, in which it recognized climate change as a common concern of mankind,

Recalling also its resolutions 45/212 of 21 December 1990, by which it established an Intergovernmental Negotiating Committee to prepare an effective framework convention on climate change, and any related legal instruments as might be agreed upon, for signature during the United Nations Conference on Environment and Development, and 46/169 of 19 December 1991, by which it provided for the contribution of work on climate change until the end of 1992,

Taking note with appreciation of the reports of the Intergovernmental Negotiating Committee for a Framework Convention on Climate Change on its work thus far in 1992[1] and the report prepared by the Chairman of the Intergovernmental Negotiating Committee for a Framework Convention on Climate Change, on behalf of the Committee, for submission to the United Nations Conference on Environment and Development,[2]

Noting resolution 15 (EC-XLIV), adopted by the Executive Council of the World Meteorological Organization at its forty-fourth session,

Noting that, in accordance with paragraph 4 of its resolution 46/169 and pursuant to resolution INC/1992/1 adopted by the Intergovernmental Negotiating Committee on 9 May 1992, arrangements are being made for the sixth session of the Intergovernmental Negotiating Committee to be held as soon as practicable, preferably before the end of 1992,

Noting also that the sixth session of the Intergovernmental Negotiating Committee will be held at Geneva from 7 to 10 December 1992,

* On behalf of the States Members of the United Nations that are members of the Group of 77.

1 A/AC.237/18 (Part I) and A/AC.237/18 (Part II) and Add.1.

2 A/CONF.151/8.

Noting further that article 21 of the United Nations Framework Convention on Climate Change provides for the secretariat established by the General Assembly in resolution 45/212 to be the interim secretariat of the Convention until the completion of the first session of the Conference of the Parties to the Convention,

Noting with appreciation the support provided for the operation of the secretariat during 1992 by the United Nations Conference on Trade and Development, the United Nations Development Programme, the United Nations Environment Programme and the World Meteorological Organization, as well as by bilateral contributors,

Having considered the report of the Secretary-General,[3] with particular reference to the possible requirements for intergovernmental and secretariat work on the implementation of the Convention in the period up to and including the first session of the Conference of the Parties to the Convention,

1. *Welcomes* the adoption, on 9 May 1992, of the United Nations Framework Convention on Climate Change by the Intergovernmental Negotiating Committee for a Framework Convention on Climate Change and its signing by a large number of States;
2. *Considers* the Convention one of the achievements of the international community working through the United Nations and a first step in a cooperative response to the common concern for the adverse effects of climate change;
3. *Calls upon* States that have not done so to sign the Convention and to ratify, accept, approve or accede to it, so that it may enter into force;
4. *Invites* signatories of the Convention to communicate to the head of the interim secretariat of the Convention, as soon as feasible, information regarding measures consistent with the provisions of the Convention, pending its entry into force;
5. *Urges* States to support and contribute to the activities at the national, regional and international levels related to the basic scientific and technical needs specified in the Convention, including those activities carried out under the World Climate Programme and the Global Climate Observing System;
6. *Decides* that the Intergovernmental Negotiating Committee shall continue to function in order to prepare for the first session of the Conference of the Parties to the Convention, as specified in the Convention, and, in that context, to contribute to the effective operation of the interim arrangements set out in article 21 of the Convention;
7. *Invites* the Committee, in this regard, to draw up an adequate plan of preparatory work at its sixth session and to implement it expeditiously thereafter, and requests the Secretary-General to make arrangements for the Committee to hold sessions as needed, if possible avoiding scheduling conflicts with the General Assembly;

[3] A/47/466.

8. *Requests* the Intergovernmental Negotiating Committee to promote a coherent and coordinated programme of activities by competent bodies aimed at supporting the entry into force and effective implementation of the Convention and strengthening the capacities of developing and other countries to prepare for their participation in the Convention;
9. *Calls upon* the organs, organizations and bodies of the United Nations system involved in the work relating to climate change, including the interim secretariat of the Convention, to initiate and strengthen such activities, where possible in collaboration with each other, and invites them to make information on these activities and on any coordination arrangements regularly available to the Intergovernmental Negotiating Committee, through its secretariat;
10. *Invites* the Intergovernmental Negotiating Committee to convey information on its work to the General Assembly as well as to the Economic and Social Council and the Commission on Sustainable Development, as appropriate, in particular in the context of chapter 9 of Agenda 21;
11. *Requests* the Secretary-General, to strengthen the secretariat established by the General Assembly in resolution 45/212 so that it may function as the interim secretariat of the Convention until the completion of the first session of the Conference of the Parties and, in that capacity, provide adequate substantive support to the evolving work of the Intergovernmental Negotiating Committee, and further requests him to make provisions for this purpose within the current and forthcoming programme budgets and up to the first session of the Conference of the Parties to the Convention;
12. *Requests* United Nations programmes and agencies, particularly the United Nations Environment Programme and the World Meteorological Organization, to contribute staff to assist the head of the interim secretariat;
13. *Requests* bilateral sources to continue to assist the interim secretariat as hitherto;
14. *Requests* the head of the interim secretariat to maximize opportunities for collaborative work with other secretariat entities, including the secretariat of the Commission on Sustainable Development;
15. *Requests* the Secretary-General to maintain the special voluntary fund established under paragraph 10 of General Assembly resolution 45/212 to support the participation of developing countries, in particular the least developed among them, as well as small island developing countries, in the work of the Intergovernmental Negotiating Committee and in the first session of the Conference of the Parties to the Convention;
16. *Also requests* the Secretary-General to maintain the trust fund established under paragraph 20 of General Assembly resolution 45/212 to contribute to the costs of the interim secretariat of the Convention;

17. *Takes note with appreciation* of the contributions made to these extrabudgetary funds and appeals to present and new contributors to make adequate and timely contributions to both funds;
18. *Invites* the Chairman of the Intergovernmental Negotiating Committee for a Framework Convention on Climate Change to submit a final report to the General Assembly on behalf of the Committee, on the completion of the Committee's work, following the conclusion of the first session of the Conference of the Parties to the Convention;
19. *Requests* the Secretary-General to report to the General Assembly at its forty-ninth session on the implementation of the present resolution;
20. *Decides* to include in the provisional agenda of its forty-ninth session an item entitled "Protection of global climate for present and future generations."

Draft Resolution A/C.2/55/L.23 of 2 November 2000 entitled "Environment and Sustainable Development: Protection of Global Climate for Present and Future Generations of Mankind"

Nigeria:* draft resolution

Protection of global climate for present and future generations of mankind

The General Assembly,

Recalling its resolution 54/222 of 22 December 1999 as well as other resolutions relating to the protection of global climate for present and future generations of mankind,

Noting with appreciation that all Member States and one regional economic integration organization have ratified or acceded to the United Nations Framework Convention on Climate Change,[4]

Concerned that global greenhouse gas emissions have continued to grow at an alarming rate and that the adverse effects of climate change are impacting negatively at the global level,

Stressing the importance for all parties to the Convention to implement their respective commitments and recognizing that provision of financial resources, technology transfer and capacity-building are important prerequisites for developing country parties of fulfilling their obligations under the Convention, bearing in mind the principle of common but differentiated responsibilities,

Welcoming the convening of the sixth session of the Conference of the Parties to the United Nations Framework Convention on Climate Change in The Hague, the Netherlands, from 13 to 24 November 2000, and expressing its deep appreciation to the Government of the Netherlands for its generous offer to host the Conference of the Parties,

* On behalf of the States Members of the United Nations that are members of the Group of 77 and China.

[4] A/AC.237/18 (Part II)/Add.1 and Corr.1, annex I.

Expressing its deep appreciation for the generous offer of the Government of Morocco to host the seventh session of the Conference of the Parties in Marrakech,

Noting the preparatory process towards the sixth session of the Conference,

1. *Calls upon* all parties to the United Nations Framework Convention on Climate Change to intensify their efforts towards reaching a successful outcome of the sixth session of the Conference of the Parties to the Convention, including the consensus necessary for the timely entry into force of the Kyoto Protocol to the United Nations Framework Convention on Climate Change;[5]
2. *Urges* all parties to the Convention that have not yet ratified or acceded to the Kyoto Protocol to do so as soon as possible with a view to ensuring its early entry into force, bearing in mind the United Nations Millennium Declaration;[6]
3. *Invites* the Conference of the Parties at its seventh session to contribute to the preparation of the ten-year review of the implementation of Agenda 21[7] and the Programme for the Further Implementation of Agenda 21[8] and requests the Executive Secretary of the United Nations Framework Convention on Climate Change to report to the Commission on Sustainable Development at its tenth session to this end;
4. *Notes with satisfaction* the steps taken to strengthen cooperation among the United Nations Framework Convention on Climate Change, the Convention on Biological Diversity[9]
   and the United Nations Convention to Combat Desertification in those Countries Experiencing Serious Drought and/or Desertification, particularly in Africa;[10]
5. *Takes note* of decision 10/CP.5 of 4 November 1999 on capacity-building in developing-country parties,[11] to the United Nations Framework Convention on Climate Change Adopted by the Conference of the Parties to the Convention at its fifth session, and invites the Global Environment Facility as the financial mechanism of the Convention as well as relevant international organizations to implement the provisions of that decision and its annex;
6. *Encourages* the Global Environment Facility to undertake appropriate measures to simplify its project cycle in order to strengthen its activities in the area

[5] FCCP/CP/1997/7/Add.1, decision 1/CP.3, annex.

[6] General Assembly resolution 55/2.

[7] *Report of the United Nations Conference on Environment and Development, Rio de Janeiro, 3–14 June 1992*, vol. I, *Resolutions Adopted by the Conference* (United Nations publication, Sales No. E.93.I.8 and corrigendum), resolution 1, annex II.

[8] General Assembly resolution S-19/2, annex.

[9] See United Nations Environment Programme, *Convention on Biological Diversity* (Environmental Law and Institution Programme Activity Centre), June 1992.

[10] A/49/84/Add.2, annex; appendix II.

[11] See FCCC/CP/1999/6/Add.1.

of the transfer of environmentally sound technologies and adaptation, consistent with the priorities of developing-country parties;

7. *Requests* the Secretary-General to make the necessary provisions to include in the calendar of conferences and meetings for the biennium 2002–2003 those sessions of the Conference of the Parties and its subsidiary bodies that the Conference of the Parties may need to convene in that period;
8. *Recalls* its request to the States parties to the United Nations Framework Convention on Climate Change, in accordance with General Assembly decision 52/445 of 18 December 1997, that, beginning in 2000, the Conference of the Parties to the Convention should take all appropriate measures to avoid convening its sessions and those of its subsidiary bodies during the sessions of the Assembly;
9. *Requests* the Secretary-General to report to the General Assembly at its fifty-sixth session on the implementation of the present resolution and the Executive Secretary of the United Nations Framework Convention on Climate Change to report on the work of the Conference of the Parties to the Convention;
10. *Decides* to include in the provisional agenda of its fifty-sixth session the item entitled "Protection of global climate for present and future generations of mankind."

Draft Resolution A/C.2/57/L.43 of 18 November 2002 entitled "Environment and Sustainable Development: Protection of Global Climate for Present and Future Generations of Mankind"

Venezuela:* draft resolution

Protection of global climate for present and future generations of mankind

The General Assembly,

Recalling its resolution 54/222 of 22 December 1999, its decision 55/443 of 20 December 2000 and its resolution 56/199 of 21 December 2001 and other resolutions relating to the protection of the global climate for present and future generations of mankind,

Noting that most States and one regional economic integration organization have acceded to the United Nations Framework Convention on Climate Change,[12]

Reaffirming that economic and social development and poverty eradication are the first and foremost overriding priorities of developing countries,

Remaining deeply concerned that all countries, in particular developing countries, including the least developed countries and small island developing States, face increased risk from the adverse impacts of climate change,

* On behalf of the States Members of the United Nations that are members of the Group of 77 and China.

[12] United Nations, *Treaty Series*, vol. 1771, No. 30822.

Noting that, to date, the Kyoto Protocol to the United Nations Framework Convention on Climate Change[13] has attracted 97 ratifications,

Taking into account the Johannesburg Declaration on Sustainable Development[14] and the Plan of Implementation of the World Summit on Sustainable Development,[15]

Expressing its deep appreciation to the Government of India for hosting the eighth session of the Conference of Parties to the United Nations Framework Convention on Climate Change at New Delhi from 23 October to 1 November 2002,

Taking note of the report of the Executive Secretary of the United Nations Framework Convention on Climate Change,[16]

1. *Recalls* the United Nations Millennium Declaration,[17] in which heads of State and Government resolved to make every effort to ensure the entry into force of the Kyoto Protocol[1] to the United Nations Framework Convention on Climate Change,[2] preferably by the tenth anniversary of the United Nations Conference on Environment and Development in 2002, and to embark on the required reduction of emissions of greenhouse gases in accordance with the provisions of the Convention and the Kyoto Protocol thereto;
2. *Urges* Parties that have not already done so to ratify the Kyoto Protocol in a timely manner;
3. *Takes note* of the Delhi Ministerial Declaration on Climate Change and Sustainable Development, adopted by the Conference of the Parties at its eighth session;
4. *Calls upon* all States parties to continue to take effective steps to implement their commitments under the Convention, in accordance with the principle of common but differentiated responsibilities;
5. *Stresses* the importance of providing technical and financial assistance and capacity-building to developing countries and countries with economies in transition in accordance with commitments under the Convention, including the Marrakech Accords;[18]
6. *Emphasizes* that technology transfer should be strengthened, including through concrete projects and capacity-building in all relevant sectors, such as energy, transport, industry, health, agriculture, biodiversity, forestry and waste management. Technological advances should be promoted through research and development, economic diversification and strengthening of relevant regional, national and local institutions for sustainable development;
7. *Emphasizes also* that adaptation to the adverse effects of climate change is of high priority for all countries. Developing countries are particularly vulnerable,

[13] FCCC/CP/1997/7/Add.1, decision 1/CP.3

[14] *Report of the World Summit on Sustainable Development, Johannesburg, South Africa, 26 August–4 September 2002* (United Nations publication, Sales No.E.02.), chap. I, resolution 1, annex.

[15] Ibid., resolution 2, annex.

[16] See A/57/359.

[17] Resolution 55/2.

[18] See FCCC/CP/2001/13/Add.1.

especially the least developed countries and Small Island Developing States. Adaptation requires urgent attention and action on the part of all countries. Effective and results-based measures should be supported for the development of approaches at all levels on vulnerability and adaptation, as well as capacity-building for the integration of adaptation concerns into sustainable development strategies. The measures should include full implementation of existing commitments under the Convention and the Marrakech Accords;

8. *Requests* the Secretary-General to make provision for the session of the Conference of the Parties to the Convention and its subsidiary bodies in his proposal for the programme budget for the biennium 2004–2005;
9. *Invites* the Executive Secretary of the Convention to report in a timely manner to the General Assembly at its fifty-eighth session on the work of the Conference of the Parties to the Convention;
10. *Invites also* the conferences of the parties to the multilateral environmental conventions, when setting the dates of their meetings, to take into consideration the schedule of meetings of the General Assembly and the Commission on Sustainable Development so as to ensure the adequate representation of developing countries at those meetings;
11. *Decides* to include in the provisional agenda of its fifty-eighth session the sub-item entitled "Protection of global climate for present and future generations of mankind."

Draft Resolution A/C.2/62/L.12 of 31 October 2007 entitled "Sustainable Development: Protection of Global Climate for Present and Future Generations of Mankind"

Pakistan:* draft resolution

Protection of global climate for present and future generations of mankind

The General Assembly,

Recalling its resolution 54/222 of 22 December 1999, its decision 55/443 of 20 December 2000, its resolutions 56/199 of 21 December 2001, 57/257 of 20 December 2002, 58/243 of 23 December 2003, 59/234 of 22 December 2004, 60/197 of 22 December 2005 and 61/201 of 20 December 2006 and other resolutions relating to the protection of the global climate for present and future generations of mankind,

Recalling also the provisions of the United Nations Framework Convention on Climate Change,[19] including the acknowledgement that the global nature of climate change calls for the widest possible cooperation by all countries and their participation in an effective and appropriate international response, in accordance with their

* On behalf of the States Members of the United Nations that are members of the Group of 77 and China.

[19] United Nations, *Treaty Series*, vol. 1771, No. 30822.

common but differentiated responsibilities and respective capabilities and their social and economic conditions,

Recalling further the United Nations Millennium Declaration,[20] in which Heads of State and Government resolved to make every effort to ensure the entry into force of the Kyoto Protocol and to embark on the required reduction in emissions of greenhouse gases,[21]

Recalling the Johannesburg Declaration on Sustainable Development,[22] the Plan of Implementation of the World Summit on Sustainable Development ("Johannesburg Plan of Implementation"),[23] the Delhi Ministerial Declaration on Climate Change and Sustainable Development, adopted by the Conference of the Parties to the United Nations Framework Convention on Climate Change at its eighth session, held in New Delhi from 23 October to 1 November 2002,[24] the outcome of the ninth session of the Conference of the Parties, held in Milan, Italy, from 1 to 12 December 2003,[25] the outcome of the tenth session of the Conference of the Parties, held in Buenos Aires from 6 to 18 December 2004,[26] the outcome of the eleventh session of the Conference of the Parties and the first session of the Conference of the Parties serving as the Meeting of the Parties to the Kyoto Protocol, held in Montreal, Canada, from 28 November to 10 December 2005,[27] and the outcome of the twelfth session of the Conference of the Parties and the second session of the Conference of the Parties serving as the Meeting of the Parties to the Kyoto Protocol, held in Nairobi from 6 to 17 November 2006,[28]

Reaffirming the Programme of Action for the Sustainable Development of Small Island Developing States,[29] the Mauritius Declaration[30] and the Mauritius Strategy for the Further Implementation of the Programme of Action for the Sustainable Development of Small Island Developing States,[31]

Recalling the 2005 World Summit Outcome,[32]

Remaining deeply concerned that all countries, in particular developing countries, including the least developed countries and small island developing States,

[20] See resolution 55/2.

[21] Ibid., para. 23.

[22] *Report of the World Summit on Sustainable Development, Johannesburg, South Africa, 26 August–4 September 2002* (United Nations publication, Sales No. E.03.II.A.1 and corrigendum), chap. 1, resolution 1, annex.

[23] Ibid., resolution 2, annex.

[24] FCCC/CP/2002/7/Add.1, decision 1/CP.8.

[25] FCCC/CP/2003/6/Add.1 and 2.

[26] FCCC/CP/2004/10/Add.1 and 2.

[27] FCCC/CP/2005/5/Add.1.

[28] FCCC/CP/2006/5 and Add.1.

[29] *Report of the Global Conference on the Sustainable Development of Small Island Developing States, Bridgetown, Barbados, 25 April–6 May 1994* (United Nations publication, Sales No. E.94.I.18 and corrigenda), chap. I, resolution I, annex II.

[30] *Report of the International Meeting to Review the Implementation of the Programme of Action for the Sustainable Development of Small Island Developing States, Port Louis, Mauritius, 10–14 January 2005* (United Nations publication, Sales No. E.05.II.A.4 and corrigendum), chap. I, resolution 1, annex I.

[31] Ibid., annex II.

[32] See resolution 60/1.

face increased risks from the negative effects of climate change, and stressing the need to address adaptation needs relating to such effects,

Noting that one hundred and ninety-one States and one regional economic integration organization have ratified the Convention,

Noting also that, to date, the Kyoto Protocol to the United Nations Framework Convention on Climate Change[33] has attracted one hundred and seventy-five ratifications, including from parties mentioned in annex I to the Convention, which account for 61.6 per cent of emissions,

Noting further the work of the Intergovernmental Panel on Climate Change and the need to build and enhance scientific and technological capabilities, inter alia, through continuing support to the Panel for the exchange of scientific data and information, especially in developing countries, and noting the significance of the release of the fourth assessment report,

Noting with appreciation the convening of the high-level thematic debate by the President of the sixty-first session of the General Assembly, from 31 July to 2 August 2007, as well as the initiative of the Secretary-General to convene the high-level event on climate change on 24 September 2007,

Reaffirming its commitment to the ultimate objective of the Convention, namely, to stabilize greenhouse gas concentrations in the atmosphere at a level that prevents dangerous anthropogenic interference with the climate system,

Taking note of the report of the Executive Secretary of the United Nations Framework Convention on Climate Change,[34]

1. *Stresses* that the seriousness of climate change calls for the implementation of the provisions of the United Nations Framework Convention on Climate Change and calls upon States to work cooperatively towards achieving the ultimate objective of the Framework Convention;
2. *Welcomes* the entry into force of the Kyoto Protocol on 16 February 2005 and strongly urges the States that have not yet done so to ratify it in a timely manner;
3. *Takes note* of the outcomes of the eleventh and twelfth sessions of the Conference of the Parties to the Framework Convention and the first and second sessions of the Conference of the Parties serving as the Meeting of the Parties to the Kyoto Protocol;[9,10]
4. *Takes note with appreciation* of the offer of the Government of Indonesia to host the thirteenth session of the Conference of the Parties and the third session of the Meeting of the Parties to the Kyoto Protocol, to be held in Bali from 3 to 14 December 2007, and looks forward to a successful outcome;
5. *Recognizes* that climate change poses serious risks and challenges to all countries, particularly to developing countries, especially least developed

[33] FCCC/CP/1997/7/Add.1, decision 1/CP.3, annex.
[34] A/62/276, annex I.

countries, landlocked developing countries, small island developing States, countries in Africa and disaster-prone developing countries, demands urgent global action to address climate change in accordance with the principles identified in the Convention, in particular the principle of common but differentiated responsibilities, and in this regard, urges all countries to fully implement their commitments under the Convention framework, to take effective and concrete actions and measures at all levels, and to enhance international cooperation in the framework of the Convention;

6. *Also recognizes* the need to ensure financial and technical resources, as well as capacity-building, access to and transfer of technologies, to assist those developing countries adversely affected by climate change;
7. *Reaffirms* that efforts to address climate change in a manner that enhances and ensures the sustainable development and sustained economic growth of the developing countries and the universal elimination of poverty should promote the integration of all three components of sustainable development, namely, economic development, social development and environmental protection, as interdependent and mutually reinforcing pillars, in an integrated, coordinated and balanced manner;
8. *Calls upon* the donor community to fulfil the commitments made during the fourth replenishment of the Global Environment Facility and urges the developed countries to allocate additional financial resources to the Global Environment Facility at its fifth replenishment;
9. *Notes* the ongoing work of the liaison group of the secretariats and offices of the relevant subsidiary bodies of the Framework Convention, the United Nations Convention to Combat Desertification in Those Countries Experiencing Serious Drought and/or Desertification, Particularly in Africa,[35] and the Convention on Biological Diversity,[36] and encourages cooperation to promote complementarities among the three secretariats while respecting their independent legal status;
10. *Requests* the Secretary-General to make provisions for the sessions of the Conference of the Parties to the United Nations Framework Convention on Climate Change and its subsidiary bodies in his proposal for the programme budget for the biennium 2008–2009;
11. *Endorses* the continuation of the institutional linkage between the secretariat of the Framework Convention and the United Nations until such time as a review is deemed necessary by the Conference of the Parties or the General Assembly;
12. *Invites* the conferences of the parties to the multilateral environmental conventions, when setting the dates of their meetings, to take into consideration the schedule of meetings of the General Assembly and the Commission

[35] United Nations, *Treaty Series*, vol. 1954, No. 33480.
[36] Ibid., vol. 1760, No. 30619.

on Sustainable Development so as to ensure the adequate representation of developing countries at those meetings;

13. *Invites* the Secretary-General to report to the General Assembly at its sixty-third session on the work of the United Nations Framework Convention on Climate Change and the Conference of the Parties;
14. *Decides* to include in the provisional agenda of its sixty-third session the sub-item entitled "Protection of global climate for present and future generations of mankind."

Draft Resolution A/C.2/64/L.39 of 16 November 2009 entitled "Sustainable Development: Protection of Global Climate for Present and Future Generations"

Sudan:* draft resolution

Protection of global climate for present and future generations

The General Assembly,

Recalling its resolutions 43/53 of 6 December 1988, 54/222 of 22 December 1999, 62/86 of 10 December 2007 and 63/32 of 26 November 2008 and other resolutions and decisions relating to the protection of the global climate for present and future generations of mankind,

Recalling also the provisions of the United Nations Framework Convention on Climate Change,[37] including the acknowledgement that the global nature of climate change calls for the widest possible cooperation by all countries and their participation in an effective and appropriate international response, in accordance with their common but differentiated responsibilities and respective capabilities and their social and economic conditions,

Noting that the largest share of historical and current global emissions of greenhouse gases has originated in developed countries, that per capita emissions in developing countries are still relatively low and that the share of global emissions originating in developing countries will grow to meet their social and development needs,

Recalling the United Nations Millennium Declaration,[38] in which Heads of State and Government resolved to make every effort to ensure the entry into force of the Kyoto Protocol and to embark on the required reduction in emissions of greenhouse gases,[39]

Recalling also the Johannesburg Declaration on Sustainable Development,[40] the Plan of Implementation of the World Summit on Sustainable Development

* On behalf of the States Members of the United Nations that are members of the Group of 77 and China.

[37] United Nations, *Treaty Series*, vol. 1771, No. 30822.

[38] See resolution 55/2.

[39] Ibid., para. 23.

[40] *Report of the World Summit on Sustainable Development, Johannesburg, South Africa, 26 August–4 September 2002* (United Nations publication, Sales No. E.03.II.A.1 and corrigendum), chap. I, resolution 1, annex.

("Johannesburg Plan of Implementation"),[41] the outcome of the thirteenth session of the Conference of the Parties to the Convention and the third session of the Conference of the Parties serving as the Meeting of the Parties to the Kyoto Protocol, held in Bali, Indonesia, from 3 to 15 December 2007,[42] the outcome of the fourteenth session of the Conference of the Parties to the Convention and the fourth session of the Conference of the Parties serving as the Meeting of the Parties to the Kyoto Protocol, held in Poznan, Poland, from 1 to 12 December 2008,[43] and the outcomes of all previous sessions,

Reaffirming the Programme of Action for the Sustainable Development of Small Island Developing States,[44] the Mauritius Declaration[45] and the Mauritius Strategy for the Further Implementation of the Programme of Action for the Sustainable Development of Small Island Developing States,[46]

Recalling the 2005 World Summit Outcome,[47]

Remaining deeply concerned that all developing countries, including the least developed countries, landlocked developing countries, small island developing States, countries in Africa and other developing countries, face increased risks from the adverse effects of climate change, and stressing the need to address adaptation needs relating to such effects,

Noting that, to date, there are one hundred and ninety-two parties to the Convention, including one hundred and ninety-one States and one regional economic integration organization,

Noting also that, currently, the Kyoto Protocol to the United Nations Framework Convention on Climate Change[48] has attracted one hundred and eighty-four ratifications, accessions, acceptances or approvals, including by thirty-nine parties included in annex I to the Convention,

Noting further the amendment to annex B to the Kyoto Protocol,[49]

Noting the work of the Intergovernmental Panel on Climate Change and the need to build and enhance scientific and technological capabilities, *inter alia,* through continuing support to the Panel for the exchange of scientific data and information, especially in developing countries,

Noting also the significance of the scientific findings of the fourth assessment report of the Intergovernmental Panel on Climate Change, providing an integrated scientific, technical and socio-economic perspective on relevant issues and

[41] Ibid., resolution 2, annex.

[42] FCCC/CP/2007/6/Add.1 and 2 and FCCC/KP/CMP/2007/9/Add.1 and 2.

[43] FCCC/CP/2008/7 and Add.1 and FCCC/KP/CMP/2008/11 and Add.1 and 2.

[44] *Report of the Global Conference on the Sustainable Development of Small Island Developing States, Bridgetown, Barbados, 25 April–6 May 1994* (United Nations publication, Sales No. E.94.I.18 and corrigenda), chap. I, resolution 1, annex II.

[45] *Report of the International Meeting to Review the Implementation of the Programme of Action for the Sustainable Development of Small Island Developing States, Port Louis, Mauritius, 10–14 January 2005* (United Nations publication, Sales No. E.05.II.A.4 and corrigendum), chap. I, resolution 1, annex I.

[46] Ibid., annex II.

[47] See resolution 60/1.

[48] United Nations, *Treaty Series*, vol. 2303, No. 30822.

[49] FCCC/KP/CMP/2006/10/Add.1, decision 10/CMP.2.

contributing positively to the discussions under the Convention and the understanding of the phenomenon of climate change, including its impacts and risks,

Reaffirming that economic and social development and poverty eradication are global priorities,

Recognizing that deep cuts in global emissions will be required to achieve the ultimate objective of the Convention,

Reaffirming its commitment to the ultimate objective of the Convention, namely, to stabilize greenhouse gas concentrations in the atmosphere at a level that prevents dangerous anthropogenic interference with the climate system, and reaffirming that such a level should be achieved within a time frame sufficient to allow ecosystems to adapt naturally to climate change, to ensure that food production is not threatened and to enable economic development to proceed in a sustainable manner,

Taking note of the initiative of the Secretary-General in convening a Summit on Climate Change on 22 September 2009,

Taking note of the holding of the third World Climate Conference at Geneva from 31 August to 4 September 2009, and the holding by the Government of Indonesia of the World Ocean Conference at Manado from 11 to 15 May 2009,

Acknowledging women as key actors in the efforts towards sustainable development, and recognizing that a gender perspective can contribute to efforts to address climate change,

Taking note of the note by the Secretary-General transmitting the report of the Executive Secretary of the United Nations Framework Convention on Climate Change,

1. *Stresses* the seriousness of climate change, and calls upon States to work cooperatively towards achieving the ultimate objective of the United Nations Framework Convention on Climate Change[1] through the urgent implementation of its provisions;
2. *Notes* that States that have ratified the Kyoto Protocol to the United Nations Framework Convention on Climate Change[1] welcome the entry into force of the Protocol on 16 February 2005 and strongly urge States that have not yet done so to ratify it in a timely manner;
3. *Takes note of the outcome* of the fourteenth session of the Conference of the Parties to the Convention and the fourth session of the Conference of the Parties serving as the Meeting of the Parties to the Kyoto Protocol, hosted by the Government of Poland from 1 to 12 December 2008;[1]
4. *Calls* for urgent global action to address climate change in accordance with the principle of common but differentiated responsibilities;
5. *Also calls for* the expeditious completion of the ongoing parallel work of the Ad Hoc Working Group on Further Commitments for Annex I Parties under the Kyoto Protocol and the Ad Hoc Working Group on Long-term Cooperative Action under the Convention towards reaching an ambitious and equitable agreed outcome under the Ad Hoc Working Group on Long-term Cooperative Action and adopting an amendment to annex B to the

Kyoto Protocol for subsequent commitment periods that reflects ambitious and enhanced commitments for annex I countries;

6. *Urges* developed countries to undertake ambitious and enhanced commitments under the Kyoto Protocol in subsequent commitment periods, and also urges the international community, as part of its commitments to developing countries, to address the consequences of climate change, in particular through new, additional and predictable financial resources, capacity-building and access to and transfer of technology;
7. *Takes note with appreciation* of the offer of the Government of Denmark to host the fifteenth session of the Conference of the Parties and the fifth session of the Meeting of the Parties to the Kyoto Protocol, to be held in Copenhagen from 7 to 18 December 2009;
8. *Also takes note with appreciation*, in this regard, of the offer of the Government of Mexico to host the sixteenth session of the Conference of the Parties and the sixth session of the Meeting of the Parties to the Kyoto Protocol, to be held in Mexico City in 2010;[50]
9. *Urges* parties to the Convention, and invites parties to the Kyoto Protocol, to continue to make use of the information contained in the fourth assessment report of the Intergovernmental Panel on Climate Change in their work;
10. *Recognizes* that climate change poses serious risks and challenges to all countries, particularly to developing countries, especially the least developed countries, landlocked developing countries, small island developing States and countries in Africa, including those that are particularly vulnerable to the adverse effects of climate change, and calls upon States to take urgent global action to address climate change in accordance with the principles identified in the Convention, including the principle of common but differentiated responsibilities and respective capabilities, and, in this regard, urges all countries to fully implement their commitments under the Convention, to take effective and concrete actions and measures at all levels, and to enhance international cooperation in the framework of the Convention;
11. *Reaffirms* that efforts to address climate change in a manner that enhances the sustainable development and sustained economic growth of the developing countries and the eradication of poverty should be carried out through promoting the integration of the three components of sustainable development, namely, economic development, social development and environmental protection, as interdependent and mutually reinforcing pillars, in an integrated, coordinated and balanced manner;
12. *Recognizes* the urgency of providing new, additional and predictable financial and technical resources, as well as capacity-building and access to and transfer of technology, to assist those developing countries adversely affected by climate change;

[50] Dates to be confirmed.

13. *Takes note* of the High-Level Conference on Climate Change: Technology Development and Transfer, held in New Delhi on 22 and 23 October 2009;
14. *Calls upon* the international community to fulfil the commitments made during the fifth replenishment of the Global Environment Facility Trust Fund, without prejudice to ongoing discussions on financial mechanisms under the Convention;
15. *Calls upon* all annex I countries to fulfil their financial obligations under the Convention and the Kyoto Protocol;
16. *Requests* the Secretary-General to make provisions for the sessions of the Conference of the Parties to the Convention and its subsidiary bodies in his proposal for the programme budget for the biennium 2010–2011;
17. *Notes* the ongoing work of the liaison group of the secretariats and offices of the relevant subsidiary bodies of the Framework Convention, the United Nations Convention to Combat Desertification in Those Countries Experiencing Serious Drought and/or Desertification, Particularly in Africa,[51] and the Convention on Biological Diversity,[52] and encourages cooperation to promote complementarities among the three secretariats while respecting their independent legal status;
18. *Invites* the conferences of the parties to the multilateral environmental conventions, when setting the dates of their meetings, to take into consideration the schedule of meetings of the General Assembly and the Commission on Sustainable Development so as to ensure the adequate representation of developing countries at those meetings;
19. *Invites* the secretariat of the Framework Convention to report, through the Secretary-General, to the General Assembly at its sixty-fifth session on the work of the Conference of the Parties;
20. *Decides* to include in the provisional agenda of its sixty-fifth session the sub-item entitled "Protection of global climate for present and future generations of humankind."

Draft Resolution A/C.2/65/L.33 of 8 November 2010 entitled "Sustainable Development: Protection of Global Climate for Present and Future Generations of Humankind"

Yemen:[*] draft resolution

Protection of global climate for present and future generations of humankind

The General Assembly,

Recalling its resolutions 43/53 of 6 December 1988, 54/222 of 22 December 1999, 62/86 of 10 December 2007, 63/32 of 26 November 2008 and 64/73 of 7 December

[51] United Nations, *Treaty Series*, vol. 1954, No. 33480.
[52] Ibid., vol. 1760, No. 30619.
[*] On behalf of the States Members of the United Nations that are members of the Group of 77 and China.

2009 and resolutions and decisions relating to the protection of the global climate for present and future generations of mankind,

Recalling also the provisions of the United Nations Framework Convention on Climate Change,[53] including the acknowledgement that the global nature of climate change calls for the widest possible cooperation by all countries and their participation in an effective and appropriate international response, in accordance with their common but differentiated responsibilities and respective capabilities and their social and economic conditions,

Recalling further the United Nations Millennium Declaration,[54] in which Heads of State and Government resolved to make every effort to ensure the entry into force of the Kyoto Protocol to the United Nations Framework Convention on Climate Change[55] and to embark on the required reduction in emissions of greenhouse gases,

Recalling the Johannesburg Declaration on Sustainable Development[56] and the Plan of Implementation of the World Summit on Sustainable Development ("Johannesburg Plan of Implementation"),[57]

Recalling also the 2005 World Summit Outcome,[58]

Recalling further the 2010 High-level Plenary meeting of the sixty-fifth session of the General Assembly on the Millennium Development Goals and its outcome,

Recalling the outcome of the thirteenth session of the Conference of the Parties to the Convention and the third session of the Conference of the Parties serving as the Meeting of the Parties to the Kyoto Protocol, held in Bali, Indonesia, from 3 to 15 December 2007,[59]

Reaffirming the Programme of Action for the Sustainable Development of Small Island Developing States,[60] the Mauritius Declaration[61] and the Mauritius Strategy for the Further Implementation of the Programme of Action for the Sustainable Development of Small Island Developing States,[62]

Remaining deeply concerned that all countries, in particular developing countries, including the least developed countries, landlocked developing countries, small island developing States and countries in Africa, face increased risks from

[53] United Nations, *Treaty Series*, vol. 1771, No. 30822.

[54] See resolution 55/2.

[55] United Nations, *Treaty Series*, vol. 2303, No. 30822.

[56] *Report of the World Summit on Sustainable Development, Johannesburg, South Africa, 26 August–4 September 2002* (United Nations publications, Sales No. E.03.II.A.1 and corrigendum), chap. I, resolution 1, annex.

[57] Ibid., resolution 2, annex.

[58] See resolution 60/1.

[59] FCCC/CP/2007/6/Add.1 and 2 and FCCC/KP/CMP/2007/9/Add.1 and 2.

[60] *Report of the Global Conference on the Sustainable Development of Small Island Developing States, Bridgetown, Barbados, 25 April–6 May 1994* (United Nations publication, Sales No. E.94.I.18 and corrigenda), chap. I, resolution 1, annex II.

[61] *Report of the International Meeting to Review the Implementation of the Programme of Action for the Sustainable Development of Small Island Developing States, Port Louis, Mauritius, 10–14 January 2005* (United Nations publication, Sales No. E.05.II.A.4 and corrigendum), chap. I, resolution 1, annex I.

[62] Ibid., annex II.

the adverse effects of climate change, and stressing the need to address adaptation needs relating to such effects,

Recognizing that low-lying and other small island countries, countries with low-lying coastal, arid and semi-arid areas or areas liable to floods, drought and desertification, and developing countries with fragile mountainous ecosystems are particularly vulnerable to the adverse effects of climate change,

Noting that, to date, there are one hundred and ninety-four parties to the Convention, including one hundred and ninety-three States and one regional economic integration organization,

Noting also that, currently, the Kyoto Protocol has attracted one hundred and ninety ratifications, accessions, acceptances or approvals, including by thirty-nine parties included in annex I to the Convention,

Noting further the amendment to annex B to the Kyoto Protocol,[63]

Noting the work of the Intergovernmental Panel on Climate Change and the need to build and enhance scientific and technological capabilities, inter alia, through continuing support to the Panel for the exchange of scientific data and information, especially in developing countries,

Noting also the significance of the scientific findings of the fourth assessment report of the Intergovernmental Panel on Climate Change, providing an integrated scientific, technical and socio-economic perspective on relevant issues and contributing positively to the discussions under the Convention and the understanding of the phenomenon of climate change, including its impacts and risks,

Reaffirming that economic and social development and poverty eradication are global priorities,

Recognizing that deep cuts in global emissions will be required to achieve the ultimate objective of the Convention,

Reaffirming its commitment to the ultimate objective of the Convention, namely, to stabilize greenhouse gas concentrations in the atmosphere at a level that prevents dangerous anthropogenic interference with the climate system, and also reaffirming that such a level should be achieved within a time frame sufficient to allow ecosystems to adapt naturally to climate change, to ensure that food production is not threatened and to enable economic development to proceed in a sustainable manner,

Reaffirming the financial obligations of developed country parties and other developed parties included in annex II under the Convention and the Kyoto Protocol,

Acknowledging women as key actors in the efforts towards sustainable development, and recognizing that a gender perspective can contribute to efforts to address climate change,

[63] FCCC/CMP/2006/10/Add.1, decision 10/CMP.2.

Taking note of the note by the Secretary-General transmitting the report of the Executive Secretary of the United Nations Framework Convention on Climate Change,[64]

1. *Recognizes* the urgency to address the challenge of climate change, and calls upon States to work cooperatively towards achieving the ultimate objective of the United Nations Framework Convention on Climate Change through the urgent implementation of its provisions;
2. *Notes* that States that have ratified the Kyoto Protocol to the United Nations Framework Convention on Climate Change[3] welcome the entry into force of the Protocol on 16 February 2005 and strongly urge States that have not yet done so to ratify it in a timely manner;
3. *Takes note* of the outcome of the fifteenth session of the Conference of the Parties to the Convention and the fifth session of the Conference of the Parties serving as the Meeting of the Parties to the Kyoto Protocol, hosted by the Government of Denmark from 6 to 18 December 2009;[65]
4. *Takes note with appreciation* of the offer of the Government of Mexico to host the sixteenth session of the Conference of the Parties to the Convention and the sixth session of the Conference of the Parties serving as the Meeting of the Parties to the Kyoto Protocol, to be held in Cancun, Mexico, from 29 November to 10 December 2010;
5. *Notes* the ongoing parallel work of the Ad Hoc Working Group on Long-term Cooperative Action under the Convention and the Ad Hoc Working Group on Further Commitments for Annex I Parties under the Kyoto Protocol, and that the respective parties to the Convention and the Kyoto Protocol call for an early completion of this work in accordance with their respective mandates and ensuring in particular that there is no gap between the first and the second commitment periods under the Kyoto Protocol;
6. *Encourages* Member States to approach Cancun with ambition, optimism and determination, with a view to achieving a substantive and ambitious outcome at the Conference of the Parties to the Convention and the Conference of Parties serving as the Meeting of the Parties to the Kyoto Protocol in accordance with the principles and objectives of the Convention and the Kyoto Protocol;
7. *Takes note with appreciation*, in this regard, of the offer of the Government of South Africa to host the seventeenth session of the Conference of the Parties to the Convention and the seventh session of the Conference of Parties serving as the Meeting of the Parties to the Kyoto Protocol, to be held in 2011;
8. *Urges* parties to the Convention, and invites parties to the Kyoto Protocol to the Convention, to continue to make use of the information contained in the

[64] See A/65/294, chap. I.
[65] FCCC/CP/2009/11/Add.1 and FCCC/KP/CMP/2009/21 and Add.1.

fourth assessment report of the Intergovernmental Panel on Climate Change in their work;

9. *Recognizes* that climate change poses serious risks and challenges to all countries, particularly developing countries, especially the least developed countries, landlocked developing countries, small island developing States and countries in Africa, including those that are particularly vulnerable to the adverse effects of climate change, and calls upon States to take urgent global action to address climate change in accordance with the principles identified in the Convention, including the principle of common but differentiated responsibilities and respective capabilities, and in this regard urges all countries to fully implement their commitments under the Convention, to take effective and concrete actions and measures at all levels and to enhance international cooperation in the framework of the Convention;
10. *Reaffirms* that efforts to address climate change in a manner that enhances the sustainable development and sustained economic growth of the developing countries and the eradication of poverty should be carried out by promoting the integration of the three components of sustainable development, namely, economic development, social development and environmental protection, as interdependent and mutually reinforcing pillars, in an integrated, coordinated and balanced manner;
11. *Recognizes* the urgent need to provide further support in the implementation of the Convention and its Kyoto Protocol;
12. *Recognizes further* the urgency of providing financial and technical resources, as well as capacity-building and access to and transfer of technology, to assist those developing countries adversely affected by climate change;
13. *Notes* the ongoing work of the liaison group of the secretariats and offices of the relevant subsidiary bodies of the Framework Convention, the United Nations Convention to Combat Desertification in Those Countries Experiencing Serious Drought and/or Desertification, Particularly in Africa,[66] and the Convention on Biological Diversity,[67] and encourages close cooperation to promote complementarities among the three secretariats while respecting their independent legal status;
14. *Invites* the conferences of the parties to the multilateral environmental conventions, when setting the dates of their meetings, to take into consideration the schedule of meetings of the General Assembly and the Commission on Sustainable Development so as to ensure the adequate representation of developing countries at those meetings;
15. *Invites* the secretariat of the Framework Convention to report, through the Secretary-General, to the General Assembly at its sixty-sixth session on the work of the Conference of the Parties;

[66] United Nations, *Treaty Series*, vol. 1954, No. 33480.
[67] Ibid., vol. 1760, No. 30619.

16. *Decides* to include in the provisional agenda of its sixty-sixth session the sub-item entitled "Protection of global climate for present and future generations of humankind."

Draft Resolution A/C.2/67/L.20 of 25 October 2012 entitled "Sustainable Development: Protection of Global Climate for Present and Future Generations of Humankind"

Algeria:* draft resolution
Protection of global climate for present and future generations of humankind
The General Assembly,

Recalling its resolutions 43/53 of 6 December 1988, 54/222 of 22 December 1999, 62/86 of 10 December 2007, 63/32 of 26 November 2008, 64/73 of 7 December 2009 and 66/200 of 22 December 2011 and other resolutions and decisions relating to the protection of the global climate for present and future generations of humankind,

Recalling also the principles and provisions of the United Nations Framework Convention on Climate Change,[68] including the acknowledgement that the global nature of climate change calls for the widest possible cooperation by all countries and their participation in an effective and appropriate international response, with a view to accelerating the reduction of global greenhouse gas emissions, on the basis of equity and in accordance with their common but differentiated responsibilities and respective capabilities,

Recalling further the United Nations Millennium Declaration,[69] the Johannesburg Declaration on Sustainable Development[70] and the Plan of Implementation of the World Summit on Sustainable Development ("Johannesburg Plan of Implementation"),[71] the 2005 World Summit Outcome,[72] the outcome of the thirteenth session of the Conference of the Parties to the United Nations Framework Convention and of the third session of the Conference of the Parties serving as the Meeting of the Parties to the Kyoto Protocol, held in Bali, Indonesia, from 3 to 15 December 2007,[73] and the outcomes of all the sessions, the Programme of Action for the Sustainable Development of Small Island Developing States,[74] the Mauritius

* On behalf of the States Members of the United Nations that are members of the Group of 77 and China.

68 United Nations, *Treaty Series*, vol. 1771, No. 30822.

69 Resolution 55/2.

70 *Report of the World Summit on Sustainable Development, Johannesburg, South Africa, 26 August–4 September 2002* (United Nations publication, Sales No. E.03.II.A.1 and corrigendum), chap. I, resolution 1, annex.

71 Ibid., resolution 2, annex.

72 Resolution 60/1.

73 FCCC/CP/2007/6/Add.1 and 2 and FCCC/KP/CMP/2007/9/Add.1 and 2.

74 *Report of the Global Conference on the Sustainable Development of Small Island Developing States, Bridgetown, Barbados, 25 April–6 May 1994* (United Nations publication, Sales No. E.94.I.18 and corrigenda), chap. I, resolution 1, annex II.

Declaration[75] and the Mauritius Strategy for the Further Implementation of the Programme of Action for the Sustainable Development of Small Island Developing States,[76] the political declaration on Africa's development needs[77] and the New Partnership for Africa's Development[78] and the Programme of Action for the Least Developed Countries for the Decade 2011–2020, adopted at the Fourth United Nations Conference on the Least Developed Countries, held in Istanbul, Turkey, from 9 to 13 May 2011,[79]

Recalling the outcome document of the United Nations Conference on Sustainable Development of 2012, entitled "The future we want,"[80]

Reaffirming its commitment to the ultimate objective of the Convention, namely, to stabilize greenhouse gas concentrations in the atmosphere at a level that prevents dangerous anthropogenic interference with the climate system, and also reaffirming that such a level should be achieved within a time frame sufficient to allow ecosystems to adapt naturally to climate change, to ensure that food production is not threatened and to enable economic development to proceed in a sustainable manner,

Reaffirming the financial obligations of developed country parties and other developed parties included in annex II to the Convention under the Convention and the Kyoto Protocol,

1. *Takes note* of the outcome of the seventeenth session of the Conference of the Parties to the United Nations Framework Convention on Climate Change and of the seventh session of the Conference of the Parties serving as the Meeting of the Parties to the Kyoto Protocol, hosted in Durban, South Africa, by the Government of South Africa from 28 November to 11 December 2011;[81]
2. *Recognizes* the need to build on the existing political momentum with a view to achieving the ultimate objective of the Convention through the urgent implementation of its provisions;
3. *Takes note* of the report of the Executive Secretary of the United Nations Framework Convention on Climate Change on the United Nations Climate Change Conference in Durban and its follow-up;[82]
4. *Reaffirms* that the United Nations Framework Convention on Climate Change is the primary international, intergovernmental forum for negotiating the global response to climate change;

[75] *Report of the International Meeting to Review the Implementation of the Programme of Action for the Sustainable Development of Small Island Developing States, Port Louis, Mauritius, 10–14 January 2005* (United Nations publication, Sales No. E.05.II.A.4 and corrigendum), chap. I, resolution 1, annex I.

[76] Ibid., annex II.

[77] Resolution 63/1.

[78] Resolution 57/2.

[79] *Report of the Fourth United Nations Conference on the Least Developed Countries, Istanbul, Turkey, 9–13 May 2011* (United Nations publication, Sales No. 11.II.A.1), chap. II.

[80] Resolution 66/288, annex.

[81] FCCC/CP/2011/9/Add.1 and 2 and FCCC/KP/CMP/2011/10/Add.1 and 2.

[82] A/67/295, sect. I.

5. *Stresses* that the international community, particularly the developed countries, given their historical responsibility, needs to take the lead in addressing this challenge within the United Nations Framework Convention on Climate Change and in accordance with its principles and provisions, in particular the principles of equity and common but differentiated responsibilities and respective capabilities, and provide financial and technological support to developing countries;
6. *Underlines* the importance of achieving an ambitious, substantive, holistic and balanced outcome through the ongoing negotiations at the Conference of the Parties to the Convention and the Meeting of the Parties to the Kyoto Protocol;
7. *Notes with appreciation* that the Government of Qatar will host the eighteenth session of the Conference of the Parties to the Convention and the eighth session of the Conference of the Parties serving as the Meeting of the Parties to the Kyoto Protocol in Doha from 26 November to 7 December 2012;
8. *Encourages* Member States to approach the United Nations Climate Change Conference in Doha with optimism and determination, with a view to achieving the full implementation of the outcome of the Conference held in Durban;
9. *Emphasizes* that a legally binding second commitment period under the Kyoto Protocol is critical and must be the key deliverable of the United Nations Climate Change Conference in Doha, and that its goals must be ambitious in terms of emission reductions and that it shall begin on 1 January 2013 in order to avoid any gap between the first and the second commitment periods;
10. *Reaffirms* the need to reach a successful and comprehensive outcome at the United Nations Conference on Climate Change in Doha, and stresses the importance of the full implementation of the delicate package endorsed by the United Nations Conference on Climate Change in Durban in all its aspects, including the achievement of a high quality, legal second commitment period under the Kyoto Protocol, as well as the successful conclusion of the work of the Ad Hoc Working Group on Long-term Cooperative Action under the Convention, in line with the Bali Action Plan[83] and the substantive progress made in the Cancun and Durban decisions, incorporating comparable ambitious targets for parties not included in annex I to the Kyoto Protocol, and addressing in a balanced and effective manner the issues of adaptation, mitigation, finance, technology and capacity-building;
11. *Calls upon* all parties to preserve the architecture of the Convention, cautions against any attempt to renegotiate or interpret the Convention or its principles, and stresses that the negotiations under the Convention should not

[83] FCCC/CP/2007/6/Add.1, decision 1/CP.13.

unravel the existing climate change architecture from binding obligations to a "pledge and review" approach for annex I parties;

12. *Emphasizes* that progress in the Durban Platform is critical for taking the Convention forward, but that work must ensure a strong linkage between mitigation, adaptation and means of implementation, in a balanced manner, as reflected in the Convention, and underlines that all tracks under the Convention must progress in an expeditious, ambitious and effective manner and that such progress should reflect the linkages between mitigation, adaptation and means of implementation that are embedded in the Convention;
13. *Calls upon* all annex I parties to fulfil their commitments relating to mitigation, adaptation, finance, technology transfer and capacity-building under the Convention and the Kyoto Protocol;
14. *Invites* the secretariat of the Convention to report, through the Secretary-General, to the General Assembly at its sixty-eighth session on the work of the Conference of the Parties;
15. *Requests* the Secretary-General to make provisions for the sessions of the Conference of the Parties to the Convention and its subsidiary bodies in his proposal for the programme budget for the biennium 2013–2014;
16. *Decides* to include in the provisional agenda of its sixty-eighth session, under the item entitled "Sustainable development," the sub-item entitled "Protection of global climate for present and future generations of humankind."

Draft Resolution A/C.2/70/L.18 of 28 October 2015 entitled: "Sustainable Development: Protection of Global Climate for Present and Future Generations of Humankind"

South Africa:* draft resolution
Protection of global climate for present and future generations of humankind
The General Assembly,

Recalling its resolutions 43/53 of 6 December 1988, 54/222 of 22 December 1999, 62/86 of 10 December 2007, 63/32 of 26 November 2008, 64/73 of 7 December 2009, 65/159 of 20 December 2010, 66/200 of 22 December 2011, 67/210 of 21 December 2012, 68/212 of 20 December 2013 and 69/220 of 19 December 2014, and other resolutions and decisions relating to the protection of the global climate for present and future generations of humankind,

Recalling also the objectives, principles and provisions of the United Nations Framework Convention on Climate Change,[84]

Recalling further that the global nature of climate change calls for the widest possible cooperation by all countries and their participation in an effective and

* On behalf of the States Members of the United Nations that are members of the Group of 77 and China.
[84] United Nations, Treaty Series, vol. 1771, No. 30822.

appropriate international response, with a view to accelerating the reduction of global greenhouse gas emissions, in the context of article 2 of the Convention, and that the United Nations Framework Convention on Climate Change provides that parties should protect the climate system for the benefit of present and future generations of humankind on the basis of equity and in accordance with their common but differentiated responsibilities and respective capabilities,

Acknowledging that the developed country parties must take the lead in combating climate change and its adverse effects,

Recalling the United Nations Millennium Declaration,[85] the Johannesburg Declaration on Sustainable Development[86] and the Plan of Implementation of the World Summit on Sustainable Development (Johannesburg Plan of Implementation),[87] the 2005 World Summit Outcome,[88] the outcomes of the thirteenth to twentieth sessions of the Conference of the Parties to the United Nations Framework Convention on Climate Change and of the third to tenth sessions of the Conference of the Parties serving as the Meeting of the Parties to the Kyoto Protocol, the Programme of Action for the Least Developed Countries for the Decade 2011–2020, adopted at the Fourth United Nations Conference on the Least Developed Countries, held in Istanbul, Turkey, from 9 to 13 May 2011,[89] the Programme of Action for the Sustainable Development of Small Island Developing States,[90] the Mauritius Declaration[91] and the Mauritius Strategy for the Further Implementation of the Programme of Action for the Sustainable Development of Small Island Developing States[92] and the SIDS Accelerated Modalities of Action (SAMOA) Pathway,[93]

Recalling also the outcome document of the United Nations Conference on Sustainable Development, held in Rio de Janeiro, Brazil, from 20 to 22 June 2012, entitled "The future we want,"[94]

Reaffirming its resolution 70/1 of 25 September 2015, entitled "Transforming our world: the 2030 Agenda for Sustainable Development," recognizing that it builds on the Millennium Development Goals and seeks to complete their unfinished business, and stressing the importance of the implementation of this new ambitious

[85] Resolution 55/2.

[86] *Report of the World Summit on Sustainable Development, Johannesburg, South Africa, 26 August–4 September 2002* (United Nations publication, Sales No. E.03.II.A.1 and corrigendum), chap. I, resolution 1, annex.

[87] Ibid., resolution 2, annex.

[88] Resolution 60/1.

[89] Report of the Fourth United Nations Conference on the Least Developed Countries, Istanbul, Turkey, 9–13 May 2011 (A/CONF.219/7), chap. II.

[90] *Report of the Global Conference on the Sustainable Development of Small Island Developing States, Bridgetown, Barbados, 25 April–6 May 1994* (United Nations publication, Sales No. E.94.I.18 and corrigenda), chap. I, resolution 1, annex II.

[91] *Report of the International Meeting to Review the Implementation of the Programme of Action for the Sustainable Development of Small Island Developing States, Port Louis, Mauritius, 10–14 January 2005* (United Nations publication, Sales No. E.05.II.A.4 and corrigendum), chap. I, resolution 1, annex I.

[92] Ibid., annex II.

[93] Resolution 69/15, annex.

[94] Resolution 66/288, annex.

Agenda, which has poverty eradication at its core and aims at promoting the social, economic and environmental dimensions of sustainable development,

Reaffirming also its resolution 69/313 of 27 July 2015 on the Addis Ababa Action Agenda of the Third International Conference on Financing for Development, which is an integral part of the 2030 Agenda for Sustainable Development, supports and complements it and helps to contextualize its means of implementation targets with concrete policies and actions within the framework of a revitalized Global Partnership for Sustainable Development,

Taking note of the successful and timely initial resource mobilization process of the Green Climate Fund, making it the largest dedicated climate fund and enabling it to start its activities in supporting developing country parties to the United Nations Framework Convention on Climate Change,

Stressing the importance of inclusiveness within the United Nations development system and that observer States be taken into account in the implementation of the present resolution,

1. *Reaffirms* that climate change is one of the greatest challenges of our time, expresses profound alarm that the emissions of greenhouse gases continue to rise globally, remains deeply concerned that all countries, particularly developing countries, are vulnerable to the adverse impacts of climate change and are already experiencing an increase in such impacts, including persistent drought and extreme weather events, sea-level rise, coastal erosion and ocean acidification, further threatening food security and efforts to eradicate poverty and achieve sustainable development, and in this regard emphasizes that adaptation to climate change represents an immediate and urgent global priority;
2. *Notes* the determination of the Conference of the Parties to the United Nations Framework Convention on Climate Change, expressed in its decision 2/CP.18,[95] to adopt a protocol, another legal instrument or an agreed outcome with legal force under the Convention applicable to all parties at its twenty-first session, to be held in Paris from 30 November to 11 December 2015, and for it to come into effect and be implemented from 2020;
3. *Takes note* of the outcome of the twentieth session of the Conference of the Parties to the United Nations Framework Convention on Climate Change and of the tenth session of the Conference of the Parties serving as the Meeting of the Parties to the Kyoto Protocol, hosted by the Government of Peru in Lima from 1 to 14 December 2014, and in particular its invitation, in its decision 1/CP.20,[96] to all parties to initiate or intensify domestic preparations for their intended nationally determined contributions, without prejudice to the legal nature of the contributions, in the context of

[95] See FCCC/CP/2012/8/Add.1.
[96] See FCCC/CP/2014/10/Add.1.

adopting a protocol, another legal instrument or an agreed outcome with legal force under the Convention applicable to all parties towards achieving the objective of the Convention, as set out in its article 2, and to communicate them well in advance of the twenty-first session of the Conference of the Parties in a manner that facilitates the clarity, transparency and understanding of the intended contributions, without prejudice to the legal nature of the contributions;

4. *Notes* the reiteration by the Conference of the Parties to the Convention that the work of the Ad Hoc Working Group on the Durban Platform for Enhanced Action shall be guided by the principles of the Convention;
5. *Acknowledges* that the United Nations Framework Convention on Climate Change is the primary international, intergovernmental forum for negotiating the global response to climate change, taking into account the work of the Ad Hoc Working Group on the Durban Platform for Enhanced Action on, inter alia, mitigation, adaptation, finance, technology development and transfer, capacity-building and transparency of action and support;
6. *Takes note* of the report of the Executive Secretary of the United Nations Framework Convention on Climate Change on the United Nations Climate Change Conference held in Lima from 1 to 14 December 2014;[97]
7. *Also takes note* of decision 2/CP.20, taken by the Conference of the Parties to the Convention at its twentieth session,[98] by which Parties agreed on the composition of the Executive Committee of the Warsaw International Mechanism for Loss and Damage associated with Climate Change Impacts, and its workplan;
8. *Notes* the work undertaken by the Lima-Paris Action Agenda with a view to galvanizing action to address climate change;
9. *Notes with appreciation* the hosting by the Government of France of the twenty-first session of the Conference of the Parties to the Convention and the eleventh session of the Conference of the Parties serving as the Meeting of the Parties to the Kyoto Protocol, in Paris from 30 November to 11 December 2015;
10. *Welcomes* the offer by the Government of Morocco to host the twenty-second session of the Conference of the Parties to the Convention in 2016;
11. *Urges* Member States to promote the integration of a gender perspective into environmental and climate change policies and strengthen mechanisms and provide adequate resources to ensure the full and equal participation of women in decision-making at all levels on environmental issues;
12. *Calls upon* the relevant organizations of the United Nations system, within their respective mandates and resources, to include observer States in the implementation of the present resolution;

[97] A/70/230, sect. I.
[98] See FCCC/CP/2014/10/Add.2.

13. *Invites* the secretariat of the Convention to report, through the Secretary-General, to the General Assembly at its seventy-first session on the work of the Conference of the Parties;
14. *Requests* the Secretary-General to make provisions for the sessions of the Conference of the Parties to the Convention and its subsidiary bodies in his proposed programme budget for the biennium 2018–2019;
15. *Decides* to include in the provisional agenda of its seventy-first session, under the item entitled "Sustainable development," the sub-item entitled "Protection of global climate for present and future generations of humankind."

II

INTERGOVERNMENTAL NEGOTIATING COMMITTEE FOR A FRAMEWORK CONVENTION ON CLIMATE CHANGE (INC-FCCC)

(a) Statements Made on Behalf of the Group of 77 and China at the Sessions of the Intergovernmental Negotiating Committee for a Framework Convention on Climate Change (INC-FCCC)

Statement by the Chairman of the Group of 77 on Financial Resources and Transfer of Technology in Working Group-I of the Intergovernmental Negotiating Committee for a Framework Convention on Climate Change (26 June 1991)

Mr. Chairman,

I make this statement on behalf of the Group of 77 and the People's Republic of China.

Mr. Chairman, as we all know, the major cause of the continuing deterioration of the global environment, particularly global warming, is the unsustainable patterns of production and consumption of the industrialized countries. Developed countries must, therefore, bear the main responsibility in the effort to combat environmental degradation at the national and international levels. Moreover, they have the resources and the technical know-how to promote environmental protection and enhancement measures.

Developing countries, on the other hand, are still grappling with difficult development problems, in an unfavourable economic environment characterized by mounting external indebtedness and adverse terms of trade, including low commodity prices, protectionism, and reverse transfer of huge resources from the developing to the developed countries. Consequently, environmental concerns must not be made a new layer of conditionality which will only distort the development priorities of the developing countries.

Mr. Chairman,

The framework convention and its protocols, when negotiated, may require developing countries to cooperate by adopting measures to combat climate change. If developing countries are to be encouraged to accept these responsibilities, which may entail additional burdens on the use and management of their natural resources, then they must receive financial transfers in compensation for the incremental cost. This is reasonable and fair because they bear little or no responsibility for global climate change.

In recognition of these realities, the General Assembly in resolution 44/228 and the INC in its decision 1/1 made specific recommendations relating to the provision of financial resources to enable developing countries to adopt appropriate measures for environmental protection and enhancement. The key words in these resolutions, Mr. Chairman, are "new, additional and adequate." Additionality must mean in addition to or over and above the target set by the United Nations for ODA flows. But, as we are all aware, the flow of ODA has stagnated over the years at 0.33 per cent of GNP. This is less than one half of the target of 0.7 per cent of GNP in

ODA flows established by the United Nations two decades ago. It cannot be that this inadequate level of assistance will be merely redeployed or reprogrammed for environmental protection and enhancement programmes. Were this to be the case, it would undoubtedly undercut the development efforts of developing countries and accelerate environmental degradation. Renewed efforts should, therefore, be made by all developed countries to attain the target for ODA flows established by the United Nations in addition to the "new" resources that must be made available to meet the incremental cost to developing countries of environmental protection measures.

In the context of the framework convention, "new" means flows of a qualitatively different sort. It is not assistance or aid, but transfers to compensate developing countries for adopting and pursuing costly measures to combat climate change, a state of affairs brought into being by the pattern of production and consumption of the developed countries. Such transfer of resources, if it is to be "adequate," must meet the full incremental cost of the measures that developing countries would adopt to meet global climate concerns.

The obligation to provide financial resources must be made an integral part of the commitments that developed countries must make under the Convention.

We must be imaginative in devising innovative mechanisms for mobilizing resources in support of global environmental programmes. The resources should be channelled to an international fund controlled by States parties to the Convention. The question of the mandatory or voluntary character of funding requires careful attention, because when funding is essentially voluntary the funds become starved of resources. Mandatory schemes for funding environmental programmes must, therefore, form an important element of any financial arrangements.

Mr. Chairman, I wish now to turn to the issue of transfer of technology. The relevant provisions of resolution 44/228 require us to examine effective modalities for favourable access to, and transfer of, environmentally sound technologies on concessional and preferential terms. The cost of technology transfer can be very expensive. If developing countries are to integrate environmental concerns into their development objectives and promote global environmental protection and enhancement measures, it is imperative that they have access to environmentally sound technologies at costs that they can afford. Hence the call by the General Assembly for technology transfer on concessional and preferential terms. This presupposes that a purely market-oriented approach will not help us achieve our common objectives. Developed countries must create the necessary policy framework, supported by appropriate incentives, to encourage technology transfer.

Quite apart from the transfer of hardware, it is important that capacity-building programmes such as the training of personnel to acquire the necessary skills and understanding of technological processes should form an integral part of the "transfer." The overall objective of technology transfer is to enable developing countries fully to internalize the technical know-how and be able to adapt and develop the technology to suit peculiar local conditions.

The availability of information on technological developments and processes to developing countries will enable them to make decisions on the choice of particular technologies. Ways would have to be found on how to make this information easily accessible, not only in terms of availability but in a language that is easily comprehensible.

Mr. Chairman, developing countries have reaffirmed, on several occasions, their commitment to the strengthening of international cooperation for the protection and enhancement of the environment. But the context in which they can do this will depend on the understanding and cooperation of the developed countries and their willingness to sacrifice some of the affluence attained at the cost of global environmental degradation. Sustainable development cannot mean the imposition of limitations on the use of the resources of developing countries in order to support unsustainable production and consumption patterns elsewhere. Environmental constraints and controls, like charity, must begin from the places where the major responsibility for the environmental degradation began, i.e., in the industrialized countries where the need arises to curb profligate consumption patterns. It must also mean that the developing countries will be provided with the necessary means, both financial and technological, to enable them to pursue their development objectives to the fullest extent possible while paying attention to the environmental concerns. Above all, it must mean that a more equitable economic climate is guaranteed for developing countries to eradicate poverty and provide living conditions that are decent. The developed countries must lead by example, not by counterproductive and self-righteous impositions.

Statement by the Spokesman of the Group of 77 on Pledge and Review Concept Proposed in the INC Process Held in Nairobi (13 September 1991)

Mr. Chairman,

I make this statement on behalf of the Group of 77. Since this is my first time in doing so at this current session of the INC process, allow me, Sir, on behalf of the Group of 77 and on my own behalf, to congratulate you most sincerely and warmly for the strong impetus and guidance you have given to this meeting.

The Group of 77 sincerely welcomes the serious efforts we continue to make towards reaching an acceptable accord on a Framework Convention on Climate Change. From the start of the INC process, the Group of 77 has approached in a very constructive, open, and objective manner the examination of the range of pertinent issues which have been proposed. This approach has ensured that the Group, whenever necessary, has made responsible proposals which have accommodated the concerns of our negotiating partners. Two meetings in the INC process have so far been held before this one. At these meetings, we have endeavoured to embrace our negotiating partners in a spirit of constructive engagement, so that together as partners we arrive at a common understanding in addressing adequately the issue of global warming and its adverse effects on life sustenance on our planet.

Mr. Chairman,

At the opening of this current session, the Group of 77, as in past meetings on the climate change negotiating process, decided to confront with a lot of hope and seriousness, the issues which were expected to be tabled before it, with the great expectation that we shall indeed be able to keep faith with the Earth Summit scheduled to be held in Rio in June 1992.

Despite this optimism, the Group has had to revert to a tactical position of cautious apprehension given the fact that an introduction of "pledge and review" concept may seriously, in the view of the Group, delay reaching agreements because of its lack of precision and transparency in the whole INC negotiating process. Given this, it is in the opinion of the Group of 77 to make known, long beforehand and in unambiguous terms, its position on this.

Mr. Chairman,

Without any attempt to implicitly draw conclusions from the concept of "pledge and review," it is the view of the Group of 77 that many aspects of that concept, at best remain very unclear. The following examples may best illustrate my point:

(a) Is the "pledge and review" mechanism, as it has been articulated, intended to supplement a framework convention, or is it presented as a substitute for a convention?
If the former is the case, can we agree on an adoption of a decision in the current session making it clear that a "pledge and review" mechanism would have no value except as part of a framework convention or as an appendix to it?

(b) Is "pledge" a supplement, or a substitute for "commitments" under a framework convention? If the former is what is meant, should we not postpone a discussion on "pledge and review" until we have reached a common understanding on commitments?

Mr. Chairman,

I would also briefly here seek some clarification from a purely conceptual viewpoint, the true or apparent interconnecting implications of "pledge." In this connection, the following may be important to know:

1. How precisely does "pledge" differ from "commitment"?
2. For developed countries, will "pledge" cover:
   (i) the provision of adequate, new, and additional financial resources, and
   (ii) technology transfer on preferential terms to developing countries?

On "Review":

3. For developed countries, will "review" cover provision of new and additional financial resources and technology transfers on preferential terms to developing countries, in addition to reductions in emissions?
4. For developing countries, will "review" be confined solely to implementation of mutually agreed projects financed through transfers of new and additional financial resources? Will "review" specifically exclude examination of national policies, programmes, and priorities?

Mr. Chairman,

These are only some few out of a myriad of points which I shall later be submitting to the Bureau which should seriously be addressed if we are to understand this concept, cleansing it of its ambiguities, before we can be sure that we are really on the right track. As a concept "pledge and review," as it stands and in the context of its operational significance, lacks clarity. It attempts to encompass everything, but yet succeeds in being honoured more by what it lacks than by what it seeks to address. In its present form, it is not helpful to all of us.

Notwithstanding this position, the Group will welcome wholeheartedly suggestions and ideas that are very clearly presented and articulated so that we can adhere to the principles of equity and fairness.

Joint Statement of the Group of 77, Made by Its Chairman (Ghana) at the Fourth Session of the Intergovernmental Negotiating Committee for a Framework Convention on Climate Change (Geneva, 9–20 December 1991)*

1. On behalf of the Group of 77 and China, I would like to make a statement which sets out certain elements which should be incorporated in the text on the Principles of this Convention, it being understood that this is without prejudice to the right of each delegation member of this group to articulate further more specific formulations on the elements dealt with here as well as to propose additional elements both individually and collectively. I would also request on behalf of the group that this statement be circulated as a text of this session of the Intergovernmental Negotiating Committee.
2. I will now read out the elements for incorporation:
   (a) The principle of the sovereignty of States shall be adhered to and strictly respected in all fields of international cooperation, including that for protection of the global climate.
   (b) The right to development is an inalienable human right. All peoples have an equal right in matters relating to living standards. Economic

* Contained in document A/AC.237/WG.1/L.8 of 19 December 1991.

development is the prerequisite for adopting measures to address climate change. The net emissions of developing countries must grow to meet their social and economic development needs.

(c) Protection of the global climate against human-induced change should proceed in an integrated manner with economic development in the light of the specific conditions of each country, without prejudice to the socio-economic development of developing countries. Measures to guard against climate change should be integrated into national development programmes taking into account that environmental standards valid for developed countries may have inappropriate and unwarranted social and economic costs in developing countries.

(d) All States have an obligation to protect the climate for the benefit of present and future generations of mankind on the basis of intra-generational as well as inter-generational equity. This obligation shall be carried out with different time frames for implementation in accordance with common but differentiated responsibilities and capabilities between developing and developed countries and taking fully into account that the largest part of emissions of greenhouse gases have been originating from developed countries and those countries have the main responsibility in combating climate change and the adverse effects thereof.

(e) The parties shall give full consideration to the specific needs and special circumstances of developing country parties, especially those developing countries which are particularly vulnerable to the adverse consequences of climate change and also those developing countries which would have to bear a disproportionate or abnormal burden under the Convention.

(f) In order to achieve sustainable development in all countries and to meet the needs of present and future generations, precautionary measures to meet the climate challenge must anticipate, prevent, attack, or minimize the causes of, and mitigate the adverse consequences of, environmental degradation that might result from climate change. Where there are threats of serious or irreversible damage, lack of full scientific certainty should not be used as a reason for postponing cost-effective measures to prevent such environmental degradation. The measures adopted should take into account different socio-economic contexts.

(g) The need to improve the international economic environment for the developing countries and to promote their sustained economic development are prerequisites for enabling developing countries to participate effectively in the international efforts to protect the global environment, including climate protection.

In this context, new, adequate, and additional financial resources and transfers of and access to environmentally safe and sound technology on most favourable, concessional, and preferential terms shall have to be channelled to developing countries in order to enable their full participation in global efforts for the protection of the climate.

States shall promote an open and balanced multilateral trading system. Except on the basis of a decision by the Conference of Parties, no country or group of countries shall introduce barriers to trade on the basis of claims related to climate change.

3. The issues of economic development and equity are vital for the conclusion of a Convention in which the developing countries can participate. Prospects for arriving at a consensus depend upon these factors being given the importance they deserve to arrive at a balanced result. The developing countries cannot be expected to accept any formulation that would institutionally help perpetuate, however well-intentioned the motives of some parties, the present economic disparity amongst the members of the international community.

Joint Statement on Behalf of the Group of 77 and China to the Fifth INC-FCCC by Mr. Tariq Osman Hyder, Director-General (Economic Coordination), Ministry of Foreign Affairs of Pakistan (New York, 24 February 1992)

Mr. Chairman,

On behalf of the Group of 77 and China, permit me to make the following statement.

International negotiations on the environment are fuelled by worldwide concerns on the part of citizens of the world, NGOs, and Governments that this common heritage of mankind must be saved from further deterioration. The fundamental objective of the UNCED process is to integrate development with environment so that a process of positive synergy can emerge. The only equitable and practical modality to bring this about is to achieve a new global impact between all States, developed and developing.

This fifth round of UN Intergovernmental Negotiations for a Framework Convention on Climate Change in which we are engaged represents a process at the cutting edge of worldwide environmental concerns and is to a large extent a model for the entire international environmental negotiations as it brings into focus the pervading central issues.

The developing countries, Mr. Chairman, are an equal partner with the developed world in its concern for the environment. Indeed, the 1972 UN Conference on the Human Environment in Stockholm was in large part held due to the initiative and apprehensions of the developing countries in regard to the world's environment. Unfortunately, the structures and programmes that emerged from that process were not adequately supported by the developed countries. Now, almost two decades further on, the developed countries in partnership with the developing countries have reacted to what needs to be done.

This has been a welcome development, but the concerns of the developed countries and the laudable concerns and actions of their citizens and NGOs need to be given operational effect. Commitment and sincerity is needed on all sides.

The Group of 77 and China is extremely dismayed and concerned, Mr. Chairman, at the slow rate of progress in these negotiations which have almost stalled. The principal reason is because the developed countries have not clearly stated and defined the commitments that they are willing to enter into under this proposed Convention. To a large extent, the developing countries have put their proposals on the table in terms of treaty language. It was our expectation after the fourth INC in Geneva in December 1991, that at this session the developed countries' common position would be before us for a consensus to emerge after negotiations. However, we are halfway in this last session with some 50 hours negotiations left, without a significant advance and without being in a position to respond optimistically to world expectations.

We need now to separate forms from realities. The heart of this Convention lies essentially in three elements. There has to be a clear definition of the commitments that all parties have to agree to further the objectives of these negotiations.

The developing countries by entering these negotiations have shown their preference for a "no regrets" strategy over a "wait and see" approach. They have accepted that tackling the environmental crisis is a common responsibility. Of course, since the developed countries have the main responsibility for the danger of global warming, this common responsibility is differentiated also in terms of what needs to be done to address the situation.

It should be recognized that each developing country has already made a commitment to its citizens to work towards providing a safer and less polluted environment with clean air and access to clean water. However, the scope and pace of these national efforts depend on the availability of scarce resources that face many competing demands. Poverty constitutes the greatest threat to the environment.

The developed countries must clearly indicate the commitments on emissions for stabilization and reduction that they are willing to enter into along with a specific timetable.

Secondly, there is the issue of financial resources. The developed countries have concentrated most of their negotiating energies on the subsidiary question of the institutional modalities for delivering these resources. What is really required as an essential first step is for the OECD countries to signal that the financial resources required to fulfil the objectives for this Convention will be available on an adequate and predictable basis without adversely affecting existing economic assistance inflows.

It should be kept in mind, to keep this matter in perspective, that in today's recessionary international economic situation, the net transfer of resources between developing and developed countries is in fact negative. Furthermore, protectionist policies have restricted developing countries from being able to increase their exports from two to ten times the amount now coming in as economic assistance inflows.

Thirdly, there is the issue of transfer of technology. The developed countries have to give their position as to their willingness to work for a solution whereby the technology needed by the developing countries to environmentalise their development becomes available at terms which will maximize its use.

Mr. Chairman,

The developing countries very much want to be in a position to see a meaningful Convention on Climate Change open for signature in Rio in June of this year. The environmental clock now stands at a quarter to midnight. We appeal to the developed countries to work for a successful, equitable, and balanced conclusion to these negotiations so that the minute hand does not inexorably go forward.

Joint Statement on Behalf of the Group of 77 and China at the Fifth INC for a Framework Convention on Climate Change by Mr. Tariq Osman Hyder, Director-General (Economic Coordination), Ministry of Foreign Affairs of Pakistan (New York, 28 February 1992)

Mr. Chairman,

As we reach the end of this first phase of the fifth INC, permit the Group of 77 and China to make a statement which attempts to take an honest and realistic stock of the situation with the objective of helping to move the negotiation process forward.

It might help, Mr. Chairman, if, at this stage, all of us were to ask, to reflect upon, and to take back to our capitals a number of questions:

First of all, what is the prognosis for a Convention being ready for Rio?
Secondly, what would be the shape of the Convention that we are likely to arrive at?
Thirdly, what are the first principles on which our mandate and task are based?
Fourthly, if we are not yet close to a consensus now, then what are the main issues, the main elements that we must collectively recognize as essential prerequisites for a resolution?
Fifthly, what have been the main developments at this meeting?
And sixthly, Mr. Chairman, can we identify the approach that is needed to resolve the still outstanding issues?

The prognosis, Mr. Chairman, for a successful conclusion of these negotiations by Rio cannot, when weighed in the balance, be assessed with confidence as optimistic. This is stated only to underline the continued need for commitment and sincerity on all sides in tackling this task in a pragmatic but equitable manner from the point of view of enlightened collective long-term self-interest rather than from a formalistic and short-term approach.

It is still not yet clear, Mr. Chairman, what will be the scope of the structure that we are working towards. To a large extent, and we say this in a purely constructive manner, the inability of the developed countries to harmonize their positions, to the same extent as has been already done by the developing countries, is responsible for this continuing uncertainty.

Hence, Mr. Chairman, it would not be out of place to go back to the first principles which circumscribe our deliberations and which are laid down in resolution 45/212. In broad terms, we are charged with preparing and completing prior to UNCED in June 1992 an effective Framework Convention on Climate Change, containing appropriate commitments, and any related instruments as might be agreed upon, taking into account proposals submitted by States participating in the negotiating process, the work of the IPCC, the results achieved at international meetings on the subject, including the Second World Climate Conference while reaffirming the principles embodied in resolutions 44/207 and 44/228 which take into account the concerns of all States and the specific needs of developing countries.

It is within these parameters, Mr. Chairman, that we can work and within which the General Assembly and indeed the world community will hold us responsible.

What are the main elements that we need to tackle to achieve progress? A list which has no pretensions to comprehensiveness, and to which we would urge all States to broaden, might provide a useful starting point. These elements would include:

- A clear, unified, and unambiguous stance on the part of the developed countries regarding their specific commitments.
- A clear commitment by developed countries that they would be willing to provide the adequate, new, and additional financial resources that would be required on a predictable basis by the developing countries within the context of this Convention.
- A clear commitment by developed countries that the technology required by the developing countries to ensure that their development is environment-friendly will be available on terms that will maximize its use, on most favourable, concessionary, and preferential terms.
- A meeting of minds between developed and developing countries on the delivery mechanisms for financial resources and technology transfers. We must together clearly define and agree upon the characteristics of any potential delivery mechanisms so that their structure, governance, eligibility, and project selection criteria, administration, implementation, and assured and adequate replenishment are defined and ruled by the Conference of Parties irrespective of any functional and cost-effective linkages that might emerge from the ongoing debate.

- Agreement by the developed countries that the commitments that might be entered into by developing countries under this Convention are contractually dependent on the fulfilment of the financial and technology transfer obligations that must be entered into by developed countries that are in the main responsible for the urgency of the present situation. An understanding of the fact that the developing countries are already totally committed to doing whatever they can with their limited resources for their own citizens to improve their local environment. While a concentration of rhetoric on global impact may be useful for the developed countries in terms of their own constituencies, this artificial distinction between local and global impact must be done away with.
- The issue of the need for a section on principles has yet to find a sufficiently positive response from the developed countries. As a statement of guiding principles will provide a foundation of what will follow, this section needs to be tackled from a position of sincerity rather than by a juridically pedantic approach.
- The issue of preparation and exchange of data and information also requires transparent and realistic treatment. In all developing countries, projects funded by external donors, be they bilateral or multilateral, naturally undergo a process of consultation in order that they can be further refined. However, the proposal for broad national reviews cannot be used as a means for institutionalizing a new form of conditionality.

During this session, Mr. Chairman, there has been a good working spirit, and because of a certain amount of flexibility that has been displayed on all sides, there have been some advances. However, in the main, progress has been painfully slow.

On all the issues and elements that we have briefly touched upon in this statement, Mr. Chairman, the positions of the developing countries have been very clearly laid out on the table. At the last INC in Geneva, and indeed in our earlier statement of 24 February 1992 at this session, we had appealed to the developed countries to define their position so that we could respond and through this dialogue the process could go forward.

In this respect, we paid great attention to the joint statement on commitments by the OECD countries on 25 February 1992 and also to the statement on commitments yesterday by the United States of America.

To that extent, we welcome the movement represented as a first step by the joint statement of the OECD presented by our respected and senior colleague, Ambassador Bo Kjellen of Sweden. To assess, even in a preliminary manner, the implications of the OECD joint statement, brings us first to the consideration of what is, and what is not, there. Secondly to the standard of conceptual consistency to which the OECD must now be held to, not only within the context of the scope of the actual declaration but also within the entire gamut of these negotiations.

To begin with, it is noteworthy and somewhat unfortunate that the OECD in its self-bracketed text has not yet been able to come up with a unified stand on their specific commitments.

As you know, Mr. Chairman, within the Group of 77 we have a variety of positions on a number of issues, although from this diversity in the totality of the package we are trying to arrive at, the Group has a common approach. Therefore, in regard to the specific commitments contained in the OECD declaration, I would only note that there is a great need for the OECD countries to harmonize their positions as soon as possible.

Secondly, Mr. Chairman, while the spirit of cost-effectiveness pervades the OECD declaration in the guise of joint implementation, it must be stressed that the potential loopholes that are left open must be effectively addressed.

Thirdly, Mr. Chairman, the statement is remarkable for its absence to any reference on a commitment for providing the financial resources that will be required for a successful Convention. It is not good enough to say that the brackets put by the developed countries in the text we have before us regarding financial commitments represents a position. That is not even a non-position but rather a negative position at variance with the declared objective of the OECD countries in various fora including their own with particular reference to the policy statement of the OECD Ministers on Environment and Development in Paris of 3 December 1991.

Fourthly, the statement is equally disappointing in terms of an absence of commitment regarding technology transfers.

Finally, Mr. Chairman, we can conclude by reflecting on the approach that we need to resolve these negotiations. There is of course a great importance attached to the outer forms of our project, the need to have clearer and more harmonious texts, the need to cautiously explore how innovative we can be in regard to mechanisms. However, of more importance is the need to focus on the hard problems that remain.

Joint Statement on Behalf of the Group of 77 and China at the Fifth Session, Second Part, of INC-FCCC (New York, 8 May 1992)

Mr. Chairman,

On behalf of the Group of 77 and China, permit me to make the following statement.

Throughout the process of the Intergovernmental Negotiating Committee for a Framework Convention on Climate Change, the G-77 and China has shared the concern that global environment must be saved from further deterioration. We also believe that the driving force of the UNCED process is to integrate development with the environment so that sustainable development is achieved. The only equitable and practical modality to achieve this is a new global compact between all States. As we entered the fifth and final round of the INC, all negotiating partners were conscious of the fact that an innovative approach was required to be introduced, as many portions of the text remained unresolved. It was against this background that you, Mr. Chairman, were requested to produce working papers to bring together elements which, in your opinion, formed areas where a minimum divergence of views existed. The Group of 77 and China found these papers to be a useful basis for further negotiations on the Framework Convention, and we, therefore, considered it desirable to continue negotiations in a spirit of achieving an agreement and consensus.

In the final stages of the negotiating process, which has taken over fifteen months, each group is adequately conscious of the concerns of the other groups. The Group of 77 and China, which constitutes a majority of the United Nations membership, has shown a great deal of flexibility and a constructive spirit to further the negotiating process. The Group of 77 and China remains committed to make sincere and positive efforts for an early finalization of the Framework Convention but would find any attempt to erode their basic concerns as unacceptable. It is in this context that the Group of 77 and China considers it important to reiterate some of the essential elements for their reflection in the Chairman's proposed text for the Framework Convention on Climate Change, which has now been brought for deliberations in the plenary.

The G-77 and China cannot accept any compromise on the concept of the sovereignty of States. The right to development is of primary importance to the developing countries. Nothing in the Convention should detract from this right. In the area of common but differentiated responsibility which has already been reflected in the Chairman's text is also an element which requires to be recognized in a partnership of States. It is important to recognize the concept of differentiated environmental standards as standards applied in some countries may be inappropriate and of unwarranted economic and social cost to other countries.

The G-77 and China would also like to stress once again the need to strike a balance between the general and specific commitments which should be based on equitable and differentiated responsibilities. The commitments of developing countries should be without detriment to their national developmental goals, policies, and poverty eradication priorities.

It is important to recognize that the implementation of measures by developing countries will depend on the provision of adequate, new, and additional financial resources and the access to and transfer of technology to developing countries on preferential, concessional, and favourable terms.

Mr. Chairman, your text on the funding mechanism is broadly acceptable because it is balanced and neutral. It is emphasized that the choice of the appropriate funding mechanism should be agreed upon by the Conference of Parties. The Conference of Parties shall exercise full authority over the funding mechanism and the funding mechanisms shall be accountable to the Conference of Parties.

Finally, it is imperative that in the context of developing countries communicating information to the Conference of Parties, national policies and strategies shall not be subject to any examination or scrutiny.

Mr. Chairman,

The G-77 and China had the occasion to discuss, in detail, the latest revised versions of your texts, specifically on articles 4, 11, and 12 pertaining to commitments, financing mechanism, and communication of information related to implementation. There is a widespread feeling in the Group that some of the vital interests of Group members have not been duly reflected. While we did not have sufficient time to suggest agreed amendments, individual delegations would in the course of this plenary meeting be suggesting amendments to various sections of these articles.

Mr. Chairman,

I would like to conclude by reiterating that the G-77 and China would continue to remain flexible in their earnest for the successful conclusion of the Convention. It is our hope that the other negotiating partners will respond positively to the core concerns of the G-77 and China and that the vital interests of the developing countries would be accommodated in the Convention. It is our expectation that, under your distinguished leadership, we would be able to achieve at an agreed text of the Convention which would attract universal adherence.

Statement on Behalf of the Group of 77 and China by H.E. Ambassador Luis Fernando Jaramillo, Permanent Representative of Colombia to the United Nations, at the Intergovernmental Negotiating Committee for a Framework Convention on Climate Change (United Nations, 17 March 1993)

Mr. Chairman,

The Group of 77 would like to present a few ideas concerning financial mechanisms, as well as the financial and technical support for those States parties which are developing countries.

Within the context of the concept of "common but differentiated responsibilities," the Group presents the enclosed document, which contains some criteria that should be considered in the deliberations about financial mechanisms. Various issues are addressed, among them, the manner in which the Conference of the Parties should handle the financial mechanism, how it should operate within an institutional structure, how it should define the policies, strategies, and priorities of the election programs and criteria that deal with the access to and use of the financial resources, and that the financial mechanism have an equal and balanced representation of the Parties within a transparent system of governance.

Mr. Chairman,

As we said this morning, the Group of 77 considers that the questions posed in document A/AC.237/26 are an important aid in establishing the recommendations that we are sending to the Global Environment Facility (GEF) for its next meeting in Beijing.

With regard to question A, what is the financial mechanism?

As provided for in article 11, the Conference of the Parties shall decide on the policies, programme priorities, and eligibility criteria related to this Convention.

The financial mechanism is a subsidiary body of the Conference of the Parties. It shall function under the guidance of and be accountable to the CoP. Its functions shall be those listed in paragraphs 3a, b, c, and d of article 11.

The Global Environment Facility is the interim operating entity insofar as it has been appropriately restructured. In providing the financial resources for the activities foreseen in the area of climate change, it shall follow the policies, priorities, and criteria established by the CoP.

With regard to question B, what types of measures are to be funded?

As mentioned in article 4.3, funding shall be provided to cover agreed full costs for compliance with the obligations under article 12.1 to communicate information.

Financial resources needed by developing country parties to meet the agreed full incremental costs of implementing measures that are covered by articles 4, 5, and 6 shall also be provided.

With regard to question C, could the GEF be the sole operating entity?

The GEF has been designated in article 21.3 as the interim operating entity, while article 11.4 indicates the steps to be followed in deciding upon a permanent arrangement.

All measures to be funded according to the terms of the Convention are deemed to produce global environmental benefits.

With regard to question D, how will the Convention affect the GEF?

The continuing compatibility between the interests and strategies of the CoP and the GEF is ensured by the fact that in all funding activities related to climate change the GEF shall apply the policies, priorities, and criteria established by the CoP.

The guidance provided by other Conventions for activities under those conventions shall not generate diverging tracks.

(i) How will the GEF function under the guidance of the CoP?

The financial mechanism shall ensure that the funded projects to address climate change are in conformity with the policies, programme, priorities, and eligibility criteria established by the CoP by analysing the reports received from the operating entities.

Pursuant to article 11.3 (b), should a party to the Convention request reconsideration of a funding decision, the financial mechanism shall consider such a request in the light of the policies, priorities, and eligibility criteria established by the CoP taking into account information provided by the operating entity.

Differences in interpreting and applying article 4.3 with respect to the determination of the agreed full incremental costs of specific measures may be referred to the CoP for resolution through consultations.

(a) What body will ensure conformity of GEF climate change projects to the guidance and decisions of the CoP, in accordance with article 11.3(a)? Would this be the task of the GEF/PA or of the STAP?

Only the CoP has the ultimate authority to "ensure conformity." In this regard, the CoP may be assisted or advised by SBSTA of the Convention (FCCC).

(b) Will there be a need to define a division of labour and specify collaborative working arrangements between the Subsidiary Body for Scientific and Technological Advice (Article 9) and the STAP?
SBSTA, which functions "under the guidance of the CoP," shall be responsible for assessing and ensuring conformity with CoP guidance and relevant decisions.

(ii) How will accountability of the GEF to the CoP operate?
The CoP shall at each session, as needed, address a report, resolution, or other communication to the GEF/PA compiling relevant guidance and decisions for consideration and action by the GEF/PA. These communications will be automatically placed on the agenda of the GEF/PA. The GEF/PA shall adapt its work in the area of climate change accordingly.
The GEF/PA shall submit to the CoP, through the financial mechanism, a separate report on its implementation of the guidance received from the CoP.

(iii) How will levels of GEF funding for the implementation of the Convention be determined?
A significant proportion of the funds available to the GEF should be earmarked to cover all activities under the Convention.
The financial mechanism should determine the amount of funding necessary for the implementation of the Convention. This shall serve as guidance to the GEF in its assignment of funds to these activities.

(iv) What GEF governance arrangements best respond to the Conventions requirements?
The governance should be transparent. It should be democratic, equitable, and balanced in nature and should reflect the notion of "partnership in additionality." There should be an equal voice for all parties. All developing countries should have access without conditionality. Membership should be universalized.

Mr. Chairman,

The answer to these queries guides us in the comments we may address to the GEF meeting in Beijing. Specifically, we are now in a position to present the GEF some recommendations, such as:

1. Regarding the issue of climate change, the GEF should base its work on the policies, priorities, programmes, and criteria for eligibility that the Conference of the Parties (CoP) of the Climate Change Convention will determine.
2. The financial mechanism, as stated in A, should be the one that defines the manner in which a specific financing decision could be reconsidered, within the framework of the policies, priorities, programmes, and criteria for eligibility previously defined.
3. The activities that the GEF should finance are the ones mentioned in article 4.3 of the Convention, including agreed full incremental costs. Similarly, the

financial resources required by the developing countries in order to fulfil the totality of the full incremental costs, with a view to implementing the activities specified in articles 4, 5, and 6.

4. The Conference of the Parties of the Convention should, in each one of its sessions, send a report, resolution, or some type of communication to the GEF/PA, as is deemed necessary, compiling the relevant guides and decisions, for consideration and action by the GEF/PA. These communications should be automatically included in the agenda of the GEF/PA, which should, in turn, adapt its work in the field of climatic changes accordingly.
5. The GEF/PA should send to the CoP, through the financial mechanism, a separate report concerning the implementation of the guides received by the CoP.

Mr. Chairman,

These are merely some of the recommendations that we could offer to the GEF for its next meeting in May, but we believe that in the following days this Committee will be able to present additional ones.

Statement by Mr. Jose Lino B. Guerrero, Minister-Counsellor, Philippines Mission to the United Nations, on Behalf of the Group of 77 and China, at the Eleventh Session of INC-FCCC on Item 7(b): Review of the Adequacy of Commitments in Article 4, Paragraph 2(a) and (b) (Working Group I) (New York, 8 February 1995)

Madam Chairperson,

I take the floor on behalf of the Group of 77 and China.

The Group of 77 and China has listened with respectful attention to the distinguished speakers of Annex I countries this morning and this afternoon.

We have contemplated—with no little anxiety—the awesome form of their combined and reiterated demands.

As you and everyone have known, Madam, the involvement of the Group of 77 and China in the drafting of the Convention was intense. Although made up of countries with varied interests, they were united in their common and cherished goals to achieve development in a safe and encouraging environment. As one, the Group of 77 and China sought to focus, not only on problems but also on the feasibility of solutions. Moved by the spirit of international cooperation, they quickly shunned attitudes of the aggrieved in the context of environmental pollution and manifested flexibility and a capacity for compromise—to the point of relinquishing the total vigour of some positions which they had considered essential to their national interests. It was this spirit of cooperation that moved them—some with understandable hesitation—to accept one early dawn of May 1992 the "package" that resulted from a very delicate process of give and take.

The Convention which we have adopted, signed, and ratified may not be the best which we had wanted, but it reflects many of the principles which guided our negotiations and which we find essential for our efforts to control climate change. Cardinal among these principles is that of "common but differentiated responsibility." It was this principle that moved us to agree on a balanced division of labour between developed, industrialized countries and the many developing countries of the world still aspiring to achieve the enviable levels of development already enjoyed by their partners.

Based on acknowledged fact, the problems of global warming and climate change—not to speak of related maladies of our environment—have arisen mainly from the quantities, over time, of greenhouse gases emitted by industrialized countries in their pursuit of economic growth. This fact, together with the principle that the repair of damage to the environment should be borne principally by those responsible for the damage, led to the categorization of distinct parties in our Convention. Each of the two major categories has well-defined responsibilities. Implementation of the Convention, therefore, should mean implementation efforts by parties according to their distinct responsibilities. Any attempt at this time to amend our Convention, to redefine categories of parties or to reassign responsibilities could be interpreted as an effort to transfer burdens on those who are incapable of bearing them and who are, in fact, the victims—not the perpetrators—of climate change. This clearly would be unfair and contrary to the spirit and letter of the Convention. This, Madam Chairperson, the Group of 77 and China cannot, will not, accept.

Madam Chairperson,

As we said yesterday, Madam, the Group of 77 and China submits this position: let's implement the Convention now. Later, when circumstances are opportune, we might improve it as necessary—without reneging on the principles which have guided our common effort.

Statement by Mr. Jose Lino B. Guerrero, Minister-Counsellor, Philippines Mission to the United Nations, on Behalf of the Group of 77 and China, at the Eleventh Session of INC-FCCC on Item 7(b): Review of the Adequacy of Commitments in Article 4, Paragraph 2(a) and (b) (Working Group I) (New York, 9 February 1995)

Mr. Chairman,

Thank you, Mr. Chairman, for giving me the floor once again.

I take the floor on behalf of the Group of 77 and China to express a sense of bewilderment.

Analysing this bewilderment epistemologically—i.e., knowing that we are indeed bewildered—we find the following elements of the "puzzlement":

- In all our negotiations prior to—and shortly after—the adoption of the Convention it was quite clear that the industrialized countries were aware of their ecological debt to the rest of the world, for their massive utilization of greenhouse-gas emitting substances for at least two centuries. The concentration of greenhouse gases in the atmosphere began with the activities of the major industrialized countries—a long, long time before the now developing countries even conceived of industrializing.
- In line with the "polluter pays" principle, the industrialized countries voluntarily included themselves among the Annex I countries with the specific responsibility of reducing and stabilizing greenhouse-gas emissions.

The Group of 77 and China—and some Annex I countries—had thought that the commitments were inadequate and had wanted more specific commitments from the Annex I countries, to be made explicit in the Convention, but these countries themselves insisted that their commitments articulated in general terms were adequate.

Now, these countries themselves tell us that the commitments are inadequate.

The thrust of the statements made yesterday was to include developing countries—according to their varied circumstances—in sharing the burden of emission control. This, in effect, was saying: in implementing the principle of "common but differentiated responsibility"—dividing labour between developed and developing countries—developing countries should participate in the task specifically assigned/undertaken by developed countries for reasons I have described.

From the reports presented by the Annex I countries, we have been told that only two of the Annex I countries seem to be close to fulfilling their commitments. This means that—even granting for the sake of argument that the commitments are inadequate—there is more urgent need now to live up to these commitments fully rather than amplify them.

The fact that there are developing countries which are on the verge of industrial take-off does not negate the fact that the emissions that have caused climate change over two centuries have proceeded from the non-industrialized world. It will take many, many years before the time-and-quantity lines, on the emission graph for developed and developing countries, could converge.

The industrialized countries—assuming that their common desire to involve developing countries in their task was valid—proceeded to describe in detail the modalities and mechanisms for such involvement. This, we think, was begging the question.

Because the status *quaestionis* remain:

- We should be concerned with the full implementation of the Convention now. If the commitments are inadequate, there is so much more reason that they be fulfilled in time.

- Concentrate on the fulfilment of Annex I country commitments, rather than expend energy on putting new burdens on countries which still have to work very hard to achieve the levels of development which the industrialized countries have already achieved. The accountability of each party should be based now on the provisions of our present Convention.
- Is the Group of 77 and China against improving the Convention? By no means. But first things first. Implement now. Discuss ways of improvement well in advance. But active negotiations for virtual amendments of the Convention should take place only when we are sure that even the present commitments—which many consider inadequate—can realistically be met. Otherwise we engage in wishful thinking.

(b) Draft Proposals, Decision, and Approach Paper Submitted by the Group of 77 to the Intergovernmental Negotiating Committee for a Framework Convention on Climate Change (INC-FCCC)

Paper No. 34
Ghana on behalf of the Group of 77*

Group of 77 Proposals on Transfer of Environmentally Sound Technology and Transfer of Financial Resources in a Framework Convention on Climate Change (Submitted on 20 September 1991)

Transfer of Environmentally Sound Technology

1. The identification with a view to the establishing of appropriate international mechanisms to promote, facilitate, and finance the transfer of environmentally sound technology on concessional and preferential terms, without prejudice to specific commitments and arrangements on transfer of technology to be adopted in specific international instruments regarding the protection of the environment. In this regard, such mechanisms should also aim at:
   (a) Supporting the development of endogenous capacity-building in developing countries through, *inter alia*, the development of human resources and the strengthening of institutional capacities in R&D, in accordance with the plans, objectives, and priorities of these countries;
   (b) Ensuring the access of developing countries to scientific and technological information, in particular in state-of-the-art technologies, through

* Contained in document A/AC.237/Misc.1/Add.15 of 22 October 1991.

the establishment of an international database, based on regional and national centres, easily accessible by potential users to information related to technological options, trading conditions, implementation costs, and technologies security;

(c) Exchanging experiences of and developing the capacity for technology assessment, environmental impact and risk assessment of technology (particularly of new technologies) in developing countries to enable them to make choices based on environmentally sound technology;

(d) Purchasing patents for their transfer to the developing countries on non-commercial terms;

(e) Developing safeguards on the transfer of technologies, especially new technologies, which have not been approved on environmental or health grounds in the country of origin;

(f) Sponsoring regular and short-term visits facilitating the permanent return of qualified experts in the field of environmentally sound technologies who are of developing-country institutions;

(g) Facilitating the maintenance and promotion of environmentally sound technologies that may have been neglected or displaced in developing countries.

2. Ways and means to promote long-term technological partnerships between the holders of environmentally sound technology and potential users in developing countries, *inter alia*, through increase of direct investment, joint ventures, and joint R&D programmes; taking into account developing countries objectives and policies.
3. The creation by developed countries of systems of incentives, fiscal or otherwise, to stimulate the transfer by companies operating under their jurisdiction, of environmentally sound technologies to developing countries.
4. The support to a global programme of cooperation and assistance, including that provided by United Nations agencies and international organizations to developing countries in the field of R&D and technological and human resources capacity-building.
5. Ways and means to promote and strengthen favourable access by the developing countries to processes, equipment, research, and expertise related to the development and use of environmentally sound technology.
6. Ways and means to support regional and national programmes of scientific research and technology development among developing countries, including through the involvement of both public and private enterprises and research facilities, as well as funding for TCDC programmes in this area.
7. The easing of the transfer of patents and know-how, including the issues of the period of patent protection.
8. To agree on incorporating the transfer of environmentally sound technologies to developing countries in the framework of the draft United Nations Code of Conduct on Transfer of Technology.

Transfer of Financial Resources

(1) Provision of adequate funding, covering the full incremental costs and not entailing any reallocation of ongoing or required developmental programmes from the developing countries' own resources: new and additional funding, in that there is no reallocation of existing multilateral or bilateral financial flows for developing purposes.
(2) There should be a separate fund for each convention or proposed convention.
(3) There should be a general fund (Fund for the Promotion of Sustainable Development/Green Fund) to cover activities not included in separate conventions. This fund should be separate from the GEF and should serve the sustainable development needs of developing countries. Predictability in the flow of funds should be guaranteed by mandatory contributions from developed countries, in accordance with their responsibilities.
(4) The governance of the funding mechanisms should be transparent and democratic in nature with an equal voice for all parties; with access to all developing countries without any conditionality; and provide for funding of activities according to the priority of the developing countries, taking into account the priorities identified in Agenda 21.
(5) These funds from the developed countries to developing countries will be to a great extent of a compensatory nature.
(6) The notion of "partnership in additionality" is to be understood as a commitment to provide new and additional financial resources to developing countries, for meeting, *inter alia*, the commitments and other sustainable development concerns.
(7) The need for a supportive international economic environment which promotes economic growth and development, particularly in developing countries, *inter alia*, through various ways such as market access, terms of trade, remunerative commodity prices, and transfer of technology on preferential and non-commercial terms, addressing efficiently and urgently debt problems and alleviation of poverty.

Matters Relating to Arrangements for the Financial Mechanism and for Technical and Financial Support to Developing Country Parties Group of 77 and China: Draft Decision*

Recommendations of the Intergovernmental Negotiating Committee for a Framework Convention on Climate Change to the Global Environment Facility
The Intergovernmental Negotiating Committee for a Framework Convention on Climate Change decides:

(a) That in accordance with article 11 and article 21.3 of the Framework Convention on Climate Chang (FCCC), the GEF shall be appropriately

* Contained in document A/AC.237/L.18 of 19 March 1993.

restructured and its membership made universal, and as an interim operating entity under the Convention, the GEF shall base its work on the policies, programme priorities, and eligibility criteria determined by the Conference of the Parties of the Climate Change Convention;

(b) That in those aspects of its work which relate to climate change, the GEF, as the interim operating entity of the FCCC, shall finance the activities specified in articles 4, 5, and 6 of the Convention, bearing in mind, in particular, the provisions of article 4.3;

(c) That in line with article 11.3 of the Convention, the Conference of the Parties will, after each one of its sessions, communicate to the GEF/PA the relevant guidance and decisions for implementation and action by the GEF/PA, which shall, accordingly, adapt its work in the field of climatic change;

(d) That the GEF/PA shall submit regular reports to the CoP on its activities in the field of climate change and in particular on the implementation of the guidance and decisions communicated by the CoP;

(e) That a special window of the GEF dedicated to the Framework Convention on Climate Change from the GEF shall be from a distinct and identifiable fund within the GEF in order to ensure adherence to article 11.

Matters Relating to Arrangements for the Financial Mechanism Implementation of Article 11 (Financial Mechanism), Paras. 1–4

Approach Paper by the Group of 77 and China on the Format for Communication of Information by non-Annex I Parties*

I. Background

The United Nations Framework Convention on Climate Change entered into force on 21 March 1994. The objective of the Convention is the stabilization of greenhouse gas concentrations in the atmosphere at a level that would prevent dangerous anthropogenic interference with the climate system. Such a level should be achieved within a timeframe sufficient to allow ecosystems to adapt naturally to climate change, to ensure that food production is not threatened, and to enable economic development to proceed in a sustainable manner (Article 2).

II. Provisions of the Convention

Article 4 of the Convention deals with "Commitments." According to this article, all Parties undertake a number of activities taking into account their common but differentiated responsibilities and their specific national and regional development

*Contained in document A/AC.237/Misc.40 of 11 November 1994.

priorities, objectives, and circumstances. Article 4.1(j) deals with communication of information to the Conference of the Parties related to implementation in accordance with Article 12. Article 12 entitled "Communication of information related to implementation" has laid down elements relevant to communication of information.

Article 12.1 reads as follows:

> "In accordance with Article 4, paragraph 1, each Party shall communicate to the Conference of the Parties, through the secretariat, the following elements of information:
> (a) A national inventory of anthropogenic emissions by sources and removals by sinks of all greenhouse gases not controlled by the Montreal Protocol, to the extent its capacities permit, using comparable methodologies to be promoted and agreed upon by the Conference of the Parties;
> (b) A general description of steps taken or envisaged by the Party to implement the Convention; and
> (c) Any other information that the Party considers relevant to the achievement of the objective of the Convention and suitable for inclusion in its communication, including, if feasible, material relevant for calculations of global emission trends."

Article 12.5 reads:

> "Each developed country Party and each other Party included in Annex I shall make its initial communication within six months of the entry into force of the Convention for that Party. Each Party not so listed shall make its initial communication within three years of the entry into force of the Convention for that Party, or of the availability of financial resources in accordance with Article 4, paragraph 3. Parties that are least developed countries may make their initial communication at their discretion. The frequency of subsequent communications by all Parties shall be determined by the Conference of the Parties, taking into account the differentiated timetable set by this paragraph."

Article 12.7 reads as below:

> "From its first session, the Conference of the Parties shall arrange for the provision to developing country Parties of technical and financial support, on request, in compiling and communicating information under this Article, as well as in identifying the technical and financial needs associated with proposed projects and response measures under Article 4. Such support may be provided by other Parties, by competent international organisations and by the secretariat, as appropriate."

III. Considerations Involved in Developing a Format for Developing Countries

At the outset, it should be stressed that since the requirement of furnishing of information of the measures taken by developing countries is only after three years, at this stage the developing countries need not be involved in a binding agreement on the format for communication of information. Further, there are several factors which make it difficult to come to any concrete conclusion on the format. Some of the issues which will have to be considered in connection with the format are mentioned below:

(a) There is wide diversity in the capacities of the developing countries which, *inter alia*, relate to:
   (i) lack of financial resources to undertake the study;
   (ii) lack of technical expertise to undertake the work;
   (iii) lack of institutional arrangements to take up the work;
   (iv) need for additional financial resources to implement policy measures aimed at reduction/stabilization of greenhouse gases;

(b) The Convention recognizes the differentiated responsibilities of countries in the mitigation of the global climate change. Thus, to be active partners in international action, the developing countries need to be extended all the necessary support to fulfil their obligations under the Convention and to which the developed country parties have already committed themselves under the Convention. In fact, the Convention clearly makes the implementation of Convention provisions by Annex I parties a precondition for implementation by non-Annex I parties;

(c) In accordance with article 12.5, the initial communication is dependent on the availability of funds under article 4.3 of the Convention;

(d) In accordance with article 4.3, developed country parties and other developed parties included in Annex II shall provide new and additional financial resources to meet the agreed full costs incurred by developing country parties in complying with their obligations under article 12, paragraph 1. It is noticed that, in this connection, this has been included as a programme priority in the report of the ninth session of the Committee (see A/AC.237/55, para. 80);

(e) Before the format is decided, there are other questions which would have to be decided especially regarding funding of incremental costs for activities under article 4.1 and 4.3 through the financial mechanism. These would have a bearing on the format as well;

(f) Many of the aspects in the format can be addressed and information collected only if developing countries are assisted in endogenous capacity building so as to enable them to actively participate in greenhouse gases stabilization. This aspect has been noted in the report of the ninth session of the Committee (see A/AC.237/55, para. 80);

(g) Transfer of technology is an area of vital importance and article 4.3, 4.5, and 4.7 would have to be an important aspect of assistance to developing countries for implementation of the Convention;
(h) Further, article 4.4 stipulates that the developed country parties and other developed parties included in Annex II shall also assist the developing countries that are particularly vulnerable to the adverse effects of climate change in meeting costs of adaptation to those adverse effects;
(i) As for least developed countries, article 12.5 provides for their initial communication to be made at their discretion. In this connection, due consideration should be given to article 4.9 of the Convention.

The above considerations clearly indicate that several specific and practical steps have to be undertaken before the developing countries can effectively develop a format and content for communication of information which addresses the problem of reduction/stabilization of greenhouse gases and implementation of the Convention.

IV. Format for Communication of Information

It would be useful to reiterate at this point that the entire exercise of reporting/communication is dependent on the availability of funds under article 4.3 read in conjunction with article 12.5 of the Convention.

In view of the above, the information from the developing countries may be provided in two stages as follows:

(i) initial evaluation of the cost of preparing the information required under article 12.1;
(ii) actual preparation of information required under article 12.1.

In this context, it would be of utility to identify those areas which could form a core set of requirements on which the developing countries could focus their activities in the next two to three years in order to furnish information to the Conference of the Parties.

The above format should incorporate all information required under article 12.1 of the Convention. These would include the following:

1. Information on a national inventory of anthropogenic emissions by sources and removals by sinks of all greenhouse gases not controlled by the Montreal Protocol, to the extent the capacities of the developing countries permit;
2. A general description of steps taken or envisaged by the party to implement the Convention.
3. Any other information that the party considers relevant to the achievement of the objective of the Convention and suitable for inclusion in its

communication, including, if feasible, material relevant for calculations of global emission trends. It could include, *inter alia*, the following:

(i) information on adaptation measures envisaged in article 4.1(b) and 4.1(e);
(ii) needs assessment related to article 4.1(g);
(iii) identification of the technical and financial needs associated with proposed projects and response measures under articles 4 and 12.4.

The rest of the information would depend on various factors and would, therefore, have to be flexible by its very nature. The flexibility for addressing issues in the format for developing countries needs to be underlined for reasons set out below:

(a) Developing countries have diversity of conditions both within and between them;
(b) The Convention embodies the principle of differentiated responsibilities and, respectively, capacities;
(c) The format for communication for developing countries depends on the ability of countries to document the necessary information;
(d) The first communication by developing countries is dependent on the timely availability of necessary financial inputs and accompanying technology transfer support;
(e) The methodology may, initially, have to be different.

While discussing communication of information under article 12, one should also keep in view article 12.4 which provides for developing country parties to voluntarily propose projects for financing with details of costs and benefits. This article is an important component of communication and should, where possible and appropriate, be reflected in the format and be fully funded by the operating entity of the financial mechanism.

Initially, developing countries would undertake further work on developing a format for the first stage as envisaged above.

Annex I
Proposal by the Group of 77 and China[1]

The Intergovernmental Negotiating Committee for a Framework Convention on Climate Change,

Having held fruitful and extensive but not conclusive discussions on the item of the criteria for joint implementation at its eighth, ninth, tenth, and eleventh sessions,

Recalling that the Conference of the Parties is mandated in conformity with Article 4.2 (d) to take decisions regarding criteria for joint implementation as indicated in Article 4.2 (a),

Recognizing that, according to the provisions of the FCCC, the commitment under Article 4.2 (a) to adopt national policies and to take corresponding measures on the mitigation of climate change applies only to Annex I Parties,

Emphasizing that, according to the provisions of the FCCC, only Annex I Parties have obligations to limit GHG emissions. Developing country parties have no such obligations,[2]

Acknowledging that joint activities to address climate change undertaken between developed country Parties and developing country Parties are different from joint implementation and basically fall under Article 4.5, that such joint activities shall be compatible with and supportive of national sustainable development priorities and strategies and shall promote technology co-operation, including technology transfer and capacity building; and to contribute to the cost-effectiveness of climate change policies and measures so as to ensure global benefits at the lowest possible cost, that the financing of joint activities shall be independent from and additional to financial obligations within the framework of the financial mechanism as well as to current Official Development Assistance (ODA) flows,

Decides to:

a) *Transmit* to the first session of the Conference of the Parties for consideration and appropriate action the comments made by Parties and other member States at the eleventh session of the Committee;
b) *Recommend* that the COP:
   - Decide that joint implementation under Article 4.2 (a) is applicable to Annex I Parties only;
   - Decide that no credits will be obtained by developed country Parties during the pilot phase;
   - Take note of the views expressed on joint implementation and joint activities aimed at addressing climate change, respectively;
   - Develop, at its first session, criteria for joint implementation according to Article 4.2 (d);
   - Take note of any information provided on a voluntary basis by Parties regarding joint activities;
   - Consider, at an appropriate later session, assessing the experience gained on joint implementation;

Requests the interim secretariat to provide the Conference of the Parties, at its first session, with a compilation of interventions and other comments on this subject which Parties and other member States will have transmitted to the interim secretariat by 17 February 1995. Documents that have been or will be submitted to the interim secretariat may, upon request by the submitting country or organization, be issued by the interim secretariat in the original language only and distributed to all delegations.

[1] Contained in document A/AC/.237/91/Add/1 of 8 March 1995 on the Report of the Intergovernmental Negotiating Committee for a Framework Convention on Climate Change on the Work of its Eleventh Session held at New York from 6 to 17 February 1995.

[2] "Noting that the largest share of historical and current global emissions of greenhouse gases has originated in developed countries, that per capita emissions in developing countries are still relatively low and that the share of global emissions originating in developing countries will grow to meet their social and development needs." (Paragraph 3 of the Preamble to the Convention).

III

UN FRAMEWORK CONVENTION ON CLIMATE CHANGE (UNFCCC)

I. Conference of Parties of the United Nations Framework Convention on Climate Change (COP) and Conference of the Parties Serving as the Meeting of the Parties to the Kyoto Protocol (CMP)

(a) Statements made on behalf of the Group of 77 and China at the sessions of the Conference of Parties of the United Nations Framework Convention on Climate Change (COP) and Conference of the Parties Serving as the Meeting of the Parties to the Kyoto Protocol (CMP)

Statement by Ms. Alison Drayton, Head of Delegation of Guyana, on Behalf of the Group of 77 and China, at the Fifth Session of the Conference of Parties to the United Nations Framework Convention on Climate Change (Bonn, Germany, 2 November 1999)

Mr. President,
Excellencies,
Distinguished Delegates,

On behalf of the Group of 77 and China, I would like to extend our congratulations on your election as President of the Conference of the Parties at its fifth session. We consider that we are well poised for a successful and productive meeting, and the

Group is working hard to contribute towards positive outcomes on all issues before us.

We were encouraged by the remarks on the opening day by Chancellor Schroeder of the Federal Republic of Germany noting the importance of climate change in this important country. Our appreciation also goes to the Executive Secretary and the Convention Secretariat for their contribution to enable all of us in discussing wide-ranging issues.

Buenos Aires Plan of Action:
The Fourth Conference of the Parties in November 1998 adopted the Buenos Aires Plan of Action for Implementation of the Kyoto Protocol. We now have to consider the question of how we are going to initiate action on these various issues and this is likely to take some time to resolve. Substantial progress in different elements of the Plan has to be achieved so that the Conference of the Parties will be in a position to adopt major decisions at its sixth session. The Group is confident that the fifth session in Bonn, under your Presidency, will make a substantial contribution in our road to The Hague meeting.

Mr. President,

I do not have to repeat that the challenge before developing countries is to catalyse sustainable development, while the Annex I countries have to curtail the enormous levels of greenhouse gases emissions in the past few decades. The UN Framework Convention on Climate Change affirms the principle of common but differentiated responsibilities between the developed and the developing countries. The Convention recognizes that the overriding priority of the developing countries are poverty eradication and social economic development, consequent to which their emissions would grow. The extent to which the developing countries can effectively implement their commitments will depend in large part on the effective implementation by our partners of their commitments relating to provision of financial resources and transfer of technology.

Recognizing the necessary urgency of action required to mitigate climate change, the Group was quick to focus on the three Kyoto mechanisms and provided its position at the Subsidiary Body meetings in June of this year.

Here, in Bonn, the Group, in accordance with the priority agreed by COP-4, has made a submission on the clean development mechanism. Differences in the nature and scope, purpose, and participation of the three mechanisms must be born in mind. The Group believes that the principles and nature and scope should be decided first; the operational, methodological, and other questions relating to modalities and institutional arrangements could then be decided accordingly. It should be left to the host governments to decide whether or not a particular project meets with their sustainable development objectives and strategies, including areas and choice of technologies.

Activities Implemented Jointly:
Concerning AIJ, one of the elements, which was identified for inclusion in the review process of the AIJ pilot phase, is the geographical imbalance in the distribution of AIJ activities. Recognizing the need to gain practical experience in the hosting of projects, the Group supports the continuation of the AIJ pilot phase.

Very few developing countries have participated in AIJ, and Africa and Small Island Developing States have been particularly disadvantaged in this respect. Even now that attempts are being made to remedy this situation, most of the projects are still in the planning stage and have yet to be implemented. We need particular focus on the necessary institutional framework for project-based activities and the support for related capacity-building measures.

On non–Annex I communications:
Mr. President,

The successful implementation of the Kyoto Protocol depends upon the provision of national communications, and the Convention provides that the full agreed cost be covered by Annex II parties. As you may have noted, the provision of financial assistance has not been a smooth affair. Most of the countries find that the resources provided have been insufficient to help them fully fulfil their commitments and many of us have had to draw from already scarce national resources in order to maintain the necessary institutional support for the communications.

Capacity-building:
Capacity-building, including education, training, public awareness, and research, is an overarching necessity at all levels for the developing countries to participate adequately in the implementation of the Convention and the Kyoto Protocol. Capacity-building in developing countries, particularly the least developed countries and the Small Island Developing States, is constrained by, among others, lack of access to necessary technologies and know-how; lack of appropriate institutions; lack of financial resources; and lack of regular forums to exchange ideas and build positions amongst ourselves. It is a continuous process that must be undertaken at all levels, including long-term planning, and strengthening relevant institutions like the FCCC focal points, centres of excellences, sub-regional and regional institutions, and human resource development in order to provide expertise in the areas relating to the implementation of the Convention and Protocol processes.

Within this context, the G-77 and China welcomes the decision to address capacity-building needs of developing countries in a comprehensive manner, while taking into account the special concerns and specific needs of the least developed countries and also the particular vulnerability of these countries and Small Island Developing States to climate change. I, therefore, wish to emphasize that we would be extremely disappointed if progress in this area were to be held up in any way.

Compliance:
The Group of 77 and China recognizes that extensive work on compliance still needs to be done before COP-6. The establishment of a comprehensive, efficient, and fair compliance system is imperative to ensure the successful implementation of the Protocol and as a first priority aim at ensuring that the emission reduction targets set out in article 3 are met by Annex B parties.

The discussions in the Joint Working Group have been substantive in nature and indeed fruitful. We do believe that the time spent here on a detailed analysis of the various positions will assist us in the future to reach agreement on a compliance system that would serve the parties and the Protocol well. It is the intention of the Group of 77 and China to participate constructively in future deliberations.

Mr. President,

The developed countries have not achieved any degree of success in fulfilling their commitments under the Convention for reduction of greenhouse gas emissions. The latest data points to the fact that, in most cases, the emissions of Annex I parties have registered significant increases in the recent years. This cannot but give rise to serious doubt regarding their willingness and capacity to adhere to the obligations under the Convention and the Protocol. There has also not been any tangible progress in their extending support to the considerable efforts of the developing countries in dealing with climate change, despite the provisions of the Convention and the Protocol relating to resource transfers and the transfer of technology. The Group of 77 and China would like to reiterate that climate change issues can be discussed only in a framework of equity. The Group stands ready to contribute to your efforts in carrying forward the process.

Statement by Ambassador Bagher Asadi, Chairman of the Group of 77 (Islamic Republic of Iran), at the Informal Consultations on the New Proposals by the President of the Sixth Session of the Conference of the Parties (COP-6) to the UN Framework Convention on Climate Change (New York, 21 April 2001)

Mr. President,
Honourable Ministers,
Distinguished Colleagues,

It is a great pleasure, and yet quite a challenge, for the Chairman of the Group of 77, the largest bloc in the universal intergovernmental body with a very diverse constituency, to address such a distinguished and certainly demanding audience, particularly under very uncertain circumstances now surrounding the discussions on and around the Kyoto Protocol and the continuing COP-6 process. I might as well have emulated the words of Mr. Cutajar yesterday evening and called it a "crisis." However, characterized, the situation under which we have gathered here to engage in initial, exploratory informal consultations on Minister Prank's new Paper is rather peculiar. The very future of an almost decade-old and tortuous negotiations for the development, adoption, and finally entry into force of the instrument for the realization of the objective of the Climate Change Convention seems to have been thrown in total jeopardy.

Mr. President,

Let me say, at the very outset, that from our point of view, the Climate Change Convention and the Kyoto Protocol are valid international instruments. And the

Protocol is not to be renegotiated. Its fundamental principles, as guided by the Convention, should be respected and remain intact. Simultaneously, work on the operationalization of its provisions, as agreed by all in Kyoto back in December 1997, should continue. Within this framework, it hardly needs to be underlined that the principle of "common but differentiated responsibilities"—as enunciated at the Rio Summit almost ten years ago as well as in the Convention—is as valid and to be equally respected. And furthermore, it should be quite clear that the developing world will not undertake any new commitments.

Over and above, immediate negative impact on the continuing COP-6 process, to which I just alluded, we in the Group of 77 are very much concerned about the unsettling repercussions of the United States policy pronouncements on the Kyoto Protocol for multilateral negotiations and processes in general. We find unilateral approaches to multilateral processes and withdrawal from commitments unacceptable. The message from the new Republican administration to the international community cannot but be considered sad and indeed disappointing.

Turning to the immediate matter at hand, that is, the "New Proposals by the President of COP-6," let me first of all express our deep appreciation and gratitude to Minister Jan Pronk for his tireless and dedicated efforts in the entire COP-6 process and also for the preparation and presentation of his new Paper. We are aware that a lot of effort has gone into its production, for which we commend Mr. Pronk and his assistants. The Group of 77 and China is fully cognizant of Minister Prank's genuine desire to move the process beyond the impasse at the end of the session in The Hague. We are sure that our informal consultations today on the New Proposals, initial and exploratory as they inevitably are, will help all of us in the intergovernmental body to arrive at a better understanding of the relevant issues involved and take a step forward. And I presume that we all agree that we are dealing with intrinsically very complex and difficult issues in this process.

It is a fact that it has not been long since the President's New Proposals became available to parties, and hence, most of us in the Group of 77 have not yet had the opportunity for an in-depth study and analysis of its content. That is exactly why I termed the approach to the Paper at this stage initial and exploratory. Nevertheless, the Group met yesterday afternoon and discussed in very broad terms the content of the Paper. The Group is appreciative of the fact that some progress is discernible in certain areas in the Paper, for example, as regards financial mechanisms, but does not find the tenor of the Paper favourable to its positions, concerns, and interests. In the eyes of our membership, these concerns and interests have not been addressed adequately, even some fundamental principles and concepts in the Convention and the Protocol appear to have been downplayed or neglected. As for the Group's negotiating platform, the positions presented in The Hague by the Group on various issues still hold.

Mr. President,

Moving from an initial assessment of the New Proposals to what lies ahead, let me say, on behalf of the Group of 77 and China, that we remain committed to a firm, active, and yet proactive pursuit of our stated goals and objectives. To this end, and despite the current state of uncertainty, the Group remains committed to the continuation of negotiation towards completing the unfinished work of the COP-6. It is our genuine hope that what is called the current "Policy Review" within the US Government will soon result in their joining the negotiating table in earnest and in a spirit of constructive dialogue. "Come back to the family fold," as the President said. It should be underscored, however, that our support for the validity of the Protocol and disposition to continue active involvement in the process depends, first and foremost and in the final analysis, on the good faith of all the negotiating partners and ultimately on their political will in actuality to work for meaningful progress in the areas of interest and priority to the developing world. As always and as in all circumstances, it takes two to tango.

And a very brief word on procedure. Looking back at The Hague experience, it should be clear that agreement on the sensitive issues we are dealing with can only be achieved through a fully participatory and transparent process. It was reassuring to hear President Pronk underline that. Regardless of any other extraneous factor, we believe that prior to the meeting in Bonn in July the negotiating text to be subsequently presented by Mr. Pronk needs to be discussed at the expert level with open-ended participation. It is our understanding that the new negotiating text will be based on the texts of the subsidiary bodies, as presented in The Hague, taking into consideration the results of political consultations by Mr. Pronk. I should thank Mr. Pronk for the reconfirmation he made of this point in his introductory remarks.

To conclude, let me just add that today's exercise is a valuable and I grant a quite costly effort. It needs, however, to be complemented by further opportunities of exchange of views where every interested country would have the chance to participate and engage in the process.

Statement by Ambassador Bagher Asadi, Chairman of the Group of 77 (Islamic Republic of Iran), at the Open-ended Informal High-level Consultations on the Resumed COP-6 of the United Nations Framework Convention on Climate Change (The Hague, 27 June 2001)

Mr. President,
Honourable Ministers,
Distinguished Colleagues,

It is indeed a great pleasure for me to express, on behalf of the Group of 77 and China, our most sincere words of appreciation to you and your distinguished colleagues for the excellent opportunity and arrangements for The Hague consultations. The countdown for the resumed COP-6 in Bonn has already started. Nevertheless, the circumstances are as uncertain as in April when we met in New York. Our colloquium here indicates, if nothing else, that we are ready and willing to go to Bonn to finish an unfinished job. And that in itself should be taken as a good omen and forward-looking approach. Every possibility should be explored and every effort should be made to ensure success of the resumed session. Let us hope that our two-day rendezvous here will make a real, substantive contribution to this end.

Mr. President,

All of the colleagues here, including your good self, remember fully well the statement I made on April 21 in New York, in which the overall approach and specific positions of the Group of 77 and China on the status of the Kyoto Protocol and the new American policy were laid out in very clear terms. There is hardly any need to repeat them today. They are as valid now as they were then. It should be added, however, that despite the continuing uncertainty and the fact that the outcome of the much-talked-about "policy review" in Washington is not out yet, the overall picture can be judged—of course with a certain degree of liberal optimism—to be less static than expected previously. Recent further reiteration of previous American pronouncements on the Kyoto Protocol along with reiteration of commitment to the Climate Change Convention seem to be at once confounding and containing some elements of positive future action.

Mr. President,

Now that your unbracketed text has been issued and studied, today I intend to present our reflections, preliminary as they are at this stage, on its provisions.

First and foremost, let me register our gratitude to you for the very valuable effort you have put into producing the new text. We consider your new text as a good tool in the course of these consultations and for the Bonn meeting. You can rest assured that it will be found useful as well as helpful in this ongoing process. What I present here now is the outcome of the two precious days of intensive exchange of views within the Group of 77 on various parts and provisions of your new text—thanks to you, the Dutch Government as well as the other European Governments supporting these consultations. In our exchanges today and tomorrow, we will be frank and forthcoming in laying out our concerns and interests. The exercise, I hope—in fact, the whole Group hopes—would be found educational and enlightening, and that our negotiating partners would reciprocate the approach and would bring to the fore their respective outlook and specific positions. In underlining our commitment to the continuation of proactive and constructive engagement in the process we would like to indicate that the developing world is serious in pursuing its interests and demands and is equally well disposed to work in concert with all the willing fellow travellers towards saving the hard-won achievements of a decade-long collective multilateral enterprise.

Mr. President,

Turning to practical aspects of our work today, I should start with the reiteration of a rather familiar, and yet critical, concept; that is, the ultimate aim of our ongoing negotiations has been, and continues to be, to fulfil the mandate established by the Buenos Aires Plan of Action. As such, the texts presented by the subsidiary bodies at The Hague last November form the basis of negotiations in Bonn in July. Moreover, compliance with that mandate also implies that no new agenda item should be introduced or injected in the work of the resumed session.

The most important, and in fact, the most pressing issue before us all, the entire international community, is to undertake with resolve and good faith to strengthen the implementation of the provisions of the Climate Change Convention. And simultaneously, we can, and indeed we should, continue our debates and deliberations on Kyoto Protocol issues with a view to resolving the outstanding issues. From our point of view, and it comes as no surprise, adaptation, technology transfer, and provision of financial resources are Convention issues, whose implementation should command priority.

Within this overall framework, our specific positions on various crunch issues will be presented. For this, with your indulgence, Mr. President, when you take up specific crunch issues, I will ask my colleague, Mr. Mohammad Reza Salamat, an old hand and a known face in climate change negotiations, to be assisted by our Core Group Facilitators, to outline the Group's positions and demands.

Statement by Ambassador Bagher Asadi, Chairman of the Group of 77 (Islamic Republic of Iran), at the Opening Meeting of the Seventh Session of the Conference of the Parties to the United Nations Framework Convention on Climate Change (Marrakech, Morocco, 29 October 2001)

Mr. President,

It is indeed a great honour and distinct pleasure for the Chairman of the Group of 77 to have the unique opportunity to address the Seventh Session of the Conference of the Parties to the United Nations Framework Convention on Climate Change, at the very beginning of its work, in this beautiful historical city and particularly under your presidency. While commending the Government and the people of Morocco for hosting this important Conference and for the excellent arrangements and extending the most sincere, heartfelt felicitations of the Group of 77 and China to you, Mr. Minister, for the prestigious office you have just assumed, let me seize the moment to assure you of our full cooperation in the collective enterprise ahead of us all. I should as well avail of this opportunity to place on record our deep gratitude and appreciation to Minister Ian Pronk, distinguished President of COP-6, for his perseverance and his tireless, indefatigable efforts throughout his tenure and, no less importantly, for his marvellous performance in shepherding the achievement of the Bonn Agreements. Thanks, are also due to Mr. Michael Zammit Cutajar and his colleagues in the Convention Secretariat for all their invaluable efforts and contribution, substantive and otherwise, for COP-7.

Mr. President,

We are just beginning a very important international gathering within the framework of an ongoing decade-old multilateral process towards implementing the Climate Change Convention. But we are meeting here under a quite different global atmosphere, when as a result of the tragic events of September 11 and its consequences the need for genuine multilateralism across the board has never been as compelling and urgent. Yes, as Mr. Pronk just said, multilateralism works, based, of course, on international cooperation, dialogue, and understanding. The fact that COP-7 is taking place under these changed and yet charged circumstances is very important in itself; what might have been considered a mission impossible, should, by the end of the next week, be a mission completed—a successful fait accompli of the international community.

Mr. President,

We have come here to Marrakech with a great, historical achievement in our hands—the Political Agreements we sealed in Bonn less than three months ago. There and then all of us, those engaged in that long marathon of negotiations, resolved to prepare the grounds for the entry into force of the Kyoto Protocol by the year 2002, and as all of us tend to understand, before the Johannesburg Summit. And once the overall Political Agreements were reached, we started with the next stage of our work; that is, translating the agreements into solid legal language on various crunch issues. Well, thanks to everybody's spirit of cooperation and sense of pragmatism and flexibility—indispensable ingredients for any successful negotiation—we managed to make progress in a number of important areas. Document FCCC/CP/2001/5/Add.1 contains decisions in those areas where negotiations were completed and consensus was reached, and which have been forwarded to this Conference for adoption. Moreover, as we all remember, there were a number of other equally important areas where progress was made but the work was not finished. Document FCCC/CP/2001/5/Add.2 contains the draft decisions which have been forwarded to COP-7 for elaboration, completion, and adoption. As you underlined, Mr. President, this is the central part of the work of COP-7.

Mr. President,

This is a rather short statement. I will not engage in a long, detailed expose of the positions of the Group of 77 and China on various issues we have before us in

COP-7. Instead, I merely suffice to lay out a number of overarching considerations, which we would like to share with you and our negotiating partners quite early on.

First and foremost, we consider the Bonn Agreements an honourable deal that should be respected by all; we remain faithful to it and call on all other partners to do so. Such an approach by all is absolutely imperative for this Conference to achieve ultimate success of this unique multilateral process and give practical effect to those Agreements.

Second, and closely related to the above assertion, is the imperative for everybody to avoid any temptation for re-opening of the Bonn Agreements, including through resort to interpretation of the agreed language. Every effort should be made to resolve the outstanding differences in a manner that would not undermine the political integrity of the Bonn Agreements. All of us are fully, and yet consciously, cognizant of the fact that some of the differences on the table, whether on Compliance, Mechanisms or LULUCF or under articles 5, 7, and 8, may seem quite difficult. Nevertheless, I remain confident that everybody in the house, both developed and developing, concurs with me on the fundamental necessity of preserving the integrity of the Agreements and completing the work here. It is do-able; hence, it should be done. As implied a little while earlier, our detailed positions will be brought to the table as soon as actual negotiations on the draft decisions and other issues commence.

Mr. President,

Your good self-represent a developing country, therefore, you are fully familiar with the concerns of your fellow members of the Group of 77. That is exactly why I deem it necessary to underline right here, on behalf of the Group of 77 and China, a point of caution—that the reports before us, or for that matter, items of the agenda, should not be utilized in any possible manner to inject into our deliberations the rather stale question of new commitments for the developing world. Neither COP-7 nor the Johannesburg Summit is the proper forum for such an untimely suggestion, which, if nothing else, would prove extremely divisive in an atmosphere requiring goodwill and disposition to consensus. Our collective endeavours here are geared towards the further effective implementation of the Climate Change Convention as well as making the Protocol ratifiable. Our expectations for the full implementation of the Agenda 21 and fulfilment of past promises and commitments are yet to be realized. It is in such a context that I have to state, in very unequivocal terms, that our disposition to compromise and consensus—based on the principle of common but differentiated responsibilities—is, as everybody knows, equally matched by our principled, if not jealous, guarding of the genuine, legitimate long-term common concerns and interests of the collectivity of the developing world. This is the indispensable platform for our unity and participation in all multilateral processes, including the climate change process. To this end, here in Marrakech, we rely on the good sense of our partners in the North and your able stewardship.

I close my statement, as always, on positive note, and with a very clear assertion. The Group of 77 and China has come to Marrakech to help crown the Bonn achievement with yet another, higher stage of international, intergovernmental agreement that would ensure the entry into force of the Kyoto Protocol by the time we walk into the Johannesburg Conference. Our success here will indeed send a potent message and make a substantive contribution to that ten-year review process. We are here to negotiate, in all earnestness and with good faith. We expect the same from our partners in the North. And none of us shall be found wanting in this great collective enterprise. To this end, we rely on dialogue and mutual understanding—so beautifully underscored in your opening statement—and equally on your diplomatic savvy and political acumen, Mr. President.

Statement by Her Excellency Dr. Massoumeh Ebtekar, Vice-President and Head of the Department of Environment (Islamic Republic of Iran), on behalf of the Group of 77, High-level Segment, COP-7, UNFCCC (Marrakech, 7 November 2001)

Mr. President,
Honourable Ministers,
Ladies and Gentlemen,

The message of the Group of 77 and China to the High-level Segment of the Seventh Session of the Conference of the Parties to the United Nations Framework Convention on Climate Change, a critical stage in this unique international process of historical significance and import, is a message of dialogue, understanding, engagement, and proactive, constructive—albeit principled—flexibility. Here, we stand at the beginning of the end of a long journey towards making the implementation of the Climate Change Convention a reality. In Bonn, the international community resolved, against all odds and an atmosphere of doubt and uncertainty, to act on the imperative of multilateralism and reach a set of overall political agreements—the Bonn Agreements—which made the ratification of the Kyoto Protocol possible by the year 2002. Those Agreements, an honourable deal indeed, needed to be translated into solid legal language and practical decisions. Part of that undertaking was completed in Bonn, the rest left for Marrakech. This Conference has the historical task of completing the remaining decisions and adopting all of them to give effect to the overall Agreements. The assembly of distinguished dignitaries and ministers, coming at the wake of a week-long intense negotiations, and representing the collective political will and determination of the entire international community, cannot but signal the necessary drive and impetus—the final green light—to all the negotiators, on both sides of the development divide, to overcome the remaining hurdles and crown the Bonn Agreements with yet a higher level of international consensus. This signifies the particular importance we in the developing world attach to our long-term destiny and the future of our environment as a prerequisite to peace and prosperity for present and future generations. And nothing should stand in the way of the actual realization of this collective resolve.

Mr. President,

Before turning to the practical aspects of our work here, I should avail of this opportunity to extend, on behalf of the Group of 77 and China, our most sincere gratitude and appreciation to you, and through you, to the Government and the people of Morocco for hosting this historical Conference and for all the excellent arrangements. I am fully cognizant of the extremely positive and critical contribution the Group of 77 and China in its entirety, and the excellent leadership of Ambassador Asadi and his colleagues, representing the Group, have been making to the process of negotiations, in Bonn and here in Marrakech. A realistic assessment of the state of negotiations indicates that the progress made thus far in COP-7, thanks to the sense of objectivity, cooperation, and compromise of the negotiators and your able, seasoned leadership, is solid and very encouraging. There is cause for satisfaction and strong optimism, but we are not out of doldrums yet. For our part, as underlined in the Group's statement last week, you can rest assured of our collective determination to stay the course and give you and the Bureau full cooperation towards the final success of the Marrakech Conference.

The occasion could hardly be more opportune for me to present the Group position of the developing world and simultaneously represent the Islamic Republic of Iran in this year of Dialogue among Civilizations, particularly in a historical city as Marrakech, an important nexus where cultures and civilizations have met and left their indelible imprint on history. The positive outlook and approach of the developing world in this process which made the achievement of the Bonn Agreements possible has brought us to this point. We will certainly continue the process along the same lines and with the same spirit till we complete our task at COP-7. I remain confident that all our negotiating partners will reciprocate this outlook and approach and lend themselves in good faith to resolving the remaining outstanding issues. The welcome agreement on compliance last night and the progress in other important areas point to a certain degree of timely realism among some of our negotiating partners. The same spirit should continue to prevail till the very end.

Mr. President,

Turning to the outstanding issues, let me just lay out, very briefly though, the negotiating positions of the Group. What you have already heard from the Group of 77 over the past week on various issues before the Conference simply need not be repeated. Rather, I merely suffice to address just a few areas which, in our view, are of a particularly political nature, and hence, call for political guidance, which the distinguished colleagues are here to provide.

First, on the legally binding nature of the compliance regime, which is intimately related to the very logic of the Kyoto Protocol. The agreement reached last night is indeed a very good outcome. Its elements provide the framework for a strong, well-defined binding compliance regime as the only effective guarantee for the meaningful pursual of the objectives of the Protocol and the implementation of its provisions, and for that matter, the objectives of the Bonn Agreements and COP-7. We believe the Ministers had already decided in Bonn that these procedures and mechanisms shall be legally binding. With the agreed elements in place, the COP-MOP-1 should proceed to finalize the necessary arrangements that would ensure implementation of the Protocol and bring these procedures into effect. The deal on compliance, including as regards eligibility requirements for participation in mechanisms, now can ensure effective, multilateral monitoring of the enforcement of the guidelines for their functioning. Also, with the robust compliance regime now in our hands, LULUCF-related activities would not simply turn into a compendium of loopholes. Moreover, what was achieved would as well help safeguard the much-cherished notion of the environmental integrity of the Protocol. And this is no small feat.

Second, implementation of past agreements, decisions, and commitments is central to our approach to the remaining outstanding issues; whether the review of the implementation of the Agenda 21 at WSSD, or the operationalization of the three Funds agreed in Bonn. The agreements on these Funds in Bonn, although followed by some positive pronouncements, still seem to be far from reality. We need to be assured in COP-7 that a substantive discussion on them in COP-8 will lead to agreement in principle on practical modalities for burden-sharing for their original replenishment. Within the same context, we emphasize the importance of the implementation of decisions on transfer of technology, capacity-building, economic diversification, and adaptation.

Third, in a general sense, success of the Marrakech Conference depends, in the final analysis, on due consideration for the priority areas of the developing community—to some of which I just referred. In the same vein, it should be reaffirmed, beyond doubt or illusion, that neither COP-7 nor the Johannesburg Summit is the proper forum for addressing the question of "new commitments for the developing countries."

And finally, ratification and entry into force of the Kyoto Protocol is the best substantive contribution we can make in this process to the World Summit on Sustainable Development. Our input to WSSD should, in a general sense, help the ongoing global drive for sustainable development as defined and understood in Rio, including as concerns climate change. We believe the Bonn Agreements properly placed the question of climate change at the heart of sustainable development. Let us hope, and more importantly, let us resolve, that the actual implementation of those Agreements will pave the way for the achievement of the goals and objectives we have collectively agreed on. With an eye to the bigger global picture, the ongoing developments as well as the still unfolding globalization process, we all need to set an example, rather now and here in COP-7, through the adoption of adequate, effective actions and measures towards promoting an equitable and democratic global governance.

Mr. President,

The distinguished audience here hardly needs to be reminded of the rather obvious fact that the disposition of the Group of 77 and China to flexibility and compromise towards reaching consensus is equally matched—if not more so—by a principled commitment to the genuine, legitimate long-term common concerns and interests of the collectivity of the developing world. As underlined in the Group's previous statement, this is the very raison d'être of the Group and the indispensable platform for its unity and solidarity.

With the foregoing in perspective, let me just add that the good sense, flexibility, and disposition to consensus exhibited so far by everybody—all negotiating partners, developed and developing—should be able to overcome the difficulties still hounding the process and save the political integrity of the Bonn Agreements, which we all tend to share and underscore rather unquestioningly. And on this positive note, I close my statement and wish you and the Conference all luck. This Conference cannot but complete its work, adopt all the decisions, and end in success. The bright end is in clear sight. Let us grasp it. We shall be going to Johannesburg with a ratified Kyoto Protocol. And our message to WSSD, a clear, potent, and unmistakable message, will be on the compelling and urgent need for genuine multilateralism across the board and international cooperation for long-term development, including the necessity of the full implementation of the Agenda 21 as well as a concomitant future-looking vision for serving the cause of sustainable development on a global scale. The ultimate success of this ten-year-old, hard-won multilateral process will no doubt carry a strong symbolic message as well; dialogue, understanding, and cooperation as the only avenue before the international community to address and resolve common problems of a global nature. This could be, and in fact, should be, the common cause of us all.

Statement of the Delegation of Morocco, on behalf of the Group of 77 and China, Delivered by Mr. Mohamed Arrouchi at the Opening of the 9th Conference of the Parties to the United Nations Framework Convention on Climate Change (Milan, 1 December 2003)

Mr. President,

On behalf of the G-77 and China, allow me, at the outset, to congratulate you for your well-deserved election to the Presidency of this very important session of this

COP-9 on climate change. I would like also to seize this opportunity to extend our sincere thanks to His Excellency Minister M.T.R. BAALU from India for the invaluable efforts he invested during the Presidency of the COP-8. Our thanks go as well to the Executive Secretary of the Convention, Mrs. Joke Waller-Hunter and all the Secretariat staff, for the continuous support they provide for the implementation of our Convention.

Mr. President,

Climate change is a process and a global challenge which necessitates an urgent global action. Reversing this trend through an effective global response is a necessary step towards the attainment of sustainability.

Since Rio, and despite the efforts made so far to meet the goals and objectives of our Convention, significant steps are still to be taken in order to ensure an effective and durable implementation of our Convention at a time the climate change continues to have enormous negative impact on the world's regions and populations, particularly in developing countries, including the least developed countries and Small Island Developing States.

The G-77 and China, therefore, believes that efforts should be doubled to translate our joint commitments into concrete and effective actions, thus meeting the objective of protecting our common global climate for present and future generations of mankind.

In this context, the G-77 and China is looking forward to see concrete progress and action-oriented decisions taken by the COP-9 while avoiding repetitive normative debate. We would like to highlight the following elements of particular importance to the Group:

1. *Different Aspects of the Kyoto Protocol and CDM (Clean Development Mechanism)*

We would like to recall that in the United Nations Millennium Declaration, Heads of State and Government resolved to make every effort to ensure the entry into force of the Kyoto Protocol and to embark on the required reduction in emissions of greenhouse gases. It is worth noting in this regard that, to date, the Kyoto Protocol to the United Nations Framework Convention on Climate Change has attracted one hundred and twenty ratifications, including from parties mentioned in Annex I to the Convention, who account for 44.2 per cent of emissions.

However, the entry into force of the KP is still awaiting particularly the ratification by the Federation of Russia.

While reiterating that the protection of the global nature of climate change calls for the widest possible cooperation by all countries and their participation in an effective and appropriate international response, in accordance with their common but differentiated responsibilities and respective capabilities and their social and economic conditions, the G-77 and China firmly calls on the parties who have not yet ratified the KP, notably the United States of America, to come back on board as soon as possible.

The Group of 77 and China notes the significant work accomplished by the CDM Executive Board since its establishment two years ago in Marrakech. In this respect, we would like to emphasize the importance of reliable support by the developed countries to the developing countries to ensure equitable geographical representation within the operational entities. Developing countries are also in need of a strong support to set up their Clean Development Mechanism (CDM) and Designated National Authority (DNA) and to master the CDM technical aspects.

The G-77 and China is looking forward to a final decision on the LULUCF (Forestation and reforestation) in the CDM process during this COP.

2. Vulnerability and adaptation

While expressing our deep concern at the enormous negative impact of climate change which continues to hinder social and economic progress, in particular in developing countries, the issue relating to vulnerability and adaptation should be given due consideration in conformity with the terms of the Convention.

In this respect, we would like to emphasize the urgency of putting all the expected funds created by the Convention and KP into operation and identifying other structural financial mechanisms where Annex I parties can comply with their commitments. This would, in particular, enable parties to implement an efficient and integrated strategy to deal with adaptation. Therefore, we expect this COP to give guidance to the GEF to develop the necessary rules and procedures to make these new funds operational.

3. IPCC's Third Assessment Report (TAR)

We would like to underline with regret that according to this report, emissions from developed countries continue, contrary to the provisions of the Convention, to increase. We, therefore, call on developed countries to take the necessary effective measures to reverse this trend.

The objective of the Global Climate Observation System is to improve the world climate observation system. We, therefore, encourage the creation of a Fund to reach this objective.

4. National Communication of Annex I Parties

The Group of G-77 and China looks forward to the evaluation of the third national communication of Annex I parties to draw conclusions on the progress accomplished by these countries in the implementation of their commitments.

5. National Communication of Non–Annex I Parties
On this aspect, COP-8 adopted new guidelines for the second national communication. GEF has also elaborated and adopted at its last Council meeting the guidelines for the use of these funds. Hence, all the practicalities are ready now for the second National Communication.

Given the complexity of the guidelines of this second national communication, we believe that the discussion of the issue of national communication frequency should be reported to a later stage.

6. Capacity-Building and Transfer of Technologies
Capacity-building and transfer of technologies are indispensable components in the implementation process of the Convention. The G-77 and China is looking forward to concrete decisions in this respect.

This COP should examine the barriers and obstacles, which prevent the transfer of technologies notably towards developing countries, and how to ensure an enabling environment for the transfer of technologies according to the Convention and KP provisions.

7. Secretariat of the Convention's Budget
The Group of 77 and China is concerned about the low level of contribution by parties to this Convention, given the increasing needs, notably related to the complex tasks that the Secretariat is entrusted with. Therefore, the G-77 and China invites parties to increase significantly their contributions and provide the Secretariat with adequate resources to deliver adequately and as expected the various programmes.

Mr. President,

The G-77 and China, while reiterating its full cooperation to the presidency for the success of this session, stands ready to engage with a constructive spirit in the forthcoming negotiations with our partners keeping in mind our common objective and guiding principle of protecting global climate for present and future generations.

Finally, let me seize this opportunity to recall here that the city of Marrakech where COP-7 took place and where important decisions were taken is going to host from 15 to 19 December 2003 a high-level conference on South-South cooperation where the issue of climate change will be addressed within the context of sustainability.

Statement by H.E. Mr. Mohamed El Yazghi, Minister of Territory Development, Water and Environment, on behalf of the G-77 and China, during the discussions of the First, Second and Third Round Tables of the High-level Segment of COP-9 on Climate Change
(Milan, 1–12 December 2003)

COP-9: Ministerial Round Table 1

Climate Change, Adaptation, Mitigation and Sustainable Development

Context:

- The conclusions of the TAR indicate clearly that the negative impacts of CC are already in action in our world, particularly in developing countries, the most vulnerable to CC.
  - This explains why developing countries are so concerned about adaptation to already unavoidable impacts of CC. This concern has not yet been given the urgent attention it deserves.
  - These impacts undermine the enormous efforts put by developing countries to achieve their sustainable development.
- Annex I countries emissions continue to grow at an alarming rate despite their Commitments under the Convention.
- Many developing countries are implementing mitigation strategies in their development plans, despite their low emissions level.

Achievements under the Convention:

- Limited progress has been made in the implementation of articles 4.8 and 4.9 of the convention since its entry in force.
- Funds created under Marrakech Accords meant to deal with adaptation, are not yet operational.
- Through their national communications, developing countries have shown their commitment to contribute to the ultimate objective of the Convention, putting efforts into mitigation.
  - Very limited efforts to mitigate GHG emissions have been made by some Annex I parties; the main tools to achieve the ultimate objective of the Convention, particularly the KP, seem to be resisted.
  - Most of developing countries have ratified the KP showing their willingness to help Annex-I countries to fulfil their emission reduction commitments.

Expectations:

- Strong support to developing countries, particularly the most vulnerable ones, with technology transfer, capacity-building, and additional financing, to cope with the negative impacts of Climate Change.
- A recognition of adaptation as a priority for developing countries and an urgent start of action, notably implementation of the NAPAs.
- Early entry into force of the Kyoto Protocol.
- Consideration to be given to the negative impacts of the implementation of response measures on concerned developing countries with support to be provided to these countries in diversifying their economies.
- A global move of the world towards Sustainable Development.

G-77 and China

COP-9: Ministerial Round Table 2

Technology, Including Technology Use and Development and Transfer of Technologies

Context: To achieve the objective of the Convention both for mitigating the effects of greenhouse gases emissions and for adapting to climate change, we require technology use and development, and rapid and widespread transfer of environmentally sound technologies (EST). These needs are particularly crucial for developing countries, which are adversely affected by climate change. However, as indicated by the various technical papers tabled during this Conference, not much progress has been done. Hopes for accelerated transfer and diffusion of EST have remained largely unfulfilled. Most government equated transfer of technology with commercialization citing private sector domain and IPR as the main reasons for such a failure. As such, developing countries continue to be lacking in scientific capacity to generate scientific inventions and produce technological innovations and to adapt and absorb technologies.

Achievements under the Convention: The Convention recognized that transfer of technologies is the basic element for developing country parties to meet their commitments. This is clearly stipulated under article 4.7 of the Convention. To facilitate such transfer, the Convention under articles 4.3 and 4.5 provides the necessary guidance for Annex II countries to carry out their commitments to ensure that transfer of technologies is carried out.

In this regard, the UNFCCC Reporting Guidelines contain a mandatory requirement for Annex II parties to provide information on technology transfer activities including activities for financing access by developing countries to soft and hard environmentally sound technologies.

We are, therefore, pleased that COP-7 has set up the Expert Group of Technology Transfer to examine the effective means for transferring technologies. We are also pleased that many developing country parties have already done their technology needs assessments.

Expectations: Although we have seen some progress in this area, we believed that there are many more things that need and can be done to ensure faster rate of transfer of technologies in particular adaptation and mitigation technologies. Among them are:

i. providing financial support to meet the full incremental cost of implementing all the technology needs identified by non–Annex I parties,
ii. disseminating information regarding existing EST;

iii. establishing concrete programs such as joint research, access to and development of technology;
iv. providing incentives to the private sectors in developed country parties to facilitate the transfer of technologies;
v. innovative financing of development and transfer of technologies;
vi. promotion of indigenous technologies; and
vii. encourage the South-South cooperation in the transfer of technologies.

COP-9:

Ministerial Round Table 3

Assessment of Progress in the National, Regional and International Levels to Fulfil the Promise and the Objective Enshrined in the Climate Change Agreements, Including the Scientific, Information, Policy and Financial Aspects

Context:

- The promise enshrined in the climate change agreements is the achievement of the ultimate objective of the United Nations Framework Convention on Climate Change in the context of sustainable development, and based on the principle of common but differentiated responsibilities.
- The G-77 and China has clearly demonstrated their willingness to fulfil the promise and objectives enshrined in the climate change agreements.
- The vast majority of their members have ratified the United Nations Framework Convention on Climate Change and the Kyoto Protocol.
- According to article 4.7 of the Convention, the extent to which developing country parties will effectively implement their commitments under the Convention will depend on the effective implementation by developed country parties of their commitments under the Convention related to financial resources and transfer of technology and will take fully into account that economic and social development and poverty eradication are the first and overriding priorities of the developing country parties.
- The Clean Development Mechanism has opened important possibilities for strengthening international cooperation, fostering capacity-building in developing countries, and creating a significant incentive for the ratification of the Kyoto Protocol.

Achievements under the Convention:

- At the policy level, several initiatives have been taken and programs put in place to address climate change in areas such as energy efficiency and technologies, cleaner technologies, waste management, and land use.
- As regards to information, important efforts have been made by G-77 and China members in the areas of education, training, and public awareness.

Through the process of elaborating the national communications to the Convention, developing countries are providing relevant information referring to emissions of greenhouse gases by sources and removals by sinks, as well as steps taken to implement the Convention.

- On the scientific side, coordinated actions have been taken in the areas of research and systematic observation and climate modelling, contributing to an improved understanding of climate change and its impacts. To the extent possible, developing countries' experts have progressively increased their participation in the work of the Subsidiary Body for Scientific and Technological Advice of the Convention and the Intergovernmental Panel on Climate Change.

Expectations: Noting that the largest share of historical and current global emissions of greenhouse gases has originated in developed countries, that per capita emissions in developing countries are still relatively low, and that the share of global emissions originating in developing countries will grow to meet their social and development needs, the main expectations of countries from G-77 and China are as follows:

- In order for developing countries to progress in their efforts to address climate change and adapt to the impact of response measures, including economic diversification, there needs to be a significant increase in the efforts by the developed country parties in the transfer of financial resources and technology, as well as the development of capacity-building and institutions, in fulfilment of their commitments under the Convention.
- There is an urgent need to allow a greater space for the participation of developing countries in the scientific efforts do address climate change. Difficulties are particularly visible in the context of the Intergovernmental Panel on Climate Change, where literature in languages other than English is not given due consideration, and the participation of experts from developing countries is still very limited.
- In order to advance in the provision of information referring to climate change, support for the preparation of national communications by developing countries needs to be improved, through simplification of procedures and increase of financial resources provided by the Global Environment Facility. Improvements are also necessary in the areas of methodology and data provision.
- The failure of some countries to ratify the Kyoto Protocol has so far prevented it from entering into force, to the detriment of the international regime for climate protection. G-77 and China urges countries that have not yet ratified the Kyoto Protocol to do so in a timely manner.

Statement on behalf of the Group of 77 and China by Mr. Marthinus Van Schalkwyk, Minister of Environmental Affairs and Tourism of the Republic of South Africa, at the Opening of the High-Level Segment of COP-12 and COP/MOP-2 of the UN Framework Convention on Climate Change (Nairobi, 15 November 2006)

Mr. President,

On behalf of the Group of 77 and China, I would like to express our full confidence in your leadership in bringing this meeting to a successful and forward-looking conclusion.

Adaptation is a top priority for developing countries. The G-77 and China Group is therefore encouraged by the agreement on activities under the Five-Year Programme of Work on impacts, vulnerability, and adaptation to climate change, as well as the completion of the principles and governance foundations that will make it possible to operationalise the Adaptation Fund during 2007, which in reality is largely funded by developing countries for developing countries.

Acknowledging the decisive action taken on adaptation in Nairobi, it is also clear that a future, strengthened climate regime would need to more fully balance our international efforts on mitigation and adaptation. Whilst continuing to build our knowledge base on adaptation needs, we must increasingly shift our focus to implementation. In order to access the required new and additional funding, we must also widen the circle of implementation beyond the narrow emphasis on mainstreaming of adaptation into the development process. Adequate and sustainable resources for adaptation are not only critically needed—it is a legally binding commitment to be implemented by developed countries.

Likewise, we must ensure that the adverse impacts of response measures as they relate to the unintended consequences of mitigation are addressed as a distinct priority in a focused and consolidated work programme.

Mr. President,

One issue that will require significant political will is the issue of unlocking and accelerating the development and transfer of adaptation and mitigation technologies, in particular addressing the intellectual property rights barriers. This will require new thinking on the institutional arrangements, cooperation, and funding mechanisms aimed at facilitating access to current technologies, stimulating the development of new technologies and expanding South-South cooperation.

In responding to the COP President's call for a more equitable distribution of CDM projects, we must facilitate the development of concrete projects on the ground—thereby ensuring that our capacity-building interventions follow a bottom-up approach in partnership with local institutions.

Mr. President,

You have challenged us to take advantage of the high-level segment to expand the creative space and give practical content and focus to the future. Broadly speaking there are two streams of thinking on future action.

The one approach, favoured by some Annex I parties, says to developing countries "cap now." The other approach says to developed countries: "cap first" and to developing countries "empower first." This second approach enables non–Annex I parties to integrate climate considerations in their development paths without compromising sustainable development, thereby ensuring meaningful contribution within their respective capabilities.

The message from developing countries is clear: it will be unfair and misguided to ignore the fact that Annex I parties achieved economic progress through more than a century of cumulative emissions; thereby building greater institutional, technological and financial capabilities and greater adaptive capacity. This historical responsibility is the moral and legal basis of Annex I parties' obligation to take the lead in "capping first" under the Kyoto Protocol, and in creating an "empower first" environment for enhanced action by all countries under the Convention.

Mr. President, this understanding underlies the expected outcomes of the Montreal two-track process:

- firstly, deeper absolute emission reductions by developed countries under the Kyoto Protocol to be agreed in the AWG by 2008; and
- secondly, building on the dialogue on long-term cooperative action to address climate change by enhancing implementation of the Convention.

Mr. President, at its core this is a process of exercising collective political will and decision-making.

We must make the link in the minds of people around the world between climate change, their development, health, and well-being, and their actions—and those of their elected representatives. The people who rely on us for new hope and a strengthened climate deal do not want to see a few countries holding our common future to ransom or retreating from commitments to address climate change.

To succeed we will have to build a new spirit of trust and solidarity, and acknowledge the legitimate fears and concerns of parties. Political will and being bold in our thinking about the future will carry us through. I think we will be surprised by the amount of goodwill, common resolve, and political vision that can be unlocked on all sides of the debate when we put our heads together. Mr. President, the G-77 and China stands ready to work with you in tackling our common challenges.

Statement by Ambassador Attiya Mahmood of Pakistan on behalf of G-77 and China at the Opening Session of the 13th Conference of the Parties to the United Nations Framework Convention on Climate Change (UNFCCC) (Bali, Indonesia, 3 December 2007)

Mr. President,

1. It is my pleasure to make this contribution on behalf of the Group of 77 and China. I would like to congratulate you and members of the Bureau on your election and assure you of our full support and cooperation in bringing our deliberations to a fruitful conclusion.
2. Let me also thank the Government and the people of the fraternal Republic of Indonesia for the warm hospitality extended to us since our arrival in this beautiful island.
3. I would like to assure you as well as our negotiating partners of the Group of 77 and China's resolve to engage constructively so as to ensure a substantive outcome of this important meeting.
4. This meeting takes place in the backdrop of the recently released Synthesis Report of the IPCC Fourth Assessment Report, which presents a stark and dire warning about climate change. The IPCC reports and the recent scientific findings demonstrate, irrefutably, that climate change is posing a very serious and immediate challenge to the efforts of developing countries.
5. The Group of 77 and China is concerned about the fact that the adverse effects of climate change and the associated phenomena threaten sustainable development, livelihoods, and the very existence of many developing countries and in particular Africa, the LDCs, the LLDCs, SIDS, and disaster-prone developing countries.

Mr. President,

6. Climate change poses serious risks and challenges to the developing countries that are least equipped to respond and therefore most vulnerable to its rising dangers.
7. According to the Fourth Assessment Report of IPCC:
   - In Africa, climate change is projected to expose between 75 and 250 million people to increased water stress and reduced yields from rain-fed agriculture by up to 50%.
   - In Asia, freshwater availability is projected to decrease, coastal areas will be at greater risk due to increased flooding, and climate change is projected to compound pressures on natural resources and public health.
   - In Latin America, climate change threatens significant loss of biodiversity through species extinction. Reduction in productivity of important crops will pose risks to food security.

- Small Islands are expected to face inundation, storm surges, erosion, and other coastal hazards, threatening vital infrastructure, settlements, and livelihoods of island communities.

8. In all developing countries, water available for human consumption, agriculture, and energy generation is likely to be significantly affected.

Mr. President,

9. In such a bleak scenario, our task becomes even more daunting given the inextricable link between sustainable development and climate change. Developing countries, which historically were not responsible for the climate change problem, have rights and priorities in meeting their present and future development needs.
10. The most formidable challenge before us in addressing climate change and its adverse effects include: lack of fulfilment of commitments during the first commitment period of the Kyoto Protocol by Annex I countries in reducing GHG emission; provision of financial resources and technology transfer to developing countries; inadequacy of financial resources for adaptation and mitigation efforts; insufficient national institutional capacity in the developing countries for participation in carbon market mechanisms.
11. The best and the most appropriate way to address the threats of climate change is to adopt and implement an integrated approach to sustainable development. Making development more sustainable can help address climate change. On the other hand, it is very likely that climate change will slow the pace of progress towards sustainable development, and could impede achievement of the Millennium Development Goals.
12. Simultaneously, we would like to reiterate that without immediate and effective cuts in GHG emissions by developed countries, all efforts to address climate change will remain fruitless. The early completion of the work of the Ad Hoc Working Group on further commitments for Annex I parties under the Kyoto Protocol is an absolute imperative.
13. Adaptation remains at the forefront of G-77 and China's concern. We look forward to the launch of the Adaptation Fund. We hope that the Nairobi Work Programme of Action will continue to be implemented in a concrete and substantive manner as part of the implementation of the Buenos Aires Plan of Action.
14. Effective mitigation and adaptation policies must take into consideration all aspects with regard to commitments at various conferences and summits, in particular the legally binding commitments under the UNFCCC and the Kyoto Protocol in accordance with the principle of Common but Differentiated Responsibilities.

15. In addition, it needs to be ensured that the adverse impacts of response measures, as they relate to the unintended consequences of mitigation, are addressed as a distinct priority in a consolidated work programme.
16. During this session the most important issues in responding to these challenges include mustering the political will to agree on a approach based upon the key principles of Rio and those in the UNFCCC and its Kyoto Protocol, especially (a) common but differentiated responsibilities and respective capabilities; (b) polluters pay principle; (c) protection of the vulnerable; (d) equal treatment of mitigation and adaptation, including legally binding instrument for adaptation and technology transfer.

Mr. President,

17. The bigger challenge is to overcome the "trust deficit" between the developing and developed countries regarding financial and technological cooperation and commitments of Annex I countries. Good faith engagement at international level will help meet the trust deficit.
18. The G-77 and China would like to emphasise that the UNFCCC and the Kyoto Protocol serve as the multilateral agreed structure, within which the international community should address the challenge of climate change. Given the intensity of the challenge, any other effort will distract and further compound the challenge.
19. The G-77 and China welcomes reports that Australia will soon be ratifying the Kyoto Protocol. We would like to reiterate our call on those states that have not yet done so, to join the Kyoto Protocol.
20. Annex I countries should undertake ambitious commitments for GHG emission reduction in the second commitment period. Deeper GHG reductions of Annex I countries will produce greater opportunities for developing countries to move onto a sustainable development pathway.

Mr. President,

21. New institutional and financial mechanisms would significantly enhance technology cooperation, development, and transfer and meet the incremental costs. Enhancing action in pursuit of this objective is fundamental to the overall climate change agenda. Notwithstanding the lack of progress, the elements and key issues have now been raised and the stage is now set for real and meaningful progress on this agenda item.
22. We are confident that our negotiating partners will move significantly beyond the current institutional and financial arrangements. UNFCCC estimates additional financial resources up to a level of US$200–210 billion by 2030 to achieve emission reductions targets. In addition, hundreds of

billions are needed to support adaptation activities. It is, thus, essential that an investment pathway is designed to secure additional financial resources for the developing countries for mitigation and adaptation and other related requirements in accordance with their national plans.

23. Capacity-building under the Convention and the Protocol remains an area of high priority for the G-77, as it has not received the attention it deserves. The Group of 77 and China hopes that the scope for activities and replenishment will be decided upon soon with regard to the LDCs Fund and steps will be taken for implementing it through concrete projects that have measurable and positive impacts.

Mr. President,

24. Climate change is indeed the most pressing challenge of our times. It is absolutely necessary that policies made in other areas and in other fora have to be looked at through the fresh lens of addressing climate change, and made consistent with the aims and measures that we are trying to implement in combating climate change.
25. Transfer of technology remains an enormous challenge to efforts for adaptation and mitigation keeping in view the issue of incremental costs and capacity-building. Addressing current and future changes in the climate system depends on early and effective development, deployment, transfer, and diffusion of environmentally friendly technologies to developing countries. A key question is also the treatment of intellectual property rights (IPRs) over climate-friendly technologies. Developing countries must also be helped, on affordable preferential and concessional terms, through technology transfer, directed R&D, and other assistance, to acquire and build capacity for the application of technologies to meet sustainable development targets and goals. The G-77 and China would like to express its disappointment about the progress made on this agenda item. Development of performance indicators to monitor if commitments have been honoured in this area will be a useful tool.
26. As reflected in the recent IPCC Reports, reducing emissions from deforestation deserves serious global attention. Further, during this process, it has become clear that implementation of relevant policy approaches and positive incentives will require new and additional financial resources that are predictable, sustainable, and at sufficient scale. The G-77 and China recognizes the interests of the parties to consider policy approaches and positive incentives that address compensated forest conservation and also forest degradation.
27. The Ad Hoc Working Group (AWG), which reflects a legal requirement of the Protocol for the second commitment period for Annex I countries, must

complete its work by 2009 so as to allow smooth transition to the second commitment period.

28. The dialogue on long-term cooperative action to address climate change by enhancing implementation of the Convention has identified elements on which we intend to engage constructively.

Statement by Ambassador Munir Akram, Permanent Representative of Pakistan to the United Nations at the Joint High-level Segment of the Thirteenth Session of the Conference of the Parties to the United Nations Framework Convention on Climate Change and the Third Session of the Meeting of the Parties to the Kyoto Protocol
(Bali, Indonesia, 12 December 2007)

Mr. President,

1. It is my honour and privilege to speak on behalf of the Group of 77 and China at the Joint High-Level Segment of the Thirteenth Conference of the Parties to the UNFCCC and the United Nations Framework Convention on Climate Change and the Third Session of the Meeting of the Parties to the Kyoto Protocol.
2. Let me avail of this opportunity to thank the Government and brotherly people of Indonesia for their generous hospitality and the warmth that they have extended to us all in this beautiful island of Bali.
3. Let me also extend our sincere felicitations to the authors of the Fourth IPCC Assessment Report on receiving the Nobel Peace Prize, which is indeed a well-deserved recognition of their good work done.
4. The Group of 77 and China would like to welcome the ratification of the Kyoto Protocol by Australia. We would also avail of this opportunity to renew our call upon all member States that have yet not done so to ratify and implement the UNFCCC and the Kyoto Protocol.

Mr. President,

5. Climate change poses serious risks and challenges particularly to developing countries and therefore demands urgent global action and response. The Group is concerned about the fact that the adverse effects of climate change and the associated phenomena threaten the sustainable development, livelihoods, and the very existence of many developing countries and in particular Africa, the LDCs, the LLDCs, SIDS, and disaster-prone developing countries.
6. The Group of 77 and China, therefore, view these discussions as an integral part of the wider sustainable development debate.

Mr. President,

7. At Bali, it is essential to redress the gap in implementation and to generate corrective actions to address the enormity of climate challenge. We must do so on the basis of equity, common but differentiated responsibilities, and respective capabilities. The major responsibility rests on the developed countries. No significant progress can be made without major and significant reductions in emissions of GHG by all Annex I countries. Therefore, the G-77 and China attaches particular significance to the new commitments, which Annex I countries are to make in the second commitment period after 2012. This will be the single most vital determinant of success or failure in meeting the climate change challenge.
8. Secondly, as the Framework Convention recognized, the first and foremost priority for the developing countries is economic and social development. Measures and steps to address climate change should assist, not impede, the goal of sustainable development. Their development momentum must be maintained and accelerated, especially in the poorest countries.
9. Thirdly, we must enhance the full, effective, and sustained implementation of the Convention. In this context, urgent action is needed to arrest and reverse the vulnerabilities of the developing countries. Consequently, the process should accord equal priority to all the four building blocks while recognizing that the existing building blocks are not exhaustive.
10. The G-77 and China considers that the provision of financial resources to the developing countries by the developed countries is a commitment under the Convention. Financing is one of the key components and one of the main building blocks also for enhancing the implementation of the Convention. There is a huge gap between the funding currently available through the financial mechanisms of the Convention and the funding needs of the developing countries. While market-based solutions are important, nonetheless, given the scale and magnitude of the resources required, the close engagement of governments and public-sector funding and intervention will remain critical.
11. The Group of 77 and China is relieved to see the finalization of the recommendation on the Adaptation Fund. This is undoubtedly an important step, which would help finance concrete adaptation projects and programmes that are country driven and are based on the needs, views and priorities of eligible parties. We look forward to the early operationalization of the Fund with immediate, adequate, and predictable resource inflows and call upon all developed countries to contribute to the Trust Fund for operating the Adaptation Fund. Moreover, transparent utilization of the Adaptation Fund, in a cost-effective manner, will be the key to making it successful.

Mr. President,

12. The development and transfer of technology to developing countries through an effective mechanism supported by adequate and predictable financial resource base is vital to enabling the developing countries to face the challenges posed by climate change.
13. We would like to express our disappointment over the manner in which we had to struggle for long hours to restore this important item on the SBI agenda. It is our hope that this subject will be given the priority that it deserves.
14. We are also extremely disappointed not to have reached agreement on having a decision at this COP that will allow the implementation of the technologies identified by developing countries. Ironically, developed country parties do state that technology development and transfer is one of the building blocks for the design of future climate change regime.

Mr. President,

15. Capacity-building under the Convention and the Protocol remains an area of high priority for the G-77. Unfortunately, this too has not received the attention it deserves. We also express our disappointment over the difficulties and hurdles that we continue to face from developed country parties on this issue. The most recent deadlock at this session is a clear manifestation of that lack of understanding and flexibility on the part of our partners.
16. The Group of 77 and China has actually participated in the ongoing consultations on the Bali Road Map including the possible establishment of an Ad Hoc Working Group on Enhancing the Implementation of the Convention.
17. The Group of 77 and China is concerned that the recommendations relating to the Ad Hoc Working Group have not progressed as much as we would have liked. We will work with others to bring our deliberations to a successful conclusion. To do so, flexibility will be required from all sides. We must use this possibility to convert the climate challenge into a climate opportunity. However, this endeavour should not result in the erosion of the Convention or the Kyoto Protocol, or the replacement of these by a less equitable instrument. We would like to reiterate that the UNFCCC, and its Kyoto Protocol, remain the central multilateral framework for cooperative actions to address climate change.

Mr. President,

18. Let me say a few words about my own country. Although Pakistan is a large country, with the fifth largest population, it is a low Greenhouse Gas (GHG) emitter. Our total annual emissions are only 0.43% of world's total, i.e., 135th among all countries. However, the low emission status of the country provides no safety from the adverse effects of changing climate.

19. Climate change is causing irrevocable damage to Pakistan, with tremendous social, environment, and economic impacts, including on forest resources and natural ecosystems of the country. Even the glaciers in Himalayas are receding faster than any other part of the world. There are fears that many may disappear by 2050.
20. I take this opportunity to state that Pakistan is deeply committed to the global efforts to mitigate climate change impacts and has taken a number of steps for the improvement and protection of the environment.
21. These measures, however, need additional financial resources to be obtained through international and regional cooperation. The worst hit countries, like Pakistan, should be allocated a major share of the Adaptation Fund, the GEF, and other resources to meet these challenges.
22. Let me also take this opportunity to highlight the increasing energy needs of Pakistan in the backdrop of our sound economic performance and high growth rates. We will have to rely on both traditional and non-traditional sources of energy including renewables to sustain the existing high growth rates and to take them to the next higher level. Use of hydel and nuclear energy would therefore be a natural option for Pakistan. We urge the international community including the private sector to support Pakistan's endeavours in this regard.

Address by Ambassador Byron Blake, Delegation of Antigua and Barbuda, to the Poznan Business Day Luncheon
(Poznan, Poland, 9 December 2008)

Mr. Moderator,

Technology and by extension business is the main cause of our current environmental dilemma.

Technology and by extension business must be leaders in the solutions to the dilemma.

I welcome this opportunity on behalf of the G-77 and China to offer some perspectives not only on how business can contribute to securing and implementing a good outcome from the Bali process in Copenhagen but more fundamentally how business can change the behaviour of the rest of society. I thank the organisers for this opportunity.

Mr. Moderator,

How can businesses contribute to securing a good outcome in Copenhagen?

The main excuse of Annex I countries for their unwillingness to move in the direction of meeting their commitment to reduce Green House Gases is that this will involve costs which will put their businesses at a competitive disadvantage.

In Rio, and again in Johannesburg, business had put forward proposals which were much more progressive and supportive of the environment than developed country governments were willing to commit to. Business was not aggressive in pushing their governments toward outcomes closer to their proposals, however. Business can make a difference in Copenhagen by making it clear and demonstrating to their governments that the protection and integrity of the environment is good for business. The development, use, and wide diffusion of environmentally friendly technology is good for both, the bottom line, and the image of business.

Delayed action in any case is more expensive action.

Further business, especially those involved in the moulding of public opinion in developed countries, can assist the process by providing more factual information to the public in developed countries. For example, factual information on issues such as:

a) The per-person GHG emissions of developing countries such as China and India in relation to that of developed countries, as a group and individual developed countries such as the United States;
b) The per capita income and poverty levels of developing countries such as China and India, in spite of improvements in their current annual growth rates; and
c) The extent to which developing countries, including China and India, are dependent on imported technology and hence the opportunity for industrialized countries to influence positively the energy intensity of their production and consumption.

They would prepare the public in developed countries for the difference in the nature of the implementation action envisaged in the Bali Action Plan from developed and developing countries in Copenhagen.

Mr. Moderator,

How can business contribute to implementing a good outcome from Copenhagen?

A good outcome from Copenhagen rests fundamentally on the determination of Annex I countries to reduce aggressively the GHG intensity of their current and future production and consumption and the availability of more environmentally friendly technology to non–Annex I countries for adaptation and mitigation actions.

Business determines production processes, technology development and technology diffusion and choice. The lion share of current patents and technology development capacity is in the large businesses as in Annex I countries.

Business can contribute to implementing the outcome of Copenhagen by re-engineering or adapting existing production technology and processes. They can also contribute by developing new, less GHG-intensive production technologies and by making these technologies available on the market at prices which will encourage their widespread deployment in Annex I and non–Annex I countries. To achieve this business might have to work more collaboratively among themselves and with public sector institutions and support.

Secondly, business can contribute to implementing the outcomes by assisting to change consumption pattern and orientation. Current consumption behaviour, driven by business advertising and practice, revolves around acquisition and waste. The outcome of Copenhagen will require a pattern of consumption based on use, reuse, and recycle.

The communication and advertising apparatus of business can be deployed to support the public education and awareness campaign that will be necessary to break and change the current pattern of over- and wasteful consumption to one based on use, reuse, and recycle. This will be important not only in private consumption but also in business consumption.

Mr. Moderator,

The implementation of a good decision out of Copenhagen, in the time frame and with the urgency required, will create many opportunities for unscrupulous business persons to exploit the situation. Opportunities will abound in the effort to meet legal requirements in developed countries for unscrupulous businesses to off-load high-GHG technologies in developing countries, in particular developing countries with limited scientific, technical, and testing capacities.

Mr. Moderator,

Business has an opportunity to avoid such practices and to self-police as well as to assist governments where others indulge in such practices. I challenge the climate and environmentally conscious businesses participating in these important discussions to take the lead in influencing the general business community to greater environmental responsibility. I also challenge you to prevail on your governments to be ambitious in Copenhagen

Statement on behalf of the Group of 77 and China by Ambassador Dr. John W. Ashe, Permanent Representative of Antigua and Barbuda to the United Nations, and Chairman of the Group of 77, at the Joint High-level Segment of the UNFCCC COP-14/CMP-4
(Poznan, Poland, 11 December 2008)

Mr. President of the COP,
Executive Secretary,
Colleagues,
Ladies and Gentlemen,
Salutations.

Mr. President,

We are one year and four meetings from our Bali meeting. In Bali, we "resolved to enhance implementation of the Convention" and to that end "we decided to launch a comprehensive process, to enable the full, effective and sustained implementation of the Convention through long-term cooperative action, now, up to and beyond 2012, in order to reach an agreed outcome and adopt a decision at our fifteenth session."

The Bali decision and the Action Plan were reached against the backdrop of, *inter alia*:

1) The Fourth IPCC Report, which undoubtedly contributed to its winning the Nobel Prize, but put beyond doubt the fact of serious climate change, perhaps beyond reversal and the role of human beings in accelerating the change;
2) The fact the GHG emissions of Annex I parties continued to increase after 2000, when under the Convention they should have peaked and begin to fall; and
3) Annex I parties have not delivered on their commitment to enhance the transfer of technology and to increase financing to developing countries, to meet the full cost of adapting to the adverse impacts of climate change and facilitate their mitigation actions.

Mr. President,

There was an atmosphere of great urgency. In Bali, our decision therefore gave a two-year work plan, but required a mid-point review of progress. We are at the end of that review. Is it therefore appropriate to ask what has the report on the past year one tells us? Where are we in the process? Are we likely, on the present trajectory, to have within the next year, the comprehensive report envisaged in the Bali Decision and Bali Action Plan?

Developing countries, encouraged by the high-level statements by some Annex I countries especially since the third meeting in Accra, came to Poznan expecting that commitments would be placed on the table to unilaterally cut its greenhouse gas emissions by 20% and to go above that if all Annex I parties made similar commitments. We are yet to hear that clear statement from this group.

In the areas under the work programme of the Subsidiary Bodies and Working Groups, the Group of 77 and China had expected here in Poznan, at a minimum we will have to make:

(i) actions and decisions to make the Adaptation Fund established under the Convention operational;
(ii) the least developed country fund operational;
(iii) the mandate of the consultative group of experts to be renewed so that the Group can resume its functions;

(iv) the Annex I parties to begin to negotiate their emission reductions for the post- 2012 commitment period;
(v) developed countries to provide initial responses to the G-77 and China submissions, especially the submissions on financial mechanism and technology transfer which were circulated since the Accra meeting; and more broadly,
(vi) a sense of commitment to negotiate in good faith and in an open transparent manner.

Mr. President, none of these expectations has been met.

Mr. President,

In the assessment of the Group, we are unlikely to achieve the Bali objective in the absence of a radical change in approach and mindset and serious effort at confidence-building. To that end, we need at a minimum to:

1) start the discussion on how Annex I parties intend to begin to reduce their emissions now and the targets they intend to commit to for 2012 to 2020 and beyond. The current approach of Annex I parties to demand as precondition for action on their long outstanding commitment, binding action by others borders on the immoral and is counterproductive;
2) begin the process of negotiations on the mechanisms and approaches for the effective provision of adequate financing and the transfer of low GHG technologies to developing countries;
3) begin to discuss cooperative approaches to research and development which could scale up and facilitate the availability of technologies which would allow sustainable development at the level required for countries to meet other Internationally Agreed Development Goals (IADGs), including the Millennium Development Goals (MDGs); and
4) see a focus on the core issues, in a balanced manner, as demanded by the Bali Action Plan.

Mr. President,

The G-77 and China is committed, and reaffirms its commitment, to the type of outcome envisaged in the Bali decision and the Bali Action Plan. To that end, the Group has submitted concrete and detailed proposals on critical elements such as a financial mechanism and a technology mechanism as well as our views on mitigation and shared vision.

Mr. President,

The Group remains committed to a decision at COP-15.

Statement on behalf of the Group of 77 and China by H. E. Ambassador Ibrahim Mirghani Ibrahim, Head of Delegation of the Republic of the Sudan, at the Opening Plenary of the Fifteenth Session of the Conference of the Parties (COP-15) (Copenhagen, Denmark, 7 December 2009)

Mr. President,

I have the honour to deliver this statement on behalf of the Group of 77 and China.
Mr. President,

Allow me at the outset to congratulate you on your election as President for the Fifteenth Session of the Conference of the Parties and the Fifth Session of the Conference of the Parties serving as a Meeting of the Parties to the Kyoto Protocol at this historical time. I would also like to express our appreciations and gratitude to the Government and the people of Denmark for hosting this historical event in the beautiful city of Copenhagen, and would also like to thank Convention's Secretariat for their excellent arrangements.

Mr. President,

Two years ago, in the beautiful Island of Bali, we all agreed to launch a comprehensive process to enable the full, effective, and sustained implementation of the Convention through long-term cooperative action, now, up to and beyond 2012, in order to reach an agreed outcome and adopt a decision at the Fifteenth Session of the Conference of the Parties. Mr. President, we are now at the Fifteenth Session, and the Group of 77 and China is ready to fulfil the mandate that we agreed upon in Bali.

Mr. President,

For the past two years, the Group of 77 and China has worked relentlessly to fulfil this mandate. As a group, as groups of countries among us, and as individual countries, we have put on the table concrete proposals that would allow us to implement this only legally binding, science-based, universally agreed Convention and its Kyoto Protocol fully and address the greatest global challenge that we confront today.

On the fundamental elements of the Bali Action Plan for the provision of financial resources, development and transfer of technology, and capacity-building, the Group of 77 and China has tabled detailed proposals that would bridge the important shortfalls in the implementation of the commitments of developed countries, and that would allow developing countries to comply entirely with their obligations under the Convention.

Mr. President,

We engaged fully in this process in an open, transparent, and inclusive manner because we, all of developing countries, bear the brunt of the adverse effects of climate change, have only meagre resources to cope with these adverse effects, and because of our constant struggle to provide for the basic needs and aspire for a decent life for our peoples.

We engaged fully because we are fighting for our survival, Mr. President, for the present and for future generations. These are recognized in the Convention where it states that poverty eradication and economic and social development are the first and overriding priorities of developing countries.

Mr. President,

We are now told that we will only get a "politically-binding agreement" in Copenhagen, that means the process will have to continue until developed countries achieve their objective of shifting the responsibilities for addressing climate change and its adverse effects are imposed upon developing countries, in another legally binding instrument that would put together the obligations of developed countries under the Kyoto Protocol and would revoke the principle of common but differentiated responsibilities under the Convention, by imposing these obligations as well to developing countries under the guise of a "shared vision."

Mr. President,

According to the recent data on greenhouse gas emissions from Annex I parties to the Convention, as contained in document FCCC/SBI/2009/9, between 2007 and 1990, GHG emissions from developed countries increased by 11.2% excluding LULUCF, and increased by 12.8% including LULUCF. Many developed countries, though realized their industrialization more than half a century ago, have yet peaked their emissions. There is a huge gap in developed countries leadership in modifying their longer-term trends in anthropogenic emissions as required by the Convention. On the contrary, developing countries are now being required to take the leadership in cutting emissions while developed countries are continuously increasing their emissions and hence continuously over-occupying the global climate space.

Mr. President,

The Group of 77 and China is looking forward for the adoption of the draft decision on the work of the Consultative Group of Experts on National Communications from parties not included in Annex I to the Convention—the CGE—which has been forwarded for the adoption at this COP session, as contained in the report of the SBI on its thirtieth session. After two years of intense negotiations, the CGE will be finally reconstituted, at least for the period 2010–2012. Nevertheless, it must be acknowledged that the time that has been lost without the assistance of the CGE cannot be recuperated and, certainly, Mr. President, the process of preparation of National Communications from non-Annex I parties has been undermined.

Mr. President,

The Group 77 and China looks forward for COP-15 to adopt a decision on reducing emissions from deforestation and forest degradation, and the role of conservation, sustainable management of forests, and enhancement of forest carbon stocks and acknowledges the need for capacity-building and technology transfer to promote readiness for REDD.

For many developing countries reducing emissions from deforestation and forest degradation is directly linked, among others, with sustainable development, improved livelihood of local communities and indigenous peoples, and conservation of biodiversity. It is fundamental that COP defines the appropriate positive incentives and policy approaches for REDD plus ensuring adequate and predictable funding for those developing countries that voluntarily decide to engage in this effort.

Finally, Mr. President, the Group of 77 and China comes to Copenhagen to engage fully and negotiate in good faith to fulfil the mandate of the Bali Action Plan and to make this historical session a real success that enable developing countries to undertake effective actions to respond to climate change and its devastating impacts, now, up to, and beyond 2012.

Statement on behalf of the Group of 77 and China by H.E. Dr. Nafie Ali Nafie, Head of Delegation of the Republic of the Sudan, at the Joint High-level Segment of the Fifteenth Session of the Conference of the Parties of the Climate Change Convention and the Fifth Conference of the Parties Serving as a Meeting of the Parties to the Kyoto Protocol (COP-15/CMP-5)
(Copenhagen, Denmark, 16 December 2009)

Madam President,
Excellencies,
Heads of State and Government,
H.E. the Prime Minister of Denmark,
H.E. the UN Secretary-General,
Honourable Ministers and Heads of Delegation,
Ladies and Gentlemen,
Good morning!

Madam President,

Sudan is honoured to make this statement on behalf of the Group 77 and China.

Let me at the outset congratulate you on your election as the President of the Fifteenth Session of the Conference of the Parties of the UN Framework Convention on Climate Change and the Fifth session of the Conference of the Parties serving as a Meeting of the Parties to the Kyoto Protocol. Let me also on behalf of the Group 77 and China to express, to the people and Government of Denmark, our thanks and appreciation for their hospitality and for hosting this historical event in the beautiful city of Copenhagen.

Madam President,

Two years ago, in Bali, all parties agreed to adopt the results of the AWG-KP work in Copenhagen at this session of the Conference of the Parties serving as the Meeting of the Parties to the Kyoto Protocol (CMP) and thereby set up a two-track negotiation process. In this regard, the Group has been working towards achieving the core mandate of the AWG-KP, which specifically focuses on the legal requirement to define the second period under the Kyoto Protocol. In line with the science, the second commitment period must inscribe ambitious quantified emission reduction targets for developed countries beyond 2012 under an improved, more efficient and effective set of rules in order to enable developed country parties to take the lead and significantly contribute to the minimization of impacts of climate change.

However, we have seen that developed country parties to the Kyoto Protocol seek to dismantle the protocol itself in favour of a "single undertaking," allegedly comprehensive, but which is in reality much weaker and will effectively undermine and reinterpret the Convention and its Kyoto Protocol. To this end, we have seen continual delays in our work, exemplified by the fact that the AWG-KP has not met a single deadline to reach conclusions on in aggregate or individual emission reductions, which were agreed to in Poznan, only a year ago. It is clear that these efforts are intended to undermine and reinterpret the Convention itself, in particular its foundational principles of equity, common but differentiated responsibilities, and respective capabilities.

Madam President,

Let us be clear that the Group of 77 and China regards the Convention together with its Kyoto Protocol and all the decisions we have taken under these instruments as the comprehensive undertaking of the international community to address the global challenge of climate change. In this regard, the Group wishes to stress the need to maintain the two-track outcome that the Kyoto Protocol is an essential instrument which elaborates the means to enable developed country parties to the Protocol to meet their legal commitment under article 4.2 of the Convention to reduce their emissions.

Madam President,

For the sake of the well-being of our planet and its people the Group 77 and China insists that a second commitment period under the Kyoto Protocol must be established beyond 2012 as the basis for comparable emission reduction commitments among all developed country parties. We will oppose an agreement in Copenhagen which in any way results in the Kyoto Protocol being superseded or made redundant. The second commitment period under the Kyoto Protocol is a minimum requirement for the Group, without which agreement in Copenhagen will not be possible.

Madam President,

In Bali, we also agreed to launch a comprehensive process to enable the full, effective, and sustained implementation of the Convention through long-term cooperative action, now, up to, and beyond 2012, in order to reach an agreed outcome and adopt a decision at the fifteenth session of the Conference of the Parties.

Mr. Chairman, we have now reached the fifteenth session and the Group of 77 and China is ready to fulfil this mandate. However, the Group's intensive efforts to engage constructively in this process were seriously hampered by a complicated and multi-layered process of consultations imposed upon us at the beginning of this second week of this COP session.

Madam President,

While we try to understand the objective of this exercise which, we suppose, was meant to generate the necessary political will to arrive at a meaningful conclusion in this conference, we feel that there is lack of transparency in the way the decisions were made to hold these high-level consultations, and the identification of the issues to be discussed in these consultations left much to be desired.

Many of the G-77 delegations have limited capacities and could not be represented in all the meetings, all of which are of great importance to the Group.

Despite this development, the Group continued to engage in the different drafting groups and informal groups that continued until the early morning hours. We made some progress in a few of the groups, but this progress remains uncertain in the light of their linkage with the ongoing informal ministerial discussions.

Madam President,

We still keep the hope that we could reach a balanced outcome for all the elements of the Bali Action Plan for this COP, and will continue to engage constructively in the negotiations, in order to reach an equitable outcome for this session. Developing countries have the most to lose at this session if there are no concrete results of our discussions, particularly if the Kyoto Protocol is undermined or dismantled. We therefore are the most concerned that we do arrive at a successful outcome at COP-15.

Madam President,

The Group of 77 and China considers our shared vision as science-based and founded on the principles, provisions of the Convention, in particular, the principles of equity and common but differentiated responsibilities and respective capabilities. Our shared vision must reflect the historical and current responsibility of developed countries for human-induced climate change, their resulting climate debt to developing countries, and establish the conditions needed for a fair and just sharing of the atmospheric resource.

Madam President,

Our shared vision, including a long-term global goal for emission reductions, is to enhance the full effective and sustained implementation of the Convention henceforth in a balanced and comprehensive manner by addressing mitigation, adaptation, technology development and transfer, financing, and capacity-building in an integrated way. It must ensure that there is an inclusive, fair, and equitable outcome that fully respects and supports the right to development and to survival of developing countries.

It recognizes and promotes the right to survival and to development, under equitable conditions, for present and future generations is a right of all countries and peoples, and that social and economic development and poverty eradication are the first and overriding priorities of developing countries.

Madam President,

The Group 77 and China calls for a comprehensive policy guidance on adaptation, effective institutional arrangements and new, additional, scaled-up, and long-term finance to enable developing countries to address their urgent, immediate as well as mid- and long-term adaptation needs.

Madam President,

We are also concerned by the way mitigation has been dealt with in Copenhagen. Issues under the Bali Action Plan subparagraph l.b.i, which deals with mitigation by Annex I countries, have essentially stopped moving. This creates a lack of balance at the heart of the negotiation process. We cannot have a Copenhagen outcome without complete and sufficient treatment of mitigation under 1.b.i.

We want a positive result in all aspects of the Bali Action Plan. We support progress of the entire set of issues. We want a process that appropriately covers all the building blocks. We cannot support a selective approach.

Madam President,

As we indicated to you at the opening of this session the Group 77 and China supports the bottom-up and party-driven process we all established and maintained over the past two years. We believe that this approach allows a balanced consideration of all issues under the Bali Action Plan and enables all parties to participate and bring in their interests and concerns regarding the expected agreed outcome of Copenhagen. It is no doubt that such approach is only way to lead us to a party-driven, fair, and agreed outcome.

Madam President,

We understand that there is a great sense of urgency and a mounting pressure to reach an agreed outcome here in Copenhagen. I would like to assure you and all parties that our group is highly committed to make this happening. However, we do have serious concerns regarding the organization of work at this level of the session and how the results of the ongoing work under the Ad Hoc Working Groups will be considered and incorporated in the outcome of this Conference.

Madam President,

The Group 77 and China stands ready to assist you in your role as the President to maintain a party-driven, open, and transparent process that ensures the right of all developing countries to participate fully in shaping the outcome of this Conference.

Statement on behalf of the Group of 77 and China by H.E. Ambassador Abdullah M. Alsaidi, Head of Delegation of the Republic of Yemen, at the Opening Plenary of the Sixteenth Session of the Conference of the Parties of the UN Framework Convention on Climate Change (COP-16) (Cancun, Mexico, 29 November 2010)

Madam President,

1. I have the distinct honour to deliver this statement on behalf of the Group of 77 and China.
2. Allow me at the outset to congratulate you on your election as President for the Sixteenth Session of the Conference of the Parties and the Sixth Session of the Conference of the Parties serving as a Meeting of the Parties to the Kyoto Protocol. The Group would also like to pay special tribute to the leadership which Mexico is providing in the negotiations. Over the last year, the work done by the Mexican side as an incoming presidency has helped restore trust amongst parties in engaging together once again since Copenhagen. This is no mean achievement.
3. We are confident that this spirit would continue during the next two weeks and that our work will remain party-driven transparent, inclusive, and open for participants. More than ever, today is the need to ensure that these principles remain fundamental to our work.
4. I would also like, on behalf of the Group, to take this opportunity to express our appreciations and gratitude to the Government and the people of Mexico for the warm hospitality since the moment we arrive to this beautiful city of Cancun, and for the excellent arrangement and facilities which will enable

us to achieve our objectives. We would also like to thank the Convention's Secretariat for the excellent arrangements.

Madam President,

5. Over the last three years, since we all agreed to launch the process to enable the full, effective, and sustained implementation of the Convention through long-term cooperative action, now, up to, and beyond 2012, the Group of 77 and China has been engaging constructively in this process and posited concrete proposals meant to facilitate the process of negotiation. We believe that it is time to secure an outcome that fulfils the mandate that we agreed upon in Bali. In this context, the Group of 77 and China stresses that balance between the two negotiating tracks, i.e., AWG-KP and AWG-LCA must be respected and that balance in the degree of details of decisions within each track must be maintained. It is also our firm belief, however, that whatever outcome we might reach in Cancun must not compromise or prejudge the overall objective of reaching a comprehensive, fair, ambitious, and legally binding outcome in the future.
6. The Group of 77 and China highlights the technical and financial difficulties that developing country parties are facing which impeded the preparation of their national communications. Predictability of funding and the provision of the agreed full costs for the preparation of National Communications from non–Annex I parties are crucial.
7. The Group of 77 and China would also like to underline the fact that developing countries continue to suffer from the adverse impacts of climate change. As we deliberate on the implementation of the financial architecture of the Convention, there is a lack of inflow of capital to the Special Climate Change Fund and the Least Developed Countries Fund, bearing in mind the fact that these funds are under-funded to start with. Therefore, we call for more contributions to these funds, and in particular for the latter, to assist developing countries to tackle the adverse impacts of climate change. In this context, we encourage our partners to show flexibility and commitment towards the adaptation needs of the developing countries, specially LDCs and SIDS, and to treat adaptation in an equal manner exactly as the case for mitigation.
8. One of the key components of Cancun outcome is an outcome on Finance. The Group of 77 and China wishes to reiterate its proposal on the New Fund and Governance and Oversight of Climate Finance and the provision by developed countries through a percentage of their GNP to address climate change in developing countries. The Group of 77 and China would like to underline that a decision on establishing a new climate change fund must address the four components, i.e., structure, scope, scale, and sources.

9. The Group strongly supports the need for establishing, under the Bali Action Plan, a Standing Committee to be supervised, at present, by the AWG-LCA and ultimately by the SBI, to provide guidance to the operating entities of the financial mechanism; make recommendations to other organization dealing with climate change finance to ensure coherence in delivering of climate finance; assure the accountability of the operating entity/entities of the FM; assess the adequacy of climate finance for the developing countries; manage the Registry for measuring, reporting, and verifying the fulfilment of contributions by developed countries; and the flow of total financial resources/commitments from the developed to the developing countries through all sources and review the contributions by the developed countries. The Group would like to reiterate its desire to immediately engage on the two issues, the establishment of the new Fund under the Convention and a mechanism for continued governance of this fund, with a view to their finalization at the earliest. We also reiterate the importance of advancing our discussions towards establishing the adequate institutional arrangements for adaptation and technology transfer.
10. Implementation of decision 1/CP10 has been a big concern for the group for many years, the group in this session, will continue its involvement, looking forward to progressive and serious consideration of its submissions, views, and concrete proposals on different elements towards the implementation of decision 1/CP10 in order to meet adaptation needs of the developing countries.

Madam President,

11. On the data related to greenhouse gas emissions from Annex I parties to the Convention, the Group of 77 and China wants to express its concerns on the trends visualized in the report on national GHG inventory data from parties included in Annex I to the Convention for the period 1990–2007 where it is demonstrated that Annex I parties increased by 11.2 per cent their emissions excluding LULUCF and by 12.8 per cent including LULUCF. This shows the tendency which goes against the commitments those parties have, according to paragraph 4.2 of the Convention. Therefore, the Group of 77 and China considers that further actions are needed, in order to assure the fulfilments of existing commitments of developed country parties and their compliance.
12. Finally, Madam President, I would like to assure you that the Group of 77 and China will continue to work constructively and in good faith during the course of this session to make Cancun a success.

Statement on behalf of the Group of 77 and China by H.E. Ambassador Abdulla M. Alsaidi, Head of Delegation of the Republic of Yemen, at the Opening Plenary

of the Sixth Session of the Conference of the Parties Serving as a Meeting of the Parties to the Kyoto Protocol (Cancun, Mexico, 29 November 2010)
Madam President,

1. I have the honour to deliver this statement on behalf of the Group of 77 and China. Allow me at the outset to express my appreciations to the Government and people of Mexico for hosting this important meeting in the beautiful city of Cancun, and to the Convention's Secretariat for the excellent arrangements.
2. The developing countries are now experiencing the very real impacts of climate change, which are undermining our development prospects and aggravating the vulnerability of our poor communities, particularly indigenous peoples. The Group of 77 and China expects the AWG- KP to forward ambitious quantified emission reduction targets for Annex I parties for the second commitment period which was mandated to be concluded one year ago as per the decision 1 CMP1.

Madam President,

3. The Group of 77 and China would also like to recall that by decision 1/CMP.1 we agreed that the AWG-KP "would aim to complete its work and have its results adopted by the COP/MOP as early as possible and in time to ensure that there is no gap between the first and second commitment periods." The central goal of our work is to define ambitious quantified emission reductions for Annex I countries for the second and subsequent commitment periods that will significantly contribute to the minimization of future impacts of climate change. This is a goal we have not yet delivered.
4. Instead, the process so far has taken us on many circular pathways which seem designed to delay agreement on new commitments from Annex I parties. During this year's sessions, the AWG-KP experienced such slow progress on its work that it has become clear that our partners seek to delay the process through continued reference to array of technical issues and perhaps to dismantle Kyoto Protocol itself. KP is the only treaty instrument that spells out the legally binding obligation for Annex I parties to reduce their emissions.
5. The Group of 77 and China strongly reaffirms its position that a second commitment period under the Kyoto Protocol must be established for a period beyond 2012 as the basis for comparable Annex I emission reduction commitments. Therefore, the Group stresses the urgency of completing the mandate of decision 1/CMP.1 to ensure emission reductions by Annex I parties and to avoid the gap between the first and second commitment periods. The AWG-KP must deliver the results of its work for adoption at CMP-6 in Cancun, in accordance with decision 1/CMP.5. The adoption of

the second commitment period of the Kyoto Protocol is the cornerstone of the successful outcomes in Cancun and will greatly facilitate the work of the AWG-LCA.

Madam President,

6. The Group notes that currently there is a big gap between the very low aggregate level of ambition being put forward by Annex I parties and what the science requires and what is needed to restore balance of our Mother Earth. In this context, the group insists that the work here in Cancun must focus on reaching agreement on the ambitious economy wide quantified emission reduction commitments of all Annex I parties.
7. The Group of 77 and China will continue to engage openly and constructively in the work of the AWG-KP to define the second and subsequent commitment periods for the Kyoto Protocol. The Group would also like to urge all parties, particularly Annex I parties, to engage faithfully in the negotiations to complete the mandate of the AWG-KP and to build a strong Kyoto Protocol which is the foundation and basis for a fair, just, effective, and equitable outcome in Cancun.

Statement on behalf of the Group of 77 and China by H.E. Mr. Abdulrahman Fadel Al-Eryani, Head of Delegation of the Republic of Yemen, at the Joint High-level Segment of the Sixteenth Session of the Conference of the Parties of the Climate Change Convention and the Sixth Session of the Conference of the Parties Serving as a Meeting of the Parties to the Kyoto Protocol (COP-16/CMP-6) (Cancun, Mexico, 7 December 2010)

Madam President,
Heads of State and Government,
H.E. the President of Mexico,
H.E. the UN Secretary-General,
Honourable Ministers and Heads of Delegation,
Excellencies,
Ladies and Gentlemen,

1. I have the distinct honour to deliver this statement on behalf of the Group of 77 and China.
2. Let me at the outset congratulate you on your election as President for the sixteenth session of the Conference of the Parties and the sixth session of the Conference of the Parties serving as the Meeting of the Parties to the Kyoto Protocol. Likewise allow me, on behalf of the Group, to express our appreciations and gratitude to the Government and people of Mexico for their hospitality and warm welcome in this beautiful city of Cancun.

3. Over the last year, Mexico as an incoming presidency has, indeed, helped restore trust amongst parties. We are confident that our work will remain party-driven transparent, inclusive, and open for participants. These principles are fundamental to our work.

Madam President,

4. Our people are suffering from the adverse effects of climate change even as we speak! A case in point would be the recent landslides and torrential rains in Venezuela, Colombia, Saint Lucia, and other places in the developing world that have killed many and forced thousands more from their homes. Indeed, addressing the challenges of climate change is a moral and existential imperative. That is why, Madam, we must succeed in Cancun.
5. The Group of 77 and China is of the conviction that time has come to secure an outcome that fulfils the mandate stipulated in Bali. In this context, the Group stresses that balance between the two negotiating tracks, i.e., AWG-KP and AWG-LCA, must be respected and that balance in the degree of details of decisions within each track must be maintained. It is also our firm belief that whatever outcome we reach here in Cancun must not compromise or prejudge the overall objective of reaching a comprehensive, fair, ambitious, and legally binding outcome in the future.
6. The central goal of the work of the AWG-KP is to define ambitious quantified emission reductions for Annex I parties for the second and subsequent commitment periods that will significantly contribute to the minimization of future impacts of climate change. We, therefore, strongly reaffirm our position that a second commitment period under the Kyoto Protocol must be established for a period beyond 2012. We, once again, stress the urgency of completing the mandate of decision 1/CMP.1 to ensure emission reductions by Annex I parties and to avoid the gap between the first and second commitment periods.
7. The AWG-KP, Madam, must deliver the results of its work for adoption at the session in Cancun, in accordance with decision 1/CMP.5. This is, indeed, the cornerstone of the successful outcome here in Cancun.
8. Developed counties, due to their historical responsibility for the accumulation of greenhouse gas emissions in the atmosphere, must show leadership by taking on ambitious, economy-wide, quantified emission reduction commitments and providing technology, capacity-building, and new and additional financial resources to developing countries parties in accordance with the relevant provisions of the Convention. Failing to do so, however, will seriously impede the achievement of the objective of the Convention, intensify the need for and cost of adaptation, increase their responsibility for their disproportionate greenhouse gas emissions, and raise the urgency for significantly increased ambition in their mitigation commitments.

9. Three years ago, in Bali, the AWG-LCA was launched with the aim of enabling "the full, effective and sustained implementation of the Convention through long-term cooperative action, now, up to and beyond 2012." Last year in Copenhagen, the mandate of this Ad Hoc Working Group was extended "to enable it to continue its work with a view to presenting the outcome of its work to the Conference of the Parties for adoption at its sixteenth session" in Cancun. Now is the time, Madam, and success is the only option for the Group of 77 and China.
10. The Group wishes to reiterate its proposal on the New Fund and Governance and Oversight of Climate Finance and the provision by developed countries through a percentage of their GNP to address climate change in developing countries. The Group of 77 and China would like to underline that a decision on establishing a new climate change fund must address the four components, i.e., structure, scope, scale, and sources.
11. It is the view of the Group that adaptation must be addressed with the same priority as mitigation and requires the establishment of institutional arrangements to enhance adaptation action and address adaptation needs in developing countries, including an Adaptation Framework for Implementation, an Adaptation Committee, and an International Mechanism to Address Loss and Damage.
12. The Group also emphasizes that capacity-building is a prerequisite for and essential to enabling developing country parties to participate fully in and to implement effectively their commitments under the Convention. The goal is to enhance the capacity of developing countries in all areas. Therefore, a body accountable to the COP shall be established to oversee, monitor, and ensure overall implementation of capacity-building activities consistent with the provisions of the Convention.

Madam President,

13. The Group of 77 and China reiterates the necessity of Palestine effective participation in the UNFCCC process, and to have the right of access to funding from different climate change sources.
14. It is of paramount importance to realize that transparency is key to success of cooperative actions. Cooperative and ambitious solutions require engagement of all parties, including our negotiating partners, to deliver results in accordance with the Bali Road Map.
15. The Group of 77 and China, once again, stresses that in order to succeed, our work process must be open, party-driven, and transparent. Likewise, the centrality of the multilateral process under the UNFCCC in addressing climate change must be respected and maintained.

Madam President,

16. The Group stresses that the AWG-LCA and AWG-KP need to continue their work in 2011. Therefore, sufficient budget should be allocated for the meetings of both Ad Hoc Working Groups' future sessions scheduled during next year.
    Finally, Madam President,
17. I would like to assure you that the Group of 77 and China will render the necessary cooperation with the Mexican presidency to make Cancun a success.

Statement on behalf of the Group of 77 and China by H.E. Ambassador Silvia Merega, Head of Delegation of the Argentine Republic, at the Opening Plenary of the Seventeenth Session of the Conference of the Parties of the UN Framework Convention on Climate Change (Durban, South Africa, 28 November 2011)

Madam President,

1. I have the distinct honour to deliver this statement on behalf of the Group of 77 and China.
2. Allow me at the outset to congratulate you on your election as President of the seventeenth session of the Conference of the Parties and the seventh session of the Conference of the Parties serving as a Meeting of the Parties to the Kyoto Protocol.
3. I would also like, on behalf of the Group, to take this opportunity to express our appreciations and gratitude to the Government and people of South Africa, one of our members, for the warm hospitality expressed since the moment we arrived in this beautiful city of Durban, and for the excellent arrangement and facilities that they have provided us and will facilitate our work to achieve our objectives. We would also like to thank the Secretariat of UNFCCC for their excellent arrangements.
4. The Group of 77 and China associates itself to the tribute this room has paid to Mr. Mama Konaté. We are deeply saddened by his sudden passing away just a few weeks ago. This is a great loss for his country, for the climate change community, and for this Group. Mr. Konaté played a key and active role from 1997, applying his wisdom, knowledge, and insight to defend and reaffirm the pursuits of developing countries and especially least developed countries. We strongly agree with the message conveyed by the UNFCCC Secretariat upon his demise: "Undoubtedly, the climate change process has lost one of its most active, dedicated and prominent leaders." Let us follow his guidance and redouble our efforts in our fight against climate change. We are certain that by making this, the Conference in Durban will deliver a successful outcome.

Madam President,

5. The Group of 77 and China would like to reiterate that—although developing countries have not contributed to the creation of the problem—we continue to suffer most from the adverse impacts of climate change, and the increasing frequency and intensity of extreme weather events. The Group also underlines the challenges faced by developing countries from the impact of response measures.
6. This has been confirmed a few days ago by the Summary for Policy Makers from the Special Report on Managing the Risks of Extreme Events and Disasters to Advance Climate Change Adaptation (SREX) that was adopted by IPCC member governments. The report highlights that "There is high confidence that both maximum and minimum daily temperatures have increased on a global scale due to the increase of greenhouse gases" and studies show that it is virtually certain that—on a global scale—hot days become even hotter and occur more often. Moreover, fatality rates and economic losses expressed as a proportion of GDP are higher in developing countries. This confirms that high ambition of emission reductions of GHG is urgently needed.
7. The report recently released continues to support the fact that developing countries will continue to be most affected by climate change. At the same time, and with fewer means, we continue to struggle to eradicate poverty and achieve sustainable development. It is therefore urgent and pressing to find solutions for the climate change challenge that at the same time address inequality issues, right here, right now.

Madam President,

8. During the informal consultations you led last October, we had the opportunity to outline our expectations for this Conference, hosted by a developing country. Durban is a key step in the climate change negotiation process. Its outcome should be satisfactory to all developing countries as well as developed countries. COP-17 must advance negotiations in both tracks, under the Convention and the Protocol, based on these fundamental tenets:
   - The Convention and the Kyoto Protocol must be preserved.
   - The Bali Road Map and the two-track negotiation are to be followed, and decision 1/CP.16 rendered operational.
   - Negotiation process and outcomes must be carried out in an open, transparent, and inclusive manner.
   - Multilateralism is a political tool that has proved beneficial to all of us, and clearly to developing countries. It must be safeguarded.
   - The second commitment period is paramount in order to contribute to the solution of climate change crisis. Significant and ambitious efforts must be made in order to achieve its adoption.

9. The Group of 77 and China trusts that we will be able to achieve in Durban an outcome that is comprehensive and balanced, enabling the full, effective, and sustained implementation of the Convention through long-term cooperative action now, up to, and beyond 2012, pursuant to the results of the thirteenth and sixteenth sessions of the Conference of the Parties, addressing both implementation tasks and issues that are still to be concluded, on the basis of equity and taking into account the principle of common but differentiated responsibilities and respective capabilities.
10. We expect that during this session, the Cancun decision regarding the Adaptation Committee, the Standing Committee for the Green Climate Fund, and the technology mechanism will be fully operationalized. We urge developed countries to show their commitment to these mechanisms in concrete terms, and to capitalize the Green Climate Fund from their public financial resources as soon as possible. As the aforementioned SREX report stresses, "sound decisions on infrastructure, urban development, public health, and insurance, as well as for planning are needed to cope with the adverse effects of climate change."
11. Developing countries are already contributing to the global response to climate change and we will continue to do so. In this regard, and following the principles of the Convention, developed countries shall provide new, additional, stable, and predictable financial resources, capacity-building, and technology transfer will allow us to scale up the mitigation and adaptation actions under way.
12. We reiterate the necessity of enabling the effective participation of Palestine in the UNFCCC process and to make every effort to grant Palestine access to funding from different sources and mechanisms.

In conclusion, Madam President,

13. Allow me to reiterate that a comprehensive and balanced outcome under the two negotiation tracks must contribute to achieve the ultimate objective of the Convention, to protect the climate system for the benefit of present and future generations, and must be firmly rooted in equity, in accordance with the principles and provisions of the Convention.
14. I would like to assure you that the Group of 77 and China will continue to support South Africa. Under your able leadership, Madam President, the Group will continue to engage constructively and in good faith during the course of this session to make Durban a much-needed success.

Statement on behalf of the Group of 77 and China by H.E. Ambassador Alberto Pedro D'Alotto, Vice-Minister of Foreign Affairs of Argentina, at the Joint High-level Segment of the Seventeenth Session of the Conference of the Parties of the Climate Change Convention and the Seventh Session of the Conference of the

Parties Serving as the Meeting of the Parties to the Kyoto Protocol (COP-17/CMP-7)
(Durban, South Africa, 6 December 2011)

His Excellency the President of South Africa, Mr. Jacob Zuma,
Her Excellency the President of the COP/CMP, Madam Maite Mashabane,
His Excellency the Secretary General of UN, Mr. Ban Ki-moon,
The Executive Secretary of the UNFCCC, Madam Christiana Figueres,
Ladies and Gentlemen,

1. At the outset, I would like to express our full confidence in your leadership, and we commend you in the conduction of this meeting through an open, transparent, and inclusive process, based on the very roots of the spirit of the INDABA, an essential element of South African participatory democracy.

Madam President,

2. We would like to emphasize once more the urgent need to address this issue that for countries within the G-77 and China is a matter of survival. At the same time, we could not emphasize more that, although developing countries have not contributed to the creation of the problem, we continue to suffer most from the adverse impacts of climate change, and the increasing frequency and intensity of extreme weather events.
3. We are also facing the challenges arising from the impact of response measures.

Madam President,

4. Developing countries are now more than ever experiencing the very real impacts of climate change, which are undermining our development prospects and aggravating pre-existing vulnerabilities.
5. This has been confirmed a few days ago by the Summary for Policy Makers from the Special Report on Managing the Risks of Extreme Events and Disasters to Advance Climate Change Adaptation (SREX) that was adopted by IPCC member governments, highlighting that fatality rates and economic losses expressed as a proportion of GDP are higher in developing countries.
6. That points to the fact that a higher ambition in emission reductions of Green House Gasses (GHG) is urgently needed. In this regard, and as you are aware, Madam President, raising the level of ambition of emission reductions is a twofold path, since parties agreed to a two-track negotiation process in 2007, the Bali Road Map.

Madam President,

7. We are here in Durban already in 2011, and we believe this process has to deliver.
8. As we stated in the opening plenary of the Ad Hoc Working Group on Further Commitments for Annex I parties under the Kyoto Protocol, the continuation of the Kyoto Protocol is the cornerstone of our efforts in addressing climate change. However, Madam President, significant and ambitious efforts are still needed to raise the level of ambition of developed countries pledges, in line with what is required by science, equity, and historical responsibilities.
9. We urge developed countries parties to show they are taking the lead, and recommitting themselves to comply with what the Convention states, namely, modifying longer-term trends in anthropogenic emissions.
10. Modifying the patterns of production and consumption should lead us to achieve to achieve the objective of the Convention, in the context of sustainable development and poverty eradication.
11. This leadership has to be demonstrated by undertaking a second commitment period under the Kyoto Protocol, fully legally binding and ratified. Non–Kyoto Protocol Annex I parties, have to also join these efforts, with comparable commitments.

Madam President,

12. On our part, developing country parties are still struggling to eradicate poverty and achieve sustainable development. These are our first and overriding priorities. However, we are already undertaking bold action in mitigation and adaptation activities, including with our own resources, in a scenario where the provisions of the Convention regarding the support of finance, technology transfer, and capacity-building by developed countries parties in addition to the ODA are far from being met.
13. We are willing to do more, but the available international cooperation for national mitigation and adaptation actions clearly needs to be scaled up. We are concerned about the slow progress of the negotiations on financing, since we believe that resolve and progress in this front could be the key to a leap forward in mitigation actions by developing countries. Madame President, putting in motion the Green Climate Fund created in Cancun must include its initial capitalization, from public financial resources as soon as possible, to appease the fears of an "empty shell" structure.
14. In looking at the implementation of the Convention and the Kyoto Protocol regarding finance so far, pledges under the Adaptation Fund have been left

unfulfilled and there has been no voluntary contributions to the Fund yet, meaning that urgent concrete adaptation projects have remained under funded or unfunded. This comes at a time when both the Least-Developed Countries Fund (LDCF) and the Special Climate Change Fund (SCCF) also face a serious lack of resources.

Madam President,

15. Adaptation is a key priority for developing countries. The historical imbalance in finance of mitigation in detriment of adaptation must be redressed. We believe that the Cancun Adaptation Framework was one of the main achievements of COP-16 in pursuing this objective and in bringing the so much needed coherent approach to adaptation under the Convention. We look forward to making the Adaptation Committee operational in this African Climate Change Summit, keeping in mind the importance of creating the proper linkages to other institutional arrangements, in particular to the operating entities of the financial mechanism, as well as to other adaptation related arrangements.
16. In such line, setting in motion the technology mechanism, as one of the key deliverables of this Conference has to address also its interaction with other institutional arrangements under the Convention, including the Climate Technology Centre Network, the Financial Mechanism, and the Adaptation Committee.

Madam President,

17. We are gathered here, hopefully infused with wisdom and Ubuntu, to achieve an outcome that is comprehensive and balanced, enabling the full, effective, and sustained implementation of the Convention through long-term cooperative action now, up to, and beyond 2012, pursuant to the results of the thirteenth and sixteenth sessions of the Conference of the Parties, addressing both implementation tasks and issues that are still to be concluded as per the agreed agenda.
18. The outcome, on the basis of equity and taking into account the principle of common but differentiated responsibilities and respective capabilities, demands a decision on establishing the commitments of the second commitment period under the Kyoto Protocol here in Durban. That was recognized by our Ministers in the G-77 Declaration in September, and we reiterate it today.
19. The Kyoto Protocol, its mechanisms, its rules, and its compliance system must be preserved and strengthened, as an essential part of the current legally binding international multilateral rules-based system created by the UNFCCC. Any decision other than the adoption of the second commitment period of the Kyoto Protocol would cast a doubt on our shared commitment

to multilateralism and to the so needed decisive action if we are to maintain a viable chance of limiting the increase in global mean temperature.

20. The Group of 77 and China reiterates the necessity of Palestine effective participation in the UNFCCC process, and to have the right of access to funding from different climate change sources.

Finally, Madam President,

21. Once again, let me reassure you that the G-77 and China will support you in a sustainable and tireless manner. We are fully committed with you in "SAVING TOMORROW, TODAY."

Statement on behalf of the G-77 and China at the Opening Plenary of the 18th Conference of the Parties to the UNFCCC
(Doha, Qatar, 26 November 2012)

Mr. President,

1. I have the honour to deliver this statement on behalf of the G-77 and China.
2. I would like to express to you my congratulations for your election as President of the COP-18 and the CMP-8. We count on your experience and wisdom to guide us towards the success we hope.
3. I would like also to express my gratitude to the Government and the people of Qatar for their warm welcome and the hospitality they have shown since our arrival in this beautiful city of Doha. My thanks are also extended to the Secretariat of the UNFCCC for the help it provided.

Mr. President,

4. The international community is facing a multitude of challenges, especially amplified by successive crises, including the climate one.
5. In addition to these challenges, many others are faced by the international community. The most important is certainly the achievement of economic and social development and the improvement of living conditions of nearly a billion people who are suffering from hunger and extreme poverty. The most ironic perhaps is that the poorest are the most affected and particularly vulnerable to climate change, while they are not the origin of this phenomenon.
6. We must be guided by the high-level political consensus reached by the leaders in Rio+20 that reaffirmed that parties to the UNFCCC and the Kyoto Protocol should protect the climate system on the basis of equity and in accordance with the principle of common but differentiated responsibilities and respective capabilities.

Mr. President,

7. In Durban, we adopted a balanced "package" based on mutual reassurances. At Doha we must. ensure that the package is fully implemented to ensure the following:
   - Strengthen the principles and provisions of the Convention and the Kyoto Protocol, in particular the principles of equity and common but differentiated responsibilities;
   - Safeguard trust in the multilateral process through an inclusive, transparent, and a party-driven process
   - Ensure a successful and meaningful conclusion of the two pillars of the Bali Road Map, i.e., AWG-KP and AWG-LCA, through formal adoption and operationalisation of a legally binding second commitment period of the Protocol Kyoto and an agreed outcome pursuant to Bali Action Plan under the AWG-LCA.

Mr. President,

8. We welcome progress made in Bonn and Bangkok, though much remains to be done.
9. We reiterate that the Kyoto Protocol is the cornerstone of the climate change regime. The second commitment period must therefore start on 1 January 2013, and the modalities of its implementation must ensure an effective transition to an ambitious and legally binding second commitment period to avoid any gap between the two commitment periods. We urge the Annex I parties to the Kyoto Protocol, who intend to join the second commitment period, particularly those who have so far not submitted their QELROs, to work collectively in this direction, and deliver ambitious commitments, given the urgency that takes the fight against climate change. In addition, we urge those Annex I parties that do not intend to join the second commitment period or that are not parties to Kyoto protocol, to take comparable mitigation commitments under the Convention with comparable accounting rules.
10. For the Long-term Action under the Convention, we remain deeply concerned about the slow progress that characterized sessions held in Bonn and Bangkok. We still believe that additional efforts must be made by developed countries regarding the implementation of decisions taken in Cancun and Durban on all the building blocks of the Bali Action Plan, especially adaptation, financing, and technology transfer. We call for a result to enhance the effective, sustained, and full implementation of the Convention that is fair, equitable, and satisfactory for all and fulfils article 4.7 of the Convention. This result should give due consideration to the Bali Action Plan, the Cancun Agreements, and the Durban decisions.

11. We remain also deeply concerned by the slow progress on a number of aspects that concern the issue of funding. This includes mid-term finance, particularly the gap from now to 2020.
12. Regarding the Durban Platform, we believe that the work in this Ad Hoc Working Group should lead to a balanced, ambitious, fair, and equitable outcome under the Convention. Progress depends on following a balanced approach that will include mitigation, adaptation, and means of implementation, in accordance with the spirit of the Convention. We consider that before engaging in a new track of negotiations, it is important to first complete the work under the other Ad Hoc Working Groups.
13. The G-77 and China reiterates the necessity of enabling the effective participation of Palestine in the UNFCCC process and to make every effort to grant Palestine access to funding from different sources and mechanisms.

Mr. President,

14. Allow me to reiterate the readiness of the G-77 and China to look forward for a successful and comprehensive outcome at the COP-18/CMP-8. We stress the need of the full implementation of the delicate package endorsed in Durban in all its aspects, including addressing in a balanced and effective manner the issues of adaptation, mitigation, finance, technology, and capacity-building.
15. I would like to assure you that the G-77 and China will continue to support Qatar, in its actions to make the current Conference a much-needed success.

Statement on behalf of the Group of 77 and China by H.E. Ambassador Latifa Benazza, Director, Ministry of Foreign Affairs of Algeria, at the Opening Plenary of the Eighth Session of the Conference of the Parties Serving as a Meeting of the Parties to the Kyoto Protocol (CMP-8)
(Doha, Qatar, 26 November 2012)

Mr. President,

1. I have the honour to deliver this statement on behalf of the Group of 77 and China. Allow me to congratulate you on your election as President of the eighteenth session of the Conference of the Parties and the eighth session of the Conference of the Parties serving as a Meeting of the Parties to the Kyoto Protocol. I would like, also, to take this opportunity to express our deep appreciation and gratitude to the Government and people of Qatar, for the warm hospitality expressed since our arrival in this beautiful and welcoming city of Doha. We also thank the Secretariat of UNFCCC for their excellent arrangements.

2. During this CMP-8, we must work together with a renewed sense of urgency and common purpose, to deliver the mandate we collectively committed to, more than six years ago, which is to complete the work of the Ad Hoc Working Group on Further Commitments for Annex I parties under the Kyoto Protocol, in time to ensure that there is no gap between the first and second commitment periods.
3. The Group of 77 and China expects the AWG-KP to put forward ambitious quantified emission reduction commitments from Annex I parties for the second commitment period.

Mr. President,

4. The Durban outcome invited Annex I parties to submit information on their mitigation commitments or QELROs, by 1 May 2012, in order to enable the (AWG-KP) to "deliver the results of its work on QELROs" in Doha.
5. However, at the opening of this COP/MOP, only some Annex I countries have expressed their intention to participate in taking mitigation commitments and presented information on their "provisional" QELROs.
6. A higher level of ambition in the scale of emission reductions in aggregate as well as joint and individual contributions of Annex I parties must be ensured in order to overcome the wide gap between the insufficient pledges that are currently on the table and what is required by science, equity, and historical responsibility.
7. Furthermore, a second commitment period under the Kyoto Protocol must be established as the basis for comparable Annex I emission reduction commitments by those parties that choose not to abide to the second phase of the Protocol.
8. In Durban, CMP-7 mandated some specific work for narrowing down technical aspects required for adopting a second commitment period under the Kyoto Protocol in Doha. While discussions during 2012 in Bonn and Bangkok reached progress, many technical and political issues remain unresolved.
9. We also stress the importance of the achievement of a quality legal second commitment period and the successful conclusion of the work of the AWG-LCA, in line with the Bali Action Plan.

Mr. President,

10. The Kyoto Protocol is the only international instrument that sets quantified legally binding targets for Annex I parties to reduce their emissions. The Protocol must be strengthened in order to ensure a meaningful multilateral response to climate change. Also, it has to constitute the basis of the new

legal instrument under the Convention respecting the principle of common but differentiated responsibilities.

11. Doha must deliver a strong and effective second commitment period of the Kyoto Protocol that preserves environmental integrity. The Group of 77 and China has presented a consolidated proposal on carry-over and surplus of units to the second commitment period. We must have the willingness to resolve the remaining legal and technical issues that will allow us to reach a multilateral consensus and to strengthen the spirit of international cooperation.
12. Before concluding, allow me, Mr. President, once again, to assure you that the G-77 and China will continue to engage constructively and productively in these negotiations. You can count with our full support and determination to contribute to make the Doha conference a successful one.

Statement on behalf of the Group of 77 and China by Mr. Amena Yauvoli, Ambassador, UNFCCC Chair of G-77 and China at the Opening Plenary of the 19th Conference of the Parties (COP-19) of the United Nations Framework Convention on Climate Change (UNFCCC)
(Warsaw, Poland, 11 November 2013)

Thank you, Mr. President,
Excellencies,
Distinguished Representatives,
Ladies and Gentlemen,

1. I have the honour to deliver the statement on behalf of the Group of 77 and China.
2. May I at the outset express the Group's sincere appreciation and delight on your appointment as the President of COP-19 and CMP-9 today. We acknowledge the efforts your government has exerted in preparing for this Conference. It is a pleasure to be in this historical city, the venue of our meeting is a marvel. Our appreciation also goes to the people and Government of Poland for the warmth of their hospitality. We would also like to thank the Secretariat of UNFCCC for the excellent arrangements for the Warsaw Conference.
3. May I also take this opportunity to sincerely thank and acknowledge the Government of Qatar and the outgoing President for the wonderful role they played as President of COP-18 and CMP-8.

Mr. President,

4. As we embark on our discussions for addressing climate change at this Conference, the Government and the good people of the Republic of the Philippines and neighbouring countries such as Vietnam and Palau are

experiencing the devastating effect of one of the most severe typhoon in recorded history. We pause to remember the victims of Typhoon Haiyan, our prayers and thoughts are with them. The same sentiments go to all victims of adverse effect of climate change in all regions of the developing word experienced throughout this year, including countries in the South and West Asia Region: Iraq, Kuwait, Iran, Jordan, and Pakistan, currently suffering from climate induced threats, including impacts of sand and dust storms in addition to countries under occupation. Climate change is real, present, and imminent. Mr. President, it is here and now and developing countries which are the least responsible for the problem of climate change remain least able to cope with its adverse effects. It behoves all of us to accomplish our tasks with a sense of urgency.

Mr. President

5. The Group of 77 and China will be articulating its views more substantively in the CMP-9 and in the plenary of the Subsidiary Bodies. But this morning, let me convey that the Group views the nineteenth Conference of the Parties to the UNFCCC as an implementation COP. The implementation of all the Bali Action Plan and the Bali Road Map, and of past decisions of the COPs in accordance with the principles and provisions of the Convention, including Cancun, Durban, and Doha, are relevant as the foundation for the future for the success and necessary for the credibility of this multilateral process. We have no room for unilateralism. This in our view will dictate the success of the Conference in Warsaw.

Mr. President,

6. Agriculture is particularly vulnerable to the adverse effects of climate change, including changes in the frequency and severity of droughts and floods. This could pose challenges for the achievement of food security, in the context of the need to feed a world growing population in the coming decades. We welcome the organization of the workshop at SBSTA 39 to exchange views on the current state of scientific knowledge on how to enhance the adaption of agriculture of climate change impacts while promoting rural development and productivity of agriculture systems and food security, particularly in developing countries. This should take into account the diversity of agricultural systems and the differences in scale as well as possible adaptation co-benefits.

In this respect, the focus of the SBSTA work must remain on adaptation, taking into consideration its co-benefits and, in light of the linkages of agriculture with livelihoods, food security and poverty eradication. This work should be based on the principles and provisions of the Convention.

In this context, the group is ready to engage constructively and in good faith in the workshop, with willingness to move forward on this matter, as parties will consider the report of the workshop at SBSTA 40 (2014).
Mr. President,

7. Very briefly, these are the priorities for the Group of 77 and China at COP-19: finance, review, loss and damage, adaptation, transfer of technology, and response measures.
8. We would like, at this Conference, to see clarity and good outcomes in the decisions to be adopted on matters relating to finance, including for the transfer of technology, and capacity-building, which is the basic foundation of any ambitious action on climate change. Three years after its launching in Durban, the Green Climate Fund remains an empty shell. It is absolutely necessary that we call for the rapid and substantial initial capitalization and an ambitious resource mobilization for the GCF for 2014. We welcome the appointment of its Executive Director, one from a developing country, and we are certain that she will effectively carry out the role and functions of an independent Secretariat to the Fund. The Fast Start period ended in 2012, and there is still no clarity on the predictable scale up of the provision of finance up to US$100 billion per year by 2020.
9. The Group reiterates the importance of the 2013–2015 Review. We look forward to concrete progress being made at this session in the work of the Review of the lost opportunity to begin work during the June session. We would also like to underscore the needs to have an inclusive and transparent process of the review.

Mr. President,

10. The Group calls for the full implementation of the decision adopted in Doha related to Loss and Damage, taking into account the principles of the Convention and the national development processes. Carrying out such actions requires the provision of adequate support and creating the appropriate arrangements and calling for meaningful activities. Fulfilling the mandate of Doha on the issue above must be considered as one of the key elements for the success of the COP-19.
11. The Group calls for the balanced treatment of all items in this Conference, in this regard adaptation remains a priority for us and it ought to be treated with commensurate urgency.
12. The modalities and procedures of the Climate Technology Centre and Network and of its Advisory Board are important to our Group, as this will further the development and transfer of technologies, removal of barriers to such development and transfer, and implementation of the technology mechanism, which is a priority for us.

Mr. President,

13. The G-77 would like to highlight the importance of this COP for the issue of policy incentives to developing countries' actions and activities in reducing emissions from forests. We call upon all countries to reach a meaningful outcome of the COP work programme on results based-payments and financing, a decision which addresses the priorities of developing countries, namely, scaling up finance and increasing the coordination of its delivery. The progress achieved in methodological issues under the subsidiary bodies can only be complete with a meaningful decision on financing.
14. The Group wishes to highlight that in our discussion of the issues reflected in the agenda of this Conference, parties ought to avoid duplication. We are cautious about the possibility of an overlap in our desire to perfect our processes. We welcome the inclusion of Gender and Climate Change in this year's COP agenda.
15. In conclusion, the G-77 and China is ready to assist and work cooperatively with all parties to ensure the success of this Conference.

Statement on behalf of the Group of 77 and China by Minister for Women, Social Welfare and Poverty Alleviation, Dr. Jiko Luveni, UNFCCC High-level Segment, Chair of G-77 and China, at the Opening of the High-level Segment of the 19th Conference of the Parties and 9th Session of Conference of the Parties Serving as the Meeting of the Parties to the Kyoto Protocol
(Warsaw, Poland, 19 November 2013)

Mr. President,
His Excellency the Secretary General of the United Nations,
Excellency President of Tanzania,
Madam Executive Secretary,
Honourable Ministers,
Excellencies,
Distinguished Representatives,
Ladies and Gentlemen,

1. This is a historic Conference. This is the first COP where the commitments on mitigation by developed country parties is lower at the end of the COP than where they started at the beginning of this Conference.
2. How much more back sliding are we going to see, not just in mitigation ambition but in areas of adaptation, finance, technology development and transfer, transparency, and capacity-building. We call on Annex I parties to shoulder your responsibilities. The developing countries are doing more than their

share. This is borne out by various studies. We call on Annex I parties to have the commitment to set right this anomaly.

3. It is highly disappointing and indeed regrettably inadequate, that at a juncture such as this, when we are so full of enthusiasm and determination to discuss, analyse, assess, and determine for ourselves, an instrument that will guide our behaviour and regulate our affairs for the benefit of this and the future generations, in as far as the climate regime is concerned, that we are now witnessing retractions by some parties from their obligation and from their leadership role, in these processes.
4. Last week, instead of increasing its emission reduction target or at the very least remain at current level, a prominent Annex I party announced its intention to substantially deviate from its promised target to a level much less compatible with previously stated pledge. In a more recent forum, Australia and Canada clearly demonstrated their unwillingness to show increased ambition by reserving their position on the Green Climate Fund, thus, conclusively confirming their unwillingness to move forward in these endeavour.
5. When we left to come to Warsaw, we were anticipating this Conference to be an Implementation COP. We anticipated that here we will see visible signs of parties exhibiting their serious desire, willingness, and commitment to implement the Bali Action Plan. The implementation of the Bali Action Plan and the Bali Road Map, as well as of the decisions from the Cancun, Durban, and Doha COPs, in accordance with the principles and provisions of the Convention are relevant as the foundation for future success and necessary for the credibility of this multilateral process.
6. After one week of intense negotiations, our technical people have advised that things are not looking promising in Warsaw. This is a source of major concern within our Group, despite the best efforts of our delegations. We urge developed country parties to show leadership. This process is at a critical juncture where leadership is desperately desired. The Convention clearly stipulates where leadership lies.
7. In this context, we recall article 3.1 of the Convention where, *inter alia*, it is also incumbent that "developed country Parties should take the lead in combating climate change and the adverse effects thereof."
8. We would also like to underline the importance of article 4.1 while dealing with the matter of commitments in the context of CBDR and national circumstances.
9. Concerning agriculture, we believe that the rich exchange of views by parties during the in-session workshop held last week and the submissions of parties and admitted observers organizations will draw the way forward on how to enhance adaptation of agriculture to climate change impacts as a priority, as well as possible adaptation co-benefits.

Mr. President,

10. The Group of 77 and China has earlier articulated its priorities for COP-19 at the opening of this session. Despite one week of negotiations, there still remains a serious lack of clarity on the predictable scale up of the provision of finance up to US$100 billion per year by 2020. Three years after its launching in Durban, the Green Climate Fund, as I speak, remains an empty shell. It is absolutely necessary that we see a rapid and substantial initial capitalization and an ambitious resource mobilization for the GCF for 2014. Clarity on finance, including for the transfer of technology and capacity-building, which is the basic foundation of any ambitious action on climate change is essential if Warsaw is to be a success.

Mr. President,

11. The full implementation of the decision adopted in Doha related to Loss and Damage, taking into account the principles of the Convention and the national development processes cannot be over-emphasized. Carrying out such actions requires the provision of adequate support and creating the appropriate arrangements and calling for meaningful activities. Fulfilling the mandate of Doha on Loss and Damage remains as a key element for the success of the COP-19. Our Group is working hard at this Conference to realize this. We request reciprocity.
12. I will reiterate once again the Group's call on the vital importance for a balanced treatment of all items in this Conference. In this regard, adaptation remains a priority for us and it ought to be treated with commensurate urgency. Last week, our Group has observed that particular emphasis on New Markets remains, the preoccupation of our partners. This too is an imbalance.

Mr. President,

13. Group of 77 and China continues to call for the entering into force, and as soon as possible of the amendments adopted in Doha in relation to the second commitment period of the Kyoto Protocol. It is paramount that the ambition mechanism launched in Doha effectively results in the increase of the ambition of Annex I parties' quantified emissions reduction and limitation commitments for the second commitment period. We therefore once again urge all Annex I parties to the Kyoto Protocol to expeditiously go through the relevant legal procedures necessary to bring the amendments into force as soon as possible, and to revisit and significantly increase their quantified emissions reduction and limitation commitments by 2014. It is crucial that we should ensure the operationalization and implementation of the 2014 Revisit Mechanism under the Kyoto Protocol in Warsaw.

14. We have agreed that the 2015 Outcome for the post-2020 period should be guided by the Principles and Provisions of the Convention, on the basis of equity and in accordance with Common but Differentiated Responsibilities, since we have agreed that the post-2020 outcome should be "under the Convention."
15. We can move to set ourselves ambitious goals for the post-2020 period only if we meet our commitments in the pre-2020 period. If not, the post-2020 agreement will not yield the results we desire by way of enhanced actions and ambition.
16. It is equally important to remember that the 2015 outcome should not result in shifting the responsibility of the developed countries to the developing countries. This cannot be the ultimate objective of the Convention. We need to ensure that there is a reaffirmation of the principles and provisions of the Convention so that we can work toward the same goal with a spirit of purpose.
17. In this week is the commencement of our High-Level Segment. It is essential that we must intensify our efforts and frankly converse with each other as Ministers, in a spirit commensurate with the level of our perceived status.
18. Finally, Mr. President, yours is a very cold country indeed. But let me assure you, that the warmth of your hospitality is acknowledged. Please, inform the good people of Poland and the kind citizens of Warsaw that we are happy to be here and will be doing our level best in these negotiations.

Statement on behalf of the Group of 77 and China by Ambassador Rene Orellana, Chair of the Group of 77 and China at the Opening Plenary of the 20th Conference of the Parties (COP-20) of the United Nations Framework Convention on Climate Change (UNFCCC) (Lima, Peru, 1 December 2014)

Excellencies,
Distinguished representatives,
Ladies and gentlemen,
I have the honour to deliver this statement on behalf of the Group of 77 and China

1. Let me congratulate the incoming presidency of Peru and express our gratitude for the excellent hospitality of your country and government. You can count on the full support of our Group to secure the successful work of this conference. We wish to assure you that the Group is willing and ready to engage meaningfully with all parties. Our support and assistance to the Presidency is reaffirmed.
2. May I also take this opportunity to sincerely thank and acknowledge the Government of Poland and the outgoing President for the wonderful role they played as President of COP-19 and CMP-9.

Mr. President,

3. The Fifth Assessment Report of the IPCC has confirmed that the warming of the climate system is unequivocal, and since the 1950s, many of the observed changes are unprecedented over decades to millennia. The atmosphere and ocean have warmed, the amounts of snow and ice have diminished, sea level has risen, and the concentrations of greenhouse gases have increased.
4. Although commitments under the Convention have been there since the past 20 years, we are seeing backsliding, delays, and low levels of ambition on mitigation, adaptation support, finance, technology development and transfer, and capacity-building provision from developed countries. Fulfilment of their obligations under the Convention has been both too little and too late on emission reductions, provision of finance, supporting technology development and transfer, building capacity. Developing countries, on the other hand, have stepped forward and taken the lead, with many announcing and implementing ambitious mitigation and adaptation actions by and large using their own scarce resources while at the same time seeking to improve their development prospects.
5. The Group of 77 and China reiterates that the urgency of the climate change situation requires that we accelerate the process and initiate more dynamic and interactive sessions. The Group is prepared to engage in negotiations with a constructive spirit, positive, dynamic, and optimistic attitude to strive for a successful outcome of our work here in Lima.
6. We welcome the full operationalization of the Green Climate Fund and urgently call for the significant capitalization of the Convention's financial mechanism, with new, additional, adequate, sustained, accessible, and predictable funding. The Group also welcomes the initial pledges made to the Fund, though still insufficient and far from the commitment made by developed countries to provide US$100 billion per year in a timely manner.
7. The lack of Annex I ambition in the pre-2020 period, including KP commitments and the compliance with them, must also be part of the discussion. We have all agreed on the importance and the necessity for Annex I parties to take the lead in addressing climate change. This requires that they raise their level of mitigation ambition, in particular through the obligation this year to revisit the level of ambition of QELROs under the Kyoto Protocol's Second Commitment Period, and through comparable efforts under the Convention by those Annex I parties not participating in the second commitment period.

Mr. President,

8. We call for a process of building consensus on the basis of the parties' inputs and proposals reiterating that the outputs of the process should reflect parties' proposals. To build consensus requires that parties interact in a negotiating process exchanging proposals and explaining the rationale behind them.
9. The Group underlines the importance of making substantial progress on elaboration of the elements for a drafting negotiating text, essential to the adoption of the 2015 agreement in Paris. The Group reiterates that the 2015 agreement must be under the Convention and based on its principles and provisions related to commitments and responsibilities with regard to mitigation, adaptation and means of implementation, in particular the principles of equity and common but differentiated responsibilities and respective capabilities. The 2015 agreement should treat the elements of mitigation, adaptation, finance, technology development and transfer, capacity-building, and transparency of action and support in a balanced manner and on an equal footing. The provisions of the 2015 agreement should focus on enhanced action related to the six core elements.
10. The Group also looks forward to advance negotiations on the information of the intended Nationally Determined Contributions. In doing so, the Group would like to reiterate that decision 1/CP.19, paragraph 2 (d) urges developed countries, the operating entities of the financial mechanism and other organizations to provide adequate support to allow for developing countries to undertake their domestic preparations for the intended Nationally Determined Contributions and for submitting information thereon and for implementing their enhanced action after 2020.

Mr. President,

11. The Group reiterates that Intended Nationally Determined Contributions represent the effort each country is willing to make in the global effort to fight climate change and therefore must be seen in a balanced and comprehensive context pursuant to the mentioned relevant decisions in accordance with the principles and provisions of the Convention. Developed country parties shall provide finance, technology development and transfer, and capacity-building support. Developing countries will require provision of adequate support for their domestic preparations of their Intended Nationally Determined Contributions and for submitting information thereon, as well as for the implementation of their enhanced action.
12. Attempts to redefine, rewrite, renegotiate, or reinterpret the Convention and its principles and provisions will complicate and delay the process.

Mr. President,

13. The output of this COP should enhance the provision of financing, technology development and transfer, and capacity-building by developed countries to developing countries, avoiding approaches that would make that provision voluntary and subject to the providers' policy control and where MRV is more extensive with respect to mitigation but weak with respect to finance, technology development and transfer, and capacity-building.
14. We welcome the work of the Adaptation Committee and the Least Developed Country Expert Group in regards to National Adaptation Plans this year and in preparation for this session. However, we wish to bring to the attention of the Presidency our concern over the slow progress and unclear path set up for turning National Adaptation Plans from a recurring discussion to a reality implemented. Key issues need to be resolved and clarified at this session.

Mr. President,

15. We ask to pay special attention to the National Adaptation Plans to be turned into a reality—to avoid a situation where the most vulnerable are being the first victims of the slow course of discussions.
16. Technology development and transfer will continue to be a key component for a successful outcome whether pre- or post-2020. Effective mitigation and adaptation actions by parties will rely in many ways on access to technology, including the development of endogenous technologies by developing countries. COP agenda items that relate to technology should therefore focus on the objective of building up the technology mechanism and creating the institutional and policy conditions that would be conducive to supporting the rapid and effective transfer of technologies to developing countries, helping them innovate and develop their own technologies.
17. We would like to see concrete enhanced actions on technology development and transfer to be accelerated and scaled up by the technology mechanism. In this regard, we believe it is crucial for the technology mechanism to strengthen its effective coordination with the financial mechanism, as well as to strengthen the system in coordination with the relevant organizations to remove barriers for the development and transfer of technology.
18. Any agreement without equity and CBDR and RC is not in accordance with the Convention. An agreement that is mitigation focused and bottom-up for developed countries will result in developed countries emitting more than they should and will not effectively address climate change at all in the soonest time possible. Time is running out—the world cannot afford half-measures or half-commitments with respect to climate actions.

19. On the matters of the Warsaw international mechanism for loss and damage associated with climate change impacts, the Group stresses the paramount need to make this mechanism functional. This mechanism must address the needs of developing countries suffering from extreme and slow-onset climate change induced events, and the urgency for this mechanism has only increased. We call for finalizing the organization and governance of the executive committee, the necessary arrangements including the financial mechanism, and the approval of a two-year work plan that responds to the expectations of particularly vulnerable developing countries.
20. The Group is particularly concerned over the financing gap that exists, both for mitigation and adaptation in the pre-2020 period. We underline that recent IPCC reports affirm that global adaptation financial estimates are substantially greater than current adaptation funding and investment, particularly in developing countries, suggesting a funding gap and a growing adaptation deficit.
21. On Response Measures, the Group reaffirms the importance of giving full consideration to what actions are necessary to meet the specific needs and concerns of developing country parties arising from the impacts of the implementation of response measures, in accordance with the principles and provisions of the Convention.

Mr. President,

22. We want to express our sincere support to your leadership and are confident that this COP will be guided towards success by your wisdom with the spirit of equity, transparency, inclusiveness through a party driven process.

Statement on behalf of the Group of 77 and China by Ambassador Rene Orellana, Chair of the Group of 77 and China at the Opening Plenary of the Conference of the Parties Serving as the Meeting of the Parties to the Kyoto Protocol (CMP-10) of the United Nations Framework Convention on Climate Change (UNFCCC) (Lima, Peru, 1 December 2014)

Thank you, Mr. President,
Excellencies,
Distinguished Representatives,
Ladies and Gentlemen,

1. I have the honour to deliver this statement on behalf of the Group of 77 and China.
2. In Doha we took a fundamental step to further enhance the international climate change regime, through the historic adoption of a fully ratifiable amendment to the Kyoto Protocol for its second commitment period. KP CP2 is an

essential part of the pre-2020 package of actions agreed to in Doha that must be implemented fully and effectively, particularly by developed countries who have QELROs under the KP CP2.

3. Back in June, ministers from the Group of 77 and China called for three specific courses of action, and we reiterate these actions as key to success.
4. First, all parties must promptly ratify the amendment on the second commitment period so as to enable its rapid entry into force. The political will of those Annex I parties that have inscribed commitments for the Protocol's second phase will not be fully demonstrated until they have presented their ratification instruments of the Doha amendment. As part of the ratification process, parties with Annex B commitments for the second commitment period should revisit these commitments and consider bringing forward greater mitigation ambition during the ratification process. The Kyoto Protocol rules provide for this, and a number of parties are in fact in a position to increase the ambition of their commitments.
5. Second, it is important to note, Mr. President, that the rapid ratification of the amendment by all Annex I parties is crucial to build trust in the context of negotiations on the Durban Platform for Enhanced Action. Ratification of the second commitment period is an important steppingstone towards the new 2015 Agreement under the Durban Platform and its entry into force and implementation from 2020. The most crucial experience learnt from the Kyoto Protocol is that the leadership by developed country parties is the fundamental basis for the global cooperation on combating climate change. This leadership should continue during both the pre-2020 and post-2020 period.

Mr. President,

6. Thirdly, it is paramount that the ambition mechanism launched in Doha produces the increase in ambition of Annex I parties' quantified emissions reduction and limitation commitments sufficient to meet the requirements of the science. This ambition mechanism was a critical element of the political compromise achieved in Doha, and Annex I parties must undertake additional action under the Kyoto Protocol with a view to closing the ambition gap by 2020. In light of the recent report of the IPCC, decisions to raise ambition cannot be delayed until the post-2020 period. The decisions in Doha required each Annex I party to revisit in 2014 its quantified emissions limitation and reduction commitment and significantly increase their ambition to at least 25–40% below 1990 level by 2020.
7. The revisit mechanism must be made more robust, and should prioritize reviewing the extent to which developed countries that are KP CP2 signatories individually and in aggregate are increasing their pre-2020 ambitions.

Mr. President,

8. We express great concern that so far, only two developed countries have ratified the KP CP2, others have made only political pledges that they will join CP2, while still yet other developed countries have not joined KP or have left KP or have stated that they will not join CP2. We call on developed countries parties to the KP to accelerate their ratification process in order in accordance to the other parties to do so.
9. The Doha amendment ratification pace needs to be picked up by all parties, particularly by developed countries that are party to the amendment.

Mr. President,

10. At the same time, those few Annex B parties that have not adopted quantified commitments for the second commitment period under column 3 of the amended Annex B should consider now whether they would like to reconsider their non-participation in the second commitment period. They are welcome to bring forward quantified commitments to the CMP for consideration and adoption, to enable them access to the benefits of the Kyoto accounting rules.

Mr. President,

11. On agenda item 8, the G-77 expects that Annex B parties will continue to revisit their commitments in 2015 and beyond, consistent with the understanding in Doha, and will make every effort to deepen their commitments. The ambition mechanism was a critical element of the political compromise achieved in Doha, and Annex I parties must take additional action under the Kyoto Protocol with a view to closing the ambition gap by 2020. This is critically important to demonstrate the leadership of Annex I parties pre-2020, and to achieve an ambitious outcome in Paris in 2015. We emphasize our disappointment and concern that none of the Annex I parties declared its intention to increase the ambition of their commitments. We therefore propose that a contact group be set up under the CMP to consider ways and means to follow-up on the high-level ministerial round table and make necessary arrangement to make sure that real increase in ambition of commitments by Annex I parties will happen before it is too late.
12. On agenda item 11, we look forward to making progress at this session—progress that has been impeded for two years now by the refusal of a minority of parties to accept the decisions taken in Doha with respect to article 3.7 ter, 'hot air', carryover and eligibility. In this regard, the G-77 underscores that progress will come most readily if all parties accept that it is our job

here in Lima to implement the rules agreed in Doha, as mandated under this agenda item.

13. In connection with the reports to facilitate the calculation of assigned amounts for the second commitment period, the G-77 underscores the need for complete transparency on how the Doha Amendment and its related rules, including those on surplus, the article 3.7 cancellation and carryover, will be applied by parties and by regional economic integration organisations.
14. Thank you, Mr. President. The Group is committed to work with you and all parties to make this CMP-10 a success.

Statement on Behalf of the Group of 77 and China H.E. President Evo Morales Ayma, Plurinational State of Bolivia on behalf of the Group of 77 and China at the Joint Session of the High-Level Segment of the 20th Conference of the Parties and the 10th Conference of the Parties Serving Kyoto Protocol of the United Nations Framework Convention on Climate Change (UNFCCC) (Lima, Peru, 9 December 2014)

Mr. President,
H.E. Manuel Pulgar-Vidal, Minister of Environment of Peru and President of the COP-20,
H.E. Ban Ki-moon, United Nations Secretary-General,
Madam Cristiana Figueres, Executive Secretary of the United Nations Framework Convention on Climate Change,
Excellencies, Heads of State and Government,
Excellencies, Ministers and Heads of Delegation,

Especially Salutations to all the International Organisations present here today, as well as all indigenous peoples, farmer communities, and social movements and organization that are participating at COP-20.

Firstly, allow me to congratulate you on your Presidency of the COP-20, and express our gratitude for your hospitality and of the people of Peru. I assure you that you can count on the support of the Group of 77 and China to achieve concrete solutions towards the climate crisis.

Climate change is one of the most serious global challenges of our times. We underscore the fact that developing countries continue to suffer the most from the adverse impacts of climate change, the increasing frequency and intensity of extreme weather events, and the impact of response measures, even though they are historically the least responsible for climate change (. . .) Climate change threatens not only the development prospects of developing countries and their achievement of sustainable development but also the very existence and survival of countries, societies and the ecosystems of our Mother Earth.

We affirm that the United Nations Framework Convention on Climate Change (UNFCCC) is the primary international, intergovernmental forum for negotiating the global response to climate change. In this regard, we stress that the international response to climate change must fully respect the principles, provisions, and ultimate objective of the Convention, in particular the principles of equity and of common but differentiated responsibilities.

Mr. President, I will like to highlight the contribution of the G-77 and China in the climate change negotiations:

- The establishment of the United Nations Framework Convention on Climate Change with a vision of solidarity, cooperation, justice, and equity must be taken as the most important achievement.
- The creation of the new climate institutions for adaptation, finance and technology suggested by the G-77 and China are also underscored. These, with a holistic vision on climate change, we consider that mitigation of and adaptation to climate change are contingent upon different sociocultural contexts, taking particular account of indigenous peoples.
- We stress the recently achieved success of COP-19 suggested by the G-77 and China, which was the launching of the Warsaw international mechanism for loss and damage associated with climate change impacts.

Statement on Behalf of the Group of 77 and China by Ambassador Rene Orellana, Chair of the Group of 77 and China at the Closing Plenary of the 20th Conference of the Parties (COP-20) of the United Nations Framework Convention on Climate Change (UNFCCC) (Lima, Peru, 14 December 2014)

Mr. President,
Excellencies,
Distinguished representatives,
Ladies and gentlemen,

I have the honour to deliver this statement on behalf of the Group of 77 and China.

1. Let me express our Group's appreciation for the hospitality of Peru and its people and to the Peruvian Government for your commitment in organizing this conference.

Mr. President,

2. The Group underlines the work achieved in Lima as essential to the adoption of the 2015 agreement in Paris. The Group reiterates that the 2015 agreement must be under the Convention and based on its principles and provisions

related to commitments and responsibilities with regard to mitigation, adaptation, and means of implementation, in particular the principles of equity and common but differentiated responsibilities and respective capabilities. The 2015 agreement should treat the elements of mitigation, adaptation, finance, technology development and transfer, capacity-building, and transparency of action and support in a balanced manner and on an equal footing. The provisions of the 2015 agreement should focus on enhanced action related to the six core elements.

3. The Group wishes to stress the importance of the following five issues as key for the 2015 agreement:
    a) Underscore the importance of the principles and provisions of the Convention in the 2015 Agreement, in particular equity and common but differentiated responsibilities and respective capabilities. The agreement shall be under the Convention.
    b) Be consistent with the Convention, including the differentiation between developed and developing countries parties.
    c) Adaptation and Loss and Damage are key to the 2015 agreement and must be given their due space.
    d) Finance, technology, and capacity-building are essential for the 2015 agreement, and it must be clear that developed countries shall provide finance, technology development and transfer, and capacity-building support to developing countries.
    e) The agreement must have a vision consistent with achieving sustainable development and poverty eradication.
4. Attempts to replace, redefine, rewrite, renegotiate, or reinterpret the Convention and its principles and provisions will complicate and delay the process.

Mr. President,

5. We welcome the full operationalization of the Green Climate Fund and urgently call for the significant capitalization of the Convention's financial mechanism with new, additional, adequate, sustained, accessible, and predictable funding by developed country parties.
6. We appreciate the hard work invested during this COP on important issues related to adaptation, including National Adaptation Plans. While much remains to be done, we welcome the much-needed progress. We also take note of the important steps achieved in Lima under the Warsaw International mechanism for loss and damage associated with climate change impacts—the Executive Committee will play a key role in guiding the work of the mechanism and we look forward to swift and significant results.

Mr. President,

7. On Response Measures, the Group expresses its disappointment over the outcome reached. As a Group we stress the importance of addressing this issue as a matter of urgency.

Mr. President,

8. We want to express to you our sincere appreciation for your leadership in guiding this COP.

Statement by Ambassador Nozipho Mxakato-Diseko from South Africa on behalf of the Group of 77 and China, at the Opening Plenary of the 21st Conference of the Parties to the United Nations Framework Convention on Climate Change (COP-21) (Paris, France, 30 November 2015)

Excellencies,
Distinguished representatives,
Ladies and gentlemen,

1. I have the honour to deliver this statement on behalf of the Group of 77 and China.
2. Let me congratulate France as the COP-21 President and express our gratitude for your warm hospitality. You can count on the full support of our Group to secure the successful work of this COP. We wish to assure you of the Group's support and our readiness to engage constructively with all parties.
3. I would also like to take this opportunity to acknowledge the excellent work done by Peru as President of COP-20 and to thank them most sincerely for their efforts over the past year.

Mr. President,

4. Warming of the climate system is unequivocal. Concentrations of greenhouse gases have increased and as a result the atmosphere and ocean have warmed, the amounts of snow and ice have diminished, sea level has risen, and the impacts are being felt in particular by developing countries.
5. Although developing countries have the least responsibility for climate change, they are the hardest hit and least able to respond.

Mr. President,

6. The implementation of existing commitments under the Convention is of crucial importance. The COP provides an opportunity every year for the parties to assess the progress made in the implementation of the Convention. In this regard, we need to use the COP to do introspection on the lessons learnt, as we are at the threshold of adopting a new universal agreement under the Convention that is set to catalyse the achievement of its objective.
7. Very important work on implementation is undertaken in the subsidiary bodies of the Convention and these should not be overshadowed by our focus on future commitments that will only take effect from 2020. We cannot lose the five years between now and 2020 by shifting our focus away from the urgent work that needs to progress in the subsidiary bodies to implement existing commitments.
8. Developed countries must take the lead in the lead up to the post-2020 era by honouring and accelerating the implementation and increase the ambition of their existing commitments on mitigation and provision of finance, technology development and transfer, and capacity-building support to developing country parties. The fact is that many commitments by developed countries, related to the pre-2020 period still, remain unrealised, including the nearly three-year delay in ratifying the Doha Amendment and increasing the emission reduction targets to at least 25–40% by 2020. There is also, as yet, no clarity on how the six-year-old commitment by developed countries of providing the US$100 billion per year by 2020 to developing countries will be achieved.
9. We take note on the progress of the work on adaptation, particularly the Nairobi Work Programme, National Adaptation Plans, and the Adaptation Committee. While we continue to assess the climate change impacts and vulnerabilities to various regions, it is important to take into account the need for planning processes and implementation of adaptation action, as well as commensurate support that is responsive to adaptation needs, and which transcend beyond planning levels and realise enhanced adaptation action at all levels. Greater focus on priorities and needs of adaptation enables a coherent and comprehensive response to climate change, not only in terms of mitigation, but also by tackling its impacts as a key variable to be considered in the Paris agreement and in national development agendas.
10. We welcome the report of the Adaptation Committee and the effort to make balanced progress in all its work areas. We take note of the future work plan of the Committee and look forward to discussing it in the Contact Group. We also welcome the work completed on means of implementation for adaptation and we hope that its outcome translates into something that can expedite support for developing countries. We are prepared to engage with

partners in reviewing the recommendations to the COP contained in the report.

11. The G-77 welcomes the report of the Executive Committee of the Warsaw International Mechanism for Loss and Damage associated with Climate Change Impacts. The work of the WIM and on loss and damage under this Convention is of critical important to the Group. In order for this mechanism to be meaningful, it must address the needs and challenges faced by developing countries emerging from extreme and slow-onset events. We urge developed country parties to make available resources in view of the ambitious nature of the of the initial two-year work plan of the Executive Committee.
12. On finance, we reiterate that nothing under this Convention will be achieved without the provision of means of implementation to enable developing country parties address climate change. Finance, including for the transfer of technology and capacity-building, is a crucial and key element of the Paris outcome. The outcome regarding finance must provide clarity on the level of financial support that will be provided by developed country parties to developing country parties to allow for enhanced implementation of the Convention in the post-2020 period, as well as existing commitment on pre-2020 finance. We require a substantial scaling up of finance from the 2020 base level of US$100 billion and Annex I country parties and other developed countries included in Annex II have the principal responsibility in providing support. This includes setting short-term collective goals for the post-2020 period that go beyond this floor, and are revised upwards every five years, while ensuring that the finance is new, additional, predictable, and sustainable with an equal allocation between adaptation and mitigation. The financial mechanism of the Convention must serve as the financial mechanism of the legal agreement. The related funds established under the Kyoto Protocol and under the financial mechanism of the Convention must also serve as instruments of the new legal agreement.
13. On long-term finance, we need a decision that sets a clear pathway towards achieving the US$100 billion goal by 2020 and flows of finance, in particular for adaptation, under the financial mechanism of the Convention and the specialised funds. These should scale up, particularly in the context of increasing climate risks faced by developing countries. The decision in Paris must lay the foundations for the Long-Term Finance Ministerial session on the agreed thematic cluster of issues to be held at COP-22 in Morocco.
14. Furthermore, in the work on transparency, it is important that progress is made on both transparency of action, as well as transparency of support, as an opportunity to improve our collective understanding of the different elements that encompass the response to climate change.

15. Various aspects of finance are discussed in a fragmented way across the Convention bodies. We believe that it will help the process if the linkages between all matters related to finance, whether it is under the Convention, the Kyoto Protocol, or under the ADP can be discussed in a more comprehensive and coherent manner.

Mr. President,

16. Technology transfer is a key component for developing countries to be able to effectively address climate change. Effective mitigation and adaptation actions will depend on access to technology, including the development of endogenous technologies by developing countries. The technology mechanism has an important role to play in order to support the rapid transfer of technologies to developing countries, helping them innovate and develop their own technologies.
17. We would like to see concrete enhanced actions on technology development and transfer, accelerated and scaled up by the technology mechanism. In this regard, we believe it is crucial for the technology mechanism to strengthen its effective coordination with the financial mechanism, as well as to strengthen the linkages with relevant organisations.
18. We reaffirm that the process and outcome of the ADP should be in faithful to the Durban mandate focusing on the pre-2020 ambition gap, as well as the conclusion of the Paris agreement, which must be under the Convention and guided by and be in full accordance with all principles and provisions of the Convention, in particular the principle of equity and common but differentiated responsibilities. The Paris agreement is to enhance the implementation of the Convention and must address the core elements mandated by the Durban decision (mitigation, adaptation, finance, technology development and transfer, capacity-building, and transparency of action and support), as well as loss and damage and response measures in a comprehensive and balanced manner. Urgent action on the pre-2020 period is essential to build trust and create a platform for the post-2020 agreement.

Finally, Mr. President

19. We want to express our support to you in guiding us to a successful conclusion of this conference through a transparent, inclusive, and party-driven process. The Group is committed to playing a positive and constructive role.

Statement by Ambassador Nozipho Mxakato-Diseko from South Africa on behalf of the Group of 77 and China, at the Opening Plenary of the 11th Conference of the Parties Serving as the Meeting of the Parties to the Kyoto Protocol (CMP-11) (Paris, France, 30 November 2015)

President of COP-21/CMP-11,
Excellencies,
Distinguished representatives,
Ladies and gentlemen,

1. The Group of 77 and China would like to share its views on the issues that are up for discussion in the Meeting of the Parties to the Kyoto Protocol. Top of the agenda is the status of ratification of the Doha Amendment to the Kyoto Protocol.

Mr. President,

2. The Kyoto Protocol remains a key component of the international climate regime and the essential and legally binding basis for addressing pre-2020 mitigation ambition. Parties are well aware that for the Doha Amendment to enter into force at least three-fourths of the parties need to accept/ratify the amendments. The agreement on the second commitment of the Kyoto Protocol was part of the Durban package and critical to the establishment of the Durban Platform for Enhanced Action. It is concerning to the Group that only 54 parties have so far ratified the amendment to the Kyoto Protocol agreed in Doha, including those of Annex B. This Group wants to urge all parties to the Kyoto Protocol to ratify the Amendment as soon as possible. We are equally concerned that the necessary rules that are needed to allow implementation of the second commitment period of the Kyoto Protocol have not been adopted by the CMP. It is our hope that CMP-11 will adopt these rules as they have been negotiated almost fully, with very few outstanding issues remaining. The Group would like to caution against reopening agreed text, as well as attempting to renegotiate the rules in a manner that would lead to further lowering of ambition in the second commitment period of the Kyoto Protocol.

Mr. President,

3. The G-77 and China is also concerned about the manner in which the discussions are proceeding in the agenda item on issues related to the Clean Development Mechanism (CDM). We note the difficulties being encountered

in reaching consensus on issues related to modalities and procedures for the CDM. We urge parties to consider adopting text on issues which have been resolved, as this will allow for the enhancement of implementation of CDM projects in developing countries. Negotiations can then continue on other more difficult issues under this agenda item.

We would also like to encourage parties to accelerate the voluntary cancellation of certified emission reduction units as another way of increasing ambition in the pre-2020 period. We thank the Executive Board of the CDM for championing this issue.

Mr. President,

4. The G-77 and China takes note of the report of the Adaptation Fund Board. It is our view that the issue of addressing the diversification of the revenue streams of the Adaptation Fund should be given urgent priority, since the global carbon market, on which the Fund depends, has collapsed due to the low levels of ambition of Annex I commitments for 2020. This Fund is practically empty, yet we know that this is the only Fund that gives poorer countries direct access. We call for voluntary pledges by developed countries to capitalise this Fund. We would also like to encourage the continuation of discussions on developing operational linkages between the Adaptation Fund and the Green Climate Fund.

Mr. President,

5. Finally, the G-77 and China reiterates its understanding of the current mitigation gap in the pre-2020 period stemming, in large part, from Annex I commitments being far lower than required by science. We are fully aware that some of the commitments that have been put forward for attainment in 2020 will be achieved way before that. We, therefore, call on Annex I parties to revisit their commitments with a view to increasing their quantified emission limitation and reduction commitments (QELRCs) under the second commitment period of the Kyoto Protocol at least 25–40% by 2020, as provided for in the Doha amendments.
6. The G-77 and China is ready to work constructively with you in seeking solutions to all the issues that we have outlined above.

Statement by Ambassador Nozipho Mxakato-Diseko from South Africa on behalf of the Group of 77 and China at the Open-ended Consultation on Finance Process (Paris, France, 2 December 2015)

President,

1. I have the honour to speak on behalf of the Group of 77 and China. We thank the COP Presidency for acting on our request to create an opportunity to have

an informal discussion on finance as an issue that cuts across different streams of work in these negotiations. The G-77 and China stresses that nothing under the UNFCCC can be achieved without the provision of means of implementation to enable developing countries to play their part to address climate change.

2. However, clarity on the complete picture of the financial arrangements for the enhanced implementation of the Convention keeps on eluding us. We believe that it will help the process if all matters related to finance, whether it is under the Convention, the Kyoto Protocol, and under the ADP can be discussed in a comprehensive and coherent manner, regardless of where they will be reflected in the end, whether in the decision or the agreement.
3. As the G-77 and China, we hope that by elevating the importance of the finance discussions under the different bodies, we can ensure that the outcome meets parties' expectations and delivers what is required. We hope, in particular, that we can build greater coherence in the negotiations across the different streams dealing with finance.
4. The Group welcomes the most recent pledges to the Least Developed Countries Fund (LDCF), which has remained under-resourced for a long time, despite repeated calls for contributions. Equally, adequate resources for the Special Climate Change Fund (SCCF) are urgently required. However, we caution against a piecemeal approach with regard to climate finance and once-off announcements. It is now time for all developed country parties to convert their pledges to the GCF into contribution agreements, as well as scaling up commitments in the ADP process. We also need to find a solution for the Adaptation Fund, as well as the issue of its resourcing in the Paris agreement.
5. Under the Convention, developed countries are obliged to provide financial resources, including technology transfer and capacity-building, to all developing countries. This is a legal obligation under the Convention. It is neither "aid" nor "charity," nor is it the same as development assistance. Finance support from developed countries relates to the impacts of historical emissions, which will only get worse with time for developing countries. The Group is, therefore, concerned about the introduction of new language, which has no basis in the Convention, such as "Parties in a position to do so" and "dynamism" that do not take into account responsibility for historical emissions.

President,

6. The G-77 and China is deeply concerned with the attempts to introduce economic conditions in the finance section currently under negotiation here in Paris. This approach is not consistent with the Convention, the mandate of the ADP, and the sovereignty of parties. Any attempt to replace the core obligation of developed countries to provide financial support to developing countries with a number of arbitrarily identified economic conditions is a violation

of the rules-based multilateral process and threatens an outcome here in Paris. We should not shift the focus of this meeting away from arresting dangerous climate change and addressing the immediate and urgent need for adaptation and loss and damage.

7. As developing countries, we find ourselves confronted with a simplistic narrative that suggests that "the world has changed since the UNFCCC was adopted in 1992" due to the dramatic economic development gains of some of our members and hence that it is time to expand the pool of so-called "donors" of climate "aid" and to narrow the list of those eligible to receive this "support" to only the "poorest of the poor." This narrative serves narrow national interests of developed countries and says little about reality. If the world has really changed so much, we ask why it is that after all these decades all our members remain developing countries with little or no voice in global decision-making processes and institutions?
8. Despite not having a finance obligation under the Convention, developing countries are already making significant contributions towards the global effort through the implementation of climate actions. It is, therefore, necessary that the new agreement provides for the recognition of the social, economic, and environmental value of actions financed voluntarily by developing country parties, including on adaptation, and their co-benefits to health and sustainable development.
9. Differentiation is, therefore, not just a finance issue, but about the overall Paris outcome. The specific outcomes on finance must also not impose on our sovereignty and should not override or displace the zero poverty goals.
10. In particular, the Paris outcome must provide clarity on the level of financial support that will be provided by developed country parties to developing country parties to allow for enhanced implementation of the Convention in the post 2020 period.
11. A substantial scaling up of finance from the 2020 base level of US$100 billion per year is required. In this regard, developed country parties, and other developed countries included in Annex II, have the main responsibility to provide finance that is new, additional, predictable, and sustainable and with an balanced allocation between adaptation and mitigation.
12. The financial mechanism of the Convention must serve as the financial mechanism of the legal agreement. The related funds established under the Kyoto Protocol and under the financial mechanism of the Convention must also serve as instruments of the legal agreement.
13. On long-term finance, we need a decision that flows of finance, particularly for adaptation, under the financial mechanism of the Convention and the specialised funds, should increase, particularly in the context of increasing climate risks facing developing countries. The decision in Paris must lay the foundations for the Long-Term Finance Ministerial session on the agreed thematic cluster of issues to be held at COP-22 in Morocco.

14. Furthermore, in the work on transparency, it is important that agreement is reached on transparency of support urgently for both the pre-2020 and post-2020 periods.

President,

15. The fact that finance for climate change is discussed in a fragmented way across the bodies of the Convention, does not allow us to get a sense of the climate finance landscape. Our sense is that we are repeating this practice in determining what needs to be done now and beyond 2020, without the complete picture. This cannot be best way to address this most crucial aspect of the fight against climate change.
16. The crucial linkages between the provision of financial resource, technology transfer, and capacity-building support have not been addressed in an integrated way in the UNFCCC system. This approach in the real world does not make any sense. It cannot continue if we are serious about addressing climate change. We need to have a coherent and comprehensive approach on means of implementation which includes the provision of finance, technology transfer, and capacity-building. We, therefore, need a process that would enable us to agree on such a comprehensive approach. We also need to understand how institutional arrangements created for delivery of means of implementation are linked to ensure a coherent policy approach to the provision of support.
17. The Group believes that this informal consultation today should be the start of a new phase where parties to the UNFCCC can discuss the provision of finance support in its broadest sense in a coherent and comprehensive manner that responds to the actual needs of developing countries to implement actions that are required to address climate change. We look forward to a fruitful and constructive discussion.

Comments on the Negotiations under the United Nations Framework Convention on Climate Change by the Chairperson of the G-77 and China, Ambassador Nozipho Mxakato-Diseko, Paris Climate Change Conference (Le Bourget, 3 December 2015)

As Chairperson of the Group of 77 and China, I have the honour to share my impressions on the status of negotiations towards the adoption of a legal agreement and key decisions under the United Nations Framework Convention on Climate Change (UNFCCC) here at the Paris Climate Change Conference.

We have now entered the last few days of a four-year long negotiation process that began at the Durban COP in 2011. The purpose of this negotiation process, which we refer to as the "Durban Platform for Enhanced Action," is—as its title suggests—to enhance action under the existing Convention.

I am confident that we will achieve this objective under the guidance of the most capable incoming French COP Presidency, with whom our delegation and Group has an excellent working relationship. I would especially like to convey our appreciation to Peru, which is a member of our Group, in its capacity as the current COP Presidency, for having guided us so effectively to this point.

This confidence in a successful outcome to the Paris Climate Change Conference is based on the reality that failure is not an option for our members for whom climate change is an issue of vital importance, or in the case of our low-lying islands a matter of national survival. It is also firmly based on the encouraging and inspiring messages we heard from the unprecedented gathering of world leaders on the opening day of this meeting.

However, I also need to convey to you that members of the Group of 77 and China are well aware of the challenges we face and that there are grave concerns over both the process and the substance in these negotiations. We have intervened as a Group on many occasions this year and at this conference to try to adjust the process and to speed up the negotiations. We have taken a leadership role in the hopes of securing the shared objectives of all parties.

The basis of our concern is that the Durban mandate is not being respected by all parties and we are witnessing repeated attempts by one group in particular—the so-called "Umbrella Group"—to rewrite or reinterpret the Convention. This Group is attacking the Convention's core principles, such as equity, historical responsibility, and differentiation of action and support.

The climate change regime is based on the need for developed countries to lead and all developing countries to undertake actions with empowering support. This basic tenant is as relevant today as it was when the Convention was adopted in 1992. This is because even after all these years all our members face pressing socio-economic challenges and acute vulnerability to climate change. Despite the considerable development gains we have made in the short time since decolonisation, none of us can truly say that we have achieved the status of being fully developed—a privilege our negotiating partners have enjoyed for a considerable period of time.

It was in recognition of this unchanged reality, as well as the equally important need to unlock the mitigation potential of developing countries, that the Durban agreement was premised on three equally important and mutually dependent pillars, namely: 1) developed countries should honour their existing commitments under the Convention; 2) a second commitment period to the Kyoto Protocol should enter into force; and 3) a new legal instrument would be adopted under the Convention that is applicable to all parties.

The Durban agreement was historic because it unblocked an impasse that had hampered action on climate change for many years. It offered a consensus on the way forward that would balance the interests of developed and developing counties and achieve the objective of the Convention to stabilise greenhouse gas concentrations in order to limit dangerous climate change within a time frame to allow ecosystems to adapt.

The context of the current negotiations as they reach their final stage is that, with only a few exceptions, developed countries have neither honoured their existing commitments, nor even provided a clear road map on how they intend to do so in the remaining years before 2020. They are silent on the support they will provide post-2020.

The leadership we were all counting on has not been translated into action on the ground and the second commitment period of the Kyoto Protocol has also not yet entered into force.

This is not a mere political statement, it is a reflection of a harsh reality that many developing countries have not received the support they require and are entitled to receive under a legal agreement to help them cope with the calamities caused by a rapidly changing climate that are occurring with increased frequency and severity. All too often we have had to respond to crises without the assistance of developed countries by using our own scarce domestic resources or with voluntary help from fellow developing countries through South-South solidarity.

There are direct implications of non-compliance with climate change commitments for basic human rights and environmental integrity. Climate finance and other means of implementation are therefore not regarded by the international community as voluntary charity or Overseas Direct Assistance (ODA), but as a legal requirement as they are vital tools for action and survival.

It is, therefore, impossible for our Group to understand why the Umbrella Group in particular is refusing to engage in the negotiations on some of the most important issues that would empower developing countries to cope with climate change and to put forward their best effort to contribute to the global response. As you will have seen, the text that is currently being discussed is littered with the Umbrella Group's "no text options" on precisely the areas that are most relevant to empowering action by developing countries, namely, means of implementation support for developing countries (financial resources, technology transfer, and capacity-building), adaptation, loss and damage, and response measures.

The Group has, therefore, decided to convene an urgent bilateral meeting with the United States immediately after this press conference to convey our concerns and to impress upon them the need to enter the negotiations on these issues and to remove all its "no text" proposals.

For its part, the G-77 and China remains fully committed to addressing climate change under the UNFCCC. The impressive number of ambitious Intended Nationally Determined Contributions (INDCs) that have been submitted by developing countries to date further testifies to the commitment of developing countries to contribute their fair share. Virtually all our members have submitted INDCs that include both mitigation and adaptation components and have announced very ambitious pledges, even though no guarantees of support have been forthcoming.

The Group has demonstrated unprecedented unity and has shown leadership in these negotiations, both on process and on substance as the generator of most of the proposals and negotiating text that are currently under consideration for the Paris

Agreement and supporting COP decisions. We intend to continue this constructive role until we secure our shared objectives.

Statement on behalf of the Group of 77 and China by Ambassador Nozipho Mxakato-Diseko at the Meeting of the Conference of the Parties to the United Nations Framework Convention on Climate Change (COP-21), Paris Climate Change Conference (Paris, France, 5 December 2015)

President,

1. I have the honour to speak on behalf of the Group of 77 and China.
2. Once again, the Group wishes to reiterate its support to the COP President and our readiness to engage constructively with all parties to reach a successful outcome here in Paris.
3. The ADP has now concluded its work with a text that is party-owned and that is now the basis of further negotiations. The Group wishes to point out that, following the invitation made in the ADP closing plenary to submit any comments and proposals on elements that were missing from the draft text, members of the G-77 and China submitted such proposals. However, not all of these are reflected in the Rev.1 document. We would, therefore appreciate it if these proposals could be included in the reflections note and released as a Rev.2 text with those comments and proposals included.
4. We now enter the next and final phase of our work under the guidance of the COP Presidency. The G-77 and China is ready to engage.
5. The Group wishes to stress the importance of clarity and predictability of the process. During this new phase, we thank you for your proposal on how we will be moving forward.
6. The process, therefore, should be clear and transparent, inclusive, and party-driven. The format you suggested is similar to the one followed in Durban, which proved to be a useful format that will enable us to have the much needed and urgent discussion on cross-cutting issues that we have been calling for. These cross-cutting and highly political issues will need ministerial discussion. We also need a central place where there can be an overview of progress made across all areas.
7. We remain open to the Presidency's suggestions on how we can use different modalities for different issues. However, we note that the utilisation of facilitation, spin-off, and informal-informal groups, although with varying degrees of effectiveness, proved to be useful tools for the development of text and we should use such tools.
8. Ministers must engage on political issues. Their role should be to make the necessary policy decisions. On the basis of these discussions, they should instruct their negotiators to develop text reflecting their instructions.

9. As Ministers start working, we must ensure that there are no parallel processes. There cannot be a situation where negotiators and Ministers are working on the same issues at the same time in parallel. The management of this process is, therefore, important. We welcome your proposal of using individual Ministers as facilitators to resolve difficult issues.

President,

10. At this historic moment, where all parties will take a significant step forward in the fight against climate change, we must remain focused on what we agreed in Durban. The Group of 77 and China wishes to re-emphasise its position that the Paris outcome must be under the Convention and in full accordance with its principles and provisions, in particular the principles of equity and common but differentiated responsibilities and respective capabilities. The purpose of the Paris outcome is to enhance the implementation of the Convention and must not replace, rewrite, or reinterpret the Convention and it must also be fully in accordance with the Durban mandate. The core elements mandated by the Durban decision (mitigation, adaptation, finance, technology development and transfer, capacity-building, and transparency of action and support), as well as loss and damage and response measures must be addressed in a comprehensive and balanced manner, both in the agreement and in the COP decisions. Adaptation and mitigation must receive the same priority. These must be supported by finance, technology development and transfer, and capacity-building by developed country parties on a scale that matches the level of action required to achieve the objective of the Convention as set out in article 2 of the Convention. In this regard, we urge developed country parties to take the lead through undertaking ambitious emission reduction commitments and providing enhanced finance, technology development and transfer, and capacity-building support to developing country parties for their ambitious mitigation and adaptation actions. We also wish to reiterate our position that a fair and ambitious outcome of our work here in Paris must address both pre-2020 ambition of actions and support, as well as the post-2020 agreement. We are ready to negotiate and work as fast as possible on the basis of the text produced by the ADP.

Finally, President,

11. The Group wishes to express its support to you in guiding us to a successful conclusion of this conference and we assure you of our commitment to play a positive and constructive role.

Statement on behalf of the Group of 77 and China by South Africa at the Opening of the High-level Segment of COP-21/CMP-11 (Paris, France, 7 December 2015)

Mr. President,
Your Excellency Mr. Secretary-General,
Madam Executive Secretary,
Excellencies,
Distinguished delegates,
Ladies and gentlemen,

1. South Africa has the honour to speak on behalf of the Group of 77 and China.
2. At the outset, the Group wishes to express its full support to you, Minister Fabius, at this historic conference as you guide us towards a fair and ambitious outcome of this conference and we thank you for the leadership role you have played throughout the year with the President of COP-20 from Peru.
3. This is indeed an historic moment for the G-77 and China that is more united than ever before. The G-77 and China represents about 85% of the world's population and there can be no meaningful agreement if the Group's concerns are not taken into account.
4. As developing countries, we share a common commitment to address the climate challenge in a manner that ensures that we achieve our goal of limiting temperature rise to safe levels, while at the same time allowing flexibility to developing countries to pursue their sustainable development priorities.
5. Our people suffer the effects of climate change first hand. In many cases, climate change threatens the very existence and survival of countries, societies, and the ecosystems of our Mother Earth. In light of this reality, developing countries have already taken ambitious steps to address climate change, mostly without adequate finance, technology, and capacity-building support, despite the fact that our countries are home to the vast majority of the world's people living in poverty. This commitment is demonstrated by the unprecedented fact that nearly all developing countries have submitted Intended Nationally Determined Contributions (INDCs) that outline the ambitious action they intend to take in the post-2020 period. Many of these INDCs include a component on adaptation: action which we have to take as a result mostly of the historical emissions by developed countries. This was done without any concrete reassurances from our partners that post-2020 support will be available.

Mr. President,

6. The starting point for the G-77 and China is that the mandate of our work is the Durban Platform for Enhanced Action. This mandate requires us to

promote the full, effective, and sustained implementation of the Convention. We are not here in Paris to renegotiate, rewrite, or reinterpret the Convention. Our objective is to strengthen the multilateral rules-based system under the Convention in accordance with its principles and provisions.

7. The Group of 77 and China reiterates that the agreement must be under the Convention, applicable to all parties and based on its principles and provisions, in particular the principles of equity and common but differentiated responsibilities and respective capabilities.
8. The core elements mandated by the Durban mandate, namely, mitigation, adaptation, finance, technology development and transfer, capacity-building, and transparency of action and support, as well as loss and damage and response measures must be addressed in a comprehensive and balanced manner, both in the agreement and in the COP decisions. Adaptation and mitigation must receive the same priority and must be supported by finance, technology development and transfer, and capacity-building by developed country parties on a scale that matches the level of action required to achieve the objective of the Convention as set out in article 2 of the Convention. We, therefore, call on developed country parties to take the lead through undertaking ambitious emission reduction commitments and providing enhanced finance, technology development and transfer, and capacity-building support to developing country parties for their ambitious mitigation and adaptation actions.
9. The Group of 77 and China regards the work on pre-2020 ambition as an integral part of the ADP that has direct bearing on the successful adoption of the 2015 agreement. Enhanced pre-2020 ambition will provide a strong basis for post-2020 cooperation.
10. The urgent entry into force of the Doha Amendment would be an important signal to the world that parties are committed to closing the pre-2020 ambition gap. Scaling up climate finance towards the goal of US$100 billion by 2020 will also provide the resources required by developing countries to enhance pre-2020 mitigation and adaptation actions.

Mr. President,

11. Finance, technology development and transfer, and capacity-building are crucial and key elements of the Paris outcome. The outcome regarding finance must provide clarity on the level of financial support that will be provided by developed country parties to developing country parties to allow for enhanced implementation of the Convention in the post-2020 period, as well as existing commitment on pre-2020 finance. We require a substantial scaling up of finance from the 2020 base level of US$100 billion and Annex I country parties and other developed countries included in Annex II have the principal responsibility in providing support, which must be new,

additional, predictable, and sustainable with an equal allocation between adaptation and mitigation.

12. Very important work on implementation is also undertaken under the Convention and the Kyoto Protocol, which should not be overshadowed by our focus on future commitments that will only take effect from 2020. We cannot lose the five years between now and 2020 by shifting our focus away from the urgent work that needs to progress in the subsidiary bodies to implement existing commitments.

Mr. President,

13. There can be no doubt that the Group of 77 and China is committed to play our part in addressing the global challenge of climate change. In order for the Group to turn this commitment into real actions, we have repeatedly called on developed countries to provide the necessary support to enable the members of the Group to take on their fair share of the global effort. This pre- and post-2020 support is essential to enable developing countries to unlock their full mitigation potential and to allow them to adapt to climate change and its associated loss and damage.

Mr. President,

14. Ministers of the G-77 and China are here in Paris ready to engage constructively to find solutions to the outstanding political issues to enable us to deliver a strong outcome.

Intervention on behalf of the Group of 77 and China by Mrs. Edna Molewa, Minister of Water and Environmental Affairs of the Republic of South Africa, at the Meeting of the Paris Committee on Capacity-Building, Paris Climate Change Conference (Paris, France, 9 December 2015)

Mr. President,

1. I am taking the floor on behalf of the Group of 77 and China.
2. The Group wishes to thank the COP Presidency, the ministerial facilitators, and the Secretariat for their work and for presenting us with a further version of the Draft Paris Outcome.
3. We have studied the text carefully and consulted with our Group and wish to highlight some initial observations. These should not be regarded as an exclusive list of the concerns of the Group.
4. The Group is concerned about the steady delinking of the text from the Convention and a dilution of its principles. In this regard, the framing of parties' commitments in many places in the text are not properly

differentiated. There are also numerous inconsistencies in the text between the Convention language and the new draft text.

5. Regarding adaptation, we are concerned that key adaptation proposals from the Group do not appear in the new text. We trust that we will be able to engage further on this critical issue for developing countries.
6. In the paragraphs dealing with the provision of the means of implementation, the Group does not see adequate reassurances that its actions on mitigation and adaptation will be sufficiently supported in the post-2020 period.
7. In particular, we are concerned that there does not appear to be a long-term vision on the provision of support, nor strong legal commitments for developed country parties to provide finance, technology transfer, and capacity-building. There is no assurance that there will be predictability and scalable funds.
8. It is not clear how the institutional mechanisms will be linked in order to deliver the necessary level of support. We also need to find a way to provide for the continued operation of and delivery by the Adaptation Fund, the Least Developed Countries Fund, and the Special Climate Change Fund.
9. On capacity-building, the Group is concerned about the lack of differentiation in the new text.
10. On loss and damage, the Group acknowledges that there will be further consultations to advance on these issues. We, however, need to reiterate our position that there should be a separate article in the agreement on loss and damage; that this article must be clearly bounded by the principles of the Convention, particularly CBDR&RC; that addresses the permanent and irreversible impacts of climate change; and that we need a permanent institution to deal with loss and damage arising from the adverse effects of climate change.
11. Moreover, the Group is concerned that the issue of unilateral measures have been omitted from the text when it is principle of the Convention. We are ready to work on language for this matter.

Mr. President,

12. Despite these concerns, the Group is of the view that the text is a good basis on which to continue our negotiations and on which a new iteration tomorrow.
13. The Group believes that addressing the key political and cross-cutting issues of differentiation, ambition, and finance will unlock progress towards and enable many other issues to be resolved and brackets to be removed.
14. On issues, where consensus is within reach, the Group is of the view that further informal-informals would be helpful to resolve outstanding matters.
15. It, however, remains important that the process of negotiations be open, transparent and party-driven.

Statement by South Africa on behalf of the Group of 77 and China, at the Closing Plenary of the 21st Conference of the Parties to the United Nations Framework Convention on Climate Change (COP-21) (Paris, France, 12 December 2015)

Mr. President,
Your Excellency, Mr. Secretary-General,
Madam Executive Secretary,
Excellencies,
Distinguished delegates,
Ladies and gentlemen,

1. I have the honour to deliver this statement on behalf of the Group of 77 and China.
2. At the outset, allow me to convey the Group's sincere appreciation for the leadership of France as COP President during this conference. The tireless efforts by Minister Fabius and the dedicated team of the Presidency inspired all parties to work constructively and in a spirit of compromise—not only on concluding the Paris Agreement but also on addressing issues that have a direct bearing on the urgent implementation of our actions to address climate change. The closing of the pre-2020 ambition gap is essential and the work of the COP in this regard must remain our main focus. Therefore, the outcomes under the COP and CMP at this session are welcomed. We have been focusing strongly on the creation of a post-2020 climate agreement and, therefore, spent less time on major tasks that would enhance our implementation pre-2020. We must now refocus our attention to the urgent tasks at hand.

Mr. President,

3. The commitment of the G-77 and China to this process has been unwavering. Climate change already has serious impacts in developing countries. Many of our members already experience untenable rising sea levels. Some countries experience the devastation of extreme weather events, such as heat waves, heavy precipitation, greater frequency and intensity of tropical cyclones, severe droughts, and water and food insecurity. These impacts are steadily eroding the development gains that we have made.
4. Our commitment to address climate change does not begin and end here in the UNFCCC. We are already taking the most ambitious measures we can to prevent further harm and to adapt to inevitable changes. However, the efforts we make on our own will not be enough. We need the cooperation of all countries to make a difference in the fight against climate change.
5. Given the exceptional nature of the Paris Climate Change Conference and our focus on securing an ambitious and fair Paris Agreement, a number of key issues related to the COP finance agenda unfortunately could not receive the

appropriate consideration, particularly issues related to long-term finance and the guidance to the Standing Committee on Finance. We expect to come back in Morocco with substantive discussions on increasing finance ambition pre-2020.

Mr. President,

6. The Convention was written with this spirit of cooperation in mind. In its principles and provisions, the Convention recognises that countries have different responsibilities and capabilities. This is still case. In addition to serious climate change impacts, developing countries also face urgent socio-economic challenges. The only way that we can address climate change and eradicate poverty is if developed countries continue to take the lead.
7. Our developed country partners argue that the world has changed since the adoption of the Convention. Indeed, there have been changes and developing countries have stepped up their actions in line with their capacity. The fact that we are here in Paris to adopt a universal agreement "agreement applicable to all" attests to this fact. This is a great leap forward for developing countries. Again, developing countries have been asked to take this leap without the firm commitments on support that we have asked for to enable us to do our fair share. For our efforts to be successful, it is critical that developed countries significantly enhance the ambition of their actions and ensure that the enhanced actions of developing countries are adequately supported. In the build-up to this conference, we have noticed and welcomed the pledges made by a number of developed country parties. This support has to be sustained if we wish to have any meaningful response.

Statement on behalf of the Group of 77 and China at the Closing Plenary of the 11th Session of the Conference of the Parties Serving as the Meeting of the Parties to the Kyoto Protocol (CMP-11) (Paris, France, 12 December 2015)

President of the CMP,
Excellencies,
Distinguished representatives,
Ladies and gentlemen,

Mr. President

1. I have the honour to deliver this statement on behalf of the Group of 77 and China. First of all, I would like to commend you for the efforts you have made during this session to advance the important work on the agenda of the eleventh Conference of the Parties serving as the Meeting of the Parties to the Kyoto Protocol (CMP-11).

Mr. President,

2. The Paris Agreement was the focus of our work and represents an ambitious step forward in our efforts to address climate change. We must, however, remind ourselves that entry into force of this Agreement will take a few years. The continuation of our work pre-2020 must therefore be prioritized. We see the Kyoto Protocol as a fundamental building block in our response and the work done under the CMP has to be concluded. In this regard, the entry into force of the Doha Amendment for a second commitment period under the Kyoto Protocol is urgently required.
3. As stated during the opening of this session, the G-77 and China believes that adaptation is an important and urgent priority for developing country parties. Financing for adaptation is critical and securing the continued role of the Adaptation Fund beyond 2020 is welcomed. The adaptation Fund has successful brought a new process into being where direct access modalities are in place and concrete adaptation activities are being implemented.
4. The Group notes that in the decision which we will adopted on the report of the Adaptation Fund Board, we will essentially proceed to undertake the work needed to prepare the Fund to serve the Paris Agreement. The G-77 and China supports this process. However, we note that the role of the Adaptation Fund is not addressed in the Paris Agreement. The Group had signalled that this matter required political discussion which did not take place here in Paris.

President,

5. We therefore draw your attention to this matter and request that this be entered into the record of this meeting. The Group of 77 and China also calls for an agenda item to be added to the next CMP agenda so that a discussion can be had on this matter of importance to our members.
6. The Group strongly believes that capacity-building should be based on and responsive to national needs, fostering country ownership. We already have ample lessons learned since the adoption of the Convention to know that the process of capacity-building must be participatory, country-driven and cross-cutting.

Mr. President,

7. On the revision of Guidelines for National Communications for Annex I parties, the Group welcomes the progress made towards the finalisation of these guidelines. We look forward to further consultative engagements at SBI44 with a view to adopting comprehensive guidelines for Annex I National Communications by COP-22.

8. The agenda item on CDM Modalities and Procedures and Guidance to the Executive Board was successfully concluded with draft conclusions. The CDM is an important tool to many in the Group and we are pleased that we were able to work constructively to reach draft conclusions.
9. Under the SBSTA's agenda items on methodological issues under the Kyoto Protocol, the Group of 77 and China worked constructively with other parties for a number of years to finalise the rules applicable for the second commitment period and has been consistently committed to maintaining the environmental integrity of the commitments agreed to in Doha. This will remove the final obstacle to the implementation of the second commitment period. The ratification of the Doha Amendment by all parties has to be done urgently in order for it to come into force. The G-77 and China has shown extraordinary flexibility in the interests of achieving some ambition through its implementation, and in the interests of carrying the legacy of the Kyoto Protocol into the new agreement.
10. On the budget for the biennium 2014–2015 and 2016–2017 we actively participated on the agenda items related to governance and the discussions on the arrangements on intergovernmental meetings as well as on administrative, financial, and institutional matters. We still reiterate that it is important that the functions and operations of the Secretariat are supported in an adequate and balanced manner for it to play its role in support of the parties.

In conclusion, President,

11. The G-77 and China conveys its appreciation to you for your leadership and looks forward to engage further with parties during the next session.

Statement by H.E. Mr. Manasvi Srisodapol, Special Representative of the Chair of the Group of 77 for Climate Change, on behalf of the Group of 77 and China, at the Joint Plenary of the 22nd Session of Conference of the Parties (COP-22) and the 12th Session of the Conference of the Parties Serving as the Meeting of the Parties to the Kyoto Protocol (CMP-12) (Marrakech, Morocco, 8 November 2016)

Mr. President,
Excellencies,
Distinguished representatives,
Ladies and gentlemen,

1. I have the honour to deliver this statement on behalf of the Group of 77 and China.
2. At the outset, the Group would like to congratulate the presidency of the Kingdom of Morocco and express our deep gratitude for the warm hospitality.

We reaffirm our support to the Presidency and stand ready to working constructively with all parties to ensure meaningful outcomes and success of our deliberations.

3. May I also take this opportunity to sincerely thank and commend the Government of France and the outgoing President for the able leadership in steering COP-21 and CMP-11.

Mr. President,

4. Climate change and sustainable development are intrinsically linked; the goals and targets under the 2030 Agenda for Sustainable Development cannot be achieved if countries continue to face with negative impacts of climate change.
5. The Group welcomes the Paris Agreement and its early entry into force, and encourages all its parties to fully implement the Agreement, and parties to the UNFCCC that have not yet done so to deposit their instruments of ratification, acceptance, approval or accession, where appropriate, as soon as possible.
6. As we are now in the implementation phase of the Paris Agreement, as applicable to parties that ratify the Agreement, it is crucial to preserve the delicate balance from Paris and ensure that no one will be left behind. In moving forward, we must ensure transparency, inclusiveness, party-driven process, and balance of all issues and across different bodies. As for enhancing the implementation of the Convention, its provisions and principles, in particular equity and common but differentiated responsibilities and respective capabilities, must be taken into account.

Mr. President,

7. The work of enhancing the pre-2020 actions is long overdue. After nearly four years, only 71 parties have deposited their instruments of acceptance to the Doha Amendment. We therefore urge all parties to ratify the Amendment expeditiously.
8. The Group also stresses the urgent need to enhance the pre-2020 ambition which will provide a strong basis for post-2020 efforts under the Paris Agreement. Any deficiency in fulfilling the pre-2020 or closure of emission of reduction gap and means of implementation gaps shall not be deferred. We call on parties that have not deposited their instruments of acceptance to announce their plans.
9. We look forward to the Facilitative Dialogue on enhancing ambition and support in Marrakech to assess progress of the pre-2020 implementation and identify opportunities to enhance the provision of financial resources, including for technology development and transfer, and capacity-building support.

10. As for the concrete road map on how to achieve a floor of the US$100 billion goal per year by 2020, we stress the significance of the source of additional, adequate, and predictable finance and call for developed country parties to enhance ambition on mitigation actions and the provision and mobilization of support.

Mr. President,

11. Developing country parties require urgent and enhanced support in order to formulate and implement their National Adaptation Plans (NAPs). Financing for adaptation is therefore critical and securing the role of the Adaptation Fund to serve the Paris Agreement is welcomed and should be enhanced. We take note of the progress made by the Nairobi Work Programme (NWP), Least Developed Countries Experts Group (LEG), and Adaptation Committee (AC), and note with concern that the current financial availability for the AC and LEG is inadequate for supporting the implementation of NAPs related activities.
12. The Group further takes note of the report of the Executive Committee of the Warsaw International Mechanism for Loss and Damage associated with Climate Change Impacts, including the implementation of its initial two-year work plan. We consider the five-year rolling work plan as the basis for developing corresponding activities and in order for this mechanism to be meaningful, it must address the needs and challenges faced by developing countries emerging from extreme and slow-onset events. We urge developed country parties to make available resources to support those activities under this new work plan.

Mr. President,

13. Means of implementation are critical for actions on mitigation and adaptation both pre-2020 and post-2020. Hence, the adequate, predictable, and sustained finance, technology, and capacity-building must be provided and delivered by developed country parties to assist developing country parties with respect to enhancing their climate actions.
14. The Group is of concern that adaptation finance provided to developing countries in 2013–2014 is still insufficient, as reflected in the report of the Standing Committee on Finance (SCF). We reiterate the need to scale up adaptation finance, particularly in the context of increasing climate risks faced by developing countries, and ensuring the balance between financing for mitigation and adaptation.
15. On enhanced transparency framework, the Group is of a belief that a more focus should be given to transparency of support as it is yet as mature as transparency of actions.

16. The Group attaches great importance to the work to be done under the APA on the preparatory work necessary to make the Adaptation Fund serve the Paris Agreement. Adaptation is a priority of developing countries in the light of increasing adverse effects of climate change. The Adaptation Fund has made operational direct access for developing countries and has financed concrete adaptation actions by developing countries. We therefore look forward to having this preparatory work done successfully in the APA.
17. The Group is concerned that the focus defined and decided by the COP has now been diluted in the programme prepared by this High-Level Ministerial Dialogue on Climate Finance. Work has been done by parties for the past two years to decide on the themes of the high-level dialogue. We would urge that the programme and focus be restored to be coherent with the COP decision on long-term finance.

Mr. President,

18. Technology development and transfer is a key component for developing countries to be able to effectively address climate change. Effective mitigation and adaptation actions will depend on access to technology, including the development of endogenous technologies by developing countries. The technology mechanism has an important role to play in order to support the rapid transfer of technologies to developing countries, helping them innovate and develop their own technologies. We would like to see concrete enhanced actions on technology development and transfer accelerated and scaled up by the technology mechanism, under the guidance of the COP through the subsidiary bodies and the Technology Framework. In this regard, we believe it is crucial for the technology mechanism to strengthen its effective linkages with the financial mechanism.
19. Capacity-building is one of the key deliverables to the success of Marrakech. Capacity-building should be based on and responsive to national needs and fostering country ownership, and the process must be participatory, party-driven, and cross-cutting. In our view, COP-22 should adopt the Terms of Reference and initial work plan for the Paris Committee on Capacity-Building (PCCB) to ensure a timely start of its work in 2017 and the nomination of the representatives of the Committee. We expect progress and early operationalization of the whole package of capacity-building, including the Capacity-Building Initiative for Transparency (CBIT). It is important to ensure that there is linkage between and no duplication of the works of PCCB and CBIT.
20. Last but not least, the Group requests the COP to instruct implementing agencies including but not limited to the Global Environment Facility (GEF) to not exclude any non–Annex I party from support regarding means of implementation, especially finance, technology transfer, and capacity-building,

in addition to preparation of national periodic reports to be submitted to the Convention and to ensure accessibility of eligible non–Annex I parties to available resources.

Mr. President,

21. The Group wishes to once again express our support to you in guiding us to a successful conclusion of this Conference through a transparent, inclusive, and party-driven process. The Group is committed to engage positively and constructively.

G-77 and China Statement at Presidency Event on the Talanoa Dialogue (Opening) (Bonn, Germany, 2 May 2018)

- The G-77 and China would like to congratulate the COP-23 Presidency and thank them for their hard work and dedication to organize and launch what we hope will be a fruitful, effective, and inclusive Talanoa Facilitative Dialogue. We believe that this format has the potential for creating a unique dynamic based on trust, empathy, and consideration, which will hopefully contribute in a positive way to the overall global effort to address climate change issues.
- The G-77 and China looks forward to this series of events and are committed not only to share their stories and narratives, but equally to listen to those of others both at the state level and at the non-state level. We all stand to benefit from this type of open exchange.
- Mr. President, we have had the opportunity to seek some clarity regarding a number of issues related to the dialogue and while some clarification has been provided, we still hope to obtain more clarity through our discussion here today, particularly regarding the nature of the outcomes of this process, as well as other organizational matters which we hope would ensure a balanced narrative coming out of the process and reflective of all perspectives. One reality which we regret is that capacity constraints have to some extent restricted the participation of civil society and other non-state actors from developing countries in this important effort. Our communities have amazing stories to tell and rich experiences, of both successes and challenges, to share. Alas, this will not be possible. We hope that we can find a way to introduce a balance when it comes to non-state party engagement as the process progresses over the year.
- Mr. President, the 2018 Talanoa Facilitative Dialogue should provide for a common understanding of where parties collectively are with regards to the Agreement's long-term goals as well as on a sense of what opportunities exist to actually achieve these long-term goals.
- To this end, we hope we can approach the process in a comprehensive and holistic manner. The Mitigation target is extremely important but we still think

that equal consideration should be given to the full gamut of issues namely mitigation, adaptation, and MOI.

- On where we are, we believe that international cooperation among all parties to address climate change has achieved positive outcomes, yet significant gaps still remain in relation to mitigation, adaptation, finance, technology transfer, and capacity-building, especially for developing countries.
- On where we want to go, we need to work hard to achieve the medium and long-term goals set by the Convention and its related agreements, while fully upholding the principles of equity, common but differentiated responsibilities and respective capabilities, in light of different national circumstances, and promoting the coordination of combating climate change with the UN's sustainable development goals 2030.
- On how we get there, we believe the key to achieving these goals is to find a feasible path for green and low-carbon development and to effectively integrate economic development with environmental protection and strengthen international cooperation.
- Mr. President, in our view, the process should nurture openness, inclusiveness and trust building among party and non-party stakeholders to be able to confront the harsh reality of climate change and its impacts. To this end, we believe that the format of the dialogue should not be prescriptive and all parties should be allowed to share their stories in the manner they deem most constructive. All voices should be captured and, while we appreciate that some logistical constraints may limit participation, we hope that we can find a formula to ensure that at least the widest possible audience can be given the opportunity to hear and benefit from the rich array of stories and experiences which will be shared.
- To conclude, allow me to assure you once again of the full commitment of the member states of the G-77 and China to the success of this worthy endeavour and our confidence that the Talanoa spirit will inspire us all and that the experiences of our communities and societies will represent a significant and novel contribution to the global effort to combat climate change and address its adverse effects.

Statement on Behalf of the Group of 77 and China by Ambassador Wael Aboulmagd, Chair of the G-77 and China for the Climate Change Process, at the Closing Plenary of the 24th Session of the COP to the UNFCCC (COP-24) (Katowice, Poland, 15 December 2018)

1. The G-77 and China acknowledges the hard work and full commitment to success at this COP which was demonstrated by the tireless efforts of the Polish Presidency, as well as ably supported by the UNFCCC Secretariat to whom all we wish to express our appreciation. We also note the significant progress made at this session towards addressing the divergences which

existed with regard to the text which we are about to approve. Nonetheless, and despite our best efforts to influence this process and push it into a more cooperative mode, one which is not based solely on stating positions and fighting for them but also on actually listening to the concerns of others, we did not succeed in that.

2. We say this because finally, and as we look at, and assess the overall package, rather than just the individual components in isolation, we do not see the balance we have consistently called for. Instead, we see a mitigation-centric regime in the making, with the urgent adaptation needs of developing countries relegated to second-class status, along with consistent resistance to meaningfully reflect the factual differentiation between developed and developing countries, as well as a diluted overall support package.
3. Unfortunately, and despite our best efforts to influence this process and push it into a more cooperative mode, one which is not based solely on starting positions but also on actually listening to the concerns of others, we did not succeed in that.
4. We say this because, finally, and as we attempted to look at, and assess the overall package, rather than just the individual components in isolation, we do not see the balance we have consistently called for. Instead, we see a blatantly mitigation centric regime in the making, with the urgent adaptation needs of developing countries relegated to second class status.
5. We are now clearly creating a regime which chose, consciously, to ignore or at least ignore the very real, factual principle of common but differentiated responsibilities. This principle is not a tactical negotiating tool. It is a reflection of a reality on the ground. It is a translation of the stark differences between countries with regard to historical and current responsibilities and their differences in capacities and their access to technologies and their urgent developmental needs and priorities and needs to pull their populations out of abject poverty.
6. Mr. Chairman, we made these remarks out of concern for the prospects of success of our collective efforts over the past years. The record will show that over the past years and since assuming our responsibility as Chair of the G-77 and China, we have NEVER not highlighted the fact that we want an outcome at Katowice—BUT not just any outcome! We want an outcome that can be accepted and embraced and implemented in good faith by all.
7. With that in mind, we are truly fearful for this regime. We all know that this agreement is defined by its "Nationally Determined Character"! It is therefore and in effect a rather fragile regime highly dependent on the goodwill of the parties. If that goodwill is dissipated and eroded due to the prevalence of short-term obsession with narrow gains and short-sighted approaches related to competitiveness, then our new regime will have very little chance of survival.

8. This causes us much concern. We are keenly aware of the existential threats posed by the negative impacts of climate change! Our peoples, particularly the poor and most vulnerable, are suffering from them daily. We are equally aware that as things stand, we remain on a dangerous path to higher increases in global temperature and therefore more, not less, needs to be done. We worry that even the perception of imbalance along with the outright rejection of the principle of equity will potentially push many countries to implement this agreement at the lowest possible level. Combine that with clear attempts to backslide, by some, on existing commitments and you have what can only be seen as an extremely worrying picture.
9. Yet the opportunity is still before us. In implementing the outcomes of this COP with regard to the Paris Agreement, we must recall the aforementioned principles of CBDR and equity. We must not gloss over the real differences between developed and developing countries both in responsibility and capability. Texts that simply deny this cannot alter the reality.
10. The stakes are too high for us all to continue on an adversarial path. We need to find a way to do this together given the elevated threat, and the increasing awareness of the gravity of the issue not only by states but also by non-state actors. We have a good chance of shifting course of taking advantage of a new spirit of advances in technology drops in some prices of inspiring commitment from youth movements around the world of small business investing in climate related micro projects of big business sometimes realizing the value of being more climate friendly—and the list goes on.
11. State parties on their part must rise to the occasion. On our part, we will continue to demonstrate full commitment to doing our fair share of the lifting. We have our legitimate development goals but will always strive to show as much ambition as possible when it comes to curbing emissions. We do not see this as a zero-sum equation. Indeed, the opposite should be the case. There is a path that allows us all to benefit. We hope that in the years to come we can find that path and follow it for the benefit of all.

Statement on behalf of the Group of 77 and China by Mr. Ahmadou Sebory Touré, Lead Negotiator, Director, Ministry of Environment, Water and Forests of the Republic of Guinea, at the Joint Plenary of the Conference of the Parties (COP-26), Conference of the Parties Serving as the Meeting of the Parties to the Kyoto Protocol (CMP-16), Conference of the Parties Serving as the Meeting of the Parties to the Paris Agreement (CMA-3), Subsidiary Body for Scientific and Technological Advice (SBSTA52–55) and Subsidiary Body for Implementation (SBI52–55) (Glasgow, United Kingdom, 31 October 2021)

1. Distinguished Mr. President, Chairs of the Subsidiary Bodies, Madame Executive Secretary, colleagues,

2. The Republic of Guinea is honoured to deliver this statement on behalf of the Group of 77 and China. We assure you of the Group's commitment to contribute constructively to the success of COP-26 for the collective benefit of our peoples and future generations. We would like to express sincere appreciation to the United Kingdom and the people of Glasgow for their generous hosting of COP-26, despite the challenges that the COVID-19 pandemic has imposed.
3. The Group looks forward to concluding the work that has been pending since COP-25 in Madrid in December 2019 despite the restrictions and limitations imposed by the pandemic on our modalities of work. In doing so, our proceedings must be balanced, inclusive, participatory, and transparent.
4. Sustainable development and poverty eradication are overriding priorities for developing countries. We come to this COP with a deep sense of urgency because we are deeply concerned about the increasing impacts of climate change on our socio-economic circumstances and development priorities and trajectories.
5. As the G-77's Ministers stated in their November 2020 Ministerial Statement in New York, the Paris Agreement, adopted under the United Nations Framework Convention on Climate Change (UNFCCC), is the collective achievement of all parties. It seeks to enhance the implementation of the Convention, in accordance with its objectives, principles, and provisions, in particular on the basis of equity, the principle of common but differentiated responsibilities and respective capabilities, in the light of different national circumstances, needs, and priorities, and the right to development, in the context of sustainable development and efforts to eradicate poverty.
6. These principles are fundamental to our work. The balanced package in the Paris Agreement with respect to mitigation, adaptation, provision of the means of implementation and support to developing countries, enhanced transparency, and international cooperation must be upheld and are not to be renegotiated nor reinterpreted.
7. The Group expects at this COP that developed countries fill deficiencies in their implementation of their pre-2020 commitments. Developed countries must undertake and increase the economy-wide absolute emission reduction targets in their NDCs and scale up their provision of support to developing countries.
8. Climate finance is key to success here at COP-26 and the effective implementation of the Paris Agreement. Long-standing climate finance commitments such as the US$100 billion goal by 2020 must now be fulfilled. We cannot rely on unfulfilled promises. We must see tangible actions from developed countries at this COP that translate into enhanced climate finance flows that are demand-driven and responsive to the needs of developing countries. These include real progress in our negotiations relating to the new finance goal. We note that the recently adopted Needs Determination Report and the Biennial Assessment and Overview on Climate Finance Flows from the Standing

Committee on Finance have given us some key benchmarks on the scale of financing that would need to be mobilized and delivered to support developing countries in implementing their NDCs.

9. For the Group, financial resources as well as technology development and transfer and capacity-building are crucial enablers of climate action. Enhanced ambition must come with enhanced support. Provision of this support from developed countries is a binding commitment under the Convention and reconfirmed in the Paris Agreement. There are nearly 15 agenda items on finance at this COP; as such, no finance negotiations under different agenda items should be organized in parallel.
10. For the Group, long-term finance discussions are not about having an agenda of workshops and dialogues but should focus on how the long-standing climate finance commitments of developed countries established under the Convention and its Paris Agreement are being implemented. We expect that COP-26 will decide on the continuation of the LTF Work Programme to contribute to scaling-up post-2020 climate financing and monitor the accomplishment of the US$100 billion goal up to 2020 and to 2025.
11. The provision and mobilization of finance, technology, and capacity-building must be done in a transparent manner, must be new, additional, and predictable, and consider the actual needs and priorities of developing countries. These must be reflected in the reporting of backward- or forward-looking information under the Convention and its Paris Agreement, as well as in the initiation of the process in Glasgow to establish a new collective quantified climate finance goal based on a floor of US$100 billion per year.
12. The reporting of the provision of finance by developed countries to developing countries should be improved, given concerns that climate finance is translating into increased external debt of developing countries. This includes improving the reporting of grant equivalency, climate specificity, and how developed countries are taking into account the needs and priorities of developing countries and the provision of grant-based public resources under articles 9.4 and 9.5 of the Paris Agreement. The needs of developing countries with respect to financial support for loss and damage should also be discussed, including reporting by developed countries on the provision of such support.
13. The establishment of the new collective quantified finance goal must be the result of a transparent and inclusive process that is party-driven, participatory, easily quantifiable, and concrete. The Group has been pressing for this process to begin since 2017. COP-26 must result in a timeline that ensures the participation of all; that the new goal will reflect the needs of developing countries; and that it includes both a quantitative and qualitative component, including specific goals for adaptation and linkages to the Adaptation Fund to ensure predictability of financing for this Fund that is very important to developing countries.

14. The Group also wishes to reiterate the importance of ensuring that climate finance is not politicized and that all eligible developing countries can access all available financial resources of the implementing entities of the financial mechanism of the Convention and its Paris Agreement.
15. Adaptation is a critical priority for developing countries and must be treated in a balanced manner compared to mitigation actions. Our work on the global goal on adaptation under the Paris Agreement must advance. Support for adaptation actions in developing countries will be increasingly crucial for developing countries as the adverse effects of climate change scale up in the future. Hence, we would like to see concrete and tangible outcomes from COP-26 on the provision of public, grant-based finance by developed countries to developing countries for adaptation action, including to formulate and implement NAPs as stipulated by the Convention.
16. Adaptation planning continues to be a priority to developing countries. It forms a critical foundation for building resilience in our countries. Progress on adaptation planning in our countries has not been encouraging as many developing countries have still not formulated or implemented their adaptation plans.
17. Fully realized technology development and transfer is of vital importance to improve resilience for developing countries. The technology mechanism must be strengthened to serve such purpose and to implement the technology framework. We are deeply concerned with the slow progress made in climate-related technology transfer to developing countries and the challenges faced by the operational arm of the technology mechanism, the CTCN, in securing stable and sustainable financial resources. We call on developed countries to enhance their efforts in technology transfer and strengthen their support to the CTCN through the provision of financial and other resources, to enable enhanced actions on technology development and transfer in implementing the Convention and its Paris Agreement. We look forward to satisfactory results from a CTCN Donor Roundtable on 8 November 2021 in Glasgow as a first step to such enhanced support.
18. Capacity-building is a critical enabler for developing countries to meet their climate actions. Significant progress has been registered at the previous sessions and we hope that we can build on that to finalise the work at hand. We look forward to engaging constructively with the view of concluding the fourth comprehensive review of the implementation of the framework for capacity-building in developing countries under the Kyoto Protocol and the annual progress report of the Paris Committee on Capacity-Building for 2020 and 2021, including its recommendations to the COP and the CMA.
19. On the Koronivia work programme on agriculture, we believe the discussions that we had for the last four years should pave the way for a tangible output after the conclusion of the Koronivia road map. Parties should report back to COP-26 on the final outcome to define the way forward for implementation

focusing on enhancing adaptation and adaptation co-benefits in agriculture, while promoting sustainable development and increasing productivity of the agricultural sector to ensure food security in all countries, particularly in developing countries, to fight hunger and eradicate poverty, taking into consideration the diversity of the agricultural systems around the globe and the differences in scale.

20. On response measures, the work plan activities of the response measure forum and the KCI should be fully implemented. Time lost to date and activities not implemented in 2020 must be fully made up. The Forum and the KCI need to be given sufficient time and space to advance their work and ensure effective treatment of response measures-related issues under the Paris Agreement.
21. The agenda items on loss and damage under the COP, CMA, and SBs are important to the Group. This includes the report of the Warsaw Implementation Mechanism on Loss and Damage and on the joint governance of the COP and CMA over the WIM. The treatment of loss- and damage-related agenda items under the COP and the CMA must be balanced to reflect their joint governance. COP-26 should deliver on ensuring that the WIM through its Executive Committee and the Santiago Network becomes an effective mechanism under the Convention and its Paris Agreement for addressing the needs of developing countries, especially for enhanced action and support in relation to loss and damage, including loss and damage-related financing and technology transfer.
22. Our work on transparency must be completed as per the mandate. Developing countries' best efforts at reporting at a higher standard of transparency, once the reporting tools are completed, must be accompanied by real support from developed countries. Access by developing countries to adequate and timely support for transparency should be facilitated. We also call for Annex I parties to submit their reports required under the Convention in a timely manner, including reports that were missing from previous reporting cycles.
23. The negotiations with respect to article 6 of the Paris Agreement should be concluded at COP-26 in a manner that ensures that there is a balanced outcome under articles 6.2, 6.4, and 6.8, ensures environmental integrity, avoids double counting, promotes sustainable development, provides adequate and predictable funds for adaptation, and enables future cooperative arrangements among parties through the nationally appropriate use of both market and non-market approaches.
24. The Group of 77 and China in the spirit of inclusiveness and leaving no one behind calls for the full and effective implementation of the Enhanced Lima

Work Programme on Gender and Climate Change and its Gender Action Plan. We call for continued efforts in ensuring gender parity in national delegations and in all constituted bodies of the Convention and its Paris Agreement.

25. The Group looks forward to the start of the first Global Stocktake under the Paris Agreement. We wish to highlight the importance of having diverse, balanced, and comprehensive inputs for the GST in all the thematic areas, particularly from developing countries and the need to facilitate the participation of non-party stakeholders from developing countries. We expect that the GST will be undertaken in a holistic, systemic, comprehensive, and facilitative manner, considering all thematic areas, including mitigation, adaptation, the means of implementation and support, the consequences of response measures, and loss and damage, in the light of equity and the best available science. The GST process should enable us to look backward at implementation gaps and challenges, including with respect to historical responsibility and pre-2020 implementation of the Convention, and to look forward in terms of what must be done and how these would be addressed in a systemic and transformative way.
26. The Group's Ministerial Statement of November 2020 reaffirmed that the imposition of coercive economic measures, including unilateral sanctions, against developing countries does not contribute to economic and social development, including dialogue and understanding among countries. These actions adversely affect the capabilities of developing countries to finance their efforts in mitigation and adaptation to climate change and hinder their right to access available resources.
27. The program budget for the biennium 2022–2023 should reflect a balance between adaptation and mitigation, with the adaptation-related budget being funded from the core budget rather than be subject to the uncertainty of the supplementary budget.
28. For the Group, it is also important to consider how to best advance ocean-climate and land-climate issues and solutions in relation to the work and processes under the UNFCCC.
29. Finally, rest assured, Mr. President, that the Group of 77 and China will work with you and our partners for the successful conclusion of COP-26, in a manner that moves us all forward in meeting the objective of the Convention and the goals of its Paris Agreement in an equitable manner that respects the principles of the Convention and the balanced package under its Paris Agreement.

(b) Draft Resolutions, Decisions, and Proposals Submitted by the Group of 77 to the Conference of the Parties of the United Nations Framework Convention on Climate Change (COP) and Conference of the Parties Serving as the Meeting of the Parties to the Kyoto Protocol (CMP): Draft List of Items Proposed by the Group of 77 and China*

Draft List of Items for Consideration of the High-Level Segment – COP-3
Participants in the high-level segment of COP-3 in Kyoto should provide the necessary guidance, particularly in the final stage of the negotiation of the Berlin Mandate process. They should be guided by the principles of the Convention and the provisions of the Berlin Mandate.

The following items shall provide the main focus for the high-level segment:

1. Guidance to the final stage of the negotiation of the Berlin Mandate process.
2. Means of implementation of the Convention:
   (a) Financial resources (resources flow);
   (b) Technology development, demonstration and diffusion of technologies, promoting technology breakthrough;
   (c) Education, training, public awareness;
   (d) Strengthening of observational networks and research to reduce scientific uncertainties.
3. Way forward:
   Cooperation in good faith, in accordance with the Convention provisions and guidance to:
   (a) Implementation of all existing commitments under the Convention;
   (b) Implementation of commitments to be agreed upon at Kyoto on limiting and reducing greenhouse gases by Annex I parties to the Convention.

Submission by Indonesia: (On Behalf of the Group of 77 and China)*
Proposal No. 1 Draft Decision of the Group of 77 and China on Additional Guidance to the Financial Mechanism

Recalling its decisions 11/CP.1; 10/CP.2; and 11/CP.2,

Recalling further that the Global Environment Facility, as stated in its Operational Principles for Development and Implementation of its Work Programme, will maintain sufficient flexibility to respond to changing circumstances, including evolving guidance of the Conference of the Parties and experience gained from monitoring and evaluation activities;

* Contained in document FCCC/CP/1997/L.1 of 14 November 1997.
* Contained in document FCCC/CP/1998/MISC.3/Add.1 of 5 November 1998.

Recognizing the need to provide clear guidance for the effective implementation of the Convention;

Expressing grave concern over the continued difficulties encountered by developing countries in complying fully with their obligations due to constraints in the availability and dispersal process of financial resources on a grant and concessional basis, including for the transfer of technology;

Expressing further continued concern over problems arising from the project cycle, the application of the concept of incremental costs, and the availability of resources through the Implementing Agencies;

Noting the need to examine and address the impacts of the implementation of response measures, in particular for those countries listed in article 4.8 of the Convention;

Decides to adopt the following additional guidance to the GEF as an interim operating entity of the financial mechanism. In this regard, the GEF shall provide the necessary financial resources to:

a) proposed projects to implement the adaptation response measures under article 4.1 of the Convention; and to move to the funding for implementation of such adaptation measures and activities envisaged in Stages II and III as stated in decision 11/CP.1, paragraph 1 (d) (iv);
b) respond to the need for improving existing, and setting up technology information centres as stated in paragraph 2(b) of decision 9/CP.3, through the establishment of dedicated, specialised information systems, comprising of enhanced national and regional centres that would, *inter alia*, facilitate national/regional access to the information provided by international centres, and strengthen national/ regional capacities to work with these centres for the dissemination of information, information services, and transfer of environmentally sound technologies and know-how in support of the Convention;
c) in accordance with article 5 of the Convention, enhance the strengthening of observational networks and research to reduce scientific uncertainties relating to the causes, effects, magnitude, and timing of climate change, including capacity to determine the economic and social consequences of various response strategies;
d) meet the agreed full costs of the preparations of subsequent national communications of non-Annex I countries, taking into account that, as stated in paragraph 1(d) of decision 11/CP.2, the preparation of national communications is a continuing process, and in accordance with article 4.3 of the Convention;
e) assist non-Annex I parties in the studies leading to the preparation of national programmes to address climate change, compatible with national plans for sustainable development, in accordance with article 4.1 (b) of the Convention and paragraph 13 of the Annex to decision 10/CP.2;

f) in implementation of article 6 of the Convention, and in accordance with decision 11/CP.1 paragraph 1 (b) (iii) under programme priorities, improve national public awareness and education on climate change and response measures, in cooperation with other relevant UN agencies where necessary;
g) implement the relevant conclusions of the workshops and other meetings for non–Annex I parties, as contained in Section IV of FCCC/SBI/1998/INF.3, for the electronic availability, translation, reproduction and dissemination of initial national communications from non–Annex I parties;
h) support capacity-building for:
   (i) the assessment of technology needs to fulfil the commitments of developing countries under the Convention, the identification of sources and suppliers of these technologies, and the determination of modalities for the acquisition and absorption thereof;
   (ii) client-oriented country-driven activities and projects to enable non–Annex I parties to design, evaluate, and manage these projects; and
   (iii) strengthen the capacity of non–Annex I parties to host projects, from project formulation, development, and implementation;
i) provide also technical support for the formulation of projects directed at minimizing the adverse effects and impacts of climate change, in particular for those countries listed in article 4.8;
j) promote and finance transfer of technology on a grant and concessional basis, in accordance with chapter 34 of Agenda 21.

Requests the GEF, for the improvement of its activities and performance, to:

(i) further streamline its project cycle with a view to making project preparation simpler, less prescriptive, more transparent, and country-driven;
(ii) further simplify and expedite procedure for approval and implementation, including disbursement for GEF-funded projects; and
(iii) make the process for the determination of incremental costs more transparent and its application more acceptable.

Requests the GEF to take the necessary steps to ensure that its Implementing Agencies are performing their obligations in accordance with the decisions adopted by the Conference of the Parties, and within the context of the principles of the Convention, following national priorities and objectives, including as a first priority the use of national experts in all aspects of the project development and implementation, whenever possible, and to establish guidelines to determine the different roles and the activities of its three Implementing Agencies;

Requests the GEF to include in its report to the Conference of the Parties the specific steps it has undertaken to implement the provisions of this decision.

Proposal No. 2

G-77 and China Draft Decision on the Review of the Financial Mechanism
The Conference of the Parties,
Recalling its decisions 9/CP.1, 11/CP.2, and 11/CP.3,

Recalling also the review process undertaken by the Subsidiary Body of Implementation in accordance with decision 11/CP.2,

Taking note of the report on the study of the Global Environment Facility's overall performance,

Decides that the restructured GEF shall be an entity entrusted, on an interim basis, with the operation of the financial mechanism referred to in article 11 of the Convention.

Decides also, in accordance with article 11.4 of the Convention, to regularly review the financial mechanism every two years, on the basis of the criteria and guidelines contained in the Annex to this decision, as well as further guidelines to be developed on actions to improve the effectiveness of the financial mechanism.

Annex II

Guidelines for the Review of the Financial Mechanism

A. Objectives

1. In accordance with paragraph 4, article 11 of the Convention, the objectives will be to review the financial mechanism and take appropriate measures regarding:
   (a) Its conformity with the provisions of article 11 of the Convention;
   (b) Its conformity with the guidance of the COP;
   (c) The effectiveness of the activities it funds in implementing the Convention;
   (d) Its effectiveness in providing financial resources on a grant or concessional basis, including for the transfer of technology, for the implementation of the Convention's objective on the basis of the guidance provided by the COP;
   (e) Its effectiveness in providing resources to developing country parties under article 4.3.

B. Methodology

2. The review shall draw upon the following sources of information:
   (a) Information provided by the parties on their experiences regarding the financial mechanism;
   (b) Annual reviews by the COP on the conformity of the activities of the financial mechanism with the guidance of the COP;

(c) The GEF annual report to the COP on its activities as the operating entity of the financial mechanism, the annual reports of the GEF, and other relevant GEF policy and information documents;
(d) Reports from the GEF monitoring and evaluation programme;
(e) Reports from the United Nations Commission on Sustainable Development and relevant bilateral and multilateral funding institutions;
(f) Relevant information provided by other intergovernmental organizations and non-governmental organizations.

C. Criteria

3. The effectiveness of the financial mechanism will be assessed taking into account the following:
   (a) The transparency of decision-making processes;
   (b) The adequacy, predictability, and timely disbursement of funds for activities in developing country parties;
   (c) The responsiveness and efficiency of the GEF project cycle and expedited procedures, including its operational strategy, as they relate to climate change;
   (d) The amount of resources provided to developing country parties, including financing for technical assistance and investment projects;
   (e) The amount of finance leveraged;
   (f) The sustainability of funded projects.

Paper No. 2: Indonesia (On behalf of the Group of 77 and China) Development and Transfer of Technologies Draft Decisions for the Fourth Session of the Conference of the Parties Proposed by the Group of 77 and China*
Technology Development and Transfer

The Conference of the Parties,

Recalling the relevant provisions of chapter 34 of Agenda 21 and the relevant provisions of the programme for the further implementation of Agenda 21, which was adopted by the United Nations General Assembly at its nineteenth special session, on the transfer of environmentally sound technologies,

Pursuant to articles 4.1, 4.5, 4.7, 4.8, 4.9, 9.2 and 11.1 of the United Nations Framework Convention on Climate Change,

Recalling its decisions 13/CP.1, 7/CP.2, and 9/CP.3 on development and transfer of technology,

Noting the slow progress of practical activities with regard to the development and transfer of technology,

* Contained in document FCCC/CP/1998/MISC.5/Add.3 of 5 November 1998.

Bearing in mind article 10, paragraph (c) of the Kyoto Protocol, which states that all parties shall "cooperate in the promotion of effective modalities for the development, application and diffusion of, and take all practicable steps to promote, facilitate and finance, as appropriate, the transfer of, or access to, environmentally sound technologies, know-how, practices and processes pertinent to climate change, in particular to developing countries, including the formulation of policies and programmes for the effective transfer of environmentally sound technologies that are publicly owned or in the private domain and the creation of an enabling environment for the private sector, to promote and enhance the transfer of, and access to environmentally sound technologies,"

1. *Reaffirms* its decisions 13/CP.1, 7/CP.2, and 9/CP.3 on transfer of technology;
2. *Urges:*
   (a) Parties listed in Annex II, as the first step, to provide a list of environmentally sound and economically viable technologies and know-how related to adaptation and mitigation of climate change that are publicly owned or in the private domain for reference by developing country parties, including report in their national communications steps taken to implement article 4.5 of the Convention;
   (b) Non-Annex I parties, in the light of their social and economic conditions and taking into account the state-of-the-art environmentally sound technologies, to submit their prioritized technology needs, especially as concerns some key technologies needed in particular sectors of their national economy conducive to addressing climate change; and
   (c) Both developed and developing country parties to create an enabling environment, including public awareness, to stimulate private sector investment in and transfer of environmentally sound technologies and know-how to developing countries, taking into full account article 10(c) of the Kyoto Protocol;
3. *Requests* the Convention Secretariat:
   (a) To prepare an inventory of environmentally sound and economically viable technologies and know-how conducive to adapting and mitigating climate change, taking into account submissions made, under subparagraphs 2 (a) and (b) above;
   (b) To submit the documents on the elaboration of the terms under which transfer of technologies and know-how could take place, through the SBSTA, to the Fifth Conference of the Parties for consideration;
4. *Decides* to define hereby a technology transfer mechanism (TTM) to address climate change. The purpose of TTM shall be to assist developing country parties to obtain their needed environmentally sound technologies and know-how conducive to addressing climate change on non-commercial, preferential terms and thus contribute to the ultimate objective of the Convention. The functions of the TTM shall be elaborated by the Conference of the

Parties, taking into account recommendations of the subsidiary bodies of the Convention. Such further elaboration may include, *inter alia*, the following:

(a) The developed country parties, in particular Annex II parties, shall take all practicable steps, including regulatory, legal, and economic instruments or incentives, to promote, facilitate, and finance the transfer of technologies and know-how to developing country parties on non-commercial, preferential terms as provided for in chapter 34 of Agenda 21;

(b) The developed country parties, in particular Annex II parties, shall also take the necessary steps to promote capacity-building in non–Annex I country parties; and

(c) The developing country parties shall create an enabling environment for those environmentally sound technologies and know-how to be transferred to them on preferential terms related to adaptation and mitigation of climate change.

5. *Further decides* to establish an Intergovernmental Technical Advisory Panel (ITAP) in accordance with decision 6/CP.1, Annex II. The functions of the ITAP will include, *inter alia*, assessing environmentally sound technologies and making recommendations to SBSTA, advising on methodological issues, and developing guidelines on the development and transfer of environmentally sound technologies;
6. *Decides* to, at the fifth session of the Conference of the Parties, and at the sessions of the Conference of the Parties thereafter, elaborate modalities and procedures for reviewing the implementation of the Annex II parties' commitments under article 4.5 of the Convention regarding technology transfer with the objective of ensuring effective transfer of environmentally sound technologies and know-how to developing country parties.

Capacity-Building

The Conference of the Parties,

Recalling its decisions 13/CP.1, 7/CP.2 and 9/CP.3 on development and transfer of technologies,

Reaffirming the ultimate objective of the United Nations Framework Convention on Climate Change as contained in its article 2,

Acknowledging that human activities since the industrial revolution have been substantially increasing the atmospheric concentrations of greenhouse gases,

Noting that the largest share of historical and current global emissions of greenhouse gases has originated from developed countries, that per capita emissions in developing countries are still low and that the share of global emissions originating from developing countries will grow to meet their social and developmental needs,

Taking note of the Kyoto Protocol to the Convention,

Recognizing that the global nature of climate change calls for the widest possible cooperation and participation by all countries in accordance with their common but differentiated responsibilities, respective capabilities, and their social and economic conditions,

Recognizing the right of all countries to promote sustainable development and the legitimate needs of the developing countries for achievement of sustained economic growth and the eradication of poverty,

Recalling the relevant provisions of the programme for the further implementation of Agenda 21 on transfer of environmentally sound technology, cooperation, and capacity-building, as adopted by the United Nations General Assembly at its nineteenth special session in 1997, and as reaffirmed by decision 9/CP.3,

Reaffirming the provisions of article 4.7 of the Convention,

1. *Agrees* that strengthening the capacities and capabilities of developing country parties to address climate change will help these parties to make their contributions to modifying the long-term trends of climate change, address climate change, achieve sustainable development and contribute to the ultimate objective of the Convention;
2. *Decides* to mobilize efforts of all relevant international organizations, particularly those of the financial institutions, to provide financial resources needed by developing country parties to meet their incremental costs, including transfer and development of technology, enhancement of endogenous capacities, implementation of such measures as improving energy efficiency, exploiting renewable energies, enhancing sinks, and preparing for adaptation to adverse effects of climate change;
3. *Requests* Annex I parties, in particular Annex II parties, to the Convention to take all practical steps to promote, facilitate, and finance the transfer and development of environmentally sound technologies, or access to environmentally sound technologies, know-how, and practices, to developing country parties. Annex I parties are also requested to support capacity-building and strengthening of national institutions to enable transfer of environmentally sound technologies;
4. *Further requests* Annex I parties, in particular Annex II parties, to the Convention:
    (a) To assist the developing country parties in their efforts to build capacity and institutional framework to improve energy efficiency and utilization of renewable energies through multilateral and bilateral cooperative efforts;
    (b) To provide assistance to developing country parties for sustainable management, conservation, and enhancement, as appropriate, of sinks and reservoirs of all greenhouse gases not controlled by the Montreal Protocol, including forests, biomass, and seas;
    (c) To assist developing country parties to build capacity to adapt to adverse effects of climate change;

(d) To assist developing country parties to strengthen their endogenous capacities and capabilities in the areas of technological, technical, and socio-economic research and systematic observation relevant to climate change and its associated adverse effects; and
(e) Taking into account article 6 of the Convention, to cooperate in and promote capacity-building of developing country parties at the international, regional, subregional, and national levels through cooperation programmes supported by multilateral, bilateral, and United Nations agencies;

Requests the Secretariat to further strengthen its activities related to technical and financial support to developing country parties with regard to strengthening of their capacity-building.

Paper No. 3: Indonesia (On behalf of the Group of 77 and China)*
Draft Decision Second Review of Article 4.2(a) and (b) of the Convention and Related Matters

The Conference of the Parties, at its fourth session,

Noting (Reaffirming) that "the largest share of historical and current global emissions of greenhouse gases has originated in developed countries, that per capita emissions in developing countries are still relatively low and that the share of global emissions originating in developing countries will grow to meet their social and development needs" (quoted from para. 3 of the Preamble to the Convention),

Basing itself on the Convention provisions, in particular article 4.2 (d) of the Convention,

Having reviewed article 4.2 (a) and (b) of the Convention in accordance with article 4.2(d) of the Convention, and having concluded that these subparagraphs are not adequate,

Deeply concerned that, according to their national communications, most of the developed country parties will not be able to honour their evidently inadequate commitments of retuning to their 1990 levels their anthropogenic emissions of the greenhouse gases as required of them under article 4.2 (b),

Decides

1. that those developed country parties that have not made demonstrable progress in returning to their 1990 levels their anthropogenic emissions of the GHGs as specified in article 4.2 (b) of the Convention, shall make efforts in good faith in honouring their commitments under article 4.2(a) and (b) by the end of the present decade (or: at the latest, by 2005 as provided for in article 3.2 of the Kyoto Protocol);

* Contained in document FCCC/CP/1998/MISC.6 of 5 October 1998.

2. that the Third Review, by the Conference of the Parties, of article 4.2(a) and (b) of the Convention shall take place at the second session of the Conference of the Parties serving as the Meeting of the Parties to the Kyoto Protocol, taking into account the timing mentioned in article 9.2 of the Kyoto Protocol;
3. that, in accordance with the provisions of article 4.2(d) of the Convention further reviews of article 4.2(a) and (b) of the Convention shall take place thereafter at regular intervals, namely, one year before the commencement of each subsequent "commitment period" for developed country parties, following their first commitment period (2008–2012), until the objective of the Convention is met;
4. that any such review shall not introduce any new commitments for developing country parties.

Submission by Venezuela: (On Behalf of the Group of 77 and China) Draft Decision of the Second Review of the Adequacy of Sub-paragraphs (a) and (b) of Paragraph 2 of Article 4 of the Convention*

The Conference of the Parties, at its Fourth Session,

Having reviewed sub-paragraphs (a) and (b) of article 4.2 of the Convention, which relate to the commitments of parties included in Annex I, in accordance with subparagraph (d) of article 4.2, and having concluded that they are inadequate,

Having ascertained that, according to the national communications submitted by parties included in Annex II of the Convention, their collective greenhouse gas emissions have increased since the entry into force of the Convention, in spite of their commitment of aiming to return, individually or jointly, to their 1990 levels by the year 2000,

Deeply concerned that current projections indicate a continued growth of the emissions of most of the parties included in Annex I,

Regretting that the Kyoto Protocol, which has yet to enter into force, provides for no reduction commitments on the part or parties included in Annex I before the year 2008,

Fearing that, if present trends are allowed to continue unchecked, eventual compliance with the Kyoto Protocol could be seriously compromised,

1. *Decides* that developed country parties shall make genuine efforts to return their greenhouse gas emissions to 1990 levels as stipulated under subparagraphs (a) and (b) of article 4.2 of the Convention.
2. *Decides* that firm guidelines shall be established, no later than the Fifth Session of the Conference of the Parties, to ensure that parties included in Annex I that have made little or no progress in stabilizing or reducing their greenhouse gas emissions achieve demonstrable progress by year 2005 at the latest.

* Contained in document FCCC/CP/1998/MISC.6/Add.2/Rev.1 of 10 November 1998.

3. *Instructs* the Subsidiary Body for Implementation and the Subsidiary Body for Scientific and Technical Advice to report on this matter to the Conference of the Parties at its Fifth Session.
4. *Requests* the Secretariat to add the decision on the timing for conducting the third review and subsequent reviews in accordance with article 4.2(d) of the Convention on the provisional agenda of COP-5.
5. *Urges* early ratification of the Kyoto Protocol by all parties.

The Group of 77 and China Draft Decision: Modalities and Procedures for a Clean Development Mechanism as Defined in Article 12 of the Kyoto Protocol*

The Conference of the Parties,

Recalling that in article 12 of the Kyoto Protocol a clean development mechanism is defined with the purpose to assist parties not included in Annex I to the Convention in achieving sustainable development and in contributing to the ultimate objective of the Convention, and to assist parties included in Annex I in achieving compliance with part of their quantified emission limitation and reduction commitments under article 3, and reflecting provisions contained in appendix X to the annex on modalities and procedures to decision,

Recalling also its decisions 1/CP.3, 7/CP.4, 8/CP.4, and 14/CP.5,

Bearing in mind the need to promote equitable geographic distribution of the clean development mechanism project activities at regional and sub-regional level,

Emphasizing that parties included in Annex I to the Convention should promote technologies and activities in parties not included in Annex I in a manner that minimizes any environmental, economic, or social adverse effects,

1. *Decides* to prompt start the clean development mechanism, in accordance with the modalities and procedures in the annex to this decision, taking into account the prior need to set up requisite institutional and related arrangements, fully capable of functioning effectively to implement the modalities and procedures, including the convening of the executive board on an interim basis, with the Conference of the Parties assuming responsibilities of the Conference of the Parties serving as the Meeting of the Parties to the Protocol related to the implementation of the clean development mechanism;
2. *Decides also* that the parties included in Annex I to the Convention should start implementing measures to assist parties not included in Annex I to the Convention, in particular the least developed and Small Island Developing States amongst them, with building capacity in order to facilitate their participation in the clean development mechanism, taking into account relevant decisions on capacity-building by the Conference of the Parties and the Conference of the

* Contained in document FCCC/CP/2000/MISC.2 of 21 November 2000.

Parties serving as the Meeting of the Parties to the Kyoto Protocol as well as decisions on guidance to the financial mechanism of the Convention;

3. *Establishes* a specific mechanism, to be facilitated, as appropriate, by the interim executive board, to assist parties not included in Annex I to the Convention, in particular the least developed and Small Island Developing States amongst them, with building capacity to participate in the clean development mechanism; keeping in view the need to build capacity for developing projects based on advanced technologies which augment energy efficiency or generate energy in a sustainable manner from biomass and renewable sources;
4. *Invites* the Subsidiary Body for Scientific and Technological Advice to prepare guidelines for baseline setting under the guidance of the executive board to determine reductions in anthropogenic emissions by sources [and anthropogenic enhancements of removals by sinks] that are additional to any that would occur in the absence of certified project activity under the CDM;
5. *Requests* the Subsidiary Body for Scientific and Technological Advice to adopt the guidelines for baseline setting and accreditation procedures not later than its fifteenth session;
6. *Requests* the executive board to include the guidelines adopted under paragraph XX in the UNFCCC clean development mechanism reference manual;
7. *Decides* that the adaptation fund shall be managed by an existing institution;
8. *Decides* to review regularly the equitable regional and subregional distribution of clean development mechanism project activities with a view to promoting equitable distribution and provide appropriate guidance to the executive board accordingly;
9. *Decides* to establish a clean development mechanism equitable distribution fund to provide financial assistance to project activities, where necessary, to address imbalances in the regional distribution of CDM project activities, to be financed by parties included in Annex II, with certified emission reductions generated by such projects to be acquired by such parties in proportion to their contribution;
10. *Elects* the members of the executive board on an interim basis, nominated in accordance with the modalities and procedures;
11. *Requests* the Secretariat of the Convention to perform any functions assigned to it in decision -/[CMP.1] and respective annexes;
12. *Decides* that the share of proceeds shall be collected and allocated, in accordance with provisions contained in appendix D, to cover administrative expenses and to the adaptation fund defined in appendix E to the annex to this decision;
13. *Invites* parties included in Annex I to contribute to the trust fund established to cover the administrative expenses of the executive board established on interim basis. Such contributions shall be reimbursed, if requested, from the share of proceeds collected for administrative expenses in accordance

with disbursement procedures and the timetable determined by the executive board;

14. *Decides* to examine the facilitation of the establishment of the clean development mechanism not later than x years from the adoption of this decision, without affecting the project activities already registered;
15. *Recommends* that the Conference of the Parties serving as the Meeting of the Parties to the Protocol, at its first session, adopt the following decision:

Decision -/[CMP.1] Modalities and Procedures for a Clean Development Mechanism as Defined in Article 12 of the Kyoto Protocol

The Conference of the Parties serving as the Meeting of the Parties to the Kyoto Protocol,

Taking into account provisions contained in articles 3 and 12 of the Kyoto Protocol,

Bearing in mind that, in accordance with article 12, the purpose of the clean development mechanism is to assist parties not included in Annex I to the Convention in achieving sustainable development and in contributing to the ultimate objective of the Convention, and to assist parties included in Annex I in achieving compliance with part of their quantified emission limitation and reduction commitments under article 3 and reflecting provisions contained in appendix X to the annex on modalities and procedures,

Acknowledging that the participation of parties not included in Annex I in certified project activities for the purpose of sustainable development makes the clean development mechanism distinctive from the other mechanisms,

Also bearing in mind the provisions contained in articles 3 and 12 of the Kyoto Protocol, in accordance with which any certified emission reductions which a party included in Annex I acquires from another party not included in Annex I shall be added to the assigned amount of the acquiring party, keeping in view that any such additions are solely for the purpose of contributing to the achievement of compliance with the quantified emission limitation and reduction commitments in article 3 of the acquiring party without altering that party's assigned amount pursuant to its quantified emission limitation and reduction commitments inscribed in Annex B,

Bearing in mind further that a share of the proceeds from certified project activities under the clean development mechanism shall be used to cover administrative expenses and to assist developing country parties that are particularly vulnerable to the adverse effects of climate change to meet the costs of adaptation,

Affirming that, in their actions to achieve the purpose of the clean development mechanism, parties shall be guided by articles 2 and 3 of the Convention and, *inter alia*,

Equity between developed and developing countries relates to equitable per capita emission entitlements for developing country parties, keeping in view that per capita emissions in developing countries are still relatively low and that the share of global emissions originating in developing countries will grow to meet their social and development needs, taking fully into account that economic and social development and poverty eradication are the first and overriding priorities of such parties, while affirming that developed country parties shall continue to limit and reduce their emissions with the aim of attaining lower levels of emissions through domestic policies and measures with a view to reducing per capita inequities in emissions between developed and developing country parties.

Additionality: Reductions in anthropogenic emissions by sources [and anthropogenic enhancement of removals by sinks] should be additional to any that would occur in the absence of the project activity, keeping in view that business-as-usual projects shall not be eligible as CDM projects, while ensuring that overseas development assistance and the other existing financial commitments of parties included in Annex I are not used for the acquisition of certified emission reductions, taking into account that the implementation of the commitment of parties included in Annex II in article 4, paragraphs 3, 5 and 7 of the Convention are distinct from the implementation of article 12 of the Protocol.

Non-discrimination, prevention of distortion of competition: All developing country parties may participate in or initiate CDM project activities on a voluntary basis. No unilateral action should preclude a party not included in Annex I from participating in or initiating any clean development mechanism project activity. Clean development mechanism project activities should not distort competitiveness in parties not included in Annex I.

Special needs of least developed country parties: Activities under the clean development mechanism shall give full consideration to the special needs of least developed countries, in particular to the identification of their special technology needs and to capacity-building.

Special vulnerabilities and character of Small Island Developing States: Activities under the clean development mechanism shall take into account the special vulnerabilities and character of Small Island Developing States, in particular capacity-building for adaptation activities and the implementation of clean development mechanism project activities.

Special situations of developing countries that are particularly vulnerable to the adverse effects of climate change: Activities under the clean development mechanism shall take into account the adverse impacts on food and agricultural sustainability, keeping in view the poorest populations which are the most vulnerable, and the need to build capacity for adaptation activities and the implementation of CDM project activities.

Special situations of developing country parties that are particularly vulnerable to the adverse impacts of mitigation activities: CDM project activities shall be implemented in such a way as to minimize adverse social, environmental, and economic impacts on developing country parties, particularly those identified under article 4, paragraphs 8 and 9 of the Convention.

Having considered decision [B/CP.6] on modalities and procedures for the clean development mechanism,

1. *Decides* to confirm and give full effect to any actions taken pursuant to decision [B/CP.6];
2. *Adopts* the modalities and procedures for the clean development mechanism contained in the annex on modalities and procedures;
3. *Decides* that possible future revisions of this decision and the annex on modalities and procedures may be considered, taking into account the experience of parties. Revisions shall not affect clean development mechanism project activities already registered. Any revisions to this decision shall be made by consensus of the parties. The first such revision shall be undertaken not less than five years after the adoption of the clean development mechanism modalities and procedures by the Conference of the Parties serving as the Meeting of the Parties to the Kyoto Protocol at its first session.

Annex
Modalities and procedures for a clean development mechanism

Definitions
For the purpose of this Annex:

(a) "Party" means, unless the context otherwise indicates, a party to this Protocol.
(b) "Protocol" means the Kyoto Protocol to the United Nations Framework Convention on Climate Change.
(c) "Article" means an article of the Protocol, unless otherwise indicated.
(d) The "assigned amount" for each party included in Annex I shall be equal to the percentage inscribed for it in Annex B of the Protocol of its aggregate anthropogenic carbon dioxide equivalent emissions of the greenhouse gases listed in Annex A of the Protocol in 1990, or the base year or period determined in accordance with article 3, paragraph 5 of the Protocol, multiplied by five.
(e) A "certified emission reduction" or "CER" is a unit issued pursuant to article 12 of the Protocol and requirements thereunder and is equal to one metric tonne of carbon dioxide equivalent, calculated using global warming potentials defined by decision 2/CP.3 or as subsequently revised in accordance with article 5.
(f) An "emission reduction unit" or "ERU" is a unit issued pursuant to article 6 of the Protocol and requirements thereunder and is equal to one metric tonne of carbon dioxide equivalent, calculated using global warming

potentials defined by decision 2/CP.3 or as subsequently revised in accordance with article 5.

(g) A "part of assigned amount" or "PAA" is a unit issued pursuant to article 17 of the Protocol and requirements thereunder, and is equal to one metric tonne of carbon dioxide equivalent emissions, calculated using global warming potentials defined by decision 2/CP.3 or as subsequently revised in accordance with article 5.

Submission No. 16: Nigeria* (On behalf of the Group of 77 and China)
G-77/China Amendment to Mr. Pronk's Note

Attached is an amendment to the note by the President of COP-6, Mr. Pronk's guidance note. The attachment only addresses the issue raised by the note and does not reflect all issues which G-77/China has stated positions. The G-77/C issues are clearly stated in the negotiating documents of SB13 and in the statements of the Minister of Environment of Nigeria, the G-77/C leader.

G-77/China Amendment to Mr. Pronk's Note

Box A. Capacity-building, technology transfer,

Implementation of Articles 4.8/4.9; 3.14, finance

Funding mechanisms (and guidance to the GEF and guidance to the Executive Board) (Guidance to the GEF, as an operating entity of the financial mechanism, is contained in doc. No. FCCC/SBI/2000/CRP. 16/Rev.1) Parties have reached general agreement on frameworks for technology transfer, capacity-building, adaptation, and impacts of response measures.

Adaptation Fund
Parties decide to create a new fund under the COP/MOP: the adaptation fund. Guidance shall be given to the fund and special consideration will be given to the needs of the LDCs and SIDS.

- An adaptation fund shall be established under the COP/MOP as a trust fund. The implementation of concrete adaptation projects in non–Annex I parties will be financed (stage III activities). Finance will be generated by the share of proceeds on the CDM (90% of 10% of the CERs generated by a project). Projects will be implemented by the UN specialized agencies. [Annex II parties will transfer [X] per cent of their assigned amount to the registry of the fund.

* Contained in document FCCC/CP/2001/MISC.1 of 7 March 2001.

Annex I parties can acquire these units, on the basis of article 17, for the purpose of meeting their commitments of article 3.1.] (moved).

- The CDM Executive Board shall manage the fund. The Board shall function under the guidance of, and be accountable to, the COP/MOP. Such guidance shall be given by COP/MOP on programs, priorities and eligibility criteria for funding of adaptation activities.
- *The following activities will be included in the category of adaptation activities, inter alia, in the areas of water resources management, prevention of deforestation, land management, agriculture, health, infrastructure development, ecosystems, integrated coastal zone management, combating land degradation and desertification, particularly in Africa, and sea-level rise.*
- UN specialized agencies shall be the trustee of this fund.

Special Fund

Parties decide to create a new Special Fund for climate change activities under the trusteeship of a UN specialized agency, such as the UNEP. The guidance shall be given to the fund by the COP and special consideration will be given to the needs of the LDCs and SIDS.

- The Special Fund shall be a separate entity under the Convention.
- Under this special fund, new and additional funding shall be made available by Annex II parties for activities in developing countries: technology transfer of and technical support for environmentally sound technology, capacity-building activities identified in the framework (contained in doc. Nos. FCCC/SB/2000/CRP.16), assistance with economic diversification.
- Sources of funding shall be new and additional mandatory contributions by Annex II parties
- The fund shall be managed under the guidance of the COP. The special fund shall function under the special guidance of, and be accountable to, the COP. This *shall* ensure more responsiveness to the needs and priorities and projects of developing countries. Ownership and "country-drivenness" in projects *shall* be enhanced.

Resources

In addition to the Adaptation and the Special Fund parties agree to increase resources for climate change funding, through other channels. They agree that the sum total of new and additional financing to be provided by Annex II parties on a grant or concessional basis should reach the level of one billion US$ on an annual basis, as soon as possible, but not later than in the year 2005. If the resources referred above in 2005 would be less than one billion US$ on an annual average basis between 2000 and 2005, parties agree to apply a levy on article 6 (Joint Implementation) and/or article 17 (emission trading) to the extent of fully covering the balance of the unfulfilled commitment referred above.

The following criteria shall apply to all funds and funding mechanisms/entities under the Convention and the Protocol: new and additional resources, on a grant or concessional basis, adequacy, predictability, agreed full costs for article 12.1 activities and agreed full incremental costs to other article 4.1 activities.

Climate Resources Committee
Parties decide to establish as a subsidiary body of the COP a Climate Resources Committee at COP-7, with the following mandate:

- To review the sufficiency of financing and institutional arrangements for climate change
- To give policy advice to existing financing channels and institutions such as the GEF, Regional Development banks, the World Bank, UNDP, and other multilateral institutions. The advice will be focused on:
  - Increasing climate funding
  - Mainstreaming (request clarification)
  - Monitoring and assessment

Capacity-building
Parties decide to establish a framework to guide capacity-building activities related to the implementation of the Convention and effective participation in the Kyoto Protocol, in order to assist non–Annex II parties. (See Draft Decisions FCCC/SB/2000/CRP.16 and FCCC/SB/2000/CRP.17.)

Technology Transfer

- Parties decide to adopt [when finalized] the framework [Annex . . .] for meaningful and effective implementation of article 4.5 of the Convention
- Parties decide to establish an intergovernmental consultative group of technical and scientific experts on technology transfer under the SBSTA

The group will:

- Facilitate the exchange and review of information by creating an information clearing house and national, subregional, and regional technology transfer centres;
- Evaluation, assessment, review, and reporting of the progress of technology transfer in relation to article 4.5;
- Advise SBSTA on further actions to be taken;
- Focus on ways and means to address the barriers for technology transfer;
- Be composed on the basis of equitable geographical distribution based on existing UN groupings;

- SBSTA will review the group's work on a regular basis, consider its advice and if necessary request the COP to take any further action, including *inter alia* programs and priorities for financing of activities.

Articles 4.8, 4.9, and 3.14: I. General Comment: The introduction of the paper on page 1 says that the paper addresses unresolved issues. Turning to the actual text, on pages 4 and 5, it addresses some resolved issues and fails to address a number of unresolved issues.

The unresolved issues are:

1. Whether one or two decisions,
2. Use of mandatory language,
3. Linkages with articles 5, 7, and 8.

Apart from the omission of the above unresolved issues, the paper addresses the following extraneous issues:

1. Avoidance of deforestation and land degradation (4th bullet under adverse effects of climate change),
2. Reference to "high energy carriers" (1st bullet under article 3.14).

II. Specific Text Proposals <u>Adverse Effects of Climate Change</u>

- Bullet 1: Replace "can" on the 1st line with "may"; on the 3rd line, after national communications, insert "and/or." This comment applies to all parts where there is a reference to national communications and other relevant information (under 4.8/4.9 decision).
- Bullet 2: Delete the word "sufficient." Add fragile mountains ecosystems.
- Bullet 3: Delete the part after the word "prevention" up to "climate change" and replace with "in the context of."
- Bullet 4: This should be deleted since it constitutes an extraneous issue that was not part of the original agreed text*.

<u>Actions to address impacts of response measures (Article 3.14)</u>

We are not in total agreement with the contents of this section and recommend the following changes, understanding that the language should comply with the language of the Protocol:

1. Chapeau should read "Each Annex I Party decides to report in their national communications and national inventory report";

*Subsequently reviewed by plenary for possible change.

2. Bullet 1 – Delete "the Efforts to limit" and replace with "What actions they have taken to address the adverse ____"; Delete the last part of Bullet 1 after (coal subsidies).
3. Insert the G-77/China position as reflected in FCCC/SB/2000/CRP.18, sections A and B, pages 15–20. The G-77/C position in sections A and B reads as follow:

Section A

1. *Decides* that Annex I parties shall provide information, as part of the necessary supplementary information to their annual inventory report, in accordance with the guidelines under article 7.1 of the Kyoto Protocol, on their actions in striving, under article 3.14 of the Kyoto Protocol, to implement their commitments mentioned in article 3.1 of the Kyoto Protocol in such a way as to minimize adverse social, environmental and economic impacts on developing country parties, particularly those identified in articles 4.8 and 4.9 of the Convention;
2. *Decides* that Annex II parties shall provide assistance to non–Annex I parties to enable them to provide information on their specific needs and concerns related to the adverse social, environmental and economic impacts that may arise from the implementation of commitments under article 3.1 of the Kyoto Protocol;
3. *Decides* that Annex I parties shall provide information, by [date], to the Conference of the Parties serving as the Meeting of the Parties to the Kyoto Protocol, through the Secretariat, on their intended policies and measures, their impacts, and suggested ways to minimize these impacts;
4. *Decides* that Annex I parties shall provide information, including the relevant information identified in the appendix to the guidelines for the preparation of information required under article 7 of the Kyoto Protocol (FCCC/SBSTA/2000/CRP.17) [, by the time of COP/MOP 2], to the Conference of the Parties serving as the Meeting of the Parties to the Kyoto Protocol, in accordance with guidelines developed under article 7 of the Kyoto Protocol through the Secretariat, on their intended policies and measures, their impacts, and measures taken to minimize these impacts;
5. *Decides* that Annex I parties shall provide information in their annual inventory report in accordance with guidelines developed under article 7.1 of the Kyoto Protocol by [COP/MOP 2], to the Conference of the Parties serving as the Meeting of the Parties to the Kyoto Protocol through the Secretariat, on, *inter alia*, progress on their reduction and phasing out of existing market imperfections, fiscal incentives, tax, and duty incentives and subsidies in their energy sector, and on their plans to reduce or phase out such distortions;

6. *Aware* that the consideration of actions under article 3.14 to address the impact of the implementation of response measures must meet the specific needs and concerns of developing country parties;
7. *Decides* to develop, by the time of COP/MOP 2, mandatory criteria to determine if Annex I parties are in compliance with their commitments to minimize adverse effects, including the adverse effects of climate change, effects on international trade, and social, environmental and economic impacts on other parties, especially developing country parties, and in particular those identified in articles 4.8 and 4.9 of the Convention;
8. *Invites* the Intergovernmental Panel on Climate Change, in cooperation with other relevant organizations, to prepare a technical paper on geological carbon storage technologies, covering current information, and report on it for its consideration at its xx session;

Section B

9. (Proposal by the Group of 77 and China, as amended by Saudi Arabia): Decides, by the time of COP/MOP 2, that Annex I parties shall start to implement the actions listed below, and shall report, in their annual inventory report, on actions related to subparagraphs (a) to (c) below, and in their national communications on actions related to subparagraphs (d) and (e) below, in accordance with guidelines developed under article 7:
   a) Restructuring their tax systems to reflect the greenhouse gas content in all greenhouse gas emitting sectors, and removing subsidies;
   b) Discouraging the production of fossil fuels in Annex I parties, and concentrating on domestic actions that will not negatively impact their fossil fuel imports from developing country parties;
   c) Discouraging the use of environmentally unsafe and unsound technologies, in particular nuclear energy, by reflecting their huge externalities, and ensuring that existing nuclear energy plants are constantly monitored to guarantee optimal safety;
   d) Removing the existing barriers (political and regulatory) to the use and import of oil, particularly in relation to the electricity sector;
   e) Encouraging wider use of carbon dioxide emission reduction, and carbon capture and storage technologies;
10. *(Group of 77 and China proposal as amended by Saudi Arabia):*
    Decides that Annex II parties shall start to implement the actions listed in subparagraphs (a) and (b) below, and shall report back in their annual inventory in accordance with guidelines developed under article 7.1 on their minimization efforts, by the time of COP/MOP 2:

a) Assisting developing country parties which are highly dependent on the export and consumption of fossil fuels in diversifying their economies;
b) Providing prompt, adequate and just compensation to developing country parties adversely impacted by the implementation of response measures by Annex I parties;

11. *Encourages* Annex I parties to adopt policies and measures that will result in reductions in emissions of greenhouse gases, as a contribution to minimizing the adverse effects of climate change, and to provide information on these policies and measures in their national communications;
12. *Decides,* on the basis of the output of the workshops referred to in this decision, and in accordance with article 3.14 of the Kyoto Protocol, and the relevant provisions of the Convention, to take actions related to compensation, funding, insurance and technology transfer, for proven adverse impacts of response measures on developing country parties;

Actions to address impacts of response measures (article 4.8)

- Bullet 1 – Replace "will" with "shall"; and in the third line, delete "energy" and in the 4th line, replace "production" with activities,
- Bullet 2 – delete entire bullet and replace with the agreed language in paragraph 11, page 8 in document FCCC/SB/2000/CRP.18. Which reads,

"Encourages non-Annex I Parties to provide information in their national communications and/or other relevant reports on their specific needs and concerns arising from the impact of the implementation of response measures."

Specific Needs of LDCs, including the Small Island Developing States – SIDS amongst them (Article 4.9)

1. Amend the title to read "Specific Needs of LDCs, including Small Island Developing States (SIDS), amongst them (article 4.9)";
2. Include the Institutional Development Fund as contained in document FCCC/SB/2000/CRP.18.
3. Include new paragraph reading: Develop expedited and streamlined procedures to provide funding to LDCs on a priority basis to: (a) Support and Promote the effective implementation by them of the capacity-building framework annexed in COP6 decision XX, and to (b) assist them in overcoming their institutional limitations which impede their effective ability to address and cope with the impact of climate change and support their activities identified in paragraph XX of COP 6 decision XX.

Box B. Mechanisms

COP/MOP <-> Executive Board

A. Composition of the Executive Board of the CDM

- Parties agree that the composition of the Executive Board is an essential element in ensuring integrity, credibility and efficient operationalisation of the system. The balance in the Executive Board will be in accordance with current UNFCCC practices (equitable geographical representation of the five UN regional groupings, taking into account the interest groups as reflected by the current practice in the UNFCCC Bureau).
- Equal numbers of members from each of the five UN regional groups, plus one representative from the group of Small Island Developing States (21 members).
- Executive Board members shall make every effort to reach agreement on any proposed decision by consensus. Any decision shall as a last resort be adopted by a three-fourths majority vote of the members present and voting at the meeting.

B. Decision-making power of the COP/MOP vis-à-vis the Executive Board

- The Executive Board shall be subject to the authority and guidance of, and be accountable to, the COP/MOP.

C. Institutions for a prompt start for the CDM

- Parties decide that a prompt start for the CDM will be operationalised by electing the Executive Board will be elected at the next session of the COP.
- The Executive Board will be served by the UNFCCC Secretariat.
- Appropriate resources shall be made available for the prompt start of the CDM.

Eligibility of Project Activities under the CDM

Regarding bullet no. 2, i.e., reference to nuclear facilities, there is no group position; a number of country parties' position is that nuclear projects should not be excluded from the CDM. The position of these parties is that the reference to nuclear projects must be deleted.

- Parties recognize that it is up to the host developing country party's discretion to judge whether a project activity is in line with its national strategy on sustainable development.
- Annex I parties will declare that they will refrain from using nuclear facilities for generating certified emission reductions under the CDM.

- The Executive Board shall define and implement an expedited procedure for small scale projects which contribute to the sustainable development of non–Annex I p arties and to the ultimate objective of the Convention.
  ~~Parties decide that because of their contribution to the ultimate objective of the convention and to sustainable development, the following activities should be given priority and will have expedited consideration within the rules, modalities and procedures of the CDM:~~
  ~~renewable energy (inter alia small-scale hydro)~~
- ~~energy efficiency improvements~~
- Under the guidance and approval of COP/MOP, the Executive Board shall further develop rules and modalities for the operationalisation of this decision.
- Public funding of a CDM project should be additional to ODA and other financial commitments.

Supplementarity

- Annex I parties shall meet their emission commitments primarily through domestic action since 1990. Participation of each party shall be contingent on that party demonstrating to the Protocol's compliance system that domestic actions constitute the principal means for achieving its article 3 commitments. Each party's use of the mechanisms under articles 6, 12, and 17 collectively shall not exceed 9 per cent of its assigned amount pursuant to their quantified emission limitation and reduction commitments as inscribed in Annex B.
  ~~Compliance with principle will be assessed by the facilitative branch of the compliance committee on the basis of qualitative and quantified information, reported in national communications and reviewed under Article 8. The facilitative branch shall advise on how to ensure the effective implementation of this provision. A first assessment should be reported to the fourth national communications of Annex I Parties due in 2005.~~

Trading modalities and liability

- Parties agree that article 17 provides opportunities for parties to fulfil their commitments in a cost-effective way. Parties also recognize that reporting, review, and a strong and enforceable compliance regime are not sufficient to prevent parties from over transferring, thereby potentially endangering the environmental integrity of the system.
- Eligibility shall be demonstrated by transferring and acquiring parties before trading. Parties must demonstrate compliance of their articles 5 and 7 commitments.
- Parties therefore decide that Annex B parties shall retain a portion of their assigned amounts in their national registries specific to that commitment

period. This portion shall be 98 per cent of their assigned amounts or the portion determined on the basis of projected or recent emissions.

- After the annual review of each party's emissions data, the part of assigned amount that must be retained shall be recalculated and, if necessary, adjusted.
- A share of the proceeds based on transactions under article 17 to assist developing country parties that are particularly vulnerable, as listed in article 4.8 of the Convention to meet the costs of adaptation.

Fungibility

- Parties should protect the climate system for the benefit of present and future generations of human kind, on the basis of equity and in accordance with their common but differentiated responsibilities and respective capabilities. Accordingly, the developed country parties should take the lead in combating climate change and the adverse effects thereof. Parties affirm that in their actions to achieve the purpose of the mechanisms, parties shall be guided by article 2 of the Convention and the principles contained in article 3 of the Convention.
- Parties note that per capita emissions in developing countries are still relatively low and that the share of global emissions originating in developing countries will grow to meet their social and developments needs, while affirming that developed country parties shall continue to limit and reduce their emissions with the aim of attaining lower levels of emissions through domestic action with a view to reducing per capita inequities in emissions between developed and developing country parties.
- Parties recognize that the Kyoto Protocol has not created or bestowed—on parties included in Annex I to the Convention and in Annex B to the Protocol—any right, title, or entitlement.
- Parties note that emissions reduction units (under "joint implementation") and parts of an assigned amount (under emissions trading) could be added to, or subtracted from, the assigned amount of a party, without altering any party's assigned amount. Parties agree that certified emissions reduction units (CDM) could be added to the assigned amount of a party and could be used for the purpose of contributing to compliance with the quantified emission limitation and reduction commitments in article 3 without altering that party's assigned amount pursuant to its commitments inscribed in Annex B.

Promotion of geographic distribution of CDM projects

- Parties agree that there should be opportunities for all parties to participate in the CDM and decide that an equitable distribution of CDM projects will be fostered. Therefore, standardized baselines, which are based on an appropriate Annex I average, may be used for small-scale projects (<XMw) and

renewable energy projects (<XMw). The Executive Board is asked to elaborate on and make recommendations on preferential treatment of these specific project types.

- Parties decide to foster LDC participation in the CDM by giving special attention to institutional capacity-building for LDCs.
- CDM projects in LDCs shall be exempt from the share of proceeds for adaptation.

Procedures for "joint implementation"

- Parties note that "joint implementation" takes place among Annex I parties with greenhouse gas emission limitation and reduction commitments. Eligibility criteria shall be demonstrated. Compliance with articles 5 and 7 shall be demonstrated by both acquiring and transferring parties before acquisitions and transfers. Projects under article 6 shall follow the same rigorous procedure as provided for under the CDM procedures.
- A share of the proceeds shall be applied to article 6 to assist developing country parties that are particularly vulnerable, as listed in article 4.8 of the Convention to meet the costs of adaptation.

Box C. Land-use, Land-use change and forestry

Definitions for afforestation, reforestation and deforestation under article 3.3 (new introduction) Parties decide that LULUCF activities will be based on the following principles:

(a) Any land-use, land-use change and forestry activity carried out in addition to the commitments made under article 4.1(d) of the Convention for the purposes of determining compliance of Annex I parties with their quantitative emission limitation and reduction objectives under the Kyoto Protocol, must not change the global effect of the Kyoto Protocol, which is to mitigate climate change in the first commitment period equivalent to reducing Annex I anthropogenic emissions by sources covered by Annex A to the Kyoto Protocol by an aggregate proportion of at least 5 per cent with reference to their 1990 levels, in accordance with article 3.1 of the Kyoto Protocol;

(b) For the purposes of determining compliance of Annex I parties with their quantitative emission limitation and reduction objectives, any land-use, land-use change and forestry activity must not result in an increase of anthropogenic emissions by sources minus removals by sinks deriving from the application of removals by sinks of carbon dioxide, indirect nitrogen fertilization effects and dynamic age structures;

(c) In view of the impact of climate change on forests and desertification, forest conservation and rehabilitation of degraded vegetation cover are potential climate change adaptation activities, and as such could be included among those activities to benefit from the share of proceeds of the mechanisms of the Protocol intended to meet the cost of adaptation. This is without prejudice to decisions on land-use, land-use change and forestry activities in the mechanisms of the Kyoto Protocol;

(d) The rules for the inclusion of land-use, land-use change and forestry activities in the accounting of Annex I countries, for purposes of compliance with their commitments under the Kyoto Protocol, must not imply a transfer of such commitments to a future commitment period;

(e) Carbon removed by land-use, land-use change and forestry activities shall be considered as a temporary removal. Any Annex I party that makes use of such removal to achieve compliance with its Kyoto Protocol commitment shall continue to be responsible for any subsequent emissions;

(f) In the methodologies to account for emissions by sources and removals by sinks in the land use, land-use change and forestry sector, no consideration shall be given to the simple presence of stocks of carbon, in line with the provisions of article 5.2 of the Kyoto Protocol,

New preamble: COP recommends to COP/MOP the following decisions:

Definitions for afforestation, reforestation and deforestation under article 3.3

1st paragraph: Delete second sentence

2nd paragraph: Parties decide to establish a process to investigate the ~~feasibility of applying~~ <u>inclusion</u> of biome-specific definitions for future commitment periods.

Additional activities and accounting under article 3.4

Option 1: Strongly held view to oppose any work on article 3.4 for first commitment period due to the fact that the article 3.4 of the Kyoto Protocol refers to the application of these activities in the second commitment period.
Option 2: Revise text by:

<u>*Eligible activities:*</u> 1st paragraph: Parties decide to establish a process under SBSTA to develop a comprehensive set of definitions for the following activities: grazing land management, cropland management, and forest management (delete reference to broadly based land management activities) and revegetation/<u>vegetation degradation</u> (new).

2nd paragraph (new): Parties will also decide to establish a process under SBSTA to assess aspects of associated with scale, uncertainties and risk associated with the above-listed activities.

Accounting Second paragraph: "Therefore parties decide that the contribution of additional activities under article 3.4, towards meeting a party's target in the first commitment period shall be limited to 3% of the party's base year emissions."

Second interval first paragraph: Parties decide that carbon stock changes accounted for in accordance with the provisions of article 3.4 shall, for the broadly defined management activities exclude the effects of:

Second paragraph: Therefore, parties shall apply a reduction of 30% of the ~~net~~ carbon stock ~~changes~~ and ~~net~~ GHG ~~emissions~~ removals that result from additional cropland and grazing land management activities and of 85% to the ~~net~~ carbon stock ~~changes~~ and ~~net~~ GHG ~~emissions~~ removals that result from additional forest management.

Additional activities under Article 3.4 in the second and consecutive commitment periods First paragraph: Parties decide that the COP/MOP shall, prior in parallel to the fixing of emission commitment periods, review the list of agreed additional activities for use in second ~~and subsequent commitment~~ periods, together with the rules, modalities, and guidelines for the accounting.

Implementation of Article 3.7

Second paragraph: Parties to decide that eligibility to make use of this provision will be determined on the basis of a reviewed national inventory review by Expert Review Team as established under Article 8.

LULUCF under the Clean Development Mechanism

Second sentence of the first paragraph: (No agreed position).

Second paragraph, second sentence: However, these activities will be labelled as ~~priority~~ potential projects to be funded under the adaptation fund in order to address drought, desertification and watershed protection, forest conservation, restoration of native forest ecosystems, restoration of salinized soils.

Fourth paragraph: Parties therefore decide to establish a process under the SBSTA at its fifteenth session to develop rules and modalities taking into account further methodological work by the IPCC, ~~where necessary~~, to deal with these issues.

Fifth paragraph (new): No afforestation and reforestation activities will be eligible under the CDM until the SBSTA and the IPCC have completed their methodological work described in paragraph 3 and have made recommendations in this regard.

Sixth paragraph (new): No afforestation and reforestation activities will be eligible under the CDM if they result in the destruction of natural forests or the loss of biological diversity.

- Seventh paragraph (new): No more than 10% of CERs validated, will come from LULUCF activities.

Additional activities and accounting under article 3.4 Eligible activities: Parties decide that a party may include the following activities: grazing land management, cropland management and forest management (broadly defined land management activities), revegetation (narrowly defined activity).

Accounting:

- Parties recognize that the scale of the activities applied could lead to major modifications in the effort for parties to meet the article 3 commitments.
- Therefore, parties decide that the contribution of additional activities under article 3.4, towards meeting a party's target in the first commitment period shall be limited to 3% of the party's base year emissions.
- In addition, parties decide that accounting for additional activities shall take place in two distinguished intervals:

First interval (full crediting up to level of 3.3 debit)

- Parties recognize the unintended outcome of article 3.3, namely that countries who have an overall increase in their total forest carbon stock, may nevertheless have their assigned amounts reduced because of accounting and definitional Conventions under article 3.3.
- Therefore, parties decide that parties may fully account for carbon stock changes and net GHG emissions in areas under forest management up to a level that is equal to the net debit incurred under the provisions of article 3.3, under the condition that the total forest carbon stock change since 1990 in that country compensates the net debit incurred under the provisions of article 3.3. This first interval shall not be more that 30 Mt CO2.

Second interval (discounted crediting in remaining interval to factor out non-direct human induced effects and to address uncertainty)

Parties decide that carbon stock changes accounted for in accordance with the provisions of article 3.4 shall, for the broadly defined management activities, exclude the effects of

- ndirect nitrogen deposition,
- elevated CO2 concentrations,

- other indirect effects and,
- (for forest ecosystems) the dynamic effects of age structure resulting from management activities before 1990,
- Therefore, parties shall apply a reduction of 30% to the net carbon stock changes and net GHG emissions that result from additional cropland and grazing land management activities and of 85% to the net carbon stock changes and net GHG emissions that result from additional forest management.

Additional activities under Article 3.4 in the second and consecutive commitment periods

- Parties decide that the COP/MOP shall, prior to the fixing of emission commitments for subsequent commitment periods, review the list of agreed additional activities for use in second and subsequent commitment periods, together with the rules, modalities, and guidelines for their accounting.
- Parties further decide that accounting of carbon stock changes and net GHG emissions shall be limited to direct human induced changes on carbon stocks and net GHG emissions. Parties therefore establish a process to periodically review the approach taken with respect to factoring out, taking into account methodological work by the IPCC on this matter.

Implementation of Article 3.7

- Parties note that, for those parties for whom land-use change and forestry constituted a net source in 1990, emissions and removals resulting from land-use change should be included in the 1990 emissions base year in accordance with the provisions of article 3.7.
- Parties decide that eligibility to make use of this provision will be determined on the basis of a reviewed national inventory

LULUCF under the Clean Development Mechanism

- Parties agree that LULUCF activities can contribute to the two-fold purpose of the CDM. Parties therefore decide to include afforestation and reforestation under the CDM. However, they also recognize the special concerns, which arise from implementing these projects.
- Parties decide that activities, preventing deforestation and land degradation, will not be eligible as credit generating projects under the CDM. However, these activities will be labelled as priority projects to be funded under the adaptation fund in order to address drought, desertification and watershed protection, forest conservation, restoration of native forest ecosystems, restoration of salinized soils.

- Parties recognize that accounting modalities and definitions for article 3.3 may need to be modified, and that the issues of non-permanence, social and environmental effects, leakage, additionality, and uncertainty should be properly addressed. LULUCF projects would also need to be in conformity with the objectives of other multilateral environmental agreements.
- Parties therefore decide to establish a process under the SBSTA to develop rules and modalities taking into account further methodological work by IPCC, where necessary, to deal with these issues.

Box D. Policies and Measures, Compliance,

Accounting, Reporting and Review

The whole paragraph below is replaced by the draft decision on "Good Practices" in policies and measures among parties included in Annex I to the Convention Policies and measures

- Parties decide to continue exchange of information on Policies and Measures.
- Parties decide to invite submissions by Annex I parties on the meaning of demonstrable progress and the need for guidelines for reporting on this progress (article 3.2 of the Kyoto Protocol) for SBSTA 14, with a view to have a further consideration at COP-7.

Add the following GENERAL NOTE:
The parties agree that the basis of negotiation is the text contained in document FCCC/2000/CRP.15/Rev 2

Compliance: consequences of non-compliance with article 3.1 Add:
Parties agreed that where the enforcement branch has determined that an Annex I party is not in compliance with article 3.1, it shall suspend the eligibility of that party to participate under articles 6, [12], and 17

- Parties decide that consequences for non-compliance with article 3.1 should be agreed in advance and should not be subject to the discretion of the enforcement branch.
- Parties recognize that subtraction of excess emissions from a party's assigned amount for the subsequent commitment period against a penalty rate guarantees environmental integrity, provided that the adoption and the entry into force of the emission commitments for subsequent commitment periods are timely.
- Parties agreed that penalty rates will be an essential element of the compliance system.

Although they will partly serve as an interest rate for the delays in the achievement of emission commitments, they should also be an incentive to comply and they should, therefore, be set at a relatively high level.

NOTE:

The acceptance of a consequence of the subtraction of excess emissions from a party's assigned amount for the subsequent commitment period is directly linked with the acceptance of the consequence of making a financial contribution in a compliance fund to be established. In the absence of such a financial contribution into a compliance fund, the penalty rates to be applied must be adjusted to a much higher level.

- Parties decide that emission commitments for the second commitment period should be adopted before the beginning of the first commitment period.
- Parties decide that, if a party has been determined as being in non-compliance with its commitments under article 3.1, the enforcement branch shall apply the following consequences in combination:
- Subtraction of excess emissions from the assigned amount of the subsequent commitment period.
- Penalty rate should be set at 2 [1.5] and be increased by 0.50 [0.25] per year for as long as that party is in non-compliance as well as in relation to the amount with which the party concerned has exceeded its target [after the subsequent commitment period if the party concerned is not in compliance at the end of the subsequent commitment period.]
- Parties concerned shall after determination of non-compliance, develop and submit to the enforcement branch for its approval a compliance action plan setting out *inter alia* how they propose to meet their commitments in the subsequent commitment period.

Compliance: differentiation between parties (in particular Annex I and non–Annex I)

- Parties decide that the mandate of the enforcement branch shall [will] be limited to obligations [that are incumbent on] of Annex I parties only.
- There will be no eligibility requirements for non–Annex I parties in respect of their participation in the CDM. [, recognizing that only parties can participate in the CDM that have ratified the Kyoto Protocol and meet commitments under article 12 of the Convention taking into account the availability of financial resources.]

NOTE: The eligibility criteria should be the same as those that have been agreed to under the CDM discussions. No discrepancies shall be allowed.

- There will be no differentiation between Annex I parties and non-Annex I parties in respect of the application of consequences by the facilitative branch.

NOTE: This is unacceptable. The differentiation between Annex I and non-Annex I should be maintained as this is a reflection of the operationalisation of the principle of common but differentiate responsibilities. Not all the consequences that have been proposed can apply to non-Annex I parties in the same manner as it applies to Annex I parties. Some of the consequences are not appropriate. For example, it is proposed as a consequence that the facilitative branch can refer a case to the enforcement branch. This is totally inappropriate where non-Annex I parties are concerned.

The concerns of the countries with economies in transition can be met without changing the structure of a differentiation between Annex I and non-Annex I parties as far as the kind of consequences that the facilitative branch can apply to them.

Compliance: relationship between the COP/MOP and the Compliance Committee Add the following:
Parties agreed that the Compliance Committee shall report to the COP/MOP

- Parties decide that the role of the COP/MOP should be [limited] to give general policy guidance to the Compliance Committee and that it should not intervene in individual cases.
- Parties decide that there is no need for an appeals procedure.

NOTE: We can accept that no appeal is needed if the procedure proposed by the G-77 and China with regard to the expert review teams reports is accepted. This procedures entail that a small panel of the COP/MOP consisting of 6 members will consider the reports of the Expert review teams in a manner that will not hamper the effective and efficient functioning of the Compliance Committee. The reasoning for this panel includes the fact that it is in line with the provisions of article 8(3) of the Protocol and will provide the necessary political overview that is lacking where experts that act in their personal capacity are involved. In the present case there will be experts acting independently in the expert review teams as well as in the Compliance Committee.

Mandates enforcement branch and facilitative branch NOTE: The position proposed here is not in line with the Group of 77 and China position. We have proposed that non-compliance with articles 5, 7, and 3.14 should also be dealt with under the enforcement branch.

- Parties decide that the mandate of the enforcement branch covers quantitative emission commitments, eligibility requirements under articles 6, 12 (only Annex I parties), and 17.

- All other cases of non-compliance fall within the mandate of the facilitative branch, including articles 2.3, 3.14, [5.1, 7.1, 7.2,]* 10, and 11, taking into account the character of commitments for Annex I and non–Annex I parties.

NOTE: Compliance with the provisions in articles 5 and 7 that is bracketed is directly related to the eligibility criteria to be dealt with by the enforcement branch. The mandate of the branches must be clearly defined and this contradiction must be addressed.

- The facilitative branch shall be responsible for providing advice, facilitation to parties in implementing the Kyoto Protocol and promoting compliance of parties with their commitments under the Protocol, taking into account the principle of common but differentiated responsibilities and capabilities of parties included in Annex I and parties not included in Annex I.

<u>Compliance: composition of the Compliance Committee</u>

- Parties decide to establish a Compliance Committee, which shall function through a plenary and two branches namely a facilitative branch and an enforcement branch.

Add:

The parties agreed that the Committee will have two co-chairpersons, one from Annex I parties and the other from non–Annex I parties and the chairmanship of each branch will rotate between the parties in such a manner that the co-chairs will never be only from one group of parties.

The parties agreed that the Committee will have a plenary that will perform certain functions in such a manner that it will not hamper the efficient functioning of the branches. The plenary will perform specific functions as outlined in paragraph 13 (c) to (h) of document CRP15/Rev 2. The plenary will also allocate questions to the appropriate branches.

Facilitative branch

- Parties decide that the balance in the facilitative branch will be in accordance with current UNFCCC practices (equitable geographical representation of the five UN regional groups, taking into account interest groups as reflected by the current practice in the UNFCCC Bureau).
- Equal numbers of members from each of the five UN regional groups, plus one representative from the group of Small Island Developing States.
- The facilitative branch shall consist of 11 members.
- Facilitative branch members shall make every effort to reach agreement on any proposed decision by consensus. Any decision shall, as a last resort, be adopted

by a three-fourths majority vote of the members present and voting at the meeting.

Enforcement branch

- Parties decide that the balance in the enforcement branch will be in accordance with current UNFCCC practices (equitable geographical representation of the five UN regional groupings, taking into account the interest groups as reflected by the current practice in the UNFCCC Bureau).
- Equal numbers of members from each of the five UN regional groups, plus one representative from the group of Small Island Developing States.
- The enforcement branch shall consist of 11 members.
- Enforcement branch members shall make every effort to reach agreement on any proposed decision by consensus. Any decision shall as a last resort be adopted by a:
- Three-fourths majority vote of the members present and voting at the meeting.
- Double majority (majority as a whole and in Annex I and non–Annex I). NOTE: There was no agreement on this. A double majority voting rule is unacceptable as it would make the effective decision making of the branch almost impossible and will in effect give a veto right to Annex I and Non–Annex I parties which is not in the interest of the effective functioning of the Committee.

Compliance: Legal basis, the form of adoption of the final result on compliance NOTE: The mode of adoption is directly linked with the kind of consequences that will be adopted. The Group strongly supports the adoption of legally binding consequences. In terms of article 18 of the Protocol this will necessitate an amendment of the Protocol. The Group does not have a common position on the format of or on how the amendment should be effected. The Group did identify certain principles that should apply to any kind of amendment as follows:

The amendment should form an integral part of the Protocol;
It shall be restricted to adopting the procedures and mechanisms on compliance and to bringing it into force;
It shall bind all parties that have ratified the Kyoto Protocol;
It shall already apply to the first commitment period.

- Parties decide that the adoption of the compliance system, including binding consequences, should be legally based on:
- An agreement supplementing the Kyoto Protocol prior to its entry into force.

Submission No. 3: India (On behalf of the Group of 77 and China)*
Annex II Modalities for Accounting of Assigned Amount and for the Compliance Assessment
I. Calculation of assigned amount pursuant to article 3, paragraphs 7 and 8[1]

1. The assigned amount pursuant to article 3, paragraphs 7 and 8, for the first commitment period, from 2008 to 2012, for each party included in Annex I with a commitment inscribed in Annex B to the Kyoto Protocol shall be equal to the percentage inscribed for it in Annex B of its aggregate anthropogenic carbon dioxide equivalent emissions of the greenhouse gases, and from the sources, listed in Annex A to the Kyoto Protocol in the base year multiplied by five, taking into account the following:
   (a) The base year shall be 1990 except for those parties included in Annex I undergoing the process of transition to a market economy that have selected a historical base year or period other than 1990, in accordance with article 3, paragraph 5, and for those parties included in Annex I that have selected 1995 as the base year for total emissions of hydrofluorocarbons, perfluorocarbons, and sulphur hexafluoride, in accordance with article 3, paragraph 8;
   (b) Those parties included in Annex I for which land-use change and forestry (all emissions by sources and removals by sinks under category 5 of the *Revised 1996 Intergovernmental Panel of Climate Change Guidelines for National Greenhouse Gas Inventories)* constituted a net source of greenhouse gas emissions in 1990 shall include in their 1990 emissions base year or period the aggregate anthropogenic carbon dioxide equivalent emissions by sources minus removals by sinks in 1990 from land-use change (all emissions by sources minus removals by sinks reported in relation to the conversion of forests (deforestation));
   (c) Those parties included in Annex I that have reached an agreement in accordance with article 4 to fulfil their commitments under article 3 jointly shall use the respective emission level allocated to each of the parties in that agreement instead of the percentage inscribed for it in Annex B.
2. Each party included in Annex I with a commitment inscribed in Annex B shall facilitate the calculation of its assigned amount pursuant to article 3, paragraphs 7 and 8, for the commitment period. To this end, each party shall submit a report containing the following information, or references to such information where it has been previously submitted to the Secretariat:
   (a) Complete inventories of anthropogenic emissions by sources and removals by sinks of greenhouse gases not controlled by the Montreal Protocol for all years from 1990, or other approved base year or period

* Contained in document FCCC/CP/2001/MISC.8 of 2 November 2001.
[1] "Article" in these modalities refers to an article of the Kyoto Protocol, unless otherwise specified.

under article 3, paragraph 5, to the most recent year available, prepared in accordance with article 5, paragraph 2, and relevant decisions of the Conference of the Parties serving as the Meeting of the Parties to the Kyoto Protocol (COP/MOP), taking into account any relevant decisions of the Conference of the Parties (COP);

(b) Identification of its selected base year for hydrofluorocarbons, perfluorocarbons, and sulphur hexafluoride in accordance with article 3, paragraph 8;

(c) The agreement under article 4, where the party included in Annex I has reached such an agreement to fulfil its commitments under article 3 jointly with other parties included in Annex I;

(d) Calculation of its assigned amount pursuant to article 3, paragraphs 7 and 8 on the basis of its inventory of anthropogenic emissions by sources and removals by sinks of greenhouse gases not controlled by the Montreal Protocol;

3. After review under article 8 and resolution of any questions of implementation relating to adjustments or assigned amounts pursuant to article 3, paragraphs 7 and 8, the assigned amount pursuant to article 3, paragraphs 7 and 8, of each party included in Annex I shall be recorded in the database for the compilation and accounting of emissions and assigned amounts referred to in paragraph 37.

3bis. Once recorded, the assigned amount shall remain fixed for the commitment period.

II. Accounting for the compliance assessment

A. Accounting of additions to, and subtractions from, assigned amount pursuant to article 3, paragraphs 7 and 8

4. Additions to the assigned amount pursuant to article 3, paragraphs 7 and 8, of a party included in Annex I shall be made for accounting of compliance assessment where:

(a) The party included in Annex I acquires emission reduction units, certified emission reductions or assigned amount units from another party in accordance with article 3, paragraphs 10 and 12, and articles 6, 12 and 17;

(b) The activities of a party included in Annex I under article 3, paragraphs 3 and/or 4, result in a net sink of greenhouse gases, as reported in accordance with article 7, reviewed in accordance with article 8, accounted in accordance with the decision -/CP.7 (land use, land-use change and forestry) and subject to any questions of implementation related to those activities having been resolved;

5. Subtractions from the assigned amount pursuant to article 3, paragraphs 7 and 8, of a party included in Annex I, shall be made for accounting of compliance assessment where:

(a) The party included in Annex I transfers emission reduction units or assigned amount units to another party included in Annex I in accordance with article 3, paragraph 11, and articles 6 and 17;
(b) The activities of a party included in Annex I under article 3, paragraphs 3 and/or 4, result in a net source of greenhouse gas emissions, as reported in accordance with article 7, reviewed in accordance with article 8 and accounted in accordance with the decision -/CP.7 (land use, land-use change and forestry);
(c) The party included in Annex I cancels emission reduction units, certified emission reductions, removal units or assigned amount units so that they may not be used in fulfilment of commitments under article 3, paragraph 1.

B. Retirement amount

6. Each party included in Annex I with a commitment inscribed in Annex B shall retain a retirement amount for each commitment period by retiring assigned amount pursuant to article 3, paragraphs 7 and 8, taking account of additions to, and subtractions from, such assigned amount under paragraphs 4 and 5 above, for the purpose of demonstrating its compliance with its commitment under article 3, paragraph 1. No part of a retirement amount may be subsequently transferred.

C. Compliance assessment

7. The assessment, after the first commitment period and the expiration of the additional period for fulfilling commitments, of the compliance of a party included in Annex I with its commitment under article 3, paragraph 1, shall be based on the comparison of its retirement amount with its aggregate anthropogenic carbon dioxide equivalent emissions of the greenhouse gases, and from the sources, listed in Annex A to the Kyoto Protocol[2] during the first commitment period as reported in accordance with article 7 and reviewed in accordance with article 8, taking into account any adjustments in accordance with article 5, paragraph 2. The aggregate emissions shall include all emissions by sources and removals by sinks of all gases that were taken into account in the calculation of the assigned amount pursuant to article 3, paragraphs 7 and 8, of that party.

[2] Including, for parties included in Annex I for which land-use change and forestry constituted a net source of greenhouse gas emissions in 1990, emissions by sources and removals by sinks from land-use change (all emissions by sources minus removals by sinks reported in relation to the conversion of forests (deforestation)).

D. Additional information for compliance assessment

7bis. Each party included in Annex I with a commitment inscribed in Annex B shall demonstrate its capacity to account for its emissions and compliance assessment. To this end, each party shall submit a report containing the following additional information, or references to such information where it has been previously submitted to the Secretariat:

(a) Calculation of its commitment period reserve in accordance with decision -/CP.7 (emissions trading);
(b) Identification of its selection of minimum values for tree crown cover, land area and tree height for use in accounting for its activities under article 3, paragraph 3, together with a demonstration of the consistency of those values with historical reporting to the Food and Agriculture Organization of the United Nations or other international bodies, and in the case of difference, an explanation of why and how such values were chosen, in accordance with decision -/CP.7 (land use, land-use change and forestry);
(c) Identification of its election of activities under article 3, paragraph 4, for inclusion in its accounting for the first commitment period, together with documentation of the specific land area associated with the activities, in accordance with decision -/CP.7 (land use, land-use change and forestry);
(d) A description of its national system in accordance with article 5, paragraph 1, reported in accordance with paragraphs 20 and 21 of the guidelines for the preparation of the information required under article 7 of the Kyoto Protocol;
(e) A description of its national registry, reported in accordance with paragraph 22 of the guidelines for the preparation of the information required under article 7 of the Kyoto Protocol.

E. Carry-over of assigned amount

8. After expiration of an additional period for fulfilling commitments and where the final compilation and accounting report referred to in paragraph 43 below indicates that the assigned amount of the party included in Annex I pursuant article 3, paragraphs 7 and 8, reduced of assigned amounts units and emission reduction units transferred to another party included in Annex I in accordance with paragraph 5 (a) above or assigned amount units cancelled in accordance with paragraph 5 (c) above, is greater than its anthropogenic carbon dioxide equivalent emissions for that commitment period, the party may carry over this difference, on its request, to the subsequent commitment period, in accordance with article 3, paragraph 13.

8bis. Each party included in Annex I may carry over to next commitment period:

(a) Emission reduction units (ERUs), held by that party up to [x]% of that party's assigned amount pursuant article 3, paragraphs 7 and 8;
(b) Certified emission reductions (CERs), held by that party up to [y]% of that party's assigned amount pursuant article 3, paragraph 7 and 8;

9. Where the Compliance Committee subsequently determines that the party included in Annex I is not in compliance with its commitment under article 3, paragraph 1, in a commitment period, the carry-over of assigned amount to the subsequent commitment period, up to the amount in tones of the excess emissions, shall be revoked.

III. REGISTRY REQUIREMENTS

A. National registries

10. Each party included in Annex I with a commitment inscribed in Annex B shall establish and maintain a national registry to ensure the accurate accounting of the issuance, holding, transfer, acquisition, cancellation and retirement of emission reduction units; certified emission reductions, units resulting from activities under article 3, paragraphs 3 and 4, and assigned amount units, where:
    (a) An "emission reduction unit" or "ERU" is a unit issued pursuant to article 6 and requirements thereunder and is equal to one metric tonne of carbon dioxide equivalent, calculated using global warming potentials defined by decision 2/CP.3 or as subsequently revised in accordance with article 5;
    (b) A "certified emission reduction" or "CER" is a unit issued pursuant to article 12 and requirements thereunder, and is equal to one metric tonne of carbon dioxide equivalent, calculated using global warming potentials defined by decision 2/CP.3 or as subsequently revised in accordance with article 5;
    (c) A "removal unit" or "RMU" is a unit issued pursuant to article 3, paragraphs 3 and/or 4, and requirements thereunder, established in accordance with paragraphs 4(b) above, and is equal to one metric tonne of carbon dioxide equivalent, calculated using global warming potentials defined by decision 2/CP.3 or as subsequently revised in accordance with article 5;
    (d) An "assigned amount unit" or "AAU" is a unit issued pursuant to article 3, paragraphs 7 and 8, and requirements thereunder, established in accordance with paragraphs 1 to 3bis above, and is equal to one metric tonne of carbon dioxide equivalent, calculated using global warming potentials defined by decision 2/CP.3 or as subsequently revised in accordance with article 5.

11. Each party included in Annex I shall designate an organization as its registry administrator to maintain the party's national registry. Any two or more such Parties may voluntarily maintain their respective national registries in a consolidated system, provided that each national registry remains distinct.
12. A national registry shall be in the form of a standardized electronic database which contains, *inter alia*, common data elements relevant to the issuance, holding, transfer, acquisition, cancellation, and retirement of ERUs, CERs, and AAUs and the issuance, holding, cancellation, and retirement of RMUs. The structure and data formats of national registries shall conform to technical standards to be adopted by the COP/MOP for the purpose of ensuring the accurate, transparent and efficient exchange of data between national registries, the clean development mechanism (CDM) registry and the independent transaction log.
13. Each ERU, CER, RMU, and AAU shall be held in only one account in one registry at a given time.
14. Each national registry shall have the following accounts:
    (a) At least one holding account for the party included in Annex I;
    (b) At least one holding account for each legal entity authorized by the party included in Annex I to hold ERUs, CERs, RMUs, and/or AAUs under its responsibility;
    (c) At least one cancellation account for each commitment period for the purposes of:
        (i) Cancelling RMUs and/or AAUs in accordance with paragraph 5 (b);
        (ii) Cancelling ERUs, CERs, RMUs, and/or AAUs in accordance with paragraph 5 (c);
    (d) One retirement account for each commitment period.
15. Each account within a national registry shall have a unique account number comprising the following elements:
    (a) party identifier: the party included in Annex I in whose national registry the account is maintained, identified by means of the two-letter country code defined by ISO 3166;
    (b) A unique number: a number unique to that account for the party included in Annex I in whose national registry the account is maintained.

B. Issuance of ERUs, RMUs, and AAUs

16. Each party included in Annex I with a commitment inscribed in Annex B shall, prior to any transactions taking place for that commitment period, issue its assigned amount pursuant to article 3, paragraphs 7 and 8, calculated in accordance with paragraphs 1 to 3bis above, into its national registry as AAUs.

17. Each AAU shall have a unique serial number comprising the following elements:
    (a) Commitment period: the commitment period for which the AAU is issued;
    (b) party of origin: the party included in Annex I issuing the AAU, identified by means of the two-letter country code defined by ISO 3166;
    (c) Type: an element identifying the unit as an AAU;
    (d) A unique number: a number unique to the AAU for the identified commitment period and party included in Annex I of origin.
18. Each party included in Annex I shall issue, at the end of the commitment period, but before the start of the additional period for fulfilling commitments, RMUs into its national registry as a result of activities under article 3, paragraphs 3 and 4, in accordance with paragraph 4 (b) above.

    18bis. Each party included in Annex I shall ensure that the total quantity of RMUs issued into its registry pursuant to article 3, paragraphs 3 and 4, over the commitment period does not exceed the limits established for that party set out in decision -/CP.7 (land-use, land-use change, and forestry).

    18ter. Each RMU shall have a unique serial number comprising the following elements:
    (a) Commitment period: the commitment period for which the RMU is issued;
    (b) Party of origin: The party included in Annex I issuing the RMU, identified by means of the two-letter country code defined by ISO 3166;
    (c) Type: an element identifying the unit as an RMU;
    (d) A unique number: a number unique to the RMU for the identified commitment period and party included in Annex I of origin.
19. Each party included in Annex I shall issue ERUs into its national registry by converting AAUs previously issued by that party and held in its national registry. An AAU shall be converted into an ERU by adding a project identifier to the serial number and changing the type indicator in the serial number to indicate an ERU. Other elements of the serial number of the AAU shall remain unchanged. The project identifier shall identify the specific article 6 project for which the ERUs are issued, using a number unique to the project for the party of origin. Upon such issuance, the party shall transfer the ERUs to the account or accounts of the project participants and parties included in Annex I specified in their distribution agreement.

    19bis. Each party included in Annex I shall ensure that the total quantity of ERUs resulting from forest management undertaken under article 6 issued into its registry over the commitment period does not exceed the limits established for that party set out in decision -/CP.7 (land-use, land-use change and forestry).

C. Transfer, acquisition, cancellation and retirement of ERUs, CERs, RMUs and AAUs

20. Each party included in Annex I with a commitment inscribed in Annex B may transfer ERUs and AAUs and acquire ERUs, CERs, and AAUs.
21. Each party included in Annex I with a commitment inscribed in Annex B:
    (a) Shall cancel, at the end of the commitment period, but before the start of the additional period for fulfilling commitments RMUs and/or AAUs equivalent to net sources of greenhouse gases from activities under article 3, paragraphs 3 and 4, in accordance with paragraph 5 (b) above, by transferring RMUs and/or AAUs to a cancellation account in its national registry;
    (b) May cancel ERUs, CERs, RMUs, and/or AAUs so they cannot be used in fulfilment of commitments under article 3, paragraph 1, in accordance with paragraph 5 (c) above, by transferring ERUs, CERs, RMUs, and/or AAUs to a cancellation account in its national registry. Legal entities, where authorized by the party included in Annex I, may also perform this function.
22. Each party included in Annex I with a commitment inscribed in Annex B shall retire ERUs, CERs, RMUs, and/or AAUs for the purpose of contributing to its retirement amount to be used in fulfilment of its commitment under article 3, paragraph 1, in accordance with paragraph 6 above, by transferring ERUs, CERs, RMUs, and/or AAUs to the retirement account in its national registry.
23. ERUs, CERs, RMUs, and AAUs transferred to cancellation or retirement accounts may not be further transferred. ERUs, CERs, RMUs, and AAUs transferred to cancellation accounts may not be used for the purpose of demonstrating the compliance of a party included in Annex I with its commitment under article 3, paragraph 1.
24. Each party included in Annex I with a commitment inscribed in Annex B may carry over AAUs, CERs, and ERUs held by that party to the subsequent commitment period, in accordance with paragraph 8 and 8bis above. Each AAU, CER, and ERU carried over in this manner shall maintain its original serial number. AAUs, CERs, and ERUs of a previous commitment period which have not been carried over in this manner as well as RMUs of a previous commitment period shall be cancelled after the end of the additional period for fulfilling commitments.
25. Where the Compliance Committee determines that the party included in Annex I is not in compliance with its commitment under article 3, paragraph 1, for a commitment period, AAUs previously carried over into the subsequent commitment period, equal to the amount in tonnes of excess emissions, shall be transferred to the retirement account of the party and for the commitment period for which such non-compliance was determined, in accordance with paragraph 9 above.

D. Transaction procedures

26. The Secretariat shall establish and maintain an independent transaction log to ensure the validity of transactions, including the issuance, transfer, acquisition, cancellation and retirement of ERUs and AAUs; the issuance, acquisition, cancellation, and retirement of CERs and the issuance, cancellation, and retirement of RMUs. The transaction log shall ensure that each ERU, CER, RMU, and AAU is held in only one account in one registry at a given time.
27. A party included in Annex I shall initiate issuance of an AAU and/or RMU by directing its national registry to issue AAUs and/or RMUs into a specific account within that registry. The executive board of the CDM shall initiate issuance of a CER by directing the CDM registry to issue CERs into its pending account in accordance with the requirements under article 12. A party included in Annex I shall initiate issuance of an ERU by directing its national registry to convert specified AAUs into ERUs within an account of that national registry. Subject to notification by the transaction log that there are no discrepancies pertaining to the issuance, the issuance shall be completed when specific ERUs, CERs, RMUs, or AAUs are recorded in the specified account and, in the case of ERUs, the specified AAUs are removed from the account.
28. A party included in Annex I shall initiate any transfer of ERUs, CERs, RMUs, and/or AAUs, including any transfer to cancellation and retirement accounts, by directing its national registry to transfer specified ERUs, CERs, RMUs, and/or AAUs to a specific account within that registry or to transfer specified ERUs and/or AAUs to a specific account within another registry. The executive board of the CDM shall initiate any transfer of CERs by directing the CDM registry to transfer specified CERs to a specific account within that registry or another registry. Subject to notification by the transaction log that there are no discrepancies pertaining to the transfer, the transfer shall be completed when the specified ERUs, CERs, RMUs, and/or AAUs are removed from the transferring account and are recorded in the acquiring account.
29. Upon the initiation of any issuance, cancellation or retirement of ERUs, CERs, RMUs, and/or AAUs, and transfer of ERUs or AAUs, and prior to the completion of those transactions:
    (a) The initiating registry shall create a unique transaction number comprising: the commitment period for which the transaction is proposed; the party identifier for the party included in Annex I initiating the transaction (using the two-letter country code defined by ISO 3166); and a number unique to that transaction for the commitment period and initiating party;

(b) The initiating registry shall send a record of the proposed transaction to the transaction log or, in the case of transfers to another registry, to the acquiring national registry. The record shall include: the transaction number; the transaction type (issuance, transfer, cancellation, or retirement, further distinguished in accordance with the categories in paragraphs 4 and 5 above); the serial numbers of the relevant ERUs, CERs, RMUs, or AAUs; and the relevant account numbers. In the case of transfers to another registry, the acquiring registry, subject to its acceptance of the proposed transaction, shall send the record to the transaction log;

(c) The transaction log shall, upon receipt of the record, conduct an automated check to ensure that there are no discrepancies with regard to units previously retired or cancelled; duplicated units; units improperly issued; units not carried over from a previous commitment period; the eligibility of parties involved in the transaction to participate in the mechanisms; the eligibility of legal entities involved in the transaction to hold ERUs, CERs, RMUs, or AAUs; and infringements on the commitment period reserve of the party included in Annex I established in the requirements under article 17 and on the maximum value inscribed in the appendix to the decision -/CP.7 (land-use, land-use change, and forestry), regarding forest management activities under article 3.4. Upon completion of the automated check, the transaction log shall notify the initiating and, in the case of transfers to another registry, the acquiring party's registry of the results of the automated check;

(d) If a discrepancy is notified by the transaction log, the initiating registry shall terminate the transaction;

(e) If no discrepancy is notified by the transaction log, the initiating registry and, in the case of transfers to another registry, the acquiring party's registry shall complete or terminate the transaction and send the record and a notification of completion or termination of the transaction to the transaction log. In the case of transfers to another registry, the initiating and acquiring parties' registries shall also send their records and notifications to each other.

30. The transaction log shall record, and make publicly available, all transaction records and the date and time of completion of each transaction, to facilitate its automated checks and the review under article 8.

E. Publicly accessible information

31. Each national registry shall record non-confidential information and provide a publicly accessible user interface through the Internet that allows interested persons to query and view it.

32. The information referred to in paragraph 31 shall include the following account information relevant to the national registry, for each account number:
    (a) Account name: the holder of the account;
    (b) Account type: the type of account (holding, cancellation or retirement);
    (c) Commitment period: the commitment period with which a cancellation or retirement account is associated;
    (d) Representative identifier: the representative of the account holder, using the party identifier (the two-letter country code defined by ISO 3166) and a number unique to that representative within the party's registry;
    (e) Representative name and contact information: the full name, mailing address, telephone number, facsimile number, and email address of the representative of the account holder.
33. The information referred to in paragraph 31 shall include the following article 6 project information, for each project identifier against which the party included in Annex I has issued ERUs:
    (a) Project name: a unique name for the project;
    (b) Project location: the party included in Annex I and town or region in which the project is located;
    (c) Years of ERU issuance: the years in which ERUs have been issued as a result of the article 6 project;
    (d) Reports: downloadable electronic versions of all documentation relating to the project, including proposals, monitoring, verification, and issuance of ERUs, where relevant, subject to confidentiality provisions in decision -/CP.1 (article 6).

    33bis. The information referred to in paragraph 31 shall include the following article 3 paragraphs 3 and 4 activity information, for each activity identifier against which the party included in Annex I has issued RMUs:
    (a) Activity type: type of the activity (afforestation, reforestation, deforestation, forest management, revegetation, cropland management, or grazing land management);
    (b) Activity location: the party included in Annex I and geographical location of the activity;
    (c) Commitment period: commitment period in which RMUs have been issued as a result of the article 3, paragraphs 3 and 4 activities;
    (d) Reports: downloadable electronic versions of all documentation relating to the activity, in accordance with decision -/CP.7 (land-use, land-use change and forestry).
34. The information referred to in paragraph 31 shall include the following holding and transaction information relevant to the national registry, by

serial numbers, for each calendar year (defined according to Greenwich Mean Time):

(a) ERUs, CERs, RMUs, and AAUs in each account at the beginning of the year;
(b) AAUs issued on the basis of assigned amount pursuant to article 3, paragraphs 7 and 8;
(c) In relation to additions:
    (i) ERUs, CERs, and AAUs acquired from other registries and the identity of the transferring accounts and national registries;
    (ii) RMUs issued on the basis of activities under article 3, paragraphs 3 and 4;
(d) In relation to subtractions:
    (i) ERUs and AAUs transferred to other registries and the identity of the acquiring accounts and national registries;
    (ii) RMUs and/or AAUs cancelled on the basis of activities under article 3, paragraphs 3 and 4;
    (iii) Other ERUs, CERs, RMUs, and AAUs cancelled;
(e) ERUs, CERs, RMUs and AAUs retired;
(f) ERUs, CERs, and AAUs carried over from the previous commitment period;
(g) Current holdings of ERUs, CERs, RMUs, and AAUs in each account.

35. The information referred to in paragraph 31 shall include a list of legal entities authorized by the party included in Annex I to hold ERUs, CERs, RMUs, and/or AAUs under its responsibility.

IV. Compilation and accounting of emission inventories and supplementary information under article 7, paragraph 1

A. Report upon expiration of the additional period for fulfilling commitments

36. Upon expiration of an additional period for fulfilling commitments, each party included in Annex I with a commitment inscribed in Annex B shall report, in a standard electronic format:
    (a) The total quantities of the categories of ERUs, CERs, RMUs, and AAUs listed in paragraph 34 (a) to (f), for the current calendar year until the end of the additional period for fulfilling commitments (defined according to Greenwich Mean Time). This information shall only include ERUs, CERs, RMUs, and AAUs valid for the previous commitment period;
    (b) The total quantity of ERUs, CERs, RMUs, and AAUs in its retirement account;

(c) The ERUs, CERs, and AAUs which the party included in Annex I requests to be added to its assigned amount for the subsequent commitment period.

B. Compilation and accounting database

37. The Secretariat shall establish a database to compile and account for emissions and assigned amounts pursuant to article 3, paragraphs 7 and 8, and additions to, and subtractions from, such assigned amount in accordance with paragraphs 4 and 5 above, including cancellations, retirement and carry-overs. A separate account shall be maintained in the database for each party included in Annex I with a commitment inscribed in Annex B for each commitment period.
38. The information on emissions recorded in the database for each party included in Annex I and each commitment period shall include:
    (a) Aggregate anthropogenic annual carbon dioxide equivalent emissions of the greenhouse gases, and from the sectors/source categories, listed in Annex A to the Kyoto Protocol[3] for each year of the commitment period that has been reported in accordance with article 7 and reviewed in accordance with article 8;
    (b) Any adjustments under article 5, paragraph 2, recorded as the difference, in carbon dioxide equivalent terms, between the adjusted estimate and the inventory estimate reported under article 7;
    (c) Aggregate anthropogenic carbon dioxide equivalent emissions in the commitment period, calculated as the sum of the amounts in subparagraphs (a) to (b) above for all years of the commitment period that have been subject to review in accordance with article 8;
    (d) Aggregate anthropogenic carbon dioxide equivalent emissions and removals of the greenhouse gases listed in Annex A to the Kyoto Protocol from activities under article 3, paragraphs 3 and 4, that have been reported in accordance with Article 7 and reviewed in accordance with article 8.
39. Where a party included in Annex I submits recalculated estimates of emissions and removals of greenhouse gases for a year of the commitment period, subject to the review in accordance with article 8, appropriate amendments

[3] Including, for parties included in Annex I for which land-use change and forestry constituted a net source of greenhouse gas emissions in 1990, emissions by sources and removals by sinks from land-use change (all emissions by sources minus removals by sinks reported in relation to the conversion of forests (deforestation)).

shall be made to the information contained in the database including, where relevant, the removal of previously applied adjustments.

40. The information recorded in the database for each party included in Annex I and each commitment period shall include:
    (a) The assigned amount pursuant article 3, paragraphs 7 and 8;
    (b) The supplementary information reported in accordance with article 7, paragraph 1, and reviewed in accordance with article 8, related to ERUs, CERs, RMUs, and AAUs;
    (c) The information reported upon expiration of the additional period for fulfilling commitments in accordance with paragraph 36 and reviewed in accordance with article 8.

C. Compilation and accounting reports

41. The Secretariat shall compile and account information contained in its database on the emission inventories and supplementary information under article 7 paragraph 1 of each party included in Annex I, on an annual basis as well as upon the expiration of an additional period for fulfilling commitments, to assist the COP/MOP and the Compliance Committee in assessing the compliance of each party included in Annex I with its commitment under article 3, paragraph 1.
42. The Secretariat shall publish an annual compilation and accounting report for each party included in Annex I and forward it to the COP/MOP, the Compliance Committee and the party concerned, indicating, *inter alia*, its current retirement amount and aggregate anthropogenic carbon dioxide equivalent emissions for all years of the commitment period that have been subject to review in accordance with article 8.
43. After the commitment period and the additional period for fulfilling commitments, the Secretariat shall publish a final compilation and accounting report for each party included in Annex I and forward it to the COP/MOP, the Compliance Committee and the party concerned, indicating:
    (a) Whether the retirement amount of the party is equivalent to its aggregate anthropogenic carbon dioxide equivalent emissions for the commitment period;
    (b) Where appropriate, the quantity of AAUs of the party which is available to be carried over to the subsequent commitment period;
    (c) Where appropriate, the amount in tones by which the aggregate anthropogenic carbon dioxide equivalent emissions exceed the retirement amount for the commitment period, expressed also as a percentage of the retirement amount.

Submission from Jamaica (On behalf of the Group of 77 and China)*
Possible Elements for Draft Decision on Article 3.9 of the Kyoto Protocol
Proposal by G-77 and China

The Conference of the Parties serving as the Meeting of the Parties to the Kyoto Protocol to the United Nations Framework Convention on Climate Change, at its first session,

Guided by the provisions and principles of the Convention, in particular article 3, paragraph I, which reads as follows: "The Parties should protect the climate system for the benefit of present and future generations of humankind, on the basis of equity and in accordance with their common but differentiated responsibilities and respective capabilities. Accordingly, the developed country Parties should take the lead in combating climate change and the adverse effects thereof,"

Recognizing the fact that the largest share of historical and current global emissions of greenhouse gases has originated in developed countries, that the per capita emissions in developing countries are still relatively low and that the share of global emissions originating in developing countries will grow to meet their social and development needs,

Recalling the Berlin Mandate adopted by decision lICP.l of the Conference of the Parties to the Convention at its first session,

Recalling also article 3, paragraph 2 of the Protocol that each party included in Annex I shall, by 2005, have made demonstrable progress in achieving its commitments under the Protocol,

Gravely concerned that the emissions of greenhouse gases from developed countries are still increasing, far beyond their 1990 levels,

Fully convinced of the need for parties to cooperate in good faith to fully implement the provisions of the Protocol,

Reaffirming that no new commitment shall be introduced under the Protocol for Parties not included in Annex I, as stated in paragraph 2(b) of the Berlin Mandate,

Pursuant to article 3, paragraph 9 of the Protocol,

1. *Decides* to initiate a process to consider further commitments for parties included in Annex I for the periods beyond 2012 through the adoption of amendments to Annex B to the Protocol; and
2. *Decides further* that the process should begin without delay and be conducted in an open-ended ad hoc group of parties to the Protocol hereby established, which will report to the second and third sessions of the Conference of the Parties serving as the Meeting of the Parties to the Protocol on the status of this process. The sessions of this group should be scheduled to ensure completion of the work as early as possible in 2008, with a view to adopting the results

* Contained in document FCCC/KP/CMP/2005/MISC.3 of 30 November 2005.

at the fourth session of the Conference of the Parties serving as the Meeting of the Parties to the Protocol.

Submission by the Group of 77 and China on the Paris Committee on Capacity-Building (PCCB)

The Group of 77 and China (G-77 and China) welcomes the opportunity to submit its views on the annual focus area or theme for the Paris Committee on Capacity-Building for 2017, and on which representatives of the bodies established under the Convention and of the operating entities of the Financial Mechanism should be invited to the first meeting of the Paris Committee on Capacity-Building, for consideration at SBI 45 (November 2016), with a view to the SBI making a recommendation on this matter for consideration and adoption at COP-22, as invited by the SBI. This submission is composed of three parts:

I. Views on the annual focus area or theme for the Paris Committee on Capacity-Building for 2017,
II. Views on representatives of the bodies established under the Convention and the
Operating Entities of the Financial Mechanism to be invited to the first meeting of the Paris Committee on Capacity-Building,
III. Views on the Third Comprehensive Review of the Capacity-Building Framework.

CONTEXT

Under the Paris Agreement (COP-21), countries agreed to enhance capacity-building activities through the Paris Committee on Capacity-Building (PCCB). The PCCB oversees a comprehensive work program for the period 2016–2020, as mentioned in paragraph 74 of decision 1/CP.21, including to the following activities:

(a) Assessing how to increase synergies through cooperation and avoid duplication among existing bodies established under the Convention that implement capacity-building activities, including through collaborating with institutions under and outside the Convention;
(b) Identifying capacity gaps and needs and recommending ways to address them;
(c) Promoting the development and dissemination of tools and methodologies for the implementation of capacity-building;
(d) Fostering international, regional, and bilateral cooperation;
(e) Identifying and collecting good practices, challenges, experiences, and lessons learned from work on capacity-building by bodies established under the Convention;

(f) Exploring how developing country parties can take ownership of building and maintaining capacity over time and space;
(g) Identifying opportunities to strengthen capacity at the national, regional, and subnational level;
(h) Fostering dialogue, coordination, collaboration, and coherence among relevant processes and initiatives under the Convention, including through exchanging information on capacity-building activities and strategies of bodies established under the Convention;
(i) Providing guidance to the Secretariat on the maintenance and further development of the web-based capacity-building portal.

Developing countries aim for strengthening capacity to implement mitigation (and the preparation of their INDCs) and adaptation priorities, as well as the enhancement to access climate finance and technology transfer, and to relevant matters of education, training, and public awareness under a gender and intercultural balance.

The Paris Agreement also recognizes the need of meeting transparency requirements as defined in article 13 of the Paris Agreement, hence the establishment of a Capacity-Building Initiative for Transparency, so countries will aim to:

(a) Strengthen national institutions for transparency-related activities in line with national priorities.
(b) Provide relevant tools, training and assistance for meeting the provisions stipulated in article 13 of the Agreement.
(c) Assist in the improvement of transparency over time.

The post-2020 international climate regime requires that all countries significantly scale up emissions-reduction efforts while simultaneously increasing resilience to climate change impacts. However, it is worth noting that, countries are at different stages of development and levels of capability. For the new international climate agreement to be universally effective, capacity-building must enable developing countries to contribute to global efforts of reducing emissions and adapting to climate change.

I. It is in this context that we believe the annual theme for the Paris Committee on Capacity-Building (PCCB) for the period 2016–2020 should place emphasis on the following capacity needs:
   - *Capacity for the mobilization, use and management of climate finance* from different sources to ensure that the Developing Countries are able to harness and effectively disburse available climate funding.
   - *Capacity to access funds and execute* them in line with national development plans and strategies.
   - *Capacity in assessing vulnerability to climate change for addressing adaptation, planning and implementation* as climate change impacts are already

manifesting themselves in the form of drought, floods and other impacts in Developing Countries and require sound adaptation measures to enhance their resilience.

- *Capacity for addressing loss and damage with regard to planning, management and implementation* where the impacts of climate change will be beyond the capacities of Developing Countries to adapt.
- *Capacity for early warning systems and instrumentation*
- *Capacity to* fully respecting human rights in climate action.
- *Capacity to prepare, update and implement Intended Nationally Determined Contributions (INDCs)/Nationally Determined Contributions (NDCs)* such that the Developing Countries are able to deliver on their obligations under the Paris Agreement.
- *Capacity for Measurement Reporting and Verification and for transparency of action* to ensure that information is communicated in timely manner and the communicated information is line with reporting requirements.
- *Capacity for mitigation actions planning and implementation* in order for Developing Countries to contribute a fair share in the global fight against climate change.
- *Capacity to develop and implement policies, legislations and measures* aimed at building resilience to climate change and to promote low carbon development pathways.
- *Capacities to formulate and implement programmes and plans* on climate change e.g. NAMAs, NAPs, REDD+ programmes, and CDM projects.
- *Capacity to develop policies, legislation, measures and plans that are gender-responsive and consider intercultural participation.*
- *Capacity to* create, articulate and strengthen national and sub-national institutional capacities.
- *Capacity to generate knowledge and information* to make informed decisions on adaptation and mitigation based on science.
- *Capacity for communication, education, and public awareness* on climate change, conservation, and sustainable use of resources to increase the commitment and participation of all stakeholders.
- *Capacity for technology needs assessment and technology transfer* and for the creation of capacity for technology development, considering learning lessons and experiences.

Considering the urge to call up for climate action, the PCCB should prioritize in 2017, the need to develop capacities to create, articulate, and strengthen national and sub-national institutional capacities to enhance the timely implementation of the Paris Agreement and Convention with respect to its principles of equity and CBDRRC.

In accordance with decision 1/CP.21, paragraph 71, the objective of the Paris Committee on Capacity-Building (PCCB) is to address gaps and needs, both current and emerging, in implementing capacity-building in developing country parties and further enhancing capacity-building efforts, including with regard to coherence and coordination in capacity-building activities under the Convention.

II. In line with the objectives of the PCCB, one representative of the following bodies established under the Convention and the Operating Entities of the Financial Mechanism to be invited to the first meeting of the Paris Committee on Capacity-Building:
   - Adaptation Fund Board (AFB) – The Adaptation Fund facilitates capacity-building of countries through development of a readiness programme to assist national and regional implementing entities to strengthen the quality of design and implementation of adaptation projects.
   - Adaptation Committee – The Adaptation Committee can contribute to the work of the PCCB related to the adaptation mandates emanated from Paris.
   - Advisory Board (AB) of the Climate Technology Centre and Network (CTCN) – The (CTCN) stimulates technology cooperation and enhances the development and transfer of technologies.
   - Board of the Green Climate Fund (GCF) – The GCF supports projects, programmes, policies and other activities in developing country parties.
   - Technology Executive Committee (TEC) – The TEC is the policy branch of the technology mechanism; analyses technology policy issues and provides recommendations to support countries in enhancing their climate technology efforts.
   - Council of the Global Environment Facility (GEF) – The GEF has the mandate from COP-21 to set the Capacity-Building Initiative for Transparency and is one of the operating entities of the Financial Mechanism.
   - Standing Committee on Finance (SCF) – Parties decided to establish a Standing Committee on Finance to assist the COP in exercising its functions in relation to the Financial Mechanism of the Convention. This involves organising of forums for communication and continued exchange of information among bodies and entities dealing with climate change finance in order to promote linkages and coherence in the delivery of climate change financing, rationalisation of the financial mechanism, mobilisation of financial resources and measurement, reporting and verification of support provided to developing country parties.

III. The third comprehensive review of the Capacity-Building Framework is an important step to enhance the capacity-building efforts under the Convention and the Kyoto Protocol. For the G-77 and China, it is a continuation of the work done in the first and second comprehensive reviews as contained in decisions 2/CP.10 and 12/CP.17, 15/CMP.7 respectively. It is therefore important that findings of the previous reviews form a basis for the third review. Over and above that, the conclusions, and recommendations of the third comprehensive review, should be used to enhance the terms of reference of the Paris Committee on Capacity-Building (PCCB) in order to pave a way for future decisions to enhance capacity-building activities and institutional arrangements as stipulated in article 11.5 of the Paris Agreement.

Proposal by the G-77 and China for a Technology Mechanism under the UNFCCC

I. Rationale Enhanced mitigation and adaptation under the UNFCCC require an acceleration in the development, deployment, adoption, diffusion, and transfer of environmentally sound technologies among all parties, particularly from Annex II parties to non–Annex I parties, in order to avoid the lock-in effects of nonenvironmentally sound technologies on developing country parties, and to promote their shift to sustainable development paths, thus enhancing the goals of the Convention. There is a critical and urgent need to provide access to technology for adaptation at a regional and national level, enabled by capacity-building and provision of new and additional funding to meet the costs of both integration of adaptation into the development process and stand-alone adaptation activities.

Currently, access to financing is limited, and should be enhanced to deliver technology development, deployment, adoption, diffusion, and transfer to non–Annex I parties. Barriers to technology transfer also inhibit the adoption of environmentally sustainable technologies in non–Annex I parties, highlighting the urgency for access to these technologies while balancing rewards for innovators with the common good of humankind, including jointly developed technology and intellectual property rights (IPR) sharing.

The immediate and urgent delivery of technology development, deployment, diffusion, and transfer to non–Annex I parties requires suitable responses, including a continued emphasis by all parties on the enhancement of enabling environments, facilitating access to technology, and financing that leverages private sector financial resources. Current institutional arrangements are insufficient to deliver immediate and urgent technology development, deployment, diffusion, and transfer to non–Annex I parties.

To address these challenges, this mechanism will build on existing activities within the Convention, including the work of the EGTT, and promote coherence by integrating expanding and ongoing activities related to technology. It will provide a means to enhance delivery on the Convention obligations on technology and related finance and capacity-building.

II. Objective of a Technology Mechanism An enhanced institutional mechanism will address all aspects of cooperation on technology research, development, diffusion, and transfer in accordance with articles 4.1(c), 4.3, 4.5, and other relevant articles of the Convention, in order to enable mitigation and adaptation under the relevant paragraphs of decision 1/CP.13.

Guiding Criteria
The technology mechanism will operate under the authority and guidance of the COP and be accountable to it. It shall aim to achieve:

- Accessibility, affordability, appropriateness, and adaptability of technologies required by developing countries for enhanced action on mitigation and adaptation.
- Provision of full costs and full incremental costs, as per article 4.3 of the Convention.
- Adequacy and predictability of funds for technology transfer.
- Removal of barriers for technology development and transfer.

III. Institutional Arrangements The mechanism comprises an Executive Body and a Multilateral Climate Technology Fund operating under the Conference of the Parties.

A. Executive Body on Technology
An Executive Body on Technology shall be established as a subsidiary body of the Convention in accordance with article 7(2)(i) to enable implementation of the Convention by enhancing action on technology development and transfer to support action on mitigation and adaptation. This subsidiary body shall comprise government representatives, elected by the COP and with balanced regional representation, who are experts on matters related to technology transfer, and be open to input from other experts. The Executive Body would comprise and be supported by:

i. Strategic Planning Committee to develop strategy; provide regular guidance; assess and elaborate technology-related matters; continuously evaluate progress; and develop updates for the Technology Action Plan, as described below, at regular intervals.
ii. Technical Panels to generate and compile current expert information related to capacity-building; policies and measures; intellectual property cooperation; sectoral, cross-sectoral, and cross-cutting cooperation; assessment, monitoring, and compliance; and other necessary topics. The Executive Body may establish additional technical expert committees, panels, or working groups or other bodies to provide scientific, technical, and operational expertise and to consolidate and provide advice to the Executive Body and COP in order to assist it in the performance of its functions. In this context, it shall take fully into account the consideration of regional balance.
iii. Verification Group to verify the financial and technological contributions made to the mechanism in accordance with the overall "measurable, reportable, verifiable" requirement of decision 1/CP.13.
iv. Secretariat to support and facilitate the activities of the Executive Body. The Secretariat will compile and prepare a final report on financial and

technological contributions made and reported by parties to the technology mechanism, in accordance with the overall "measurable, reportable, verifiable" requirement of decision 1/CP.13.

B. Multilateral Climate Technology Fund (MCTF)
This fund will provide technology-related financial requirements as determined by the Executive Body. The fund will operate under the COP as part of the enhanced multilateral financial mechanism described in the relevant G-77 and China proposal.

- The MCTF shall be financed by assessed contributions from Annex II parties. Contributions to the mechanism shall be additional to other financial transfers to non–Annex I parties and shall meet the costs incurred by such parties.
- An agreed proportion of contributions by developed country parties and other parties included in Annex II of the Convention to bilateral and regional co-operation may be considered as contributions to the MCTF, provided that such co-operation is consistent with the policies and scope of the mechanism.
- Financial transfers to the MCTF shall be counted as measurable, reportable, and verifiable commitments under paragraph 1.b(ii) of the Bali Action Plan. Any funding not under the authority and guidance of the UNFCCC shall not be regarded as the fulfilment of commitments by developed countries under article 4.3 of the Convention or decision 1/CP.13.
- The MCTF shall cover, *inter alia*, eligible costs of activities approved by the Executive Body; administrative costs of the Executive Body, Secretariat, and Trustee or Trustees; and costs associated with other specific decisions of the Conference of the Parties.
- In the context of the enhanced multilateral financial mechanism proposed by the Group of 77 and China, the MCTF shall be managed by a Trustee or Trustees, selected through a process of open bidding, who shall have fiduciary responsibility and administrative competence to manage the MCTF, and shall hold in trust, the funds, assets, and receipts that constitute the fund, and shall comply with the principles and modalities for their management and disbursement as stipulated by the Conference of the Parties.

V. Technology Action Plan A Technology Action Plan shall serve as a starting point for the work of the Executive Body. It will include clear actions and dates for the first three years and will be updated for successive three-year periods. To realize the full potential of technology, the Action Plan shall support all stages of the technology cycle, including:

- Research. The Action Plan will accelerate research and invention through scientific and technical cooperation at all levels, including that of scientists and institutions.
- Development. The Action Plan will accelerate the rate at which technologies are developed and brought into effect.

- Transfer and diffusion. The Action Plan will ensure financing for technology transfer (including all available means to ensure the affordability of technologies, products, and related services).

The Technology Action Plan will define specific policies, actions, and funding requirements for all relevant technologies under the following classifications:

- Public domain technologies. The Action Plan will identify needs and establish an international cooperation system to ensure lowest cost options, as well as transferring know-how to use and maintain the technologies and adapt them to local conditions, including endogenous technologies.
- Patented technologies. The Action Plan will ensure that privately owned technologies are available on an affordable basis including through measures to resolve the barriers posed by intellectual property rights and addressing compulsory licensing of patented technologies. Technologies with shared ownership (government and private) will be made available on an affordable basis by facilitating transfer of the government proportion on a reduced or no-cost basis. Technologies that are government owned will be made available on an affordable basis by facilitating transfer at reduced or no-cost basis.
- Future technologies. The Action Plan will support the establishment of national and regional technology excellence centres and will reinforce North-South, South-South, and triangular cooperation, including joint research and development.

VI. Eligible Activities The mechanism will cover technologies in all relevant sectors and endeavour to remove barriers to effective technology development, deployment, diffusion, and transfer. It will articulate with the overarching financial mechanism of the Convention to secure necessary financing. The following list of activities and costs eligible for support by the mechanism is indicative and may be modified by the COP at any time.

Activities eligible for support from the mechanism include, *inter alia*:

- Promotion, facilitation, and implementation of activities along the entire technology cycle to enable the accelerated adoption of ESTs.
- Support for research, development, manufacture, commercialization, deployment, and diffusion of technologies for adaptation and mitigation in accordance with decision 1/CP.13.
- Adaptation technologies to address the adverse effects of climate change and finance the removal of barriers to the large-scale transfer of technologies for adaptation.
- Technologies to address the adverse impact of response measures, and finance the removal of barriers to the large-scale transfer of technologies for reducing the adverse impact of response measures.

- Capacity-building to manage and generate technological change, enhance absorptive capacity, create enabling conditions in developing countries, *inter alia*, costs of:
  - Research, development, and demonstration of new technologies.
  - Enhancing human and institutional capacity.
  - Guarantees on foreign direct investment for environmentally sound technologies.
- Commercialization of new and emerging technologies, *inter alia*:
  - Venture capital, with public investment leveraging private capital markets for emerging technologies.
  - Research, development, and demonstration of new technologies, financed by venture capital and other sources.
  - Joint technology development.
- Creation of manufacturing facilities for EST, including low-GHG emission technologies, *inter alia*, costs of:
  - Compulsory licensing, cost associated with patents, designs, and royalties.
  - Conversion of existing manufacturing facilities or of establishing new facilities.
  - Research and development activities, including joint research, development, design, and demonstration.
  - Technology adaptation.
  - Retraining and dissemination of know-how.
  - Operation; and
  - Monitoring and verification.
- Procurement of low-GHG emission technologies, including software and hardware, *inter alia*:
  - Cost of premature modification or of replacement of existing equipment, as well as the cost of new equipment.
  - Cost of retraining and dissemination of know-how.
  - Cost of technical assistance for the design, installation, and stable operation of the technology.
  - Cost of fuel and other operational costs.
  - Cost of technologies for fuel switching.
  - Cost of monitoring and verification.

G-77 and China Proposal Financial Mechanism for Meeting Financial Commitments under the Convention

Objective

The G-77 and China proposes the operationalisation of an effective financial mechanism under the COP. This mechanism is to ensure the full, effective, and sustained implementation of the Convention, in relation to implementation of commitments for the provision of financial resources. This is mandated under articles 4.3, 4.4, 4.5, 4.8, and 4.9 of the Convention in accordance with article 11 defining the financial mechanism.

Principles

The following are principles for enhanced action on the provision of financial resources and investment to support action on mitigation and adaptation and technology development and transfer.

The mechanism shall:

1. Be underpinned by the principle of equity and common but differentiated responsibilities
2. Operate under the authority and guidance, and be fully accountable, to the COP.
3. Have an equitable and geographically balanced representation of all parties within a transparent and efficient system of governance (article 11.2);
4. Enable direct access to funding by the recipients; and
5. Ensure recipient country involvement during the stages of identification, definition, and implementation, rendering it truly demand driven.

The goal is to bring about coherence in the global financial architecture for financing under the authority and governance of the COP.

Elements

Elements for enhanced financial resources provided under the Convention include the following:

Aims

1. The mechanism will recognise, promote, and strengthen the significance of engagement at the country level, in order to give effect to the principles of a country-driven approach, and direct access to funding and enable the implementation of this.
2. The mechanisms should enable a shift from a project-based approach when dealing with proposals for funding, to a programmatic approach, where appropriate, in order to make optimal use of the full range of means of implementation available and to allow for implementation at scale.
3. The mechanism would facilitate linkages between the various funding sources and separate funds in order to promote access to the variety of available funding sources and reduce fragmentation.
4. The mechanism would maintain consistency with the policies, programme priorities, and eligibility criteria adopted by the decisions of the COP and

all "activities (including those related to funding) relevant to climate change undertaken outside the framework of the financial mechanism" consistent with decision 11/CP.1, op. paragraph 2(a).

Sources of Funding

5. The main source of funding will be through the implementation of commitments under article 4.3. The funding will be "new and additional" financial resources, which is over and above ODA. The major source of funds would be the public sector.
6. Any funding pledged outside of the UNFCCC shall not be regarded as the fulfilment of commitments by developed countries under article 4.3 of the Convention, and their commitments for measurable, reportable, and verifiable means of implementation, that is, finance, technology, and capacity-building, in terms of paragraph 1.b (ii) of the Bali Action Plan.
7. It should be ensured that there be predictability, stability, and timeliness of funding.
8. The resources shall be essentially grant-based (particularly for adaptation), without prejudice to certain concessional loan arrangements in appropriate form, to meet the needs of a specific programme.
9. The level of the new funding can be set at 0.5% to 1% of the GNP of Annex I Parties. Quantified commitments by developed countries to adequate and predictable funding for mitigation and adaptation must be addressed. The portion of funding that must be allocated to adaptation and mitigation and their respective means of implementation shall be decided by the Board and periodically reviewed, taking especially into account the historical imbalances in and the urgency of funding for adaptation.

Activities to be funded

10. The mechanism will fund the agreed full incremental costs for the implementation of developing countries' commitments under article 4.1, including:
    a) Mitigation
    b) Deployment and diffusion of low-carbon technologies
    c) Research and development for technologies
    d) Capacity-building
    e) Preparations of national action plans and implementation
    f) Patents
    g) Adaptation in accordance with articles 4.4 and 4.9
11. The mechanism will fund the agreed full costs for the preparations of national communications.
12. In accordance with article 4.3, developing country Parties are to be provided with new and additional financial resources, including for the transfer

of technology, to comply with their obligations under article 4.1 of the Convention. The funds can be used for (i) adaptation and its means of implementation; and (ii) mitigation and its means of implementation. Meeting these two funding objectives may include technology development, deployment and transfer, capacity-building, and risk management, including insurance, etc. It will cover financing the implementation of action programmes developed under the Convention, such as the NAPAs and TNAs.

Design and Structure

1. The COP is the supreme decision-making body of the Convention, under whose authority and guidance the mechanism will operate. The COP shall decide on the policies, programme priorities, and eligibility criteria.
2. The COP will appoint a Board, which shall have an equitable and balanced representation of all parties within a transparent and efficient system of governance. The Board shall be assisted by a Secretariat of professional staff contracted by the Board.
3. The COP and Board shall establish specialized funds, and funding windows under its governance, and a mechanism to link various funds.
4. Funds would be administered by a Trustee or Trustees selected through a process of open bidding.
5. Each of the separate funds may be advised by an expert group or committee, which could also be supported by a technical panel or panels addressing specific issues addressed by the fund.
6. To ensure transparent and efficient governance, other possible components of the structure include a consultative/advisory group of all relevant stakeholders, and an independent assessment panel.
7. Modalities for the determination of the role of existing funds and entity/ies for the operation of the financial mechanism will have to be worked out.

Proposal by the G-77 and China on a Draft Decision on Agenda Item 3 of COP (Forum and Work Programme on the Impact of the Implementation of Response Measures), Warsaw, 19th Conference of the Parties

The Conference of the Parties,

Recalling decisions 5/CP.7, 1/CP.10, 1/CP.13, 1/CP.16, 2/CP.17, 8/CP.17, 1/CP.18, and 31/CMP.1, the objective, principles, and provisions of the Convention, in particular article 3, paragraphs 1 and 5, and article 4, paragraphs 1(g) and (h), 8, 9, and 10, of the Convention, and article 2, paragraph 3, and article 3, paragraph 14, of the Kyoto Protocol,

Reaffirming that economic and social development and poverty eradication are the first and overriding priorities of developing countries, and that developing country parties face economic and social consequences of response measures to climate change

Stressing the need for an effective mechanism for enhanced action to address the social and economic consequences of the implementation of response measures,

Acknowledging that the objective of enhanced action to deal with the social and economic consequences of the implementation of response measures is to address the negative social and economic consequences of response measures taken by developed country parties on developing country parties,

Affirming that parties should cooperate fully to enhance understanding of the economic and social consequences of response measures, and further reaffirming the need to consider how existing channels, such as national communications and biennial reports by developed country parties, could be improved, and built upon,

Recalling the constructive discussions that took place during the meetings under the work programme on the impact of the implementation of response measures held in conjunction with the thirty-sixth, thirty-seventh, thirty-eighth, and thirty-ninth sessions of the subsidiary bodies

Acknowledging that the work of the forum on the impact of the implementation of response measures has provided opportunities to engage in in-forum workshops, an expert meeting, and valuable initial discussions by parties, in order to improve the understanding of the impact of the implementation of response measures in the areas of the work programme referred to in decision 8/CP.17, paragraph 1.

Noting that the review pursuant to decision 8/CP.17, paragraph 5, indicates that it is important to improve the need for a more focused consideration of the effectiveness of the process and the substantive consideration of the issues,

Recognizing the need to focus future work under the forum on the impact of the implementation of response measures on expert input, the provision of concrete examples, case studies and practices, in order to enhance the capacity of developing country parties to deal with the negative impacts of the implementation of response measures,

Welcoming the progress made in the work of the forum on the impact of the implementation of response measures convened under the Subsidiary Body for Implementation and the Subsidiary Body for Scientific and Technological Advice, and recognizing the need for parties to continue to participate in the forum, including the sharing of views on policy issues of concern, such as unilateral measures,

Recognizing the need to give full consideration to what actions are necessary under the Convention, including actions related to funding, insurance, and the transfer of technology, to meet the specific needs and concerns of developing country parties arising from the impact of the implementation of response measures,

Affirming that there are still gaps in implementation related to how developed country parties are implementing their policies and measures to respond to climate change in such a way as to avoid negative social and economic consequences for developing country parties and that there is a need for further work, building on the forum on the impact of the implementation of response measures and its work programme,

1. *Decides* to hereby continue the forum on the impact of the implementation of response measures in order for it to provide a platform allowing parties to share, in an interactive manner, information, experiences, case studies, best practices, and views.
2. *Decides* that the forum shall be convened by the Chairs of the subsidiary bodies to implement the work programme included in the Annex A and meet twice a year in conjunction with the sessions of the subsidiary bodies.
3. *Reiterates* that the forum will be convened under a joint agenda item of the subsidiary bodies and will operate in accordance with the procedures applicable to contact groups.
4. Requests the subsidiary bodies to review, at their forty-third sessions (December 2015), the work of the forum, with a view to providing recommendations to the Conference of the Parties at its twenty-first session.
5. *Adopts* the modalities for the operationalization of the work programme on the impact of the implementation of response measures, which could include, as appropriate and subject to the availability of financial resources, convening workshops and meetings, receiving inputs from experts, practitioners, and relevant organizations, and preparing reports and technical papers.
6. *Requests* participants in the forum to focus on enhancing understanding and building the capacity of developing countries to deal with the negative economic and social consequences of response measures on those countries through the provision of support and discussion of concrete examples, case studies, and practices.
7. *Decides* to establish a Mechanism for Enhanced Action on Response Measures under the Conference of the Parties to facilitate implementation of enhanced action to address the negative social and economic consequences of response measures taken by developed country parties on developing country parties and to recommend specific actions, including in terms of support to developing countries, to avoid and minimize those consequences, and to deliver the functions as included in Annex B.
8. *Decides* that the forum will report to the mechanism and that the mechanism will make recommendations and report to the Conference of the Parties annually on its work with a view for adopting relevant decisions.
9. *Further decides* that the mechanism will report to the Conference of the Parties on its review of its work, including functions and further actions that may be required, starting in COP-24 and every five years thereafter, with a view to provide recommendations and adopt relevant decisions.
10. *Decides* that the mechanism will meet for the first time in the first quarter of 2015.

11. *Decides* that the mechanism will engage and develop linkages and synergies with relevant work programmes, bodies, and institutions under the Convention.
12. *Further decides* that the mechanism will collaborate with relevant intergovernmental, regional, national, and subnational level institutions, organizations, networks and centres.
13. *Requests* parties to undertake the necessary arrangements at the fortieth sessions of the Subsidiary Bodies (June 2014) for the development of the terms of reference and the modalities of operationalization of the mechanism with the view to providing recommendations to the Conference of the Parties.

Annex A: Elements to be included in the new work programme of the forum

- Dialogue on assessment and analysis of adverse impacts of response measures, including unilateral ones, in terms of their consequences for, *inter alia*, employment, income, economic growth rates and living standards in developing countries; and explore ways to minimize adverse impacts of response measures
- Ways to strengthen multilateral cooperation, in opposition to unilateral measures
- Overview of progress on activities to address adverse economic and social consequences of response measures on developing countries made at various levels, including bilateral, regional and multilateral.
- Economic diversification and resilience-building in developing country parties, to deal with the adverse impacts of response measures.
- Exchange of views on just transition and creation of decent work, in accordance with nationally defined development priorities and strategies.
- Dialogue on how developed countries report on actions and impacts related to the implementation of response measures, in such a way as to minimize adverse impacts.

Annex B: Functions of the mechanism (to be further elaborated in TORs)

- Development of methodologies and tools for the assessment and analysis of adverse impacts of response measures, including unilateral ones, in terms of their consequences for, *inter alia*, employment, income, economic growth rates, and living standards in developing countries; and explore ways to minimize adverse impacts of response measures.
- Provision of specific support by developed country parties to developing country parties in terms of transfer of technology, financial resources, and capacity-building, in order for the latter to be able to deal with the adverse economic and social effects of response measures.

- Capacity-building and support for developing countries for economic diversification and resilience-building to deal with the adverse impacts of response measures.
- Capacity-building and assessments on ways to ensuring a just transition and creation of decent work, in accordance with nationally defined priorities.
- Capacity-building related to economic modelling, studies, methodology development, scenario-setting, and technology transfer to assist developing country parties in addressing the negative economic and social consequences of response measures.
- Development of specific guidelines for developed countries on how to report on actions and impacts related to the implementation of response measures, in such a way as to minimize adverse impacts.
- Cooperation at various levels, including at bilateral level, with regional and multilateral organizations, experts and institutions, to address adverse economic and social consequences of response measures on developing countries.
- Secretariat to develop a structured and user-friendly repository of information on response measures.

Input from the G-77 and China in preparation for COP-19 on loss and damage associated with climate change impacts in developing countries that are particularly vulnerable to the adverse effects of climate change

1. The G-77 and China takes this opportunity to present views in preparation for COP-19 for achieving the mandate set out in 3/CP18.
2. Climate change and related loss and damage is happening now—at different scales on the national, regional, and international levels, that will require additional resources. At the heart of the challenge of loss and damage is comprehensively addressing the needs and aspirations of communities and people, who have contributed least to the causes of climate change yet are among its first and worst victims. The urgency and importance of responding to these challenges are beyond dispute and requires real action. We call for an approach that considers needs to address loss and damage in order to develop the functions and modalities of the international mechanism.
3. The recent IPCC AR5 SPM points to irreversible negative consequences for physical and social systems that will set back or reverse human welfare. Addressing loss and damage will require diverse of tools to manage climate risks, and entirely new approaches at different and greater scales. The scientific certainty of the IPCC AR5 SPM bolsters the need for a systematic response to address loss and damage and to soften the consequences of loss and damage from the adverse impacts of climate change on socioeconomic development and ecosystems.

4. The G-77 and China reiterates that the COP "invited Parties, taking into account common but differentiated responsibilities and respective capabilities and specific national and regional development priorities, objectives and circumstances, to enhance action on addressing loss and damage associated with the adverse effects of climate change, taking into account national development processes." Carrying out such actions requires the provision of adequate support and creating the appropriate mechanism and calling for meaningful activities. In this context, the Group reiterates the "request (to) developed country Parties to provide developing country Parties with finance, technology, and capacity-building, in accordance with decision 1/CP.16 and other relevant decisions of the Conference of the Parties." There are clear gaps in multiple areas, particularly in the area of slow onset events. Filling the knowledge gaps requires guidance and oversight from the UNFCCC, even though the expertise may exist outside the Convention. However, it is also not possible to wait for all knowledge gaps to be addressed before acting, including under the Convention.
5. Leadership from the UNFCCC is critical, and the UNFCCC is the primary international, intergovernmental forum for negotiating the global response to climate change. The frequency of occurrence and magnitude of climate change-related events and their resulting impacts cannot be predicted. Therefore, there are limits to adaptation planning and the mainstreaming of adaptation concerns. As the policy-relevant forum for climate change, the UNFCCC must take a leading role in managing the problem of loss and damage and signalling to other bodies what assistance is required.
6. At COP-18, we decided to establish, at COP-19, institutional arrangements, such as an international mechanism, to address loss and damage associated with the impacts of climate change, and fulfilling this mandate is key for the success of Warsaw. The G-77 and China has been calling for the establishment of an international mechanism, under the Convention, on loss and damage that addresses the needs of developing countries as a result of extreme and slow-onset events, and the urgency for this mechanism has only increased. This mechanism cannot be an empty shell and addressing loss and damage under the Convention cannot be done through talk-shops, in the form of forums, platforms, or any other similar arrangements that does not clearly support implementation on the ground. The mechanism has to ensure enhanced action on addressing loss and damage associated with the adverse effects of climate change through the provision of new, predictable, and reliable financial support for the assessment of, and responses to, loss and damage through an appropriate financial mechanism.
7. The G-77 and China reiterates its call for international mechanism to address loss and damage associated with the adverse effects of climate change from

extreme and slow onset events by developing country parties, especially the least developed countries and Small Island Developing States and other developing countries particularly vulnerable to the adverse effects of climate change by, *inter alia*:

- provide global oversight and coordination on the assessment and implementation of actions related to loss and damage associated with the adverse effects of climate change.
- promote cooperation, linkages, and enhanced action to address loss and damage, and strengthen engagement between national, regional, and international organizations, centres, and networks involved in assessing and addressing loss and damage.
- develop and, as appropriate, strengthen the knowledge base at multiple levels on loss and damage to the adverse effects of climate change, including on slow onset events, non-economic losses, migration, and displacement.
- develop innovative measures, approaches, and modalities to assess and address permanent losses and irreversible damage, including non-economic losses.
- enhance action to address loss and damage associated with the adverse effects of climate change through provision of technical support and guidance to national governments on comprehensive approaches to risk assessment and risk management for extreme and slow onset events, including socioeconomic and non-economic impacts.
- support for the efficient development and operationalization of approaches, at all levels, to address loss and damage from extreme weather events and slow onset events.
- support the establishment of social safety net and social protection programmes to address damage to or loss of livelihoods associated with the adverse effects of climate change.
- support the development and ensure that a spectrum of risk transfer tools is available to parties and regional bodies, including insurance, to address loss and damage associated with the adverse effects of climate change.

8. Further, the G-77 and China believes that the SBI work programme on loss and damage should continue contributing to the systematic work under the Convention on loss and damage including, *inter alia*, assessing the risk of loss and damage associated with the adverse effects of climate change and the current knowledge on the same; exploring a range of approaches to address loss and damage associated with the adverse effects of climate change, including impacts related to extreme weather events and slow onset events, taking into consideration experience at all levels; and on the role of the Convention in enhancing the implementation of approaches to address loss and damage associated with the adverse effects of climate change.

9. The G-77 and China is committed to work constructively and expediently to achieve the mandate set for Warsaw to strengthen the actions undertaken under the Convention to address loss and damage associated with climate change impacts in developing countries.

Conference Room Paper submission by the G-77 and China

The submission by G-77 and China provides its views on the agenda item in accordance with decision 1/CP.21 paragraph 57 and on paragraph 7 of article 9 on the Paris Agreement,

These views are presented as a CRP, as the outcome of the work related to the development of modalities for the accounting of financial resources provided and mobilized through public interventions in accordance with article 9, paragraph 7 of the Paris Agreement, which stipulates that developed country parties shall provide transparent and consistent information on support for developing country parties provided and mobilized through public interventions biennially.

The G-77 and China highlights the importance of this transparent and consistent information as crucial in the work related to the accounting and fulfilment of the financial commitments of developed countries and the provision of support for the implementation of the Paris Agreement, in relation to articles 2, 3, 4.5, 7.13, 8, 9, 10, 11, and 13.

The Group of G-77 and China notes that discussions related to paragraph 7, article 9 of the Paris Agreement have taken current reports as the basis for deliberations and for the development of the modalities mandated by paragraph 57 or decision 1/CP.21 and that an informal note has been developed in the context of this work. This submission takes current work into consideration.

It is crucial to remember that the Paris Agreement recognizes a need to support developing country parties for its effective implementation, which clearly implies that without such support, the Agreement cannot be implemented fully and effectively, and it also recognizes that support shall be provided to developing country parties for the implementation of articles 2, 4, 7, 8, 10, 11, and 13. It is also important to state that the modalities that paragraph 57 has mandated are to be based on current arrangements.

SBSTA should strive for a combination of a top-down and bottom-up approach when adopting modalities for which finance flows count towards the financial commitments under articles 9.1 and 9.3.

While parties are requested to report on their methodologies, assumptions and definitions used, the aim is to reach a level of standardisation over time.

The SBSTA accounting modalities should adopt some overarching parameters/principles for establishing climate relevance.

In addition, the SBSTA/CMA could consider to use the reporting on methodologies, definitions, and assumptions used to inform an assessment by a technical body and recommendations for standardisation over time.

Draft Decision The Conference of the Parties serving as the Meeting of the Parties to the Paris Agreement Based on the Mandate Contained in Decision 1/CP.21, paragraph 57, Recalling Articles 4 and 11 of the Convention.

Further recalling articles 2, 3, 4, 7, 9, 8, 10, 11, 13 of the Paris Agreement

1. *Endorses* the modalities for the accounting of financial resources provided and mobilized through public interventions in accordance with article 9, paragraph 7, applicable to the information to be reported under article 13 of the Paris Agreement, as included in Annex I to this decision,
2. *Decides* that these modalities shall be applicable as of the first report of developed country parties under the transparency framework.
3. *Encourages* other parties that provide support to implement these modalities when voluntarily reporting such support, if applicable and to the extent possible.

Annex I:

Modalities for the accounting of financial resources provided and mobilized through public interventions in accordance with article 9, paragraph 7 of the Paris Agreement
The modalities that follow build on existing reporting guidelines for developed country parties, including those specified in decision 2/CP.17 and decision 9/CP.21.

1. The following modalities apply to the information that developed country parties shall provide under the transparency framework to enhance understanding, transparency, accuracy, consistency, comparability, and completeness of the information reported, as well as definitions and methodologies used.
2. Developed country parties shall report biennially information on year, currency, status, funding source, financial instrument, type of support, sector, channel, and amount for all categories of support provided.

Cross-cutting considerations

x. In providing information in accordance with article 9, paragraph 7, the following cross-cutting elements shall be reported:

Table 1 Reporting Parameters and Guidance for Reporting on Support Provided

	Parameter	Guidance for reporting
Minimum reporting parameters (based in current system)	Year	Parties shall provide biennial information on annual contributions without overlapping with the previous reporting periods. Methodologies for calculation of annualized information shall be included. In case projects' implementations span for a period longer than the period of reporting, only the disbursements done during the reporting period should be reflected.
	Currency (USD)	Parties shall provide an explanation on methodology used for currency exchange rate in the documentation box. Domestic currency reporting is optional.
	Status	Parties shall explain, in their biennial reports, definitions and methodologies used to specify the funds as committed, provided, and disbursed.
	Funding Source	Parties shall specify the definition and methodologies used to classify the funding source as ODA, OOF, or other. Funding sources shall include definitions, methodologies, and assumptions for accounting climate finance.
	Financial instrument	Parties shall report the definitions of instruments used. Parties shall provide definitions and methodologies for reporting grant equivalent, net value, face value.
	Type of support	Parties shall specify the definition and methodology to classify the type of support understood as mitigation finance, adaptation finance, loss and damage, and cross-cutting. There shall be a description of how support has been targeted at NDCs/NAPs countries needs incl. for loss and damage and how it has facilitated the implementation of the Paris Agreement.
	Sector	Parties shall describe the methodology and definitions used to identify sectors and subsectors reported.

Table 1 Continued

	Parameter	Guidance for reporting
	Amount	Parties shall report both face value and grant – equivalent value. Only the grant-equivalent value shall be counted towards resources provided and mobilised in accordance with Art. 9.1 and 9.3.
	Climate-specific	Only climate-relevant flows shall be counted as climate finance towards
		resources provided and mobilised in accordance with Art. 9.1 and 9.3. The following general parameters shall be applied to determine climate-relevance of flows: 1) Alignment with Art. 2.1c. Consideration of a negative list of activities that are not aligned with Art. 2.1c 2) Mitigation parameters 3) Adaptation parameters In addition, Parties shall explain in their biennial communication the definitions and methodologies to determine climate specificity/relevance and detail any changes made overtime.
	New and additional	Parties shall provide information on how support provided is new and additional and how it represents a progression between previous levels. Only financial resources consistent with a pathway towards low greenhouse gas emissions and climate resilient development are reported and counted, consistent with Art. 2.1 (c) of the Paris Agreement. Information on progress on the fulfilment of the finance goals.
Additional reporting parameters applicable to finance provided through bilateral,	Recipient country/ region/project/ programme/activity	Parties shall report information on recipient country and region. Parties shall provide information on project and

(*continued*)

Table 1 Continued

	Parameter	**Guidance for reporting**
regional and other channels		activity level, to the extent possible, to improve the level of granularity. Parties shall provide information on implementing agency, including percentage of funding channelled through executing agencies and implementers and suppliers of the developed country party. There shall be a mutual agreement/ cross-checking with recipients before submitting information. Parties shall provide information on how resources effectively address the needs and priorities of developing countries are linked to the implementation of the Paris Agreement. In case a project involves more than one country, clear information should be presented on the amount of funding disbursed per each beneficiary country.
	Capacity-building and technology transfer component	Parties shall report information on activities with capacity-building and technology transfer components to facilitate better tracking and avoid double counting according to build options.
	Provision of information on transaction and overhead costs, loan repayments, and return on investments	Parties shall provide information on transaction and overhead costs, loan repayments (grant-equivalent), and return on investments. Parties shall provide information on terms of conditions of loans provided.
	Link to mobilized resources	Party shall provide information on whether the activity mobilized additional financial support from a private source (potential link with Table 4).

Table 1 Continued

	Parameter	Guidance for reporting
Climate finance provided through multilateral channels	Multilateral climate change funds, as well as other climate change funds; multilateral financial institutions, including regional development banks; and specialized United Nations bodies	
	Core/General	Description of definition, methodology, and assumption used to assess the core/general contribution and description of which proportion or share of these are considered and reported as climate financing, including parameters and methodologies. Loan repayments done by recipient countries during the period of reporting should be reported to identify the net finance provided. (Potentially report % of core contribution that climate specific represents.) Provision of information on bilateral funds provided through multilateral channels.
	Outflows	Parties shall provide information to improve the understanding on the outflow of finance from multilateral channels to developing country Parties, including methodologies, information from financial institutions by financial instrument and recipient. Criteria used by Parties and international financial institutions to identify contributions and outflows as being climate specific.

Table 2 Reporting Parameters and Guidance for Reporting on Support Mobilized through Public Interventions

Parameter	Information
Type of public intervention used to mobilize the support reported (grant, concessional loan, non-concessional loan, equity, policy intervention, capacity-building, technology transfer, technical assistance)	Parties shall provide information on methodologies and assumptions used to define climate finance mobilized through public interventions. Leveraging factor to per type of public intervention reported
Amount of resources used to mobilize the support	Parties shall report methodologies and assumptions to calculate the amount of resources used to mobilize the support.
Information on boundaries for tracking mobilized finance through public interventions	Parties shall provide in their definition of climate finance mobilized through public interventions information on the methodologies and assumptions used to establish causality between a public intervention and mobilized finance. Provide evidence for causality.
Amount of climate-specific private resources mobilized	
Recipient country share of mobilization	
Criteria to avoid double counting	Parties shall provide information on methodology used to avoid double counting among multiple actors involved in the mobilization of support.
Good practice and public policies/regulatory framework	Parties shall provide qualitative information such as good practices on public policy and regulatory frameworks to incentivize further private climate financing and investments.
Additional information	Parties may provide additional information.

a) Information on how the resources used through emission trading schemes with developing countries were not counted as support provided or mobilized.

b) When applicable, official documentation on the status of funds.

y. There shall be a mutual agreement/cross-checking with recipients before submitting information.

z. A common tabular reporting format shall be developed to facilitate the accounting of financial resources provided and mobilized through public interventions in accordance with article 9, paragraph 7 of the Paris Agreement.

The Group of 77 and China
15 June 2011
Draft Decision on the Standing Committee of the Financial Mechanism of the Convention
The Conference of the Parties at Its Seventeenth Session,

Recalling articles 4 and 11 of the Convention,

Also recalling article 7 of the Convention, in particular 7.2 (h) and (i),

Pursuant to the Bali Action Plan (decision 1/CP.13), which recognizes the need for enhanced action on the provision of financial resources and investment to support action on mitigation and adaptation and technology cooperation,

Having established the Standing Committee under the Conference of the Parties as provided for in paragraph 112 of decision 1/CP.16,

Reiterating the need for enhanced *and urgent* action on the provision of financing resources and investment to support action on mitigation, adaptation, and technology cooperation to developing country parties,

ON ROLES AND FUNCTIONS

1. *Reaffirms* that the Standing Committee is established under the Conference of the Parties to assist the Conference of the Parties in exercising its functions with respect to the financial mechanism of the Convention in terms of:
   a) improving coherence and coordination in the delivery of climate change financing, including through, *inter alia*:
      (i) the development of recommendations to the COP for the coordination of all current and future funds under the Convention to ensure coherence in the delivery of climate change finance.
      (ii) the provision of a forum for the exchange of information with relevant financial institutions, bilateral aid agencies, and UN agencies dealing with climate change financing, as well as the provision of assistance to the COP in analysing relevant information to ensure coherence and coordination; and
      (iii) the establishment of a communication platform to advice coordination and coherence of operating entities of the financial mechanism under the Convention, as well as coordination with other thematic bodies of the Convention to identify the gaps in implementation related to financial support.

b) rationalization of the financial mechanism, including through, *inter alia*, developing recommendations to rationalize the financial mechanism of the Convention and existing funds under it, for achieving cost-effectiveness and efficiency.
c) mobilization of financial resources, including through, *inter alia*, the preparation of recommendations to the COP on the technical feasibility and enhancing accessibility of the mobilization of resources from a wide variety new and additional sources, including public and private, bilateral, multilateral, and alternative sources, taking into account the financial needs identified by developing country parties, including those contained in their national communications.
d) measurement, reporting and verification of support provided to developing country parties, including through, *inter alia*,
   (i) the assessment of information related to the measurement, reporting and verification of support and enabling means provided to developing country parties under the Convention, including through the information contained in Annex I national communications and information received from developing countries.
   (ii) the development of recommendations on indicators for an assessed scale of contributions for Annex II countries, where applicable.

2. *Requests* the Standing Committee to elaborate an initial programme of work on all the elements identified in paragraph 1 for the consideration of the Conference of the parties at its eighteenth session, as well as other elements that may be identified by the Standing Committee.

Decides

3. that the Standing Committee shall be composed of members nominated by parties for approval of the Conference of the Parties, with expertise and competence in areas relevant to the work of the Standing Committee
4. that the Standing Committee shall consist of 16 members and be composed as follows:
   a) 2 representatives from each of the 5 UN regional groups
   b) 1 representative of the Small Island Developing States
   c) 1 representative of the least-developed country parties
   d) 2 representatives from parties included in Annex I to the Convention
   e) 2 representatives from parties not included in Annex I to the Convention
5. that the parties shall also nominate an alternate for each member of the Standing Committee on the same criteria as set out in paragraphs 3 and 4 above, and that the nomination of a candidate member shall be accompanied by a nomination of a candidate alternate member from the same group.

6. that Standing Committee members and alternates shall serve for two years. No member or alternate may serve in the Standing Committee for [more] than two consecutive terms.
7. that the Standing Committee shall be open to representatives of the existing and future operating entities of the financial mechanism of the Convention, representatives of relevant bilateral, regional, and multilateral funding entities, and representatives of observer organizations accredited to the UNFCCC.
8. *Encourages* the Standing Committee to draw upon additional expertise from all levels, national, sub-regional, regional, and multilateral institutions, as it may deem necessary.
9. *Decides* that the Standing Committee shall meet at least twice a year, or more if necessary, and that its first meeting shall take place not later than the (date) of (month) 2012.
10. *Also decides* that the Standing Committee shall report and make recommendations to the Conference of the Parties at each ordinary COP session, on all aspects of its work, for decisions to be taken by the COP as may be necessary.
11. *Also decides* that the Standing Committee shall perform any other functions that may be assigned to it by the COP.
12. *Further decides* that the cost of meetings and the participation of members and alternates from developing country parties shall be covered by the budget of the Convention.
13. *Decides* that the UNFCCC Secretariat shall also serve the Standing Committee.

(c) Excerpts from the G-77 Ministerial Declarations on the Conference of the Parties of the United Nations Framework Convention on Climate Change (COP) and Conference of the Parties Serving as the Meeting of the Parties to the Kyoto Protocol (CMP)

Twenty-Second Annual Meeting of the Ministers for Foreign Affairs of the Group of 77 was held in New York on 25 September 1998

Excerpts from the Ministerial Declaration

48. The Ministers expressed their commitment to strengthen institutional effectiveness within the United Nations system and the relevant international bodies to promote the programme of action and called the early ratification of the Kyoto Protocol to the United Nations Framework Convention on Climate Change.

Twenty-Third Annual Meeting of the Ministers for Foreign Affairs of the Group of 77 was held in New York on 24 September 1999

Excerpts from the Ministerial Declaration

53. The Ministers welcomed the Kyoto Protocol on legally binding commitments for the parties to the Framework Convention on Climate Change to reduce their emission of Greenhouse Gases as contained in Annex-B of the Kyoto Protocol. They urged developed countries to undertake urgent and effective steps to implement these commitments including domestic action. Emission trading for implementation of such commitments can only commence after issues relating to the principles, modalities etc. of such trading, including the initial allocation of emission entitlement on an equitable basis to all countries has been agreed upon by the parties to the Framework Convention on Climate Change. The Ministers categorically reject all attempts by some developed countries to link their ratification of the Kyoto Protocol with the question of participation by developing countries in the reduction of Greenhouse Gases emissions. The Ministers also called for immediate measures to provide the developing countries with necessary financial resources and clean technology to enable them to meet their existing commitments under the Framework Convention on Climate change, including *inter alia*, inventorization of national emissions and dissemination of knowledge of climate change. The ministers also urged developed countries to avoid misuses of the "flexibility mechanisms" envisaged in the Kyoto Protocol to evade, *inter alia*, domestic commitments to reduce greenhouse gas emissions.

Twenty-Fifth Annual Meeting of the Ministers for Foreign Affairs of the Group of 77 was held in New York on 16 November 2001

Excerpts from the Ministerial Declaration

26. We note the outcome of the seventh Conference of the Parties to the United Nations Framework Convention on Climate Change held in Marrakech, Morocco, from 29 October to 9 November 2001, which finalized the operational details of the Kyoto Protocol opening the way to widespread ratification by Governments and for the Protocol's early entry into force. We also welcome the Marrakech Ministerial Declaration as an input to the preparatory process of the World Summit on Sustainable Development, especially as regards the contribution that action on climate change can make to sustainable development and emphasize the importance of providing adequate financial resources, capacity-building, technology innovation and transfer to developing countries and cooperation with the biodiversity and desertification Conventions

Thirty-First Annual Meeting of the Ministers of Foreign Affairs of the Group of 77 and China, New York, 27 September 2007

Excerpts from the Ministerial Declaration

26 The Ministers recognized that Climate Change poses serious risks and challenges particularly to developing countries and therefore demanded urgent global action and response. In this regard, the Ministers reaffirmed the Rio Principles, in particular Principle 7 on the Common but Differentiated Responsibilities. All three pillars of sustainable development, namely economic development, social development, and environmental protection, should be addressed in an integrated, coordinated, interdependent and mutually reinforcing manner. The ministers also recognized the need to identify new, additional, and predictable resources, as well as additional innovative resources for financing for development, as a special assistance to those developing countries adversely affected by climate change.

27. The Ministers looked forward to the 13th Session of the Conference of the Parties to the United Nations Conventions on Climate Change and the Third Session of the Meeting of the Parties to the Kyoto Protocol, to be held in Bali, Indonesia, in December 2007.

28. The Ministers also welcomed the initiative of the President of the 61st session of the General Assembly to convene a thematic debate on climate change from 31st July to 2 August 2007 and the initiative of the Secretary-General to convene a High-level event on climate change on 24 September 2007.

Thirty-Second Annual Meeting of the Ministers of Foreign Affairs of the Group of 77 and China, New York, 26 September 2008

Excerpts from the Ministerial Declaration

29. The Ministers acknowledged that the global nature of climate change calls for the widest possible cooperation by all countries and their participation in an effective and appropriate international response, in accordance with their common but differentiated responsibilities and respective capabilities and their social and economic conditions. In this regard the Ministers reiterated that UNFCCC and its Kyoto Protocol remain the central multilateral framework for cooperative action to address climate change.

30. The Ministers remained deeply concerned that the developing countries, in particular LDCs, SIDS and African countries, face increased risks from the negative effects of climate change and further stressed the need to urgently address adaptation needs related to such effects.

31. The Ministers reaffirmed that responses to climate change should be coordinated with social and economic development in an integrated manner, with a view to avoiding adverse impact on the latter, taking into account the legitimate priority needs of developing countries for the achievement of sustained economic

growth and the eradication of poverty. They welcomed the decisions adopted during the Thirteenth Conference of the Parties to UNFCCC held in Bali and called for urgent global action to address climate change in accordance with the principle of common but differentiated responsibilities. They particularly urged developed countries to undertake ambitious and enhanced commitments under the Kyoto Protocol in subsequent commitment periods. They also urged the international community to assist developing countries to address the consequences of climate change particularly through new, additional, and predictable financial resources, capacity-building, and access to and transfer of technology.

Thirty-Third Annual Meeting of the Ministers for Foreign of the Member States of the Group of 77, New York, 25 September 2009

Excerpts from the Ministerial Declaration

26. The Ministers acknowledged that the global nature of climate change calls for the widest possible cooperation by all countries and their participation in an effective and appropriate international response, in accordance with their common but differentiated responsibilities and respective capabilities as well as their social and economic conditions. In this regard, the Ministers reiterated that UN Framework Convention on Climate Change and its Kyoto Protocol remains the central multilateral framework for cooperative action to address climate change.

27. The Ministers also urged developed countries to undertake ambitious and enhanced commitments under the Kyoto Protocol in subsequent commitment periods. They also urged the international community to assist developing countries to address the consequences of climate change, particularly through new, additional, and predictable financial resources, capacity-building, and access to and transfer of technology.

28. The Ministers reaffirmed that responses to climate change should be coordinated with social and economic development in an integrated manner, with a view to avoiding adverse impact on the latter, taking into account the legitimate priority needs of developing countries for the achievement of sustained economic growth and the eradication of poverty. In this context, the Ministers look forward to the positive outcomes of the Fifteenth Session of the Conference of the Parties to the United Nations Framework Conventions on Climate Change and the Fifth Session of the Meeting of the Parties to the Kyoto Protocol, to be held in Copenhagen, Denmark from 7 to 18 December 2009.

Thirty-Fourth Annual Meeting of the Ministers for Foreign of the Member States of the Group of 77, New York, 28 September 2010

Excerpts from the Ministerial Declaration

30. The Ministers acknowledged that the global nature of climate change calls for the widest possible cooperation by all countries and their participation

in an effective and appropriate international response, in accordance with their common but differentiated responsibilities and respective capabilities as well as their social and economic conditions. In this regard, the Ministers reiterated that UN Framework Convention on Climate Change and its Kyoto Protocol remains the central multilateral framework for cooperative action to address climate change. Ministers further stressed that the process of work under the UNFCCC must be open, party-driven, inclusive, and transparent.

31. The Ministers urged developed countries to undertake ambitious and enhanced commitments under the Kyoto Protocol in subsequent commitment periods and to ensure that there is no gap between the first and subsequent commitment periods. They also urged the international community to assist developing countries to address the consequences of climate change, particularly through new, additional, and predictable financial resources, capacity-building, and access to and transfer of technology.

32. The Ministers looked forward to positive outcomes at the sixteenth Conference of the Parties (COP16) and the sixth Conference of the Parties serving as the Meeting of the Parties to the Kyoto Protocol (CMP6) to be held in Cancun, Mexico, from 29 November to 10 December 2010.

33. The Ministers welcomed with appreciation South Africa's commitment to host the Seventeenth Conference of the Parties (COP 17) to the United Nations Framework Convention on Climate Change (UNFCCC) and the seventh Conference of the Parties serving as the Meeting of the Parties to the Kyoto Protocol (CMP7) in 2011.

34. The Ministers took note of the offer made by the Government of the State of Qatar to host in 2012 the Eighteenth Conference of the Parties to the United Nations Framework Convention on Climate Change (COP-18) and the eighth Conference of the Parties serving as the Meeting of the Parties to the Kyoto Protocol (CMP8) while at the same time the Ministers will not be prejudging the final decision by the Asian group in the UNFCCC.

Thirty-Fifth Annual Meeting of Ministers for Foreign Affairs of the Group of 77, New York, 23 September 2011

Excerpts from the Ministerial Declaration

66. The Ministers underlined the importance of mitigation as part of a balanced and ambitious outcome in Durban. They reiterated that appropriate treatment of mitigation, as determined in the Bali Roadmap, demanded a decision, at CMP 7, in Durban on establishing the commitments of the second commitment period under the Kyoto Protocol. In this regard, the Ministers expressed their concern that, current mitigation pledges from developed countries parties in the UNFCCC negotiations are not adequate enough to reduce global greenhouse gas emissions so as to hold the increase in global average temperature according with what is

required by science, and they urged developed countries to raise their level of ambition.

67. The Ministers reiterated the need for enhanced and urgent actions on the provision of financial resources and investments to support actions on mitigation, adaptation, and technology cooperation to developing countries. The Ministers called for the full operationalization of the Standing Committee of the Financial Mechanism of the Convention, the Technology Mechanism, and the Adaptation Committee in Durban.

68. The Ministers reiterated their call on parties included in Annex II of the Convention to intensify their efforts aimed at fulfilling their commitments on the provision of adequate, predictable, new and additional financial resources, enhancing technology development and transfer, meeting costs of adaptation, and strengthening capacity-building in developing country parties in accordance with articles 4, paragraphs 3, 4, and 5 of the Convention. The historical imbalance in financing to the detriment of adaptation must be redressed, and adaptation financing be treated in an equal manner as for mitigation. The Ministers recalled that according to decision 1/CP16, a significant share of new multilateral funding for adaptation should flow through the Green Climate Fund.

Thirty-Sixth Annual Meeting of the Ministers for Foreign Affairs of the Member States of the Group of 77 held in New York on 28 September 2012

Excerpts from the Ministerial Declaration

59. The Ministers stressed that the international community, particularly the developed countries, given their historical responsibility, need to take the lead in addressing this challenge within the United Nations Framework Convention on Climate Change (UNFCCC) and its principles and provisions, particularly, the principles of equity and common but differentiated responsibilities and respective capabilities, and provide financial and technological support to developing countries. The Ministers emphasized that a legally binding second commitment period under the Kyoto Protocol is critical and must be the key deliverable of the 18th meeting of the Conference of the Parties to the United Nations Framework Convention on Climate Change (COP 18) and the 8th session of the Conference of the Parties serving as the Meeting of the Parties to the Kyoto Protocol (CMP-8) at Doha, and must be ambitious in terms of the emission reductions and shall begin on 1 January 2013, in order to avoid any gap between the first and the second commitment periods. Ministers stressed the need to urgently close the ambition gap and expressed their concern with the lack of fulfilment of commitments by developed countries. They emphasized that developed countries must take robust and ambitious mitigation commitments, with ambitious

quantitative emissions limitation reduction targets, as required by science and mandated by the Convention.

60. In this context, the Ministers looked forward for a successful and comprehensive outcome at the COP 18/ CMP 8, and stressed the importance of the full implementation of the delicate package endorsed in COP17/CMP 7 in Durban in all its aspects, including the achievement of a quality legal second commitment period for the Kyoto Protocol, the successful conclusion of the work of the AWGLCA, in line with the Bali Action Plan and the substantive progress made in the Cancun and Durban decisions, incorporating comparable ambitious targets for Annex-I non-KP parties, and addressing in a balanced and effective manner the issues of adaptation, mitigation, finance, technology, and capacity-building.

61. The Ministers called on all parties to preserve the architectures of the Convention and its Kyoto Protocol developed over almost two decades and cautioned against any attempt to renegotiate or interpret the Convention or its principles and warned against the unravelling of the international climate change architecture into a weaker regime based on "pledge and review" for Annex I parties.

62. The Ministers considered that progress in the Durban Platform is critical for taking the Convention forward. However, work must ensure a strong linkage between mitigation, adaptation and means of implementation, in a balanced manner, as is reflected in the Convention. The Ministers held the view that all tracks under the Convention must progress in an expedite, ambitious and effective manner. Such progress should reflect the linkages between mitigation, adaptation and means of implementation. This relationship is embedded in the Convention.

63. The Ministers called on all Annex I parties to fulfil their commitments relating to mitigation, adaptation, finance, technology transfer, capacity-building under the UNFCCC and its Kyoto Protocol.

64. The Ministers stressed that the treatment of climate change in IMO and ICAO needs to be coherent with UNFCCC and KP principles and provisions.

Thirty-Seventh Annual Meeting of the Ministers for Foreign Affairs of the Member States of the Group of 77 held in New York on 26 September 2013

Excerpts from the Ministerial Declaration

86. The Ministers affirmed that the United Nations Framework Convention on Climate Change is the primary international intergovernmental forum for negotiating the global response to climate change.

87. The Ministers recalled once again that climate change is one of the most serious global challenges of our times. They underscored the fact that

developing countries continue to suffer the most from the adverse impacts of climate change, the increasing frequency and intensity of extreme weather events and the impact of response measures, even though they are the least responsible for climate change. Accordingly, they called for developed countries to take the lead in responding to climate change. Climate change threatens not only the development prospects of developing countries and their achievement of sustainable development, but also the very existence and survival of countries and societies.

88. The Ministers stressed that the developed countries, given their historical responsibility, need to take the lead in addressing this challenge in accordance with the principles and provisions of the United Nations Framework Convention on Climate Change, in particular the principles of equity and common but differentiated responsibilities and respective capabilities, and to provide financial and technological support to developing countries.

89. The Ministers noted the progress made towards addressing climate change at the eighteenth meeting of the Conference of the Parties to the United Nations Framework Convention on Climate Change, held in 2012 in Doha, through concrete decisions on remaining work under the Bali Action Plan, a plan of work under the Durban Platform and a second commitment period of the Kyoto Protocol, with a clear timeline. With respect to the second commitment period of the Kyoto Protocol, however, ambition is lacking; they hoped that its level would be enhanced in 2014 as agreed at the eighteenth meeting of the Conference of the Parties.

90. The Ministers reiterated that the extent to which developing countries will effectively implement their commitments under the Convention will depend on the effective implementation by developed countries of their commitments under the Convention related to financial resources and transfer of technology and that economic and social development and poverty eradication are the first and overriding priorities of the developing countries.

91. The Ministers noted the progress in the work of the Ad Hoc Working Group on the Durban Platform for Enhanced Action and emphasized that the outcome of the Working Group must enable further enhancement of the full, effective, and sustained implementation of the Convention. Ministers reiterated that the work of the Working Group and its outcome must be in accordance with the objective, principles and provisions stipulated in the Convention, including the principles of equity and common but differentiated responsibilities and respective capabilities. The process under the Working Group must not lead to a reinterpretation or a rewriting of the Convention.

92. The Ministers stressed the need to urgently close the ambition gap and expressed their concern with the lack of fulfilment of commitments by developed countries. In addressing this gap, the focus must not be limited to mitigation but

must also include gaps relating to finance, technology, and support for capacity-building. They emphasized that developed countries must make robust and ambitious mitigation commitments, with ambitious quantitative emissions limitation reduction targets, as required by science and mandated by the Convention. In this context, the Ministers looked forward to a successful and comprehensive outcome of the nineteenth session of the Conference of the Parties/ninth session of the Conference of the Parties serving as the Meeting of the Parties to the Kyoto Protocol.

Thirty-Eighth Annual Meeting of the Ministers for Foreign Affairs of the States Members of the Group of 77 held in New York on 26 September 2014

Excerpts from the Ministerial Declaration

51. The Ministers recalled once again that climate change was one of the most serious global challenges of the times. They underscored the fact that developing countries continued to suffer the most from the adverse impacts of climate change and the increasing frequency and intensity of extreme weather events and the impact of response measures, even though they were the least responsible for climate change. Accordingly, they called for developed countries to take the lead in responding to climate change. Climate change threatens not only the development prospects of developing countries and their achievement of sustainable development but also the very existence and survival of countries and societies.

52. The Ministers stressed that the developed countries, given their historical responsibility, needed to take the lead in addressing this challenge in accordance with the principles and provisions of the United Nations Framework Convention on Climate Change, particularly the principles of equity and common but differentiated responsibilities and respective capabilities, and provide financial and technological support to developing countries.

53. The Ministers reiterated that the extent to which developing countries would effectively implement their commitments under the Framework Convention would depend on the effective implementation by developed countries of their commitments under the Convention related to financial resources and transfer of technology and would take fully into account that economic and social development and poverty eradication were the first and overriding priorities of the developing countries.

54. The Ministers reiterated their support for the success of the twentieth Conference of the Parties to the United Nations Framework Convention on Climate Change (UNFCCC), to be held in Lima, Peru. The Ministers reaffirmed the need to achieve progress in Lima towards the adoption at the twenty-first Conference of the Parties to the UNFCCC in 2015 of a protocol, another legal

instrument, or an agreed outcome with legal force under the Convention that is in accordance with its principles and provisions, in particular CBDR, and that will strengthen the multilateral rules-based system. The Ministers also reiterated their support for constructive discussions at the Social Pre-COP meeting in Venezuela ahead of Lima. In this regard, the Ministers expressed their support to the Governments of Peru and Venezuela for the successful steering of the work of these meetings.

Thirty-Ninth Annual Meeting of the Ministers for Foreign Affairs of the States Members of the Group of 77 held in New York on 24 September 2015

Excerpts from the Ministerial Declaration

40. The Ministers recalled that the United Nations Framework Convention on Climate Change is the primary international, intergovernmental forum for negotiating the global response to climate change. The global nature of climate change calls for the widest possible international cooperation aimed at holding the increase in global average temperature below 2 degrees or 1.5 degrees Celsius above pre-industrial levels by accelerating the reduction of global greenhouse gas emissions and to adapt to the impacts of climate change. Looking ahead to COP21 to be held in Paris, France in December 2015, the Ministers called on all States to work for a comprehensive and ambitious climate protocol, another legal instrument or agreed outcome with legal force under the Convention that will strengthen the multilateral rules-based system and address all the elements mandated by the Durban decision (mitigation, adaptation, finance, technology development and transfer, capacity-building and transparency of action and support), as well as loss and damage and response measures, in a balanced manner. The Ministers stressed that the developed countries, given their historical responsibility, need to take the lead in addressing this challenge in accordance with UNFCCC principles and provisions, particularly, the principles of equity and common but differentiated responsibilities and respective

II. CONFERENCE OF THE PARTIES SERVING AS THE MEETING OF THE PARTIES TO THE PARIS AGREEMENT (CMA)

(a) Statements at the Sessions of the Conference of the Parties Serving as the Meeting of the Parties to the Paris Agreement (CMA) [2016]

Statement by H.E. Mr. Manasvi Srisodapol, Special Representative of the Chair of the Group of 77 and China for Climate Change on behalf of the Group of 77 and

China at the Opening Meeting of the Bonn Climate Change Conference (Bonn, Germany, 16 May 2016)

Madam President,
Madam Executive Secretary,

1. I have the honour to deliver this statement on behalf of the Group of 77 and China.
2. At the outset, allow me to congratulate you upon your appointment as the President of COP-21 and express our appreciation for the work you have already done. The Group of 77 and China stands ready to commence our work and to work closely with you at this session as well as in the upcoming months.
3. The Paris Agreement is a result of collective and tireless efforts of all parties working constructively in a spirit of compromise for our efforts on climate change, through enhancing the implementation of the Convention, including its provisions and principles, in particular equity and common but differentiated responsibilities and respective capabilities. As we move into the implementation phase, the delicate balance of all issues which we have achieved in Paris as well as the principles and provisions of the Convention must be preserved. We also expect developed countries to continue taking the lead role in addressing climate change, particular in the implementation of the Paris Agreement, in accordance with their historical responsibilities and their respective capabilities.
4. As we move forward, we reiterate the urgent need to enhance the pre-2020 ambition, including the ratification of the Doha amendment to the Kyoto Protocol, which will provide a strong basis for post-2020 efforts under Paris Agreement. We also need to address the significant gap between the aggregate effect of parties' mitigation pledges by 2020 and aggregate emission pathways consistent with holding the increase in the global average temperature to well below 2°C above pre-industrial levels and pursuing efforts to limit the temperature increase to 1.5°C. The focus now should be on delivering major tasks to enhance pre-2020 implementation including action on adaptation and loss and damage, which is an urgent priority for developing countries. We would like to underline that any deficiency in fulfilling such commitments or in closure of emissions reduction gap shall not be deferred to commitments under the Paris Agreement post-2020.
5. While the Group of 77 and China remains committed to addressing climate change, the group has been the most affected by the adverse impacts of climate change which are eroding our development gains and undermining and delaying the achievement of the goals under the 2030 Agenda on Sustainable Development. We are already taking ambitious measures in line with our

capacities. Nonetheless, for our endeavours to be achieved, enhanced, and adequate financial and technology support as well as capacity-building must be provided to allow for effective action both pre-2020 and beyond. In the context of implementation, we believe parties should respect, promote, and consider their respective obligations including the right of people in vulnerable situations.

Madam President,

6. We appreciate the efforts of the COP-21 President and the incoming COP-22 President for their reflections note and do agree that our work program must move forward in a comprehensive, coherent, and balanced manner. Last year, the COP requested its subsidiary bodies to take forward different parts of the work. The Group of 77 and China would like to stress the need for coherence between the SBI, SBSTA, and APA. Due attention, in both time allocation and facilitation support, should be equally given to the long-standing agenda items and the new mandates coming from Paris. In this regard, we welcome the initiative of the COP President to convene two special stocktaking events. We believe that they could be useful to ensure progress under each body, ensure balance across different bodies and among cross-cutting issues.
7. In order to prepare for our work at COP-22, in particular for the facilitative dialogue to assess the progress in implementing decision 1/CP.19 paragraphs 3 and 4, and identify relevant opportunities to enhance the provision of financial resources, including for technology development and transfer, and capacity-building support, the Group believes that we could benefit from an early consultation at this session on the modality and scope of work of the said dialogue.

Madam President,

8. As I have already stated, the Group stands ready and eager to commence our work as soon as possible. Nonetheless, in order to ensure balance among all issues and stay true to the mandates given to us at Paris, we would like to propose some concise surgical amendment to the agendas of SBI, SBSTA, and APA. We have submitted our amendment proposals and look forward to that our suggestion be taken into account by the Chairs and Co-Chairs of the respective bodies.

Statement by H.E. Mr. Manasvi Srisodapol, Special Representative of the Chair of the Group of 77 and China for Climate Change on Behalf of the Group of 77 and

China at the Opening Plenary of 1st Session of the Ad Hoc Working Group on the Paris Agreement (APA1) (Bonn, Germany, 17 May 2016)

Co-Chairs,

1. I have the honour to deliver this statement on behalf of the Group of 77 and China at the 1st Session of the Ad Hoc Working Group on the Paris Agreement.
2. At the outset, the Group would like to congratulate both of you on your election as the Co-Chairs of the APA. Having two ladies chair this important working group is a clear indication of the seriousness with which parties take their undertakings on gender in the Paris Agreement. We trust that, under your guidance and leadership, the meeting will be able to move constructively towards a successful outcome. The Group is ready to work closely with you.
3. In recent years, all parties have worked collectively and tirelessly, in a constructive manner and a spirit of compromise, to negotiate and adopt the Paris Agreement. Now, as we move into the implementation phase, there is a lot of work ahead to achieve the objectives of the Convention. The APA has a crucial task ahead to prepare for the entry into force of the Paris Agreement. The Group stands ready to commence our task immediately and to work closely with our partners to fulfil the mandates given to us by the COP. Being mindful of the work that is going on in other subsidiary bodies, we would like to emphasize the need for coherence of our work in APA and those in SBSTA and SBI.

Co-Chairs,

4. In Paris, we achieved a balanced Agreement among all elements needed to address the threat of climate change, including the issues of Adaptation and Loss and Damage that are of so much importance to developing country parties. This successful balanced approach to the Paris outcome needs to feed the spirit of the current discussion on the implementation starting here in Bonn among all parties. The Group believes that the work of the APA should be undertaken in a well-structured, balanced, comprehensive, and coherent manner. We stress that no crucial element to the Paris outcome and their interlinkages with other elements, are left behind. All issues under the APA must be given equal attention, in both time allocation and facilitation support. Moreover, we must ensure that the agenda reflects the clarity of the

tasks and reflects faithfully the mandates, as well as the balanced outcome of the Paris Agreement.

5. The Group has submitted our concise surgical amendments to the agenda on Sunday. We recognize the effort made by COP-21 and COP-22 Presidents and two incoming Co-Chairs in carrying out consultations with all Groups yesterday to find a balanced solution on the agenda. We hope to further engage in the discussion in order to move the process forward.

Co-Chairs,

6. The Group would like to underline again the need to close the emission gap and enhance ambition in the pre-2020 period, particularly by developed countries, consistent with holding the increases in the global average temperature to well below 2°C above pre-industrial levels and pursuing efforts to limit the temperature increase to 1.5°C. Actions shall not be deferred to post-2020 implementation under the Paris Agreement. In the implementation of the Paris Agreement, the Group expects developed countries to continue taking the lead role in addressing climate change.
7. The Group acknowledges the importance of CBDR-RC and of providing developing country parties with flexibility in the transparency framework for action and support under article 13 of the Paris Agreement, taking into account parties' different capacities. Support shall be provided to developing countries for the implementation of article 13 and for the building of transparency-related capacity on a continuous basis. The Group reiterates that modalities, procedures, and guidelines under article 13 should be built on and draw from experiences from existing arrangements related to transparency under the Convention and ensure balanced treatment of all areas indicated under the article.
8. In order to ensure comprehensiveness of the Global Stocktake, the Group emphasizes that due attention should be given to the discussion on transparency of support to enable clarity of relevant input that will inform the Global Stocktake process defined in article 14 of the Paris Agreement. Such clarity will be a crucial basis for ensuring that adequate finance, technology, and capacity-building supports are provided to developing countries to allow for effective action beyond 2020.

Co-Chairs,

9. Developing countries' efforts towards the achievement of the goals under the 2030 Agenda on Sustainable Development, especially of those that are

considered most impacted and vulnerable, are being seriously undermined by the adverse impacts of climate change. Urgent actions are needed, so let's get to work.

Statement by H.E. Mr. Manasvi Srisodapol, Special Representative of the Chair of the Group of 77 and China for Climate Change on behalf of the Group of 77 and China at the Stocktaking Event (Bonn, Germany, 21 May 2016)
Madam President,

1. I have the honour to deliver this statement on behalf of the Group of 77 and China.
2. At the outset, I would like to thank you, Madam President, for holding this stocktaking event today. The Group believes that it could be useful for ensuring coherence among different bodies and progress under each body.
3. The Group is delighted that now APA can move forward and join SBI and SBSTA in pursuing those tasks mandated to us at Paris. We would like to express our appreciation for your effort, as well as those of the Chairs and Co-Chairs of all bodies, in facilitating our discussion and providing us with necessary space that is needed in reaching an agreement under this party-driven process. Even though we had to spend some time during this past week discussing about the agendas of all bodies, but the conversation was essential for us in order to gain more clarity and to reach common understanding. As we are in the implementation phase, it is important to get the agendas right to define the scope of our work and to be a tool to organize our deliberation in the post-Paris era.
4. The Group believes that the spirit of balance and coherence, among APA, SBI and SBSTA, is critical in driving our work forward and it must be maintained throughout this session and beyond.

Madam President,

5. Under the APA, the Group stresses that the delicate balance achieved in the Paris Agreement and accompanying decisions requires a balanced progress of all issues in a context of implementation. While recognizing the urgency of mitigation, we also stress the importance of adaptation, especially to developing countries which are particularly vulnerable to the adverse effects of climate change, as well as the provision of the necessary means of implementation to developing countries for their climate actions, both for adaptation and mitigation. The Group stands ready to engage with all parties based on the APA agenda as adopted. We believe it gives assurances to the need for a balanced, coherent, and cross-cutting approach to address the APA issues.

6. The Group is of the view that modalities, procedures, and guidelines for the transparency framework for action and support should be based on relevant paragraphs in decision 1/CP.21 and article 13 of the Paris Agreement. We recognize interlinkages of the transparency framework with other provisions in the Paris Agreement, and the magnitude of works to be carried out in developing common modalities, procedures, and guidelines. Therefore, we urge APA to aim at producing program of work on modalities, procedures, and guidelines for further deliberation in COP-22 and beyond.
7. The Group welcomes the progress made so far in SBI and SBSTA in various agenda items as well as in the mandated in-session events.
8. For SBI, the ICA should aim to identify capacity-building needs of developing countries in order to facilitate the reporting of information in the subsequent BURs and ICA.
9. On the Terms of Reference for the 3rd review of the Adaptation Fund, the Group believes that it should address the effectiveness and sustainability of the operation of the Fund including its resources. This is in line with the spirit of the Paris Agreement which we should be careful to maintain. With a view to achieving this objective, we must therefore reflect on the status of its resources, access modalities, approval procedures, amongst other innovative features of the Fund. At the same time, we must focus on the coherence of the Fund with other institutions under the Convention as well as reflect upon its institutional arrangements.
10. The Group welcomes the fifth meeting of the Durban Forum on Capacity-Building. We appreciate the technical paper elaborated by the Secretariat to support parties in conducting the third comprehensive review of the implementation of the framework for capacity-building in developing countries. The Group welcomes the progress made in the consultations regarding the PCCB, a key element for the implementation of the Paris Agreement. We would like to see the composition of the PCCB completed in such a way that it is balanced and equitable in terms of geographical representation and gender. It should include a wide range of parties to reflect the diversity of capacity-building providers and recipients and take into account the specific needs, concerns, and circumstances of developing country parties.
11. Regarding the forum and work programme on the impact of the implementation of response measures, by the closing of this Bonn session, we expect the operationalization of three following core tasks, namely the development of the work programme of the improved forum, the elaboration of the Terms of Reference for the Technical Expert Group, and the list of activities with specific timelines to implement the work programme.
12. For SBSTA, the Group notes the progress made on the elaboration of the Technology Framework under article 10, paragraph 4, of the Paris

Agreement, highlighting that the Technology Framework should play a strategic role in the implementation of the Paris Agreement, particularly its article 10, and its guidance to the technology mechanism should be flexible, balanced, systematic, and comprehensive in order to respond the evolving needs of climate technology development and dissemination in developing countries. In addition, we hope that the results of the workshop on linkages between technology mechanism and financial mechanism will lead to enhanced mobilization of financial resources to support technology development and transfer.

13. The Group reiterates that adaptation of agriculture to the adverse effects of climate change continues to be the key priority for developing countries for SBSTA work, in light of the particular vulnerabilities of the agriculture sector and its relationship with livelihood, food security and poverty eradication. This is in line with the Paris Agreement, which recognizes the fundamental priority of safeguarding food security and ending hunger, and the particular vulnerabilities of food production systems to the adverse effects of climate change. As well, it is important to recall that the Agreement states in its objective that food production is not to be threatened. We are engaging constructively in informal consultation to continue the consideration of the reports of the first two workshops held at SBSTA42, as well as in its participation in the two workshops mandated for this session. We look forward to discussing the report of the four workshops at SBSTA45, as agreed in Paris, and to continue considering work that will serve to increase the adaptive capacity of agriculture.

Madam President,

14. The Group would like to express our appreciation to the COP Presidencies for their initiative to organize the informal group consultations on issues related to COP-22 review of the WIM, and the special event by the Presidencies on issues related to the WIM in the lead up to, and beyond COP-22, to provide a platform for parties to engage in conversation in preparation for the review of the WIM, which is an issue of importance to our Group. Additionally, in order to prepare for the facilitative dialogue to assess the progress in implementing decision 1/CP.19 paragraphs 3 and 4, and to identify relevant opportunities to enhance the provision of financial resources, the groups reiterate our request to have an early consultation in this session on the modality and scope of work. We also would like to highlight the priority assigned to pre-2020 action as the basis for post-2020 ambitious action. We expect this topic is properly included in the agenda in the next session
15. In moving forward, the Group of 77 and China stresses the need to ensure transparency and inclusiveness. We request that constraint of small

delegations should be taken into consideration when scheduling meetings to ensure efficient and meaningful participation. The Group also expects to see substantial progress in the elaboration of the terms of reference for PCCB in the remaining days to prepare solid groundwork for its adoption at COP-22. We urge all parties to continue working in a collaborative manner and to work expeditiously, especially in APA, to ensure comparable progress in all bodies which is essential for successful preparation for the entry into force of the Paris Agreement and for the convening sofCMA1.

Statement by H.E. Mr. Manasvi Srisodapol, Special Representative of the Chair of the Group of 77 and China for Climate Change on behalf of the Group of 77 and China at the Closing Plenary of 1st Session of the Ad HocWorking Group on the Paris Agreement (APA1)
(Bonn, Germany, 26 May 2016)
Madam Co-Chairs,

1. I have the honour to deliver this statement on behalf of the Group of 77 and China.
2. At the outset, I would like to thank you, Madam Co-Chairs, for your efforts during the first session of the APA. The Group believes that this is a very important first step of our work to prepare for the entry into force of the Paris Agreement and for the convening of the CMA-1. We appreciate the opportunity to exchange views to enhance clarity and understanding in this party-driven process. We believe that the guiding questions of the Co-Chairs have been useful in framing the focus of our discussions.
3. Whereas the various issues under the APA are equally important, the Group takes note of different levels of maturity of the issues on the agenda. We, therefore, stress that appropriate methods must be tailored in response to the nature and maturity of each issue. Due to the interlinking nature of issues, we reiterate that the spirit of coherence and balance among all bodies, which we have adhered to, must be carried forward to Marrakech and beyond.

Madam Co-Chairs,

4. The Group of 77 and China would like to recap some of the points that have arisen from the discussions in the APA during the past few days.
5. The Paris Agreement was reached in the spirit of compromise, achieving a delicate balance of all issues. We reiterate that Nationally Determined Contributions (NDCs) encompass not only mitigation. Regarding further guidance in relation to mitigation section of decision 1/CP.21, we must recognize their nationally determined nature, and the guidance must accommodate the diversity of submitted INDCs.

6. While we all recognize the urgency of mitigation with leadership by developed countries, the Group emphasizes the importance of adaptation, especially since developing countries are particularly vulnerable to adverse impacts of climate change. We underline the different natures of mitigation, adaptation and means of implementation components. We are of the view that further guidance in relation to adaptation communication should reflect the county-driven nature of adaptation and aim to enhance the adaptive capacity of developing countries parties without creating addition burden and contribute to the global goal on adaptation.
7. The Group emphasizes that the provision of necessary means of implementation to developing countries is crucial to our climate actions in both mitigation and adaptation. We reiterate our concern on the access to adequate finance, especially from the financial-related constituted bodies serving under the Convention and stress its linkage to both pre-2020 actions and the successful preparation for the Paris Agreement.
8. We recognize the interlinkages of the transparency framework with other provisions in the Paris Agreement, both on actions and supports, where coherence of work among them is necessary. We stress the relevance of flexibility for developing countries in the modalities, procedures, and guidelines to be developed under article 13. Support shall be provided to developing countries for the implementation of article 13 and for the building of transparency-related capacity.
9. The Global Stocktake will serve an important function in tracking our progress towards achieving the purpose of the Paris Agreement and its long-term goals. The Group stresses that the Global Stocktake shall be comprehensive and facilitative, covering mitigation, adaptation, and the means of implementation and support, in the light of equity and the best available science. Inputs and modalities of the Global Stocktake are important issues that must be identified in a facilitative manner referring to Global Stocktake section of decision 1/CP.21.
10. The Group recognizes the importance of the compliance mechanism for the implementation of the Paris Agreement. We reaffirm that the mechanism shall be facilitative in nature and functions in a manner that is transparent, non-adversarial, and non-punitive as we have agreed in Paris, while also taking into account the respective national capability and circumstance of parties.
11. Acknowledging the possibility of the Paris Agreement entering into force earlier than we had previously anticipated, the Group stresses the need for necessary technical work to continue. Under such circumstance, we emphasize that the work should be carried out in an inclusive manner.

Madam Co-Chairs,

12. The Group of 77 and China would like to, once again, underscore the importance of accelerated pre-2020 actions as a solid foundation for our post-2020

efforts under the Paris Agreement. We look forward to having this issue adequately addressed in the upcoming sessions, including through the facilitative dialogue to be conducted in Marrakech.

13. In moving forward, we reiterate our call for coherence among all issues under APA and of our work here and those in other bodies. Also, the constraint of small delegations should be taken into consideration when scheduling meetings so that no more than two contact groups be conducted in parallel in future sessions.
14. We are looking forward very much to working closely with both of you, the incoming-Presidency, and all delegates in the upcoming months and at Marrakech.

Statement by H.E. Mr. Manasvi Srisodapol, Special Representative of the Chair of the Group of 77 and China for Climate Change, on behalf of the Group of 77 and China, at the Opening Plenary of the Second Part of the first Session of the Ad Hoc Working Group on the Paris Agreement (APA 1.2) (Marrakech, Morocco, 7 November 2016)

Madam Co-Chairs,
Excellencies,
Distinguished representatives,
Ladies and Gentlemen,

1. I have the honour to deliver this statement on behalf of the Group of 77 and China.
2. At the outset, the Group would like to thank Co-Chairs, for the scenario note which provides a helpful outline for our work at this session, especially since we are working under a time constraint. We are looking forward to working closely with you and to engaging actively and constructively.
3. In moving forward, we reiterate that the work of APA should be party-driven and undertaken in a balanced and coherent manner. Transparency and inclusiveness must be ensured. We appreciate the Co-Chairs' efforts to take into account the constraint of small delegations when scheduling meetings. The Group highlights the importance of guidance given to facilitators to ensure comparable treatment and even progress for all issues.

Madam Co-Chairs,

4. The Paris Agreement achieved a delicate balance of all issues. In this regard, the Group reiterates that Nationally Determined Contributions (NDCs) are a key vehicle to deliver enhanced action under the Paris Agreement to achieve its long-term goals on all issues, including mitigation, adaptation and means of implementation.

5. On further guidance in relation to the mitigation section of decision 1/CP.21, the Group stresses that national determination is one of the features of NDCs and that the further guidance should take into account such character. The guidance should assist parties with the preparation and communication of their NDCs in order to facilitate clarity, transparency, and understanding of parties' contributions. Nonetheless, it should be developed in a flexible manner to accommodate the diversity of NDCs and the national circumstances of developing country parties. Developed country parties should continue to take the lead in applying the guidance for accounting. Implementation of NDCs, by parties who have presented them, should reflect the principle of common but differentiated responsibilities and respective capabilities, in light of different national circumstances.
6. On further guidance in relation to the adaptation communication, the Group emphasizes the importance of adaptation especially since climate change has adversely impacted on our members and sees this as opportunity to raise the profile of adaptation and position it at an equal footing with mitigation, and as a tool to help us achieve the Global Goal on Adaptation. The balance between adaptation and mitigation should continue to be pursued in the implementation of the Paris Agreement. The Group stresses that the guidance must reflect the country-driven nature of adaptation and aim to enhance the adaptive capacity, reduce vulnerability, and increase resilience without creating additional burdens on developing countries, be comprehensive and have optional elements help guide parties' Adaptation communication. We emphasize that all vehicles outlined in article 7, paragraph 11, of the Paris Agreement can be used. The Group considers the adaptation communications as an essential input to the Global Stocktake and adequate action and support for adaptation.
7. On modalities, procedures, and guidelines for the transparency framework for action and support, the Group believes that given the tight timeline for this work to be considered by the CMA in 2018, it is important to get started on the technical work which will be party-driven and guided by the key principles of the enhanced transparency framework. The Group also emphasizes that the work should progress in a balanced manner across all elements of the enhanced transparency framework, recognizing there is less experience to draw upon for transparency of support. On the notion of flexibility, the Group highlights that flexibility applies to all aspects of the enhanced transparency framework—reporting, review, and multilateral consideration—for developing countries in light of their capacities. The Group is of the view that agreeing on a work programme will be a good start to the work ahead.
8. On matters relating to the Global Stocktake, the Group believes that modalities of the Global Stocktake shall be done in comprehensive and facilitative manner, considering mitigation, adaptation and the means of implementation and support, and in light of equity and the best available science. Further discussion on the scope of Global Stocktake is important for reaching a common

understand and will provide a strong basis for addressing its designs including sources of input and modalities and ensure that it assists parties in enhancing and/or updating action and support.

9. On modalities and procedures for the effective operation of the committee to facilitate implementation and promote compliance, the Group reaffirms that the Committee shall be facilitative in nature and function in a transparent, non-adversarial and non-punitive manner. National capabilities and circumstances of parties shall be reflected, and the adequate participation of parties concerned is important for its effective operation. Self-triggering could be an important mechanism to trigger the work of the Committee. The Group stands ready to engage based on the guiding questions by the Co-Chairs.
10. The Paris Agreement has entered into force at an unprecedented speed which marks the level of importance the global community attached to climate change. This momentum must be maintained. As we now embark on the implementation phase of the Paris Agreement, in particular with the convening of the CMA1, we must ensure that no one will be left behind and that the implementation of the Paris Agreement only apply to the parties that have ratified the Agreement. The Group believes that our work should have a clear timeline in order to send a positive signal to the international community that work is progressing.

Madam Co-Chairs,

11. The Group of 77 and China would like to, once again, underscore the importance of accelerating the implementation of pre-2020 commitments and actions, including the ratification of the Doha amendment, and the need to address the significant gap between the aggregate effect of parties' mitigation pledges by 2020 and aggregate emission pathways. We therefore emphasize the urgency to revisit and increase the emission reduction targets under the Convention and its Kyoto Protocol. We also emphasize the importance of implementing and enhancing the provision of finance, technology development and transfer and capacity-building support by developed country parties for developing countries, including the implementation of the road map to achieve the goal of providing US$100 billion annually by 2020.
12. We are looking forward to working closely with both of you, and all delegates, during this session.

Statement by H.E. Mr. Manasvi Srisodapol, Special Representative of the Chair of the Group of 77 and China for Climate Change, on behalf of the Group of 77 and China, at the Closing Plenary of the Second Part of the First Session of the Ad

Hoc Working Group on the Paris Agreement (APA 1.2) (Marrakech, Morocco, 14 November 2016)

Madam Co-Chairs,

1. I have the honour to deliver this statement on behalf of the Group of 77 and China.
2. At the outset, the Group would like to thank you, Madam Co-Chairs, and all the facilitators for your hard works during this session of the APA.
3. With the early entry into force of the Paris Agreement, which happened at an unprecedented speed, it is important that the APA sends a positive signal to the international community that work is progressing. The Group reiterates

   that the delicate balance of all issues we achieved in Paris must be preserved. The Nationally Determined Contributions (NDCs) are a key vehicle to deliver enhanced action under the Paris Agreement to achieve its long-term goals on all issues, including mitigation, adaptation and means of implementation.

Madam Co-Chairs,

4. The Group of 77 and China would like to recap some of the points that we made in this session during the past few days.
5. On further guidance in relation to the mitigation section of decision 1/CP. 21, the Group supports the proposal to hold a roundtable discussion and a call for submissions. We, once again, stress that it should be developed in a flexible manner to accommodate the diversity of NDCs and the national circumstances of developing country parties and take into account the nationally determined nature of contributions should be taken into account.
6. On further guidance in relation to the adaptation communication, the Group has demonstrated its constructive engagement during the informal consultations bearing in mind that adaptation communication is one important part in the process of implementing the adaptation provisions of the Paris Agreement. We had an interesting discussion about the purpose, possible elements, linkages, and flexibility of the adaptation communication. The progress made so far is reflected in the table attached to the co-facilitators' note. The Group understands the table is a basis for the work that will continue in the next session. The Group has advanced its understanding of the positions that include purpose of the adaptation communication, as well as some common elements and the importance of implementing the flexibility of the vehicles as reflected in the Paris Agreement. parties need this flexibility in order to accommodate different capacities and circumstances of our countries, as well as avoiding generating additional burden for developing countries.

7. On modalities, procedures, and guidelines for the transparency framework for action and support, the Group hopes that the agreed next steps as reflected in the informal note are accurately captured in the APA conclusions. We would also like to highlight that balanced progress across all APA agenda items does not necessarily mean equal progress. We are pleased with the good progress made under this agenda item and hope to continue making progress in future sessions. On the agreed next steps, the Group is of the view that the targeted submissions will allow all parties to express their views on the specific issues identified thus facilitating understanding of our respective positions. We believe that action and support form one cohesive whole, therefore, our work on both halves of the transparency framework must therefore progress together and enabled by the work plan. We look forward to the workshop ahead of the next APA session which will provide us with the opportunity to elaborate on our views and start work on developing the modalities, procedures, and guidelines of the enhanced transparency framework for action and support in a balanced manner. All previous and ongoing processes under the Convention, on transparency of support must inform the work. The Group stands ready to start technical work as soon as possible.

8. On matters relating to the Global Stocktake, the Group believes that focused submissions ahead of the May 2017 session could contribution to reaching a common understanding on this issue.
9. On modalities and procedures for the effective operation of the committee to facilitate implementation and promote compliance, the Group welcomes a call for focused submissions ahead of the May 2017 session. We would like to thank the co-facilitators for their guiding questions but wish highlight that parties should be able to put forward their views on any issues or aspects in relation to the operationalization of article 15 as they deem relevant.
10. On Adaptation Fund, the Group reiterates that adaptation funding is essential to enable developing countries to be enabled to cope with the increasing adverse effects of climate change, and to undertake enhanced actions under the Paris Agreement, without excluding enhanced actions of developing country parties of the Convention and non-parties of the Paris Agreement. We, therefore, are greatly concerned that preparatory work for the Adaptation Fund to serve the Paris Agreement has been delayed, despite the Group's efforts to address all the concerns raised by the developed country parties. We hope that further efforts will allow us to progress in the negotiations on this item.

Madam Co-Chairs,

11. The Group of 77 and China would like to reiterate, once again, the importance of accelerating the implementation of pre-2020 commitments and actions, including the ratification of the Doha amendment, and the need to address the significant gap between the aggregate effect of parties' mitigation pledges by 2020 and aggregate emission pathways. This gap should be addressed now rather than later. We also emphasize the importance of implementing and enhancing the provision of finance, technology development and transfer and capacity-building support by developed country parties for developing countries. We look forward to having this issue adequately addressed in the upcoming sessions.
12. In moving forward, we reiterate our call for transparency and inclusiveness. The work of APA should be party-driven and undertaken in a balanced and coherent manner among all issues and with other bodies.
13. The Group of 77 and China will continue engage actively and constructively in the upcoming months and at the resumed APA session.

Statement on behalf of the Group of 77 and China by H.E. General Surasak Karnjanarat, Minister of Natural Resources and Environment of the Kingdom of Thailand, at the Joint High-level Segment of the 22nd Session of Conference of the Parties (COP22), the 12th Session of the Conference of the Parties Serving as the Meeting of the Parties to the Kyoto Protocol (CMP-12) and the 1st Session of the Conference of the Parties Serving as the Meeting of the Parties to the Paris Agreement (CMA1)
(Marrakech, Morocco, 16 November 2016)

Mr. President,

1. I have the honour to deliver this statement on behalf of the Group of 77 and China.
2. We would like to express our full support to you and thank for your leadership.
3. The Group welcomes the early entry into force of the Paris Agreement which signifies the high level of political commitment the global community attaches to climate change. We must maintain this momentum.
4. COP-22 is the "COP for action." We need enhanced actions and ambitions, on both mitigation and adaptation, as well as support.

Mr. President,

5. Countries of the Group of 77 and China have been the most affected by the adverse impacts of climate change. Yet we are taking ambitious measures in line with our capacities. Developed countries must support our endeavours.

6. The Group would like to highlight the following points on the implementation phase of the Paris Agreement, as applicable to parties that ratify the Agreement:
7. First, the delicate balance achieved in Paris must be preserved. It is crucial to ensure transparency, inclusiveness, party-driven process, and balance of all issues and across all work plans of subsidiary bodies. We must reaffirm the provisions and principles of the Convention, in particular, equity and common but differentiated responsibilities and respective capabilities as reflected in the Paris Agreement.
8. Second, there is an urgent need to enhance the pre-2020 ambition, including the expeditious ratification of the Doha Amendment to the Kyoto Protocol to provide a strong basis for post-2020 efforts under the Paris Agreement.
9. Third, capacity-building support for climate action is critical for developing countries and should be based on and responsive to national needs, foster country ownership, participatory, and cross-cutting.
10. Fourth, developing countries require additional, adequate, predictable, and sustainable climate financing to transform our economies to climate resilience and low greenhouse gas emissions. The Group notes the efforts by developed countries for the formulation of a road map to achieve the floor of US$100 billion per year by 2020. We reiterate our call for developed country parties to enhance ambition on the provision and mobilization of support, and to achieve a balance between adaptation and mitigation finance, including by setting a target to quadruple resources allocated to adaptation from public and grant-based sources by 2020.
11. Fifth, technology development and transfer are also vital. Technology mechanism needs to be enhanced to support the rapid transfer of technologies from developed countries to developing countries, helping them to innovate and develop their own technologies. Concrete enhanced actions on technology development and transfer and strengthening of the linkages between the technology mechanism and the financial mechanism is required.
12. Direct access of all developing country parties of the Convention and Paris Agreement to means of implementation including finance, technology transfer and capacity-building provided by multilateral supporting mechanism should be simplified and granted.
13. For us, adaptation remains a priority. Developing countries are the least contributors to climate change, however, we are the most affected. In order to increase adaptive capacity and resilience, we require the implementation of guarantees of the Paris Agreement in terms of the means of implementation.
14. The Group remains ever committed to addressing climate change and looks forward to a clear and strong outcome of COP22.

Statement by H.E. Mr. Manasvi Srisodapol, Special Representative of the Chair of the Group of 77 for Climate Change, on behalf of the Group of 77 and China, at the Joint Closing Plenary of the 22nd Session of Conference of the Parties (COP-22), the 12th Session of the Conference of the Parties Serving as the Meeting of the Parties to the Kyoto Protocol (CMP-12) and the 1st Session of the Conference of the Parties Serving as the Meeting of the Parties to the Paris Agreement (CMA-1) (Marrakech, Morocco, 18 November 2016)

Mr. President,

1. I have the honour to deliver this statement on behalf of the Group of 77 and China.
2. The Group would like to extend our deep gratitude to the Presidency of Morocco for the hard work and the warm hospitality extended to all parties.
3. We also thank the Executive Secretary and the Secretariat for their relentless support and contribution to the organization of the Conference and in servicing the Group of 77 and China coordination meetings. We are also grateful to all parties for their efforts and cooperation in working constructively with us to reach meaningful outcomes and maintain the Paris spirit at this Conference.

Mr. President,

4. We came to Marrakech with a challenging task, the challenge of turning agreements into action. COP-22 can indeed be considered a "COP for action." The speedy and unprecedented entry into force of the Paris Agreement signals the level of urgency and importance with which our leaders and the international community attach to combating climate change. We are here to accelerate climate actions, and this has been underscored by the Marrakech Action Proclamation which we endorsed yesterday and the tireless efforts of the High-Level Champions over the past year.

Mr. President,

5. While the Paris Agreement has entered into force at an unprecedented speed, it is regrettable that the same cannot be said about the Doha Amendment. After nearly four years, only 73 parties have deposited their instruments of acceptance to the Doha Amendment. The Group reiterates that the unfinished business of the pre-2020 actions and ambition, which are long overdue, must be urgently addressed. The Group sees the Kyoto Protocol as a fundamental building block in our post-2020 efforts. We urge all parties that have not done so to ratify the Doha Amendment expeditiously.
6. The Group would like to reiterate the relevance and priority we attach to adaptation. Adaptation is a matter of urgency for developing countries whose capacities to carry out actions to cope with the adverse impacts of climate

change are limited. We therefore urge that progress in implementing the Paris Agreement must reflect balance between adaptation and mitigation.

Mr. President,

7. It is of utmost importance for us to send a clear message to the global community that we must all be part of the global climate solution. We are pleased that the Marrakech Conference was able to achieve some clarity and good progress has been made. This include the adoption of the Terms of Reference and initial work plan for the Paris Committee on Capacity-Building (PCCB), the established linkage between technology mechanism and the financial mechanism, the indicative framework for the five-year rolling work plan of the Executive Committee of the Warsaw International Mechanism for Loss and Damage (WIM), the conclusion of the Third Comprehensive Review of the implementation of the framework for capacity-building under the Convention and under the Kyoto Protocol.
8. Nonetheless, there remain outstanding issues which require further discussion after Marrakech. The Group places a priority on scaling up of finance, in particular adaptation finance. There can be no enhanced action without enhanced support. Support enables action and action needs support. Enhanced action needs enhanced support in the provision of scaled-up financial resources, technology, and capacity-building. Action must cover both adaptation and mitigation.
9. Developing country parties are bearing the brunt of the increasing adverse effects of climate change and are the least equipped to cope with this problem on our own. The extent to which we can undertake our actions depends on the implementation by developed country parties of their obligations related to finance, technology, and capacity-building.
10. The provision of scaled-up financial resources should cover all developing country parties undertaking climate change actions under the Convention. To this end, we have adopted decisions on guidance to the two operating entities of the financial mechanism, the Green Climate Fund, and the Global Environment Facility, as well as on guidance to the Standing Committee on Finance.
11. We are pleased that much work has been done during this Conference on finance. There has been good guidance to the operating entities although much more work remains for all issues to finance. We note the adoption of the decision on long-term finance, but we have yet to see clarity or assurances on the mobilization and provision of scaled up financial resources for developing countries, in particular for achieving a balance of financing for mitigation and adaptation.
12. The strong and united call of the Group of 77 and China for certainty that the Adaptation Fund serves the Paris Agreement has not been fully heard.

Despite our call, against it, the conditions required for this to be triggered are still in the decision. Hence, the predictability and adequacy of financing for adaptation remain important difficulties to be resolved.

13. The Group reiterates that means of implementation are critical for actions on mitigation and adaptation both pre- and post-2020. Adequate, predictable, and sustained finance, technology and capacity-building must be ensured to assist developing country parties to enhance our climate actions.

Mr. President,

14. In closing, the Group wishes to thank you once again in guiding us to a successful conclusion of this Conference. The Group is committed to engaging positively and constructively and look forward to a smooth transition to the next COP Presidency. On this note, the Group extends its sincere congratulations to Fiji and reiterates the Group's full support and cooperation to Fiji and our full confidence in the leadership that Fiji will bring to our work next year. We also appreciate the announcement by Poland to host COP-24 and look forward to building up momentum together as we approach 2018.

Statement on behalf of the Group of 77 and China by Ms. Carola Iñiguez, Under-Secretary of Multilateral Affairs of Ecuador, at the Opening Plenary of the Third Part of the First Session of the Ad Hoc Working Group of the Paris Agreement (APA 1–3) (Bonn, Germany, 8 May 2017)

Distinguished Co-Chairs,
Ecuador has the honour to deliver this statement on behalf of the Group of 77 and China.

1. The Paris Agreement adopted under the UNFCCC is the collective achievement of all parties, which seeks to enhance the implementation of the United Nations Framework Convention on Climate Change, in accordance with its principles and provisions, in particular equity and common but differentiated responsibilities and respective capabilities, in the light of different national circumstances, and the right to development, in the context of sustainable development and efforts to eradicate poverty. The global effort to fight climate change is an irreversible process that cannot be postponed. We reiterate that the implementation of the Paris Agreement will reflect equity and the principle of common but differentiated responsibilities and respective capabilities, in the light of different national circumstances.
2. As we continue the work to develop and agree on the set of decisions for the implementation of the Paris Agreement's various provisions, we reiterate

the importance of preserving the delicate balance of all the issues that was achieved in Paris at COP-21 and in Marrakech at COP-22. These outcomes are not to be renegotiated nor reinterpreted, as the process under the Paris Agreement is irreversible. We stress the importance of moving from conceptual discussions to textual negotiations by COP-23 while maintaining the balance struck in the Paris Agreement between mitigation, adaptation and means of implementation.

3. The work of APA should be party-driven and undertaken in a transparent, inclusive, balanced, and coherent manner. All elements of the Paris Agreement, including mitigation, adaptation, finance, technology development and transfer, capacity-building, transparency of actions and support, and the mechanism to facilitate the implementation and promotion of compliance, must advance. There must be the appropriate coordination to generate synergies while carefully analysing overlaps with different bodies, in particular the SBSTA and SBI.
4. The G-77 and China recognizes that Nationally Determined Contributions (NDCs) are a key vehicle to deliver enhanced action under the Paris Agreement and to achieve the Agreement's long-term goals on all issues, including mitigation, adaptation and means of implementation in support to developing countries. National determination is a fundamental characteristic of NDCs. Appropriate and further guidance on features, information, and accounting for NDCs as well as further guidance in relation to the adaptation communication, including, *inter alia*, as a component of NDCs, is welcomed; in this regard, we urge developed country parties to provide finance, technology development and transfer, and capacity-building support to developing country parties for the preparation, communication, and implementation of their NDCs.
5. The Group highlights the importance of adaptation. The Group further highlights the importance of achieving the global goal on adaptation, especially since climate change is adversely impacting our countries. Further guidance in relation to the adaptation communication would therefore enhance adaptation action and support and also be an essential input to the Global Stocktake and as an opportunity to balance the profile of adaptation with mitigation while implementing the Paris Agreement. Such guidance must reflect the country-driven nature of adaptation and aim to enhance the adaptive capacity, reduce vulnerability, and increase resilience without creating additional burdens on developing countries. In this regard, we urge developed countries to provide adequate support to developing countries in meeting the cost of their adaptation actions.
6. The Group recognizes the importance of the work on the modalities, procedures, and guidelines for the transparency framework for actions and support, given the imminent timeline of 2018, for this work to be considered by the Conference of the Parties serving as the Meeting of the Parties to the

Paris Agreement (CMA). This technical work needs to be party-driven, balanced and guided by the principles of the enhanced transparency framework, which should build on the existing arrangements under the Convention. Flexibility for developing countries in light of their capacities must be discussed as part of the enhanced transparency framework, including reporting, technical expert review, and facilitative multilateral consideration. Complying with the set timeline will send a positive signal to the international community that work is progressing.

7. The Group believes that sources of input and modalities of the Global Stocktake should be comprehensive and facilitative, considering mitigation, adaptation, and the means of implementation and support, in light of equity and the best available science. Further discussion on the linkage between actions and support in the modalities of the Global Stocktake is important for reaching a common understanding and for providing a strong basis for addressing its design.
8. The Group reaffirms that the Committee to facilitate implementation and promote compliance must be facilitative in nature and function in a transparent, non-adversarial, and non-punitive manner. National capabilities and circumstances of parties should be reflected, and the adequate participation of parties concerned is important for its effective operation.
9. On Response Measures, the Group reaffirm the importance of giving full consideration to identifying the necessary actions to meet the specific needs and concerns of developing country parties arising from the impact of the implementation of response measures and avoid the negative economic and social consequences of response measures on developing countries. In this regard, we look forward to enhanced actions through strengthening institutional arrangements and the establishment of a cooperative mechanism to address the adverse impacts of the implementation of response measures on developing countries. The Group welcomes the first technical expert group meeting on the impact of implementation of response measures and looks forward to the inputs and recommendations from the experts to support the work of the improved forum. We should provide sufficient space and time for TEG members to make their contributions, which will allow the improved forum to achieve concrete outcomes as envisaged by parties. The Group also emphasizes the importance of working on the modalities, functions, and work programs for the forum under the Paris Agreement.

Distinguished Co-Chairs,

10. The Group of 77 and China stresses the importance of developed countries to take the lead in accordance with their historical responsibilities including by reducing their emissions and providing support to developing countries. We recall the importance on honouring their commitment to undertake

pre-2020 action, particularly by ratifying the Doha Amendment to the Kyoto Protocol by the end of this year so that it can enter into force, and ensure support, including finance for adaptation action, as an urgent priority for developing countries.

11. The Group emphasizes the importance of developed countries to provide new and additional climate finance, including the goal of mobilizing US$100 billion annually by 2020 from all sources to address the needs of developing countries; technology development and transfer; cooperation; participatory, country-driven and cross-cutting capacity-building; and all the needed support and means of implementation for developing countries, which have ambition to improve performance over time but currently lack capacities to do so. We emphasize the need for further clarity and robust methodologies to track and account for the provision of finance by developed countries. We also stress the importance that the Adaptation Fund definitively serve the Paris Agreement as of 2018.
12. On accounting of financial resources, the Group reaffirms that the modalities for accounting of financial resources by developed country parties to developing country parties, mobilized through public interventions, in accordance with article 9, paragraph 7, of the Paris Agreement, must aim to provide transparency and consistency. The reported information must also be comparable and verifiable. No developing countries are to be excluded from receiving financial support for their enhanced climate change actions whether they have or have not ratified the Paris Agreement.
13. Direct access of all developing country parties of the Convention and the Paris Agreement to means of implementation including finance, technology transfer, and capacity-building provided by developed country parties through relevant multilateral entities should be simplified and granted to ensure proper implementation of climate action plans and the achievement of the objectives of the Convention and the purpose of the Paris Agreement.
14. The G-77 and China reaffirms its full support to you, Co-Chairs, and will continue to engage in this ongoing process constructively.

Statement on behalf of the Group of 77 and China by Mr. Walter Schuldt, Deputy Special Representative of the Chair of the Group of 77 and China for Climate Change at the Closing Plenary of the Ad Hoc Working Group on the Paris Agreement, Third Part of the First Session (Bonn, Germany, 18 May 2017)

Madam Co-Chairs,

I have the honour to deliver this statement on behalf of the Group of 77 and China. At the outset, the Group would like to thank you, Madame Co-Chairs, and all the facilitators under your able leadership, for your efforts during this session.

After the early entry into force of the Paris Agreement and the important decisions adopted at COP-22 in Marrakech, it is essential that the international community realizes that this Ad Hoc Working Group has being able to make progress in concrete textual work. To that effect, we have been engaged constructively with a view to maintain the delicate balance achieved in Paris and to ensure that the implementation of the Paris Agreement reflects equity and the principle of common but differentiated responsibilities and respective capabilities, in the light of different national circumstances.

1. On further guidance in relation to the mitigation section of decision 1/CP.21, the Group takes note of the invitation to present focused submissions based on the elements and issues outlined in the informal note prepared by the co-facilitators, without prejudice to further work under this agenda item, as well as the request for an in-session round table during the COP-23. In any case, we stress that this guidance should be developed in a flexible manner to accommodate the diversity of NDCs and the national circumstances of developing country parties and the nationally determined nature of contributions.
2. On further guidance in relation to the adaptation communication, the Group of 77 and China took an active and constructive position during the informal consultations. We had an interesting discussion about the purpose, possible elements, linkages, vehicles, and flexibility of the communication, as well on the possible "skeleton" or structure of the outcome on this agenda item. The G-77 and China provided specifics written inputs for purpose, elements and "skeleton" or structure. The Group also expects that the roundtables address the linkages with support by developed country parties, transparency, and Global Stocktake. The informal note of the facilitators captures the debate and the views of parties during the session, and we are happy to find in the draft conclusions some possible ways to advance our work to COP-23. We would like to recall that adaptation is a priority of developing countries as evidenced by our active involvement in this issue, and a key component of the implementation of the Paris Agreement.
3. On modalities, procedures, and guidelines for the transparency framework for action and support, the Group is pleased with the progress made, recognizing that there is still much work to be done. We look forward to preparing our targeted submissions, which will give us the opportunity to provide our views on these elements contained in the informal note prepared by the co-facilitators and detail substantive options under each of these elements, without limiting the continuation of discussion during the next session. With respect to the framework for transparency of support, we stress the need that all financial flows provided and mobilized should take into account the needs, priorities, and flexibilities to be provided to developing country parties. We insist that the objective of this framework should be to clarify

information on financial support that developed countries provide and mobilize to developing countries for their implementation of climate actions under the Paris Agreement; and enable developing countries to evaluate their needs and define their finance priorities. We look forward to participating in the pre-sessional roundtable and we hope it will allow inclusive, open, and broad participation of all parties and facilitate technical discussions on how cross cutting issues listed in article 13, including paragraphs 2–4 are considered in parties' submissions.

4. On matters relating to the Global Stocktake, the Group believes that we have made some progress at this session, with greater understanding emerging from our discussions with respect to the context, linkages, scope, purpose, modalities, information needs, sources of inputs, and outcome of the GST. However, we continue to look for convergence because much divergence remains. The issues and elements that have been raised by parties with respect to the GST have been reflected in the informal note on agenda item 6, without prejudice to parties' reflections on various aspects of the specific contents in the informal note, including on the possible outline. The Group wishes to stress, in this connection, that the comprehensive scope, its facilitative nature, its outcome, and the role of the GST in the implementation of the Paris Agreement as stated in the Paris Agreement should be fully reflected in the results of our negotiations going forward.
5. On modalities and procedures for the effective operation of the committee to facilitate implementation and promote compliance, the Group welcomes the call for focused submissions by 15 September 2017 session. We would like to thank the co-facilitators for their informal note, but also highlight that parties should continue putting forward their views on any issues or aspects in relation to the operationalization of article 15 as they seem relevant. The Group considers that further discussions need to be taken on the manner in which the measures to be taken by the Committee could be related with financial, technology development and transfer, and capacity-building mechanisms that provides guidance or assistance developing country parties. The G-77 and China is willing to work constructively with all parties to move towards a negotiating text on the item at the end of COP-23, laying a solid foundation for the timely completion of the work in 2018.
6. On the Adaptation Fund, the Group reiterates that the Adaptation Fund shall serve the Paris Agreement. During the session, the group actively participated in the discussions promoted by the co-facilitators on the mandate given by CMA-1 regarding governance and institutional arrangements, safeguards, and operating modalities of the Adaptation Fund to serve the Paris Agreement. We provided concrete ideas regarding the possible elements to be included under these titles, as well as the options of governance and legal questions regarding the implications of these aspects. These points have been collected in the informal note of co-facilitators. Notwithstanding, the Group

highlights that the Adaptation Fund's decision to serve the Paris Agreement should address procedural matters as well as reflect the high relevance of the matter which calls for a prompt response. The Group is expecting concrete actions in that direction during the COP-23. In this vein, access of developing country parties to means of implementation including finance, technology transfer, and capacity-building should always be guaranteed in order to meet their reporting obligation and implement their climate action plans.

7. On Response Measures, the Group reaffirms the importance of giving full consideration to identify the necessary actions to meet the specific needs and concerns of developing country parties arising from the impact of the implementation of response measures and avoid its negative economic and social consequences, including with regard to equitable access to sustainable development and poverty eradication. The group welcomes the findings of the first meeting of the TEC, which would help to enhance the work of the Forum. In this regard, we look forward to enhanced actions through strengthening institutional arrangements and the establishment of a cooperative mechanism to address the adverse impacts of the implementation of response measures on developing countries. Moreover, following decision 11/CP.21 it is important to move towards the implementation of an enhanced forum and technical group of experts to allow for an institutional arrangement post-2020 in the context of the Paris Agreement.
8. The Group recognizes the continuation of the discussions on the possible additional matters, in particular on financial support by developed country parties under agenda item 8. In this regard, the APA should take finance as a significant issue in the November session.
9. The work under SBI, SBSTA, and other bodies under the UNFCCC, and its Kyoto Protocol has a direct impact for both the post-2020 implementation and the enhancement of the pre-2020 action, and in that regard, we would like to reemphasize the urgent need to enhance pre-2020 action and support, as a solid foundation for post-2020 implementation. On the path to COP-23, we look forward to a constructive engagement in adequately addressed in the upcoming sessions the need to enhance the provision of financial resources, including for technology development and transfer, and capacity-building support for pre-2020 action. We need to send a signal that we are committed with pre-2020, otherwise we fear that if we don´t address this, the gap may widen.

The Group of 77 and China will continue to engage actively and constructively in the upcoming months and at the resumed APA session in November. Statement of the Group of 77 and China, delivered by Mr. Walter Schuldt, Deputy Special Representative of the Chair of the Group of 77 and China for Climate Change, at the Joint Opening Plenary of the 23rd Session of the Conference of the Parties (COP-23), 13th Session of the Conference of the Parties Serving as the Meeting of the Parties to the Kyoto Protocol (CMP-13) and Second Part of the 1st Session of the Conference of the Parties Serving as the Meeting of the Parties to the Paris Agreement (CMA1.2) (Bonn, Germany, 6 November 2017)

Mr. President,

I have the honour to deliver this statement on behalf of the Group of 77 and China.

At the outset, the Group would like to express its gratitude to Morocco for a successful presidency of COP-22 while congratulating Fiji, for taking the historic role as the first Small Island Developing State presiding a COP. We are very proud that a former Chair of the G-77 will lead us in this COP and we are sure that the Bula spirit which means inclusiveness, friendliness, and solidarity and the Pacific concept of Talanoa of inclusiveness, participatory and transparent dialogue that builds empathy and leads to decision making for the collective good, and that both concepts will influence a successful outcome at the end of this two weeks and during its entire presidency.

At the same time, allow me to express our deepest sympathy and solidarity with all countries that have faced extreme weather events during this intersessional period in different parts of the world, that have endured serious human and economic losses, demonstrating that the impacts of climate change will not wait until 2020, and that we need to address urgently its growing impacts to our peoples, our development as well as our cultures, ecosystems, and biodiversity. The best way to honour these victims will be to achieve concrete progress during this COP including the fulfilment of the pre-2020 agenda and the development of more effective mechanisms to address the loses and damages and the provision of sufficient financial, technology, and capacity-building support.

We are ready to engage constructively in the textual work that is needed for the operationalization of the Paris Agreement in a manner that reflects equity and the principle of common but differentiated responsibilities and respective capabilities, in the light of different national circumstances, while continuing to enhance the full implementation of the Convention and its Kyoto Protocol, without any renegotiation or reinterpretation of their principles and provisions.

COP-23 must continue to advance the Work Program of the Paris Agreement, towards its completion in 2018. It also must provide clarity on the design of the 2018 Facilitative Dialogue referred by the Fijian Presidency as Talanoa Dialogue.

We stress the need to fully implement article 8 of the Paris Agreement as a matter of urgency, in order to allow a better integration of loss and damage issues into the broader ongoing work of the UNFCCC, to identify and implement concrete alternatives of support and cooperation for developing country parties that are increasingly experiencing losses and damages resulting from extreme weather events to facilitate this fully implementation. The G-77 and China calls for loss and damages to be included as a permanent item on the agendas of the subsidiary bodies, with a broader and more inclusive scope of inputs from all parties that will be available at regular meetings of the subsidiary bodies, including the Warsaw International Mechanism for Loss and Damage and its five-year work program. In this regard we stress further our need for special financial resources from developed country parties to cover activities and further actions in our countries.

As we continue being in the implementation phase of the Paris Agreement, it is crucial to preserve its delicate balance and ensure that no one will be left behind. We must ensure transparency, inclusiveness, a party-driven process on the basis of consensus and balance of all issues and across different bodies.

Mr. President,

The Group stresses the need to enhance the pre-2020 ambition providing a strong basis for post-2020 efforts under the Paris Agreement. We would also call further for the ratification of the Doha Amendment by parties that have not yet done so, so as to enable its prompt entry into force and the implementation of the Kyoto Protocol second commitment period expeditiously.

On another issue, we would expect a concrete outcome of this COP to be the confirmation that the Adaptation Fund will serve the Paris Agreement, via decisions from the CMP and the CMA so that the following sessions of the bodies of the COP and the next COP can decide on the arrangements pending for this to happen.

It is important to recognize that adaptation efforts by developing country parties contribute to combating adverse effects of global climate change. In this regard the group proposes to construct the proper way to recognize and register adaptation efforts and measures. We also emphasize the importance of the work under APA in relation to further guidance to the adaptation communication in order to enhance support for adaptation in developing countries. It is crucial that TEP-Adaptation provides a better understanding for parties to be prepared for the 2018 Facilitative Dialogue.

The advances of the Committee of Adaptation reflected in the report are very welcome; however expert guidance for modalities and procedures under APA should be reviewed in a comprehensive and holistic manner.

We see with concern the flows to finance adaptation actions through specific multilateral funds, rapidly declining. Funds under the guidance of the COP are demanding additional unwarranted requirements that have not being agreed under the Convention and place an additional burden to developing countries.

We would like to stress the importance of having substantial and concrete advancement at this COP. We expect that the discussions on long-term finance will help to identify the needs and priorities of developing countries, in particular on adaptation, financing, technology, and capacity-building, which could also assist in the establishment of a new long-term financial goal, including through a new collective quantified goal beyond the already committed but yet insufficient floor of US$100 billion per year, in line with decision 1/CP.21.

Guidance to the Green Climate Fund has to include filling the policy gaps, in particular on eligibility criteria, the start of a replenishment process, and the linkage with the UN system so as to facilitate direct access to GCF funds. The sixth review of the financial mechanism will provide the opportunity to promote coherence in the climate finance architecture.

On the provision on financial and technical support, the Group regrets to bring to your attention the increasing difficulties and conditionalities faced by several developing countries in accessing financial resources from the GEF, including through the establishment of program priorities and eligibility criteria that have not been agreed at the intergovernmental level. The Group is deeply concerned about the no response from GEF to continued communication of these parties.

The Group also expresses its deepest concern that some developed countries are unilaterally applying into the decision-making processes eligibility criteria that are not agreed to and that limit the access of funding to developing countries under the GCF; such criteria is not compatible with guidance from the COP and is a clear departure from the letter and spirit of the Convention and the Paris Agreement. We also feel that the process and procedures of these institutions are creating continuous additional barriers to access financial resources for climate action, which severely undermine the level of ambition of developing countries in the global effort against climate change. Also, we expect this issue to be clearly addressed in the guidance of the COP to the financial mechanism.

On response measures, the Group reaffirms the importance of giving full consideration to identify necessary actions to meet the specific needs and concerns of developing country parties arising from the impact of the implementation of response measures and to avoid the negative economic and social consequences of response measures on developing countries. The Group welcomes the invitation to the pre-sessional workshop on modalities, work programme and functions under the Paris Agreement of the forum on the impact of the implementation of response measures and looks forward to the report, inputs and recommendations from the roundtable to support the work of the improved forum. The group also emphasizes the importance of fulfilling the mandate of decision 11/CP21 and advancing the work on the pre-2020 and post-2020 tracks on the modalities, functions, and work programs for the forum under the Paris Agreement.

It is crucial to guarantee the participation of developing countries in the work of the bodies of the Convention, including the Standing Committee on Finance, making the necessary adjustments so that the system works effectively and efficiently.

In the face of increasing number and intensity of extreme weather events, there is an urgent need for effective action on the provision of financial resources, including for technology development and transfer and capacity-building to developing countries.

Mr. President,

We recall that capacity-building should be based on national needs and foster country-ownership, the process must be participatory as well as cross-cutting.

We also express our concern on negative implications resulting out of unilateral coercive economic measures for climate action in developing countries, to avoid undermining developing countries capacities to fight climate change and the rights to live of our peoples.

Finally, the G-77 and China conveys its deep appreciation to you Mr. Chair, and reaffirm its commitment to continue engaging constructively under your guidance in order to achieve a successful outcome at the end of this COP.

Statement on behalf of the Group of 77 and China, delivered by Mr. Walter Schuldt, Deputy Special Representative of the Chair of the Group of 77 and China for Climate Change, at the Opening Plenary of the Ad Hoc Working Group of the Paris Agreement, Fourth Part of the First Session (Bonn, Germany, 7 November 2017)

Madame Co-Chairs,

I have the honour to deliver this statement on behalf of the Group of 77 and China. At the outset, the Group would like to thank the Co-Chairs for the Reflection Note which provides a helpful outline for our work at this session. We look forward to continue to engage constructively in the textual work that is needed for the operationalization of the Paris Agreement in a manner that reflects equity and the principle of common but differentiated responsibilities and respective capabilities, in the light of different national circumstances, and in the context of sustainable development and efforts to eradicate poverty; while continuing to enhance the full implementation of the Convention and its Kyoto Protocol, without any renegotiation or reinterpretation of their principles and provisions.

In that process, we reiterate that the work of APA should be party-driven and undertaken in a comprehensive, balanced, and coherent manner, addressing mitigation, adaptation, finance, technology development and transfer, and capacity-building in a single package. To that effect, our Group and its different constituencies have provided an important number of submissions with concrete substantive proposals and inputs that together with the submissions from the rest of our partners, should be the basis for our negotiations, of course, without limiting the opportunities for parties to provide additional inputs that may have been omitted or that may result from the round tables or the negotiations, ensuring therefore that no one is left behind.

On agenda item 3, the Group stresses that the guidance should respect both the diversity and the nationally determined character of NDCs, and that it should assist parties with the preparation and communications of their NDCs in order to facilitate clarity, transparency and understanding of parties' contributions. In this regard we welcome an appropriate and further guidance on features, information, and accounting for NDCs as well as further guidance in in relation to the adaptation communication, including, *inter alia*, as a component of the NDC. We stress that this guidance should be develop in a flexible manner to accommodate the diversity of NDCs, their nationally determined nature, and the national circumstances of developing country parties. We urge developed countries to provide finance, technology development and transfer, and capacity-building support to developing country parties for the preparation, communication, and implementation of their NDCs.

The Group emphasizes the extreme importance of adaptation especially since climate change is increasingly impacting our members and limiting our overall capacities to achieve sustainable development. On agenda item 4, we believe that adaptation communications would enhance adaptation action and support and at the same time they will serve as a clear input to the Global Stocktake and as a tool to achieve the global goal on adaptation. The guidance must reflect the country-driven nature of adaptation and aim to enhance the adaptive capacity, reduce vulnerability, and increase resilience without creating additional burdens on developing countries, while being comprehensive and have optional elements to help guide parties' Adaptation communication. We urge developed country parties to provide adequate support to developing country parties in meeting the cost of their adaptation actions.

On agenda item 5, we consider that the MPGs for enhanced transparency framework need to reflect the different and nationally determined nature of the NDCs and should be developed on the basis of the existing differentiated transparency arrangements under the Convention, with a view to enhance them. The Group highlights that flexibility applies to all aspects of the enhanced transparency framework-reporting, review, and multilateral consideration, for developing countries in light of their capacities. We stress the need that all finance provided and mobilized by developed country parties should take into account the needs and priorities of developing country parties. In this regard, we believe that one the purposes of this framework should be to clarify information on financial support that developed countries provide and mobilize to developing countries for their implementation of climate actions under the Paris Agreement; and also to enable developing countries to evaluate their needs and define their finance priorities.

On agenda item 6, the Group would like to recall the comprehensive, transparent, and facilitative nature of the Global Stocktake, and in that regard its modalities and the sources of its inputs should include mitigation, adaptation, and all the means of implementation, in light of equity and the best available science, enabling a clear linkage between action and support. Therefore, such modalities should facilitate a Global Stocktake of the collective progress made in the achievement of the objective purpose and goals of the Convention and its Paris Agreement, so that the outcome as established on the article 14.3 informs parties in updating and enhancing, in a nationally determined manner, their actions and support in accordance with the relevant provisions of the Agreement, as well as in enhancing cooperation for climate action. In this regard, we wish to highlight the importance of addressing loss and damage for developing countries, and the importance of the specific needs and concerns of developing countries arising from the impacts of the implementation of response measures, in line with the objective of achieving the purpose of the Paris Agreement and its long-term goals.

On agenda item 7, the Group reaffirms that the article 15 Committee to promote compliance and facilitate implementation shall be facilitative in nature and function in a transparent, non-adversarial and non-punitive manner, reflecting the different responsibilities, national circumstances, and capacities of developed and developing country parties under the Convention and its Paris Agreement. At the same time, the work of the Committee should be comprehensive and consultative with a view to guidance or assistance in all aspects, including mitigation, adaptation, finance, technology development and transfer, capacity-building and response measures.

On agenda item 8, we would like to recall that there are a number of additional issues—some of which are mandated issues to CMA to address—that deserve further consultations, and therefore we reiterate the urgent need to decide on their different processes including, *inter alia*, in relation to the communication of information on public finance by developed country parties, the Forum on the Impact of the Implementation of Responses Measures to serve the Paris Agreement, the Adaptation Fund to serve the Paris Agreement, the Financial Mechanism as well as the LDC Fund and the SCCF under the Paris Agreement, and the establishment of a new long-term financial goal, taking into account the needs and priorities of developing countries. On the Adaptation Fund's decision to serve the Paris Agreement, the Group considers it should address procedural matters and reflect the high relevance of the matter which calls for a prompt response. The Group is expecting concrete actions in that direction during this COP.

Finally, we also express our concern on the negative implications resulting out of unilateral coercive economic measures for climate action in developing countries, to avoid undermining developing countries capacities to fight climate change and the rights to live of our peoples.

Madame Co-Chairs, we reiterate our continued constructive engagement with you and with all the rest of the delegations to achieve a successful and balanced outcome on all the agenda items.

Statement of the Group of 77 and China delivered by Mr. Walter Schuldt, Deputy Special Representative of the Chair of the Group of 77 and China for Climate Change at the Stocktaking Session of COP-23, CMP-13, CMA-1.4, SBI-47, SBSTA-47, and APA-1.4 (Bonn, Germany, 11 November 2017)

Distinguished Chairs and Co-Chairs,

I have the honour to deliver the following remarks on behalf of the Group of 77 and China, at this mid-term Stocktake session:

At the outset, the G-77 and China appreciates your work Chairs and Co-Chairs as well as the efforts of the Co-Facilitators to guide us towards the concrete progress that we came here to achieve at this COP in all the agenda items.

We thank you all for your reports and we reaffirm our full support to you, while reiterating our will to continue engaging constructively in the textual work that is needed for the operationalization of the Paris Agreement and the enhancement of the full implementation of the Convention and its Kyoto Protocol.

During the opening plenaries at the beginning of this week, we reaffirmed, *inter alia*, the need for a balanced treatment of mitigation, adaptation and means of implementation throughout the different agenda items; the need to avoid any attempt of reinterpretation of the Convention and of the Paris Agreement; the need to respect the differentiation between developed and developing country parties reflected in the Convention and in the Paris Agreement.

However, we regret to transmit our concern about certain procedural and substantial issues. On process, our Group thank you for the diagram as an effort to address the challenge of identifying all the interlinkages between the different tracks and components of the implementation of the Paris Agreement under the different bodies. We hope that this tool will help us to better address the situations in which there is an unequal treatment of certain elements within the agenda items, unequal modalities and guidance followed by parties in the discussions, and also different levels of engagement and preference in terms of how and when to capture the outcomes of the discussions.

The G-77 and China would like also to re-emphasize the urgent need to enhance pre-2020 action and support in finance, technology, and capacity-building from developed country to developing country parties, as a solid foundation for post-2020 implementation. In that regard we look forward for the assessment of the progress of implementation of decision 1 C.P/19, paragraphs 3 and 4 to accelerate the implementation of the commitments and obligations in relation to the provision of means of implementation, including technology, finance, and capacity-building support for developing country parties. We stress the need to take stock of the collective progress made in implementing the pre-2020 commitments and actions and increasing ambition, in particular on the provision of support. We recognize the efforts of the Presidency of COP-23 for the ongoing consultations, we remain open to exploring news options in that regard, while reaffirming the high importance that we attach to this issue, in particular in the context of the twentieth anniversary of the Kyoto Protocol and the increasing adverse impacts of climate change in our countries, that keep reminding us that we need climate action and support now, and not only after 2020.

Precisely, on finance, the Group is greatly concerned over the lack of progress on all finance and finance-related issues, faced with the lack of political will to advance on these issues. We are also concerned over the very short time provided for negotiations of these very important agenda items. The G-77 and China do not have an inter-sessional forum to discuss the preparations for the COP and can only meet during COPs. Moreover, most of us have small delegations and cannot be present at all negotiating discussions and need coordinating time. In essence, time is important, but even more important is the political will needed to advance on items related to finance as the enabler to move towards the operationalization of the Paris Agreement.

The Group also believes that one of the most important issues is the eligibility criteria for the GEF, on this vein on COP agenda item 10.d. the Group has presented written inputs to the Co-Facilitators in the form of a draft decision, based on the text provided by the Standing Committee on Finance and its appendix, while also having taken into consideration the important views of the parties. It is imperative to stress that the SCF's work should not limit the discussion on the guidance to the GEF, as all parties are entitled to introduce their concerns and views for discussion, especially at the COP, which task is to provide guidance to the entity on eligibility, programming priorities, and policies. The group would like to stress that access to financial resources must be granted to all developing country parties. We look forward to having constructive discussion over this and other important matters, such as access modalities, in order to achieve a result that accommodates all parties concerns.

On the Green Climate Fund, we reiterate our concern that the Board has started to apply categories of developing country parties that are neither recognized by the Convention nor within the scope of the governing instrument of the Fund, these categories are in clear violation of the eligibility criteria of the Fund and cannot be the basis for the Secretariat giving guidance to parties suggesting they do not apply for grants or concessional financing for climate change. We will insist this be solved in GCF guidance and reject this type of behaviour.

On the review of the functions of the SCF, we recognize that the committee has made great efforts to enhance participation of observers and that it has a key role in assisting the COP in all finance related issues. However, due to the difficulties related to climate change extreme weather events, and other economic and political shocks, developing country members have not been able to guarantee their participation for every session, and for this reason our Group had proposed a system of alternates so that when a member is not able to attend the meetings, its alternate would be able to do so. This proposal has no budgetary implications whatsoever and nonetheless it has been objected by developed country parties without a clear argument, which demonstrates that there is no real interest in ensuring a full participation of developing countries in the Committee.

On COP agenda item 10(f) on the process to identify the information that developed countries will present under article 9.5 of the PA, we note the willingness of our partners to limit discussions on the types of information already being reported under biennial reports and under biennial submissions, on strategies and approaches to mobilize climate finance. However, we see the lack of will to discuss modalities to report that information, which was a proposal of our Group presented under APA agenda item 8. Without these modalities, like common formats, definitions, underlying assumptions and methodologies, the information that will be presented on expected levels of financial support will be rendered incomparable, impossible to aggregate and useless to have a global picture of climate finance to be provided, which limits developing countries planning on their implementation of the Paris Agreement and their NDCs.

On the Adaptation Fund serving the Paris Agreement, we regret to see lack of will to have a decision saying the Fund shall serve the Agreement. We are stuck in discussions on the strategic role of the Fund within the broader climate finance panorama, or on the conditions to engage in these discussions, like the definition of every detail and arrangement for the Fund to serve the Agreement, when these arrangements can be developed until 2020. We urge developed country parties to demonstrate their political will for a decision at this COP, particularly taking into account the importance of this Fund to developing countries and SIDS in particular.

On adaptation, we reiterate the high priority that our countries assign to adaptation, particularly in the current context of the increasing occurrence and severity of extreme weather events and the costs involved. Therefore, our Group has worked hard in this session to continue having a common position on adaptation and especially with regard to adaptation communication. We have reached a document that attempts to advance aspects of the guidance of adaptation communication in the understanding that this is the time to generate substantive progress. One of the key points of this guidance is the support needed from developed to developing country parties, in order to implement article 7.13 of the Paris Agreement, considering the need for public and grant-based resources for adaptation under article 9.4. We hope that this session will result in a skeleton where headings, subheadings, and textual inputs are clearly identified in the informal consultations based on the submissions or proposals from country parties.

On National Adaptation Plans, we would like to reiterate that, addressing medium and long-term adaptation challenges in developing country parties are extremely important. There are still multiple challenges that developing country parties face in accessing financial support for the development and implementation of NAPs from the Green Climate Fund and would therefore call for easy and simplified procedures by the GCF for the NAPs readiness and implementation facilities.

With regard to Loss and Damage, our Group has confirmed with great concern how extreme weather events unprecedentedly affects our countries in a more frequent and destructive manner than ever before, while there's not either an effective approach to address the loss and damage associated with slow onset events related to climate change. For those reasons we call for the full implementation of article 8 of the Paris Agreement and relevant decisions of the UNFCCC. Special financial resources from developed country parties for activities and actions in developing countries need to be provided urgently. Loss and Damage requires a permanent item on the agendas of the SBs, in order to count on a more inclusive space of negotiations that allows all parties to express their approaches in relation to the full operationalization of the Warsaw International Mechanism. Relevant mandates of this Convention need to be urgently undertaken in order to provide the support developing countries need as a matter of survival.

With regard to agriculture, our Group has been working hard for several years in the objective of reaching an agreement that allows the implementation in agriculture. However, the SBSTA work on this agenda item is only meaningful if it feeds SBI and other implementation bodies under the Convention. For this, we want to achieve a COP decision that opens the door for implementation and a synergistic work between SBSTA and SBI, including other implementation bodies. We also need to renew our work in SBSTA with new topics to fulfil our mandate. Until now we have progressed a lot in that direction, but difficulties still remain, due to the resistance of Annex I parties to accept a COP decision that includes SBI. Tomorrow is the last day we have for this, and our partners are still reluctant. Nevertheless, we are optimistic that an agreement can be found, and the Group has shown a great flexibility for this. Not arriving to any outcome again, would be a very bad sign, being agriculture the most vulnerable sector and the basis of food security.

On the article 15 Committee, the G-77 and China believes that in general all elements and provisions of the Paris Agreement shall be covered by the work of the committee, while the scope may differ in respect to the function of facilitating implementation and promoting compliance. The Group is also the view that establishing linkage with supporting mechanism is critical for fulfilling the facilitative role of the committee. In addition, the Committee shall pay particular attention to the respective national capabilities and circumstances of parties both in procedures and outcomes of the Committee.

On Transparency, our Group recognizes the progress made in the development of the modalities procedures and guidelines for the transparency framework on action and support. We participate on the basis of the mandate given in article 13 of the Paris Agreement which clearly provides different purposes for transparency of actions and support, in accordance with the relevant articles of the Paris Agreement. We have stated that enhanced support enables enhanced action, and that enhanced action requires enhanced support. Both must progress in a balanced manner.

On Global Stocktake, our Group emphasizes the need for a clear idea of the landing zone that we will arrive at, when this COP-23 ends. The Group feels that we need to move this process forward in a way that will enable us to arrive at a draft negotiating text for the CMA decision on the GST. The use of the revised template containing various possible building blocks for the GST modalities and other issues is useful, but there are other elements that should also be included such as context, coverage, principles, sources of inputs, modalities including activities to be undertaken, institutional arrangements, form of the output, and nature of the outcome. Equally important is reflecting equity, in an operational manner, in the

GST. The group appreciates the substantial time that has been allotted at this session for parties to focus on equity and its reflection in the GST and expects that similar attention will be provided to this issue specifically as negotiations progress. Other issues such as loss and damage and impacts of response measures are also important to highlight in this context. The Group feels that to move our process forward and accelerate our work, it would help to be clearer about what we are trying to design, capture the diversity as well as convergence of views and options presented by parties, and conclude at this session with a clear general structured outline for the various elements for the mandate, coverage, principles, process, institutional arrangements, inputs and activity modalities, and results of the GST.

On response measures, the Group reaffirms the importance of giving full consideration to identifying necessary actions to meet the specific needs and concerns of developing country parties arising from the impact of the implementation of response measures, and to avoid the negative economic and social consequences of response measures on developing countries. The Group also emphasizes the importance of fulfilling the mandate of decision 11/CP.21 and advancing the work on the pre-2020 and post-2020 tracks on the modalities, functions, and work programs for the forum under the Paris Agreement. The Group welcomes the progress made in this session and looks forward to progressing with this momentum.

On capacity-building the Group welcomes the synthesis report prepared to facilitate the annual monitoring and evaluation of the implementation of the framework for capacity-building in developing countries established under decision 2/CP7, and the summary report of the sixth meeting of the Durban Forum on capacity-building. However, there are still gaps with regards to strengthening work on capacity-building priority areas as outlined in the framework for capacity-building in developing countries and other emerging areas from the Paris Agreement. We would like to register our disappointment with lack of progress in finalizing textual proposals, with some parties seeming to block progress. The current resource constraints have an effect on the mandate of the Paris Committee on Capacity-Building (PCCB) to fully implement its work plan, aimed at achieving the goals as set out in article 2 of the Paris Agreement.

On common metrics, our Group acknowledges the draft conclusions agreed on SBSTA agenda item "Common metrics to calculate the carbon dioxide equivalence of greenhouse gases" and reiterates its acknowledgement of the relevance of common metrics to climate change policy.

Finally, our Group wants to reaffirm the spirit of openness to further explore innovative ways to move forward, and in that regard we welcome the continuation of your regular internal coordination, the allocation of two-hour slots, we accept the extension of hours of negotiation, but one component is still missing, not from you, but from our developed country parties, and that is the political will to engage constructively towards the highest priority of ensuring a balanced progress in all agenda items.

Statement on behalf of the Group of 77 and China by Mr. Walter Schuldt, Deputy special Representative of the Chair of the Group of 77 and China for Climate Change, at the Closing Plenary of COP-23, CMP-13, and CMA-1.2 (Bonn, Germany, 17 November 2017)

Mr. President,

I have the honour to deliver this statement on behalf of the Group of 77 and China.

The Group would like to extend its deepest gratitude to you, Honourable Prime Minister Baininarama, and to the entire team of the Presidency of Fiji for all your hard work, personal commitment, and engagement during these weeks, as well as for the demonstration of the Talanoa Spirit and warmth extended to all parties.

We also thank Germany for having hosted this COP-23 in partnership with Fiji and we thank the Executive Secretary for the continuous support and contribution to the successful organization of this Conference.

Mr. President,

The Group would like to reiterate its constructive engagement in all the negotiations of the APA agenda during this past two weeks, with the responsibility of advancing the work programme for the implementation of the Paris Agreement under the Convention, and the achievement of its purpose and objective respectively.

As we are entering into a new phase, we need to keep the political momentum and the level of political engagement that allowed the adoption and early entry into force of the Paris Agreement. In the same vain, we need to ensure that the delicate balance achieved in the Paris Agreement is maintained, in accordance with the principles of equity and common but differentiated responsibilities and respective capabilities, in light of the different national circumstances, the provision of flexibility for developing countries in all the different tracks of the design of the work programme under the Paris Agreement, and the provision of means of implementation, especially finance, technology development and transfer, and capacity-building for developing countries.

All these elements should be taken into account transversally in the work programme and the level of substantive progress in the negotiations must be indeed accelerated to ensure a synergetic, coordinated, and coherent progress within all the APA agenda items and the items under SBSTA, SBI, and COP.

In that regard, we acknowledge the importance of tools developed by the Secretariat to provide an overview of the work that is needed and to facilitate the identification of all the linkages and interlinkages between the work of COP and the bodies, in relation to the work programme of the Paris Agreement. Nevertheless, we believe that most importantly, the way forward to advance such work programme, must be determined by the outcomes of the work of the APA, the SBI, the SBSTA, and the COP on all matters related to the work programme, contained in the informal notes prepared at this session reflecting the views and proposals that we as parties put forward at this session and in our submissions.

We look forward for the reflections note to be presented with an overview of this session and options for the way forward on the basis mentioned above, to reflect all parties' views and options in a balanced manner.

Mr. President,

We believe that this COP has achieved the objective of continue to advance the textual work of the work programme of the Paris Agreement, and several deliverables that are very important for developing countries and for our peoples, and that we are proud to have contributed to shape.

Among those elements of success, we want to highlight the important decision on pre-2020 implementation and ambition, that includes a stock take on where we are, in relation to the pre-2020 work, recognizing that the enhancement of pre-2020 action and support in finance, technology, and capacity-building from developed country to developing country parties, is the solid foundation for post-2020 implementation. Pre-2020 is back and we are very proud to have contributed to that. In that regard we look forward for the assessment of the progress of implementation of decision 1 C.P/19, paragraphs 3 and 4 to accelerate the implementation of the commitments and obligations in relation to the provision of means of implementation for developing country parties. This is of particular importance for our countries, including in particular context of the twentieth anniversary of the Kyoto Protocol and the increasing adverse impacts of climate change in our countries, that keep reminding us that we need climate action and support now, and not only after 2020.

Under your leadership, Mr. President, we have undergone a constructive work towards the operationalization of the Warsaw International Mechanism for Loss and Damage, coherently with the need to tackle the consequences of extreme and slow onset weather events related to climate change that have affected different regions of the world, resulting in human and economic losses. We welcome the strengthening of the five years rolling work plan of the ExCom and the call for the establishment of the Suva Expert Dialogue, as the first step to the future establishment of an expert group on action and support, and the call for mobilization of resources for averting, minimizing, and addressing loss and damage. However, it still remains a long way to achieve the full implementation of the WIM under article 8 of the Paris Agreement.

Likewise, the Group of 77 and China is also very proud that our countries were able to contribute to a longstanding aspiration of our local communities and indigenous peoples, so that no longer are they considered mere observers of climate change but have the opportunity to become real actors of the solution, including through the exchange of experiences and sharing of best practices on climate change action in a holistic and integrated manner. The establishment of the Facilitative Working Group and the development of its work plan are fundamental and concrete steps towards for the full operationalization of the Platform.

We are also very satisfied about the progress achieved in agriculture after several years without any result. In this regard, we welcome the decision achieved, as an important first step for implementation and a synergistic work between SBSTA and SBI, including other implementation bodies, in the sector of agriculture that is one of the most vulnerable areas in our countries and one of the main bases of our food security.

Likewise, our Group share the same sentiment of pride and satisfaction with regard to the establishment of the first Gender Action Plan in relation to climate change, and several other important decisions on capacity-building, education, training and public awareness, public participation and public access to information, common metrics, and several other important areas of our countries.

Mr. President,

In spite of that good part of the storytelling of this COP-23, the story on financing is not necessarily a happy one. On such an important area, we have not seen progress on core elements such as in resolving the eligibility criteria adopted by the GEF through a draft decision, based on the text provided by the Standing Committee on Finance and its Appendix, and also taking into consideration the important views of the parties. It is imperative to stress that the SCF's work should not limit the discussion on the guidance to the GEF as we have continuously been observing. We reiterate that the access to financial resources must be granted to all developing country parties.

With relation to the discussions that were held on the Green Climate Fund, the Group reiterates its complete rejection to the usage of criteria outside of the scope of the UNFCCC or the governing instrument of the Fund in the assessment and discussion of developing countries funding proposals. Although we proposed the inclusion of language to this specific objective in guidance to the GCF, we understand that the compromise reached makes reference to requesting the Board to ensure that all developing country parties have access to all financial instruments available through the GCF, in line with the eligibility criteria referred to in the Governing Instrument and relevant COP decisions and to ensure application of the agreed policies of the Fund, but we insist on the issue behind this decision and hope that these situations are not repeated, they are completely out of the scope of what the executive board of the GCF should do and not in line with what the GCF was created to do.

On the other hand, no attention has been given to the proposal to adopt a system of alternates so that when a member is not able to attend the meetings of the SCF, its alternate would be able to do so.

On long-term finance we have identified the needs and priorities of developing countries, in particular on adaptation, financing, technology, and capacity-building, which could also assist in the establishment of a new long-term financial goal, including through a new collective quantified goal beyond the already committed but yet insufficient floor of US$100 billion per year, in line with decision 1/CP.21.

On adaptation, work has advanced. However, we have different challenges, such as refining the skeleton, advancing on the placement of information, and continuing the discussion on linkages. The G-77 and China stress that adaptation communication should not be prescriptive but should be anchored in the flexibility with a view of achieving the necessary support according to our priorities and needs.

We see with concern the flows to finance adaptation actions through specific multilateral funds, rapidly declining. Funds under the guidance of the COP are demanding additional unwarranted requirements that have not being agreed under the Convention and place an additional burden to developing countries.

The Group reaffirms the importance of giving full consideration to meet the specific needs and concerns of developing country parties arising from the impact of the implementation of response measures and to avoid the negative economic and social consequences of response measures on developing countries. The Group welcomes the invitation to the pre-sessional workshop on modalities, work programme, and functions under the Paris Agreement of the forum on the impact of the implementation of response measures and looks forward to the report, inputs and recommendations from the roundtable to support the work of the improved forum. The group also emphasizes the importance of fulfilling the mandate of decision 11/CP21 and advancing the work on the pre-2020 and post-2020 tracks on the modalities, functions, and work programs for the Forum under the Paris Agreement.

At the same time, we wanted to congratulate you for the successful Open Dialogue between parties and non-party stakeholders held last week, and we highlight that many reminded us that we have a responsibility to enhance transparency, as called for in the conclusions parties agreed earlier this year at SBI 46, alongside openness and inclusiveness. In this regard, we believe that existing frameworks, principles, and rules in other areas of the UNFCCC as well as in other organizations, can serve as good examples to promote enhanced participation while addressing the realities of the different constituencies, and specifically the capacity of some to unduly influence outcomes to serve their own vested interests.

We stress the need to preserve the delicate balance achieved in Paris and ensure that no one will be left behind. We must also ensure transparency, inclusiveness, a party-driven process on the basis of consensus and as the obligation of developed countries to provide towards its completion in 2018.

Finally, we also express our concern on negative implications resulting out of unilateral coercive economic measures for climate action in developing countries, to avoid undermining developing countries capacities to fight climate change and the rights to live of our peoples.

Mr. President,

The G-77 and China is pleased to reiterate its commitment to continue on your side in this journey until COP-24, so that together with all the rest of the delegations, we can achieve a successful and balanced outcome. We look forward for any advanced information in relation to additional negotiation time between the forty-eighth session of the subsidiary bodies and COP-24, highlighting the importance of continue to ensure an open and inclusive, transparent, effective, and party-driven process, allowing for the participation of delegates from developing countries.

Statement of the Group of 77 and China delivered by Mr. Walter Schuldt, Deputy Special Representative of the Chair of the Group of 77 and China for Climate Change at the Closing Session of APA1.4 (Bonn, Germany, 17 November 2017)

Distinguished Chairs and Co-Chairs,

Ecuador has the honour to deliver this statement on behalf of the Group of 77 and China. At the outset, the Group would like to thank you, Madame Co-Chairs, and all the facilitators under your able leadership, for your efforts during this session.

The Group would like to reiterate its constructive engagement in all the negotiations of the APA agenda during this past two weeks, with the responsibility of advancing the work program me for the implementation of the Paris Agreement under the Convention, and the achievement of its purpose and objective respectively.

As the adverse effects of climate change are more and more evident, we need to keep the political momentum, recalling that this level of political engagement allowed the adoption and early entry into force of the Paris Agreement.

We need to maintain the delicate balance achieved in the Paris Agreement, the principles of equity and common but differentiated responsibilities and respective capabilities, in light of the different national circumstances, the provision of flexibility for developing countries in all the different tracks of the design of the work programme under the Paris Agreement, and the provision of means of implementation, especially finance, technology development and transfer, and capacity-building for developing countries.

These elements should be taken into account transversally in the work programme and the level of substantive progress in the negotiations must be indeed accelerated to ensure a successful conclusion of the work programme under SBSTA, SBI, and APA by COP-24.

In that regard, we acknowledge the importance of the tools developed by the Secretariat to provide an overview of the work that is needed and to facilitate the identification of all the linkages and interlinkages between the work of COP and the bodies, in relation to the work programme of the Paris Agreement.

To advance such work programme, we believe that the informal notes prepared at this session reflecting the views and proposals that we as parties have worked on, must reflect faithfully the outcomes of the work undertaken by the APA, the SBI, the SBSTA, and the COP on all matters related to that programme. We look forward for the reflections note to be presented with an overview of this session and options for the way forward on the basis mentioned above, reflecting the inputs and options from all parties in a balanced manner.

On agenda item 3, we reiterate our view that the guidance should respect both the diversity and the nationally determined character of NDCs, as well as the national circumstances of developing countries, and that it should assist parties with the preparation and communications of their NDCs in order to facilitate clarity, transparency, and understanding of parties' contributions. This guidance should be developed in a flexible manner to accommodate the diversity of NDCs, their nationally determined nature, and the national circumstances of developing country parties. At the same time, we call upon developed countries to provide finance, technology development and transfer, and capacity-building support to developing country parties for the preparation, communication, and implementation of their NDCs.

On item 4 of the APA agenda, our group continues to support the priority of adaptation and the urgency of action in terms of the growing needs of developing countries. We have maintained our common position as a contribution to advance the work under this agenda item, reaffirming that adaptation communication should not be prescriptive, but anchored in the flexibility and with a view to achieve the necessary support according to our priorities and needs. We consider that this session has been fruitful to the extent that the advances were accurate. However, we have different challenges, such as refining the skeleton, advancing on the placement of information, and continuing the discussion on linkages between adaptation efforts by developing country parties and support provided by developed countries.

On agenda item 5, our Group recognizes the progress made in the development of the modality's procedures and guidelines for the transparency framework on action and support. We participated on the basis of the mandate given in article 13 of the Paris Agreement which clearly provides different purposes for transparency of actions and support, in accordance with the relevant articles of the Paris Agreement. Nevertheless, one of the main purposes of this framework should be to clarify information on financial, technological, and capacity-building support that developed countries provide and mobilize to developing countries for their implementation of climate actions under the Paris Agreement; and also to enable developing countries to evaluate their needs and define their priorities in terms of finance, technology, and capacity-building. In that regard, we reaffirm that enhanced support enables enhanced action, and that enhanced action requires enhanced support. Therefore, both transparency of actions and transparency of support must progress in a balanced manner.

On agenda item 6, our Group appreciates the constructive and participatory manner in which the consultations were undertaken. In particular, because of the importance that the Group attaches to the inclusion of equity considerations into the GST, the Group appreciates the substantial amount of time allotted and the informative engagement by all parties on the issue of how to reflect and make equity operational in the process and outcome of the GST. The informal note containing the co-facilitators' understanding of parties' views and options with respect to the possible building blocks for the GST provides parties with a good tool for moving forward in the next resumed session of the APA to substantive discussions and the development of a negotiating text on the GST, although we should note that it can still be improved because it does not fully capture the wide range and diversity of the views and inputs provided by parties at this and previous sessions nor the output of previous sessions.

On agenda item 7, we recall the nature of the article 15 Committee to promote compliance and facilitate implementation which shall be facilitative in nature and function in a transparent, non-adversarial, and non-punitive manner, reflecting the different responsibilities, national circumstances, and capacities of developed and developing country parties under the Convention and its Paris Agreement. In this regard, we reaffirm that the Committee shall pay particular attention to the respective national capabilities and circumstances of parties, and its guidance and assistance must include all the elements and provisions of the Paris Agreement.

On agenda item 8, we reiterate the urgent need to decide on their different processes including, *inter alia*, in relation to the communication of information on public finance by developed country parties, the Forum on the Impact of the Implementation of Responses Measures to serve the Paris Agreement, the Adaptation Fund to serve the Paris Agreement, the Financial Mechanism as well as the LDC Fund and the SCCF under the Paris Agreement, the establishment of a new long-term financial goal, taking into account the needs and priorities of developing countries. We further stress the importance and significance of the modalities to communicate the information on provision of finance by developed country parties in accordance with article 9.5 of the Paris Agreement, which deserve more attention and balanced treatment in 2018.

Madame Co-Chairs, we reiterate our continued constructive engagement with you and with all the rest of the delegations to achieve a successful and balanced outcome on all the agenda items, and we look forward for any advanced information in relation to additional negotiation time between the forty-eighth session of the subsidiary bodies and COP-24, highlighting the importance of continue to ensure an open and inclusive, transparent, effective, and party-driven process, allowing for the participation of delegates from developing countries.

Statement of the Group of 77 and China, delivered by Ambassador Wael Aboulmagd, Chair of the G-77 and China for the Climate Change Process, at the Opening Plenary of the Ad Hoc Working Group of the Paris Agreement, Bonn, 30 April 2018

It is my honour to deliver this statement on behalf of the Group of 77 and China. I would like to begin by thanking the Co-Chairs on their continued commitment and professionalism, as well as for their latest Reflection Note, which provides in our view a clear and succinct blueprint for our way ahead at this important session.

As we embark on this first round of our work in this final year of the completion of the Paris Agreement Work Program related to the implementation of the Paris Agreement, allow me to assure you that the Group of 77 and China is fully committed to the success of our work, and has every intention to engage constructively with all concerned to achieve our shared goal of fully and effectively implementing the Paris Agreement.

We are fully aware that this will be a challenging task. There are varying and often divergent views on most of the agreement's provisions. This is normal and we can assure you that we take the concerns and views of all delegations seriously and will not dismiss any party's view as irrelevant. We trust that this sentiment will be reciprocated.

The PA is a landmark agreement. If effectively implemented, it will have far-reaching implications on nearly every aspect of every country's sustainable development and could ultimately transform the development model espoused by most developed countries for more than a century and a half—with devastating consequences—to a more sustainable one. With this in mind, it should come as no surprise that developing countries on behalf of whom I speak today, attach the utmost importance to the key principles of equity and common but differentiated responsibilities and respective capabilities, in light of national circumstances, and will seek to ensure that these principles are preserved and reflected in the outcome of the PAWP as a manifestation of both the principles and provisions of the Convention and the provisions of its Paris Agreement and in the context of sustainable development and in line with efforts to eradicate poverty.

The Group wishes to recall the importance of ensuring the legitimate right of all developing country parties to access available financial resources through different financing mechanisms including but not limited to GEF, GCF, and others.

The G-77 and China would also stress that as we navigate this process it is crucial not to overlook, postpone or otherwise sideline any of the agenda items, whether this is in the context of the APA, SBI, or SBSTA, rather we should adopt a holistic, coherent, comprehensive, and balanced approach which addresses the full gamut of topics including mitigation, adaptation, finance, technology development and transfer, capacity-building, and loss and damage. In this regard, the G-77 and China stresses the importance of maintaining the balance that was structured by the Paris Agreement and expect reasonably balanced and comparable progress to be made on all agenda items throughout this and future sessions, while reminding everyone that no issue should be left behind and that only a fair and balanced outcome in Katowice—in particular as it relates to action and support—can move us forward in the operationalization of the PA. To this end, we hope that at the end of this session, we will have come up with texts that could serve as the basis for negotiation for all issues in the PAWP. We underline that the output for this session should reflect all parties' views and concerns in a neutral and balanced manner, through clear options to be developed in the informal notes.

The Group would like to draw attention to the fact that several agenda items under consideration are interlinked and in many cases progress on a given agenda item relies on progress of another. In particular, progress on the transparency framework on action and support needs to be aligned with progress on issues related to NDCs, Adaptation Communications, and means of implementation (finance, technology development and transfer, and capacity-building).

On response measures, the Group reaffirms the importance of giving full consideration to identify necessary actions to meet the specific needs and concerns of developing country parties arising from the impact of the implementation of response measures and to avoid the negative economic and social consequences of response measures on developing countries. The Group welcomes the in-forum training workshop on the use of economic modelling tools related to economic diversification and just transition of workforce. The Group also emphasizes the importance of fulfilling the mandate of decision 11/CP21 and advancing the work on the pre-2020 and post-2020 on the modalities, functions, and work programs for the permanent forum under the Paris Agreement.

On agenda item 3, the Group wishes to draw special attention to the importance of maintaining the nationally determined nature of NDCs in light of equity, common but differentiated responsibilities and respective capabilities, in light of national circumstances. We would also like to confirm that NDCs include mitigation, adaptation, and means of implementation (finance, technology development and transfer, and capacity-building) components as per article 3 of the Paris Agreement. Guidance developed under this agenda item should respect the diversity arising from the nationally determined nature of NDCs. It should assist parties in preparing and communicating their NDCs in order to facilitate clarity, transparency, and understanding of parties' contributions. In this regard, we are looking forward to achieving progress on further guidance for NDCs as well as further guidance in relation to the adaptation communication, including, *inter alia*, as a component of NDCs. This guidance should be developed in a flexible manner to accommodate the diversity of NDCs, their nationally determined nature, and the national circumstances of developing country parties. Furthermore, we urge developed countries to provide finance, technology development and transfer, and capacity-building support to developing country parties for the preparation and implementation of their NDCs.

The Group would also wish to stress that adaptation efforts under the Paris Agreement should be given sufficient attention reflecting the adaptation-mitigation parity under the Paris Agreement. In addition, under agenda item 4, the adaptation communications will continue to play a crucial role in enhancing adaptation action to achieve the global goal on adaptation and help developing countries deal with the significant additional burden borne from dealing with the repercussions of anthropogenic GHG emissions. The IPCC has validated these assertions in its latest reports by showing that developing countries will remain on the frontlines of the human-induced climate change over this century. To this end, the G-77 is determined to move towards the implementation of all adaptation provisions included in the PA. Moreover, the discussion of agenda item 4 should consider further guidance in relation to the adaptation communication, including, *inter alia*, as a component of NDCs as well as interlinkages with transparency, GST and means of implementation and other related items discussed under the subsidiary bodies.

Regarding agenda item 5, the Group looks forward to making progress on developing the modalities, procedures, and guidelines for the Enhanced Transparency Framework for Action and Support, in a balanced fashion recognizing the importance of both transparency of action, which has achieved significant progress, and transparency of support, which continues to lag behind. In this regard, the Group highlights the importance of achieving comparable progress on both transparency of action and support. In our view, the Transparency Framework should take into consideration the realities of national circumstances and limited capacities of developing country parties compared to those of developed countries, which have been in the process of developing their national MRV systems for more than 15 years. Consequently, sufficient time and support should be afforded to developing countries to increase their capacities to implement the enhanced transparency framework over time.

On agenda item 6, noting the Global Stocktake's role under the different elements of the Paris architecture, it must be conducted in the light of the equity and the best available science, and continuing to recognize the transparent, comprehensive, and facilitative nature of the Global Stocktake. In this regard, the Group calls for the inclusion of mitigation, adaptation and means of implementation (finance, technology development and transfer, and capacity-building) within the scope of the modalities, sources of inputs, and planned outcomes of the Global Stocktake. Moreover, the Group strongly insists that the Global Stocktake process in its role of informing the updating and enhancing parties actions shall not lead to any type of mandatory approach to increase ambition.

On APA item 7 on article 15 Committee, the G-77 and China believes that in general all elements and provisions of the Paris Agreement shall be covered by the work of the Committee, while the scope may differ in respect to the function of facilitating implementation and promoting compliance. The Group is also of the view that establishing the relevant linkages with support arrangements is key for fulfilling the facilitative role of the Committee. In addition, the Committee shall pay particular attention to the respective national capabilities and circumstances of parties, in particular developing country parties both in procedures and outcomes of the Committee. Engagement with the party concerned is a crucial element in this regard.

On agenda item 8, the Group would like to stress that further matters related to the implementation of the PA are vital in securing the balance envisaged in the outcome at the end of this year, as they relate to the full package of the Paris Agreement Work Program. With this in mind, we reiterate the urgent need to decide on the agreed processes including, *inter alia*, in relation to the communication of information on public finance by developed country parties, the Forum on the Impact of the Implementation of Responses Measures to serve the Paris Agreement, the Adaptation Fund to serve the Paris Agreement, the Financial Mechanism, as well as the LDC Fund and the SCCF under the Paris Agreement, and the establishment of a new long-term financial goal, taking into account the needs and priorities of developing countries. Financial support is of fundamental importance to developing countries, in particular in the implementation of the Paris Agreement and their NDCs. However, there is nothing concrete on the table on financial support from our developed country partners in the post-2020 period. Therefore, we must acknowledge the urgent need to scale up financial resources for developing countries in order to implement ambitious mitigation and adaptation actions. The current goal is not enough.

The Group remains concerned over the lack of progress on all finance issues and the reluctance of our partners to advance on these issues. We are equally concerned by the application of unilateral coercive economic measures that affect the capacities of developing countries to finance their efforts in mitigation and adaption to climate change. In this context, it is of utmost importance for all necessary measures to be undertaken to depoliticize the flow of international financial resources such as through the GEF mechanism.

At COP-23, the G-77 and China advocated for a standalone SBI item on the identification of the information to be provided by developed country parties in accordance with article 9.5. For the G-77 and China, concluding work under the new SBI item is a key and necessary element of the implementation of the Paris Agreement Work Program. Developing country parties consider that this information on the pathway to scaling up the mobilization of financial resources is essential for enhancing predictability and effectiveness of Climate Finance in responding to the needs and priorities of Developing Countries as reflected, *inter alia*, in our NDCs and National Adaptation Plans, as well as support needs to avert, minimize, and address loss and damage.

APA agenda item 8(b) is intended separately to address the modalities for biennially communicating finance information in accordance with article 9.5 and we will address the potential linkages with other items of the Paris Agreement Work Programme, such as transparency and the Global Stocktake, for the effective implementation of the Agreement.

The G-77 and China has, for the past several years, attached great importance to the long-term finance process, and we look forward to contributing to the in-session workshop to be held during this session. Our deliberations on finance and LTF in particular come at a time when the Global Environment Facility's seventh replenishment concluded recently in Stockholm with a total of US$4.1 billion pledged, out of which only US$3.3 billion is actually new funding. However, we noted that climate change will see a 47% decrease in developing country allocations and an aggregate 37% decrease compared to GEF 6. Coupled with the lack of clarity on resources for the Adaptation Fund and a delayed start to the Green Climate Fund's replenishment, the outcome in Stockholm does not reflect the progression of ambition as articulated in COP decisions and the Paris Agreement.

The G-77 and China attaches great importance to concluding our work on the Adaptation Fund serving the Paris Agreement in 2018. We request the Co-Chairs, in the organization of work, to ensure due time is provided for negotiations to conclude this matter and for us to finalize arrangements for the Adaptation Fund to take its rightful place in the climate finance architecture of the Paris Agreement.

In conclusion, allow me to once again assure you that we will spare no effort towards making our work this year a success. The G-77 and China is committed to this objective. But here I must be clear. We want an outcome but not just any outcome . . . rather one that everyone can subscribe to, embrace, and implement in good faith. Any alternative scenario may seem attractive, but in reality, may have the opposite effect. To this end, you have our assurances that we will work with you, Madame Co-Chairs, and with all other groups towards our shared objective of a balanced outcome at Katowice.

Statement on behalf of the G-77 and China at the APA HoD Meeting, 3 May 2018

Thank you very much for convening this meeting.

Allow me to start with a few general remarks and then to move to the specific items under consideration.

We believe it is important that the APA Co-Chairs work closely with the Chairs of SBI and SBSTA to ensure that there is balanced progress on all aspects of the Paris Agreement Work Programme. We hope we will be in a position, by the end of COP-24, to adopt a balanced package for operationalizing the PA. To this end, we wish to emphasize that means of implementation are extremely important to the G-77 and China and addressing them in an adequate manner will in fact contribute to the ability of all developing countries to increase their levels of ambition.

On the operational level, we think it would be desirable to see the co-facilitators on all agenda items produce a streamlined text. But most importantly, one that is inclusive of the views of all parties.

Lastly, I wish to indicate that perhaps in the future there will be an opportunity to also address the linkages between APA 3 and APA 5

1. Progress on APA item 4 and its linkage to APA item 5

- The G-77 and China has had a proactive approach in adaptation, given the priority that our countries assign to this issue.
- As a demonstration of the G-77 and China's commitment to progress in this regard we have presented at APA 4a structure for the discussion on the adaptation communication that colleagues have accepted to work on.
- The co-facilitators have reordered the information of the last iteration of the informal note last year based on this structure. The tool provided by the co-facilitators based on the structure of the G-77 and China is acceptable, and we consider it a good basis. While at the same time it is important that we do not miss the clear reference to SUPPORT that is missing. Our Group has been very emphatic in the importance of support for the entire adaptation communication cycle, which involves its preparation, elaboration, implementation, and updating.
- It is good to have now a more manageable text where ideas appear more clearly, but at the same time, we need to move towards the narrative of the text that as agreed for this session and the Group is especially interested in advancing.

We think reporting on adaptation information is extremely important, including both *ex ante* information and *ex post* information, as well as corresponding financial, technology, and capacity-building support received and needed on adaptation.

In reply to some of the specific questions:

- On what would help to accelerate the development of further guidance on adaptation communications? We believe that it is best to continue in a party-driven process, trying not to balloon the structure built so far, and including all the inputs in a comprehensive approach.
- How can we reduce the risks of duplication of work between items 4 and 5, and, at the same time, ensure that everything that needs to be developed is developed, and that nothing is left behind because parties are not certain where to address it? We believe that it would be useful to have joint consultation meetings between APA item 4 and APA item 5 negotiators, that include clear questions to be worked and the necessary time to coordinate internally in the country groups. So, it is suggested to have at least two meetings of one hour each. The output of the joint session should be informal paper from co-facilitators including recommendations from the floor.

2. Progress on APA item 3
At this session, we want to move towards an agreed basis for negotiations and, for item 3, we need material on substantive elements to help us get there. What approach would best assist us with this and allow technical work for progress.

- First allow me to state once again that it is our view that NDCs under article 3, include mitigation, adaptation, and MOI as per the PA.
- We came out of COP-23 with an informal note. We support this informal note as a good starting point for this item to move forward. It seems like a lengthy outcome, nonetheless after closer consideration it may appear that the document does contain some duplication within the subheadings and the various bullet points as well as the level of detail of elements presented by some parties. We therefore see much potential in the effort this session to streamline this note and we hope to see some progress at the end of this session.
- We welcome the arrangement of discussion on the substantive elements during informal consultations at this session. We have been provided with a clear picture by the co-facilitators on how to organize this session and the time allocations for different issues. We have been informed that yesterday good progress was made, and the first three slots have been put to good use and they witnessed a good exchange of views.
- We of course acknowledge that there continue to be significant areas of divergence amongst delegations and groups. This simply means that we must exert more effort and to continue to seek agreement to resolve those outstanding issues. It also means that we should continue to address the substantive issues at the consultations while at the same time encouraging individual parties as well as groups to attempt to streamline the text with the aim of reaching a text which if not perfect, is at least acceptable to all parties.

Statement by the G-77 and China at the Joint Stocktaking Meeting, 5 May 2018

Madame Co-Chairs,
Distinguished Chairs,

I would like to begin by thanking you for your continued support throughout our work here in Bonn. The G-77 and China welcomes this opportunity to pause and take stock of our work thus far and to build on whatever positive elements we see and rectify whatever impediments to progress may exist. To this end, allow me to make a few remarks which reflect some general observations regarding our work so far and how we hope to see our process moved forward regarding the totality of our work be it under the APA or equally importantly under the SBs.

Distinguished Chairs,

As I and several other representatives of regional and negotiating groups within our Group have highlighted on previous occasions, the G-77 and China remains somewhat disconcerted by the lack of progress on certain agenda items, while other items are seemingly moving forward at a faster pace. We have in the past stressed that this is not simply a matter of allocating time equally but perhaps a political matter that must be attended to.

A holistic package approach and our agreement that no issue should be left behind should be manifested in the level of progress we make on various tracks and across the rooms. Again, allow me to clarify that what we are seeking is comparable progress to assure everyone that their priorities are not being ignored nor marginalized. We believe that this is in the full interest of the process and more conducive to making real progress.

And here again, allow me to stress that in our view it is essential to see progress on the entire PAWP. And that the work should be carried out in accordance with the principles of the Convention, its Kyoto Protocol and Paris Agreement, in particular the principle of common but differentiated responsibilities and respective capabilities. The coherence and harmony of the various decisions under these bodies must be maintained. To this end, we believe that the process should be iterative and merge similar views, without pre-judging the final outcome and with equal treatment being granted to the views of all parties.

Furthermore, and as our work progresses in this and future sessions, we truly hope that attitudes will change and that the negotiations process will not be held up by procedural obstacles. This round we've seen quite a few. In the future we hope to see less. It is crucial that this process remains transparent and party-driven. The reality, and the perception of co facilitators as completely impartial in the performance of their duties must be preserved and ensured.

Madame Co-Chairs,
Distinguished Chairs,

At this stage, we are concerned that the discussions on the implementation of the finance arrangements to implement the Paris Agreement are still focusing on further elaborations and adding details to the informal notes, despite a number of CRP documents being submitted by the G-77 and China and also by G-77 members. It will be important for us to shift to negotiating mode as soon as possible, ideally if we can leave Bonn with draft negotiating text so we can start negotiations in earnest at our next session.

On the issue of parallel tracks discussing climate change, namely the IMO and ICAO, we recognize the importance and value of efforts to address emission reduction efforts throughout the UN system. However, we expect such efforts to complement and support our work here rather than conflict with or distort it. It is vital that such efforts remain faithful to and consistent with the Convention, its Kyoto Protocol, and the Paris Agreement, while conforming to their key principles, including CBDR-RC.

It is essential that time be allocated this session to a substantive discussion on the need for these and other sectoral bodies to ensure that their decisions are fully compatible with the core principles and provisions of the United Nations Framework Convention on Climate Change and that adequate means of implementation are provided to developing countries.

Lastly, and regrettably I find it necessary to address a matter of concern once again to the G-77 and China which has been on the table for quite a while without a satisfactory resolution . . . indeed not even an attempt to resolve it and that is the issue of access to GEF resources which is currently and inexplicably being denied to certain legally eligible developing country parties. In this regard, the G-77 and China once again finds it necessary to express our concern over the unresponsiveness of the Global Environment Facility to the continued communications from developing country parties as well as ignoring the COP guidance in this regard.

Finally, allow me to stress that we bring these issues, at this time, and at this stocktake opportunity in an attempt to resolve some of these outstanding issues be they substantive or procedural while, as always, assuring you distinguished Chairs of our full commitment to the success of our work towards the achievement of our shared goal regarding the operationalization of the Paris Agreement.

Statement on behalf of the Group of 77 and China by Ambassador Wael Aboulmagd, Chair of the G-77 and China for the Climate Change Process, at the Joint Closing Plenary of APA 1-5, SBI and SBSTA-48, Bonn, 10 May 2018

Madame Co-Chairs,
Distinguished Chairs,

It is my pleasure to deliver this statement on behalf of the Group of 77 and China.

At the outset, the Group would like to extend its gratitude to the distinguished Chairs, Co-Chairs, and various co-facilitators for their untiring, diligent efforts here in Bonn, noting the hard work that was required of each and every one of them to carry out this challenging task.

We would also like to thank the Executive Secretary and her staff at the UNFCCC for their support and contribution to the successful organization of the session.

The G-77 and China has done its utmost to engage constructively in all the negotiations of the APA, SBI, and SBSTA during these past two weeks, realizing the responsibility we all share in advancing the work program for the implementation of the Paris Agreement under the Convention, and remaining true to its purpose and principles.

We welcome progress achieved this session in a number of areas of the PAWP, while noting that, to some extent, the outcomes have been uneven. It is therefore of utmost importance that we strive for greater balance in future work, which we believe can be achieved through closer coordination amongst work between the APA, SBI, and SBSTA. In the same vein, we hope that the increasing resort to procedural means to hold back work do not represent a recurring trend. We truly wish to maintain the level of trust needed to push the process forward. It is also vital that the process remain transparent, and party-driven, and that no issue is left behind. Furthermore, we wish to stress once more that the indispensable role of co-facilitators can only be helped if we maintain the sense of impartiality and even-handedness which they have consistently demonstrated over the years.

Madame Co-Chairs,
Distinguished Chairs,

Before addressing a few items on the agendas of the three bodies, allow me to share a brief thought regarding pre-2020 issues. The Group of 77 and China has consistently stressed that enhanced post-2020 ambition and action are inextricably linked to enhanced pre-2020 ambition and actions. We therefore wish to remind that there is an urgent need to enhance pre-2020 action, as well as provision of support in terms of finance, technology development and transfer, and capacity-building.

Madame Co-Chairs,
Distinguished Chairs,

Allow me now to highlight a few points regarding the work carried out at this session starting with the APA:

The Group welcomes the conclusions of APA 1-5 which acknowledge and stress the need for progress on all items in a balanced manner to ensure that the consideration of all matters relating to the Paris Agreement Work Programme by the SBI, SBSTA, and the APA are closely coordinated. We also welcome the intention of the Co-Chairs of APA, in consultation with Chairs of SBSTA and SBI, to prepare, by 1 August 2018, a joint reflection note addressing progress on all matters pertaining to the PAWP. The Group would once again wish to highlight our understanding that this process will reflect the unanimous view calling for all options to remain on the table, and that no option will be removed unless explicitly called for by the party concerned.

On Finance, the Group looks forward to making progress in Bangkok with a view to negotiate an outcome in Katowice on articles 9.5, 9.7, and 13 and APA agenda item 8. Together these elements will be a critical part of the overall Katowice package. Finance is an integral element of the PAWP and the means of implementation-adequate capacity-building, technology transfer, and financing support for developing countries is critical and should be based on and respond to national needs, and foster country ownership.

Enhanced financial support from developed countries will allow for effective implementation and enhanced ambition of developing countries. Multilaterally agreed modalities are needed to track the delivery of support, including the US$100 billion per year in climate finance by 2020 and additional and scaled up finance that is secure, predictable, and sustainable is crucial for developing countries in the post-2020 context. For the G-77, the Katowice finance outcome must be complemented by increased efforts to mobilize, and enhance access to, climate finance.

On a related issue, and as we have mentioned several times throughout the session, we wish to recall the importance of ensuring the legitimate right of all developing country parties to access available financial resources through different financing mechanisms including but not limited to the GEF and GCF. As highlighted before, we are particularly concerned by the issue of access to GEF resources, which are currently being denied to unquestionably eligible developing country parties. The mere fact that the Global Environment Facility has chosen to simply ignore all communications in this regard is added reason for concern.

On APA 4, the Group would like to underline the utmost relevance that adaptation has for developing countries. For that reason, we understand the further guidance in relation to the adaptation communication is an important part in the process of implementing the Paris Agreement. Bangkok should advance the work using the progress made during this session as a starting point.

On APA agenda item 5, the Group is pleased with the progress made so far. All parties engaged in substantive discussions in a constructive manner, and we hope this continues in future sessions. However, the Group would like to emphasize that more time needs to be allocated to this agenda item given the volume of work ahead. We would seek to deepen our understanding and work on the modalities, procedures, and guidelines of the Enhanced Transparency Framework in all of its elements. Allocating more time will ensure that all aspects of the Enhanced Transparency Framework for Action and Support can be discussed in a comprehensive and balanced manner.

On the Global Stocktake (APA agenda item 6) we are pleased to note that our work at this session in Bonn has been productive and has enabled us to arrive at a good basis for moving forward in Bangkok and COP-24. The G-77's views, especially the importance of reflecting equity as an integral, essential, and cross-cutting basis for the GST, have been incorporated into the document and we look forward to working with our partners in further developing the modalities for the GST under the Paris Agreement. We would expect such modalities to reflect the provisions of the Paris Agreement and to be workable, implementation-oriented, simple, sustainable, and effective, especially in enabling the parties to have a solid and robust collective assessment of progress in the implementation of the Paris Agreement towards the achievement of the long-term goals and the objective of the Convention and in strengthening international cooperation on climate change.

On APA item 7 on the article 15 Committee, the G-77 and China believes that the discussion during the session has been constructive, and the informal note produced by co-facilitators is inclusive and helpful. The Group looks forward to work with all parties to develop elaborated texts with more clarity in future, while keeping the facilitative nature and full scope of the committee and reflect national circumstances and capabilities in designing the process and measures of the work of the committee.

Madame Co-Chairs, Distinguished Chairs, I would now like to move on to the Group's comments on a number of agenda items under SBI and SBSTA:

On the work of Consultative Group of Experts on National Communication from non–Annex I (SBI agenda item 4b.), I would like to begin by referencing the statement I made earlier today at the closing plenary of the SBI. On this important matter, I would like to reiterate the Group's disappointment that some parties appear to be unwilling to continue the CGE's work after 2020, which will bring a great deal of uncertainty to the body's future and will definitely undermine its supporting role for developing countries. The renewal of the mandate of the CGE is vital to build trust between parties as we finalize the new Paris Agreement transparency system. The renewal of the mandate of the CGE is vital to build trust between parties as we finalize the new Paris Agreement transparency system.

On response measures, the Group reaffirms the importance of giving full consideration to identify necessary actions to meet the specific needs and concerns of developing country parties arising from the impact of the implementation of response measures, and to avoid the negative economic and social consequences of response measures on developing countries. The Group looks forward to the pre-sessional workshop on the review of the work of the improved forum. The Group also emphasizes the importance of fulfilling the mandate of decision 11/CP21 and advancing the work on the modalities, functions and work programs and establishing a permanent body for response measures under the CMA.

On the issues related to technology, the Group believes that the Technology Framework can provide the much-needed guidance to the work of the technology mechanism, especially in providing support for actions on technology development and transfer to developing countries to implement the Convention and its Paris Agreement. In this regard, operationalizing the Technology Framework is crucial, while ensuring that it continues to evolve.

The Group welcomes the management response of the UNEP on the relevant findings and recommendations of the independent review of the effective implementation of the Climate Technology Centre and Network (CTCN) and look forward to the enhanced provision of support for strengthening the capacity of national designated entities of developing country parties.

On the issue of parallel tracks discussing climate change, namely, the IMO and ICAO. We recognize the importance and value of efforts to address emission reduction efforts and ensure environmental integrity throughout the UN system, however we expect such efforts to complement and support our work here and by all means not to conflict with or distort it. It is vital that such efforts remain faithful to and consistent with the Convention, its Kyoto Protocol, and the Paris Agreement, while conforming to their key principles.

On SBI15, we welcome the exchanges with the identification of the information to be provided by parties in accordance with article 9, paragraph 5 of the Paris Agreement. Nonetheless, further deliberations are needed regarding the linkages of this topic with other tracks of negotiations.

On SBSTA7, I would like to refer to our statement this afternoon at the closing plenary of the SBSTA. The Local Communities and Indigenous Peoples Platform is of particular importance to the G-77 and China. Despite efforts to reach a consensus at this session not succeeding, we are hopeful that the co-facilitators' draft decision text will help achieve a positive outcome in Katowice, and ultimately enhance the inclusion and engagement of indigenous peoples and local communities in the UNFCCC process.

Madame Co-Chairs,
Distinguished Chairs,

We are fully aware that the final stretch of operationalizing the PA will be a challenging one. There are varying and often divergent views on many of the agreement's provisions. This is normal and we can assure you that we have and will continue to come to the table with an open mind and all willingness to reach accommodations. If this is the prevailing sentiment and attitude, we have every reason to hope that whatever obstacles we may meet on the road to Katowice will be overcome.

Statement on behalf of the Group of 77 and China by Ambassador Wael Aboulmagd, Chair of the G-77 and China for the Climate Change Process at the Joint Opening Plenary of APA 1-6 and the Resumed SBs 48-2, Bangkok, 4 September 2018

Madame Co-Chairs,
Distinguished Chairs,

I have the honour to deliver this statement on behalf of the Group of 77 and China. In the interest preserving as much time as possible for negotiations on the outstanding issues, the Group has decided to use the opportunity of this general debate to make a few political and procedural remarks.

Distinguished delegates, if there is one thing, we can all agree on, it is that this session here in exciting, vibrant Bangkok is an added opportunity for us all to advance our work and to hopefully resolve the remaining outstanding issues before we go to Katowice. We have every hope that this session, if conducted efficiently and effectively will lay the foundation for a successful outcome in Katowice.

We are fully aware that this final stretch of operationalizing the PA will be a challenging one. Varying and often divergent views still persist on many of the agreement's provisions. However, we can assure you that we will continue to come to the table with an open mind and with full willingness to reach consensus. We trust that if this is the prevailing sentiment and attitude, whatever obstacles we face on the road to Katowice can be overcome.

We also recognize that despite the reasonable progress we made at the Bonn session, much remains to be done. The convening yesterday of the round table on interlinkages was a useful exercise which highlighted the intrinsic relationship between the various tracks and various issues under consideration, and we believe that it paved the way for further coordination, in particular as it relates to achieving progress on substantive linkages on APA agenda items 3, 4, and 5. In this regard, we wish to stress the importance we attach to the linkages between all of the support-related provisions across the agenda of the APA, SBI, and SBSTA, as well as the linkages between adaptation on the one hand and finance, technology, capacity-building, transparency of action and support, the different items on registry and the GST on the other.

The G-77 and China welcomes the joint reflections note prepared by the Presiding Officers of APA, SBSTA, and SBI and particularly as it reflected a holistic, bird's-eye view of the progress achieved, and perhaps more importantly, the areas where progress remains lacking. In this context we welcome the Presiding Officers' acknowledgement that the progress of work has been uneven, and that it remains insufficient for completing the mandated work by Katowice. With this in mind, it is incumbent upon us all to ramp up progress here in Bangkok across the board. The Group of 77 and China believes that it is vital for this progress to:

a) Ensure that operationalization of the various elements of the PA is coherent, complete, and balanced in form and content, while bearing in mind the particularities of each issue, with comparable progress across the board to pave the way for enhanced ambition in both action and support, whilst ensuring differentiation and flexibility for developing countries.
b) Ensure that the level of detail in the outcome of the PAWP is sufficient to enable all mechanisms, institutions, and processes under the PA to operate effectively and efficiently. Achieving this will require careful consideration as to the degree of detail needed in the outcome of each item of the PAWP.

Madame Co-Chairs,
Distinguished Chairs,

The Group expects to achieve significant progress in this session regarding the expected *form* of the COP-24 outcome so as to avoid encumbering parties in Katowice with this discussion at the last minute.

In light of time constraints, we believe that the modality of work in Bangkok should allow for a more constructive, effective, and focused discussion to formulate draft negotiation texts, including through informal-informal sessions should the need arise.

Further to this, and in order to achieve greater balance between the various elements of the Paris Agreement Work Program (PAWP), the session should consider allocating more time to agenda items which have achieved relatively less progress and/or which are more complex in nature, bearing in mind the need to secure balanced progress between action and support and that many of our countries have small delegations. In this context, some items, namely, adaptation communications, finance-related issues, and transparency of action and support, will most likely require a greater time allocation.

Adaptation continues to be a priority for developing countries. We hope that this session will provide the opportunity to move forward, in a meaningful and substantive manner, on all aspects of adaptation included in the PAWP. In this context, the Group is prepared to advance the technical and political work on the adaptation communication, whilst underlining the centrality of support for all stages, including the process of preparation, implementation, and presentation of the communication.

Moreover, we believe that progress in this area must complemented by meaningful progress on the AC Report and the Mandates of Paris to the AC and LEG with the collaboration of the SCF. We hope that the specific proposals presented by our Group at the previous session can provide a solid basis for further progress here in Bangkok

Madame Co-Chairs,
Distinguished Chairs,

On the topic of finance, we note with deep concern the US$3 billion shortfall of resources at the Green Climate Fund. In this regard, we stress the urgency of initiating a replenishment process guided by the relevant arrangements between the COP and the GCF, particularly paragraphs 17 (a) and (b). We further stress the need to move towards draft negotiating text as soon as possible on the finance issues, and we believe that the draft text submitted by the G-77 on article 9.7 provides a reasonable and balanced basis for negotiations at this session.

We also believe that it is important for us to begin preparations here in Bangkok aimed at reaching an agreement in Katowice on the process and modalities for the establishment of a new global goal on finance. Delaying this process further may jeopardize the level of confidence in the financing framework of the Paris Agreement.

We are also concerned by the application of unilateral coercive economic measures that affect the capacities of developing countries to finance their efforts in mitigation and adaptation to climate change.

The Group also wishes to recall the importance of ensuring the legitimate right of all developing country parties to access available financial resources through different financing mechanisms including but not limited to GEF, GCF, and others

Madame Co-Chairs,
Distinguished Chairs,

On NDCs, the Group reaffirms the importance of maintaining the comprehensive full scope of NDCs, as agreed in Paris, not exclusively focusing on mitigation. Thus, NDCs should include mitigation, adaptation, and means of implementation (finance, technology development and transfer, and capacity-building) components as per article 3 of the Paris Agreement. The Group stresses the importance of maintaining the nationally determined nature of NDCs in light of equity, common but differentiated responsibilities and respective capabilities, in light of national circumstances. In this context, we believe parties should be free to determine whether the adaptation communication is part of their NDC. The Group recalls that Nationally Determined Contributions communicated by parties shall be recorded in a public registry, referred to in article 4.12, maintained by the Secretariat and that article 7.12 establishes the same provision for the adaptation communications.

For the GST within the modalities and the identification of the sources of input, it is important that these are further elaborated to appropriately reflect the activities to be undertaken, institutional arrangements, form of the output, and nature of the outcome, as well as the importance of reflecting equity. Furthermore, there are other elements that need to be considered such as context, coverage, and principles.

On transparency, the Group welcomes the progress made in the new version of agenda item 5 tool that was developed for the Bangkok session. However, we wish to stress the importance of both transparency of action, which has achieved significant progress, and transparency of support, which still continues to lag behind. The transparency framework should reflect the realities of national circumstances and limited capacities of developing country parties compared to those of developed countries. Therefore, the new framework should aim at reporting requirements that are implementable and must afford sufficient time and support to developing countries to increase their capacities to implement the enhanced transparency framework over time.

As for response measures, the Group highlights the importance of identifying the necessary actions to meet the specific needs and concerns of developing countries arising from the impact of the implementation of response measures. To this end the Group hopes to leave Bangkok with a draft text on work program, functions, and modalities on the forum serving the Paris Agreement which would be the basis for negotiation in Katowice.

Madame Co-Chairs,
Distinguished Chairs,

As we are all aware, actual negotiating time will be extremely limited at Katowice. With this in mind, the Group believes that it is necessary that the APA Co-Chairs, guided by parties' discussions and based on parties' inputs and submissions where available, and of course with the assistance of the co-facilitators, strive to prepare at least two iterations of all the texts of the PAWP during this session, covering all the elements of the PAWP, with the aim of mainstreaming ideas and reflecting clear options on points of divergence. We believe this would be the practical manifestation of the assertion made by the Presiding Officers in their reflections note that the outcome of Bangkok should present "clear and streamlined" options. This should, of course, be done while ensuring that no idea is left out, that no party is left behind and no issue left un-addressed.

Moreover, we see value in allocating a time slot at the Bangkok session to discuss the format of the outcome of COP-24 without prejudice to its progress in substance. A formal space to discuss how the different PAWP elements will be structured, and whether the Katowice outcome will take the form of a single "omnibus" decision or multiple decisions may help the presiding officers advance the work to ensure that we arrive in Katowice with a party-owned draft negotiation text.

Madame Co-Chairs,
Distinguished Chairs,

As I wrap up, it would be remiss of me not to share a brief thought regarding pre-2020 issues. While the G-77 and China recognizes that this session is focused on operationalizing the PA it is vital to reiterate that enhanced post-2020 ambition and action are inextricably linked to enhanced pre-2020 ambition and actions. There remains a pressing need to enhance pre-2020 action, as well as provision of support in terms of finance, technology development and transfer, and capacity-building in order to pave the way for enhanced ambition, and in any event, we must ensure that the burden of unfulfilled commitments should not be passed on to developing countries.

To conclude, allow me to assure you that the G-77 and China will continue to engage constructively, actively, and tirelessly in all the negotiating tracks here in Bangkok, recognizing our shared responsibility in advancing the PAWP whilst remaining faithful to the Convention, its purpose and principles.

Statement on behalf of the Group of 77 and China by Ambassador Wael Aboulmagd, Chair of the G-77 and China for the Climate Change Process, at the Joint Closing Plenary of APA 1-6 and the Resumed SBs 48-2, Bangkok, 9 September 2018

Madame Co-Chairs,
Distinguished Chairs,

I have the honour to deliver this statement on behalf of the Group of 77 and China. As we wrap up our work here in Bangkok, please allow me to make a few overarching political and procedural remarks on this additional session's level of progress, and as the case may be, where we are concerned to see that insufficient progress has been made.

At the outset, please allow me to thank our gracious host—Thailand—for their generous hospitality. I would also like to thank, on behalf of the Group, the Secretariat, the presiding officers, and of course, the various co-facilitators for their round-the-clock, diligent work in undertaking this immensely challenging task.

Distinguished Delegates, I believe that all of us arrived at this session fully aware of the magnitude of the task before us and how critical this session would be if we were to realize our ultimate objective: finalizing the PAWP in Katowice at the end of this year, particularly in light of the time constraints we are all contending with.

Madame Co-Chairs,
Distinguished Chairs,

Throughout this session, our Group spared no effort to engage on the various negotiating tracks with an open mind and with full willingness to reach agreement, particularly on the contentious issues.

As the Presiding Officers acknowledged in their previous joint reflections note, and as we have stated on every occasion, progress of work has been uneven, and remains to date insufficient for completing the mandated work by Katowice. Furthermore, we have continued to witness a certain level of rigidity in some tracks of the negotiations. Our Group has repeatedly called for maintaining reasonable comparability in the levels of progress achieved across the board, while ensuring coherence, completeness, and balance in form and content. We believe this to be key for genuine buy-in by all parties and consequently provides the best chance for increased ambition by all.

We welcome the approach taken this session to highlight the interlinkages across the various tracks of negotiations, re-affirming the holistic, cross-cutting nature of the various tracks and the fact that they must be viewed in their totality as parts of a whole within a single package, as was laid out clearly by the PA.

Madame Co-Chairs,
Distinguished Chairs,

We welcome all efforts by parties here in Bangkok to engage in constructive, effective, and focused discussions and to formulate draft negotiation texts, including through informal-informal sessions, and believe that these efforts have paid off in several of the negotiating tracks which have witnessed relatively mature textual narratives. Again, we would like to stress here the importance of balance and the treatment of the PAWP as a package.

Regarding the overall assessment of the work done at this session, and while acknowledging that progress has been made on many tracks, we believe that it still falls short compared to our expectations for this session. As we stated at the start of the session, we came to Bangkok with the hope of leaving with a textual basis for negotiations to start from at the beginning of the COP-24 session. Alas, this is certainly not the case. And at Katowice we will have no choice but to deal with a heavy and complex workload. In addition, we would like to draw attention to an issue we have noted with some concern during this session. And that is the attempt by some to undermine the core principle of CBDR-RC by blocking references to developed/developing countries in the proposed text for some of the modalities and procedures of our work for the PAWP.

In this regard, I wish to highlight a few of the concerns we have regarding our work thus far with the hope that addressing them would facilitate expedited progress and pave the way for success at COP-24.

On the issue of finance, the Group once again wishes to stress its centrality to the PAWP. All means of implementation are essential to assist and enable developing parties to make their contributions under the Paris Agreement. Developing countries are already making significant efforts and with more resources they can certainly do more. However, without adequate support, some developing countries will be limited in the implementation of climate action, and yet others will not show the necessary ambition. With this in mind, we note with concern that engagement on finance here in Bangkok has not been sufficient to resolve the outstanding differences and, ultimately, move the process forward. We once again stress the need to move towards draft negotiating text as soon as possible on finance issues and believe that the draft text submitted by the G-77 on article 9.7 provides a reasonable and balanced basis for negotiations.

We also believe that it is important to move forward towards an agreement in Katowice on the process and modalities for the establishment of a new global goal on finance. Delaying this process may jeopardize the level of confidence in the financing framework of the Paris Agreement.

On adaptation, and in the context of its critical relevance for developing countries, the group would like to highlight that progress has been made in this session in terms of the further guidance of the adaptation communication as well as AC Mandates under the SBs. Under APA agenda item 4, the text is more streamlined and in some cases language, concepts, and ideas were clarified. We are happy to see that the organization of the text continues to be the one provided by our Group. Moreover, we are pleased to see the options submitted by the G-77 and China. We consider the tool workable and are prepared to move the process forward in Katowice.

As for the AC Report, we believe significant progress has been made in terms of paragraphs 41 and 42 and some improvement in paragraph 45 of decision 1/CP.21, transitioning to decision text based on the proposals of the parties as well as taking into account the recommendations made by bodies in this regard. We had a good opportunity to interact with our colleagues in many formats. The Group emphasizes that Paris Mandates are a very important adaptation component of the Katowice outcome.

On APA item 3, the Group regrets that despite some engagement between parties, we are leaving Bangkok without the required progress to achieve what is required under the PA. We continue to stress the importance of maintaining the comprehensive full scope of NDCs. The Group again stresses the importance of maintaining the nationally determined nature of NDCs in light of equity, common but differentiated responsibilities and respective capabilities, in light of national circumstances.

On transparency, the Group notes that parties worked constructively during this session on APA agenda item 5. As we work through the technical details of the Enhanced Transparency Framework for Action and Support, we would like to highlight three key principles that we hope all parties keep in mind:

1. First, the principle of no backsliding. As the Paris Agreement states that we build on and enhance the existing arrangements under the Convention.
2. Second, the principle of recognizing different starting points. The Paris Agreement provides flexibility to developing countries because it recognizes our different starting points with regard to capacities in comparison to developed countries.
3. Third, the principle of improvement over time. The Paris Agreement calls for an enhancement to transparency and states that support will be provided to developing country parties on a continuous basis to build transparency-related capacity over time.

On Response Measures, the Group reaffirms the importance of fully considering and identifying the necessary actions to meet the specific needs and concerns of developing countries arising from the impact of the implementation of response measures, while avoiding its negative economic and social consequences, including with regard to equitable access to sustainable development and poverty eradication.

On the Global Stocktake, issues relating to how equity will be reflected and made operational in the GST as well as to the scope of the GST in order to include loss and damage and response measures continue to remain unresolved. Once resolved, we believe that we may see the needed progress regarding the discussions on the actual design of the GST mechanism.

We highlight the need for the outcome of the GST to provide clarity on collective progress towards the achievement of the long-term goals and in doing so, inform the updating and enhancing of parties efforts in accordance with the Paris Agreement.

Madame Co-Chairs,
Distinguished Chairs,

Before concluding, allow me to stress the full support of the G-77 and China to the incoming Polish Presidency of COP-24, and our full confidence in the wisdom of the Presidency as it leads our work at this most crucial juncture. With this in mind, we wish to highlight the importance of finding the right balance between the important array of events which will be held at the high level, and the most critical task of successfully completing the operationalization of the PAWP. For the G-77, the priority is to focus political messaging on reaffirming support for the multilateral approach to addressing the pressing global challenge of climate change, with the UNFCCC as the lead, and to secure full implementation of the Paris Agreement. The priority task of the Katowice Climate Conference is to finalize the Paris Agreement Work Programme (PAWP) and to hold successful mandated events, such as the Talanoa Dialogue and high-level events on the pre-2020 agenda and finance. The G-77 and China trusts that the Polish Presidency is keenly aware of these priorities and that the ongoing planning for the COP will most certainly reflect them.

Finally, allow me to once again assure you first and foremost of our continued commitment to the success of our work and our full intention to continue to engage constructively, actively, and tirelessly with all parties. We also wish to reiterate our full confidence and unreserved support to the various Chairs, Co-Chairs, and co-facilitators. We firmly believe that we all share great responsibility to make the upcoming COP a success, recognizing our shared responsibility in advancing the PAWP whilst remaining faithful to the Convention, its purpose, and principles.

Statement on behalf of the Group of 77 and China by Ambassador Wael Aboulmagd, Chair of the G-77 and China for the Climate Change Process, at the Joint Closing Plenary of the APA, SBI and SBSTA, Katowice, 8 December 2018

Madame Co-Chairs,
Distinguished Chairs,

At the outset, please allow me to express our appreciation to you all on behalf of the G-77 and China for your dedicated efforts to guide our work at this very delicate moment as we all prepare for the next, and final phase of our work. We do understand the complexity of your respective tasks and as ever will continue to be as constructive as possible.

Distinguished Presiding Officers,

As we have stated on multiple occasions, the G-77 and China are fully committed to a successful outcome at COP-24. We have in the past and will continue throughout the remaining days to demonstrate this commitment not only through our words but more importantly through our positions.

Throughout the year, the G-77 and China has worked closely with the Presiding Officers, The incoming Presidency and the Executive Secretary and all of her team to build bridges and to reach out to others with an eye on facilitating a balanced, comprehensive, and fully implementable PAWP. One which would enjoy not only the acceptance of all parties, but most importantly will withstand the test of time and be subscribed to fully and wholeheartedly by all. Anything less than that, and particularly any outcome perceived by any party as unfair or over burdening will only lead to undesired outcomes down the road.

Distinguished Delegates,

With that in mind, we must share with you our concern at the fact that some positions as well as some proposals being put forward do not appreciate nor perhaps share these sentiments.

This is regrettable since the general consensus among all parties was that we should strive to move forward in the second week with texts as clean as possible. We took it that these texts would capture the fundamental positions of all parties and address all critical elements of the overall package, leaving only a handful of issues to be resolved at the political level. Alas, this is not the case and despite some encouraging progress on a number of issues, several core elements remain unresolved and even more disconcerting, many fundamental basic principles of the process continue to be questioned in what is tantamount in some instances to a re-negotiation of the very PA which we are purportedly attempting to operationalize.

Distinguished Chairs, despite this being the case we still have every hope that we can all rise to the occasion and show the necessary political will to reach a balanced outcome. Time is limited but the opportunity is still before us.

Allow me now to highlight the views of the G-77 and China on a few of the central issues in the negotiations:

ON FINANCE

As we have stressed on every occasion, issues of finance are of utmost importance to the G-77 and China. In addition to being the cornerstone of the support side of the equation, we firmly believe that adequately and comprehensively addressing issues of finance has the potential of unlocking other issues across the PAWP.

The PA is about enhancing implementation of the Convention and its objectives and as such the finance negotiations should not be about rewriting the PA, nor be an opportunity to try to dilute the obligation of developed countries to provide finance and in particular new and additional finance nor an occasion to introduce new notions with regard to established obligations. Indeed, we believe that the obligations to communicate indicative information under article 9.5 and to report support provided and mobilized under article 9.7 are at the core of the PAWP and their implementation should not be contingent on the availability of resources nor be tied to an imposition of a fragmented view of the Paris Agreement.

ON ADAPTATION

Needless to say, adaptation is also of utmost importance to all developing countries. Our countries are paying on a daily basis a disproportionate price and are enduring disproportionate hardships for centuries of unsustainable economic policies by others. With this in mind, we regretfully had no choice but to reject the second iteration of the draft decision in relation to paragraphs 41, 42, and 45 of decision 1/CP.21 earlier today. This rejection was due to our deep discomfort with regard to the evolution of this draft from its first iteration. In that first iteration the G-77 and China had made significant concessions in many important topics in the hope that that would facilitate progress particularly with regard to "adaptation related institutional arrangements," the recognition of adaptation efforts and the methodology for assessing adaptation needs.

We underscored that the second iteration did not reflect the conversations that took place. A new iteration has been prepared according to the first iterations and other options of other groups. We remain to be prepared and fully willing to engage but we need assurances that our main concerns will be taken on board and that the result will be balanced. We also wish to reaffirm that the Paris Mandates to AC LEG in collaboration with SCF is a full and important part of the PAWP.

ON THE ADAPTATION COMMUNICATION

Our Group is seriously concerned by the limited progress captured in the latest iteration of the drafts after the informal consultation held yesterday, as well as the informal-informal meeting where we had the opportunity to have rich discussions, in particular about the annex.

Some of the sections where the Group wishes to express a clear concern are "the purpose" where some critical issues have been left out and the chapeau language which remains extremely vague. We would also wish to express our serious concern at the fact that the very "principles and provisions" of the Convention are still double bracketed.

Finally, the paragraphs on support are extremely weak and in effect ignore the significant challenges that developing countries will face when preparing and implementing their adaptation communications.

ON NDCs

The Group once again wishes to stress the importance of maintaining the comprehensive full scope of NDCs as well as upholding and respecting the nationally determined nature of NDCs in light of equity, common but differentiated responsibilities and respective capabilities, in light of national circumstances. We also stress the need for the guidance being developed under this agenda item with respect to the features, information, and accounting of NDCs faithfully reflect the provisions of the Paris Agreement and the aforementioned principles under which it was developed.

ON TRANSPARENCY

The Group would like to thank the APA Co-Chairs for their bold attempt to streamline the text. We note that several options proposed by members of our Groups were deleted from the latest text. We also welcome the deletion of the extremely problematic concept of timebound flexibility. We appreciate the balance the APA Co-Chairs tried to strike and thus remain willing to engage on this text on the basis that this concept is not reintroduced. As we have mentioned several times before, we would like the Enhanced Transparency Framework for Action and Support (ETF) to facilitate universal participation and should thus bear in mind developing country parties' different capacities and national circumstances. The Group would also like to highlight article 13.14 of the Paris Agreement, which clearly stipulates that "support shall be provided to developing countries" for the implementation of the ETF.

ON THE GLOBAL STOCKTAKE (GST)

On GST, the G-77 has been extremely constructive, putting forward text proposals on scope, equity, information needs, and sources of inputs, as well as proposals to find textual landing zones with our partners. We will continue to do so. We expect to see our inputs being reflected in the Co-Chairs' text on GST, particularly on the operationalization of equity in the GST and the scope of the GST to also reflect loss and damage and impacts of response measures and economic diversification. This is extremely important because both scope and equity together in the GST will help us all move together towards ambition in our climate actions and support through the implementation of the Paris Agreement. It is also important that the definition of GST scope, inputs, and modalities keep a clear focus on ensuring collective progress in the context of the purpose of the Paris Agreement and its long-term goals, in light of equity and based on the best available science.

In addition, the Group is concerned that our numerous textual proposals on the GST have either not been reflected in the text or else reflected inadequately. We are also deeply concerned at the discernible lack of willingness to directly engage on our G-77 texts on the part of our partners.

ON COMPLIANCE

The Group is of the view that good progress has been made on this item and we are willing to further engage to finalize the work in Katowice. The Group would expect the article 15 committee would be able to take effective facilitation measures to assist parties in implementation.

ON TECHNOLOGY TRANSFER

The assessment on the adequacy of support, namely the gap between the support needed by the TM to support the implementation of PA on Technology development and transfer, and the scale of the existing support received, is the core of the Periodic Assessment and is essential to inform future flow of sustainable and enhanced support to enable concrete outcome in realizing the shared long-term Vision on Technology development and transfer.

On TM: The Technology Framework, as overarching guidance to the technology mechanism, must reflect the special needs of the developing country parties, and facilitate the enhanced support provided to them for strengthening cooperative actions on technology development and transfer.

ON CAPACITY-BUILDING

We welcomed the annual technical progress report of the Paris Committee on Capacity-Building for 2018, taking note of the recommendations contained therein. Particularly with regard to provision of adequate support and resources to enable the PCCB to carry out its mandate effectively. We look forward to the review of the PCCB at COP-25, need for extension, the effectiveness and enhancement with a view to make recommendations to the CMA on enhancing institutional arrangements for capacity-building consistent with article 11, paragraph 5, of the Paris Agreement.

ON THE CONSULTATIVE GROUP OF EXPERTS (CGE)

The Group of 77 and China would like to express its concerns on the issue of the review of the Terms of Reference of the Consultative Group of Experts on National Communications for parties not included in the Annex I of the Convention (CGE). Our Group believes that it is necessary to extend the mandate of the CGE, which ends in December 2018, and guarantee that it will also serve the CMA. CGE is reaching next year 20 years of experience on capacity-building for non–Annex I country parties under the Convention. By concluding agenda item 4b on a positive note, the parties under the SBI acknowledge the good work of the CGE during this five-year mandate, including in the support of developing countries under the MRV arrangements under the Convention; and considering the enhanced reporting requirements for developing countries under the Paris Agreement, revising CGE mandate is more needed than ever before. The negotiations this week under the SBI progressed and we reached almost a clean text. By that we suggest opening this issue under the COP agenda so we can reach a conclusion for extending the mandate of CGE as a legacy from Katowice.

ON SBI AGENDA ITEM 4d

Once again, and despite efforts exerted on our part, the G-77 and China remains disappointed by the complete unwillingness to engage on the issue of access to GEF resources for financial and technical support by eligible developing country parties.

This lack of engagement on the issue is certainly not aligned with the constructive spirit we hoped would define this session.

ON RESPONSE MEASURES

On response measures, the Group reaffirms the importance of giving full consideration to identifying the necessary actions to meet the specific needs and concerns of developing countries arising from the impact of the implementation of response measures, while avoiding its negative economic and social consequences, including with regard to equitable access to sustainable development and poverty eradication. By the end of COP-24, it is our ambition to have in place improved modalities, functions, and mechanisms, as well as the requisite work program and governance arrangements to allow for the technical work to understand the impact of implementation of response measures and to take action accordingly.

ON INDIGENOUS PEOPLES

On SBSTA agenda item 7 on Local Communities and Indigenous Peoples Platform, our Group is very glad that this was one of the first agreements reached here in Katowice, and we hope that it will provide a good example and a positive influence in the rest of the outcomes of this COP. The G-77 and China played a key role by listening to all and presenting constructive proposals during the last 2–3 years of negotiations, that enabled us to find solutions and compromises, especially when negotiations seemed to be blocked around a number of complex and sensitive issues. We are really pleased that this decision will enable the operationalization of the Platform and its functions, by providing a Facilitative Working Group where indigenous peoples and local communities can have a permanent space for the enhancement of their participation, the exchange of knowledge and best practices, and the identification of synergies with the UNFCCC mechanisms. Finally, we thank and congratulate indigenous peoples and local communities present here at COP-24 and all over the world, for this important accomplishment that will certainly open a new phase and mode of interaction between them and party representatives towards a more inclusive and holistic climate action at all levels.

CONCLUSION

To conclude, allow me to stress that while highlighting the aforementioned areas of concern we have every intention to continue to be as constructive as possible. We will continue to engage with our interlocutors effectively and with an open mind. We will pursue compromises whenever possible, and we will continue to support the Polish Presidency in every manner possible. Their success is a success for us all.

We are also confident that our Ministers once seized with some of these issues will continue to cooperate and seek solutions. But we insist as we have in the past that we expect reciprocal treatment from our interlocutors and an equal commitment on their part to a balanced package as the only acceptable outcome of this most important COP. We are confident that with the requisite political will everyone can gradually realize that a fair and equitable outcome is not and should never be seen as a zero-sum equation. Everyone needs to realize the benefits of this new regime and to appreciate that notwithstanding whatever responsibilities and contributions each of us will take upon ourselves, the short- and long-term benefits far outweigh whatever contribution will be made.

Statement on behalf of the Group of 77 and China by Ambassador Wael Aboulmagd, Chair of the G-77 and China for the Climate Change Process, at the Joint Opening Plenary of the 24th Session of the COP to the UNFCCC (COP24); the 14th Session of the CMP; and the Third Part of the 1st Session of the CMA, Katowice, Poland, 2018

Excellencies,
Ladies and Gentlemen,

Climate change is one of the greatest challenges of our time and its widespread, unprecedented impacts disproportionately burden all developing countries and in particular the poorest and most vulnerable among them. The year 2017 was one of the three warmest years on record at a full 1.1 degrees Celsius above pre-industrial levels.

The devastating effects of climate change are real and sudden. Extreme natural disasters can affect the environment, the economy and society and reverse hard-earned developmental gains overnight. The massive humanitarian consequences that follow are even more catastrophic.

Distinguished Delegates,

As we start our work here at Katowice, it is useful to remember that we are at perhaps the most crucial moment of the Climate Change process. Paris was a historical milestone. But without the successful completion of the task of operationalizing the Paris Agreement here in Poland the opportunity to turn the tide will be missed.

And while doing so, we must also maintain focus on the implementation of existing commitments by developed countries in the pre-2020 period, including increasing their ambition and revising their emission reduction targets, as well as providing means of implementation for developing countries, and to enhance action to address loss and damage and the adverse effects of climate change from extreme and slow onset events, including through the Warsaw International Mechanism for Loss and Damage associated with Climate Change Impacts.

Distinguished Delegates,

While engaging with the technical negotiating process we should always remain aware of the broader global picture. Unfortunately, and despite the growing awareness of the perils caused by climate change and the rise of a supporting public opinion, we are regrettably witnessing increased challenges to the very science underlying this effort as well as rising hostility towards collective multilateral efforts, particularly with regard to climate change.

On our part the G-77 and China has never wavered in its commitment to effectively combatting climate change and dealing with its adverse impacts already witnessed across the world. We have spared no effort to support the process and have approached the negotiations with an open mind and a full willingness to achieve success here in Katowice. We have made it a point to avoid entrenchment and maximalism, and we have done our utmost to build bridges and engage sincerely.

While we are optimistic that this spirit will prevail, we must also caution against inflexibility. While no one can deny that we have made real progress in moving the PAWP further towards maturity, we must reiterate, as we have done at all opportunities presented thus far, that a lopsided or unbalanced outcome is not sustainable. What we expect at the end of this COP is an outcome which can and will be embraced and implemented in good faith by all.

The Paris Agreement was crafted with a delicate balance in mind between action on the one hand, both in mitigation and adaptation, and support on the other. We remain concerned by the lack of progress on many of the pivotal tracks in the negotiations, particularly on the support side. While no one can reasonably expect all tracks to achieve identical progress, given the specifics and particularities of each of them, we are still concerned that our calls for reasonable comparability in the levels of progress achieved across the board remain unfulfilled. We once again stress that reasonable comparability is essential and that the only guarantee for complete buy-in by all parties is a package which leaves no issue behind.

Distinguished Delegates,

We cannot stress enough that the guiding principle, as set out by the Convention and its Paris Agreement, of common but differentiated responsibilities and respective capabilities, in light national circumstances must be upheld in the outcome of our work here in Katowice. We must also respect the core tenets of undertaking the climate agenda in line with efforts to achieve sustainable development and poverty eradication. The parity clearly outlined in the PA between mitigation and adaptation efforts must also be safeguarded and upheld, recognizing the pressing and existential threats we are facing here and now, and subsequently the resources we are already spending on facing them.

As developing countries, our pressing needs for development and the betterment of lives by lifting people out of poverty must be respected and safeguarded in this process. Herein lies the criticality of support. As developing countries, we committed to this most crucial cause of facing climate change collectively as we genuinely recognized that the existential threat it poses looms upon all of us. However, we also undertook it in light of a clear commitment laid out by Paris that the means of implementation would be readily available.

Distinguished Delegates,

The G-77 and China believes that Katowice provides us with an opportunity to deliver a balanced and robust outcome which would responsibly and adequately respond to the serious challenges of climate change, most recently highlighted by the IPCC special report on the impacts of global warming of 1.5 °C which underscored the urgent need for enhanced action.

Allow me now to highlight the views of the G-77 and China on a number of the central issues in the negotiations:

FINANCE

On the finance side, in light of the deep concern regarding the shortfall of resources within the Green Climate Fund, we note with appreciation the initiation of the GCF's first formal replenishment and will continue to seek a substantial and ambitious replenishment. The first formal replenishment process must be informed by the needs and priorities of developing countries and guided by ambitious potential mitigation and ambition scenarios drawing on the NDCs, NAPs, and country strategies as well as by the relevant elements of the arrangements between the COP and the GCF in particular paragraphs 17 (a) and (b).

As for reporting and communication of finance in terms of article 9, key issues are yet to be resolved regarding the modalities and vehicles to be used, as well as of what is done with the information to be reported on as part of the obligation of developed country parties to provide finance and how it is assessed under the enhanced transparency regime.

Finally, it is critical that we in Katowice reach agreement on the process for the establishment of a new global goal on finance which needs to be initiated now. This will contribute to the enhancement of trust and confidence among parties and contribute to the aim of increasing the predictability of finance for the implementation of the Paris Agreement. As we have said before, we believe that the issues of finance are of utmost priority. Addressing them in a comprehensive, satisfactory manner will create in our view favourable conditions that could potentially unlock a broad array of related and linked issues under our negotiations.

We are also concerned by the application of unilateral coercive economic measures that affect the capabilities of developing countries to finance their efforts in mitigation and adaptation to climate change. The Group also reiterates its deep concern at the lack of response from GEF to communications from parties and once again insists on the necessity of making all financial resources accessible to all eligible country parties.

TECHNOLOGY TRANSFER

The Group firmly believes that technology development and transfer is vital for the implementation of mitigation and adaptation actions under the Convention and its Paris Agreement. With robust and overarching guidance provided by the Technology Framework, which reflects the basic Principles of the Convention and its PA, namely, equity and the principle of CBDR and RC, in light of different national circumstances, and with the Periodic Assessment to ensure its effectiveness, adequacy, and predictability on support, the technical mechanism will better serve all parties, especially developing country parties, to improve resilience and to reduce greenhouse gas emissions towards achieving the goals of the Paris Agreement. In this regard, a clear and effective linkage between the technology mechanism and the financial mechanism shall be strengthened in practically operational ways to support endeavours to enable concrete and scalable adaptation and mitigation results.

ADAPTATION

We consider that the tools provided by the Co-Chairs regarding the adaptation guidance of the PAWP, in particular, APA 4 and the Paris Mandates to the AC-LEG are acceptable and have evolved positively since their last version in Bangkok, especially towards decision text format with clearer options. In any case, several brackets remain in the text that we will have to solve in our technical work of the first week.

The G-77 and China will continue to emphasize that the final outcome of this COP should give adaptation a key role in line with our challenges. To this end, support for adaptation actions in terms of the preparation of the adaptation communication, as well as the preparation and implementation of national strategies, plans, and programs in accordance with the nationally determined needs of developing countries is a critical element of an acceptable outcome of this COP in Katowice.

TRANSPARENCY

On APA agenda item 5 on the MPGs for the Enhanced Transparency Framework for Action and Support (ETF), the G-77 and China believes that we can make progress if we adhere to the following three principles. First, no backsliding. This means that parties should build on their current standard of transparency, and the ETF shall build on and enhance the existing transparency arrangements under the Convention. Second, recognize that developing country parties have different starting points and the MPGs should have built-in flexibility and allow developing country parties to self-determine which flexibilities we will apply. Third, enable improvement over time. The ETF should ensure that all parties improve over time and in the case of developing country parties this will require support. The Group believes that we can successfully conclude negotiations if the MPGs establish an Enhanced Transparency Framework that is equally robust for Action and Support.

NDCs

Under APA agenda item 3 on the NDCs, the Group continues to stress the importance of maintaining the comprehensive full scope of NDCs. The Group again stresses the importance of maintaining the nationally determined nature of NDCs in light of equity, common but differentiated responsibilities and respective capabilities, in light of national circumstances. We also stress the need for the guidance being developed under this agenda item with respect to the features, information, and accounting of NDCs faithfully reflect the provisions of the Paris Agreement and the aforementioned principles under which it was developed.

GST

Under APA agenda item 6 on the Global Stocktake (GST), the modalities for the GST should ensure that the scope be comprehensive so as to allow for a full and fair treatment of issues relating to the implementation of the Paris Agreement, and that it is conducted in the light of equity and the best available science, which must be made operational in the modalities for the GST. The modalities should also ensure that parties have control over the GST process and that the GST outputs and outcome are developed within an appropriate time frame that allows parties to effectively consider the information inputs for the GST and take stock of the collective progress towards achieving the long-term goals, thereby having the GST outcome inform parties with respect to their future climate actions and international cooperation under the Convention and its Paris Agreement.

LOSS AND DAMAGE

For article 8 of the Paris Agreement to be implemented effectively, we need to strengthen the information base to understand climate change impacts and loss and damage being suffered. This information base will also serve as an important barometer on the adequacy of mitigation ambition and action, as well as adaptation action—which in turn, is critical for assessing progress towards the Paris Agreement's long-term goals. Guidance for reporting on loss and damage under the transparency framework, and information on loss and damage as inputs to the GST, are relevant for the implementation of the Paris Agreement, including its articles 8.3 and 8.4.

The G-77 and China looks forward to engaging with the recommendations in the 2018 annual report of the WIM ExCom, especially because they include the substantial outcomes of the work of the Task Force on Displacement. We are pleased that parties have expressed a willingness to address the report of the ExCom via COP-24 agenda item 7. The G-77 and China notes that the annotated agenda does not accurately reflect that this is the focus of work under this agenda item. The G-77 is prepared to consider the matter of future governance of the WIM as early as next year and looks forward to these discussions, while not prejudging the outcome.

RESPONSE MEASURES

On response measures, the Group once again stresses the importance of fully considering and identifying the necessary actions to meet the specific needs and concerns of developing countries arising from the impact of the implementation of response measures, while avoiding its negative economic and social consequences, including with regard to equitable access to sustainable development and poverty eradication.

By the end of COP-24, it is our ambition to have in place improved modalities, functions, and mechanisms, as well as the requisite work program and governance arrangements to allow for the technical work to understand the impact of implementation of response measures and to take action accordingly.

PRE-2020

Once again, we must stress that enhanced post-2020 ambition and action are inextricably linked to enhanced pre-2020 ambition and actions. Living up to the commitments under pre-2020 action, in particular raising ambition and revising emission reduction targets as well as the provision of support in terms of finance, technology development and transfer, and capacity, by developed country parties is needed to pave the way for enhanced ambition. We also remain concerned by the notion that the burden of unfulfilled commitments may somehow be passed on to developing countries.

TALANOA

We would like to take this opportunity to express our sincere thanks to the Fijian Presidency of COP-23 for their tireless work in pushing the climate change process forward. Their diligent efforts to encourage parties to come to the table with an open mind and to espouse the Talanoa spirit has infused our work with the much-needed notions of empathy, understanding, and trust-building, as well as expanding the process beyond the conference rooms by bringing in the voices and stories of actual people facing the real impacts of climate change on the ground.

(b) Draft Resolutions, Decisions, and Proposals Submitted by the Group of 77 to the Conference of the Parties Serving as the Meeting of the Parties to the Paris Agreement (CMA)

G-77 and China on APA Item 8

Recalling article 2 of the Paris agreement,

Recalling paragraphs 59 and 60 of decision 1/CP.21,

Further recalling decision 1/CMP.11,

Highlighting the importance of the Adaptation fund as an important funding institution of the Convention and Protocol Kyoto, and welcoming the work it has done for supporting developing countries with regards to adaptation, including through enhancing direct access modalities,

Recognizes that the adaptation fund would enhance the implementation of the Paris Agreement, in particular with regards to supporting developing country parties' actions with regards to adaptation in line with article 2 of the Paris Agreement,

Recommends that the adaptation fund in accordance with decision 1/CP.21 shall also serve the Paris agreement, on interim basis, and requests the Adaptation fund board to take the necessary actions as appropriate,

Decides to mandate the SBI to further discuss legal and institutional issues related to expanding the mandate of the AF to serve the Paris Agreement, based on proposals to be provided by the parties and a technical paper to be prepared by the Secretariat with a view to provide recommendations to the CMP and CMA for their consideration,

Requests the Secretariat to take the necessary action for the implementation of the decision, in preparation for the first meeting of the CMA consideration of the issue.

Submission by Group of 77 and China on the Paris Committee on Capacity-Building by Ecuador, 31 July 2017

At the first meeting of the Paris Committee on Capacity-building (PCCB), held in Bonn, Germany, from 11 to 13 May 2017 in conjunction with the forty-sixth session of the Subsidiary Body for Implementation, the PCCB agreed to launch a call for submissions from parties and other stakeholders with a view to, *inter alia*, advancing the work on its 2017/2018 focus area or theme on "capacity-building activities for the implementation of nationally determined contributions in the context of the Paris Agreement." Ecuador on behalf of the Group of 77 and China (G-77 and China), welcomes the opportunity to submit its views on the following topics:

a) Information on capacity-building activities for the implementation of Nationally Determined Contributions in the context of the Paris Agreement.
b) Information and suggestions regarding the web-based capacity-building portal.

CONTEXT

The adoption of the Paris Agreement was a victory for the multilateral effort to curb climate change. It provided a universal platform for all countries to take action towards a common agreed goal in the form of Nationally Determined Contributions (NDCs). These NDCs are to represent countries' best effort, and to be progressively enhanced over time. For developing countries, the implementation of the NDCs has the potential to support the achievement of the Sustainable Development Goals (SDGs), and other internationally agreed goals, across all sectors and levels of government. However, it is worth noting that countries are at different levels of climate change policy development and implementation, as such would require capacity to fulfil the mandate of the Paris Agreement.

Developing Countries are required to take on new roles—focusing on implementation. Therefore, capacity-building is a central enabler in achieving a low-carbon climate-resilient world for the reduction of greenhouse gas emissions and for adapting to climate impacts. The following are capacity needs activities identified to be addressed urgently to increase the capacity of developing countries in implementing the Nationally Determined Contributions (NDCs) and relevant policies to be implemented in the future:

A) Enhanced Human Capacity

- Develop and create capacity to analyse, develop and implement climate policy.
- Capacity to develop a baseline of capacities (among public actors and other stakeholders), identify technical gaps, and prioritize action areas for capacity-building in developing countries.
- Promote the creation of institutional and human resilience programs.
- Harness and learn from best practices on institutional knowledge for identifying mitigation actions in relevant government bodies.
- Promote the use of tools and methodologies for developing scenarios for mitigating climate change.
- Promote gender-base and rights approaches as a tool to achieve inclusive and transformative outcome.

Institutional Arrangements for Communication and Information Sharing

- Promote a specialized dialogue and build awareness on the need for, and benefits of, coordinated action among stakeholders, between key government ministries, climate change policy coordinating bodies, the private sector and national focal points.
- Mainstream and integrate climate change into national and local planning, budgets and development processes, at least up to a 2050 horizon.
- Strengthen the links between regional, national and subnational government policies, plans and actions on climate change.
- Include peer-to-peer training initiatives and generate with recommendations to the PCCB in order to create links between potential offers and requests of cooperation.
- Compile the information on barriers, gaps and needs of parties with similar circumstances and recommend to the PCCB the creation of a work programme or focalized action at the regional level or between groups of countries.
- Establish a mandate for coordinating actions around NDCs and driving implementation.

- Establish processes of public awareness, participation and access to information.
- Promote knowledge sharing and open communication platforms that enhance public engagement.
- Share best practices in designing and communicating national climate change strategies to the wider public.
- Ensure the continued participation of a representative of the CTCN in the annual meetings of the PCCB, given the close relationship between technology transfer and capacity-building and development.

Measuring, Reporting and Verification

- Support the development of systems to track implementation and application of lessons learned, thus enhancing analytical capacity and understanding of policies and actions that work best, and why.
- Enhance transparency in measuring, reporting and verification systems.
- Explore potential ways to further enhance the monitoring and review of the effectiveness of capacity-building with a view to achieve enhanced transparency.
- Consider the theme of the capacity-building for the implementation of MRV mechanisms in the development and implementation of NDCs, as one of the thematic areas of action of the PCCB for the period 2018/2019.

Capacity to Assess Resources

- Address resource constraints for developing and implementing climate change policy.
- Enhance capacity to mobilize, access and execute funds.

B)

The capacity-building portal is a web-based platform which, through an interactive world map, enables users to search, identify, and download capacity-building information submitted since 2008 by United Nations organizations, its specialized agencies, and related institutions. Its objective is to contribute to the annual monitoring and review of the progress on the implementation of the framework for capacity-building in developing countries, enshrined in decision 2/CP.7. Furthermore, in line with the provisions of decision 1/CP.21, the Paris Committee on Capacity-Building will provide guidance to the Secretariat on the maintenance and further development of the web-based capacity-building portal as contained in the 2016–2020 capacity-building work plan.[4]

The web-based capacity-building portal can be enhanced in the following manner:

- Promote the exchange of knowledge by encouraging participation in capacity-building activities with interactive functions such as a calendar view of up-coming activities.
- Notifications and announcements of new activities.
- Include a user manual for the use of the capacity-building portal with all its functions.
- Serve as a resource hub for climate change-related data, information and knowledge.
- Inform and educate users on best practices and successful case studies.
- Promote the voluntary publication of information on methodologies and technologies used or applied for climate change mitigation and adaptation actions, with contact information of those in charge of developing and managing such methodologies and technologies, or links to access them in order to avoid duplication of efforts.
- Further analysis of information and presentation in a more user-friendly manner (e.g., using examples such as NAZCA platform).
- Provide links to expertise, partners, literature, and resources, including contact details for participation in or further information on listed activities.
- Systematic linkages with and inclusion of information from other UFCCC constituted bodies as well as from different UN agencies that engage in climate capacity-building activities.
- Develop and promote open-source online tools and instrument, such as presentation modules.
- Ensure and promote inclusiveness, openness and transparency mechanisms.
- Facilitate continued communication and collaboration of countries across capacity-building networks, including the establishment of a registry of capacity-building focal points.

[4] Decision 1/CP.21, paragraph 73 (i).

G-77 Inputs to Building Blocks for GST Submitted by the Philippines on behalf of the G-77 and China 13 November 2017

- Design principles—simple, practical, pragmatic, facilitative, collective, party-driven

Elements to be considered	Main common ideas in G-77 Group and party submissions
• Overarching elements	
• Mandate and objective of GST • Context and linkages and guiding principles • Coverage	Provide appropriate references to Art. 2 and 14 PA and paras. 99 and 101, 1/CP.21, including all operative articles of the PA as the mandate Identify the linkages between GST and other provisions of the PA that would be relevant to be considered to get a complete global picture of implementation of PA and LD and RM and collective progress to achieving PA purpose and LTGs; and reiterate role of GST in Art. 14.3 to inform parties their PA actions and support and enhance international cooperation; process is in the light of equity and best available science as important considerations to be reflected. Reflect equity as cross-cutting and overarching principle that applies to MA+MOI and other operational articles of the PA in the GST process and will inform parties in nationally determined manner with respect to their actions and support. Questions for parties: • Is this where principles like equity, CBDRRC, party-driven and facilitative nature, collective aggregate consideration (not individual party consideration) to guide GST process can be placed? • Is this where overarching questions to be addressed by GST can be placed?

Elements to be considered	Main common ideas in G-77 Group and party submissions
• Institutional arrangements (governance)	Comprehensive and facilitative per Art. 14.1 PA (MA+MOI) LD and RM are key issues for consideration in the GST and should be key features in the outcome Questions for parties: • How to reflect LD and RM appropriately as among issues that fall within coverage of GST? • Do LD and RM come in Activity A, B, and/or C? CMA has overall oversight over entire GST process CMA to mandate SBs to set up joint contact group (JCG) to oversee implementation of GST Activities A and B, and be the venue for negotiation on the output under Activity C (implying that JCG reports to SB chairs and for SB chairs to jointly report to CMA on progress and output of JCG) Questions for parties: • CMA to set up structured technical expert dialogue process guided by SBs (similar to Review) to implement Activities A and B and report to JCG its output for consideration by JCG under Activity C? What would be arrangements for SED—similar to Review?

Elements to be considered	Main common ideas in G-77 Group and party submissions
• Sources of input	Listing of sources of input by copying or reference to para. 99, 1/CP.21 Questions for parties: • Various groups also suggest reports submitted by parties under UNFCCC/PA processes, information on how to understand collective progress, information on equity (including synthesis reports on aggregate effects of INDCs FCCC/CP/2016/2, other analysis on equity that comes from various regions), guidance from SBs on criteria for comprehensive analysis under GST in order to analyse all the workstreams and focus on aggregate synthesis report as output of Activity B, information on regional impacts from regional agencies, LD information, RM information, economic and social science information, information on development gaps and poverty eradication, report from next Review, reports from other international organizations, other peer-reviewed information from scientific community not considered by IPCC, inputs from non-state actors. How should these be considered? • How to identify the information needed for the GST? • Make list of sources of input non-exhaustive—i.e., use "inter alia" or "including" rather than make it closed list? What criteria for additional sources of input not included in the list?

Elements to be considered	**Main common ideas in G-77 Group and party submissions**
• Modalities for GST • Activity A – Information-gathering, compilation, consolidation	This refers to the activities to be undertaken under GST process: • Activity A: Information gathering, compilation, consolidation—process under joint contact group for getting information from the sources of inputs for parties to consider under Activity B Questions for parties: • Timeline – start in 2021, July 2022, or mid-2023? • How to synthesize the information and how parties can interact in a facilitative manner with those who will have synthesized the information? • Should this be undertaken by a structured expert dialogue? • How to reflect and operationalize equity under this activity?
• Activity B – technical expert consideration of the inputs	• Activity B: Technical expert consideration of the inputs—process under joint contact group by which parties undertake a structured technical exercise to consider and exchange views on the information obtained under Activity A Questions for parties: • Timeline—when to start? end in mid-2023? • How can a comprehensive approach in this activity be ensured? • Should this be undertaken by a structured expert dialogue? • How to reflect and operationalize equity under this activity?

Elements to be considered	Main common ideas in G-77 Group and party submissions
• Activity C – Political consideration of the output	• Activity C: Political consideration of the output—process by which parties through a joint contact group, on the basis of the results of Activity B, undertake a political consideration to make recommendations on the conclusions and form of the output of the GST for adoption by CMA Questions for parties: • Timeline—when to start? • How to reflect and operationalize equity under this activity? • How can outcome of GST inform parties and international cooperation?
• Output	The options in the cofacs' revised table covers the various options for output suggested by parties; and how parties can enhance international cooperation (reflection of Art. 14.3)
• Nature of outcome	Highlight that when GST output informs parties under Art. 14.3, the updating and enhancement of climate actions and support shall be done by parties in a nationally determined manner, while recognizing obligations and leadership by developed countries

Key Ideas of G-77 on Equity in the GST Submitted by the Philippines on behalf of the G-77 and China, 14 November 2017

- Equity is a cross-cutting and overarching consideration in the GST (article 14.1):
  - It is to reflect and link to the purpose and principles of implementation of PA (article 2)
  - About including fairness in both process and outcome of GST, to contribute to implementing article 14.3
- Operational rather than abstract concept; needs to be operationalized in the GST in two parts:
- Part 1 (GST process) – Can be reflected and made operational in the different activities of the GST:
  - Activity A (information gathering and compilation)

    - Call for information related to equity in MAMOI and other issues related to implementation of PA (LD, RM, etc.)—e.g., information that identifies implementation gaps (e.g., how much has been done vis-à-vis previous commitments made), information on ways in which equity can be considered in implementation of PA such as information on linkages between the various MAMOI and other elements/issues covered by the GST in order to get a global picture of collective progress in PA implementation
    - Information to be balanced, obtained from sources that are geographically representative (also in different languages) particularly from developing countries
  - Activity B (technical consideration of inputs)
    - Equity could be looked at in terms of various indicative (not prescriptive) reference benchmarks or indicators, including but not limited to historical responsibility for temperature increase, capacity to act due to development levels, sustainable development, etc.; and in terms of ensuring integration of PA implementation with national sustainable development and poverty eradication objectives at the national level
  - Activity C (political consideration of output of Activity B)
    - Focus on stocktake of collective progress; no individual party focus (no name and shame)
    - Non-policy prescriptive consideration of collective progress that parties can use to inform the updating and enhancement of their successive climate actions and support and further international cooperation
- Part 2 (Use of the GST outcome by parties nationally and internationally) – Can be reflected when parties take the outcome of GST and use that outcome to inform in a nationally determined way updating and enhancement of their NDCs and undertake actions to enhance international cooperation, while recognizing obligations and leadership by developed countries

Text Proposals by G-77 and China on the Impact of the Implementation of Response Measures for the Draft Agreement and Decision Presented by Co-Facilitators G-77 and China Alternative Proposal for Article 2, Paragraph 9 of the Draft Agreement:

In accordance with the principles and provisions of the Convention, parties shall give full consideration to what actions are necessary under the Convention, including actions related to funding, insurance, and the transfer of technology, to meet the specific needs and concerns of developing country parties arising from the impacts of the implementation of response measures, and taking into consideration that poverty eradication and social and economic development are the first and overriding priorities of developing country parties. The COP shall strengthen institutional arrangements through a cooperative mechanism to address the adverse impacts of the implementation of response measures on developing country parties, as included in decision 1/CP 21.

Paragraph 33 of the draft decision text – G-77 and China proposal for the provision on response measures:

Parties decide to establish a cooperative mechanism by COP xx to address the specific needs and concerns of developing country parties arising from the impacts of the implementation of response measures, by building on the work of the forum to develop a specific work program to be undertaken by the mechanism that shall be implemented with the view of recommending specific tools, actions, and programs to address the impacts and the implementation gaps to avoid and minimize adverse effects on developing country parties.

Workshop on Cooperative Sectoral Approaches and Sector-Specific Actions, in Order to Enhance Implementation of Article 4, Paragraph 1(c), of the Convention

Bernardits Muller
G-77 and China
UNFCCC article 4.1(c)

- Promote and cooperate in the development, application, and diffusion, including transfer of technologies, practices and policies that control, reduce or prevent anthropogenic emissions of greenhouse gases not controlled by the Montreal Protocol in all relevant sectors, including the energy, transport, industry, agriculture, forestry, and waste management sectors

"Development, application and diffusion, including transfer"

- Article 4.1(c) covers all stages of the technology cycle:
  - Development
  - Application
  - Transfer
  - Diffusion
- Information on available technologies, conditions of access to, and financing transfers of these technologies
- Effective modalities for the implementation of these different stages
- Formulation of policies and programs for the effective transfer for ESTs that are publicly owned or in the public domain
- Creation of an enabling environment for the private sector to promote and enhance the transfer of and access to ESTs

"Technologies, practices and processes"

- Implementation covers:
  - Technologies

- Practices
- Processes
- Know-how
- Achieving this requires enhancement of endogenous capacities and technologies of developing countries
- Other parties and organizations in a position to do so may also assist in facilitating the transfer or access to these technologies

"Control, reduce or prevent"

- Article 4.1(c) covers a wide scope of technologies, including those that:
  - Control emissions
  - Reduce emissions
  - Prevent emissions
- Technologies for abatement of increases in emissions and enhancement of and removal by sinks
- Technologies that are publicly owned or in the public domain or are held by the private sector
- Technologies for mitigation and adaptation

Sectoral approaches

- Distinguish sectoral *efforts* and *agreements*
- Aim of sectoral closely related to technology (Art. 4.1c)
  - development, application, and diffusion, including transfer, of technologies, practices and processes
  - Not to develop global sector-specific standards
  - Includes long-term R&D, but not limited to it
- Not undermine founding principles of UNFCCC, notably equity and common but differentiated responsibilities and respective capabilities

Parameters on sectoral

- For developed countries:
  - Sectoral efforts can contribute to, but must not replace, legally binding absolute emission reduction targets (QELRCs) for all Annex I countries
  - Competitiveness and leakage concerns dealt with elsewhere
- For developing countries
  - Transnational sectoral agreements not acceptable
  - Sectoral agreements at the international level should not be used to impose targets on developing countries
  - Domestic sectoral efforts are ONE option in the toolbox for national mitigation actions
  - Not a basis to impose trade barriers, punitive trade measures, benchmarking, or standards, for developing countries

(c) Excerpts from the G-77 Ministerial Declarations on the Conference of the Parties Serving as the Meeting of the Parties to the Paris Agreement (CMA) [2016]

Fortieth Annual Meeting of the Ministers for Foreign Affairs of the States Members of the Group of 77 held in New York on 23 September 2016

Excerpts from the Ministerial Declaration

96. The Ministers stressed that the Paris Agreement was a result of the collective and tireless efforts of all parties to the United Nations Framework Convention on Climate Change working constructively in a spirit of compromise for our efforts to address climate change, through enhancing the implementation of the Convention, including its provisions and principles, in particular equity and common but differentiated responsibilities and respective capabilities. As the Paris Agreement moves towards its implementation phase, they reiterated the importance of preserving the delicate balance of all of the issues which were resolved in Paris as well as the principles and provisions of the Convention. They also recognized the importance of developed countries continuing to take the lead in addressing climate change, particularly in the implementation of the Paris Agreement in accordance with historical responsibilities and their respective capabilities.

97. The Ministers emphasized that developed countries shall continue to take the key leading role on mitigation by undertaking and increasing economy-wide absolute emission reduction targets for their pledges and Nationally Determined Contributions (NDCs). For developing countries, capacity-building support for climate action is critical and should be based on and responsive to national needs and foster country ownership. The process of capacity-building must be participatory, country-driven, and cross-cutting. Enhanced financial and technological support from developed countries will allow for effective implementation and enhanced ambition of developing countries.

98. The Ministers stressed the need to address adverse impacts of and reduce vulnerability to climate change; they look forward to the mobilization of new and predictable additional resources, with developed countries continuing to take the lead through provision of finance, technology transfer and capacity-building to developing countries.

Forty-First Annual Meeting of the Ministers for Foreign Affairs of the States Members of the Group of 77 held in New York on 22 September 2017

Excerpts from the Ministerial Declaration

83. The Ministers reaffirmed that the Paris Agreement, adopted under the United Nations Framework Convention on Climate Change (UNFCCC), was the

collective achievement of all parties, which seeks to enhance the implementation of the United Nations Framework Convention on Climate Change, in accordance with its objectives, principles and provisions, in particular equity and common but differentiated responsibilities and respective capabilities, in the light of different national circumstances, and the right to development, in the context of sustainable development and efforts to eradicate poverty. It is also essential to maintain focus on the implementation of existing commitments by developed countries in the pre-2020 period, including the ratification of the Doha amendment to the Kyoto protocol. They stressed that global effort to fight climate change is an irreversible process that cannot be overlooked nor postponed. The Ministers also called for increased action to address loss and damage and the adverse effects of climate change from extreme and slow onset events, including through the Warsaw International Mechanism for Loss and Damage associated with Climate Change Impacts.

84. The Ministers called for mobilizing further action and support for climate change mitigation, adaptation and loss and damage, taking into account the specific needs and special circumstances of developing countries, especially, those particularly vulnerable to the adverse effects of climate change. They also called for increased efforts to mobilize, and enhance access to, climate finance, including public and private, domestic, and international, bilateral and multilateral, as well as alternative sources of finance.

85. The Ministers emphasized that developed countries shall continue to take the key leading role on mitigation by undertaking and increasing economy-wide absolute emission reduction targets for their pledges and Nationally Determined Contributions (NDCs). For developing countries adaptation to climate change is a priority, and a key component of the implementation of the Paris Agreement. In this regard adequate capacity-building, transfer of technology and financing support for developing countries according to historic responsibilities and common but differentiated responsibilities and respective capabilities for climate action is critical and should be based on and respond to national needs, and foster country ownership. The process of capacity-building must be participatory, country-driven, and cross-cutting. Enhanced financial and technological support coupled with knowledge and skills transfer from developed countries will allow for effective implementation and enhanced ambition of developing countries. Multilaterally agreed modalities are needed to track the delivery of US$100 billion per year in climate finance by 2020. Furthermore, additional and scaled-up finance that is secure, predictable, and sustainable is crucial for developing countries in the post-2020 context. In concrete baseline target for post-2020 financing with progression from US$100 billion per year is needed to prevent backsliding and build trust.

86. The Ministers reiterated the importance of preserving the delicate balance of all the issues of the Paris Agreement that was achieved in Paris at COP-21 and in Marrakech at COP-22, as delegations continue the work to develop and agree

on the set of decisions for the implementation of the Paris Agreement's various provisions. They stressed the fact that these outcomes are not to be renegotiated nor reinterpreted, as the process under the Paris Agreement is irreversible. They emphasized the importance of moving from conceptual discussions to textual negotiations by COP-23 while maintaining the balance struck in the Paris Agreement between mitigation, adaptation and means of implementation.

87. The Ministers encouraged all parties to fully implement the Paris Agreement and parties of the UNFCCC that have not yet done so to deposit their instruments of ratification, acceptance, approval, or accession, where appropriate, as soon as possible. They also highlighted the importance to hold the increase in the global average temperature to well below 2°C above pre-industrial levels and pursuing efforts to limit the temperature increase to 1.5°C above pre-industrial levels, recognizing that this would significantly reduce the risks and impacts of climate change. Parties aim to reach global peaking of greenhouse gas emissions as soon as possible, recognizing that peaking will take longer for developing country parties, and to undertake rapid reductions thereafter in accordance with best available science, so as to achieve a balance between anthropogenic emissions by sources and removals by sinks of greenhouse gases in the second half of this century, on the basis of equity, and in the context of sustainable development and efforts to eradicate poverty.

Forty-second Annual Meeting of the Ministers for Foreign Affairs of the States Members of the Group of 77 held in New York on 27 September 2018

Excerpts from the Ministerial Declaration

43. The Ministers stressed that climate change is one of the greatest challenges of our time and its widespread, unprecedented impacts disproportionately burden all developing countries and in particular the poorest and most vulnerable among them. They recalled that the year 2017 was one of the three warmest years on record and was 1.1 degree Celsius above pre-historical levels. They reiterated the need for an effective and progressive response to the urgent threat of climate change on the basis of the best available scientific knowledge. Welcoming the Paris Agreement and its early entry into force. The Ministers reiterated that the unfinished business of the pre-2020 actions and ambition, which are long overdue, must be urgently addressed. They stressed the Kyoto Protocol is a fundamental building block in our post-2020 efforts; They urged all parties that have not done so to ratify the Doha Amendment expeditiously.

44. The Ministers reaffirmed that humanitarian emergencies arising out of natural and man-made disasters and other causes and outbreak of epidemics and other global health threats, deserve to be given the same level of attention as those arising out of armed conflicts. The devastating effects of climate change are real and sudden. Extreme natural disasters can affect the environment, the economy and society and reverse hard-earned developmental gains overnight. The massive

humanitarian consequences that follow are even more catastrophic. Millions of lives are lost while many are forcibly displaced and separated from their families. In a similar vein, the devastating humanitarian emergencies resulting from other forced displacement equally deserves the attention of the international community which should spare no effort investing in durable solutions.

45. The Ministers look forward for the full operationalization of the local communities and indigenous people's platform for the acknowledgement of their valuable voice and support of the spreading of their knowledge in the fight of climate change.

46. The Ministers reaffirmed that the Paris Agreement, adopted under the United Nations Framework Convention on Climate Change (UNFCCC), was the collective achievement of all parties, which seeks to enhance the implementation of the United Nations Framework Convention on Climate Change, in accordance with its objectives, principles and provisions, in particular equity and common but differentiated responsibilities and respective capabilities, in the light of different national circumstances, and the right to development, in the context of sustainable development and efforts to eradicate poverty. It is also essential to maintain focus on the implementation of existing commitments by developed countries in the pre-2020 period, including the ratification of the Doha amendment to the Kyoto Protocol. They stressed that global effort to fight climate change is an irreversible process that cannot be overlooked nor postponed. The Ministers also called for increased action to address loss and damage and the adverse effects of climate change from extreme and slow onset events, including through the Warsaw International Mechanism for Loss and Damage associated with Climate Change Impacts.

47. The Ministers encouraged all parties to fully implement the Paris Agreement and parties of the UNFCCC that have not yet done so to deposit their instruments of ratification, acceptance, approval, or accession, where appropriate, as soon as possible. They also highlighted the importance to hold the increase in the global average temperature to well below 2°C above pre-industrial levels and pursuing efforts to limit the temperature increase to 1.5°C above pre-industrial levels, recognizing that this would significantly reduce the risks and impacts of climate change. Parties aim to reach global peaking of greenhouse gas emissions as soon as possible, recognizing that peaking will take longer for developing country parties, and to undertake rapid reductions thereafter in accordance with best available science, so as to achieve a balance between anthropogenic emissions by sources and removals by sinks of greenhouse gases in the second half of this century, on the basis of equity, and in the context of sustainable development and efforts to eradicate poverty.

48. The Ministers reiterated the importance of preserving the delicate balance of all the issues of the Paris Agreement that was achieved in Paris at COP-21, and they noted the significant advancement of the Paris Agreement work program in Marrakech at COP-22 and in Bonn at COP-23 as delegations continue the work

to develop and agree on the set of decisions for the implementation of the Paris Agreement's various provisions. They stressed the fact that these outcomes are not to be renegotiated nor reinterpreted, as the process under the Paris Agreement is irreversible. They emphasized the importance of having clear options for textual negotiations at COP-24 while maintaining the balance struck in the Paris Agreement between adaptation, mitigation, and means of implementation.

49. The Ministers welcomed the holding of the COP-24 in Katowice, Poland, and stressed the importance of ensuring that the outcome is both fully operationalized and reflects the delicate balance of the Paris Agreement, including issues related to Adaptation, mitigation, means of implementation. The Ministers highlighted the importance of reflecting the commitment of all parties to fully implement the Agreement within their respective responsibilities and capabilities with developed countries taking the lead both on action and support, in line with the UNFCCC.

50. The Ministers called for mobilizing further action and support, in line with the Convention and its Paris Agreement, for climate change adaptation, mitigation, and loss and damage, taking into account the specific needs and special circumstances of developing countries, especially, those particularly vulnerable to the adverse effects of climate change. They also called for increased efforts to mobilize, and enhance access to, climate finance, including public and private, domestic, and international, bilateral and multilateral, as well as alternative sources of finance.

51. The Ministers stressed the importance of provisions of adequate, predictable, and sustainable financial resources to developing countries, in line with the Convention and its Paris Agreement, to enhance developing countries actions in mitigation and adaptation, all means of implementation are essential to assist and enable developing parties to make their contributions under the Paris Agreement. Developing countries are already making significant efforts but with more resources they can certainly do more. They reiterated that it is important to move forward towards an agreement in Katowice on the process and modalities for the establishment of a new global goal on finance. The Ministers expressed their deep concern of the shortfalls in resources of the financial mechanism of the UNFCCC, in particular the GCF and the GEF, the Ministers further stressed on importance of finance as a corner stone to ensure the success and effective implementation of the Paris Agreement in particular in relation to enhancing ambition of action, and the urgency of initiating a replenishment process guided by the relevant arrangements between the COPs and the GCF.

52. The Ministers expressed their deep concern on the recent development in some developed countries in relation to fulfilling their commitments under the Paris Agreement, in particular the announcement of withdrawal from the Agreement, they stressed that the global effort to combat climate change is an irreversible process that should not be undermined or weakened, and highlighted the expectation that developed countries should fulfil their leadership role through

more ambitious mitigation targets and financial support to developing countries in line with priorities of developing countries.

53. The Ministers emphasized that developed countries shall continue to take the key leading role on mitigation by undertaking and increasing economy-wide absolute emission reduction targets for their pledges and Nationally Determined Contributions (NDCs). For developing countries adaptation to climate change is a priority, and a key component of the implementation of the Paris Agreement. In this regard, adequate capacity-building, transfer of technology and financing support for developing countries according to historic responsibilities and common but differentiated responsibilities and respective capabilities for climate action is critical and should be based on and respond to national needs, and foster country ownership. The process of capacity-building must be participatory, country-driven, and cross-cutting. Enhanced financial and technological support coupled with knowledge and skills transfer from developed countries will allow for effective implementation and enhanced ambition of developing countries. Multilaterally agreed modalities are needed to track the delivery of US$100 billion per year in climate finance by 2020. Furthermore, additional and scaled up finance that is secure, predictable, and sustainable is crucial for developing countries in the post-2020 context. In concrete baseline target for post-2020 financing with progression from US$100 billion per year is needed to prevent backsliding and build trust.

III. SUBSIDIARY BODIES

A. Subsidiary Body for Implementation (SBI)

(a) Statements Made on behalf of the Group of 77 at the Sessions of the Subsidiary Body for Implementation (SBI)

Statement on behalf of the Group of 77 and China by Ms. Alison Drayton of the Delegation of Guyana, at the Opening of the 10th Session of the Subsidiary Bodies of the United Nations Framework Convention on Climate Change (Bonn, 1 June 1999)

Distinguished Chairmen of the Subsidiary Bodies,
Distinguished Delegates,

I have the honour to speak on behalf of the Group of 77 and China.

I would like first of all to express our gratitude to the City of Bonn for providing us with the facilities for the pre-sessional meetings we held last Saturday and Sunday, and to the Secretariat for making the necessary arrangements. These meetings are invaluable for the Group to exchange information and to consolidate our approach to the important work before us in these next two weeks.

Mr. Chairmen,

In undertaking the forthcoming discussions, the Group reiterates the importance of taking a balanced approach—a balance between the need to continue to implement the Convention effectively and the work needed to prepare an eventual entry into force of the Kyoto Protocol. We view this approach as particularly important with respect to the discharge of Annex I responsibilities, in view of the very low targets reached under the Kyoto Protocol. Scientific assessments show that now and, in the future, adverse effects of climate change will continue to be borne, most particularly by developing countries and the most vulnerable among us. Adaptation and capacity-building are among the cross-cutting issues that we will underline in these next two weeks in all agenda items.

We also stress the need for the continuity of the intergovernmental process that we, parties to this Convention, are undertaking, as a treaty body, and as the supreme body of this Convention. We left Buenos Aires last November with a Buenos Aires Plan of Action. Priority should be accorded to the implementation of this Plan of Action, which contains specific decisions and indicative time frames. The Group of 77 and China reiterates decision 1/CP.4 which resolves to demonstrate substantial progress on each of the issues in the Buenos Aires Plan of Action, in accordance with their respective time frames. We consider national communications as an essential obligation of all parties to the Convention. We must see to it that their contents, manner of consideration, and timing of submissions conform to the provisions of the Convention and the decisions taken by the Conference of the Parties.

Annex I communications should inform on the implementation of commitments under the Convention, in particular as provided for in article 12.2 and 12.3 of the Convention, on policies and measures taken to demonstrate that developed countries are taking the lead in modifying longer-term trends in anthropogenic emissions consistent with the objective of the Convention, and details of measures taken in accordance with article 4, paragraph 3, on the provision of new and additional financial resources; paragraph 4 on assistance on meeting costs of adaptation, and paragraph 5 on transfer of technology and enhancement of endogenous capacities, of developing country parties.

On non–Annex I parties' national communications, the guidelines as contained in decision 10/CP.2, shall remain valid for the developing country parties' national communications, and shall also continue to serve as policy guidance for the operating entity of the financial mechanism, the Global Environment Facility. It is of primary importance to the G-77 and China that the provision of the agreed full costs of the preparation of non–Annex I initial and subsequent national communications be met by the operating entity of the financial mechanism, in particular for the maintenance and enhancement of relevant national capacity, taking into account the guidelines adopted by the Conference of the Parties. We underline the need to move forward in the effective transfer of technology to developing countries, and the implementation of decision 4/CP.4 which would ensure the full participation of developing countries in the consultative process and strengthening endogenous capacities and capabilities in developing countries.

The Group reiterates that a common understanding on the mechanisms under articles 6, 12, and 17 of the Kyoto Protocol must be reached among the parties, and that the nature and scope of the mechanisms must be defined at the outset. Hence, due effort is required to identify and define the principles for the mechanisms and the other fundamental parameters. This work must commence soon so that the methodological and operational questions pertaining to the mechanisms can be guided accordingly. The G-77 and China wishes to emphasize the importance of following the Work Programme on the Mechanisms of the Kyoto Protocol defined in decision 7/CP.4. These elements must be addressed with priority to be given to the Clean Development Mechanism.

The Group reaffirms its position that domestic action by the developed countries should be their primary means of greenhouse gas limitation and reduction. Not until the Kyoto Protocol has entered into force and domestic compliance measures are undertaken can these mechanisms be availed of to meet targets of developed countries. The objective of sustainable development for developing countries in the CDM can only be defined by these countries at the national level. These articles relate to the serious concerns of all developing countries, in particular the least developed countries, arising from adverse effects of climate change and the impacts of the implementation of response measures 2E. The Group underlines the importance of the implementation of the Programme of Work contained in decision 5/CP.4. The Group abides by decision 6/CP.4, which decides to continue the pilot phase, to provide all developing countries with the opportunity to enhance their capacity-building, and all parties to gain further experience with AIJ. We are prepared to begin discussions on the preparations for a review process of the pilot phase at these tenth sessions. The Conference of the Parties, the Subsidiary Bodies, and the Secretariat should function in accordance with the provisions of the Convention regarding their responsibilities and division of labour. Activities should be undertaken in accordance with decisions of the COP and guided by the intergovernmental process of this treaty body. Resources should be focused on supporting capacity-building in developing countries and their full participation in the Convention process.

Mr. Chairmen,

Capacity-building for developing countries is an essential component in the implementation of the Buenos Aires Plan of Action. The Group of 77 and China stresses that capacity-building must be accomplished for, by, and in developing countries. Transfer of and access to technology, including information technology and enhancement of endogenous technologies, and the provision of financial resources, in particular for the full participation of developing countries in the implementation of these decisions, are necessary for developing countries to build their institutional and human capacities.

In closing, Mr. Chairmen, the Group of 77 and China would like to reassure you of their usual full cooperation and support in the accomplishment of the tasks before us in these next two weeks.

Statement by Mr. Jamil Ahmad of Pakistan on behalf of G-77 and China at the Opening Session of Subsidiary Body on Implementation (SBI 27) (Bali, Indonesia, 3 December 2007)

Mr. Chairman,

1. It is my pleasure to make this contribution on behalf of the Group of 77 and China. I would like to assure you of support and cooperation in the discharge of your responsibilities and to make this meeting successful.
2. I would like to assure our negotiating partners, the Group of 77 and China's resolve, to engage constructively so as to ensure a substantive outcome of this important meeting.
3. We are meeting in the backdrop of the recently released Synthesis Report of the IPCC Fourth Assessment Report, which presents a stark and dire warning about climate change. The IPCC reports and the recent scientific findings demonstrate, irrefutably, that climate change is posing a very serious and immediate challenge to the efforts of developing countries, who are least equipped to respond and therefore most vulnerable to its rising dangers.
4. We would like to reiterate that without immediate, deeper, and effective cuts in greenhouse gases (GHG) emissions by developed countries, all efforts to address climate change would remain fruitless.
5. Adverse effects of climate change and the associated phenomena threaten the sustainable development, livelihoods, and the very existence of many developing countries and in particular Africa, the LDCs, the LLDCs, SIDS, and disaster-prone developing countries.
6. According to the Fourth Assessment Report of the IPCC:
    - In Africa, climate change is projected to expose between 75 and 250 million people to increased water stress and reduced yields from rain-fed agriculture by up to 50%.
    - In Asia, freshwater availability is projected to decrease, coastal areas will be at greater risk due to increased flooding, and climate change is projected to compound pressures on natural resources and public health.
    - In Latin America, climate change threatens significant loss of biodiversity through species extinction. Reduction in productivity of important crops will pose risks to food security.
    - Small Islands are expected to face inundation, storm surges, erosion, and other coastal hazards, threatening vital infrastructure, settlements, and livelihoods of island communities.

7. In all developing countries water available for human consumption, agriculture, and energy generation is likely to be significantly affected.

Mr. Chairman,

8. In such a bleak scenario, our task becomes even more daunting given the inextricable link between sustainable development and climate change. The most formidable challenge before us in addressing climate change and its adverse effects include: lack of fulfilment of commitments during the first commitment period of the Kyoto Protocol by Annex I countries in reducing GHG emission; provision of financial resources and technology transfer to developing countries; inadequacy of financial resources for adaptation and mitigation efforts; insufficient national institutional capacity in the developing countries for participation in carbon market mechanisms.
9. Adaptation is at the forefront of the concerns of developing countries and provides the means to particularly assist developing countries. As pointed out in the recent scientific findings, more extensive adaptation than is currently occurring is required to reduce vulnerability to climate change.
10. The Adaptation Fund, if not operationalized immediately with adequate and predictable resource base, will not be able to contribute significantly to meeting our objectives. In this context, we also hope that the Nairobi Work Programme of Action will continue to be implemented in a concrete and substantive manner as part of the implementation of the Buenos Aires Plan of Action.
11. The G-77 and China would like to emphasise that the UNFCCC and the Kyoto Protocol serve as the multilateral agreed structure within which the international community should address the challenge of climate change. Given the intensity of the challenge, any other effort will distract and compound the challenge further.

Mr. Chairman,

12. New institutional and financial mechanisms would significantly enhance technology cooperation, development, and transfer and meet the incremental costs. Enhancing action in pursuit of this objective is fundamental to the overall climate change agenda. Notwithstanding the lack of progress, the elements and key issues have now been raised and the stage is now set for real and meaningful progress on this agenda item.
13. UNFCCC estimates additional financial resources up to a level of US$200–210 billion by 2030 to achieve emission reductions targets. In addition, hundreds of billions are needed to support adaptation activities. It is essential that an "investment pathway" is designed to secure additional financial

resources for the developing countries for mitigation and adaptation and other related requirements in accordance with their national plans.

14. Capacity-building under the Convention and the Protocol remains an area of high priority for the G-77, as it has not received the attention it deserves. The Group of 77 and China hopes that the scope for activities and replenishment will be decided upon soon in regard to the LDCs Fund and steps taken for implementing it through concrete projects that have measurable and positive impacts.

Opening Statement on behalf of the Group of 77 and China by Ambassador Byron Blake, Delegate of Antigua and Barbuda, at the Opening Plenary of the Twenty-Eighth Session of the Subsidiary Body for Implementation (SBI) of the UN Framework Convention on Climate Change (Bonn, Germany, 4 June 2008)

Mr. Chairman,

The Group of 77 and China would like to express its appreciation to the Government and the people of Germany for the excellent arrangements provided for our meetings. We would also take this opportunity to thank the Secretariat of the UNFCCC for all the hard work that it puts in during the preparation and execution of these meetings. The Chair of the Group of 77 and China would like to assure you of its support and cooperation in the discharge of your responsibilities. We look forward to working in the spirit of openness, transparency, and cooperation to make this meeting successful. The Group would like to assure our negotiating partners, the Group of 77 and China's resolve, to engage constructively so as to ensure a substantive outcome of this important meeting.

Mr. Chairman,

The Group of 77 and China attaches very high priority to the actual implementation of measures that reduce emissions of greenhouse gasses and measures that strengthen the capacity of States to adapt to the consequences of past actions and inaction in accordance with the principles of the Convention. We have spent significant time defining and refining the problem while the level of emissions and the costs of adaptation keep increasing. We must now move expeditiously to implement the provisions of the Convention in a comprehensive and balanced manner, on the basis of our common but differentiated responsibilities.

Mr. Chairman,

The limitations in financing and in access to technology have been the major constraints to the implementation by developing countries. In this regard, the Group of 77 and China considers this fourth review of the financial mechanism very important to the Convention's future work and full implementation. In Bali, the Group worked for widening the review so as to open the way for finding solutions to financing problems that have continuously constrain developing countries in their efforts to implement the Convention. All the papers so far produced for this review have confirmed that financing for developing countries implementation of the Convention has been inadequate. We sincerely hope that the review will assist us in increasing the financial resources available for implementation of the Convention.

Mr. Chairman,

Agreement on the Adaptation Fund was an important development in the effort to assist developing countries adapt to climate change. The Group of 77 and China is aware that the Adaptation Fund under the Kyoto Protocol reports directly to the COP/MOP. However, given the importance of implementation, we would be pleased to have an opportunity to be informed of the progress in the operationalization of the Fund. We are aware that the Board held its first meeting last March and will hold its second meeting immediately after these sessions. The Group of 77 and China is of the opinion that we as the CMP might give some direction to the Board, in advance of its next meeting.

Parties will recall that in Bali by its decision 4/CP.13, the COP requested the Global Environmental Facility, as an operational entity of the financial mechanism under the Convention, in consultation with interested parties, international financial institutions, other relevant multilateral institutional and representatives of the private financial community, to elaborate a strategic programme to scale up the level of investment for technology transfer to help developing countries address their needs for environmentally sound technologies, and to report on its findings to the twenty-eighth session of the Subsidiary Body for Implementation for consideration by parties.

The Group of 77 and China is greatly disappointed by the response and work carried out by the GEF, as a result of the decision of the GEF Council. This is completely opposite to the expectations of the parties—at least the developing country parties—and brings into question whether the GEF takes guidance for parties or vice versa.

Mr. Chairman,

The Group of 77 and China is increasingly convinced that the GEF is unable to deliver out expectations as an effective financial mechanism for the Convention. This leads us to conclude that a new financial mechanism may need to be put in place to service the needs of the Convention.

Mr. Chairman,

One of the most regrettable outcomes at SBI 27 for developing countries was the lack of consensus on renewing the mandate of the Consultative Group of Experts (CGE). At this session, the Group of 77 and China would like to reiterate its willingness to renew the CGE mandate and have fruitful discussions under this agenda item. We must be clear, however, that the review of the CGE mandate cannot lead to any kind of reviewing of the process of National Communications from non-Annex 1 parties.

Mr. Chairman,

It is of the view of the Group that Reducing Emissions from Deforestation and Forest Degradation (REDD) is an important mitigation alternative, and in addition there is the need to treat it in a comprehensive manner discussing the contribution of forest conservation, sustainable management of forest, and enhancement of forest carbon stocks.

Finally, Mr. Chairman, let me indicate that, due to the multiplicity of meetings anticipated to deliver our mandate over the next year and a half, developing countries will find it extremely difficult to finance the level of representation needed to effectively participate in the process. The Group is therefore requesting additional funding to allow and effective inclusive participation of all member states.

Statement on behalf of the Group of 77 and China by H.E. Ambassador Ibrahim Mirghani, Delegation of the Republic of the Sudan, at the Closing Plenary of the 30th Session of the Subsidiary Body for Implementation (SBI) (Bonn, Germany, 10 June 2009)

Madam Chair,

I have the honour to deliver this statement on behalf of the Group of 77 and China.

The Group reiterates its sincere appreciations to the Government of Germany and the Climate Change Secretariat for the excellent arrangements made for this session.

Madam Chair,

We are distressed that during the whole session, issues of great importance to the Group are being subject to conditionalities and delay by our negotiating partners. It is very disappointing and frustrating to note that in the ongoing negotiations under many agenda items, our partners have shown their unwillingness to even continue discussing issues, trying to find every opportunity to ensure that it does not even appear on the COP-15 agenda.

The Group of 77 and China is greatly concerned with the lack of progress on capacity-building under the Convention and Kyoto Protocol and lack of flexibility to address the factual capacity-building needs for developing countries. Capacity-building is a prerequisite and a key building block for the implementation of the Convention and participation in the Kyoto Protocol by developing countries. It is clear from the synthesis report for the second comprehensive review that capacity-building support in developing countries has so far concentrated on meetings, workshops, and seminars. Decision 2/CP.7 clearly shows the scope of capacity-building needs that must be supported and many of these have not received concrete support.

The G-77 and China needs to ensure that capacity-building support is undertaken as agreed and there should be the use of performance indicators for the evaluation and monitoring of capacity-building support consistent with the agreed areas. Capacity-building needs arising from the Convention processes must also be supported. We look forward to a decision at COP-15 that will conclude the second review and consider a more robust mechanism to ensure that capacity-building for developing countries is supported as agreed.

Madam Chair,

The Group of G-77 and China notes that the EGTT report on performance indicators will contribute to the work of the SBI relating to the review of the effectiveness of the implementation of articles 4.1(c) and 4.5 of the Convention and call on the Secretariat to prepare a template that will allow parties to provide structured information for the purposes of the review. The Group also likes to recognize the handbook for technology needs assessment (TNAs), which has been updated by the UNDP. This handbook would assist developing countries in preparing and updating their technology needs assessment. We would like to urge the GEF to expedite access to funding for developing countries to prepare their TNAs.

In a more positive note, the Group of 77 and China would like to recognise that an agreement on the terms and the mandate of the CGE was finally reached here in Bonn, at this SBI session. The draft decision that SBI must be forwarding for the adoption of the next COP on this issue is a significant breakthrough. We would like to reiterate the dear need of the developing countries for the technical support and advice of CGE, as many of them are now preparing their second national communications. We are looking forward for effective engagement with the CGE after its mandate has been renewed.

The implementation of adaptation activities represents a high priority for all developing countries, particularly the most vulnerable among us. Therefore, the Group looks forward for the implementation of 1/CP.10. During this session some progress has been achieved, however, for the next SBI session we envisage to obtain more substantive outcomes from the negotiations with our partners on this important agenda item.

Finally, Madam Chair, the Group would like to assure you its commitment to continue to work constructively with you and our partners to make real progress in future sessions.

Statement on behalf of the Group of 77 and China by H.E. Ambassador Ibrahim Mirghani Ibrahim, Head of the Delegation of the Republic of the Sudan at the Opening Plenary of the 31st Session of the Subsidiary Body for Implementation (SBI 31) of the UN Framework Convention on Climate Change (Copenhagen, Denmark, 8 December 2009)

Madam Chair,
Excellencies, Dear Colleagues,
Good morning!
Madam Chair,

I have the honour to deliver this statement on behalf of the Group of 77 and China.

The Group reiterates its sincere appreciation to the Government of Denmark and the Climate Change Secretariat for the excellent arrangements made for this session.

Madam Chair,

The Group of 77 and China is greatly concerned with the lack of progress on capacity-building under the Convention and Kyoto Protocol and lack of flexibility to address the factual capacity-building needs. For developing countries capacity-building remains one of the most important issues to be agreed in the new climate change regime. The Group would like to reaffirm that the enhanced action on capacity-building should be guided by provisions of the Convention and relevant decisions of the Conference of the Parties

Madam Chair,

The application and use of environmentally sound technologies continue to be the surest way that the global community will be able to address the problem of climate change in a carbon constrained world. In this light the G-77 and China would like to express its appreciation to the EGTT for preparing the report on the performance indicators The Group looks forward for considering the report which would guide parties' work on assessing the delivery of technology development and transfer going forward.

The Group is also looking forward for the consideration of the two-year rolling programme of work of the EGTT for 2010–2011.

Madam Chair,

The G-77 and China appreciates the Secretariat for preparing the information on national communications and greenhouse gas emissions from Annex I parties. Developed countries committed themselves under articles 3.1, 4.2 (a), 4.3, 4.5, and 4.7 of the Convention on taking the lead in cutting emissions and provision of financial support and transfer of technology to developing countries.

However, there are huge gaps with regard to the commitments of developed countries. The in-depth reviews of the fourth national communications from Annex I parties indicated that developed countries have failed in meeting their commitments on provision of financial support and technology transfer.

Madam Chair,

The G-77 and China expresses its great concern on the existing huge gap with regard to the fulfilment of developed countries' commitments. The Group strongly urges developed countries to take concrete actions now to meet their commitments under the Convention and the Kyoto Protocol in taking the lead in modifying the longer-term trends in their greenhouse gas emissions and providing financial support and transferring technology to developing countries.

Madam Chair,

Regarding National Communications, non–Annex I parties have constantly faced several technical and financial constraints in the process of preparation of their national communications. The best way to make progress in this SBI agenda item is to ensure adequate technical assistance and funding to meet the agreed full costs incurred by developing country parties in complying with the obligations contained in article 12 of the UNFCCC.

Madam Chair,

The implementation of adaptation activities represents a high priority for all developing countries, particularly the most vulnerable among us. Therefore, the Group looks forward for the implementation of 1/CP.10. During the last session some progress has been achieved, by discussing the way forward. During this SBI session we look forward to negotiating, in a contact group, the proposed Chair's text based on the submissions by parties and groups.

Finally, Madam Chair,

We understand that this SBI session will be short; however, we expect more efficient allocation of time and engagement in a constructive discussion with our partners to make real progress in all issues under the SBI.

The Group would like to assure you its commitment to continue to work constructively with you and our partners to make real progress in this session.

Statement on behalf of the Group of 77 and China by Mr. Haroldo de Oliveira Machado Filho, Delegate of Brazil, at the Thirty-First Session of the Subsidiary Body for Implementation (SBI) of the UN Framework Convention on Climate Change (Copenhagen, Denmark, 8 December 2009)

Madam Chair,

I have the honour and the responsibility of speaking on behalf of the Group of 77 and China on this agenda item. Although agenda sub-items 4(a) and 4(c) have been deferred and sub-item 4(b) has been kept in the base, I would like to make a statement on behalf of the Group.

Madam Chair,

National communications are one of the dearest issues for non–Annex I parties, not only because it is a commitment for all parties but also because it represents a valuable opportunity for developing countries, enabling us to better understand the problems related to climate change. At the opening plenary of every session of the SBI, the Group of 77 and China makes a statement highlighting that non–Annex I parties still face several technical and financial constraints in the process of preparation of national communications. It is not a political statement, Madam Chair. It is a sincere appeal to the organ, the COP, in the assessment and review of the effective implementation of the Convention to take appropriate measures ensuring that article 4.3 of the Convention is adequately implemented.

One of the main difficulties that developing countries face in this regard is the access to funding through the GEF, which is an operating entity of the financial mechanism of the Convention. In our previous statement, Madam Chair, we raised many concerns related to the role of the GEF in financing national communications and although the efforts that have been made, unfortunately, the GEF has not been very responsive to the requests of developing countries.

Our more recent concern is the ongoing discussion on the Fifth Replenishment of the GEF, especially on the related discussions on national communications from non–Annex I parties. During the last meeting of the GEF Council, there was a discussion on increasing the amount of money for the expedited procedures of national communications from non–Annex I parties from US$405,000 to US$500,000.

Madam Chair,

With all due respect, donors seem that they have not understood the crux of the question. It is not an increase of 20 per cent of the budget for each national communication that will solve the problems of most countries. What non–Annex I parties want is to have ensured new and additional financial resources to meet the agreed full costs incurred by them in complying with their obligations under article 12, paragraph 2, of the Convention.

Operational procedures for expediting the finance of national communications from non–Annex I parties establishing a maximum amount for those countries that wish to speed up the disbursement of such funds actually deny the right of agreed full cost. Moreover, a fixed amount of money for the expedited procedure for big or small countries regardless indicates the GEF has not been able to deal with different national realities of countries. The process of preparation of national communications from non–Annex I parties must be controlled by the countries, defined by the existing guidelines for this purpose and not imposed to them. No criteria must be applied beyond what has been agreed to in these guidelines. Furthermore, it must be in line with article 12.5 of the Convention, which stipulates that least developed countries may present their national communications at their discretion.

In sum, the replenishment of the GEF is a discussion that must be driven by all parties and not only by the GEF Council. The Group, in its proposal on Fifth Replenishment, in fact calls on ensuring active participation of recipient partners in the replenishment process.

Madam Chair,

The Group of 77 and China has confidently reiterated that the best way to make progress in this SBI agenda is to ensure timely disbursement of funds to meet the agreed full costs incurred by developing countries in complying with the obligations contained in article 12 of the Convention. The financial support that is currently available is certainly not sufficient and the procedures in having access to them are inadequate. Before starting any discussion on additional obligations related to national communications from non–Annex I parties, not only financing must be provided in a timely manner and significantly scaled up, but also technical support under the Convention must be provided in a sustainable manner.

Statement on behalf of the Group of 77 and China by H.E. Ambassador Abdullah M. Alsaidi, Head of Delegation of the Republic of Yemen, at the Closing Plenary of the 32nd Session of the Subsidiary Body for Implementation (SBI) under the UN Framework Convention on Climate Change (Bonn, Germany, 9 June 2010)

Mr. Chairman,

I have the honour to deliver this statement on behalf of the Group of 77 and China. The Group of 77 and China was constructively engaged in the work this session and therefore, has shown a lot of flexibility in many issues with the aim of achieving progress.

The Group of 77 and China wants to express their concerns on the trends visualized in the report on national GHG inventory data from parties included in Annex I to the Convention for the period 1990–2007 where it is demonstrated that Annex I parties increased by 11.2 per cent their emissions excluding LULUCF and by 12.8 per cent including LULUCF. This shows the tendency which goes against the commitments those parties have, according to paragraph 4.2 of the Convention. Therefore, the G-77 and China considers that further actions are needed in order to assure the fulfilments of commitments of developed country parties and their compliance.

Mr. Chairman,

As we indicated earlier that developing country parties are facing many difficulties in terms of lack of support, technically and financially, to enable them to prepare their national communications. In this connection, the Group would like to reiterate that predictability of funding and the provision of the agreed full costs for the preparation of National Communications from non–Annex I parties are crucial.

The G-77 and China regrets that no conclusions have been reached on item 3, which SBI has the mandate to fix a date of the submission of the sixth national communications from Annex I parties. In a time when non–Annex I parties are being pushed to increase the frequency of their national communications, Annex I parties are delaying the process of fixing the date of their national communications and are not willing to increase the frequency of their submissions. This is unfair to non–Annex I parties, and it is contradictory to the provision of article 12.5 of the Convention and the principle of common but differentiated responsibilities.

The Group of 77 and China is glad to note that the work programme prepared by the reconstituted CGE in its first meeting has been endorsed and, therefore, CGE can start working. However, we regret that no conclusion was reached on the further implementation of article 12.5 of the Convention under the SBI.

Mr. Chairman,

Implementation of decision 1/CP10 based on the G-77 and China's submissions and views on different elements has been a big concern for the Group for many years. Although little progress has achieved during this session in this respect, the Group will continue its involvement towards progressive and serious consideration of our concrete proposals in order to meet adaptation needs of the developing countries, especially those most vulnerable, particularly LDCs and SIDS through implementation of decision 1/CP10.

There is a lack of inflow of fund to the Special Climate Change Fund and the Least Developed Countries Fund, bearing in mind the fact that these funds are under-funded to start with. Therefore, we call for more contributions to assist developing countries to tackle the adverse impacts of climate change.

Mr. Chairman,

During these two weeks, we exchanged views on the review of the financial mechanism of the Convention on which we reiterate our readiness to build on and continue working in order to undertake appropriate actions and decisions that would reinvigorate a financial mechanism. Such mechanism will be an effective channel for the implementation of commitments for financial resources under the Convention, and fully respond to the needs of developing countries.

Although parties could not come to a clear outcome on the review of the Adaptation Fund during this session, as it was envisaged, some steps have already been undertaken. In this context, the Group of 77 and China will continue to constructively engage in the next session. The Adaptation Fund is a solidarity fund among developing countries, mainly funded through the shares of proceeds from the Clean Development Mechanism project activities. It is also open to other contributions, and we would like to acknowledge the contributions made by Spain to this Fund. We consider the Fund to be a model of governance of funds under this Convention, and bring this model, among other models, forward in our discussions of a new fund under this Convention. An adaptation needs assessment would be necessary in order to determine the adequacy of existing and other possible sources of financing for adaptation. We endorse the progress made in the operationalization of the Adaptation Fund, in particular on the legal capacity for the Board that would allow direct access to the Fund.

We are concluding the fourth review of the financial mechanism, which would allow us to assess the operations of current financing institutions providing financial resources to developing countries. We note that the current channels of financing lack adequacy as well predictability of financing required by the Convention. We continue to have concerns over the accessibility of these funds, as well as the conditionalities attached to provision of resources under existing channels. We hope to have a review that would pave the way for an effective operationalization of the financial mechanism of the Convention, under the authority of the Conference of the Parties, one that would be a truly effective channel through which implementation of obligations of developed countries to provide new and additional financial resources to developing countries, to meet costs of adaptation as well as for development and transfer of technology, would be implemented.

Mr. Chairman,

The Group of 77 and China would like to assure you that it will continue to work constructively with you and our partners to make concrete progress during the next and subsequent sessions in order to achieve the objectives of the Convention and the Protocol.

Statement on behalf of the Group of 77 and China by H.E. Ambassador Abdullah M. Alsaidi, Head of Delegation of the Republic of Yemen, at the Closing Plenary of the 33rd Session of the Subsidiary Body for Implementation (SBI) (Cancun, Mexico, 4 December 2010)

Mr. Chairman,

1. I have the honour to deliver this statement on behalf of the Group of 77 and China.
2. Although the time allocated for this SBI session was quite short, we found it to be effective and useful under your able leadership and guidance. It allowed parties, particularly the G-77 and China member countries, to be engaged constructively in discussions in order to achieve real progress on different issues under the SBI. In this context, Mr. Chairman, the Group of 77 and China assures you that it will similarly continue to engage in future sessions.
3. SBI is the body responsible for implementing climate change related activities, and I underline the word implementation. Therefore, the Group of 77 and China, in this context, would like to see more efforts towards implementation oriented decisions and conclusions on important issues to be adopted by the COP, in order to enable developing countries to deal with the difficulties they are facing in terms of lack of technical and financial support, predictability of funding and the provision of the agreed full costs. This will eventually allow them to overcome the barriers on implementing activities and programmes on adaptation and mitigation of climate change.

Mr. Chairman,

4. The Group of 77 and China considers the operation of the Adaptation Fund and the direct access to funding to be an excellent example of successes that we have achieved, which will help pave the road for an equal and balanced treatment of adaptation, in providing funding as it has been historically given to mitigation.
5. In this context, the review process of the Adaptation Fund and its institutional arrangements that will be conducted in 2011 are also important steps that the G-77 and China is looking forward to.
6. I have no intension to repeat the Group's concerns that we clearly articulated in our opening statement on last Tuesday; but allow me, however, to highlight some of these key issues, namely, review of financial mechanism, governance of long-term finance, review of Adaptation Fund and its institutional arrangements, Implementation of decision 1/CP10, lack of inflow

of capital to the Special Climate Change Fund and the Least Developed Countries Fund to enable developing countries to deal with the adverse impacts of climate change, predictability of funding and the provision of the agreed full costs for the preparation of National Communications from non–Annex I, which are all big concerns for the Group.

7. SBI agenda item No 8, development and transfer of technology is a key element for developing countries as they have the right for development, which will not be achieved without paving the road through the creation of a technology mechanism consisting of the key elements that are necessary for scaling up of development and transfer of technology for adaptation and mitigation by the developed countries. Here once again, it is important that financing technology transfer should come from public resources of developed countries.
8. We recognize the work that GEF is carrying out under the Poznan Strategic Program on development and transfer of technologies. However, in the planning of its future activities, the Group strongly recommends the GEF to align these activities with those of the technology mechanism to be established under the UNFCCC.
9. The Group accentuates the importance, in future sessions of the SBI, of switching from the habitual "to take note of documents" to a proactive action to raise COP decision for the parties included in Annex I with increase trends of GHG emissions in the period 1990–2007, to adopt national policies and take corresponding measures on the mitigation of climate change, by limiting and effectively reducing its anthropogenic emissions of greenhouse gases and protecting and enhancing its greenhouse gas sinks and reservoirs and the guidelines to establish mechanism to ensure compliance.
10. At the same time, the Group considers that it is urgent to adopt COP decision to implement the recommendations, prepared by the Consultative Group of Experts on National Communications from parties not included in Annex I to the Convention, to cope with the constraints and gaps affecting non–Annex I parties in the process of and preparation of their national communications and the assessment of their capacity-building needs.

Mr. Chairman,

11. Since the Cancun Conference will not be able to complete the negotiation under the mandate of Bali Road Map, the AWG-LCA and AWG-KP need to continue their work in 2011 in order to achieve an outcome in South Africa. As a result, sufficient budget should be allocated for the meetings of the AWG-LCA and AWG-KP scheduled in next year.
12. The Group of 77 and China reiterates the necessity of Palestine's effective participation in the UNFCCC process, and to have the right of access to funding from different climate change sources. Furthermore, we request the

SBI to provide financial support for the participation of the Palestinian delegation in the meetings of the Convention and its Protocol.

13. Finally, Mr. Chairman, the Group of 77 and China would like to reassure you of its commitments to make concrete progress during the next and subsequent sessions consolidated, with the compromise of all parties, in conclusions and decisions in all SBI agenda items in order to achieve the main goal and objectives of the Convention and its Protocol.

Statement on behalf of the Group of 77 and China by H.E. Ambassador Jorge Arguello, Permanent Representative of Argentina to the Unit6ed Nations and Chair of G-77 and China at the Opening Plenary of the 34th Session of the Subsidiary Body for Implementation (SBI 34) of the UN Framework Convention of Climate Change (Bonn, Germany, 6 June 2011)

Mr. Chairman,

1. I have the honour to deliver this statement on behalf of the Group of 77 and China. The Group of 77 and China would like to assure you of our full support and cooperation. Allow me at the outset to express my deep appreciation to the Government and people of Germany for hosting this important meeting in the historical city of Bonn. We also thank the Secretariat for their excellent work regarding the arrangements for this meeting.
2. The Group of 77 and China would like to reiterate its readiness to engage constructively in substantive work, in a party-driven manner, so that concrete progress can be achieved during this session on the many issues under the SBI.

Mr. Chairman,

3. The Group of 77 and China would like to emphasize that the mandate for AWG-LCA is the full, effective, and sustained implementation of the Convention, as per the Bali Action Plan and, in this regard, the Subsidiary Bodies should play an important complementary role.
4. We are aware that Cancun outcomes introduced new issues under the Subsidiary Body on Scientific and Technical Advice, as per decision 1CP/16, and, consequently, the SBI agenda has been enlarged. Some assignments to the SBI agenda following Cancun are clear enough, yet the new processes needing further political development therefore must be kept under the AWG-LCA sphere. In this sense, we believe that discussions on unresolved issues should continue in the AWG-LCA track, and not be transferred to other bodies, since that would not be in line with the Convention nor with the mandate given by parties to the

AWG-LCA, which was extended in Cancun. We further emphasize that the AWG-LCA must maintain an overview of the specific issues that were mandated to SBI through decision 1CP/16, and that the progress made under SBI must feed into the comprehensive and balanced outcome of the AWG-LCA.

Mr. Chairman,

5. The Group would like to emphasize the shared difficulties faced by developing country parties in terms of lack of technical and financial support to enable them to prepare their national communications. Moreover, the Cancun decisions contained additional reporting obligations for developing countries, as well as more frequent timelines for the submission of reports, in particular on inventories of greenhouse gas emissions which require specific technical and technological inputs, as well as increased human and institutional capacities.
6. Predictability of funding and the provision of the agreed full costs for the preparation of National Communications from non–Annex I parties are crucial, currently subject to limited financing allocations under expedited procedures. We also urge Annex I parties to provide detailed information or make available in their national communications the level of improvement in emissions reductions, or lack thereof. In this sense, it is important to maintain and strengthen Annual reports on the technical review of greenhouse gas inventories from parties included in Annex I to the Convention as well as the monitor, report, and evaluation of their domestic mitigation action. As repeatedly stated in the synthesis of Annex I communications, standard formats of reporting on the provision of financial resources, including for transfer of technology and adaptation should be utilized in fulfilment of obligations under article 12.3 of the Convention.
7. The Group would like to underline the fact that developing countries continue to suffer from the adverse impacts of climate change, and the increasing frequency and intensity of extreme weather events. The Group also underlines the challenges faced by developing countries from the impact of response measures. Therefore, we call for more contributions to the funds under the Convention, in particular the Special Climate Change Fund, the Least Developed Countries Fund, and the Adaptation Fund under the Kyoto Protocol.
8. There must be fewer conditions attached to the allocation and use of the funds that are managed through the Global Environment Facility as an operating entity of the financial mechanism of the Convention, in particular the requirement of co-financing for the use of these funds, and to treat adaptation in an equal manner as the case for mitigation. Balanced allocation of

resources for adaptation, including for the design of the Green Climate Fund, as well as direct access as operationalized in the Adaptation Fund, are strong positions of the Group of 77 and China that we will continue to pursue in these negotiations.

Mr. Chairman,

9. The adoption of the agenda helped us to clarify the work ahead of us towards Durban. However, time is limited and therefore, the G-77 and China, request the Secretariat to strive not to schedule parallel meetings in order to allow for effective participation by small delegations from developing countries, as well as to ensure that there will be no clash of meetings of negotiating groups dealing with closely interlinked, or similar issues.
10. On the other hand, the Group of 77 and China is convinced that even with the best use of the time available to us, these sessions cannot be the last ones before convening in Durban, and there is a clear necessity for an additional session to be held in the fall. In this regard, we expect to receive further clarity on the preparations under way and definitions of such meeting at the earliest possible time, and before we adjourn our work this session.
11. Accordingly, the Group will work to ensure that the budget and administrative matters to be considered during this session will be commensurate with the political will needed and with the urgency and importance of the issues under UNFCCC, as well as the additional responsibilities required for the implementation of decision 1/CP.16. Additionally, and no less importantly, decisions over global issues can only be made at the global level, and in this regard, it is fundamental to maintain adequate funding to ensure the full and effective participation of all developing countries in these processes.
12. The Group of 77 and China reiterates the necessity of Palestine active participation in the UNFCCC process and to make every effort to grant Palestine access to funding from different Climate Change sources.
13. We acknowledge decision 1/CP.16 was adopted over the explicit objection of one party. We expect this to be on the record.

Finally, Mr. Chairman,

14. The Group of 77 and China would like to assure you that it will continue to work constructively with you and all parties to make concrete progress during this session in order to advance towards a balanced and comprehensive outcome in Durban.

Statement on behalf of the Group of 77 and China by H.E. Ambassador Silvia Merega, Chair of the G-77 and China at the Closing Plenary of the 34th Session of the Subsidiary Body for Implementation (SBI 34) (Bonn, Germany, 16 June 2011)

Mr. Chairman,

1. I have the honour to deliver this statement on behalf of the Group of 77 and China.
2. Allow me to say that under your guidance we worked intensively during this session, and we interchanged ideas that helped the parties to understand each other's position. This constructive engagement has been very useful, and we are ready to continue in this fashion in future sessions.

Mr. Chairman,

3. According to the Compilation and Synthesis of fifth national communications from parties included in Annex I to the Convention, over the period 1990–2008, the total aggregate of greenhouse gas (GHG) emissions from Annex I parties that are not economies in transition, excluding LULUCF, increased by 8%. Moreover, according to projected data, the GHG emissions of Annex I parties, excluding emissions and removals from the LULUCF sector are expected to increase by 7.8% between 2010 and 2020.

Mr. Chairman,

4. The Group of 77 and China is very concerned about the facts and the trend contained in the reports FCCC/SBI/2011/INF.1, Add. 1 and Add. 2. The Group strongly urges Annex I parties to intensify their efforts aimed at reducing their GHG emissions in accordance with the principles and provisions, the objective of the Convention and their commitments under the Convention and the Kyoto Protocol.
5. With reference to the same document on the "Compilation and Synthesis of Fifth National Communications of Annex I Parties," on financing, it states, in Section III covering the implementation of commitments for financial resources, transfer of technologies, and capacity-building, that "many data gaps and inconsistencies in reporting approaches among Annex II countries and across periods still persist, which was also noted in the previous synthesis report."
6. We therefore urge Annex I parties, first, to provide detailed information or make available in their national communications the level of improvement in emissions reductions, or lack thereof. In this sense, it is important to maintain and strengthen Annual reports on the technical review of greenhouse gas inventories from parties included in Annex I to the Convention as well as the

monitor, report, and evaluation of their domestic mitigation action. Secondly, as repeatedly stated in the synthesis of Annex I communications, standard formats of reporting on the provision of financial resources, including for transfer of technology and adaptation should be utilized in fulfilment of obligations under article 12.3 of the Convention.

7. At a time when more and more responsibilities on reporting are placed on developing country parties, it is incumbent on developed country parties who have the obligation to provide financial resources at agree full costs basis to developing country parties, to clarify whether they are meeting their commitments under the Convention related to financing.
8. We underline our call on parties included in Annex II of the Convention to intensify their efforts aimed at fulfilling their commitments on the provision of financial resources, enhancing technology development and transfer, meeting costs of adaptation, and strengthening capacity-building in developing country parties in accordance with article 4, paragraphs 3, 4, and 5 of the Convention. To this end, the accuracy, comparability, and level of detail of information regarding the provision of support of financial resources, technology development and transfer, and capacity-building reported in National Communications of Annex II parties must be further defined and enhanced.
9. The G-77 and China considers that verifiable, concrete actions are needed in order to assure the fulfilment of commitments of developed country parties and their compliance.

Mr. Chairman,

10. The Group would like to reiterate the shared difficulties faced by developing country parties in terms of lack of technical and financial support to enable them to prepare their national communications. As we are all aware, the Cancun decisions contain additional reporting obligations for developing countries as well as provisions on more frequent timelines for the submission of reports. Decision 1/CP.16 clearly specifies that "developing countries, consistent with their capabilities and the level of support provided for reporting should also submit biennial reports . . ." (para. 60 (c)). The submission of biennial reports is therefore contingent on support, and would therefore require specific technical and technological inputs, as well as increased human and institutional capacities.
11. Predictability of funding and the provision of the agreed full costs for the preparation of national communications from non–Annex I parties are crucial. Financing of non–Annex I national communications are currently subject to limited allocations and other conditions.
12. We also reiterate our call for more contributions to the funds devoted to adaptation under the Convention, in particular the Special Climate Change Fund, the Least Developed Countries Fund, and the Adaptation Fund under

the Kyoto Protocol. Not only are they hugely underfunded, and most of them dependent on voluntary funding, they are also the only main sources of financing adaptation under the Convention.

13. In addition, we urge that conditions attached to the allocation and use of the funds that are managed through the Global Environment Facility as an operating entity of the financial mechanism of the Convention should not be applied to these funds, in particular the requirement of co-financing prior to accessing funding. The historical imbalance in financing to the detriment of adaptation must be redressed, and adaptation financing be treated in an equal manner as for mitigation. Balanced allocation of resources for adaptation, including for the design of the Green Climate Fund, as well as direct access as operationalized in the Adaptation Fund, are basic principles and are strong positions of the Group of 77 and China. We will continue to pursue these positions firmly in these negotiations.
14. Still on financing, Mr. Chairman, we deeply regret that the developed country parties refuse the continuation of the National Economic, Environment and Development Study (NEEDS) project for climate change that have benefited 11 developing country parties in undertaking their financial needs assessment, and to allow us to extend this project to other developing countries. Such financial needs assessment would have enabled us to determine how we can fully implement the Cancun decisions.

Mr. Chairman,

15. The G-77 and China expects that the process for the formulation and implementation of National Adaptation Plans modalities and guidelines will truly enable developing countries to address adaptation needs. We seek to clearly establish a process to enable least developed country parties to formulate and implement national adaptation plans. In addition, we seek to develop the modalities for particularly vulnerable developing countries. We require a clear way forward to support LDCs and other particularly vulnerable developing countries to formulate and implement their National Adaptation Plans.

Mr. Chairman,

16. On article 6 of the Convention, we would like to emphasize that education, training, and public awareness about climate change are essential for all countries and even more for developing countries, to enable them to formulate and implement mitigation and adaptation programmes and actions. It is so important that it deserved a specific article in the Convention, in addition to being an activity in article 4.1(i) subject to financing at agreed full incremental costs basis

17. In this SBI session the Terms of Reference for the review of the Implementation of the Amended New Delhi Work Programme were agreed. This will be key for collecting proposals in order to design the new article 6 Programme after 2012.
18. Mr. Chairman, your support was decisive. We specially congratulate your proposal to organize an event at COP-17, in Durban, to define the opportunities to both strengthen and promote article 6. We are sure that under your leadership we will have a new article 6 Programme, that will be funded with new and additional resources.

Mr. Chairman,

19. On activities to be undertaken by the Work Programme on Loss and Damage, the G-77 and China reaffirms the need to strengthen international cooperation, to enhance knowledge and capacity directed to reduce adverse effects of climate change, and to provide support for its implementation.

Mr. Chairman,

20. The G-77 and China welcomes the forum on the impact of the implementation of response measures and its special event convened by the Chairs of the SBI and SBSTA at this session under paragraph 93 of 1.CP/16, to be continued at the thirty-fifth session of the subsidiary bodies, with the objective of developing a work programme under the subsidiary bodies to address these impacts, and with a view to adopting, at the seventeenth session of the Conference of the Parties, modalities for the operationalization of the work programme and a possible forum on response measures.
21. The Group of 77 and China reiterates the necessity of enabling the active participation of Palestine in the UNFCCC process and to make every effort to grant Palestine access to funding from sources of climate change financing.

Finally, Mr. Chairman,

22. The Group of 77 and China would like to reassure you of its commitment to make concrete progress in order to achieve the main goal and objectives of the Convention and its Kyoto Protocol, thereby ensuring the success of the seventeenth session of the Conference of the Parties in Durban, South Africa.

Statement on behalf of the Group of 77 and China by Counsellor Valeria González Posse, Argentina Republic, at the Opening Plenary of the 35th Session of the Subsidiary Body for Implementation (SBI 35) (Durban, South Africa, 29 November 2011)

Mr. Chairman,

1. I have the honour to deliver this statement on behalf of the Group of 77 and China.
2. At the outset, the Group of 77 and China would like to assure you of our full support and cooperation. We are ready to engage constructively in substantive work, in a party-driven manner, so that concrete progress can be achieved during this session on the many issues under the Subsidiary Body for Implementation.

Mr. Chairman,

3. According to the Compilation and Synthesis of fifth national communications from parties included in Annex I to the Convention, over the period 1990–2008, the total aggregate of greenhouse gas (GHG) emissions from Annex I parties that are not economies in transition, excluding LULUCF, increased by 8%. Moreover, according to projected data, the GHG emissions of Annex I parties, excluding emissions and removals from the LULUCF sector are expected to increase by 7.8% between 2010 and 2020. We continue to be very concerned about the facts and the trend contained in the reports FCCC/SBI/2011/INF.1, Add. 1 and Add. 2.
4. We expect that the decision adopted by the COP on this matter reflects a strong call to Annex I parties to intensify their efforts aimed at reducing their GHG emissions in accordance with the principles and provisions, the objective of the Convention and their commitments under the Convention and the Kyoto Protocol.

Mr. Chairman,

5. With reference to the above-mentioned document, that states that "many data gaps and inconsistencies in reporting approaches among Annex II countries and across periods still persist," we urge Annex I parties, first, to provide detailed information or make available in their national communications the level of improvement in emissions reductions, or lack thereof. In this sense, it is important to maintain and strengthen annual reports on the technical review of greenhouse gas inventories from parties included in Annex I to the Convention as well as the monitor, report, and evaluation of their domestic mitigation action. Secondly, as repeatedly stated in the synthesis of Annex I communications, standard formats of reporting on the provision of financial resources, including

for transfer of technology and adaptation should be utilized in fulfilment of obligations under article 12.3 of the Convention. Therefore, a COP decision under this agenda item must take all these elements on board.

6. At a time when more and more responsibilities on reporting are placed on developing country parties, it is incumbent on developed country parties that have the obligation to provide financial resources at agreed full costs basis to developing country parties, to clarify whether they are meeting their commitments under the Convention related to financing.
7. We underline our call on parties included in Annex II of the Convention to intensify their efforts aimed at fulfilling their commitments on the provision of financial resources, enhancing technology development and transfer, meeting costs of adaptation, and strengthening capacity-building in developing country parties in accordance with article 4, paragraphs 3, 4, and 5 of the Convention. To this end, the accuracy, comparability, and level of detail of information regarding the provision of support of financial resources, technology development and transfer, and capacity-building reported in National Communications of Annex II parties must be further defined and enhanced.
8. The conclusions forwarded by the SBI to COP must include the abovementioned elements for adoption by this COP.

Mr. Chairman,

9. The Group would like to recall the Cancun decisions contain additional reporting obligations for developing countries, as well as provisions on more frequent timelines for the submission of reports, which represent an added burden to the difficulties faced by developing country parties in terms of lack of technical and financial support when it comes to prepare their national communications. As we are all aware, paragraph 60 (c) of decision 1/CP.16 clearly establishes a link between the level of support provided and the submission of biennial reports by developing countries. Therefore, it requires specific technical and technological inputs, as well as increased human and institutional capacities.
10. Regarding the preparation of national communications from non–Annex I parties, predictability of funding and the provision of the agreed full costs is also to be met. Unfortunately, we are currently faced with a situation where national communications are subject to limited allocations and other conditions.
11. We also reiterate our call for more contributions to the funds devoted to adaptation under the Convention, in particular the Special Climate Change Fund, the Least Developed Countries Fund, and the Adaptation Fund under the Kyoto Protocol. Not only are they hugely underfunded, and most of them dependent on voluntary funding, they are also the only main sources of financing adaptation under the Convention.

12. The Group of 77 and China insists that conditions attached to the allocation and use of the funds that are managed through the Global Environment Facility as an operating entity of the financial mechanism of the Convention should not be applied to these funds, in particular the requirement of co-financing prior to accessing funding. Also, the Group reiterates its position that adaptation efforts must be treated in an equal manner as mitigation. Adaptation has historically been underfunded, a situation that must be reversed. The Group will continue to insist firmly on a balanced allocation of resources for adaptation, including for the design and capitalization of the Green Climate Fund, as well as direct access as operationalized in the Adaptation Fund, which are fundamental principles of the Group of 77 and China.

Mr. Chairman,

13. The G-77 and China expects a successful outcome for a clear and well-supported LDC process for the formulation and implementation of National Adaptation Plans (NAPs), including on the modalities and guidelines that may be employed by other particularly vulnerable developing countries.
14. We must also agree on the necessary institutional linkages to support this process, stressing the important role that the Adaptation Committee and the LDC Expert Group should have in the preparation and implementation of NAPs.
15. We believe that NAPs without the adequate means of implementation create new responsibilities for developing countries and we need to make progress to ensure that the formulation and the implementation of NAPS is not an additional burden, but an implementation-driven process to respond to climate change.
16. The Group consider the Work Programme on Loss and Damage as one of the key aspects to advance the implementation of adaptation in order to cope with the adverse impacts of climate change in developing countries. We welcome the progress made since the establishment of the Work Programme on Loss and Damage at COP-16 and we look forward to further advance in this important issue here with a view to making recommendations on loss and damage to the Conference of the Parties for its consideration at its eighteenth session.
17. On the activities to be undertaken by the Work Programme on Loss and Damage, the G-77 and China reaffirms the need to strengthen international cooperation, to enhance knowledge and capacity directed to reduce adverse effects of climate change, and to provide support for its implementation.

Mr. Chairman,

18. The G-77 and China looks forward to engaging constructively in the forum on the impact of the implementation of response measures at the Subsidiary Bodies, with the objective of developing a work programme under the SBSTA and the SBI to address these impacts, and to adopt at the seventeenth COP modalities for the operationalization of the work programme and a forum on response measures. Even if there is a need to make progress in the SBs in this matter specifically related to paragraph 93 of 1.CP/16, it is important to note that there is also a mandate to continuing discussions in the AWG-LCA on all the elements of economic and social consequences of response measures, in order to establish the political parameters that are required to meet the specific needs and concerns of developing countries in relation to this issue.
19. The G-77 and China acknowledges the work done by the Technology Executive Committee in its first and only meeting so far. We expect next year the TEC can meet as often as necessary and have enough time and resources to develop and implement a program of work that fulfils its functions as were adopted by the COP in Cancun, last year.
20. The Group of 77 and China reiterates the necessity of enabling the active participation of Palestine in the UNFCCC process and to make every effort to grant Palestine access to funding from sources of climate change financing.

Finally, Mr. Chairman,

21. The Group of 77 and China would like to reassure you of its commitment to make concrete progress to ensure the success of the seventeenth session of the Conference of the Parties and the seventh Meeting of the Parties here in Durban.

Statement on behalf of the Group of 77 and China by Ambassador Silvia Merega, Head of Delegation of the Argentine Republic, at the Closing Plenary of the 35th Session of the Subsidiary Body for Implementation (SBI 35) (Durban, South Africa, 3 December 2011)

Mr. Chairman,

1. I have the honour to deliver this statement on behalf of the Group of 77 and China.
2. Although our expectations on the agenda items under the SBI were higher on the results the work at this session should have achieved, we believe there has been progress in moving the issues forward.

Mr. Chairman,

3. The Group notes with concern that according to projected data the GHG emissions of Annex I parties, excluding LULUCF, are expected to increase by 7.8% between 2010 and 2020. In this regard, we call on Annex I parties to intensify their efforts aimed at reducing their GHG emissions in accordance with the principles and provisions, the objective of the Convention, and their commitments under the Convention and the Kyoto Protocol.
4. We call on Annex I Countries to further enhance the completeness, comparability, accuracy, and level of detail of the reported information. We also call on parties included in Annex II to enhance further the completeness, comparability, accuracy, and level of detail of the reported information regarding the provision of support of financial resources, technology development and transfer, and capacity-building to developing country parties, and regarding progress made to meet the specific needs and concerns arising from the impacts of implementation of response measures.
5. The Group notes with concern that twenty-four Annex I parties have submitted their Fifth National Communication behind the due date, and even one party has yet to submit it. In this sense, we urge the Annex I parties to take the necessary actions to comply with the obligation of submitting them by relevant due date in the future.
6. We look forward to the discussions on further implementation of article 12.5 at the thirty-sixth session of SBI.

Mr. Chairman,

7. The Group of 77 and China wish to highlight the value and the positive impact of the work programme of the Consultative Group of Experts on National Communications from parties not included in Annex I to the Convention (CGE). For this reason, the group has reiterated the importance of ensuring continued financial support for the implementation of the CGE's work programme and we especially urge parties included in Annex II to the Convention to make every effort to provide the necessary resources for the CGE to continue operating at its full capacity to play its role in improving the process of and the preparation of National Communications.
8. The Group of 77 and China has also reiterated that any consideration on further implementation of article 12.5 must fully take into account the principle of common but differentiated responsibilities, and that the process of reporting for non–Annex I parties cannot be as onerous as that of Annex I parties. We also believe that any future reporting framework needs to reflect the enormous diversity in national circumstances between parties, and that enhanced reporting will require a substantial increase in funding and technical resources. At a time when more and more responsibilities on

reporting are placed on developing country parties, we are faced with a difficult situation when national communications are subject to limited allocation of funding and other conditions.

9. We would like to express our deep concern over the grave situation of the Adaptation Fund of the Kyoto Protocol. Not only have there been no voluntary contributions to the Fund, with pledges that are left unfulfilled, but also the price of certified emission reduction units have gone down drastically in the last few months. This means of course that urgent concrete adaptation projects have remained underfunded or unfunded. In this sense, Mr. Chairman, we believe it is worthy to recall that the Adaptation Fund is the only fund that provides funding for concrete adaptation activities in particularly vulnerable developing countries.
10. This comes at a time when the Least Developed Countries Fund (LDCF), which mainly provides funding for the preparation of National Adaptation Plans of Action, also faces a serious lack of resources, and their activities are not allowed funding under the Global Environment Facility Trust Fund for Climate. This situation is also true of the Special Climate Change Fund (SCCF). Moreover, both the SCCF and the LDCF remains subject to co-financing, as well as the application of the concept of global benefits, imposed by the Global Environment Facility as manager of the LDCF. These Funds are voluntary Funds and the main sources of financing for adaptation for developing countries under the Convention and the Kyoto Protocol.

Mr. Chairman,

11. The future of the Adaptation Fund is moreover uncertain, until clarity is reached on the future of the Kyoto Protocol and the financial mechanism of the Convention. It likewise remains unclear as to whether there is indeed a balanced allocation of resources between mitigation and adaptation under the fast-start finance, which is now entering its final year.
12. Adaptation financing still remains clearly to be defined and implemented through the Green Climate Fund. This is a key priority for developing countries.
13. All these come at a time when extreme weather events have affected many countries around the developing world. The time for us has come to act urgently in terms of providing adequate and predictable financing for adaptation.

Mr. Chairman,

14. The G-77 and China stresses that the LDCs process for the formulation and implementation of National Adaptation Plans (NAPs) be supported adequately.

15. We must now make the institutional linkages to support this process, stressing the important role that the Adaptation Committee and the LDCs Expert Group should have in the preparation and implementation of NAPs.
16. We believe that NAPs need the adequate means of implementation. We need to make progress to ensure that the formulation and the implementation of NAPS are viable and an implementation-driven process.
17. The Group considers the Work Program on loss and damage as one of the key aspects to advance the implementation of adaptation in order to cope with the adverse impacts of climate change in developing countries. We welcome the work achieved in this session and look forward to seeing enough time dedicated to this issue over the next year for the adoption of a successful outcome at COP1-8.
18. The G-77 and China engaged constructively in the forum on the impact of the implementation of response measures at the Subsidiary Bodies, with the objective of developing a work programme under the SBSTA and the SBI to address these impacts, and to adopt at this seventeenth COP modalities for the operationalization of the work programme and a forum on response measures, as mandated by paragraph 93 of 1.CP/16.
19. However, the G-77 and China expresses its disappointment to the lack of agreement for a draft decision on the development of the work programme, modalities for its operationalization and a forum on the impact of implementation of response measures. We look forward to the full implementation of paragraph 93 of decision 1.CP/16.
20. The G-77 and China acknowledges the report of the Global Environment Facility (GEF) on the Poznan Strategic Programme on technology transfer. In this regard we would like to see the future activities of GEF under this program to be aligned with activities under the technology mechanism of the Convention. In addition, we would like to request the GEF to assess its capacity to provide support for the short-term activities of the Climate Technology Centre Network.
21. The G-77 and China recognizes the activities done by the TEC during 2011 and urges parties to ensure the adequate financial resources for the implementation of the TEC's program of work for 2012.
22. G-77 and China expresses thanks for the SBI to conclude the second comprehensive review which is of paramount importance in the implementation of the capacity-building framework according to decision 2/CP.7. However, the G-77 and China feels that the process has taken so long and future guidance by the SBI may be required to enable timely completion of such work in the future.
23. The Group of 77 and China reiterates the necessity of enabling the active participation of Palestine in the UNFCCC process and to make every effort to grant Palestine access to funding from sources of climate change financing.

Finally, Mr. Chairman,

24. The Group of 77 and China would like to reassure you of its commitment to make concrete progress to ensure the success of the seventeenth session of the Conference of the Parties and the seventh Meeting of the Parties here in Durban.

Statement by Mr. Abdelghani Merabet, Third Secretary at the Permanent Mission of Algeria to the United Nations on behalf of the G-77 and China, at the Closing Plenary of the Thirty-sixth Session of the Subsidiary Body for Implementation (SBI) of the UN Framework Convention on Climate Change (Bonn, Germany, 25 May 2012)

Mr. Chairman,

1. I have the honour to deliver this statement on behalf of the Group of 77 and China.
2. Let me first congratulate you for your efforts as a chairman of this important subsidiary body during this session in order to paving the way to a real progress in implementing all items of its agenda in a constructive manner taking into account the concerns and interests of parties, particularly the G-77 and China members.

Mr. Chairman,

3. With respect to the National Communications from parties included in Annex I to the Convention and the Status of submission and review of the fifth national communications, the G-77 and China urges them to improve reporting information in accordance with all elements of "Guidelines for the preparation of national communications by Annex I parties to the Convention." It also calls Annex I parties to enhance the completeness, comparability, and level of detail of the reported information.
4. The Group calls developed country parties to submit their sixth national communications by 1 January 2014, and to submit their national inventories using the "Revised reporting guidelines on annual inventories for Parties included in Annex I to the Convention." In this context, it urges those parties to intensify their efforts in reducing their GHG emissions in accordance with the principles and provisions of the Convention and the Kyoto Protocol.

Mr. Chairman,

5. The Group stresses on the necessity for developed countries to enhance their support to parties not included in Annex I of the Convention and providing

them with appropriate technical assistance to facilitate the preparation of their national communications and biennial update reports by identifying problems, constraints, and difficulties encountered in the use of guidelines and methodologies for their preparation. In this regard, the continuation of the Consultative Group of Experts on non–Annex I National Communications will be essential in providing necessary support to the members of our group.

6. The G-77 and China recommend the COP at its eighteenth session to request the GEF to provide funds for technical support for the preparation of biennial update reports from non–Annex I parties, similar to that provided by the National Communications Support Programme, recognizing that the costs of such technical support are not deducted from the funds provided to non–Annex I parties for the preparation of their biennial update reports. The Group invites the GEF to report on this matter in its report to the COP at its nineteenth session.
7. The Group would like to recall that since Cancun, additional reporting obligations for developing countries were established, which represent a new burden for them. Such burden cannot be supported by developing countries without adequate, appropriate, and predictable means of implementation.

Mr. Chairman,

8. With respect to mitigation action by developing countries, the Group stresses the importance of establishing an MRV system of support to ensure better information and implementation of support actions received from developed countries. It also recommends to start a new process with a view to enable developing countries to elaborate their own MRV for NAMAs, which will be implemented at the national level taking into account relevant and specific elements of mitigation actions as well as national circumstances.
9. The G-77 and China recalls the need to operationalize ICA in a non-intrusive and non-punitive manner to the national sovereignty of the developing country parties through an appropriate support from developed countries. The members of the team of technical experts referred to in decision 2/CP.17, Annex IV, must be selected with a view to achieving a balance between experts from Annex I parties and non–Annex I parties in the overall composition of the team.
10. We consider that the participation in the registry shall be voluntary, and its elaboration must take into account the diversity of the nationally appropriate mitigation actions of developing country parties. The G-77 and China took note of information provided by the Secretariat on the design of the prototype of the registry, including that, in accordance with decision 2/CP17, this design includes separate sections for nationally appropriate actions (NAMAs) seeking international support and for other NAMAs submitted for recognition.

Mr. Chairman,

11. The G-77 and China welcomes your approach for the Forum and work programme on the impact of the implementation of response measures in accordance with the decision 8/CP.17, with the objective of improving the understanding of the impact of the implementation of response measures.
12. We are at the beginning of an important process, and we welcome the constructive work done in this session in order to finalizing all modalities to operationalise the forum on the impact of the implementation of response measures and to start implementing its work programme and defining relevant and specific elements to structure its activities on the basis of decision 8/CP.17. We celebrate the conclusion of an agreement on the activities to implement the work programme, and we look forward to engaging constructively in the in-forum workshops and discussions at the forum planned for the thirty-seventh, thirty-eighth, and thirty-ninth session of the Subsidiary Bodies, taking into account the specific needs and concerns of developing country parties in relation to the impact of the implementation of response measures taken by developed country parties.
13. We are pleased with the progress under the work programme on loss and damage associated with climate change impacts in developing countries that are particularly vulnerable to the adverse effects of climate change, including on points relevant to assessing the risk of loss and damage on, *inter alia*, technical, and financial assistance. The group stresses the importance on continuing to advance the work on matters related to non-economic losses. We hope to see this issue advance in Doha and to reach a decision then, including establishing an international mechanism to address loss and damage.

Mr. Chairman,

14. The adaptation is an issue of central concern to members of the Group of 77 and China. The Group is particularly concerned by the diminishing of resources of the Adaptation Fund due to the current low market prices of certified emission reductions. Such situation is liable to affect the necessary balance between adaptation and mitigation in providing the means of implementation to developing country parties. The group considers any effort to ensuring sustainability, predictability, and adequacy of the resources of the Adaptation Fund as a priority.
15. The Group took note with appreciation of the efforts of the Adaptation Fund Board to promote the accreditation of national implementing entities, the direct access to its resources and initiatives taken by it to explore options for raising additional resources.
16. The G-77 and China encourages the SBI to continue its consideration of the initial review of the Adaptation Fund in accordance with the annex to decision

6/CMP.6 with a view to preparing a draft decision on the outcome of the initial review of the Adaptation Fund for adoption by the CMP at its eighth session.

17. The G-77 and China urges developed country parties to mobilize financial support for the national adaptation plans for LDC parties through bilateral and multilateral channels, including the Least Developed Countries Fund (LDCF) in accordance with decision 1/CP.16 and 1/CP.17 and took note the work of the Least Developed Countries Expert Group (LEG) and other experts groups under the Convention.

Mr. Chairman,

18. The G-77 and China recognizes the activities done by the Technology Executive Committee (TEC) during 2012 and welcomes its rolling work plan for 2012– 2013. The group emphasized the necessity for the TEC to structure its work plan in short and medium term, including the organisation of a thematic dialogue on enabling environment and on barriers to technology development and transfer.
19. We recommend the TEC to establish an interaction with other institutional arrangements under the Convention, including the Climate Technology Centre Network (CTCN), the Financial Mechanism, and the Adaptation Committee as part of its programme of work.
20. The G-77 and China calls the Global Environment Facility to continue to provide as appropriate financial resources to non–Annex I parties, to support the implementation of the Doha work programme on article 6 of the Convention relating to education, training, and public awareness in order to achieve the goals of the Convention and a full implementation of adaptation and mitigation actions. It is highly important that the new work programme on article 6 of the Convention has the technical and financial support necessary to achieve the goals of the Convention and a full implementation of adaptation and mitigation actions.

Mr. Chairman

21. The Group of 77 and China reiterates the necessity of an effective participation of Palestine in the UNFCCC process, and to have the right of access to funding from different climate change sources. Furthermore, we request the SBI to provide financial support for the participation of the Palestinian delegation in the meetings of the Convention and the Kyoto Protocol.

Finally, Mr. Chairman,

22. The Group of 77 and China is fully committed to achieve a success of the thirty-seven session of the Subsidiary Body for Implementation (SBI) and all other bodies of the Convention during the eighteenth session of the Conference of the Parties which will be held in Doha.

Statement by Minister Counselor Djacta Larbi, Permanent Mission of Algeria to the United Nations on Behalf of the Group of 77 and China at the Closing Plenary of the 37th Session of the SBI (Doha, Qatar, 1 December 2012)

Mr. Chairman,

1. I have the honour to deliver this statement on behalf of the G-77 and China.
2. I would like to thank you for the efforts you have made to push the process forward.

Mr. Chairman,

3. The G-77 and China welcomes the adoption of the new Work Programme on article 6 of the Convention, related to education, training and public awareness.
4. The Group stresses however that the following elements must be considered as benchmarks for the next steps:
   - Providing financial resources to support the activities related to the implementation of article 6 of the Convention.
   - Enhancing the support of Annex I to non–Annex I parties, by providing technical assistance to facilitate the preparation of their national communications and biennial update report. The work of the Consultative Group of Experts on Non–Annex I National Communications will be essential in providing necessary support requested by developing countries.
   - Submitting by Annex I parties of their sixth national communications, by 1 January 2014, and their national inventories using the "Revised reporting guidelines on annual inventories for Annex-I Parties."
   - Intensifying the efforts of Annex I parties in reducing their GHG emissions in accordance with the principles and provisions of the Convention and the Kyoto Protocol.
   - The operationalization of the ICA in a non-intrusive and non-punitive manner to the national sovereignty of developing country parties through the provision of adequate financial resources by developed countries.
   - The participation in the Registry shall be on a voluntary basis, and its elaboration must take into account the diversity of the nationally appropriate mitigation actions of developing countries.
   - The establishment of an international mechanism under the Convention on loss and damage that addresses the needs of developing countries emerging from extreme and slow-onset events. This mechanism will be a key step to support multiple approaches on loss and damage to respond to this complex issue.
   - Continuing of activities related the Work Programme under the Forum on economic and social consequences of response measures, as well as the review of the work of the forum and preparation of recommendations to the Conference of the Parties, in accordance with the Work Programme.

- The structuration of the Work Plan of the Technology Executive Committee in short and medium terms.
- The mobilization of financial support for the national adaptation plans of LDCs and developing country parties that are not LDCs, through bilateral and multilateral channels, in accordance with the decisions 1/CP.16, 1/CP.17, and 5/CP.17.

5. Finally, the G-77 and China looks forward to engage during the next session of the SBI in a constructive manner to enhance the implementation of the Convention and its Kyoto Protocol.

Statement on behalf of the Group of 77 and China by Ambassador Amena Yauvoli, Permanent Secretary of Foreign Affairs and International Cooperation of the Republic of Fiji, Chair of the Group of 77 and China, at the Opening Plenary of the 38th Session of the Subsidiary Body for Implementation (SBI 38) of the United Nations Framework Convention on Climate Change (UNFCCC) (Bonn, Germany, 3 June 2013)

Thank you, Mr. Chairman,
Excellencies,
Distinguished representatives,
Ladies and gentlemen,

1. I have the honour to deliver this statement on behalf of the Group of 77 and China in the Opening Plenary of the Thirty-eighth Session of the Subsidiary Body on Implementation.
2. The Group is ready to engage meaningfully with all members and I assure you, Mr. Chairman, of our support.

Mr. Chairman,

3. These are the views of the Group in relation to the following agenda items under SBI. On National Communications from parties included in Annex I, the Group of 77 and China reiterates its point of view expressed in Doha, that the above parties are urged to submit, by 1 January 2014, their sixth national communications and their national inventories using the revised reporting guidelines on annual inventories for Annex I parties. On national communications from Parties not included in Annex I to the Convention, the Group calls developed countries to enhance their financial support to parties not included in Annex I of the Convention technical assistance and capacity-building to facilitate the preparation of national communications and biennial updates.
4. The Group considers also that the work of the Consultative Group of Experts on Non–Annex I National Communications will be crucial in providing necessary support requested by developing countries.

5. The Group is of the view that the provision of financial support is essential to allow developing countries to meet their obligations in submitting national communications by 1 January 2014.
6. On agenda item 5, the G-77 and China welcomes considerations to enhance the work programmes to further the understanding of the diversity of nationally appropriate mitigation actions and calls for more support from developed countries for helping developing countries to accomplish their obligations in this regard.

Mr. Chairman,

7. On agenda item 8, the Group appreciates the work of the Least Developed Countries Expert Group (LEG) and its report and work programme. It is now very important that the national adaptation programme of actions (NAPAs) prepared by the 47 LDCs are fully implemented along with rest of the elements of LDC work programme and the NAP process without any delay.
8. On agenda item 9, National Adaptation Plans, the Group believes that for developing countries, adaptation is an urgent and high priority. Despite the clear mandate of the Cancun Adaptation Framework on the launching of national adaptation plan process for the least developed countries and modalities for other developing countries, the Group deplores the lack of funding as of today to start NAP process. The question of urgency and priority is glossed over. Our Group needs expedited funding to kick off the NAP process.

Mr. Chairman,

9. On the issue of loss and damage, the Group calls for the full implementation of the decision adopted in Doha related to this matter. It calls also for the operationalization of the mechanism established by this decision, taking into account the principles of the Convention and the national development processes. Carrying out such actions requires the provision of adequate support and creating the appropriate arrangements and calling for meaningful activities. Fulfilling the mandate of Doha on the issue above must be considered as one of the key elements for the success of the COP-19, which will be held in Warsaw.
10. Then, the Group has been calling for the establishment of an international mechanism under the Convention on loss and damage that addresses the needs of developing countries emerging from extreme and slow-onset events, and the urgency for this mechanism has only increased. This mechanism cannot be an empty shell, and we expect substantive movement on this matter at this session.

Mr. Chairman,

11. The Group considers that the effectiveness and the sustainability of the resources of the Adaptation fund are the main challenges for making the institutional mechanism dedicated to the adaptation operational. It is essential that a large debate must be engaged in order to resolve effectively the lack of functioning which characterizes this mechanism.

Mr. Chairman,

12. On Development and Transfer of Technologies, the Group of 77 and China took note of the first meeting of the Advisory Board of the Climate Technology Centre and Network and the ongoing efforts to set the modalities and procedures of CTCN and its Advisory Board. In order to fully implement the technology mechanism to enhance the action of technology development and transfer, we believe it is of crucial importance to ensure coordination between the two bodies of technology mechanism, the Technology Executive Committee and the CTCN. We look forward to the tangible development and transfer of technologies to developing countries for climate change.

Mr. Chairman,

13. The Group is of the view that capacity-building is an integral element, and essential to enable developing country parties to participate fully in addressing the challenges of climate change, and to implement effectively their commitments under the Convention.
14. Capacity-building is one of the basic foundations of any mitigation or adaptation effort by both developed and developing countries to deal with the effects of climate change. From the Bali Action Plan to the Doha Climate Gateway, capacity-building has made a lot of progress, but not resolved all the issues raised by the BAP, especially institutional arrangements for capacity-building and enhancement of monitoring and review of capacity-building.
15. The Group acknowledges the organization of the Durban Forum for In-depth Discussion on Capacity-Building by the SBI, which was a result of colleagues' hard work in response to paragraphs 136 and 137 of 1/CP.16.
16. We had agreed to its establishment in Durban on the understanding that its output would help improve the capacity-building support received by developing countries, and further enhance the monitoring and review of the

effectiveness of capacity-building. However, it remains unclear what the SBI intends to do with the information from the Durban Forum and other information provided by non–Annex I parties, besides including it in the SBI's comprehensive reviews of the implementation of the framework for capacity-building in developing countries.

17. A two-year work programme should be prepared under SBI with a view to further strengthening the monitoring and review of the effectiveness of capacity-building, developing a comprehensive, integrated, and balanced set of evaluation indicators, and assessing the activities by developed countries in supporting developing countries capacity-building. Pursuant to paragraph 144 of FCCC/CP/2011/9/Add.1, the objective of the Durban Forum is to further strengthen the monitoring and review of the effectiveness of capacity-building.
18. The specific issues to be considered at the second and subsequent meetings of the Durban Forum should be identified annually with a view to formalizing measures and the way for and forward for enhanced capacity-building in the ADP. Pursuant to paragraph 5 of decision 1/CP.17, capacity-building is one of the elements in the Durban Platform process, which requires equal treatment with the other elements

Mr. Chairman,

19. Finally, on item 14, the Group of 77 and China looks forward to continuing engaging constructively in the forum on the impact of the implementation of response measures at the Subsidiary Bodies and its work program to address these impacts. In particular, we welcome the activities that will take place in these sessions in the areas of the work programme related to the assessment of impacts; the just transition of the workforce; economic diversification; and modelling. In addition, as mandated by decision 1.CP.18, we also look forward to sharing views in the forum on policy issues of concern, such as unilateral measures.
20. In this respect, we attach great importance to this issue as all developing countries will be affected by economic and social consequences of response measures taken by developed countries. Therefore, there is a need to take full consideration on the specific needs and concerns of developing countries arising from the impact of the implementation of response measures, in accordance with the provisions and principles of the Convention.
21. In conclusion, Mr. Chairman, the Group of 77 and China reserves its position on the remaining agenda item not articulated in this statement.

Statement on behalf of the Group of 77 and China by Mr. Amena Yauvoli, Ambassador, UNFCCC Chair of G-77 and China at the Opening Plenary of the 39th Session of the Subsidiary Body for Implementation (SBI 39) of the United Nations Framework Convention on Climate Change (UNFCCC) (Warsaw, Poland, 11 November 2013)

Thank you, Mr. Chairman,
Excellencies,
Distinguished representatives,
Ladies and gentlemen,

1. I have the honor to deliver this statement on behalf of the Group of 77 and China in the Opening Plenary of the Thirty-ninth Session of the Subsidiary Body on Implementation.
2. With this Subsidiary Body not meeting in the last Session, I wish to assure you that the Group is willing and ready to engage meaningfully with all parties. Our support and assistance to you is rendered and reaffirmed.

Mr. Chairman,

3. These are the views of the Group in relation to the following agenda items under SBI. On National Communications from parties included in Annex I, the Group of 77 and China reiterates its point of view expressed in Doha, that the above parties are urged to submit, by 1 January 2014, their sixth national communications and their national inventories using the revised reporting guidelines on annual inventories for Annex I parties. On national communications from parties not included in Annex I to the Convention, the Group calls developed countries to enhance their financial support and technical assistance to parties not included in Annex I of the Convention, in order to build the capacities needed to facilitate the preparation of national communications and biennial updates.
4. The Group considers also that the continuation of the work of the Consultative Group of Experts on Non–Annex I National Communications will be crucial in providing necessary support requested by developing countries.
5. The Group is of the view that the provision of financial and technical support is essential to allow developing countries to meet their obligations in submitting national communications by every four years.
6. On agenda item 5, the G-77 and China welcomes considerations to enhance the work programmes to further the understanding of the diversity of nationally appropriate mitigation actions, and calls for more support from developed countries for helping developing countries to accomplish their obligations in this regard.

Mr. Chairman,

7. On agenda item 9, the Group appreciates the work of the Least Developed Countries Expert Group (LEG) and its report and work programme. It is now very important that the national adaptation programme of actions (NAPAs) prepared by the 47 LDCs are fully implemented along with the rest of the elements of LDC work programme and the NAP process without any delay.
8. On agenda item 10, National Adaptation Plans (NAPs), the Group believes that for developing countries, adaptation is an urgent and high priority. Despite the clear mandate of the Cancun Adaptation Framework on the launching of national adaptation plan process for the least developed countries and modalities for other developing countries, the Group deplores the lack of funding as of today to start NAP process. The question of urgency and priority is glossed over. Our Group needs expedited funding to kick off the NAP process. The Group also appreciates the work done by the Adaptation Committee on the NAPs for other developing countries and believes that funding and technical supports are needed by other developing countries to prepare and implement their NAPs.

Mr. Chairman,

9. On the issue of loss and damage, the Group calls for the full implementation of the decision adopted in Doha related to this matter. It calls also for the operationalization of the mechanism established by this decision, taking into account the principles of the Convention and the national development processes. Carrying out such actions requires the provision of adequate support and creating the appropriate arrangements and calling for meaningful activities. Fulfilling the mandate of Doha on the issue above must be considered as one of the key elements for the success of the COP-19, which will be held in Warsaw.
10. Then, the Group has been calling for the establishment of an international mechanism under the Convention on loss and damage that addresses the needs of developing countries emerging from extreme and slow onset events, and the urgency for this mechanism has only increased. This mechanism cannot be an empty shell, and we expect substantive movement on this matter at this session.

Mr. Chairman,

11. The Group considers that the effectiveness and the sustainability of the resources of the Adaptation Fund are the main challenges for making the institutional mechanism dedicated to the adaptation operational. It is essential that a large debate must be engaged in order to resolve effectively the lack of functioning, which characterizes this mechanism.

Mr. Chairman,

12. On Development and Transfer of Technologies, the Group of 77 and China took note of the first meeting of the Advisory Board of the Climate Technology Center and Network and the ongoing efforts to set the modalities and procedures of CTCN and its Advisory Board. In order to fully implement the technology mechanism to enhance the action of technology development and transfer, we believe it is of crucial importance to ensure coordination between the two bodies of technology mechanism, the Technology Executive Committee and the CTCN. We look forward to the tangible development and transfer of technologies to developing countries for climate change.

Mr. Chairman,

13. The Group is of the view that capacity-building is an integral element, and essential to enable developing country parties to participate fully in addressing the challenges of climate change, and to implement effectively their commitments under the Convention.
14. Capacity-building is one of the basic foundations of any mitigation or adaptation effort by both developed and developing countries to deal with the effects of climate change. From the Bali Action Plan to the Doha Climate Gateway, capacity-building has made a lot of progress, but not resolved all the issues raised by the BAP, especially institutional arrangements for capacity-building and enhancement of monitoring and review of capacity-building.
15. The Group acknowledges the organization of the Durban Forum for In-depth Discussion on Capacity-Building by the SBI, which was a result of colleagues' hard work in response to paragraphs 136 and 137 of 1/CP.16.
16. We had agreed to its establishment in Durban on the understanding that its output would help improve the capacity-building support received by developing countries, and further enhance the monitoring and review of the effectiveness of capacity-building. However, it remains unclear what the SBI intends to do with the information from the Durban Forum and other information provided by non–Annex I parties, besides including it in the SBI's comprehensive reviews of the implementation of the framework for capacity-building in developing countries.
17. A two-year work programme should be prepared under SBI with a view to further strengthening the monitoring and review of the effectiveness of capacity-building, developing a comprehensive, integrated, and balanced set of evaluation indicators, and assessing the activities by developed countries in supporting developing countries capacity-building. Pursuant to paragraph 144 of FCCC/CP/2011/9/Add.1, the objective of the Durban Forum

is to further strengthen the monitoring and review of the effectiveness of capacity-building.

18. The specific issues to be considered at the second and subsequent meetings of the Durban Forum should be identified annually with a view to formalizing measures and the way forward for enhanced capacity-building in the ADP. Pursuant to paragraph 5 of decision 1/CP.17, capacity-building is one of the elements in the Durban Platform process, which requires equal treatment with the other elements.

Mr. Chairman,

19. The G-77 and China reaffirms the importance of the forum on the impact of the implementation of response measures at the Subsidiary Bodies and its work program to address these impacts. In particular, we welcome the organization for this session of the workshop on area b of the work programme (cooperation on response strategies) and, as mandated by decision 1.CP.18, we also look forward to sharing views in the forum on policy issues of concern, such as unilateral measures.
20. In this respect, all developing country parties will be affected in different ways by negative economic and social consequences of response measures taken by developed country parties. Therefore, we affirm the importance of the continuation of the forum, as there is a need to take full consideration to what actions are necessary to meet the specific needs and concerns of developing country parties arising from the impact of the implementation of response measures, in accordance with the provisions and principles of the Convention. In this regard, we look forward to continuing working in the forum, in COP-19 and beyond, in order to address specifically how developed countries parties are minimizing the adverse economic and social effects of their response measures on developing countries parties.
21. Finally, on item 16, the Group wishes to reiterate the importance of the 2013–2015 Review. We look forward to concrete progress being made at this session in the work of the Review in light of the lost opportunity to begin work during the June session.
22. The Group welcomes the progress achieved in Doha on advancing the implementation of article 6 of the Convention through the adoption of the Doha work programme and the establishment of the Dialogue on article 6. Concerted action on education, public awareness and public participation is a pre-condition to any meaningful action on adaptation and mitigation. The first Dialogue held in June this year proved to be a useful platform for exchanging experiences and approaches to climate change education and training. The Group considers that the organization of the Dialogue needs to be further enhanced to better support efforts of parties to implement article 6. The Group considers it fundamental to provide further guidance for the

organization of the next Dialogue and we are ready to work on that. Thank you, Mr. Chair, for your permanent support to this issue.

23. In conclusion, Mr. Chairman, the Group of 77 and China reserves its position on the remaining agenda items not articulated in this statement.

Statement on behalf of the Group of 77 and China by Ambassador Rene Orellana, Chair of the Group of 77 and China, at the Opening Plenary of the 40th Session of the Subsidiary Body for Implementation (SBI 40) of the United Nations Framework Convention on Climate Change (UNFCCC) (Bonn, Germany, 4 June 2014)

Thank you, Mr. Chairman,
Excellencies, Ministers,
Distinguished representatives,
Ladies and gentlemen,

1. I have the honour to deliver this statement on behalf of the Group of 77 and China during the Opening Plenary of the Fortieth Session of the Subsidiary Body on Implementation. I wish to assure you that the Group is willing and ready to engage meaningfully with all parties. Our support and assistance to you is rendered and reaffirmed.

These are the views of the Group in relation to the following agenda items under SBI,

2. The G-77 and China would like to express its concern on agenda item 3 (c), regarding the additional period for fulfilling commitments, or the so-called true-up period. As we know, it has been agreed that parties will be allowed a period of 100 days after the completion of the review of the final annual report for the commitment period to continue to make transactions of Kyoto units, including transfers, acquisitions, issuances, replacements, and retirements. The party's compliance with its commitment under the Kyoto Protocol will be determined after the review of the true-up period. For the G-77 and China, it is essential to know the compliance status of the Kyoto Protocol parties to their article 3, paragraph 1 commitments during the first commitment period of the Kyoto Protocol. We note with grave concern that a party has chosen to withdraw from their legal commitments under the KP in the hope to avoid compliance issues—and further note that those legal obligations should be fulfilled until their last day as a party to the Kyoto Protocol.

Mr. Chairman,

3. Setting the date for completion of the expert review process in time for an informed process in Paris will entail understanding the historical difficulties in

completing the review process, as well as understanding the importance to the G-77 and China of knowing the compliance status of the KP parties in the first Commitment Period. We should not allow technical excuses to delay this very important and politically sensitive issue. The Group highlights that this matter is paramount to trust-building among parties to the ADP negotiations—one cannot expect parties to agree on new obligations without knowledge of their Partners' compliance with previous commitments.

Mr. Chairman,

4, On National Communications from parties included in Annex I, the Group of 77 and China reiterates its point of view expressed in Doha, that the above parties were urged to submit, by 1 January 2014, their sixth national communications and their national inventories using the revised reporting guidelines on annual inventories for Annex I parties. On national communications from parties not included in Annex I to the Convention, the Group calls on developed countries to enhance their financial support and technical assistance to parties not included in Annex I of the Convention, in order to build the capacities needed to facilitate the preparation of national communications and biennial updates.
5. The Group considers also that the continuation of the work of the Consultative Group of Experts on Non–Annex I National Communications will be crucial in providing necessary support requested by developing countries. The Group is of the view that the provision of financial and technical support is essential to allow developing countries to meet their obligations in submitting national communications every four years.

Mr. Chairman,

6. We welcome the report of the LEG from its twenty-fifth meeting held in Dar es Salaam, United Republic of Tanzania, on 27 and 28 February. We also welcome the progress achieved in the implementation of its 2013–2014 work and new activities as part of its two-year rolling work programme for 2014–2015.
7. We also appreciate the Least Developed Countries Independent Expert Group efforts in supporting the LDCs for the National Adaptation Plan process, especially trainings on NAPs and ongoing progress on the development of NAP Central.
8. Let us underscore that the LDCs are still waiting for support to ensure the implementation of the full LDC work programme, in particular the remaining elements of the work program other than NAPAs.
9. On National Adaptation Plans (NAPS), the Group believes that for developing countries, adaptation is an urgent and high priority and the Group

deplores the lack of funding and technical support as of today to start the NAP process. The question of urgency and priority is glossed over. Support for the LDCs has been unacceptably slow, and the situation for the non-LDC NAPS is no different. Our Group needs expedited funding to kick off the NAP process.

10. The mandate for SB40 regarding NAPS focuses on the review of the NAPS guidelines. It is the view of the Group that it is too early to revise them given that only a few countries have begun the process. However, there might be a few lessons already that can be already addressed, particularly those that can be directed to the GCF so that they can be addressed in financing the formulation and implementation of NAPS, as well as requests to the LEG, AC, and other bodies to address issues challenging the formulation and implementation of NAPS.

Mr. Chairman,

11. The Group welcomes the outcome of the 2/CP.19 on the Warsaw international mechanism for loss and damage associated with climate change impacts. The need to make this mechanism functional is paramount. This mechanism must address the needs of developing countries emerging from extreme and slow-onset events. The urgency for this mechanism has only increased. This mechanism cannot be an empty shell, and it is therefore with great concern that the Group finds itself isolated from the work on the development of the Mechanism plan by interim Executive Committee. We call for an immediate solution to the unprecedented lack of transparency on this matter of survival and development for the group. The Group also calls for the operationalization of the mechanism established by this decision, taking into account the principles of the Convention and national development processes. Carrying out these actions requires the provision of adequate support, creating the appropriate arrangements, and setting out meaningful activities.
12. For this session, we look forward to engage in discussing the composition and procedures for the Executive Committee. We call for a composition that is equitable with membership of this Convention, with a majority from developing countries and a similar membership structure as the Adaptation Committee. On procedures, it is important to think of procedures appropriate to the work of a mechanism, for example, the integration of outside experts on key issues such as migration, humanitarian issues, recovery and rehabilitation and insurance. We call for the provision of adequate support to implement the work of the mechanism, including the activities of the two-year work plan.

Mr. Chairman,

13. On item 4(b) on financial and technical support, the Group notes that the sixth replenishment process for the GEF was concluded and also notes that there are some new recommendations regarding GEF funding and star allocation. In this regard the Group stresses the fact that the main aim of support provided by the GEF should be focused on implementing projects related to climate change and not only focus on funding reporting processes.
14. Regarding the second review of the Adaptation Fund, the Group welcomes the pledges by Annex II countries amounting to around US$100 million. However, the group believes that the main concerns regarding the sustainability, predictability and adequacy of resources to the Adaptation Fund are still not dealt with. The Group believes that the second review should provide recommendations to ensure that adequate and sustainable resources be available for the Adaptation Fund, which is until now the only fund dedicated to adaptation in developing countries.
15. On item 18 regarding the Program Budget, the Group notes that the program budget adopted by the parties in Warsaw included addition of new postings in the Secretariat. However, the Group highlights that the imbalance between adaptation and mitigation allocations within the budget and within the regular postings within the Secretariat still exists. The G-77 stresses that this imbalance should be reviewed and further consideration to adaptation-related issues should be provided in the incoming proposed program budget.
16. On Development and Transfer of Technologies, the Group of 77 and China believes that in order to fully implement the technology mechanism to enhance the action of technology development and transfer, it is crucial to ensure coordination between the two bodies of the technology mechanism, the Technology Executive Committee and the CTCN. We look forward to the tangible development and transfer of technologies to developing countries for climate change. The Group emphasizes the necessity for the TEC to structure its work plan for the short and medium term, including the organisation of a thematic dialogue on enabling environments for technology development and transfer, including the mechanisms needed to address all barriers, such as IPR.
17. Capacity-building is of utmost importance to the Group of 77 and China. While we support the Durban Forum on Capacity-Building, our experience is that it does not go far enough to adequately address our current needs and concerns. Therefore, we are urging our negotiating Partners to accept our proposal for a two-year work programme that we are confident will resolve many of the problems relating to capacity-building in developing countries in a manner that will be beneficial to all.

18. The Group is of the view that capacity-building is an integral element, and essential to enable developing country parties to participate fully in addressing the challenges of climate change, and to implement effectively their commitments under the Convention.

Mr. Chairman,

19. On Response Measures, the G-77 and China reaffirms the importance to give full consideration to what actions are necessary to meet the specific needs and concerns of developing country parties arising from the impacts of the implementation of response measures, in accordance with the principles and provisions of the Convention. In this regard, we regret the lack of progress made in Warsaw on the matter, however, we still look forward to the favourable consideration of the issue in these Subsidiary Body sessions, towards the adoption of a decision at COP-20 for the continuation of the Forum and the establishment of a mechanism to address the negative economic and social consequences of response measures taken by developed country parties on developing country parties. In this regard, we recall the contents of the submission that the G-77 and China tabled in Warsaw on the matter, and we believe our proposal has key substantive elements towards the achievement of progress in these sessions,
20. The G-77 and China looks forward to the progress to be made at this session towards the 2013–2015 review. We underscore the importance of continuing the work under this agenda item in an inclusive, transparent, and balanced manner.

Mr. Chairman,

21. Article 6 is crucial for achieving the ultimate objective of the Convention and for the effective implementation of adaptation and mitigation action. Therefore, the G-77 and China welcomes the Second Dialogue on article 6 of the Convention that will take place in this session. It will focus on public awareness, public access to information, and public participation, as well as international cooperation on these matters. At its fortieth session the SBI will consider the issue of subsequent meetings of the Dialogue. The Group of 77 and China considers that it is fundamental to strengthen and support the work of the national focal points for article 6 of the Convention. Therefore, we are working to adopt a decision in Lima in this regard, as well as for enhancing stakeholder participation to address climate change.
22. In conclusion, Mr. Chairman, the Group of 77 and China reserves its position on the remaining agenda items not articulated in this statement and wishes to reiterate our commitment for a fruitful session.

Statement on behalf of the Group of 77 and China, Ambassador Rene Orellana, Chair of the Group of 77 and China at the Opening Plenary of the 41st Session of the Subsidiary Body for Implementation (SBI 41) of the United Nations Framework Convention on Climate Change (UNFCCC) (Lima, Peru, 1 December 2014)

Thank you, Mr. Chairman,
Excellencies, Ministers,
Distinguished representatives,
Ladies and gentlemen,

1. I have the honour to deliver this statement on behalf of the Group of 77 and China during the Opening Plenary of the Forty-first Session of the Subsidiary Body on Implementation. I wish to assure you that the Group is willing and ready to engage meaningfully with all parties. Our support and assistance to you is rendered and reaffirmed.
2. Setting the date for completion of the expert review process in time for an informed process in Paris will entail understanding the historical difficulties in completing the review process, as well as understanding the importance to the G-77 and China of knowing the compliance status of the KP parties in the first Commitment Period. We should not allow technical excuses to delay this very important and politically sensitive issue. The Group highlights that this matter is paramount to trust building among parties to the ADP negotiations.
3. We appreciate the work that the LEG and the Adaptation Committee have been doing in relation to NAPs and in particular the technical support for LDCs and other developing countries.
4. However, we believe that the current pace of efforts needs to be improved to respond to the urgency of issues related to adaptation. It is important to ensure that there is coherence between the activities under the national adaptation plan process by developing countries and the provision of support by the operating entities of the financial mechanism. Countries which have also formulated their national adaptation plans need funding for implementation. There is therefore the need for clear guidance on finance for the implementation of national adaptation plans.
5. The Group believes that for developing countries, adaptation is an urgent and high priority and deplores the lack of funding and technical support as of today to start the NAP process. The question of urgency and priority is glossed over. Support for the LDCs has been unacceptably slow, and the situation for the non-LDC NAPs is no different. Our Group needs expedited funding to accelerate the NAP process. At this session, we have identified key elements to assist in taking stock of the application of the initial guidelines and look forward to further engagement at the next session.

6. On the matters of the Warsaw international mechanism for loss and damage associated with climate change impacts, the Group stresses the paramount need to make this mechanism functional. This mechanism must address the needs of developing countries suffering from extreme and slow-onset climate change induced events, and the urgency for this mechanism has only increased. We call for finalizing the organization and governance of the executive committee, the necessary arrangements including the financial mechanism, and the approval of a two-year work plan that responds to the expectations of particularly vulnerable developing countries.

Mr. Chairman,

7. G-77 and China welcome the progress made under item 5 on the work programme to further understanding of the diversity of NAMAs. The Group noticed the mandate from decision 1/CP.18 requesting the SBI to report to the COP-21 on the outcome of the programme, and the SBI-40 agreed to prepare conclusions at SBI-41, including activities conducted, information on issues addressed and experiences shared during the work programme. However, the Group expresses its concern on the lack of progress on financial, technology, and capacity-building support available and provided from developed country parties, and the extent of the matching mitigation actions with supports under the registry, and would like to address this issue during this session. The Group assures you to work actively on the unfinished work under this mandate.
8. The Group would like to highlight the Warsaw Framework for REDD+, as the methodological guidance for the activities referred to in decision 1/CP.16, paragraph 70 seeking to obtain and receive results-based payments for results-based actions, expressed in tons of carbon dioxide equivalent per year (9/CP.19).
9. The Group would also like to recognize that alternative policy approaches, such as joint mitigation and adaptation approaches, need differentiated methodological guidance, in accordance to national circumstances and national policies, in the context of sustainable development supported by financial, technical, capacity-building within the context of the Convention.
10. On Response Measures, the G-77 and China reaffirms the importance to give full consideration on what actions are necessary to meet the specific needs and concerns of developing country parties arising from the impact of the implementation of response measures, in accordance with the principles and provisions of the Convention. In this regard, we welcome the process agreed in the fortieth session of the Subsidiary Bodies for submissions and the preparation of the technical paper and synthesis report by the Secretariat, with the aim for the Abs to providing recommendations to COP-20.

11. In this regard, we reaffirm the contents of the recent G-77 and China submissions for the continuation of the forum and the establishment of a mechanism to avoid and minimize the negative economic and social consequences of response measures taken by developed country parties on developing country parties, and in particular to address policy issues of concern, such as unilateral measures. We believe our proposal has key substantive elements towards the achievement of progress in these sessions and we trust parties will continue to engage constructively towards the adoption of a decision on the issue in Lima
12. On Development and Transfer of Technologies, the Group of 77 and China believes that in order to fully implement the technology mechanism to enhance the action of technology development and transfer, it is crucial to ensure coordination between the two bodies of technology mechanism, the Technology Executive Committee and the CTCN. We look forward to the tangible development and transfer of technologies to developing countries for climate change. The Group emphasizes the necessity for the TEC to structure its work plan for the short and medium term, including the organisation of a thematic dialogue on enabling environments for technology development and transfer, including the mechanisms needed to address all barriers.

Mr. Chairman,

13. Setting the date for completion of the expert review process in time for an informed process in Paris will entail understanding the historical difficulties in completing the review process, as well as understanding the importance to the G-77 and China of knowing the compliance status of the KP parties in the first Commitment Period.

Mr. Chairman,

14. Regarding the second review of the Adaptation Fund, the Group welcomes the pledges by Annex II countries amounting to around US$100 million. However, the group believes that the main concerns regarding the sustainability, predictability and adequacy of resources to the Adaptation Fund are still not dealt with. The Group believes that the second review should provide recommendations to ensure that adequate and sustainable resources be available for the Adaptation Fund, which is until now the only fund dedicated to adaptation in developing countries.
15. Capacity-building is of utmost importance to the Group of 77 and China. We acknowledge the successful outcome of the Durban Forum for in-depth discussion on capacity-building. However, current exchange of experiences taking place through the Durban forum requires further

strengthening. Capacity-building activities crossing in different issues need an effective institutional arrangement for coordination. Therefore, we are urging our negotiating partners to accept our proposal for the establishment of Capacity-Building Committee under the Convention, to enhance capacity of developing countries to implement mitigation and adaptation actions under the Convention, including education, human skills training for planning, implementation, and domestic institution-building, and technology innovation and development of endogenous technology. We are confident it will resolve many of the problems relating to capacity-building in developing countries in a manner that will be beneficial to all.

16. The Group of 77 and China looks forward to continuing to engage constructively at this session in the discussions related to the framework for various approaches, new-market mechanism and non-market-based approaches in a balanced manner thereafter, noting the importance of this discussion for the 2015 Agreement. Also, the Group recognizes that non-market-based approaches are important to ensure the implementation of the objective of the Convention, according to its principles and provisions.

Mr. Chairman,

17. The G-77 and China consider the Multilateral Assessment under the IAR process as one of the most crucial activities of the SBI41. The group welcomes the efforts made by the SBI chair support by the Secretariat to organise the working group session and we look forward to meaningful outcomes from the MA working group sessions in Lima, which we believe is crucial to ensure the fully implementing the Bali Action Plan outcomes and also build confidence to reach a successful 2015 agreements in Paris.
18. In conclusion, Mr. Chairman, the Group of 77 and China reserves its position on the remaining agenda items not articulated in this statement and wishes to reiterate our commitment for a fruitful session.

Statement on behalf of the G-77 and China by Ambassador Nozipho Mxakato-Diseko, Deputy Director-General, Multilateral Branch, Department of International Relations and Cooperation of the Republic of South Africa, at the Opening Plenary of the 42nd Session of the Subsidiary Body for Implementation (SBI 42) (Bonn, Germany, 1 June 2015)

Excellencies,
Distinguished representatives,
Ladies and gentlemen,
Mr. Chair,

1. I have the honour to deliver this statement on behalf of the Group of 77 and China and to assure you that the Group is willing and ready to engage constructively. We also stand ready to support and be of assistance to you Mr. Chair.
2. The Group of 77 and China believes that it is critical that the work under the subsidiary bodies continue to be accelerated in the period before the new agreement comes into force in 2020 and beyond. The work of the subsidiary bodies, in particular the SBI, assist all parties to enhance the implementation of their commitments under both the Convention and the Kyoto Protocol and of great importance to the Group.

Mr. Chair,

3. Adaptation is an important and urgent priority for the Group of 77 and China. We therefore call for the urgent and immediate implementation the NAPs process, but are particularly concerned about the lack of adequate funding for this process. For accessing funding from the GCF for the process to formulate and implement the NAPs, including simplifying the procedures for accessing finance and technical support, it is important that the work of the Adaptation Committee and the LEG, in collaboration with GCF, address how best to support developing country parties.
4. We would like to underline the essential need to consider strengthened activities under LDC Work Programme including the continuity of the LDC Expert Group with an expanded mandate, and the urgent replenishment of LDC Fund to implement the long pending projects identified in NAPAs.
5. The Group hopes that nominations for the Warsaw International Mechanism's Executive Committee are finalised before the end of this session so implementation of its two-year work plan can begin as soon as possible.
6. The Group of 77 and China believes that the SBI should be more engaged on the issue of technology transfer so that the technology mechanism could enhance action on technology development and transfer. It is extremely important for the Technology Executive Committee as well as the Climate Technology Centre and Network to work under the guidance of the Conference of the Parties through the subsidiary bodies, including the implementation of Poznan strategic programme. We look forward to the tangible transfer of technologies to developing countries to address climate change.
7. As developing countries, capacity-building is of utmost importance to us as a key component of the means of implementation and is a necessity for the implementation of the Convention. The current capacity-building work involved in all fields should be coordinated within an international

institutional arrangement which can bring equity and transparency to this process. We reiterate our call for the establishment of an effective international mechanism on capacity-building. Such a mechanism is essential for developing country parties to participate fully in addressing the challenges of climate change, and to effectively implement their commitments under the Convention. It is for this reason that we are committed to working with our partners to ensure that the Third Comprehensive Review on the implementation of the Capacity-Building Framework is initiated with the urgency it deserves.

8. One often overlooked but all-important item is article 6 of the Convention on education, training, and public awareness. Concrete actions can only be undertaken if the people on the ground are fully involved in the development of policies and their implementation. Ensuring the full participation of the people and the civil society in climate change policymaking and implementation is part of the obligations of parties in this Convention. Climate change impacts are borne by all, and only the full awareness and participation by all would allow us to face this increasing challenge.
9. Regarding the Multilateral Assessment Working Group Session, the G-77 and China calls for interactive discussions among parties during this session. It is our firm belief that these discussions are crucial for building trust and to move the process forward. We look forward to the completion of the Working Group Session in a timely manner so that the SBI can consider its conclusions.
10. On National Communications from Annex I parties, it is the view of the Group that it is imperative that Annex I parties submit their inventories using the revised reporting guidelines. The compilation and synthesis of the Sixth National Communications and First Biennial Reports from Annex I parties to the Convention is critical to ensure that Annex I parties meet their reporting obligations under the Convention.
11. The G-77 and China is concerned that the Revision of the Guidelines for the preparation of National Communications by Annex I was not concluded in Lima, thereby delaying the reporting by Annex I parties. It is thus our view that the conclusion of this item here in Bonn is of critical so as to ensure that Annex I parties meet their reporting obligations under the Convention.

Mr. Chair,

12. Since COP-18, the SBSTA and SBI supported by the Structured Expert Dialogue (SED) considered under the 2013–2015 review the adequacy of the long-term global goal and the overall progress toward achieving it. The Group

appreciates the work of the SED and welcomes its final report. The Group expects that a thorough consideration will be made of the report in order for COP-21 to take forward the work of the SED, as well as on linkages with work under the ADP.

13. On Response Measures, the G-77 and China reaffirms the importance of giving full consideration to what actions are necessary to meet the specific needs and concerns of developing country parties arising from the impact of the implementation of response measures, in accordance with the principles and provisions of the Convention. In this regard, we look forward to engage constructively on the text of the draft decision forwarded from Lima in order to adopt a decision at COP-21 for the establishment of a mechanism on enhanced action on the impact of the implementation of response measures. The G-77 and China position remains firm that the negative economic and social consequences of response measures taken by developed country parties on developing country parties must be avoided and minimised. Policy issues, such as unilateral measures, must be addressed.

Mr. Chair,

14. The UNFCCC is the primary international, intergovernmental forum for addressing the global response to climate change, and as such we are particularly interested in seeing to it that, the UNFCCC as administered by the Secretariat, serves the interests of all parties in a balanced manner. In line with this we will actively participate on the agenda items related to governance including in the discussions on the arrangements on intergovernmental meetings and on administrative, financial and institutional matters, as we look to the next biennium budget for 2016–2017. It is important that the functions and operations of the Secretariat are supported in an adequate, balanced manner in order for it to play its role in support of the parties, equally in the areas of adaptation and mitigation.
15. Furthermore, the Group looks forward to participating at the gender-responsive climate policy in session workshop. Considering that the impacts of climate affect men and women differently and their roles in addressing climate change vary based on their cultural values and responsibilities, the findings of workshop should guide us on how we address gender and climate change related issues.
16. In conclusion, the group wants to assure you that it will participate effectively in all the mandated events at this session.

Statement by Ambassador Nozipho Mxakato-Diseko from South Africa on behalf of the Group of 77 and China, at the Opening Plenary of 43rd Session of the Subsidiary Body for Implementation (SBI 43) (Paris, France, 1 December 2015)

Mr. Chair,
Excellencies,
Distinguished representatives,
Ladies and gentlemen,

1. I have the honour to deliver this statement on behalf of the Group of 77 and China. The Group wishes to express its full support towards a successful outcome to these negotiations.
2. The Group of 77 and China believes that it is critical that the work under the subsidiary bodies continue to be accelerated in the period before the new agreement comes into force in 2020 and beyond. The work of the subsidiary bodies, in particular the SBI, assists all parties to enhance the implementation of their commitments under both the Convention and the Kyoto Protocol and of great importance to the Group.
3. The G-77 welcomes the report of the Executive Committee of the Warsaw International Mechanism for Loss and Damage associated with Climate Change Impacts. The work of the WIM on loss and damage under this Convention is of critical important to the Group, and we take note of the adjustments relating to the terms of office of the members and Co-Chairs of the Executive Committee. In line with urgency of this matter, the G-77 also notes the need for resources for the successful and timely implementation of the initial two-year work plan of the Executive Committee and we urge developed country parties to make available resources in view of the ambitious nature of the work plan.

Mr. Chair,

4. Adaptation is an important and urgent priority for the Group of 77 and China. We therefore call for the urgent and immediate implementation of the NAPs process, but are particularly concerned about the lack of adequate funding for this process. In order to facilitate access to funding from the GCF for the process to formulate and implement the NAPs, including simplifying the procedures for accessing finance and technical support, it is important that the work of the Adaptation Committee and the LEG, in collaboration with GCF, address how best to support developing country parties. In this regard, we look forward to engage constructively on this item and to recommend a draft decision for adoption by the COP.
5. The G-77 welcomes the Report of the Adaptation Committee and the effort to make balanced progress in all its work areas. We take note of the future

work plan of the Adaptation Committee, and look forward to discussing it in the Contact Group. The Group also welcomes the work completed related to means of implementation for adaptation and hopes that its outcome translates into something that can expedite support for developing countries. We are prepared to engage with partners in reviewing the recommendations to the COP contained in the report.

6. We would like to underline the essential need to consider strengthened activities under LDC Work Programme including the continuity of the LDC Expert Group with an expanded mandate, and the urgent replenishment of LDC Fund to implement the long-pending projects identified in NAPAs.
7. The Group of 77 and China believes that the SBI should be more engaged on the issue of technology transfer so that the technology mechanism could enhance action on technology development and transfer. It is extremely important for the Technology Executive Committee as well as the Climate Technology Centre and Network to work under the guidance of the COP through the subsidiary bodies, including the implementation of Poznań strategic programme. We look forward to the tangible transfer of technologies to developing countries to address climate change.
8. As developing countries, capacity-building is of great importance to us as a key component of the means of implementation and is a necessity for the implementation of the Convention. In our view, the current capacity-building work undertaken in all fields should be coordinated within an international institutional arrangement which can bring equity and transparency to this process. We reiterate our call for the establishment of an effective international mechanism on capacity-building. Such a mechanism is essential for developing country parties to participate fully in addressing the challenges of climate change, and to effectively implement their commitments under the Convention. It is for this reason that we are committed to working with our partners to ensure that the Third Comprehensive Review of the implementation of the Capacity-Building Framework is initiated with the urgency it deserves.
9. Regarding the Multilateral Assessment Working Group Session, the G-77 and China calls for interactive discussions among parties during this session. It is our firm belief that these discussions are crucial for building trust and to move the process forward. We look forward to the completion of the Working Group Session in a timely manner so that the SBI can consider its conclusions.
10. On National Communications from Annex I parties, it is the view of the Group that it is imperative that Annex I parties submit their inventories using the revised reporting guidelines. The compilation and synthesis of the Sixth National Communications and First Biennial Reports from Annex I parties to the Convention is critical to ensure that Annex I parties meet their reporting obligations under the Convention.

11. The G-77 and China is concerned that the Revision of the Guidelines for the preparation of National Communications by Annex I was not concluded in Lima, thereby delaying the reporting by Annex I parties. It is thus our view that the conclusion of this item here in Paris is of critical so as to ensure that Annex I parties meet their reporting obligations under the Convention.
12. The Group appreciates the work of the Structured Expert Dialogue (SED) that is considered under the 2013–2015 review of the adequacy of the long-term global goal. The Group expects hat a thorough consideration will be made of the report in order for COP-21 to take forward the work of the SED, as well as on linkages with work under the ADP. This work is important as it relates to ambition as well as requisite support, particularly to developing countries towards the realisation of the ultimate objective of the Convention.
13. On Response Measures, the G-77 and China reaffirms the importance of giving full consideration to what actions are necessary to meet the specific needs and concerns of developing country parties arising from the impact of the implementation of response measures, in accordance with the principles and provisions of the Convention. In this regard, we look forward to engaging constructively on the text of the draft decision forwarded from the forty-second session of the SBs in order to adopt a decision at COP-21. The G-77 and China position remains firm that the negative economic and social consequences of response measures taken by developed country parties on developing country parties must be avoided and minimised. Policy issues, such as unilateral measures, must also be addressed.

Mr. Chair,

14. The UNFCCC is the primary international, intergovernmental forum for addressing the global response to climate change, and as such we are particularly interested in seeing to it that the UNFCCC, as administered by the Secretariat, serves the interests of all parties in a balanced manner. In line with this we will actively participate on the agenda items related to governance including in the discussions on the arrangements on intergovernmental meetings and on administrative, financial and institutional matters, as we look to the next biennium budget for 2016–2017. It is important that the functions and operations of the Secretariat are supported in an adequate and balanced manner in order for it to play its role in support of the parties, equally in the areas of adaptation and mitigation.
15. In conclusion, the Group wants to assure you that it will participate constructively and efficiently in all the mandated events at this session.

Statement on behalf of the Group of 77 and China by Ms. Carola Iñiguez, Under-Secretary for Multilateral Affairs of Ecuador, at the Opening Plenary of the 46th Session of the Subsidiary Body for Implementation (SBI 46) (Bonn, Germany, 8 May 2017)

Mr. Chairman,

Ecuador has the honor to deliver this statement on behalf of the Group of 77 and China.

The Group would like to express its willingness to work constructively throughout this session, to remain fully involved with the process while it stresses the need to continue to move forward with the implementation of the Convention and its Kyoto Protocol and Paris Agreement, by increasing ambition of actions and support and strengthening the global response to the threat of climate change in accordance with the principles of equity, common but differentiated responsibilities and respective capabilities and in the context of sustainable development and efforts to eradicate poverty.

Mr. Chairman,

The Group is of the view that the SBI must work in an open, transparent, balanced, party-driven, and inclusive manner and for that objective, the Group would like to express its view on the following items of the agenda, having in mind that by defining clearly our objectives for each agenda item, we will make progress, including, for fulfilling our mandate for 2018.

1. Regarding the international consultation and analysis (ICA) process (item 2), the Group reiterates the facilitative nature and the importance of this process to lead to the identification of capacity-building needs of developing countries, in order to enhance capacities for the reporting of information in subsequent biennial update reports BURs.
2. On the operation and use of a public registry for NDCs and Adaptation Communications, the Group stresses the need for these discussions to be coordinated and maintain coherence with those that deal with similar issues under other bodies and between themselves.
3. Regarding the modalities and procedures for the Clean Development Mechanism (CDM) (item 7), the Group believes that we should avoid duplication and overlapping of discussions by focusing on the essentials taking into account SBSTA work under agenda item 10.
4. With regards to National Adaptation Plans NAPs, the group expects to further explore the interlinkages between NAPs (item 9) and Means of Implementation (MOIs); particularly with regards to financial resources for planning and implementing adaptation actions as well as for evaluating

and determining priorities and needs of developing countries. Furthermore, we urge developed country parties to provide adequate support to developing country parties in meeting the cost of their adaptation actions.

5. Regarding the development and transfer of technologies (item 10), the Group would like to emphasize the importance of the financial support by developed countries in line with their obligations under the Convention and the Paris Agreement so as to enable technology transfer. The work of the SBI should focus on technology development and transfer, as well as transparency so that the technology mechanism could enhance actions on technology development and support the implementation of the Convention and its Paris Agreement. The Group would further like to have deliberate enhanced support for the implementation of the outcome of the Technology Needs Assessment and facilitated access to technologies.
6. The Group believes that the review of the role and the functions of the Standing Committee on Finance (SCF) (item 11) should be aimed at allowing the SCF to fully achieve its mandate of assisting the COP with respect to the Financial Mechanism of the Convention, including on the measurement, reporting and verification of financial support and mobilization of financial resources and to oversee all financial flows that are provided and mobilized for the implementation of obligations under the Convention and the Paris Agreement. On the Adaptation Fund, we note that the only concern raised in the first two reviews of the Fund has been on the issue of sustainability and predictability of Funds and note that the outcome of this Third Review is crucial for the decision pending on the Fund definitely serving the Agreement as of 2018.

   These financial matters need to be advanced, notwithstanding the current uncertainty regarding the scale, flow, and novelty and additionality of climate finance from developed countries to developing countries, which has a direct impact on the ability of developing countries to fully implement their commitments under the Convention and the Paris Agreement.
7. On response measures, the Group reaffirms the importance of giving full consideration to identify necessary actions to meet the specific needs and concerns of developing country parties arising from the impact of the implementation of response measures and to avoid the negative economic and social consequences of response measures on developing countries. The Group welcomes the first technical expert group meeting on the impact of implementation of response measures and looks forward to the inputs and recommendations from the experts to support the work of the improved forum. We should provide sufficient space and time for TEG members to make their contributions, which will allow the improved forum to achieve concrete outcomes as envisaged by parties. The group also emphasizes the importance of working on the modalities, functions, and work programmes for the forum under the Paris Agreement.

8. Regarding the Arrangements for Intergovernmental Meetings (AIM) (item 15), the Group would like to emphasize the urgent need to define the role of non-state actors within the process of UNFCCC ensuring the full consistency with its country-driven nature, including the need to have a clear, legal, policy framework to protect the objective, purpose, and principles of the Convention and the Paris Agreement from conflicts of interest.
9. Direct access of all developing country parties of the Convention and Paris Agreement to means of implementation including finance, technology transfer, and capacity-building provided by multilateral supporting mechanism should be simplified and granted to ensure proper implementation of climate action plans and the achievement of the objectives of the Convention.
10. Regarding the financial matters on agenda item 16, the Group stresses its concern on the actual budget allocation and the capacity of the Secretariat to fulfil with its mandates and work programmes so as to pursue the objectives of the Convention. We stress our concern regarding the current state of the budget and the need to think strategically on the way forward so that this process continues to be based on science. The Group insists on the key role of the IPCC, and it troubles us that a wrong message could be sent from this process if the institution that generates the science we claim to base our work on is thwarted in its capacity to work effectively at this time of geopolitical uncertainty.
11. G-77 and China welcomes the Marrakech decision to further the Lima work programme on gender and climate change. We view gender as a cross-cutting issue that affects the response to climate change and sustainable development. Gender responsiveness is very critical with regards to the global quest for sustainable and inclusive development in the context of climate change. Hence, the call to develop a gender action plan to support the implementation of gender related decisions and mandates under the UNFCCC process is timeous.
12. The important work carried out by the SBI has always played a fundamental role in strengthening the implementation of the Convention. As we are now preparing the groundwork for the Paris Agreement, that applies only to the parties that have ratified it, the tasks mandated to this Subsidiary Body will therefore contribute tremendously to enhancing the implementation of the Convention.
13. On accounting of financial resources, the Group reaffirms that the modalities for accounting of financial resources by developed country parties to developing country parties, mobilized through public interventions, in accordance with article 9, paragraph 7, of the Paris Agreement, must aim to provide transparency and consistency. The reported information must also be comparable and verifiable. No developing countries are to be excluded from receiving financial support for their enhanced climate change actions whether they have or have not ratified the Paris Agreement.

14. We would also like to begin exploring the possibility of considering loss and damage at these inter-sessional meetings, not just once a year at COP meetings, as is the current procedure. We hope to be able to discuss this with the current and incoming presidencies at this session for decision at COP-23.
15. Mr. Chairman, the Group would like to express the urgent need to accelerate the implementation of pre-2020 commitments and actions for a solid foundation for the post-2020 implementation, including the ratification of the Doha amendment. We request all developed country parties to increase the ambition of their pre-2020 mitigation efforts and to enhance the provision of finance, technology development and transfer, and capacity-building.
16. Finally, we reiterate the importance of the synergy in all the bodies of the UNFCCC and the need to respect different national capacities and circumstances. We are committed to achieve the long-term global goal including on mitigation, adaptation, finance, technology transfer, and capacity-building and we assure you, Mr. Chair, of our trust in your leadership and our willingness to have fruitful discussions during this session.

Statement of the Group of 77 and China, delivered by Ambassador Wael Aboulmagd, Chair of the G-77 and China for the Climate Change Process, at the Opening Plenary of the Subsidiary Body for Implementation, Bonn, 30 April 2018

Distinguished Chair,

It is my honor to deliver this statement on behalf of the Group of 77 and China.

Allow me at the outset, Chair, to assure you of the full commitment of the Group to achieving progress and reaching satisfactory outcomes on the various agenda items, and we welcome the commitment of the Chair to comprehensively cover all aspects of implementation under the Convention, its Kyoto Protocol, and its Paris Agreement. The Group highlights the importance of the mandated events under the SBI as part of the efforts to fully operationalize our decisions.

The Group would like to share its views on some of the agenda items as follows:

On agenda item 2c, we congratulate Chile, Namibia, Singapore, and Tunisia for undergoing the Facilitative Sharing of Views. We encourage all parties to follow the session and seize the opportunity to exchange experiences on the elaboration of BURs and learn best practices on communication and transparency.

On agenda item 3a, regarding "Status of submission and review of seventh National Communications and third biennial reports from Annex I Parties," we note with concern that in the Third Biennial Report, several developed country parties have not fully complied with reporting guidelines for finance provided, particularly in terms of clarifying definitions and methodologies. Some developed country parties have not even submitted their BR3, due to be submitted on 1 January 2018. Without clarity and transparency, no comparability can be made and the report will be of limited use. We urge developed country parties to fully observe current reporting guidelines and work together to reach common understandings of basic parameters of the CTF tables, particularly concerning climate-specific finance and new and additional financial resources.

On agenda item 3b, the Group expects conclusions in relation to the consideration of the Secretariat Synthesis Report on the information provided by Annex I parties of the Convention in their second biennial reports. The Group would like to draw special attention to the issue of biennial reports and biennial submissions on strategies and approaches to mobilize climate finance. It is vital to raise ambition on common modalities that provide clarity, transparency, comparability, and aggregable information, including information on quantitative and qualitative elements of a pathway, to ensure a clear global picture of climate finance is provided while ensuring the balance between adaptation and mitigation, thereby allowing developing countries to confidently plan for their implementation of the Paris Agreement and their NDCs.

On agenda item 4, it is crucial to identify and cater to the capacity-building needs of developing countries in order to facilitate reporting of information in the context of the Convention in general and specifically in preparing future BURs.

On agenda item 4b, the Group will be looking forward to extending the work of the Consultative Group of Experts as it has been instrumental in building capacities in developing country parties on transparency through workshops and training material. We must ensure that they continue to provide this technical assistance and be strengthened in coming years as the implementation of the enhanced transparency framework for action and support unfolds.

On agenda item 4c, the Group regrets having to once again express its concern regarding the fact that some developing countries are still unable to access the financial and technical support supposedly available for the preparation of NCs and BURs.

On agenda item 5 on common time frames, the Group welcomes the relative progress made by the SBI at the previous session and supports the intention to continue the discussion of common time frames at this forty-eighth session with a view to reporting back to the CMA.

On agenda item 6, on the development of modalities and procedures for the operation and use of a public registry referred to in article 4.12 of the Paris Agreement (NDC), the Group recalls that Nationally Determined Contributions communicated by parties shall be recorded in a public registry maintained by the Secretariat and that article 7.12 establishes the same provision for the adaptation communications. We also believe that the registration needs to be made by the focal point, and that the registry must be clear and transparent, ensure security, and avoid any possible manipulation.

On agenda item 8, the Group hopes that progress can be made on reviewing the modalities and procedures of the CDM this session.

On agenda item 9, the Group stresses the importance of assuring that new and additional, scaled-up, and predictable financial incentives are made available to developing country parties to support the implementation of forest mitigation and adaptation activities. Our Group thinks that the mandate of SBI allows to continue with the voluntary meetings on coordination of support facilitated by the Secretariat and will like to have more clarity on this. Decision 10/CP.19, does not set a deadline for this meeting and on previous sessions parties have not come to any agreement on this matter.

On agenda item 10, the Group welcomes the breakthrough achieved with regard to the Koronivia work programme on agriculture, and in the context of sustainable development and poverty eradication (most notably as it relates to food security), the Group believes that adaptation in agriculture, including its associated health and socioeconomic co-benefits, and the development of climate resilient agriculture are key priorities for developing country parties who continue to contend with increased vulnerabilities and challenges in their efforts to end hunger.

On agenda item 11, the Group takes note of the report of the Adaptation Committee and welcomes further work on the implementation of the flexible work plan of the Committee for the years 2016–2018. The Group is working on specific suggestions to address the gaps in the recommendations made by AC, LEG with the collaboration of SCF since we recognize the Paris Mandates to the bodies are an important part in the implementation of the adaptation provisions of the Paris Agreement.

On agenda item 13, the Group recognizes the key role of adaptation planning, specifically through the development of National Adaptation Plans (NAPs), in building climate resilience for local communities and reducing vulnerabilities. We call for greater transparency and availability of finance, technological support, and capacity-building to enhance efforts tying national adaptation plans to their means of implementation in the context of NAPs.

On agenda item 14, the Group takes note of the UNEP response to the independent review of the Climate Technology Center and Network and will be working towards an outcome that will ensure the enhancement of the role of the CTCN, allowing for facilitating the technology transfer and dissemination on preferential and concessional terms to developing countries.

On agenda item 15, progress in the area of climate finance, in particular as it relates to defining, increasing certainty, predictability, and sustainability remains seriously lacking. On the implementation of article 9.5 of the PA, the Group highlights the importance of fully operationalizing this article as an enabler to increase predictability and effectiveness of climate finance in responding to the needs and priorities of developing countries as reflected *inter alia* in our nationally determined contributions and national adaptation plans, as well as support needs to avert, minimize, and address loss and damage. The Group calls for greater ambition in this regard, in line with the requirements of the Convention and its Paris Agreement. Moreover, the Group calls for greater efforts when it comes to building on and enhancing the existing communication by developed countries on strategies and approaches for scaling up climate finance.

On agenda item 16, the Group reaffirms the importance of capacity-building as an inextricable component of the Convention, its Kyoto Protocol, and its Paris Agreement and a vital element of the overall package that must take form in the operationalization of the Paris Agreement. In this regard, the Group emphasizes the relevance of the work of the Paris Committee on Capacity-Building to take on board previous work on this area and to move forward in the development of capacities for developing countries whilst taking into account their particular contexts in terms of resource needs, planning, and monitoring requirements.

We welcome the second meeting of the PCCB that will continue with the 2017 focus area of capacity-building activities for the implementation of nationally determined contributions in the context of the Paris Agreement, as well as the seventh meeting of the Durban Forum. We recognize that the Durban Forum is a means of effective and continuous sharing of information, good practices and lessons learned among a wide spectrum of stakeholders operating within and outside the Convention, and its meetings contribute to the monitoring and review of the effectiveness of capacity-building in the Developing Countries. In this regard, we look forward to discuss the annual monitoring and evaluation of progress in the implementation of the framework for capacity-building in developing countries established under decision 2/CP.7.

On agenda item 17 concerning response measures, the Group reaffirms the importance of giving full consideration to identify necessary actions to meet the specific needs and concerns of developing country parties arising from the impact of the implementation of response measures and to avoid the negative economic and social consequences of response measures on developing countries. The Group welcomes the in-forum training workshop on the use of economic modeling tools related to economic diversification and just transition of workforce. The Group also emphasizes the importance of fulfilling the mandate of decision 11/CP21 and advancing the work on the pre-2020 and post-2020 on the modalities, functions, and work programs for the permanent forum under the Paris Agreement.

On agenda item 18, the Group would like to draw attention to the importance of working on ways of enhancing the implementation of Action on Climate Empowerment (ACE) activities so as to enhance actions under the Paris Agreement. ACE should be taken into consideration with other work streams under the APA and SBSTA to secure its integrity under the PA. In this sense the Group welcomes the organization of the in-session workshop to discuss these matters and the sixth dialogue on ACE.

On agenda item 19, the Group fully recognizes the importance of protecting groups in vulnerable situations from the adverse impacts of climate change. The Group also notes the differentiated impacts of climate change on women and men, girls and boys, and consequently views the integration of gender considerations into climate adaptation, mitigation, capacity-building, technology and finance policies, plans and actions as fundamental in addressing climate change related gender inequalities and achieving sustainable development.

On agenda item 20, the Group wishes to express its serious concern regarding the availability of accommodation and other logistical matters relating to the participation of representatives of developing countries in COP-24. The Group requests the host country together with the current presidency to update parties on measures envisioned to ensure the participation of developing country representatives in the meetings, taking into account the specific constraints and challenges those participants face.

On non-party stakeholders, the Group welcomes active engagement of non-party stakeholders in the process in a manner that ensures the transparency of such engagement and the integrity of the negotiation process, and highlights the importance of ensuring equitable participation of stakeholders from developed and developing parties, while maintaining that this is a party-driven process with states having the legal responsibilities and obligations in relation to the implementation of the relevant decisions.

On agenda item 21, the G-77 and China acknowledges the challenge facing the Secretariat in securing resources for the implementation of the mandates given by parties, and in this regard highlights that any action taken by the Secretariat to enhance its capacities should ensure the neutrality of the Secretariat and allow for balanced representation from developing and developed countries within it.

(b) Draft Resolutions, Decisions, and Proposals Submitted by the Group of 77 to the Subsidiary Body for Implementation (SBI)

Position Paper of Group of 77 and China*

Recommendations on Guidelines and Format for Preparation of Initial Communications from non–Annex I Parties

Basis for Commitment

1. Article 12.1, 12.5, and 12.7, read with relevant portions of article 4.1, of the FCCC are the basis of the commitment for submission of initial communications by all parties to the Convention. These articles should guide the non–Annex I parties for recommendations regarding guidelines and for developing a format for initial communications.
2. Article 4.1 clearly provides that commitments under that article would be undertaken "taking into account their common but differentiated responsibilities and their specific national and regional development priorities, objectives and circumstances."

* Contained in document FCCC/SB/1996/MISC.1/Add.1 of 1March 1996.

General obligations

Keeping article 4.3 in mind, it is important that the in-depth reviews of the communications of the Annex I parties clearly reflect the fulfilment of the commitments of the developed country parties especially towards developing countries.

Considerations for non–Annex I Parties

(a) Other obligations of developed country parties Articles 4.7, 4.4, and 4.5 are relevant in this connection.

(b) Specific national circumstances Articles 4.8 and 4.9 are relevant.

(c) Vulnerability Articles 4.10 and 4.4 are relevant. Keeping in view the various provisions in the Convention for developing country parties and the clear recognition of the common but differentiated responsibilities and priorities, objectives and circumstance of each party, there is a need to take into full consideration the circumstances and vulnerabilities of developing country parties. Further, the Convention makes the implementation of the Convention by Annex I parties a pre-condition for the fulfilment of the obligations of developing country parties/non–Annex I parties.

(d) Timing of submission of initial communication

I. The timing for submission of initial communication for non–Annex I parties is, in accordance with article 12.5, to be submitted within three years of entry into force for that party or/of the availability of financial resources in accordance with article 4.3. The timing of submission of initial communications should not, therefore, be fixed arbitrarily but follow the above provisions of the Convention.

Scope

(a) Inventory

1. Article 12.1 (a) provides that the initial communication could include information relating to a national inventory of anthropogenic emissions by sources and removals by sinks of all greenhouse gases not controlled by the Montreal Protocol, to the extent it capacities permit.
2. We should recognize that in order to prepare information relating to a national inventory, the capacity of developing countries vary widely in relation to their technical, financial as well as institutional capacities. In this connection, there is a clear need for adequate and additional financial resources, technical support and technology transfer to supplement the effort towards capacity-building and preparation of a national inventory.

3. In view of above, the nature of methodology used should be flexible.
4. The base for inventories should be the year 1994. However, countries which have prepared the inventory for the year 1990 may present the data in their initial communication.

(d) General description of steps The general description of steps set out within the context of sustainable development efforts of non-Annex I parties may include one or more of the following:

- Measures relating to adaption
- Information on emissions by sources and removal by sinks
- Financial resources and technical support given and required
- Capacity-building and training needs
- Requirements for technology transfer

(c) Any other information The non–Annex I parties may include any other relevant information including projects for financing, material relevant for calculation of global emission trends, constraints and obstacles etc.

Format for initial communications from non–Annex I parties
A format for initial communications from non–Annex I parties has been developed by the experts of non–Annex I parties and is given in the annexure to this document. This would be the basis for further work on initial communications from non–Annex I parties.

Observations and policy guidance
While finalising the recommendation for guidelines and format for initial communications as well as the process for further consideration, the COP must take fully into account the views expressed in this position paper. Towards this end, it is a matter of disappointment that the Annex I parties and other developed country parties have not been able to fulfil their commitments regarding provision of financial resources and transfer of technology as stipulated under the Convention. This position paper should serve as policy guidance to the interim operating entity of the financial mechanism in meeting the agreed full costs incurred by the developing country parties.

Future consideration

1. It is clearly recognised that the process of consideration of the information communicated by the non–Annex I parties under article 10 (2) (a) is different from the process envisaged for Annex I parties under article 10 (2) (b). There should not be any individual country reviews for non–Annex I parties but only the overall aggregate effect should be assessed for all parties to the Convention.

2. In accordance with article 12.7 and article 8.2(c), the Group of 77 and China shall request the necessary assistance be provided to developing country parties in the compilation and communication of information of non–Annex I parties, including for the holding of any future workshops that may be found necessary. In this connection, the Group of 77 and China express their intention to hold a workshop as a follow up to the present one in conjunction with the next meetings of SBSTA and SBI.

Format for initial national communications from non–Annex-I parties

1. This format is intended to provide a common set of guidelines for the presentation of the initial national communications by non–Annex I parties to the UNFCCC, under its article 12.1.
2. The Guidelines for the National Greenhouse Gas Inventories and Technical Guidelines for Assessing Climate Change Impacts and Adaptations or the simplified default methodologies adopted by the Intergovernmental Panel on Climate Change may be used by non–Annex I parties, as appropriate and to the extent possible, in the fulfilment of their commitments under the Convention.
3. The year 1994 should be the base year for inventories. However, countries which have prepared their inventory for the year 1990 may present this data in their initial communication, with a view to including the best available data.
4. It was recognized that the preparation of the initial communication will depend on the provision of financial resources and transfer of technology in accordance with article 4.7.
5. National Circumstances

5(a). General Circumstances

Criteria	1994
Population	
Relevant areas (square kilometres)	
GDP (1994 US$)	
GDP per capita (1994 US$)	
Estimated share of the informal sector in the economy in GDP (percentage)	
Share of industry in GDP (percentage)	
Share of services in GDP (percentage)	
Share of agriculture in GDP (percentage)	
Land area used for agricultural purposes (square kilometres)	
Urban population as per cent of total population	

Criteria	1994
Livestock population (disaggregate as appropriate)	
Forest area (square kilometres, define as appropriate)	
Population in absolute poverty	
Life expectancy at birth (years)	
Literacy rate	

Notes:

(1) In addition to the above information which can be conveniently presented in a table, non–Annex I parties may present basic geographical and climatic information, as well as other factors relevant to climate change of any nature such as, for example, peculiarities of its economy which may affect its ability to deal with climate change.
(2) Non–Annex I parties may provide a brief description of existing institutional arrangements which are relevant to the preparation of the inventory on a continuing basis, or a list of perceived deficiencies in this area.

5(b). Special Circumstances Specific needs and concerns arising from the adverse effects of climate change and/or the impact of the implementation of response measures, specially on

- Small Island Countries;
- Countries with low-lying coastal area;
- Countries with and semi-arid areas, forested areas, and areas liable to forest decay;
- Countries with areas prone to natural disasters;
- Countries with areas liable to drought and desertification;
- Countries with areas of high urban atmospheric pollution;
- Countries with fragile ecosystems, including mountainous ecosystems;
- Countries with economies highly dependent on income generated from the production, processing, and export, and/or on consumption of fossil fuels and associated energy-intensive products;
- Land-locked and transit countries; and
- Other special considerations foreseen in paragraphs 4.9 (least developed countries) and 4.10 (fossil-fuel dependency), as appropriate.

Note: Wherever applicable non–Annex I parties should present numerical indicators. For example, they might use a classification in terms of percentage of the land area, percentage of the population affected, and/or percentage of GDP, etc.

6. Inventory

6.1 Non–Annex I parties should strive to present the best available data, to the extent their capacity permits, and try to identify the areas where the data may be further improved in the future communications by national capacity-building.

6.2 The methodology for the national inventories of emissions by sources and removals by sinks of greenhouse gases to be used is that developed by the IPCC. Special note is taken of the fact that such methodology will be reviewed during 1996, with three workshops scheduled in the March–April time frame, on land-use changes, rice methane and energy and industry with completion scheduled for September.

6(a). Inventory of CO_2 emissions by sources and removals by sinks in 1994 (gigagrams/year)

Energy Fuel Combustion Activities	Energy and Transformation	
	Industry	
	Transport	
	Commercial and institutional	
	Residential	
	Other	
Land-Use Change and Forestry	Changes in Forest and other woody Biomas stock	
	Forest and grassland Conversion	
	Abandonment of Managed Lands	
Others		
Total		

Note: For conversion factors for apparent consumption and the carbon emission actors state whether the default values of the IPCC have been used or locally available values were used.

6(b). Inventory of CH, emissions by sources in 1994 (gigagrams/year)

Energy	Biomass burned for energy	
	Other	
Fugitive Fuel Emissions	Oil and natural gas systems	
	Coalmining	
Agriculture	Rice Cultivation[5]	
	Enteric Fermentation	
	Additional Burning of Savannas	
	Others	
Others		
Total		

Notes:

(1) Three-year average figures be given.
(2) For conversion factors for apparent consumption and the carbon emission factors state whether the default values of the IPCC have been used or locally available values were used.

6(c). Inventory of NO emissions by sources in 1994 (gigagrams/year)

Energy	
Industrial Processes	
Agriculture	
Total	

Notes:

(1) Non-Annex I parties which have difficulties in providing the above data may provide aggregate data.
(2) For conversion factors for apparent consumption and the carbon emission factors state whether the default values of the IPCC have been used or locally available values were used.

6(d). Other greenhouse gases Non-Annex I parties are encouraged to include in their national inventories the fully fluorinated compounds, as appropriate. Other greenhouse gases included in the IPCC methodology may be included at the discretion of the parties.

[5] Including all emissions and removals, taking account of the underlying complex chemical processes

6(e). Summary

Summary of emissions by sources and removals by sinks for all gases may be provided, including additional information such as, for example, expression of the results in terms of socio-economic-geographical indicators deemed relevant by each country.

According to the IPCC methodology, emissions from bunker fuels (aviation and Marine) should be reported in addition to national emissions.

7. General Description of Steps

A general description of steps taken or envisaged to implement the Convention. This may include:

(a) Programs related to sustainable development, research and systematic observation, education and public awareness, training, etc.;
(b) Policy options for adequate monitoring systems and response strategies for climate change impacts on terrestrial and marine ecosystems;
(c) Policy frameworks for implementing adaptation measures and response strategies in the context of coastal zone management, disaster preparedness, agriculture, fisheries, and forestry, with a view to integrating climate change impact information, as appropriate, into national strategic planning processes;
(d) In the context of undertaking national communications, building of national, regional, and/or subregional capacity, as appropriate, to integrate climate change concerns in medium- and long-term planning.

8. Financial and Technological Needs and Constraints

8.1 Non–Annex I parties may describe the financial and technological needs and constraints associated with the communication of information. In particular and following the evolving recommendations of the Conference of the Parties through its Subsidiary Bodies, the description may cover the needs and constraints associated with the further improvement of national communications, including the reduction of the margin of uncertainty in emission and removal variables through appropriate institutional and capacity-building.

8.2 According to national priorities, a description may include financial and technological needs associated with activities and measures envisaged under the Convention.

8.3 Information on measures to facilitate adequate adaptation to climate change may be added, indicating national technological needs.

8.4 Assessment of national, regional, and/or subregional vulnerability to climate change; may be added, including, where appropriate, reliance on related data-gathering systems to measure climate change effects in particularly vulnerable countries or regions and strengthening of such systems as necessary; and identification of a near-term research and development agenda to understand sensitivity to climate change, indicating relevant financial and technological needs.

9. Other Information

9.1 Any other information which non–Annex I parties may wish to provide including projects for financing, material relevant for calculation of global emission trends, constraints and obstacles etc.

Guidelines for Preparation of Initial Communications from non–Annex I Parties

Draft Decision Submitted by the Group of 77 and China*

The Subsidiary Body for Scientific and Technological Advice,
The Subsidiary Body for Implementation,

Recalling articles 4.1(a), 12.1, 12.5, and 12.7 of the United Nations Framework Convention on Climate Change, and decision 8/CP.1 on first communications from parties not included in Annex I to the Convention,

Recalling also decision 4/CP.1 on Methodological issues,

Noting that in accordance with article 12.5, each party not included in Annex I shall make its initial communication within three years of the entry into force of the Convention for that party, or of the availability of financial resources in accordance with article 4, paragraph 3, and that, parties that are least developed may make their initial communication at their discretion,

Recognizing that, in accordance with article 4.7, the extent to which developing country parties will effectively implement their commitments under the Convention will depend on the effective implementation by developed country parties of their commitments under the Convention related to financial resources and transfer of technology and will take fully into account that economic and social development and poverty eradication are the first and overriding priorities of the developing country parties,

Considering that from its first session, in accordance with article 12.7, the Conference of the parties shall arrange for the provision to developing country parties of

* Contained in document FCCC/SB/1996/L.2 of 11 July 1996.

technical and financial support, on request, in compiling and communicating information under this article, as well as in identifying the technical and financial needs associated with proposed projects and response measures under article 4. Such support may be provided by other parties, by competent international organisations and by the Secretariat, as appropriate,

1. *Request*

(a) The Secretariat, in accordance with article 8.2(c), to facilitate assistance to the parties, particularly developing country parties, in the preparation of their initial communications, through the organisation of workshops at the regional level, to provide a forum for the exchange of experiences in the development of emission factors and activity data for the estimation of the inventory, as well as, on request, for other elements of information in the initial communication, and provide a report to the Subsidiary Body for Scientific and Technological Advice at each of its sessions; and

(b) The Secretariat to make available to the Subsidiary Body for Implementation at each of its sessions, details of the financial support made available to parties not included in Annex I from the interim operating entity of the financial mechanism for the preparation of their initial communication, including projects proposed by each party, the funding decision and the date and amount of funds made available to the party.

2. *Recommend*

(a) That the second session of the Conference of the Parties adopt the guidelines for the preparation of initial communication from parties not included in Annex I;

(b) That the parties not included in Annex I to the Convention should use the guidelines contained in the annex to the present decision when preparing their initial communications under the Convention;

(c) That the national and regional development priorities, objectives, and circumstances of the parties not included in Annex I should, in accordance with article 4.1, and the provisions of article 3 and articles 4.3, 4.5, 4.7, 4.8, 4.9, and 4.10, be taken into account by the Conference of the Parties (COP); and

(d) That the parties not included in Annex I and who wish to submit voluntarily additional information may use elements from the guidelines approved for parties included in Annex I when preparing their initial communications;

Annex I to decision . . .

Guidelines for the Preparation of Initial Communications from Parties Not Included in Annex I

1. The guidelines for the preparation of initial communications by parties not included in Annex I have five principal objectives, taking into account article 4.7:
   (a) To assist parties not included in Annex I in meeting their commitments under article 12.1;
   (b) To encourage the presentation of information in ways that are, to the extent possible, consistent, transparent, and comparable as well as flexible, to take into account specific national situations and requirements for support to improve the completeness and reliability of activity data, emission factors, and estimations;
   (c) To serve as policy guidance to the interim operating entity of the financial mechanism for the timely provision of financial support, including for the transfer of technology, needed by the developing country parties to meet the agreed full costs in complying with their obligations under article 12.1;
   (d) To facilitate the process of preparation, compilation and consideration of the communications, including the preparation of compilation and synthesis documentation; and
   (e) To ensure that the COP has sufficient information to carry out its responsibilities to assess the overall aggregated effects of the steps taken by the parties in the light of the latest scientific assessments concerning climate change, and of the implementation of the Convention.

Scope

2. In accordance with article 12.1, the communication should include:
   (a) A national inventory of anthropogenic emissions by sources and removals by sinks of all greenhouse gases not controlled by the Montreal Protocol, to the extent its capacities permit, using comparable methodologies to be promoted and agreed upon by the Conference of the Parties;
   (b) A general description of steps taken or envisaged by the party to implement the Convention; and
   (c) Any other information that the party considers relevant to the achievement of the objective of the Convention and suitable for inclusion in its communication, including, if feasible, material relevant for calculations of global emission trends.

National circumstances

3. In presenting the information, parties not included in Annex I should specify their national and regional development priorities, objectives, and

circumstances on the basis of which they will address the adverse impacts of climate change. The description of these circumstances can cover a wide range of information. In addition to information which can be conveniently presented in a table (Table I), parties may present basic geographical and climatic information, as well as other factors relevant to climate change of any nature such as, for example, features of their economy which may affect their ability to deal with climate change.

4. Parties not included in Annex I may provide a brief description of existing institutional arrangements which are relevant to the preparation of the inventory on a continuing basis, or a list of perceived deficiencies in this area.
5. Parties not included in Annex I may also present information on their specific needs and concerns arising from the adverse effects of climate change and/or the impact of the implementation of response measures, specially on:
   (a) Small Island Countries;
   (b) Countries with low-lying coastal area;
   (c) Countries with arid and semi-arid areas, forested areas and areas liable to forest decay;
   (d) Countries with areas prone to natural disasters;
   (e) Countries with areas liable to drought and desertification;
   (f) Countries with areas of high urban atmospheric pollution;
   (g) Countries with areas with fragile ecosystems, including mountainous ecosystems;
   (h) Countries whose economies are highly dependent on income generated from the production, processing and export, and/or on consumption of fossil fuels and associated energy-intensive products;
   (i) Landlocked and transit countries; and
   (j) Other special considerations foreseen in paragraphs 4.9 (least developed countries) and 4.10 (fossil-fuel dependency), as appropriate.
6. In presenting the information, wherever applicable, parties not included in Annex I should present numerical indicators. For example, they might use a classification in terms of percentage of the land area, percentage of the population affected, and/or percentage of gross domestic product (GDP), etc.

Inventory

7. The Guidelines for the National Greenhouse Gas Inventories and Technical Guidelines for Assessing Climate Change Impacts and Adaptations or the simplified default methodologies adopted by the Intergovernmental Panel on Climate Change (IPCC) should be used by non–Annex I parties, as appropriate and to the extent possible, in the fulfilment of their commitments under the Convention.
8. We should recognize that in order to prepare information relating to a national inventory, the capacity of developing countries vary widely in relation

to their technical, financial as well as institutional capacities. In this connection, there is a clear need for adequate and additional financing resources, technical support and technology transfer to supplement the efforts towards capacity-building and preparation of a national inventory.

9. Parties not included in Annex I should strive to present the best available, to the extent their capacity permits, and try to identify the areas where the data may be further improved in the future communications by national capacity-building.
10. The methodology for the national inventories of emissions by sources and removals by sinks of greenhouse gases to be used is that developed by the IPCC. Special note is taken of the fact that such methodology will be reviewed during 1996. Additional information such as, for example, expression of the results in terms of socio-economic, geographical indicators deemed relevant by each country may also be provided.
11. As recognized by the IPCC in its Second Assessment Report, anthropogenic emissions from non-fossil origins are still the object of greater uncertainty than those of fossil origin, and also because such non-fossil emissions tend to play a relatively greater role in national emissions of parties not included in Annex I, such parties should make efforts to obtain field observational data to decrease the uncertainties associated with the inventory of emissions of N_2O in all relevant sectors; CH_4 from fugitive emissions from fuel, industrial processes, agriculture, land-use change and forestry, and waste sectors; and CO_2 emissions from industrial processes, land-use change and forestry, and waste sectors.
12. It is further recognized that such improvement of the quality of emission data, in addition to improving the transparency and comparability of national emission inventories, also brings about a global benefit by improving knowledge of the relationship between global emissions and resulting atmospheric concentration of greenhouse gases, and therefore aids significantly the task of estimating the emission limitations or reductions required to achieve a given concentration level the same greenhouse gases, the ultimate objective of the Convention.
13. Non–Annex I parties are thus encouraged to formulate national, and where appropriate, regional programs aiming at the improvement of the quality of local emission factors and extensive data-gathering, and to submit requests for financial and technical assistance to the financial mechanism of the Convention in association with their request for support for the preparation of the national communications.
14. Parties not included in Annex I are encouraged to include in their national inventories the fully-fluorinated compounds, as appropriate. Other greenhouse gases included in the IPCC methodology may be included at the discretion of the parties.

15. According to the IPCC methodology, emissions from bunker fuels (aviation and marine) should be reported in addition to national emissions.
16. The year 1994 should be the base year for inventories. However, parties not included in Annex I who have prepared their inventory for the year 1990 may present this data in their initial communication, with a view to including the best available data.

General description of steps

17. The initial communication should contain a general description of steps taken or envisaged to implement the Convention. This may include:
    (a) Programmes related to sustainable development, research and systematic observation, education and public awareness, training, etc.
    (b) Policy options for adequate monitoring systems and response strategies for climate change impacts on terrestrial and marine ecosystems;
    (c) Policy frameworks for implementing adaptation measures and response strategies in the context of coastal zone management, disaster preparedness, agriculture, fisheries, and forestry, with a view to integrating climate change impact information, as appropriate, into national planning processes;
    (d) In the context of undertaking national communications, building of national, regional, and/or sub-regional capacity, as appropriate, to integrate climate change concerns in medium and long-term planning.

Financial and technological needs and constraints

18. Non–Annex I parties may describe the financial and technological needs and constraints associated with the communication of information. In particular, and following the evolving recommendations of the COP through its subsidiary bodies, the description may cover the needs and constraints associated with the further improvement of national communications, including the reduction of the margin of uncertainty in emission and removal variables through appropriate institutional and capacity-building.
19. According to national priorities, parties not included in Annex I may include a description of financial and technological needs associated with activities and measures envisaged under the Convention.
20. Information on measures to facilitate adequate adaptation to climate change may be added, indicating national technological needs.
21. Assessment of national, regional, and/or sub-regional vulnerability to climate change may be added, including, where appropriate, reliance on related data-gathering systems to measure climate change effects in particularly vulnerable countries or regions and strengthening of such systems as necessary; and identification of a near-term research and development agenda

to understand sensitivity to climate change, indicating relevant financial and technological needs.

Other information

22. The initial communication may identify programmes containing measures the party believes contribute to addressing the adverse impacts of climate change, including abatement of increase in greenhouse gas emissions and enhancement of removals by sinks, so that the COP, in accordance with article 12.7, can arrange for the provision of financial and technical needs associated with proposed projects and response measures under article 4. These actions need not have as a primary objective the limitation of greenhouse gas emissions.
23. Developing country parties may, in accordance with article 12.4, on a voluntary basis, propose projects for financing, including specific technologies, materials, equipment, techniques, or practices that would be needed to implement such projects, along with, if possible, an estimate of all incremental costs, of the reductions of emissions and increments of removals of greenhouse gases, as well as an estimate of the consequent benefits.
24. Parties not included in Annex I may provide any other information relevant to the achievement of the objective of the Convention, including, if feasible, material relevant for calculation of global emission trends, constraints and obstacles, etc.

Vulnerability

25. There is a need to take into full consideration the circumstances and vulnerabilities of developing countries parties, keeping in mind that the Convention stipulates that the implementation of the commitments by Annex I parties is a pre-condition for the fulfilment of the obligations of developing country parties.

Timing of submission of initial communication

26. In accordance with article 12.5, the timing for submission of initial communications is within three years of entry into force for that party or of the availability of financial resources in accordance with article 4.3.

Structure and executive summary

27. The information provided in accordance with these guidelines should be communicated by a party to the COP in a single document. Any additional or supporting information may be supplied through other documents such as a technical annex.

28. The initial communication should include an executive summary that would present the key information and data from the full document. The executive summary will be translated and distributed widely. It would be useful to envisage an executive summary of no more than ten pages.

Language

29. The communications may be submitted in one of the official languages of the United Nations. Parties not included in Annex I are also encouraged to submit, to the extent possible and where relevant, a translation of their communication into English.

Table I National Circumstances

Criteria	**1994**
Population	
Relevant areas (square kilometres)	
GDP (1994 US$)	
GDP per capita (1994 US$)	
Estimated share of the informal sector in the economy in GDP (percentage)	
Share of industry in GDP (percentage)	
Share of services in GDP (percentage)	
Share of agriculture in GDP (percentage)	
Land area used for agricultural purposes (square kilometres)	
Urban population as per cent of total population	
Livestock population (disaggregate as appropriate)	
Forest area (square kilometres, define as appropriate)	
Population in absolute poverty	
Life expectancy at birth (years)	
Literacy rate	

Table II Initial National Greenhouse Gas Inventories

Initial National Greenhouse Gas Inventories (Gigagram per year)			
Greenhouse Gas Source and Sink Categories	CO_2	CH_4	N_2O
Total (Net) National Emission	X	X	X
1. All Energy	X	X	X
Fuel Combustion			
Energy and Transformation Industries	X		X
Industry	X		
Transport	X		
Commercial-Institutional	X		
Residential	X		
Other	X	X	
Biomass Burned for Energy		X	
Fugitive Fuel Emission			
Oil and Natural Gas Systems		X	
Coal Mining		X	
2. Industrial Processes	X		X
3. Agriculture		X	X
Enteric Fermentation		X	
Rice Cultivation		X	
Savannah Burning		X	
Others		X	X
4. Land-Use Change and Forestry	X		
Changes in Forest and other woody biomass stock	X		
Forest and Grassland Conversion	X		
Abandonment of Managed Lands	X		
5. Other Sources as appropriate and to the extent possible	X	X	

Note 1: X – Data to be presented to the extent the party's capacities permit (article 12.1(a)).

Note 2: Non–Annex I national communications will include the information in this table, and a description of assumptions and methods used, and the values of emission coefficients, where these differ from IPCC assumptions, methods and values.

Financial and Technical Cooperation

Financial Mechanism: Guidance to the Global Environment Facility

Arrangements between the Conference of the Parties and the Operating Entity or Entities of the Financial Mechanism

Draft Decision Submitted by the Group of 77 and China*

The Conference of the Parties,

Recalling article 11.3 of the United Nations Framework Convention on Climate Change,

Recalling also articles 12.5, 4.3, and 4.7 of the Convention,

Bearing in mind decision 10/CP.1 of the first session of the Conference of the Parties and its conclusions reached at its second session,

Noting the Report of the Global Environment Facility to the second session of the Conference of the Parties (FCCC/CP/1996/8),

Expressing deep concern over the difficulties encountered by developing country parties in receiving the necessary financial assistance from the Global Environment Facility due to, *inter alia*, the GEF operational policies on eligibility criteria, disbursement, project cycle, and approval, the application of its concept of incremental costs, and guidelines which impose considerable administrative and financial costs on developing country parties,

Expressing also serious concern over the difficulties encountered by parties not included in Annex I of the Convention in seeking funds from the GEF, as the interim operating entity of the financial mechanism of the Convention, for the preparations of their initial national communications,

Decides that the Global Environment Facility, as the interim operating entity of the financial mechanism of the Convention,

1. In the initial period, should finance its strategies on enabling activities which facilitate endogenous capacity-building, and data collection and archiving, consistent with the policy guidance, programme priorities and eligibility

* Contained in document FCCC/SBI/1996/L.2 of 12 July 1996.

criteria provided to it by the Conference of the Parties as contained in decision 11/CP.1 of the first session of the Conference of the Parties,

2. In providing the financial resources needed by developing country parties to meet the agreed full incremental costs in implementing measures covered by article 4.1 of the Convention, should take steps to facilitate this provision of financial resources, including through the enhancement of the transparency and the simplification of the application of its concept of incremental costs,
3. Should, together with its implementing agencies, expedite the approval and the disbursement of financial resources to meet the agreed full costs incurred by developing country parties in complying with their obligations under article 12.1 of the Convention, in accordance with article 4.3, in particular the initial and subsequent preparations of national communications of non–Annex I parties. In this regard, the guidelines and format adopted by the Conference of the Parties at its second session on the preparation of initial national communications by non–Annex I parties, contained in decision ___/CP.2, shall form the only basis for funding of communications from non–Annex I parties under article 12.1;
4. Should consider country-specific needs, but could also consider approaches which may be used for several countries with similar needs, upon request, and taking into account that the preparation of national communications is a continuing process,
5. Decides that the GEF, in funding the preparation of national communications, should refrain from imposing upon recipient countries the financing of other obligations contained in the Convention,
6. Decides also that the GEF should only finance the implementation of commitments on non–Annex I countries in an integrated manner upon request by recipient countries; and
7. Requests GEF as the interim operating entity of the financial mechanism, to report to the Conference of the Parties at its third session.

Financial Mechanism

Memorandum of Understanding between the Conference of the Parties and the Global Environment Facility

Annex to the Memorandum of Understanding: Determination of Funding Necessary and Available for the Implementation of the Convention

Draft Proposal Submitted by the Group of 77 and China*

Recalling article 11.1 of the Convention which, in the relevant part, states that the financial mechanism of the Convention shall function under the guidance of and

* Contained in document FCCC/SBI/1996/L.4/Rev.1 of 11 December 1996.

be accountable to the Conference of the Parties, as well as articles 4.7 and 4.8 of the Convention;

Mindful that, in accordance with article 11.3(d) of the Convention, the amount of funding necessary and available for the implementation of the Convention and the conditions under which that amount is to be reviewed, shall be determined in a predictable and identifiable manner;

The aggregate GEF funding requirements for the purpose of the Convention shall be determined in accordance with the following procedures.

Determination of funds necessary

1. In anticipation of a replenishment of the GEF, the COP will make an assessment of the amount of funds that are necessary to assist developing countries, in accordance with the guidance provided by the COP, in fulfilling their commitments under the Convention over the next GEF replenishment cycle, taking into account:
   (a) The amount of funds necessary to meet the agreed full costs to be incurred by developing country parties in order to prepare their national communications under article 12.1 of the Convention on the basis of the guidelines for national communications of non–Annex I parties adopted by the Conference of the Parties at its second session;
   (b) Financial resources requested by developing country parties to meet the agreed full incremental costs of measures covered by article 4.1 of the Convention;
   (c) Financial resources requested by developing country parties to meet the costs of adaptation to the adverse effects of climate change;
   (d) Information communicated to the COP from the GEF on the number of eligible programmes and projects that were submitted to the GEF, the number that were approved for funding, and the number that were turned down owing to lack of resources.

Availability of funding

2. The GEF will intimate to the COP the funds that are likely to be available over the next replenishment period.
3. The GEF replenishment will be based on the COP's assessment.
4. On the occasion of each replenishment, the GEF will, in its regular report to the COP as provided for in paragraphs 6 and 7 of this Memorandum of Understanding, indicate how it has responded during the replenishment cycle to the COP's previous assessment prepared in accordance with paragraph 1 of this annex, inform the COP of the conclusion of replenishment negotiations

and indicate the amount of new and additional funding to be contributed to the GEF trust fund in the next replenishment cycle for the purposes of the GEF, including the implementation of the Convention. The GEF shall clearly indicate the rationale by which the amount described as "new and additional" is regarded as such, vis-à-vis other sources of Official Development Assistance.

Review by the Conference of the Parties

5. The COP shall review the amount of funding necessary and available for the implementation of the Convention on the occasion of each replenishment of the financial mechanism.

Annex

Draft Proposal by the Group of 77 and China*

Consideration of Initial Communications from Parties Not Included in Annex I to the Convention

The Conference of the Parties,

Recalling articles 12.1, 12.5, and 12.7 of the United Nations Framework Convention on Climate Change,

Recalling also its decisions 8/CP.1 and 10/CP.2 on first communications from parties not included in Annex I to the Convention,

Noting that each developing country party shall make its initial communication within three years of the entry into force of the Convention for that party, or of the availability of financial resources in accordance with article 4.3 and that parties that are least developed may make their submission at their discretion,

Recognizing that the initial communications from parties not included in Annex I of the Convention shall be submitted in a staggered manner because of the different timing of the provision of funding from the interim financial mechanism,

Recognizing further that the initial communications from parties not included in the Annex I of the Convention shall be considered on overall and aggregate basis in accordance with article 10.2 (a).

* Contained in document FCCC/SBI/1997/CRP.4 of 4 August 1997.

1. *Decides* that the Conference of the Parties,
   (a) Shall consider the overall aggregate effects of measures taken pursuant to the Convention, in accordance with article 10.2 (a), taking into account article 4.7 and information communicated under article 12.3;
   (b) Shall compile a list of projects for financing submitted by parties not included in the Annex I of the Convention in accordance with article 12.4;
   (c) Shall seek funding from the financial mechanism in accordance with policy guidance, programme priorities and eligibility criteria provided under decision 11/CP.1 and the guidance provided in decision 11/CP.2, based on the list of projects submitted;
   (d) Shall consider the communications from parties not included in Annex I in a facilitative, non-confrontational, open, and transparent manner.
2. *Decides also* that the Subsidiary Body for Implementation,
   (a) Shall conduct consideration of initial communications from non–Annex I parties, on an annual or biennial basis, depending on the submission received in any particular year,
   (b) Shall submit a synthesis report to the Conference of the Parties updating the overall aggregate effects of measures taken pursuant to the Convention, in accordance with article 10.2 (a).
3. *Decides further* that the Subsidiary Body for Scientific and Technological Advice conduct scientific assessments of the overall aggregate effects of measures taken in accordance with article 9.2 (b).
4. *Requests* the Secretariat,
   (a) Drawing on the experience on the overall aggregate compilation of initial communications of parties not included in Annex I, to prepare a report on the guidelines for the preparation of initial communications with a view, among other things, to further enhancing the comparability and focus of the communications;
   (b) To provide any other assistance that may be required by non–Annex I parties for the periodic preparation of national communications, in accordance with article 8.2 (c).

Appendix I

Draft Proposal by the Group of 77 and China: Consideration of Initial Communications from Parties Not Included in Annex I to the Convention*

The Conference of the Parties,

Recalling articles 12.1, 12.5, and 12.7 of the United Nations Framework Convention on Climate Change,

* Contained in document FCCC/SBI/1997/16 of 29 August 1997.

Recalling also its decisions 8/CP.1 and 10/CP.2 on first communications from parties not included in Annex I to the Convention,

Noting that each developing country party shall make its initial communication within three years of the entry into force of the Convention for that party, or of the availability of financial resources in accordance with article 4.3, and that parties that are least developed may make their submission at their discretion,

Recognizing that the initial communications from parties not included in Annex I to the Convention shall be submitted in a staggered manner because of the different timing of the provision of funding from the interim financial mechanism,

Recognizing further that the initial communications from parties not included in Annex I of the Convention shall be considered on overall and aggregate basis in accordance with article 10.2(a),

1. *Decides that the Conference of the Parties,*
   (a) Shall consider the overall aggregate effects of measures taken pursuant to the Convention, in accordance with article 10.2(a), taking into account article 4.7 and information communicated under article 12.3;
   (b) Shall compile a list of projects for financing submitted by parties not included in Annex I to the Convention in accordance with article 12.4;
   (c) Shall seek funding from the financial mechanism in accordance with policy guidance, programme priorities and eligibility criteria provided under decision 11/CP.1 and the guidance provided in decision 11/CP.2, based on the list of projects submitted; and
   (d) Shall consider the communications from parties not included in Annex I in a facilitative, non-confrontational, open, and transparent manner.
2. *Decides also* that the Subsidiary Body for Implementation,
   (a) Shall conduct consideration of initial communications from non–Annex I parties, on an annual or biennial basis, depending on the submission received in any particular year; and
   (b) Shall submit a synthesis report to the Conference of the Parties updating the overall aggregate effects of measures taken pursuant to the Convention, in accordance with article 10.2(a).
3. *Decides further* that the Subsidiary Body for Scientific and Technological Advice conduct scientific assessments of the overall aggregate effects of measures taken in accordance with article 9.2(b).
4. *Requests* the Secretariat,
   (a) Drawing on the experience on the overall aggregate compilation of initial communications from parties not included in Annex I, to prepare a report on the guidelines for the preparation of initial communications with

a view, among other things, to further enhancing the comparability and focus of the communications; and

(b) To provide any other assistance that may be required by non–Annex I parties for the periodic preparation of national communications, in accordance with article 8.2(c).

Paper No. 1: Indonesia

(On behalf of the Group of 77 and China)

Position Paper of the Group of 77 and China on the Mechanism of the Kyoto Protocol for the Second Meeting of the Contact Group on Mechanism*

The Group of 77 and China recalls the principles of the United Nations Framework Convention on Climate Change, and affirms that any international mechanism being introduced through the Convention or the Kyoto Protocol to the Convention should be in conformity with the principles of the Convention. The rules governing the mechanisms, namely, activities implemented jointly, joint implementation, clean development mechanism, and emission trading should be determined on the basis of equity, sustainable development, and the other principles of the Convention. The mechanisms are off-shore measures. It has to be ensured that their design does not in any way compromise the modification of longer-term trends in anthropogenic emissions, consistent with the objective of the Convention. The mechanisms should be supplemental to domestic action. The greenhouse gas reductions achieved should be real and verifiable.

2. The new mechanisms indicated in the Kyoto Protocol are yet to be defined in terms of principles and modalities, rules, and guidelines. Presently, these mechanisms are immersed in uncertainty. An important reason why this is so is because preparatory work was lacking on these mechanisms during the negotiations related to the Kyoto Protocol. With respect to the clean development mechanism and emission trading, there was no preparatory work. In any case, there are very complex and intricate methodological, technical, legal, and institutional questions requiring addressal.
3. It was in this background that the Group of 77 and China had taken the position during the Kyoto negotiations that until these questions were resolved, joint implementation, and emission trading should not be introduced. In respect of emission trading, the Group of 77 and China had stated that until the question of emission rights and entitlements is addressed equitably, it would not be possible to have emission trading. The question of the legal and

* Contained in document FCCC/SB/1998/MISC.1/Add.3 of 5 June 1998.

equitable basis of entitlements continues to occupy a central position. In view of the highly complicated nature of the issues confronting the parties, the course of action should be to make due endeavour to identify the questions for the purpose of discussion and resolution. For this, preparatory work is needed.

4. The Convention Secretariat can contribute to this preparatory work. It was in this light that the Chairmen of the Subsidiary Bodies were requested (decision 1/CP.3) to give guidance to the Secretariat on the preparatory work needed for consideration by the Conference of the Parties. Due thought and effort is needed to identify the issues. This cannot and should not be rushed. A significant disadvantage confronting developing countries is that they lack know-how. Discussion and debate cannot proceed if the parties lack the requisite understanding of the issues being negotiated. It is imperative that the Group of 77 and China have an understanding of the issues because the Group, which combines the insights and perceptions of a very large body of developing economies, is, as always, keen to contribute to discussions on climate change. More preparatory work will help in this regard.
5. The preparatory work should be conducted so that the methodological questions are addressed first. The prevailing uncertainties must be removed. Without proper addressal of the methodological questions, it will not be possible to have discussions on substantive issues. The time for discussions on substantive issues will come later. The methodological questions should be addressed and responded to by the Subsidiary Body for Scientific and Technological Advice.
6. There should be no prioritisation or hierarchy assigned to the mechanisms. All the mechanisms have to be examined on the basis of the principles of equity, sustainable development, the other principles of the Convention, and in the light of the objectives of the Convention.
7. AIJ is in the pilot phase, a comprehensive review of which should take place in accordance with COP decisions, with further course of action to be decided subsequent to review by the COP.
8. The conception and design of the mechanisms should rest with the Conference of the Parties to the Convention, assisted by the SBSTA and the SBI in accordance with their division of labour in the Convention. The COP is the highest decision-making body of the Convention. The COP also has valuable experience in respect of the implementation of the Convention and its requirements. Very importantly, the COP has the fuller-term insights of the parties to the Convention. The merging trend, wherein other international multilateral agencies are also getting involved in the conduct of workshops, etc. on the mechanisms is viewed with concern by the Group of 77 and China. This trend is pre-judging the outcome of the Convention process.

Position Papers on Matters before the Eighth Sessions of the Subsidiary Bodies Submitted by the Group of 77 and China*

Position Paper No. 1

Position Paper of the G-77 and China on Issues before the 8th Session of the Subsidiary Body on Implementation, 2–12 June 1998, Bonn

General strategic approach: The Convention contains the basic principles which guide our deliberations, and our work as the supreme body of the Convention, the Conference of the Parties, in particular the principle of common but differentiated responsibilities. On this is based the delicate balance of commitments in the Convention, and any other related instruments.

The ultimate objective of this Convention and any other related instruments, which is the stabilization of greenhouse gas concentrations in the atmosphere, at such a level that would:

- Prevent dangerous anthropogenic interference with the climate system;
- Allow ecosystems to adapt naturally to climate change;
- Ensure that food production is not threatened; and
- Enable economic development to proceed in a sustainable manner.

The Group of 77 and China will remain consistent with these principles and work towards the ultimate objective as set out in the Convention, in implementing the Convention.

These sessions of the Subsidiary Bodies of the FCCC are held to prepare for the Fourth Meeting of the Conference of the Parties –

1. The COP, in accordance with article 7.2, as the supreme body of the Convention, shall keep under regular review of the implementation of the Convention and any other related legal instruments, and to make the decisions necessary to promote the effective implementation of the Convention.
2. In Kyoto, we adopted 18 decisions, two of which are related to the Kyoto Protocol, and the rest related to the implementation of the Convention. G-77 and China will ensure that COP-4 will take decisions to implement the Convention and will be submitting draft decisions for the issues under consideration.
3. COP-4 is taking place before the end of 1998 because the Convention, in its article 4.2(d), stipulates that a "second review of 4.2(a) and 4.2(b) shall take place not later than December 1998, and thereafter at regular intervals to be

* Contained in document FCCC/SB/1998/MISC.4 of 5 June 1998.

determined by the COP until the objective of the Convention is met." The issue of the second review is now in the agenda of COP-4. G-77 and China will submit a decision for the COP on this subject.

4. This is line with our general strategy to ensure that COP reviews the implementation of the Convention as its principal task.
5. In line with this general approach, and in SBI, the Group of 77 and China will pursue decisions on the provision of new and additional financial resources to be identified by the operating entity of the financial mechanism, now that the annex to the Memorandum of Understanding has been approved, in accordance with article 11.3(d) and article 4.3 of the Convention.
6. We will also pursue the issue of transfer of technology, article 4.5 of the Convention, and decisions 13/CP.1; 7/CP.2; and 9/CP.3 of the three previous COPs, which have been very inadequately implemented so far we will ensure that the necessary guidance is given to the operating entity of the financial, mechanism, so that, at last, the provision contained in article 11, paragraph 1 can be operationalised.
7. These decisions state that at COP-3, and at each session of the COP thereafter, the implementation article 4.5 and 4.1(c) of he Convention will be reviewed as separate agenda item under "matters relating to commitments." We will focus our decisions on strengthening endogenous capabilities and institutional capacities. We, therefore, request that this be put on the agenda of COP-4 as "matters relating to commitments."

The extreme relevance and importance for the G-77 and China of article 4.7 of the Convention, which states that the extent to which developing countries will implement their commitments depend on the extent to which developed countries will implement 4.3 and 4.5.

The main task remains for COP to implement all existing commitments; to implement all the decisions that we have taken so far. We will not be distracted from this important task by undefined new commitments, which almost derailed the negotiations in Kyoto. We shall instead examine how the close interrelationships of existing commitments under the Convention will indeed help COP to move forward in the achievement of our objectives.

Position Paper No. 2

Position Paper of the Group of 77 and China at the Subsidiary Body for Scientific and Technological Advice, 2 June 1998, Bonn

General strategic approach: The Group of 77 and China reaffirms that, in these discussions, the Group will continue to be guided by the basic principles of this Convention, in particular the principle of common but differentiated responsibilities. The Group will likewise continue to uphold the balance in the commitments in this Convention and in any related instrument, as it has always done.

The COP is faced with attempts to upset and deform this delicate balance, based on scientific findings, on environmental considerations, and on equity. A Protocol was adopted in Kyoto, a Protocol which is focused on the strengthening of commitments of Annex I countries, found to be inadequate in Berlin in 1995. This is in line with the principles and objective of the Convention.

1. It is necessary that COP ensures that the Kyoto Protocol enters into force as early as possible, and for there to be a clear proof that it is implemented, prior to any other moves to distract the COP from this essential task of the implementation of the Convention. Many members of G-77 and China have signed the Protocol. In this SBSTA, the Group of 77 and China will follow closely the decisions taken in Kyoto, decisions 1 and 2/CP3 on what to take up insofar as this Protocol is concerned.
2. Developing countries have commitments under this Convention. National communications are the first of these commitments, and we have moved to implement this commitment.
3. We continue to advance in the implementation of these commitments under the Kyoto Protocol, as the contribution of developing countries to the achievement of the ultimate objective of the Convention. These contributions of the G-77 and China are contained in articles 10, 11, and 12 of the Protocol.
4. In Kyoto, and in the negotiations leading to Kyoto, the Group of 77 and China have shown how much developing countries are doing to address climate change and to meet the adverse effects of climate change.
   We were, however, extremely disappointed with the very low targets agreed upon in Kyoto. We, therefore, feel that the time has come for us to face squarely, and as a leading priority, the need to address adaptation and to study the impacts of response measures agreed upon in the Kyoto. These items are in the agenda before us in these sessions. These are moves toward an effective implementation of the Convention.
5. We will pursue the issue of transfer of technology in this Subsidiary Body, and the decisions taken by the COP which have been very inadequately implemented so far. This includes the establishment of the intergovernmental technical advisory panels, essential for the effective functioning of this Subsidiary Body, and to look into adaptation measures together with the Intergovernmental Panel on Climate Change.
6. The first two of the 18 decisions taken in Kyoto refer to the Kyoto Protocol. The G-77 and China will, in its usual manner, participate constructively and in good faith in the discussions of these two decisions. The Group strongly

feels that in order for us to move forward effectively, the methodological issues have to be addressed as a first priority. It is clear that the decisions have been made by the COP to deal with methodological issues before anything else. This stands to reason, because form follows substance, and all the other decisions would have to be taken by the COP/MOP, which will only meet when the Kyoto Protocol enters into force.

7. Methodological issues of other items in the agenda for these sessions would also have to be discussed, including for such issues as the implementation of article 6 of the Convention on education, training and public awareness; as well as the consideration of articles 4.8 and 4.9 impacts of response measures and minimizing adverse effects. We request the inclusion of an item in SBSTA's agenda on methodological (under other matters) of articles 4.8 and 4.9 of the Convention.
8. The Group would like to recapitulate the importance of article 4.7 of the Convention to developing countries. article 4.7 states that the extent to which developing countries will implement their commitments depend on the extent to which developed countries will implement their own commitments related to provision of financial resources and transfer of technology, taking into account that the first and overriding priorities for developing countries are economic and social development and poverty eradication.
9. It should also be made clear that the Group is not in favour of any entity outside the Convention process to deal with in any manner with this mechanism by establishing any new bodies. Only the COP is mandated to do this.
10. The Group is of the view that the CDM, as proposed by the G-77 and agreed by consensus, is first and foremost a mechanism to promote sustainable development, rather than merely a market-based mechanism. A balance must be achieved between the objective set out for Annex I countries, that of obtaining certified emission reduction units, and the objective of non-Annex I countries is to achieve sustainable development, as set out in article 12.2 of the Protocol. This article is very clear, and no confusion is possible.
11. The determination of the methodological issues and the subsequent modalities must remain in the hands of the supreme body of the Convention, the COP and its Subsidiary Bodies, as well as the IPCC, which provides the COP with scientific and technical advice, through SBSTA.
12. Priorities must be given to Convention-based items in these meetings. This is the task of the COP. We must abide by the decisions taken at Kyoto on the work of these Subsidiary Bodies. The balance of the Convention, based on the principles of common but differentiated responsibilities must be maintained. The Group of 77 and China will take this approach in these discussions.

Position Paper No. 3

Position Paper of the Group of 77 and China on Issues Taken Up at the Joint Session of the SBI/SBSTA on Mechanisms of the Kyoto Protocol

1. The Group of 77 and China reiterates the principles which guide us in this Convention, in particular the principle of common but differentiated responsibilities. Under this principle, developed countries must take the lead of modifying longer-term trends in anthropogenic emissions consistent with the objective of the Convention.
2. This is what we adopted in Kyoto as a first step, the Kyoto Protocol rendering adequate those commitments found to be inadequate in 1995 in Berlin. This was the focus on the work we did in Kyoto, to strengthen commitments of developed country parties as the first in series of review of adequacy of commitments.
   The second review, in accordance with the Convention, will take place at the Fourth Meeting of the Conference of the Parties, before the end of 1998.
3. The Protocol contains some mechanisms for "Overseas compliance" with the targets, in particular one which was based on a proposal by the Group of 77 and China, the clean development mechanism.
4. New mechanisms bring about new uncertainties, technical as well as political, which we have to settle before we discuss any activities under these mechanisms. There is a need for us to come to a common understanding on what these mechanisms are as defined in the Protocol, to study the methodological issues of each, their differences and their common characteristics, before we come to a determination of any modalities. These modalities would be determined, in accordance with the provisions of the relevant articles by the COP serving as the Meeting of the Parties.
5. We have to proceed on a step-by-step basis on mechanisms in a Protocol that has yet to enter into force in the first place adoption of a Protocol is a long way from taking the lead in modifying longer-term trends by developed countries. As stated in the Convention, policies and measures will have to demonstrate that indeed developed countries are taking the lead of this matter.
6. These mechanisms are supplemental to domestic action. Let us first see proof of what is achieved by domestic action, then determine compliance with this action, before adding the "supplement." In the meanwhile, we have important activities to undertake in implementation of the Convention, as we have articulated this morning before the two Subsidiary Bodies.
7. The Group is becoming increasingly alarmed at the various interpretations that have been given to the clean development mechanism. The CDM is not a "cleaner production mechanism," nor is it to be assimilated to a "global carbon initiative or fund," prototype or otherwise, or any other such

schemes. To call this a mechanism for cooperative implementation is likewise incorrect, as we have pointed out earlier these are mechanisms of the Kyoto Protocol and should be referred to as that, without any qualifiers which prejudge their nature.

8. We would urge those entities outside the Convention seeking to define the CDM through these terms to be guided by what the Conference of the Parties agreed in the Convention and in the Protocol. We would call on them to refrain from misleading themselves and others, as this will serve no useful purpose and will only hinder rather than assist forward movement. We do not welcome them, since they serve to confuse the pending discussions by the only body mandated to discuss these issues, the Conference of the Parties.
9. It should also be made clear that the Group is not in favour of any entity outside the Convention process to deal with in any manner with this mechanism by establishing any new bodies. Only the COP is mandated to do this.
10. The Group is of the view that the CDM, as proposed by the G-77 and agreed by consensus, is first and foremost a mechanism to promote sustainable development, rather than merely a market-based mechanism. A balance must be achieved between the objective set out for Annex I countries, that of obtaining certified emission reduction units, and the objective of non-Annex I countries is to achieve sustainable development, as set out in article 12.2 of the Protocol. This article is very clear, and no confusion is possible.
11. The determination of the methodological issues and the subsequent modalities must remain in the hands of the supreme body of the Convention, the COP and its Subsidiary Bodies, as well as the IPCC which provides the COP with scientific and technical advice, through SBSTA.
12. Priorities must be given Convention-based items in these meetings. This is the task of the COP. We must abide by the decisions taken at Kyoto on the work of these Subsidiary Bodies. The balance of the Convention, based on the principles of common but differentiated responsibilities must be maintained. The Group of 77 and China will take this approach in these discussions.

Position Paper No. 4 – Indonesia

(On behalf of the Group of 77 and China)

Response of the Group to the Proposals of the Executive Director of UNEP and the Executive Secretary of the FCCC to the Joint Session of the SBI and SBSTA on Agenda Item 8

1. The Group of 77 and China do not support the establishment of an intergovernmental body on economic instruments for environmental Conventions as proposed by the Executive Director of UNEP for the following reasons:

i. Working Group III (WGIII) of the Intergovernmental Panel on Climate Change (IPCC) already deals with all of the issues that could conceivably be covered by such a Panel. In addition, WGIII, which will have a key role to play in the development of the IPCC's Third Assessment Report, provides an interdisciplinary approach with the participation of outstanding professionals from both developed and developing countries in the technical and social sciences fields including economics;
ii. a key recommendation of the 1992 United Nations Conference on Environment and Development (UNCED), the so-called "Earth Summit" was that there should be no new institutions;
iii. UNEP in partnership with WMO is a host institution of the IPCC. Rather than strive to create another new institution that would only duplicate work already carried out elsewhere, UNEP would be better serve to allocate its increasingly scare resources to the efforts of the IPCC in general and its Working Group III in particular;
iv. Developing countries are already making a big effort to participate in the meetings of the IPCC; they will not have the manpower or resources to participate in the work of another intergovernmental body.

2. The Group of 77 and China do not support the suggestion of the Executive Secretary that the SBSTA invite UNEP to address issues relating to land-use change and forestry that cut across the Kyoto Protocol and other legal instruments, since this would be covered by the IPCC in either its Special Report or its Third Assessment Report.
3. Decisions on the allocation of work to organizations outside the Convention process can only be made under the authority of the Conference of the Parties as the supreme body of the FCCC and its Kyoto Protocol.

Proposals on Financial Mechanism

Submission by the Group of 77 and China

Proposal No. 1

G-77 and China Draft Decision on the Review of the Financial Mechanism*

The Conference of the Parties,

Recalling its decisions 9/CP.1, 11/CP.2, and 11/CP.3,

Recalling also the review process undertaken by the SBI in accordance with decision 11/CP.2,

* Contained in document FCCC/SBI/1998/MISC.4 of 10 June 1998.

Taking note of the report of the study of the GEF's overall performance,

Decides that the restructured GEF shall be an entity on an interim basis entrusted with the operation of the financial mechanism referred to in article 11 of the Convention,

Decides, in accordance with article 11.4 of the Convention, to regularly review the financial mechanism every four years, in accordance with criteria and guidelines to be established by the SBI, with a view towards taking appropriate measures.

Proposal No. 2

Draft Decision of the Group of 77 and China on Additional Guidance to the Financial Mechanism

Recalling its decisions 11/CP.1; 10/CP.2; and 11/CP.2;

Recalling further that the Global Environment Facility, as stated in its Operational Principles for Development and Implementation of its Work Programme, will maintain sufficient flexibility to respond to changing circumstances, including evolving guidance of the Conference of the Parties and experience gained from monitoring and evaluation activities;

Recognizing the need to provide clear guidance for the effective implementation of the Convention;

Expressing grave concern over the continued difficulties encountered by developing countries in complying fully with their obligations due to constraints in the availability and dispersal process of financial resources on a grant and concessional basis, including for the transfer of technology;

Expressing further continued concern over problems arising from the project cycle, the application of the concept of incremental costs, and the availability of resources through the Implementing Agencies;

Noting the need to examine and address the impacts of the implementation of response measures, in particular for those countries listed in article 4.8 of the Convention;

1. *Decides* to request the Global Environment Facility, as an operating entity of the financial mechanism, to provide the necessary financial resources to developing country parties to:

a. implement the adaptation measures such as, the analysis of a adaptation options, including the need for development of new technologies and opportunities for adapting existing technologies in new settings; the development of adaptive management strategies for use in vulnerable areas, including advanced planning to avoid worst impacts, the protection of threatened ecosystems, pilot hazard insurance schemes; and the implementation of effective measures that emphasize defence of vulnerable areas, population centres, economic activities, and natural resources;
b. respond to the need for improving existing, and setting up technology information centres as stated in paragraph 2 (b) of decision 9/CP.3, through the establishment of dedicated/ specialised information systems, compromising of enhanced national and regional centres, that would, *inter alia*, facilitate national/regional access to the information provided by international centres, and strengthen national/regional capacities to work with these centres for the dissemination of information, information services, and transfer of environmentally sound technologies, and know-how in support of the Convention;
c. in accordance with article 5 of the Convention, enhance the strengthening of observational networks and research to reduce scientific uncertainties relating to the causes, effects, magnitude, and timing of climate change, including capacity to determine the economic and social consequences of various response strategies;
d. meet the agreed full costs of the preparations of subsequent national communications of non–Annex I countries, taking into account that, as stated in paragraph I (d) of decision 11/CP.2, the preparation of national communications is a continuing process, and in accordance with article 4.3 of the Convention;
e. assist non–Annex I parties in the studies leading to the preparation of national programmes to address climate change in accordance with article 4.1 (b) of the Convention, and paragraph 13 of the Annex to decision 10/CP.2;
f. in implementation of article 6 of the Convention, and in accordance with paragraph 1 (b) (iii) under programme priorities, improve national public awareness and education on climate change and response measures, in cooperation with other relevant UN agencies where necessary;
g. implement the relevant conclusions of the workshops and other meetings for non–Annex I parties, as contained in Section IV of FCCC/SBI/1998/INF.3, for the electronic availability, translation, reproduction, and dissemination of initial national communications from non–Annex I parties; and
h. provide the necessary financial and technical support for assisting and addressing the impacts of the implementation of response measures in particular for those countries listed in article 4.8, as a first step through the identification of these impacts at national level.

2. *Requests* the Global Environment Facility to take the necessary steps to ensure that its Implementing Agencies are performing their obligations in accordance with the decisions adopted by the Conference of the Parties, and within the context of the principles of the Convention, following national priorities and objectives, including as a first priority the use of national experts in all aspects of the project development and implementation, whenever possible;
3. *Requests* the Secretariat, in accordance with article 8.2 (c), to provide the necessary assistance to developing country parties to avail themselves of the financial resources being made available from the financial mechanism for such purposes;
4. *Requests* the GEF to include in its report to the Conference of the Parties the specific steps it has undertaken to implement the provisions of this decision.

Position Paper and Draft Decision Submitted by the Group of 77 and China*

Position Paper
On Second Review of the Adequacy of Article 4, Subparagraphs 2 (a) and (b)

1. The fourth session of the Conference of the Parties (COP-4), in carrying out its second review of the adequacy of article 4, subparagraphs 2 (a) and (b) of the Convention, must respect the mandate of the Convention, as set forth in subparagraph 2 (d) of that article.
2. COP-4 must not be distracted from carrying out that review as mandated by the Convention by the introduction of any extraneous matters such as the consideration of new commitments for parties not included in Annex I.
3. COP-4 should decide that the next review take place at the same time as the review that is to be carried out at the second session of the Conference of the Parties serving as the Meeting of the Parties, in accordance with article 9.2 of the Kyoto Protocol.
4. Subsequent review should take place in the year preceding the termination of each successive commitment period under the Kyoto Protocol.

Draft Decision
On Second Review of Article 4.2(a) and (b) of the Convention and Related Matters

The Conference of the Parties, at its fourth session,

Noting (Reaffirming) that "the largest share of historical and current global emissions of greenhouse gases has originated in developed countries, that per capita emissions in developing countries are still relatively low and that the share of global emissions originating in developing countries will grow to meet their social and development needs" (quoted from para. 3 of Preamble to the Convention),

* Contained in document FCCC/SBI/1998/MISC.5 of 11 June 1998.

Basing itself on the Convention provisions, in particular article 4.2(d) of the Convention,

Having reviewed article 4.2(a) and (b) of the Convention in accordance with article 4.2(d) of the Convention, and having concluded that these subparagraphs are not adequate,

Deeply concerned that, according to their national communications, most of the developed country parties will not be able to honour their evidently inadequate commitments of returning to their 1990 levels their anthropogenic emissions of the greenhouse gases as required of them under article 4.2(b),

Decides

1. that those developed country parties that have not made demonstrable progress in returning to their 1990 levels their anthropogenic emissions of the GHGs as specified in article 4.2(b) of the Convention, shall make efforts in good faith in honouring their commitments under article 4.2(a) and (b) by the end of the present decade (or: at the latest, by 2005, as provided for in article 3.2 of the Kyoto Protocol);
2. that the Third Review, by the Conference of the Parties, of article 4.2(a) and (b) of the Convention shall take place at the second session of the Conference of the Parties serving as the Meeting of the Parties to the Kyoto Protocol, taking into account the timing mentioned in article 9.2 of the Kyoto Protocol;
3. that, in accordance with the provisions of article 4.2(d) of the Convention further reviews of article 4.2(a) and (b) of the Convention shall take place thereafter at regular intervals, namely, one year before the commencement of each subsequent "commitment period" for developed country parties, following their first commitment period (2008–2012), until the objective of the Convention is met.
4. that any such review shall not introduce any new commitments for developing country parties.

Indonesia (On behalf of the Group of 77 and China)

Position Paper of the G-77 and China at the Third Meeting of the Joint SBI/SBSTA Contact Group on the Mechanisms of the Kyoto Protocol*

1. The G-77 and China's initial list of questions on issues is the Group's contribution to the first part of the tasks assigned to SBSTA-SBI at its eighth session under paragraph 5 of decision 1/CP.3, that is, to give guidance to the Secretariat on the preparatory work needed for consideration of COP-4.

* Contained in document FCCC/SB/1998/MISC.1/Add.5 of 11 June 1998.

2. On the basis of these list of issues, the Group then worked on the "draft proposed schedule on mechanisms" prepared by the Co-Chairs, starting with the list of issues related to the mandate in paragraph 5 of decision 1/CP.3.
3. In the consideration of this draft, the Group was guided by the following basic positions:
   a. that we have to proceed on a step-by-step basis on mechanisms in a protocol that has yet to enter into force and that a common understanding has to be reached on the nature of these mechanisms. The study of methodological issues is a first step to be taken.
   b. that the above must be accomplished under the sole authority of the Conference of the Parties with the assistance of its subsidiary bodies, and other relevant bodies which have defined relationships with the Convention, such as the IPCC, working through its subsidiary bodies. In this regard, there must be a clear delineation of functions between the two subsidiary bodies, consistent with the mandate given to them by article 9 (SBSTA) and article 10 (SBI) of the Convention.
   c. that these two first items are what is expected of us at this session, in preparation for COP-4, namely, guidance to the Secretariat for preparatory work, and allocation of work. Timing of this work comes at a later stage, and also depends upon the other articles of the Protocol. Timing and scheduling should be dealt with by SBI/SBSTA at their ninth session.
4. There are likewise different priorities, as well as linkages, mentioned in each article concerning the mechanisms in the Protocol. Issues of the CDM (article 12) should be addressed first.
5. As to paragraph 6 of decision 1/CP.3, the task is for allocation of work between the two subsidiary bodies. The draft conclusions prepared, presumably under the guidance of the two Chairs of the subsidiary bodies, do not reflect the full range of opinions expressed during the general discussions of these mechanisms. These conclusions, and the timing proposed therein, are not acceptable to the Group of 77 and China.

In particular, the work programme laid out in the annex to the draft decision is duplicative of the work being done already in the joint contact group on mechanisms. The articles of the Protocol that would be dealt with under this paragraph (articles 5, 7, 8, and 18, and relevant sub-paragraphs of articles 2 and 3) are closely interlinked with those of the mechanisms. They therefore cannot be considered separately from the work being accomplished by the Joint Contact Group on mechanisms.

The Group proposes that only one contact group, the joint contact group co-chaired by the Netherlands and Brazil, work on these matters, which would also allow effective participation of small delegations in the work being done in these sessions.

6. The Group would like to reiterate that for COP-4, important tasks dealing with the implementation of the Convention have to be accomplished. Focus of the work at these June sessions, and in COP-4 should be on these tasks.

Proposed Work Programme on Mechanisms of the Kyoto Protocol

– Group of 77 and China

Article 12 – clean development mechanism

Methodological /Technical Work

1. Purpose of CDM projects
2. Supplementarity to domestic action
3. Part of Annex I commitments
4. Additionality criteria in funding
5 Criteria for real, measurable, and long-term benefits related to climate change
6. Compatibility with sustainable development priorities/strategies
7. Criteria for project eligibility
8. Criteria for certification
9. Criteria for project baseline
10. Definition of the concept of certified emission reductions
11. Acquisition and transfer of certified emission reduction
12. Systems for independent auditing and verification of project activities
13. Format for reporting
14. Identification/ determination of share of proceeds
15. Adaptation
16. Implication of article 12.10 of the Kyoto Protocol
17. Outcome of methodological work on articles 3.3 and 3.4 of the Protocol

Institutional Issues

1. Authority and guidance of the COP
2. Executive Board – Constitution, Composition, and Functions
3. Accountability of the Executive Board to the COP/MOP
4. Functions/provision of guidance
5. Procedure
6. Identification and designation of operational entities
7. Monitoring and auditing of operational entities

Participation in projects

1. Private and/or public entities
2. Responsibility of parties
3. Guidance to be provided by the executive board

Process

1. Approval by both parties
2. Procedure to attain certification of project activities
3. Certification of emission reductions

4. Acquisition and transfer of certified emission reduction
5. Assistance in arranging funding for projects assistance
6. Rules to guarantee transparency, non-discrimination and to prevent distortion of competition

Linkage

1. With contribution to compliance with part of commitments under article 3 of Annex I parties
2. With contribution to meet the costs of adaptation
3. With article 6 projects
4. CERs and ERUs accruing from projects
5. Work related to article 18 of the Kyoto Protocol

Article 6 projects

Methodological/Technical Work

1. Supplementarity to domestic action
2. Criteria for article 6 projects
3. Criteria for project baselines
4. Acquisition and transfer of emission reduction units
5. Compliance with articles 5 and 7 of the Kyoto Protocol
6. Verification
7. Reporting
8. Non-compliance
9. Outcome of methodological work on articles 3.3 and 3.4

Process

1. Approval by parties of projects
2. Assessment of additionality
3. Compliance with articles 5 and 7
4. Acquisition and transfer of emission reduction units

Institutional

1. Role of COP/MOP, SBSTA, and SBI
2. Work on non-compliance
3. Elaboration of guidelines as per article 6.2
4. Involvement of legal entities operating under the responsibility of a party
5. Definition of institutional authority

Linkage

1. With article 5
2. With article 7
3. With article 8

4. With article 18
5. With article 12, in particular article 12.8
6. With article 17

Activities Implemented Jointly

Activities Implemented Jointly (AIJ) cannot be part of this work programme. AIJ will be governed by COP decisions, namely, 5/CP.1, 8/CP.2 and 10/CP.3. According to decision 5/CP.1, the COP shall take into consideration the need for a comprehensive review of the pilot phase in order to take a conclusive decision on the pilot phase and the progression beyond that, no later than the end of the present decade. The Secretariat should prepare an update on information about the pilot phase of AIJ.

Article 17 – emissions trading between Annex I parties

Issues for Work Programme

1. Basis of rights and entitlements of Annex I parties for trading emissions
2. Determination and creation of such rights and entitlements
3. Supplementarity to domestic action for the purpose of meeting quantified emission limitation and reduction commitments under article 3
4. Conformity with the principle of equity in the Convention
5. Real and verifiable reduction of GHG emissions
6. Elements of principles, modalities, rules and guidelines for any trading in emissions
7. Elaboration of principles, modalities, rules, and guidelines, including the funding of adaptation
8. Matters relating to verification, reporting, and accountability
9. Whether any commonality with other mechanisms

Initial list of issues on Mechanisms of the Kyoto Protocol Group of 77 and China

The following is an initial list of issues from the Group of 77 and China on "mechanisms." The issues are listed as: (1) General, (2) Article 6 projects, (3) Article 12 – clean development mechanism, (4) Article 17 – emissions trading between developed country parties. These issues need to be properly addressed to enable progress.

General

1. What are the points of difference and points of similarity among the three mechanisms provided for in the Kyoto Protocol to the Convention.
2. How to ensure that domestic actions by developed countries are their primary means of GHG limitation and reduction, and that the overseas mechanisms remain supplemental to such domestic actions by developed countries for the purpose of meeting their quantified emission limitation and reduction commitments.

3. How can it be ensured that these mechanisms lead to real and verifiable limitation and reduction of GHG emissions by developed countries.
4. How to ensure that the COP or COP/MOP will maintain the responsibility for every stage of defining, developing, structuring, and institutionalizing the mechanisms.
5. What are the specific roles of the SBSTA and the SBI with regard to these mechanisms.
6. What will be the systems for ensuring independent auditing, verification, and accountability of the working of these mechanisms.

Article 6 projects

1. What will be the elements of the guidelines for projects under article 6, in particular, for ensuring transparency, accountability, reporting, and verification.
2. What will be the criteria for deciding the baseline of projects.
3. How can compliance with articles 5 and 7 of the Protocol be ensured, and how is this related to the work to be accomplished under article 18.
4. What will be the procedure for transferring or acquiring emission reduction units resulting from projects under article 6.
5. What will be the system for auditing and verifying projects under article 6.
6. How will "legal entities," to be involved in these projects, be defined, and how will the responsibility of the party over "legal entities" for the purpose of the projects be ensured.
7. How will the benefits of a project under article 6 be equitably shared between the participating parties.
8. What will be the reporting criteria of a project under article 6 to the COP/MOP.

Article 12 – Clean Development Mechanism

1. What will be the criteria for ensuring a balance wherein each CDM project attains the objective of assisting developing country parties in achieving sustainable development in accordance with their national priorities and strategy, and assisting developed country parties in achieving compliance with their commitments under article 3.
2. How to ensure that the CDM shall be subject to the authority and guidance of the Conference of the Parties serving as the Meeting of the Parties to the Protocol.
3. How to ensure that the executive board of the CDM shall function under the authority and guidance of the Conference of the Parties serving as the Meeting of the Parties to the Protocol.
4. What will be the constitution, character, and functions of the executive board of the CDM.

5. How will the emission reductions of a CDM project be certified? What will be the certification procedure, and by whom will this be done.
6. How to define and quantify "part" in ". . . part of quantified emission limitation and reduction commitments" in article 12.3 (b) of the Protocol.
7. How to ensure the responsibility and role of governments at each stage of the CDM projects.
8. How will it be ensured that the operational entity of the CDM, as designated by the COP, functions under the authority of the COP, and that its governance is separate from those of existing institutions.
9. How will article 12.6 of the Protocol be implemented? What will be the criteria and processes for the CDM for arranging due funding.
10. How to ensure the independent auditing and verification of CDM project activities.
11. What will be the criteria for deciding the baseline of projects.
12. When should the benefits of CDM projects accrue to the participating developed country parties.
13. What will be the action for non-compliance if a CDM project goes against the CDM criteria.
14. How to define "a share of the proceeds," and how will this share be apportioned for administrative expenses and adaptation.
15. How will the responsibility of a party be ensured over the private/public entities authorized by the party to be involved in CDM projects.
16. How to ensure that CDM projects are equitably distributed so as to benefit all developing country parties, in particular the least developed country parties, and that the distribution of projects does not exacerbate existing regional/sub regional imbalances.
17. How will it be ensured that the financing for CDM projects shall be additional to ODA and other international funding, additional to and separate from the financial obligations under GEF and additional to the financial obligation of the parties as provided in the Convention and the Protocol.
18. How will the additional economic benefits, if any, of a CDM project be shared equitably between the participating parties.
19. How will the participating parties report their CDM projects to the COP/MOP.
20. What are the implications of article 12.10 of the Protocol.

Article 17 – Emissions Trading between developed country parties

1. How will the emission rights and entitlements of developed country parties be determined and created for trading emissions? Will this be consistent with the principle of equity keeping in view the historical and current responsibility of developed countries to climate change and the ultimate objective of the Convention.

2. How to ensure that any emissions trading between the developed country parties shall be supplemental to domestic actions for the purpose of meeting their quantified emission limitation and reduction commitments.
3. How to ensure that emissions trading between developed country parties will lead to real and verifiable limitation and reduction of GHG emissions for meeting the objective of the Convention and contributing to the protection of the environment.
4. What will be the environmental or economic impacts in any area due to emissions trading between developed country parties.
5. How to ensure that any emissions trading between developed country parties fully reflects the principle of equity between developed and developing countries.
6. How to ensure that emissions trading between developed country parties shall conform to the principles, modalities, rules and guidelines including any compliance procedure to be defined by the COP.

Initial Views of the G-77 and China on Procedures and Mechanisms Relating to Compliance under the Kyoto Protocol*

The Group of 77 and China has identified the following elements relevant to procedures and mechanism relating to compliance under the Kyoto Protocol. These represent the initial views of the Group on this matter and will be developed further as discussions evolve. The list of questions attached hereto, in addition to those compiled by the Secretariat, will be a useful tool in the preparation of further submissions. It is envisaged that such submissions made by members of the Group of 77 and China on the basis hereof would aid the Group to further develop its position on procedures and mechanisms relating to compliance.

ELEMENTS

Elements that need to be taken into account in the development of a compliance regime are, *inter alia*, -

- The objective of the compliance regime should be in line with the objective of the Convention and should as a first priority aim at ensuring that the emission reduction commitments are met by Annex B parties.
- A comprehensive, strong, efficient and effective compliance system is of vital importance for the successful implementation of the Kyoto Protocol and is therefore imperative for the credibility and integrity of the processes to be developed under the Protocol.

* Contained in document FCCC/SB/1999/MISC.4/Add.3 of 7 June 1999.

- In line with the provisions of the Convention and the Protocol the principle of common but differentiated responsibility is regarded as a cornerstone in the design and implementation of the compliance regime.
- In the design of the compliance regime due cognizance should be given to the principle of the need for adequate and effective national compliance regimes and enforcement measures in Annex B parties and how these can support and strengthen the international regime.
- The adoption of legally binding and quantified commitments and the introduction of the Kyoto Protocol mechanisms make the development of non-compliance procedures imperative.
- The Protocol must be assessed in its totality with a view to identify the essential elements and tools for anticipating, preventing, identifying, and responding to non-compliance.
- Compliance rules, procedures, and institutions should be such that it would enable the climate change regime to anticipate, prevent, identify, and respond to situations of non-compliance.
- The procedures and mechanisms should be effective, fair, and equitable and operate in a transparent, timely, and efficient manner.
- Aspects to be considered in the development of the compliance regime are the need for, *inter alia*, -
    - the elaboration of relevant principles, modalities, and guidelines for the verification, reporting, and accountability under the Protocol's mechanisms;
    - the potential application to the Protocol of any MCP adopted under the Convention;
    - a critical evaluation of the Convention and the Protocol's financial mechanism as a means of assessing both the obligations of Annex I parties, and the adequacy of the mechanism in assisting non–Annex I parties to comply with the Protocol.
- Only parties that are in compliance with their obligations and are bound by a compliance regime should be allowed to participate in the Kyoto Protocol mechanisms.
- Binding consequences for non-compliance are essential. This will enhance the parties collective ability to deter non-compliance.
- Consequences resulting from non-compliance should be proportional and responsive to the case at hand.
- In dealing with cases of non-compliance, facilitative as well as enforcement measures should be employed.
- It may be desirable to identify cases and/or activities that may constitute non-compliance.
- An indicative list of non-compliance consequences, depending on the cause, type, degree and frequency of non-compliance should be devised. These could include *inter alia* –

  - Appropriate assistance, including technical and financial expertise and capacity-building;
  - Issuing cautions;
  - Suspension of rights, including ability to participate in articles 6, 12, and 17;
  - Penalties, including financial penalties for Annex B parties.
- Financial penalties resulting from a non-compliance procedure should be made available to meet the cost of adaptation.
- If necessary, an appropriate institution or body may be required to consider each case of non-compliance. Relevant procedures and the review process will need to be determined. The application of the principle of due process should be fully taken into account. The constitution of such an institution or body shall be based on the principle of equitable geographical representation.
- The benefits of establishing procedures for imposing automatic consequences in certain circumstances to cases of non-compliance should be explored.
- The compliance regime will be essential to strengthen the domestic and regional arrangements of Annex B parties.

List of questions related to a compliance system

<u>Note:</u> These questions are submitted to be used in addition to the list of questions in Annex III of the Non-Paper by the Secretariat.

1. What should be the principles that guide the development of the procedures and mechanisms to implement article 18 of the Kyoto Protocol?
2. What procedures and mechanisms under article 18 entail binding consequences? What are the implications of "binding consequences" vis-à-vis other consequences of non-compliance, and the amendment of the Protocol?
3. Should procedures and mechanisms "entailing binding consequences" be adopted concerning non-compliance with respect to:
   a. "Guidelines" for the national systems for estimating emissions of greenhouse gases and removals by sinks, which may be established pursuant to article 5.1; or "guidelines" for the implementation of article 6, as provided for in article 6.2; or "guidelines" for the reporting of certain information in national communications, as provided for in article 7.4?
   b. "Modalities, rules and guidelines" adopted pursuant to article 3.4, concerning how, and which, additional categories of sinks may be added to those contained in article 3.3?
   c. "Modalities and procedures" concerning the Clean Development Mechanisms, which may be adopted pursuant to article 12.7?
   d. "Principles, modalities, rules and guidelines" concerning emissions trading, which may be adopted pursuant to article 17?

4. The expert review teams contemplated by article 8 of the Kyoto Protocol review "information submitted under article 7 by each party included in Annex I." In this regard –
   (a) Should we integrate the requirements of articles 8.3 and 8.5 with the procedures that may be developed to implement articles 18, 16, and 19? If so, how?
   (b) Although the expert review teams may provide information relevant to whether an Annex I party is at risk of non-compliance or may not be in compliance, do the teams have authority to make any determination (initial, provisional, or otherwise) that such party is in non-compliance?
   (c) If the report of the review team (issued after the end of a commitment period of an Annex I party) does not indicate non-compliance by the Annex I party with its emissions imitation/ reduction commitment under article 3 of the Protocol, does that preclude any party from being able to raise an issue of non-compliance?
   (d) Should a review team possess authority to initiate, by its own determination, a procedure adopted pursuant to article 18 that could result in binding consequences to a party?
   (e) Should a review team possess authority to initiate, by its own determination, a procedure that may be developed to implement article 16?
5. Should the idea of "automatic" penalties be used? If so, in what cases?
6. Should financial penalties be used? If so, in what cases? Elaborate, including a description of how and for what purposes the proceeds of financial penalties should be used.

Group of 77 and China

Initial Submission on Article 12 of the Kyoto Protocol: The Clean Development Mechanism*

All the paragraphs below are subject to further elaboration by the Group of 77 and China.

Introduction

1. Article 12 of the Kyoto Protocol to the UN Framework Convention on Climate Change (FCCC) has defined a clean development mechanism (CDM) with the following two-fold purpose: (1) to assist developing country parties in achieving sustainable development and in contributing to the ultimate objective of the Convention, and (2) to assist developed country parties in achieving compliance with part of their quantified emission limitation and

* Contained in document FCCC/SB/1999/MISC.3/Add.5 of 8 June 1999.

reduction commitments under article 3, and therefore each CDM project activity should meet the above two-fold purpose.

2. Decision 7/CP.4 has stipulated a work programme on the mechanisms of the Kyoto Protocol, including a list of elements. The programme has given priority to the CDM. The CDM must be taken up first for discussion and decision.
3. This submission is following the format in the earlier submission made by the Group of 77 and China on 12 November, 1998: "Initial Work programme on Mechanisms of the Kyoto Protocol" (FCCC/CP/1998/MISC.7/Add.3).

Principles

4. The principles for the CDM and other basic elements must be decided first. These principles must be in keeping with article 3 of the FCCC. These principles for the CDM are, *inter alia*: the nature and scope of the mechanisms; equity and transparency; supplementarity; climate change effectiveness; institutional framework; capacity-building; adaptation; compliance; purpose of CDM projects; supplementarity to domestic action for achieving compliance with reduction commitments under article 3; compatibility with sustainable development priorities/strategies; special needs of least developed countries; criteria for project eligibility; adaptation; and transparency, non-discrimination, prevention of distortion of competition. The methodological and operational questions will be guided accordingly.

Nature and Scope of CDM

5. The CDM is a project-based mechanism conceived and introduced in the Protocol with a two-fold purpose (see paragraph 1). Unlike the other mechanisms provided for in the Kyoto Protocol, the CDM is the only mechanism of the Protocol which involves the participation in CDM project activities by both the developed and developing country parties. Developed country parties will fund projects in developing country parties which will assist sustainable development. Developed country parties may involve private and/or public entities for such funding. In return, the developed country party, funding the project, will be enabled to meet part of its emission reduction commitment. The Protocol has made provision for certifying the emissions reduced from a CDM project. Accordingly, "certified emission reductions" (CERs) will accrue. The CERs will enable the participating developed country party to contribute to compliance with part of its quantified emission limitation and reduction commitments under article 3 to the extent permissible under the principle of "supplementarity" to be decided. It must be ensured that "a share of the proceeds from certified project activities" is used to meet costs of adaptation. For this purpose, *inter alia*, a CDM adaptation fund should be established.

Equity and transparency

6. The principle of equity in the Convention must apply to all aspects of the CDM based on equitable developmental rights and balanced regional activity. The principle of transparency must be observed in the design and application of all CDM activities including project identification and approval, certification and verification, establishment of baselines, and the operations of the executive board.

Supplementarity

7. The design and implementation of the CDM must not in any way compromise the modification of longer-term trends in greenhouse gas anthropogenic emissions and concentrations. All the mechanisms, including the CDM, must be supplemental to domestic actions for GHG limitation and reduction. Guidelines on supplementarity must be developed taking into account articles 2 and 3.2 of the Kyoto Protocol. Commensurate non-compliance processes must be put in place. Developed country access to the CDM mechanism should be contingent on satisfaction of prescribed domestic effort in fulfilment of commitments under article 3.

Climate Change Effectiveness

8. Climate change effectiveness must be in terms of real, measurable and long-term benefits related to the mitigation of climate change at the project level.

Institutional Framework

9. The institutions as provided for in article 12 of the Kyoto Protocol shall follow the principles and the nature and scope of the CDM. At the same time, it is recognized that the institutional framework will be based on representativity.

Capacity-Building

10. Capacity-building is central for ensuring wider participation, and should be incorporated in all CDM project activities. Capacity-building should include the build-up of endogenous expertise for identifying technology needs and helping enhance capacities for assimilation of technology. Developing country parties will also need to develop capacity in monitoring, reporting, and verifying emissions; and in the design, implementation, and evaluation of CDM project activities. In implementation of the CDM project activities, to the extent possible, the capacity and

capability of developing country parties at the national, sub-regional, and regional levels, through bilateral and multilateral approaches should be explored. At the national level, these approaches should be informed by the widest possible participation.

Adaptation

11. As provided for and listed in article 4.8 of the Convention, and article 12.8 of the Protocol, developing country parties that are particularly vulnerable will be assisted to meet the costs of adaptation. For this purpose, *inter alia*, a CDM adaptation fund should be established. The institutional and organizational aspects related to adaptation in the context of certified project activities require elaboration in detail. Developing country parties should identify adaptation projects for funding, and should follow a process of adaptation options identification. Consideration of this aspect should be consistent with ongoing work on adaptation under the Convention. Developing country parties should be assisted with capacity-building at all levels in order to be able to carry out such activities.

Compliance

12. Appropriate and effective procedures and mechanisms to determine and to address cases of non-compliance with the provisions of this Protocol should be established. The procedures and mechanisms should be underpinned by the principles of the Convention. These need further elaboration.

Purpose of CDM projects

13. See paragraph 1, above.

Supplementarity to domestic action for achieving compliance, etc.

14. The design and implementation of the CDM must not in any way compromise the modification of longer-term trends in greenhouse gas anthropogenic emissions and concentrations. All the mechanisms, including the CDM, must be supplemental to domestic actions for GHG limitation and reduction. Guidelines on supplementarity must be developed taking into account articles 2 and 3.2 of the Kyoto Protocol. Commensurate non-compliance processes must be put in place. Developed country parties' participation in CDM project: activities should be contingent on satisfaction of prescribed domestic effort in fulfilment of commitments under article 3. This will be further elaborated.

Sustainable Development priorities

15. Sustainable development priorities are set by national authorities. The priorities depend upon the specific requirements of a developing country party. CDM project activities must contribute to sustainable development. The developing country party where the CDM project activity is proposed to be set up shall be the sole judge for deciding whether that project activity meets its national sustainable development objectives and priorities.

Special needs of least developed countries

16. The special needs of least developed countries have to be addressed both from the point of view of identifying their special technology needs and of capacity-building. The capacity-building effort should be in the direction of build-up of endogenous expertise for identifying technology needs and helping enhance capacities for assimilation of technology. Least developed country parties need assistance to build up capacity in monitoring, reporting, and verifying emissions; and in the selection, design, and evaluation of CDM project activities.

Criteria for Project Eligibility

17. Eligible project activities, apart from meeting national sustainable development priorities, must ensure access to environmentally sound technology needed by the developing country party participating in the CDM project activity. This will be elaborated further.

Transparency, non-discrimination, prevention of distortion of competition

18. All developing country parties can participate in CDM project activities. No unilateral measures for CDM participation should preclude a developing country party from participating in any CDM project activity. Transparency should be encouraged in all CDM project activities, including for project identification, design and implementation; and verification, monitoring, and reporting, as well as regarding all costs, risks, and liabilities to be incurred by the developing country party.

Part of Annex I Commitments

19. It must be ensured that CDM project activities shall be supplemental to domestic actions by developed country parties to meet part of their quantified emission limitation or reduction commitments. Further elaboration will be made by the Group.

Additionality criteria in project funding

20. Funding for the CDM project shall be additional to ODA, GEF, and other financial commitments of the developed country parties.

Criteria for real, measurable, and long-term benefits related to climate change

21. This issue, which is related to paragraph 8 above, should be addressed by taking into account the additional reduction in emissions at the CDM project level as against the baseline of the CDM project activity. The benefits related to a project activity would be recognized as real if the actual greenhouse gas (GHG) emissions can be shown to be less than the project baseline. The benefits would be recognized as measurable if the actual level of GHG emissions of the project case and the level of GHG emissions in the project baseline can be established with a reasonable degree of certainty. The benefits of a project activity would be recognized as long-term if the emission reduction persists over an appropriate period of time taking into account the differences in the life-spans of different CDM project activities, and bearing in mind article 2 of the Convention.

Criteria for certification

22. The operational entities to be designated by the COP/MOP shall certify the emission reductions resulting from each project activity on the basis laid out in article 12.5 of the Protocol. Guidelines to carry out the certification should be elaborated.

Criteria for project baseline

23. The establishment of baselines for the determination of emissions reduction should be made on a project-by-project basis. The establishment of the baseline will quantify the level of emissions that most likely would have occurred in the absence of the certified CDM project activity. This will be further elaborated.

Definition of the concept of certified emissions reductions

24. The Protocol has made provision for certification of the emission reductions resulting from each CDM project activity. Accordingly, "certified emission reductions" (CERs) will accrue to the developed country party participating in the project activity, to enable that country to contribute to compliance with quantified emission limitation and reduction commitments under article 3.

Systems for independent auditing and verification of project activities

25. Independent auditing of project activities may be done by public or private sector entities not involved in the identification, development, or management of the project. There is need to develop uniform auditing practices. Verification has to be carried out by independent entities that have had no operational or financial links with the project, and that are fully accountable to COP/MOP which shall exercise authority and guidance over all aspects of the CDM. The composition of any team should be approved by the developing country party participating in the CDM project activity.

Format for Reporting

26. The format for reporting must be in a standardized format across all CDM projects. The reporting requirements should be as simple as possible so as to enable local human resources to fulfil these requirements.

Implication of article 12.10 of the Protocol

27. SBSTA should be requested to study the implications of article 12.10 of the Protocol and to propose recommendations. Submissions from parties could be requested by SBSTA on their views on these implications.

Outcome of methodological work on articles 3.3 and 3.4

28. The outcome shall be awaited.

Acquisition of certified emission reduction units

29. Article 3.12 of the Protocol states: "Any certified emission reductions which a party acquires from another Party in accordance with the provisions of Article 12 shall be added to the assigned amount for the acquiring Party."

Determination of share of proceeds from certified project activity for adaptation

30. Developing country parties that are particularly vulnerable, as listed in article 4.8 of the Convention, will be assisted to meet the costs of adaptation from, *inter alia*, a CDM adaptation fund. The COP/MOP of the Protocol shall ensure that a share of the proceeds from certified project activities is used to cover these costs. Detailed modalities will be required.

Determination of share of proceeds from certified project activity for administration

31. The COP/MOP shall also ensure that a share of the proceeds from certified project activities is used to cover administrative expenses for these activities. Detailed modalities will be required.

Approval by involved parties of sustainable development

32. The developing country party participating in the project activity should be the sole judge for determining whether any CDM project under consideration meets its sustainable development requirements.

Authority guidance of the COP

33. As stated in article 7 of the FCCC, the COP is the supreme body of the Convention which shall keep under regular review the implementation of the Convention and any related legal instruments that the COP may adopt, such as the Kyoto Protocol.

Accountability of the Executive Board to the COP/MOP

34. There shall be full accountability of the executive board to the COP/MOP which shall exercise authority and guidance over all aspects of the CDM.

Functions of, relationship among and operational procedures of the COP, COP/MOP, etc.

35. The COP, as stated in paragraph 33 above, shall keep under regular review the implementation of the Protocol. The COP, in implementation of decision 1/CP.3, started work on items related to specific provisions of the Kyoto Protocol. Accordingly, the COP adopted decisions 5/CP.4 (Implementation of article 4.8 and 4.9 of the Convention, decision 3/CP.3 and articles 2.3 and 3.14 of the Kyoto Protocol); 7/CP.4 on the Work programme on mechanisms of the Kyoto Protocol; and decision 8/CP.4 on Preparations for the first session of the COP/MOP. The CDM shall be subject to the authority and guidance of the COP/MOP and be supervised by an executive board of the CDM. The COP/MOP shall review periodically the implementation of CDM project activities and their geographical spread, and take appropriate action to promote the principle of equity.

Executive Board – constitution, composition, etc.

36. The executive board shall be fully accountable to the COP/MOP. Its composition shall be on the basis of equitable geographical representation, and it

should be functionally small. Under the authority and guidance of the COP/MOP the executive board shall supervise the CDM, and shall provide guidance for the involvement of private and/or public entities in CDM project activities.

Guidance regarding involvement of public and/or private entities

37. Parties are responsible for the involvement of their private and/or public entities in CDM project activities subject to the guidance provided by the executive board.

Operational entities – identification/designation/accreditation, etc.

38. Operational entities to certify emissions reductions resulting from each CDM project activity shall be designated by the COP/MOP.

Responsibility of parties

39. The parties participating in the CDM project activities must be responsible at all stages and in all aspects for the project activity in which they are participating. Any costs, risks or liabilities that have not been expressly accepted by the developing country party before approval of the CDM project activity shall be assumed to be the responsibility of the participating developed country party.

Group of 77 and China

Initial Submission on Article 6 of the Kyoto Protocol Article 6 Projects*

Further elaboration will be made on the paragraphs below.

1. Article 6 of the Kyoto Protocol to the Convention has provided that "For the purpose of meeting its commitments under Article 3, any Party included in Annex I may transfer or acquire from any other such Party emission reduction units resulting from projects aimed at reducing anthropogenic emissions . . . , provided that:
   (a) Any such projects has the approval of the parties involved;
   (b) Any such projects provides a reduction in emissions by sources, or an enhancement of removals by sinks, that is additional to any that would otherwise occur;
   (c) It does not acquire any emission reduction units if it is not in compliance with its obligations under articles 5 and 7; and

* Contained in document FCCC/SB/1999/MISC.3/Add.6 of 9 June 1999.

The acquisition of emission reduction units shall be supplemental to domestic actions for the purpose of meeting commitments under article 3. Accordingly, during COP-4, the G-77 and China submitted relevant Elements, *inter alia*, on "Article 6 projects," as contained in FCCC/CP/1998/MISC.7/Add.3.

2. Due to time constraints, the G-77 and China has not yet been able to elaborate its views on "Article 6 projects." However, the G-77 and China is of the view that the following Elements are basic and need to be addressed first, so as to enable the COP/MOP to "further elaborate guidelines for the implementation of this Article . . ." (article 6.2 of the Kyoto Protocol):
   (1) Participation of parties in article 6 projects
   (2) Supplementarity to domestic actions by the participating Annex I parties
   (3) Criteria for article 6 projects
   (4) Climate change effectiveness
   (5) Transparency
   (6) Criteria for project baselines
   (7) Acquisition and transfer of emission reduction units (ERUs), as provided for under articles 3.10 and 3.11
   (8) Parties' authorization and involvement of legal entities
   (9) Guidelines for monitoring, verification, and reporting
   (10) Consequences of non-compliance
   (11) Guidelines for review of implementation of article 6 of the Kyoto Protocol.

Group of 77 and China

Initial Submission on Article 17 of the Kyoto Protocol

Further elaboration will be made on the paragraphs below.

Introduction

1. The purpose of "emissions trading" under article 17 of the Kyoto Protocol is to assist parties included in Annex B in fulfilling part of their commitments under article 3. Article 17 states: "Any such trading shall be supplemental to domestic actions for the purpose of meeting quantified emission limitation and reduction commitments" under that article.

Principles

2. The principles for article 17 and the other basic elements pertaining to this article must be decided first and formulated accordingly. These principles

and basic elements must be in conformity with article 3 of the Convention. The methodological and operational issues must be guided accordingly. Of fundamental importance is the environmental integrity of the system to be brought in place under article 17 and its credibility. It must be ensured that the system does not have dormant any possibility or potential of freezing or perpetuating existing inequities between Annex B parties and developing country parties. The right to development of developing countries must not be affected adversely in any way. It is recognized that the Protocol has not created or bestowed any right, title or entitlement.

Nature and Scope of Article 17

3. Annex B parties have quantified greenhouse gas (GHG) emission limitation and reduction commitments stipulated in Annex B of the Protocol. Annex B parties, individually or jointly, have to ensure that their aggregate anthropogenic carbon dioxide equivalent emissions of the GHGs listed in Annex A of the Protocol do not exceed their assigned amounts, calculated pursuant to their quantified emission limitation and reduction commitments inscribed in Annex B, with a view to reducing their overall emissions of such gases by at least 5 per cent below 1990 levels in the quantified emission limitation and reduction commitment period, from 2008 to 2012. The assigned amount for each such party, in the commitment period from 2008 to 2012, shall be equal to the percentage inscribed for it in Annex B of its aggregate anthropogenic carbon dioxide equivalent emissions of the greenhouse gases (GHGs) listed in Annex A of the Protocol in 1990, or the base year or period determined in accordance with paragraph 5 of article 3 of the Protocol, multiplied by five. If an Annex B party is able to limit or reduce its GHG emissions over and above its commitment, such excess limitation or reduction can be transferred to any other Annex B party under the provisions of article 17. Such excess limitation and reduction of emissions shall be subtracted from the assigned amount for the transferring party, and be added to the assigned amount for the acquiring party.

Eligibility

4. Parties included in Annex B shall be eligible to "transfer" or "acquire" part of the assigned amount, if they:
   (a) are in compliance with articles 3, 5, and 7 of the Protocol and are responsible for meeting their commitments under the Protocol;
   (b) are not in violation of the compliance procedures as referred to in article 18 of the Protocol;
   (c) have a transparent national system for registration and verification of such "transfers" and "acquisitions."

Supplementarity

5. The design and implementation of any system under article 17 must not in any way compromise the modification of longer-term trends in GHG anthropogenic emissions and concentrations. Commensurate non-compliance processes must be put in place. Annex B parties access to article 17 should be contingent on satisfaction of prescribed domestic effort in fulfilment of commitments under article 3.

Climate Change Effectiveness

6. Any system established under article 17 of the Protocol shall contribute to and bring about real, measurable, and long-term benefits related to mitigation of climate change. It should not lead to overall increase in the GHG emissions of the developed country parties.

Rules

7. The rules to be formulated must conform to the principles. Rules have to determine that part of the assigned amount which would be transferable by an Annex B party to another acquiring Annex B party under article 17. The rules will lay down the conditions which must be fulfilled before any such transfers and acquisitions can occur. The rules will ensure that no right, title, or entitlement in any manner gets attached to the assigned amount or any part of the assigned amount which is transferred or acquired.

Modalities

8. Any Annex B party participating in the system to be established under article 17 shall establish and maintain a transparent national registration of "transfers" and "acquisitions." Such information shall be communicated regularly to the Convention Secretariat. Annex B parties participating in the transfers and acquisitions of parts of assigned amounts under article 17 of the Protocol, shall include in their national inventory, to be communicated to the Secretariat under article 7.1 of the Protocol, information on any part of an assigned amount added to or removed from its national registration during the relevant year. If an Annex B party is in non-compliance with its commitments, that part of the assigned amount that has been "transferred" shall be invalidated.

Draft Decision by the Group of 77 and China*

Initial and Subsequent National Communications from Parties Not Included in Annex I to the Convention

The Conference of the Parties

Basing itself on articles 4.3, 4.7, 12.1, and 10.2 (a) of the Convention,

Reiterating the primary important of the provision of financial and technical support, and related technology transfer, as a means for capacity-building for the preparations of national communications;

Recalling its decisions on communications from parties not included in Annex Ito the Convention, in particular decisions 10/CP.2, 11/CP.2, 2/CP.4, and 12/CP.4,

Underlining paragraph 1 (d) of decision 11/CP.2 which states that the Global Environment Facility should take into account that the preparation of national communications is a continuing process,

Underlining also the grave concern of non–Annex I parties that lack of support for post national communication activities has resulted in serious disruption of the implementation of the Convention at the national level,

Deploring the use of workshops on non–Annex I national communications, outside the UNFCCC Secretariat process, for purposes which are not compatible with the Convention and contrary to its decisions,

Decides

On guidelines and guidance,

1. that, until full information on the use of these guidelines by all parties not included in Annex I is obtained from the compilation and synthesis of initial and second national communications as called for in decision 12/CP.4, and a decision taken by the Conference of the Parties to revise these guidelines, the Guidelines for the preparations of initial national communications by parties not included in Annex I to the Convention, contained in the Annex to

* Contained in document FCCC/SBI/1999/L.8 of 9 June 1999.

decision 10/CP.2, shall remain valid, together with the guidance given to the Global Environment Facility in decision 11/CP.2;

2. that the use of these guidelines shall be the basis of any workshop on non-Annex I communications to be held for the purpose of responding to the needs of developing countries for the preparations of their national communications;
3. that, as stated in paragraph 2 (c) of decision 10/CP.2, non-Annex I parties which wish to submit voluntarily, additional information may use elements from the guidelines approved for parties included in Annex I to the Convention when preparing their initial communications, and that they may likewise do so when preparing their subsequent national communications;

On timing of submissions of non-Annex I national communications

4. that, given the small number of developing countries which have as yet submitted their national communications, and given the provision of article 12.5 stating that the COP shall take into account the differentiated timetable set by that article in determining the frequency of subsequent communications, as well as the timing of the submissions of first and second national communications from non-Annex I parties, timetables for submission of subsequent national communications shall differ for each non-Annex I party. Full information from the operating entity of the financial mechanism on the effective availability of financial resources to the party, and the timing of the disbursement of these resources to developing countries for the preparations of their initial and second national communications would be necessary to the determination of each non-Annex I party's timing of submissions, in accordance with article 4.3 and article 12.5 of the Convention;

On financial and technical support

5. that a non-Annex I Group of Experts shall be set up, on the basis of nominations received from Governments of non-Annex I parties in order to assess the availability of financial resources and technical support, to identify gaps, and also for the purposes of exchange of experiences and information, with the objective of enhancing support to preparations, and identifying the difficulties encountered by developing countries in the use of the guidelines, so as to improve the national communications of non-Annex I countries. This Group shall meet regularly, and be given the necessary resources to do so. Results of their meetings, and any recommendations from this Group shall be taken into account by the Subsidiary Bodies in their deliberations, and for any

decisions to be taken by the Conference of the parties on the national communications from non–annex i parties *(see Annex)*;

6. that the Secretariat shall provide the necessary assistance to convene the meetings of the non–Annex I Experts' Group for non–Annex I communications, in accordance with article 8.2 (c) of the Convention, and as called for in paragraph 1(a) of decision 10/CP.2; and

On matters related to consideration of non–Annex I national communications

7. that, as provided for in paragraph 2 (b) of decision 10/CP.2, and paragraph I (c) of decision 12/CP.4, any consideration of matters related to their national communications should take, into account information on the implementation of articles 4.1, 4.3, 4.4., 4.5, 4.7, 4.8, 4.9, and 4.10, in the light of the provisions of article 3;
8. that information as compiled and syn thesized by the Secretariat on non–Annex I, communications as stated in paragraph 7 of decision 12/CP.4, should be taken with the relevant information provided in Annex I parties' national communications in order to allow the SBI to consider the information communicated in, accordance with article 12, paragraph 1 of the FCCC, to assess the overall aggregated effect of the steps taken by the parties in the light of the latest scientific assessments concerning climate change as provided by the SBSTA in accordance with article 9.2 (a) of the FCCC;
9. that this compilation and synthesis shall be accomplished along the lines of the guidelines contained in decision 10/CP.2, in particular the information to be given in response to paragraphs 19 to 22 of the Annex to these Guidelines, on the identification of financial and technological needs;

On the review of the enabling activities of the Global Environment Facility

10. that the consistency of these enabling activities with the guidelines for the preparations of initial national communications from parties not included in Annex I to the Convention, as contained in decision 10/CP.2, and the guidance to the Global Environment Facility as contained in decision 11/CP.2, as well as with previous and subsequent guidance provided by the Conference of the Parties to the Global Environment Facility as an operating entity of the financial mechanism of the Convention, shall be fully examined and demonstrated in the review of the enabling activities of the GEF, and
11. that a report shall be requested from the GEF to the Conference of the Parties on the results of this review.

Annex

NON-ANNEX I EXPERT GROUP

STEERING COMMITTEE

Tasks:

1. Define work plan
2. Meet quarterly
3. Define agendas for the Expert Group Meetings

Members:	Regional representations (4 per region) Annex I experts as observers

4 EXPERT GROUP MEETINGS ALONG THEMATIC LINES

Participation: Experts nominated by parties and selected (if necessary) by the steering committee

Themes:	Greenhouse gas inventory Vulnerability assessment and adaption options Abatement issues Preparation of national communications
Duration:	Minimum 7 days
Frequency:	Each thematic group would meet once a year
Number:	±50 participants/region

Feedback to the process:

- each thematic meeting would breakdown work in regional working groups
- recommendations and conclusions would be made available to the COP/SBS
- recommendations would have “regional” perspectives/dimensions and where appropriate “global” perspectives

Draft Decision Proposed by the Group of 77 and China*

Initial and Subsequent National Communications from Parties Not Included in Annex I to the Convention

The Conference of the Parties

Basing itself on articles 4.3, 4.7, 12.1, and 10.2 (a) of the Convention,

Reiterating the primary important of the provision of financial and technical support, and related technology transfer, as a means for capacity-building for the preparations of national communications,

Recalling its decisions on communications from parties not included in Annex I to the Convention, in particular decisions 10/CP.2, 11/CP.2, 2/CP.4, and 12/CP.4,

Underlining paragraph 1 (d) of decision 11/CP.2 which states that the Global Environment Facility should take into account that the preparation of national communications is a continuing process,

Underlining also the grave concern of non–Annex I parties that lack of support for post-national communication activities has resulted in serious disruption of the implementation of the Convention at the national level,

Deploring the use of workshops on non–Annex I national communications, outside the UNFCCC Secretariat process, for purposes which are not compatible with the Convention and contrary to its decisions,

Decides

On guidelines and guidance,

1. that, until full information on the use of these guidelines by all parties not included in Annex I is obtained from the compilation and synthesis of initial and second national communications as called for in decision 12/CP.4, and a decision taken by the Conference of the Parties to revise these guidelines, the Guidelines for the preparations of initial national communications by parties not included in Annex I to the Convention, contained in the Annex to decision 10/CP.2, shall remain valid, together with the guidance given to the Global Environment Facility in decision 11/CP.2;
2. that the use of these guidelines shall be the basis of any workshop on non–Annex I communications to be held for the purpose of responding to

* Contained in document FCCC/SBI/1999/CRP.6 of 10 June 1999.

the needs of developing countries for the preparations of their national communications;

3. that, as stated in paragraph 2 (c) of decision 10/CP.2, non-Annex I parties which wish to submit voluntarily additional information may use elements from the guidelines approved for parties included in Annex I to the Convention when preparing their initial communications, and that they may likewise do so when preparing their subsequent national communications;

On timing of submissions of non-Annex I national communications

4. that, given the small number of developing countries which have as yet submitted their national communications, and given the provision of article 12.5 stating that the COP shall take into account the differentiated timetable set by that article in determining the frequency of subsequent communications, as well as the timing of the submissions of first and second national communications from non-Annex I parties, timetables for submission of subsequent national communications shall differ for each non-Annex I party. Full information from the operating entity of the financial mechanism on the effective availability of financial resources to the party, and the timing of the disbursement of these resources to developing countries for the preparations of their initial and second national communications would be necessary to the determination of each non-Annex I party's timing of submissions, in accordance with article 4.3 and article 12.5 of the Convention;

On financial and technical support

5. that a non-Annex I Group of Experts shall be set up, on the basis of nominations received from Governments of non-Annex I parties in order to assess the availability of financial resources and technical support, to identify gaps, and also for the purposes of exchange of experiences and information, with the objective of enhancing support to preparations, and identifying the difficulties encountered by developing countries in the use of the guidelines, so as to improve the national communications of non-Annex I countries. This Group shall meet regularly and be given the necessary resources to do so. Results of their meetings, and any recommendations from this Group shall be taken into account by the Subsidiary Bodies in their deliberations, and for any decisions to be taken by the Conference of the Parties on the national communications from non-Annex I parties *(see Reference)*;
6. that the Secretariat shall provide the necessary assistance to convene the meetings of the non-Annex I Experts' Group for non-Annex I communications, in accordance with article 8.2 (c) of the Convention, and as called for in paragraph 1 (a) of decision 10/CP.2; and

On matters related to consideration of non-Annex I national communications

7. that, as provided for in paragraph 2 (b) of decision 10/CP.2, and paragraph 1 (c) of decision 12/CP.4, any consideration of matters related to their national communications should take into account information on the implementation of articles 4.1, 4.3, 4.4., 4.5, 4.7, 4.8, 4.9, and 4.10, in the light of the provisions of article 3;
8. that information as compiled and synthesized by the Secretariat on non-Annex I communications as stated in paragraph 7 of decision 12/CP.4, should be taken with the relevant information provided in Annex I parties' national communications in order to allow the SBI to consider the information communicated in accordance with article 12, paragraph 1 of the FCCC, to assess the overall aggregated effect of the steps taken by the parties in the light of the latest scientific assessments concerning climate change as provided by the SBSTA in accordance with article 9.2 (a) of the FCCC;
9. that this compilation and synthesis shall be accomplished along the lines of the guidelines contained in decision 10/CP.2, in particular the information to be given in response to paragraphs 19 to 22 of the Annex to these Guidelines, on the identification of financial and technological needs;

On the review of the enabling activities of the Global Environment Facility

10. that the consistency of these enabling activities with the guidelines for the preparations of initial national communications from parties not included in Annex I to the Convention, as contained in decision 10/CP.2, and the guidance to the Global Environment Facility as contained in decision 11/CP.2, as well as with previous and subsequent guidance provided by the Conference of the Parties to the Global Environment Facility as an operating entity of the financial mechanism of the Convention, shall be fully examined and demonstrated in the review of the enabling activities of the GEF, and
11. that a report shall be requested from the GEF to the Conference of the Parties on the results of this review.

Reference

Non-Annex I Expert Group

Steering Committee

Tasks:

1. Define work plan
2. Meet quarterly
3. Define agendas for the Expert Group Meetings

Members: Regional representations (4 per region)
Annex I experts as observers

4 Expert Group Meetings along Thematic Lines

Participation: Experts nominated by parties and selected (if necessary) by the steering committee

Themes: Greenhouse gas inventory
Vulnerability assessment and adaption options
Abatement issues
Preparation of national communications

Duration: Minimum 7 days

Frequency: Each thematic group would meet once a year

Number: ±50 participants/region

Feedback to the process:

- each thematic meeting would breakdown work in regional working groups
- recommendations and conclusions would be made available to the COP/SBS
- recommendations would have "regional" perspectives/dimensions and where appropriate "global" perspectives

Position Papers on Draft Decisions for COP-5 Submitted by the Group of 77 and China*

Paper No. 1: Philippines
(On behalf of the Group 77 and China)

Initial and Subsequent National Communications from Parties Not Included in Annex I to the Convention

The Conference of the Parties

Basing itself on articles 4.3, 4.7, 12.1, and 10.2 (a) of the Convention,

Reiterating the primary important of the provision of financial and technical support, and

* Contained in document FCCC/SBI/1999/MISC.3 of 6 July 1999.

related technology transfer, as a means for capacity-building for the preparations of national communications,

Recalling its decisions on communications from parties not included in Annex I to the Convention, in particular decisions 10/CP.2, 11/CP.2, 2/CP.4, and 12/CP.4,

Underlining paragraph 1 (d) of decision 11/CP.2, which states that the Global Environment Facility should take into account that the preparation of national communications is a continuing process,

Underlining also the grave concern of non–Annex I parties that lack of support for post-national communication activities has resulted in serious disruption of the implementation of the Convention at the national level,

Deploring the use of workshops on non–Annex I national communications, outside the UNFCCC Secretariat process, for purposes which are not compatible with the Convention and contrary to its decisions,

Decides

On guidelines and guidance,

1. that, until full information on the use of these guidelines by all parties not included in Annex I is obtained from the compilation and synthesis of initial and second national communications as called for in decision 12/CP.4, and a decision taken by the Conference of the Parties to revise these guidelines, the Guidelines for the preparations of initial national communications by parties not included in Annex I to the Convention, contained in the Annex to decision 10/CP.2, shall remain valid, together with the guidance given to the Global Environment Facility in decision 11/CP.2;
2. that the use of these guidelines shall be the basis of any workshop on non–Annex I communications to be held for the purpose of responding to the needs of developing countries for the preparations of their national communications;
3. that, as stated in paragraph 2 (c) of decision 10/CP.2, non–Annex I parties which wish to submit voluntarily additional information may use elements from the guidelines approved for parties included in Annex I to the Convention when preparing their initial communications, and that they may likewise do so when preparing their subsequent national communications;

On timing of submissions of non–Annex I national communications

4. that, given the small number of developing countries which have as yet submitted their national communications, and given the provision of article 12.5 stating that the COP shall take into account the differentiated timetable

set by that article in determining the frequency of subsequent communications, as well as the timing of the submissions of first and second national communications from non–Annex I parties, timetables for submission of subsequent national communications shall differ for each non–Annex I party. Full information from the operating entity of the financial mechanism on the effective availability of financial resources to the party, and the timing of the disbursement of these resources to developing countries for the preparations of their initial and second national communications would be necessary to the determination of each non–Annex I party's timing of submissions, in accordance with article 4.3 and article 12.5 of the Convention;

On financial and technical support

5. that a non–Annex I Group of Experts shall be set up, on the basis of nominations received from Governments of non–Annex I parties in order to assess the availability of financial resources and technical support, to identify gaps, and also for the purposes of exchange of experiences and information, with the objective of enhancing support to preparations, and identifying the difficulties encountered by developing countries in the use of the guidelines, so as to improve the national communications of non–Annex I countries. This Group shall meet regularly, and be given the necessary resources to do so. Results of their meetings, and any recommendations from this Group shall be taken into account by the Subsidiary Bodies in their deliberations, and for any decisions to be taken by the Conference of the Parties on the national communications from non–Annex I parties *(see Reference)*;
6. that the Secretariat shall provide the necessary assistance to convene the meetings of the non–Annex I Experts' Group for non–Annex I communications, in accordance with article 8.2 (c) of the Convention, and as called for in paragraph 1 (a) of decision 10/CP.2; and

On matters related to consideration of non–Annex I national communications

7. that, as provided for in paragraph 2 (b) of decision 10/CP.2, and paragraph 1 (c) of decision 12/CP.4, any consideration of matters related to their national communications should take into account information on the implementation of articles 4.1, 4.3, 4.4., 4.5, 4.7, 4.8, 4.9, and 4.10, in the light of the provisions of article 3;
8. that information as compiled and synthesized by the Secretariat on non–Annex I communications as stated in paragraph 7 of decision 12/CP.4, should be taken with the relevant information provided in Annex I parties' national communications in order to allow the SBI to consider the information communicated in accordance with article 12, paragraph 1 of the FCCC, to assess the overall aggregated effect of the steps taken by the parties in the light of the latest scientific assessments concerning climate change as provided by the SBSTA in accordance with article 9.2 (a) of the FCCC;

9. that this compilation and synthesis shall be accomplished along the lines of the guidelines contained in decision 10/CP.2, in particular the information to be given in response to paragraphs 19 to 22 of the Annex to these Guidelines, on the identification of financial and technological needs;

On the review of the enabling activities of the Global Environment Facility

10. that the consistency of these enabling activities with the guidelines for the preparations of initial national communications from parties not included in Annex I to the Convention, as contained in decision 10/CP.2, and the guidance to the Global Environment Facility as contained in decision 11/CP.2, as well as with previous and subsequent guidance provided by the Conference of the Parties to the Global Environment Facility as an operating entity of the financial mechanism of the Convention, shall be fully examined and demonstrated in the review of the enabling activities of the GEF; and
11. that a report shall be requested from the GEF to the Conference of the Parties on the results of this review.

Reference

Non–Annex I Expert Group

Steering Committee

Tasks:

1. Define work plan
2. Meet quarterly
3. Define agendas for the Expert Group Meetings

Members: Regional representations (4 per region)
Annex I experts as observers

4. Expert Group Meetings along Thematic Lines

Participation: Experts nominated by parties and selected (if necessary) by the steering committee

Themes: Greenhouse gas inventory
Vulnerability assessment and adaption options
Abatement issues
Preparation of national communications

Duration: Minimum 7 days

Frequency: Each thematic group would meet once a year

Number: ±50 participants/region

Feedback to the process:

- each thematic meeting would break down work in regional working groups
- recommendations and conclusions would be made available to the COP/SBS
- recommendations would have "regional" perspectives/dimensions and where appropriate "global" perspective

Proposal by The Gambia

(On behalf of the Group of 77 and China)*

Draft Decision on Capacity-Building for Developing Countries

The Conference of the Parties,

Recalling articles 4.1, 4.3, 4.5, and 4.7, taken within the context of article 3, and also articles 5(c) and 6(b) of the Convention;

Recalling further the provisions for capacity-building for developing countries contained in decision 7/CP.4 (Work Programme on Mechanisms of the Kyoto Protocol); decisions 10/CP.2 and 12/CP.4 (National Communications of non–Annex I parties); decisions 9/CP.3 and 4/CP.4 (Development and Transfer of Technologies); decision 5/CP.4 (Implementation of article 4.8 and 4.9 of the Convention); decision 6/CP.4 (Activities Implemented Jointly under the pilot phase); decision 14/CP.4 (Research and systematic Observation); and decisions 11/CP.2 and 2/CP.4 (on Guidance to the Global Environment Facility);

Underlining that capacity-building is for and by developing countries, and activities for capacity-building are to be undertaken in developing countries, within the context of the FCCC, and under the guidance of the intergovernmental process of the Convention;

Recognising that the developing countries, in particular the least developed countries and the Small Island Developing States amongst them, because of their

* Contained in document FCCC/SB/1999/MISC.9 of 24 August 1999.

vulnerability to the adverse effects of climate change and exposure to natural disasters, require special capacity-building initiatives;

Recognising further that the main constraints to capacity-building in developing countries, in particular the least developed countries and Small Island Developing States amongst them, include lack of access to necessary technologies and know-how, including information technology, lack of appropriate institutions, the lack of financial resources, including for participation in meetings, workshops and seminars, and lack of a regular forum for exchange of information and development of positions among developing countries;

Emphasising that capacity-building, including education, training, public awareness, and research are pre-requisites for the meaningful participation of developing countries in the FCCC and the Kyoto Protocol processes, which participation should require the cooperation of the public and private sectors, civil society, relevant financial institutions, and development partners;

Emphasising further that capacity-building is a continuous process to be undertaken at all levels, including long-term planning, and aiming at strengthening relevant institutions such as FCCC national focal points or national authorities designated to handle climate change activities, universities, sub-regional, and regional institutions, as well as human resources development, in order to provide a critical mass of specialists in all areas relating to the implementation of the Convention;

Decides,

1. to conduct capacity-building activities for the implementation of the Convention in accordance with the provisions of this decision, and the prioritised capacity-building needs for developing country parties, contained in the Annex to this decision;
2. to provide the necessary financial and technical support to strengthen UNFCCC national focal points or national authorities designated to handle climate change, including training, exchange programmes, and equipment;
3. to support national activities to develop and promote climate-related research and studies for the implementation of the FCCC through:
   - the development and strengthening of national centres of excellence;
   - assistance to these centres to enable them provide information on climate change with the use of information technology;
   - the identification of developing country institutions that can undertake activities at sub-regional, regional, and international levels; and
   - support for the networking of these developing institutions among themselves, and between them and relevant institutions in developed country parties;

4. to promote capacity-building of national institutions and expertise through:
   - the use of national experts or consultants to undertake studies, design, and implementation of projects at national level;
   - the setting-up of collaborating centres on climate change–related activities in developing countries at sub-regional or regional levels, and to use these centres to promote national capacity-building; and
   - training, seminars, and exchange programmes for the personnel of developing country institutions, in relevant institutions of other developing countries or in developed countries; and
5. to ensure that workshops for capacity-building are undertaken with the participation of developing country parties concerned, including the approval of the programmes, the presentation of technical papers, and the drawing up of conclusions.
6. to request the Chairman of the Subsidiary Body for Implementation (SBI) and the Chairman of the Subsidiary Body for Scientific and Technological Advice (SBSTA):
   (a) to examine the conformity of capacity-building activities undertaken under the Convention with the provisions contained in this decision; and
   (b) to consider capacity-building for the implementation of the Convention as a regular item in its agenda;
7. to request the Secretariat:
   (a) to prepare, for the consideration of the subsidiary bodies at their twelfth session, a plan to facilitate capacity-building activities for developing countries under this Convention, taking into account the prioritised list of needs contained in the Annex to this decision;
   (b) to continue to coordinate with the secretariats of relevant UN agencies and international organisations, and bilateral and multilateral institutions on their climate change capacity-building activities in support of the implementation of the Convention, and to report on this coordination, including information on the financing of these activities; and
   (c) to report on the implementation of the provisions of this decision on a regular basis.

Annex
List of capacity-building needs of developing country parties

1. Institutional Capacity-Building
   - Strengthening of national FCCC Focal Points or national authorities designated to coordinate climate change activities.
   - Strengthening of relevant and key academic, research, and NGO institutions.

2. Capacity-Building under CDM
    - Establishment of institutional linkages required for implementation of the CDM.
    - Project identification, formulation, and design.
    - Monitoring, verification, auditing, and certification of project activities.
    - Development of criteria including for sustainable development indicators, e.g., for adaptation.
    - Development of baselines.
    - Project negotiation skills.
    - CDM demonstration projects to enhance capacity-building (learning by doing), including assessment of costs/risks (long- and short-term).
    - Data acquisition and sharing.
3. Human Resource Development
    - Fellowships and scholarships for formal training at higher levels, specialized training and informal training.
    - Development of a "pool" of expertise and skills.
    - Climate change and other relevant studies such as climate change detection and climate variability, impact assessment, vulnerability, and adaptation studies, policy analysis.
    - Workshops (including workshops to discuss the implementation plan).
    - Exchange programmes among parties.
    - Integration of climate change into educational curricula.
    - Networking and coordination at local, national, regional, and international levels.
4. Technology Transfer
    - Identification and assessment of appropriate technologies.
    - Appropriate technology information needs including support for office and other relevant equipment.
    - Analysis of constraints to the transfer of technology (non–Annex I and Annex I).
    - Exchange programmes.
5. National Communications
    - Development of local emission factors.
    - Data collection, analysis and archiving.
    - Establishment of a Technical Assistance Group, e.g., non–Annex I expert group.
    - Vulnerability assessments, including scoping, modelling, analysis, method selection, and reporting.
6. Adaptation
    - Development of Adaptation project guidelines.
    - Case studies of extreme weather events, documentation, and dissemination of study reports.

- Capacity-building/enhancement in the marine sector, such as coastal zone management.
- Identification and promotion of traditional knowledge, skills, and practices which enhance adaptation.

7. Public Awareness
   - Develop public awareness programmes.
   - Development and production of public awareness materials.
   - Workshops.
   - Involvement and consultation.
8. Coordination and Cooperation
   - Coordination programmes at the individual, community, local, government, non-government, national, and regional levels.
   - Involvement and consultation.
   - Linking and learning.
9. Improved Decision-Making
   - Awareness and knowledge.
   - Research, data, and information.
   - Technical and policy.
   - Integrating climate change policies into national development strategies/plans.

Group of 77 and China

Submission on Article 12 of the Kyoto Protocol: The Clean Development Mechanism*

I. Nature and scope

A. Purpose

1. Article 12 of the Kyoto Protocol to the U.N. Framework Convention on Climate Change (FCCC) has defined a clean development mechanism (CDM) with the following two-fold purpose: (a) to assist developing country parties in achieving sustainable development and in contributing to the ultimate objective of the Convention, and (b) to assist developed country parties in achieving compliance with part of their quantified emission limitation and reduction commitments under article 3, and therefore each CDM project activity should meet the above two-fold purpose.

B. Principles

2. Decision 7/CP.4 has given priority to the CDM. The CDM must be taken up first for discussion and decision.

* Contained in document FCCC/SB/1999/MISC.10/Add.2 of 30 October 1999.

3. The principles for the CDM and other basic elements must be decided first. The methodological and operational questions will be guided accordingly. These principles must be in keeping with article 3 of the Convention.
4. The principles for the CDM are as follows:

(a) Nature and Scope:

1) The CDM is a project-based mechanism conceived and introduced in the Protocol with a two-fold purpose: (a) to assist developing country parties in achieving sustainable development and in contributing to the ultimate objective of the Convention, and (b) to assist developed country parties in achieving compliance with part of their quantified emission limitation and reduction commitments under article 3.
2) Unlike the other mechanisms provided for in the Kyoto Protocol, the CDM is the only mechanism of the Protocol which involves the participation in CDM project activities by both the developed and developing country parties.
3) Developed country parties will fund projects in developing country parties which will assist sustainable development.
4) Developed country parties may involve private and/or public entities for such funding. In return, the developed country party, funding the project, will be enabled to meet part of its emission reduction commitment.
5) The Protocol has made provision for certifying the emissions reduced from a CDM project. Accordingly, "certified emission reductions" (CERs) will accrue. The CERs will enable the participating developed country party to contribute to compliance with part of its quantified emission limitation and reduction commitments under article 3 to the extent permissible under the principle of "supplementarity" to be decided.
6) It must be ensured that "a share of the proceeds from certified project activities" is used to meet costs of adaptation. For this purpose, *inter alia*, a CDM adaptation fund should be established.

(b) Equity:
The principle of equity in the Convention must apply to all aspects of the CDM based on equitable developmental rights and balanced regional activity. The right to development of developing countries must not be affected adversely in any way. It must be ensured that the CDM does not have dormant any possibility or potential of freezing or perpetuating existing inequities between developed and developing countries.

The COP/MOP shall review periodically the implementation of CDM project activities and their geographical spread, and take appropriate action to promote the principle of equity.

(c) Climate Change Effectiveness:
Climate change effectiveness must be in terms of real, measurable and long-term benefits related to the mitigation of climate change at the project level. This should be addressed by taking into account the additional reduction in emissions at the CDM project level as against the baseline of the CDM project activity. The benefits related to a project activity would be recognized as real if the actual greenhouse gas (GHG) emissions can be shown to be less than the project baseline. The benefits would be recognized as measurable if the actual level of GHG emissions of the project case and the level of GHG emissions in the project baseline can be established with a reasonable degree of certainty. The benefits of a project activity would be recognized as long-term if the emission reduction persists over an appropriate period of time taking into account the differences in the lifespans of different CDM project activities, and bearing in mind article 2 of the Convention.

(d) Sustainable Development Priorities:
Sustainable development priorities must be set by national authorities. The priorities depend upon the specific requirements of a developing country party. CDM project activities must contribute to sustainable development. The developing country party where the CDM project activity is proposed to be set up shall be the sole judge for deciding whether that project activity meets its national sustainable development objectives and priorities.

(e) Funding Additionality:
Funding for CDM project activity shall be additional to ODA, GEF, and other financial commitments of the developed country parties.

(f) Transparency:
The principle of transparency must be observed in the design and application of all CDM activities, including project identification, design, and implementation; and approval, certification, monitoring, and verification, establishment of baselines, operations of the executive board, as well as regarding all costs, risks, and liabilities to be incurred by the developing country party.

(g) Special Needs of Least Developed Countries:
The special needs of least developed countries have to be addressed both from the point of view of identifying their special technology needs and of capacity-building. The capacity-building effort should be in the direction of build-up of endogenous expertise for identifying technology needs and helping enhance capacities for assimilation of technology. Least developed country parties need assistance to build up capacity in monitoring, reporting, and verifying emissions; and in the selection, design, and evaluation of CDM project activities.

(h) Capacity-Building:
Capacity-building is central for ensuring wider participation, and should be incorporated in all CDM project activities. Capacity-building should include the build-up of endogenous expertise for identifying technology needs and helping enhance capacities for assimilation of technology. Developing country parties will also need to develop capacity in monitoring, reporting, and verifying emissions; and in the design, implementation, and evaluation of CDM project activities. In implementation of the CDM project activities, to the extent possible, the capacity and capability of developing country parties at the national, sub-regional, and regional levels, through bilateral and multilateral should be explored. At the national level, these approaches should be informed by the widest possible participation.

(i) Adaptation:
As provided for and listed in article 4.8 of the Convention and article 12.8 of the Protocol, developing country parties that are particularly vulnerable will be assisted to meet the costs of adaptation. The COP/MOP of the Protocol shall ensure that a share of the proceeds from certified project activities is used to cover these costs. For this purpose, *inter alia*, a CDM adaptation fund should be established. The institutional and organizational aspects related to adaptation in the context of certified project activities require elaboration in detail. Developing country parties should identify adaptation projects for funding, and should follow a process of adaptation options identification. Consideration of this aspect should be consistent with ongoing work on adaptation under the Convention. Developing country parties should be assisted with capacity-building at all levels in order to be able to carry out such activities.

(j) Compliance:
Appropriate and effective procedures and mechanisms to determine and to address cases of non-compliance with the provisions of this Protocol should be established. The procedures and mechanisms should be underpinned by the principles of the Convention.

(k) Criteria for Project Eligibility:
Eligible project activities, apart from meeting national sustainable development priorities, must ensure access to environmentally sound technology needed by the developing country party participating in the CDM project activity.

(l) Transparency, Non-Discrimination, Prevention of Distortion of Competition:
All developing country parties can participate in CDM project activities. No unilateral measures for CDM participation should preclude a developing country party from participating in any CDM project activity. Transparency should be encouraged in all CDM project activities, including for project identification, design, and

implementation; and verification, monitoring, and reporting, as well as regarding all costs, risks, and liabilities to be incurred by the developing country party.

(m) Institutional Framework:
The institutions as provided for in article 12 of the Kyoto Protocol shall follow the principles and the nature and scope of the CDM. At the same time, it is recognized that the institutional framework will be based on representativity.

C. "Part of"/supplementarity

5. It must be ensured that CDM project activities shall be supplemental to domestic actions by developed country parties to meet "part of" their quantified emission limitation or reduction commitments. The design and implementation of the CDM must not in any way compromise the modification of longer-term trends in greenhouse gas anthropogenic emissions and concentrations. All the mechanisms, including the CDM, must be supplemental to domestic actions for GHG limitation and reduction. Guidelines on supplementarity must be developed taking into account articles 2 and 3.2 of the Kyoto Protocol. Commensurate non-compliance processes must be put in place. Developed country access to the CDM mechanism should be contingent on satisfaction of prescribed domestic effort in fulfilment of commitments under article 3.

D. Participation

6. Unlike the other mechanisms provided for in the Kyoto Protocol, the CDM is the only mechanism of the Protocol which involves the participation in CDM project activities by both the developed and developing country parties. Developed country parties will fund projects in developing country parties which will assist sustainable development. Parties are responsible for the involvement of their private and/or public entities in CDM project activities subject to guidance provided by the executive board.
   6.1. The parties participating in the CDM project activities must be responsible at all stages and in all aspects for the project activity in which they are participating. Any costs, risks or liabilities that have not been expressly accepted by the developing country party before approval of the CDM project activity shall be assumed to be the responsibility of the participating developed country party.

E. Share of Proceeds

7. Developing country parties that are particularly vulnerable, as listed in article 4.8 of the Convention, will be assisted to meet the costs of adaptation from, *inter alia*, a CDM adaptation fund. The COP/MOP of the Protocol shall ensure that a share of the proceeds from certified project activities is used to cover these costs. Detailed modalities will be required. The COP/MOP shall

also ensure that a share of the proceeds from certified project activities is used to cover administrative expenses for these activities.

II. Methodological and operational issues

A. Project validation/registration

8. The CDM is a project-based mechanism conceived and introduced in the Protocol with a two-fold purpose. Eligible project activities, apart from meeting national sustainable development priorities, must ensure access to environmentally-sound technology needed by the developing country party participating in the CDM project activity. The Protocol has made provision for certification of the emission reductions resulting from each CDM project activity. Accordingly, "certified emission reductions" (CERs) will accrue to the developed country party participating in the project activity, to enable that country to contribute to compliance with quantified emission limitation and reduction commitments under article 3.
   - 8.1 The establishment of baselines for the determination of emissions reduction should be made on a project-by-project basis. The establishment of the baseline will quantify the level of emissions that most likely would have occurred in the absence of the certified CDM project activity.
   - 8.2 Independent auditing of project activities may be done by public or private sector entities not involved in the identification, development or management of the project. There is need to develop uniform auditing practices. Verification has to be carried out by independent entities that have had no operational or financial links with the project, and that are fully accountable to COP/MOP which shall exercise authority and guidance over all aspects of the CDM. The composition of any team should be approved by the developing country party participating in the CDM project activity.
   - 8.3 The developing country party participating in the project activity should be the sole judge for determining whether any CDM project under consideration meets the country's sustainable development requirements.

B. Project financing

9. Developed country parties will fund projects in developing country parties which will assist sustainable development. Developed country parties may involve private and/or public entities for such funding. In return, the developed country party, funding the project, will be enabled to meet part of its emission reduction commitment. The Protocol has made provision for certifying the emissions reduced from a CDM project. Accordingly, "certified emission reductions" (CERs) will accrue. Funding of CDM projects by developed countries shall be additional to ODA, GEF, and other financial commitments of the developed country parties.

C. Project Monitoring

10. Independent auditing of project activities may be done by public or private sector entities not involved in the identification, development or management of the project. There is need to develop uniform auditing practices.

D. Project Verification

11. Verification has to be carried out by independent entities that have had no operational or financial links with the project, and that are fully accountable to COP/MOP, which shall exercise authority and guidance over all aspects of the CDM. The composition of any team should be approved by the developing country party participating in the CDM project activity.

E. Certification/issuance of CERs

12. The Protocol has made provision for certification of the emission reductions resulting from each CDM project activity. Accordingly, "certified emission reductions" (CERs) will accrue to the developed country party participating in the project activity, to enable that country to contribute to compliance with its quantified emission limitation and reduction commitments under article 3.
    - 12.1 According to article 3.12 of the Protocol: "Any certified emission reductions which a party acquires from another Party in accordance with the provisions of Article 12 shall be added to the assigned amount for the acquiring Party." The assigned amount is the quantified greenhouse gas (GHG) emission limitation and reduction commitment of Annex B parties for the commitment period from 2008 to 2012, which shall be equal to the percentage inscribed for it in Annex B of its aggregate anthropogenic carbon dioxide equivalent emissions of the GHGs listed in Annex A of the Protocol in 1990, or the base year or period determined in accordance with paragraph 5 of article 3 of the Protocol, multiplied by five.
    - 12.2 The operational entities to be designated by the COP/MOP shall certify the emission reductions resulting from each project activity on the basis laid out in article 12.5 of the Protocol. Guidelines to carry out the certification should be elaborated.

F. Issues Related to Compliance

13. Appropriate and effective procedures and mechanisms to determine and to address cases of non-compliance with the provisions of this Protocol should be established. The procedures and mechanisms should be underpinned by the principles of the Convention. These need further elaboration. The design and implementation of the CDM must not in any way compromise the modification of longer-term trends in greenhouse gas anthropogenic emissions and concentrations.

13.1 All the mechanisms, including the CDM, must be supplemental to domestic actions for GHG limitation and reduction. Guidelines on supplementarity must be developed taking into account articles 2 and 3.2 of the Kyoto Protocol. Commensurate non-compliance processes must be put in place. Developed country parties' participation in CDM project activities should be contingent on satisfaction of prescribed domestic effort in fulfilment of commitments under article 3.

G. Adaptation Assistance

14. As provided for, and listed in article 4.8 of the Convention, and Article 12.8 of the Protocol, developing country parties that are particularly vulnerable will be assisted to meet the costs of adaptation. For this purpose, *inter alia*, a CDM adaptation fund should be established. The institutional and organizational aspects related to adaptation in the context of certified project activities require elaboration in detail. Developing country parties should identify adaptation projects for funding, and follow a process of adaptation options identification. Consideration of this aspect should be consistent with ongoing work on adaptation under the Convention. Developing country parties should be assisted with capacity-building at all levels in order to be able to carry out such activities.

H. Registries

I. Reporting by Parties

15. The format for reporting must be in a standardized format across all CDM projects. The reporting requirements should be as simple as possible so as to enable local human resources to fulfil these requirements.

III. Institutional issues

A. Role of the COP/MOP

16. As stated in article 7 of the Convention, the COP is the supreme body of the Convention which shall keep under regular review the implementation of the Convention and any related legal instruments that the COP may adopt, such as the Kyoto Protocol. There shall be full accountability of the executive board to the COP/MOP which shall exercise authority and guidance over all aspects of the CDM.

16.1 The COP, in implementation of decision 1/CP.3, started work on items related to specific provisions of the Kyoto Protocol. Accordingly, the COP adopted decisions 5/CP.4 (Implementation of articles 4.8 and 4.9 of the Convention, decision 3/CP.3 and articles 2.3 and 3.14 of the Kyoto Protocol); 7/CP.4 on the Work programme on mechanisms of the Kyoto Protocol; and decision 8/CP.4 on Preparations for the first session of the COP/MOP. The CDM shall be subject to the authority and guidance of the COP/MOP and be supervised by an executive board of the CDM.

The COP/MOP shall review periodically the implementation of CDM project activities and their geographical spread, and take appropriate action to promote the principle of equity.

16.2 The COP/MOP shall also ensure that a share of the proceeds from certified project activities is used to cover administrative expenses for these activities. Detailed modalities will be required.

B. Executive Board

17. The executive board shall be fully accountable to the COP/MOP. Its composition shall be on the basis of equitable geographical representation, and it should be functionally small. Under the authority and guidance of the COP/MOP the executive board shall supervise the CDM, and shall provide guidance for the involvement of private and/or public entities in CDM project activities.

C. Operational Entities

18. Operational entities to certify emissions reductions resulting from each CDM project activity shall be designated by the COP/MOP.

D. Parties

19. The parties participating in the CDM project activities must be responsible at all stages and in all aspects for the project activity in which they are participating. Any costs, risks, or liabilities that have not been expressly accepted by the developing country party before approval of the CDM project activity shall be assumed to be the responsibility of the participating developed country party.

E. Administrative support

20. The COP/MOP shall also ensure that a share of the proceeds from certified project activities is used to cover administrative expenses for these activities. Detailed modalities will be required.

F. Review

21. As stated in article 7 of the Convention, the COP is the supreme body of the Convention which shall keep under regular review the implementation of the Convention and any related legal instruments that the COP may adopt, such as the Kyoto Protocol.

    21.1 SBSTA should be requested to study the implications of article 12.10 of the Protocol and to propose recommendations. Submissions from parties could be requested by SBSTA on their views on these implications.

    21.2 The outcome of the methodological work on articles 3.3 and 3.4 of the Protocol shall be awaited.

Note: Further elaboration will be made on this submission.

Group of 77 and China Submission on Article 17 of the Kyoto Protocol*

Nature and Scope

A. Purpose

1. The purpose of "emissions trading" under article 17 of the Kyoto Protocol is to assist parties included in Annex B in fulfilling part of their commitments under article 3. According to article 3, the parties included in Annex I shall, individually or jointly ensure that their aggregate anthropogenic carbon dioxide equivalent emissions of the greenhouse gases listed in Annex A do not exceed their assigned amounts, calculated pursuant to their quantified emission limitation and reduction commitments inscribed in Annex B, with a view to reducing their overall emissions of such gases by at least 5 per cent below 1990 levels in the quantified emission limitation and reduction commitment period, from 2008 to 2012. If an Annex B party is able to limit or reduce its GHG emissions to an extent which exceeds its quantified limitation and reduction objectives, such excess limitation or reduction can be transferred to any other Annex B party under the provisions of article 17. Such excess limitation and reduction of emissions shall be subtracted from the assigned amount for the transferring party, and be added to the assigned amount for the acquiring party.

B. Principles

2. The principles for article 17 and the other basic elements pertaining to this article must be decided first and formulated accordingly. These principles and basic elements must be in conformity with article 3 of the Convention. The methodological and operational issues must be guided accordingly.
   2.1 According to article 3, the parties included in Annex I shall, individually or jointly, ensure that their aggregate anthropogenic carbon dioxide equivalent emissions of the greenhouse gases listed in Annex A do not exceed their assigned amounts, calculated pursuant to their quantified emission limitation and reduction commitments inscribed in Annex B, with a view to reducing their overall emissions of such gases by at least 5 per cent below 1990 levels in the quantified emission limitation and reduction commitment period, from 2008 to 2012. The assigned amount is the quantified greenhouse gas emission limitation and reduction commitment of Annex B parties for the commitment period from 2008 to 2012, which shall be equal to the percentage inscribed for it in Annex B of its aggregate anthropogenic carbon dioxide equivalent emissions of the greenhouse gases listed in Annex A of the Protocol in 1990, or the base

* Contained in document FCCC/SB/1999/MISC.10/Add.4 of 5 November 1999.

year or period determined in accordance with paragraph 5 of article 3 of the Protocol, multiplied by five.

2.2 Of fundamental importance is the environmental integrity of the system to be brought in place under article 17 and its credibility. It must be ensured that the system does not have dormant any possibility or potential of freezing or perpetuating existing inequities between Annex B parties on the one hand and developing country parties on the other. The right to development of developing countries must not be affected adversely in any way. It is recognized that the Protocol has not created or bestowed any right, title or entitlement. The rules to be formulated must conform to the principles.

2.3 Any Annex B party participating in the system to be established under article 17 shall establish and maintain a transparent national registration of "transfers" and "acquisitions." Such information shall be communicated regularly to the Convention Secretariat. Annex B parties participating in the transfers and acquisitions of parts of assigned amounts under article 17 of the Protocol, shall include in their national inventory, to be communicated to the Secretariat under article 7.1 of the Protocol, information on any part of an assigned amount added to or removed from its national registration during the relevant year. If an Annex B party is in non-compliance with its commitments, that part of the assigned amount that has been "transferred" shall be invalidated.

2.4 Any system established under article 17 of the Protocol shall contribute to and bring about real, measurable, and long-term benefits related to mitigation of climate change. It should not lead to overall increase in the GHG emissions of the developed country parties.

C. Supplementarity

3. Article 17 states: "Any such trading shall be supplemental to domestic actions for the purpose of meeting quantified emission limitation and reduction commitments under that Article."

3.1 The design and implementation of any system under article 17 must not in any way compromise the modification of longer-term trends in greenhouse gas anthropogenic emissions and concentrations. Commensurate non-compliance processes must be put in place. Annex B parties access to article 17 should be contingent on satisfaction of prescribed domestic effort in fulfilment of commitments under article 3. The rules will lay down the conditions which must be fulfilled before any such transfers and acquisitions can occur.

D. Participation

4. Article 17 states: "The Parties included in Annex B may participate in emissions trading for the purposes of fulfilling their commitments under Article 3."

Annex B parties have quantified greenhouse gas emission limitation and reduction commitments stipulated in Annex B of the Protocol. Annex B parties, individually or jointly, have to ensure that their aggregate anthropogenic carbon dioxide equivalent emissions of the GHGs listed in Annex A of the Protocol do not exceed their assigned amounts, which is the emission limitation and reduction commitment of Annex B parties for the commitment period from 2008 to 2012.

4.1 Parties included in Annex B shall be eligible to "transfer" or "acquire" part of the assigned amount, if they:
   (a) are in compliance with articles 3, 5, and 7 of the Protocol and are responsible for meeting their commitments under the Protocol;
   (b) are not in violation of the compliance procedures as referred to in article 18 of the Protocol;
   (c) have a transparent national system for registration and verification of such "transfers" and "acquisitions."

Note: Further elaboration will be made on this submission.

Financial Mechanism

Draft Decision Submitted of the Group of 77 and China*

The Philippines (On behalf of the Group of 77 and China)

Additional guidance to the operating entity of the financial mechanism

The Conference of the Parties,

Recalling its decisions 11/CP.1, 10/CP.2, 11/CP.2, 12/CP.2, and 2/CP.4;

Welcoming the launch of negotiations on the third replenishment of GEF, and urging the Annex II parties to increase their contributions to the GEF Trust Fund;

1. *Decides* that, in accordance with articles 4.3, 4.5, and 11.1 of the Convention, the GEF, as an operating entity of the financial mechanism, shall provide financial resources to developing country parties, in particular the least developed and the Small Island Developing States amongst them, to:
   (a) implement country-driven Stage II adaptation activities that build upon work done at the national level, either in preparation of national communications or from in-depth national studies, and develop demonstration

* Contained in document FCCC/SBI/2000/MISC.1 of 11 September 2000.

projects ("learning-by-doing") aimed at identifying and subsequently implementing viable options for Stage III adaptation activities;

(b) support the continuation of the "country-team" approach which enhances the collection, analysis, interpretation, and dissemination of data on climate change issues and increases national commitment to the implementation of the objective of the Convention;

(c) establish and/or strengthen national, subregional, or regional databases on climate change;

(d) develop and implement prioritized projects identified in their national communications;

(e) enhance the capacity of their subregional and/or regional information networks to enable such networks to serve as repositories of climate change related information on vulnerability and adaptation assessments and geographic information systems;

(f) improve climate change related data collection (e.g., local emission factors) and information-gathering, as well as the analysis, interpretation, and dissemination of this data to national policymakers and other end-users;

(g) establish and/or strengthen subregional and/or regional climate change related institutions and "centers of excellence," to enable these centers and institutions to provide a supportive framework, including for information retrieval and technical support;

(h) on submission of their initial national communications, to undertake, in the preparation of their subsequent national communications, more in depth public awareness and education activities and community involvement and participation in climate change issues;

(i) capacity-building for disaster preparedness and disaster management, including contingency planning for droughts and floods in areas prone to extreme weather events;

(j) strengthen existing and, where appropriate, establish early warning systems for extreme weather events in an integrated and interdisciplinary manner to assist particularly vulnerable parties.

2. Requests the GEF to:

(a) continue its efforts aimed at minimizing the time between approval of project concepts, development and approval of the related projects, and the disbursement of funds by its Implementing Agencies to the recipient countries of those projects;

(b) ensure that its Implementing Agencies are more responsive to requests for GEF assistance from developing country parties for climate change related project activities aimed at implementing the guidance of the COP;

(c) further enhance the use of national experts and/or consultants in all aspects of project development and implementation. In this regard, it should make its roster of experts available to developing country parties through the institutions referred to in paragraphs 1 (e and/or g) above;

(d) further streamline its project cycle with a view to ensuring that there is only one GEF project cycle for all GEF activities within its Implementing Agencies;

(e) give consideration to recommending that its Second Assembly increases the number of Implementing Agencies, thereby ensuring that developing country parties have more opportunities available to them for accessing GEF funds for climate change activities aimed at implementing the guidance of the COP.

3. Further requests the GEF to include in its report to the seventh session of the Conference of the Parties the specific steps it has taken to implement the provisions of this decision.

Paper No. 3:
Submission by Ghana on behalf of the Group of 77 and China*
Accra, 4 September 2002

Capacity-Building in Non–Annex I Parties

Ghana on behalf of the G-77 and China considers the review of the activities of the GEF in relation to capacity-building in Non–Annex I countries as timely, and welcomes the opportunity to express her views on the extent to which the implementation of the capacity needs self-assessment projects addresses activities identified under the initial scope of needs and areas for capacity-building listed in the annex to decision 2/CP.7

The Group of 77 and China acknowledges the importance of the decision made in Marrakech at COP-7 in relation to capacity-building in developing countries (decision 2/CP.7). From decision 2/CP.7 and other relevant decisions, the COP urged Global Environment Facility (GEF) to adopt a streamlined and expedited approach in financing activities within the framework on capacity-building.

The COP further requested the GEF as an operating entity of the financial mechanism to report on its progress in support of the implementation of the capacity-building in its report to the Conference of the Parties.

In the annex to decision 2/CP.7 parties agreed that the framework for capacity-building should be implemented promptly and developing countries which have already identified their capacity-building priorities through ongoing work aimed at the implementation of the Convention should be able to promptly implement capacity-building activities under the framework.

* Contained in document FCCC/SBI/2002/MISC.7 of 13 September 2002.

The Group of 77 and China welcomes the creation of the special climate change fund to finance capacity-building activities adopted under the Marrakech Accords and urges the GEF to facilitate the operationalisation of the fund so that capacity-building activities under the Convention and the Kyoto Protocol would receive additional financial support for effective implementation.

The G-77 and China have noted that the GEF is providing funds to implement decision 2/CP4 and the National Capacity Self-Assessment (NCSA) programme. We do not see direct action by GEF to assist developing countries in implementing decision 2/CP7. We therefore urge the GEF to do more in complying fully with the guidance provided by the decision 2/CP7 and 3/CP.7, in particular the capacity-building activities relating to the preparation of national inventories and establishment of national systems. The extent to which developing countries can contribute to addressing the global problem of climate change and also effectively participate in the climate change negotiation process will depend on the level of capacities in our countries.

Financial Mechanism: Funding under the Convention

Position of G-77 and China on Funding under the Convention*

The UNFCCC is based upon few key pillars that include the principle of common but differentiated responsibilities and respective capabilities of the parties, with developed country parties taking the lead, as well as access to financial and technological resources for developing country parties. The explicit requirement in the UNFCCC concerning the developed country parties to "take the lead" is the very soul of the Convention in attaining the goals of combating climate change and the adverse effects thereof.

The relevant provisions of the UNFCCC, especially articles 4 and 11, as well as the relevant decisions 11 and 15 of COP-1 and decision 7 of COP-7 need to be taken into account as regards funding under the Convention.

Furthermore, decision 7 of COP-7 is explicit on the need for "new and additional" financial contributions to the climate change focal area of the GEF, as well as that "predictable and adequate level of funding shall be made available to Parties not included in Annex I."

It is our view that the time-bound and effective implementation of relevant decisions of the Conference of the Parties on funding including decision 7 of COP-7 is essential to take the Convention process forward by a concrete step on the part of the developed country parties to take an effective lead in this direction.

We consider that the following steps are essential to realizing the aspirations of the developing country parties and their confidence in the Convention process:

* Contained in document FCCC/SBI/2002/MISC.9 of 29 October 2002.

STEPS

(i) Provide specific guidance to GEF for effective operationalization of the recently established funds and greater effectiveness of the existing funds.
(ii) Ensure automaticity and enhance contributions to the recently established funds to address vulnerability and adaptation.
(iii) Ensure that the project cycle is streamlined, make project identification country-driven, and the procedures simple and transparent.
(iv) Ensure that there is a quantum jump in the GEF trust funds, which have been stagnating at US$2–3 billion per cycle, in respect of the climate change focal area.
(v) Provide guidance to GEF for funding projects involving technologies with large potential for replication in non–Annex I countries, including adaptation technologies.
(vi) Ensure that GEF funding is not tied implicitly or explicitly to particular co-financing sources, including implementing agencies.
(vii) Establish norms for funding adaptation projects as distinct from GHG abatement projects.
(viii) Ensure adequate funding for effective implementation of capacity-building needs.

In order to ensure that the Convention process in this respect is expedited and for effective compliance of the above-mentioned decisions of the COP, we are of the view that there is need for setting up an "Expert Group on Funding" (EGF) under the Convention. The EGF could be established by virtue of decision of the COP and may comprise ten members with equal participation of expert nominated by Annex I and non–Annex I countries. These experts, apart from usual conditions related to conflict of interest, should be independent of GEF as well as the implementing agencies. The Terms of Reference of the EFG would relate to the above steps.

Since the funding under the Convention is a cross-cutting issue, the developing country concerns on other relevant agenda items concerning financial mechanism, must be duly reflected and incorporated in the final decisions of the Conference of the Parties.

Paper No. 8:
Tanzania on behalf of the Group of 77 and China

Submission by the Group of 77 and China on Views Regarding Capacity-Building Issues (FCCC/SBI/2002/17 para. 35)*

The United Republic of Tanzania, on behalf of the Group of 77 and China, welcomes this opportunity to submit its views on issues relating to capacity-building. The

* Contained in document FCCC/SBI/2003/MISC.5 of 8 May 2003.

group considers the review of the implementation of 2/CP.7 as an important process in laying out the foundation for the effective implementation of the provisions of the decision. In this regard, the Group of 77 and China expresses its views on the following:

1. *The progress report prepared by the Secretariat on the status of activities to implement decisions 2/CP.7 and 3/CP.7 (FCCC/SBI/2002/INF.15).*

The Group of 77 and China welcomes the preparation of the document as an initial progress report by the Secretariat on the status of capacity-building activities by parties and international organizations. The G-77 and China, however, express the view some of the activities identified were not implemented in response to capacity-building decisions since these activities have been in the pipeline before the adoption of the decisions. In this regard, the group wishes to take note of the questions raised in paragraph 70 of the document, in particular, paragraph 70(c) which deals on the question of identifying the specific scope of activities in each priority area.

In preparing future progress reports, the G-77 and China proposed that the Secretariat should develop a methodology for assessing the quality of implementation of capacity-building activities to include their effectiveness and identify possible areas for improvements.

2. *Detailed elements, methodologies and guidelines for the comprehensive review of the implementation of the capacity-building framework for developing countries and information on implementation of decision 2/CP.7 by developing country parties.*

The G-77 and China is of the view that a thorough review process of the implementation of the Capacity-Building Framework for developing countries should be conducted. Attention should be given on projects and programmes that have been launched by parties, bilateral and multilateral agencies, the Global Environment Facility and international organizations in response to decision 2/CP.7. An analysis on the effectiveness of these capacity-building activities in building and sustaining the capacities of developing countries to effectively participate in the Convention and Kyoto Protocol.

The comprehensive review process should contain the following elements:

a. An analysis of current implementation of projects and programmes implemented in response to decision 2/CP.7 and other related activities. The analysis may involve identifying success stories, challenges, and opportunities for effective implementation. Information may be drawn from national communications and submissions from parties, reports from the GEF, bilateral and multilateral agencies, international organizations, and non-government organizations.
b. Identify gaps in implementation and possible areas for further improvement in implementation. Particular focus should be given to the issue of

sustainability of capacity-building activities, allocation of resources, and participation of NGOs and private sector entities.

c. Outline steps to be undertaken by the Subsidiary Body for Implementation, with the assistance of the Secretariat, in monitoring capacity-building activities related to 2/CP.7. Related to this is establishing a process whereby the SBI and the financial mechanism of the Convention are able to respond to the capacity-building needs identified by developing countries but are not identified in decision 2/CP.7.

The G-77 and China proposed that methodologies to be used in conducting the comprehensive review should involve, *inter alia*, direct financial contributions to capacity-building activities by developed country parties, effectiveness of projects and programmes, number of impacted beneficiaries, and project and programme sustainability. There are various tools available to come up with an objective analysis of the aforementioned areas.

To accomplish the task of conducting a comprehensive review of the implementation of decision 2/CP.7, the Group of 77 and China proposes that the Chair of SBI, with the assistance of the Secretariat, convenes an expert meeting before the nineteenth session of the Subsidiary Body for Implementation to discuss the issues and processes outlined above. The expert meeting will be an opportunity for parties to interact with field practitioners, donor agencies, international organizations, private sector, and NGOs and discuss the various issues concerning the implementation of capacity-building and other related activities, e.g., National Capacity Self-Assessment, and establish possible synergy to work towards common goal of achieving objectives of the framework for capacity-building for developing countries.

Paper Submitted by Nigeria on behalf of the Group of 77 and China

Financial Matters Relating to Parties Not Included in Annex I to the Convention

Financial Mechanism: The Special Climate Change Fund Draft Conclusions

Proposed by the Group of 77 and China*

1. The Subsidiary Body for Implementation (SBI), at its eighteenth session, took note of the summary and analysis of views from parties on the activities, programmes and measures to be funded under the Special Climate Change Fund prepared by the Secretariat (FCCC/SBI/2003/INF.3) based on nine submissions representing 67 parties (FCCC/SBI/2003/MISC.1) and a submission by the Least Developed Countries Expert Group (FCCC/SBI/2003/

* Contained in document FCCC/SBI/2003/MISC.1/Add.1 of 12 June 2003.

INF.12). It also noted the submission by the Expert Group on Technology Transfer contained in document FCCC/SBI/2003/INF.12/Add.1, as a result, *inter alia*, of its third meeting held in Bonn, on 30–31 May 2003.

2. The SBI noted, that based on the analysis of views submitted so far by parties, there is convergence of opinion that activities to be funded should be country-driven, cost-effective, and integrated into national sustainable development and poverty-reduction strategies.
3. The SBI also noted that parties support the prioritization of funding for adaptation activities and their associated technology transfer and capacity-building needs. Technology transfer activities and their associated capacity-building needs, as they relate to energy-related mitigation activities, were also noted as priority areas. Economic diversification was also noted as a concern by some parties.
4. The SBI requests COP-9 to have final decision on this issue based on elements in the Annex.

Annex

Input by the Group of 77 and China for a draft decision of the COP on the SCCF

Preambular section

- recalling article 4, paragraph 8,
- having considered the decisions 4/CP.7, 5/CP.7, 7/CP.7, and 7/CP.8 and the views submitted by parties on a further definition of the prioritized activities, programmes, and measures to be funded under the Special Climate Change Fund
- reiterating decision 7/CP.8 in particular paragraph 1(a)–(d)
- stressing the importance of bilateral and multilateral funding in support of the implementation of activities, programmes, and measures in the climate change area
- recognizing that the provision of clear guidance on the LDC fund facilitated its early operationalization and that it is important to learn from this
- recognizing that the SCCF supports the implementation of the Convention and contributes to the achievement of the objectives of the WSSD

Principles Guiding the Implementation of the Special Climate Change Fund (SCCF)

1. The Special Climate Change Fund should be used to finance activities, programmes, and measures, relating to climate change, that are complementary to those funded by the resources allocated to the climate change focal area of GEF, LDC Fund, and by bilateral and multilateral funding.
2. Activities to be financed under SCCF include:
   a. Adaptation, in accordance with paragraph 8 of decision 5/CP.7;

b. Transfer of technologies, in accordance with decision 4/CP.7;
c. Energy, transport, industry, agriculture, forestry, and waste management;
d. Activities to assist developing country parties referred to under article 4, paragraph 8(h), in diversifying their economies, in accordance with decision 5/CP.7

3. Adaptation should be given the top priority.
4. Projects to be financed under this Fund should be country-driven and be consistent with sustainable development needs and goals of each country.
5. Paragraph 8 of decision 5/CP.7 highlighted eligible adaptation projects to be funded by SCCF. Implementation of such project activities requires development of innovative technology in, as well as hardware technology transfer to, the developing countries.
6. Non–Annex parties that are not included in LDCs should be given resources to prepare their adaptation plans and strategies under the SCCF.
7. The Operational guidelines for SCCF implementation should allow easy access to the Fund in order to expedite implementation of adaptation project activities.
8. Adaptation projects are of global benefit
9. Small scale, including pilot and demonstration projects should have expedited access to the SCCF.

Priority Areas

Adaptation activities in accordance with decision 5/CP.7, paragraphs 7 and 8

1. Improving the monitoring of diseases and vectors affected by climate change and related forecasting and early-warning systems, and in this context improving disease control and prevention
2. Capacity-building, including institutional capacity, for preventive measures, planning, preparedness, and management of disasters relating to climate change, including contingency planning, in particular, for droughts and floods in areas prone to extreme weather events
3. Strengthening existing and, where needed, establishing national and regional centres and information networks for rapid response to extreme weather events, utilizing information technology as much as possible
4. Based on available information, promptly implementing activities on, *inter alia*:
   a. Water resources management
   b. Land management
   c. Agriculture
   d. Infrastructure development
   e. Fragile ecosystems, including mountainous ecosystems
   f. Integrated coastal zone management

5. Enabling activities for vulnerability and adaptation assessments, including mathematical modelling
6. Support for Project Development in the areas of vulnerability and adaptation assessment resulting from Non–Annex I National Communications and/or NAPAs

Transfer of Technologies in Accordance with Decision 4/CP.7

The following activities, programmes, and measures should be considered as priority areas for transfer of technologies for funding under the special climate change fund:

Technology needs assessments

- Support the organization of regional workshops including one for Small Island States in order to advance the implementation of the results of the country-driven activities on technology needs assessments. The workshops are to be organized under the guidance of the Expert Group on Technology Transfer (EGTT).
- Support the strengthening and/or establishment of regional, sub-regional, and/or national centres of excellence, as appropriate, that would enhance the capacities of non–Annex I parties and countries with economies in transition to update and implement the results of their technology needs assessments.
- Contribute to buying down the initial investment costs or risks associated with prioritised technologies as determined by the technology needs assessments to enhance the transfer of technologies.
- Support technology transfer programmes as determined by the technology needs assessments including investment projects, feasibility studies, training and demonstration programmes.

Technology Information

- Support the strengthening of national climate change focal points and/or other appropriate national institutions for accessing and disseminating technology information as a support to the technology transfer process.
- Support the strengthening and establishment, as appropriate, of regional and national networks to facilitate the flows of technology information.

Capacity-Building

- Support capacity-building programmes aimed at strengthening the negotiation skills (business and legal) that would lead to fair terms for technology transfer.
- Strengthen institutions involved in technology assessments, acquisition, and development.

- Provide support for training, expert exchange, scholarship, and cooperative research programmes in relevant national and regional institutions for the transfer, operation, maintenance, adaptation, diffusion, and development of environmentally sound technologies with special attention to adaptation technologies.
- Support programmes that enhance the awareness of financial institutions, of the need to evaluate environmentally sound technologies on an equal footing with other technology options.
- Support the strengthening of endogenous capacities and capabilities in research, development, technological innovation, adoption, and adaptation, and technology for systematic observation relevant to climate change and its associated impacts.

Enabling Environments

- Provide support for the development of integrated and country-driven national technology transfer plan/strategy that addresses policy, institutional, and legal frameworks in the context of climate change and sustainable development.
- Provide support for projects that enhance regional cooperation on enabling environments, such as harmonization of policies, incentives, standards, legal instruments, and institutional arrangements.

Energy, Transport, Industry, Agriculture, Forestry, and Waste Management

Mitigation of climate change in the numerous relevant sectors such as energy, transport, industry, agriculture, forestry, and waste management is critical to poverty reduction.

For example, in the energy sector, there is need for

- Support for research into, and the development and use of, renewable energy including solar and wind energy in developing country parties;
- Development, diffusion, and transfer of less greenhouse gas-emitting advanced fossil fuel technologies, and/or technologies relating to fossil fuels, that capture and store greenhouse gases;
- Support developing country parties in the development, production, distribution, and transport of indigenous, less greenhouse-gas-emitting, environmentally sound, energy sources, including natural gas, according to the national circumstances of each of these parties.

Other Sectors will be further elaborated

Economic Diversification for Parties under Article 4, Paragraph 8 (h)

Assisting developing countries, in particular those most vulnerable to the impact of the implementation of response measures, in meeting their capacity-building needs for the implementation of programmes that address these impacts;

Cooperation in creating favourable conditions for investment in sectors where such investment can contribute to economic diversification; and

Technological development of non-energy uses of fossil fuels.

Consideration of appropriate technological options in addressing the impact of response measures, consistent with national priorities and indigenous resources;

Development, diffusion and transfer of less greenhouse gas–emitting advanced fossil fuel technologies, and/or technologies relating to fossil fuels, that capture and store greenhouse gases and new and renewable energy technologies.

Paper No. 5:
United Republic of Tanzania on behalf of the Group of 77 and China*

Additional Information on Capacity-Building by the United Republic of Tanzania on behalf of the G-77 and China

The United Republic of Tanzania wishes to submit the following contributions towards the implementation of the review of the Capacity-Building Framework as respond to decision .../CP.9: Capacity-Building.

Tanzania on behalf of the G-77 and China, feels that so far there has not been adequate implementation of decisions 2/CP.7 and 3/CP.7.

The agreed scope of the capacity-building activities that needed implementation has not been addressed adequately. The following is the analysis of some of the weakness into the implementation of decision 2/CP 7:

I. *Institutional capacity-building, including the strengthening or establishment, as appropriate, of national climate change Secretariats or national focal points (para. 8)*
   1. As it was noted by the G-77 and China at COP-8 and -9, it appears that most of the activities/programme contained in the Marrakech Accords have not been adequately implemented
   2. Most developing country UNFCCC Focal Points still have no capacity. In most developing countries, there is no difference in terms of institutional capacity that can be attributed towards decision 2/CP 7. Capacity-building assistance in the context of decision 2/CP7 must be over and above the available ODA. However, in reality ODA is going down. In any case immediate support is still a problem and institutional capacity-building to address climate change in a comprehensive manner still suffer from uncoordinated and insufficient both technical and financial assistance.

* Contained in document FCCC/SBI/2004/MISC.1 of 23 March 2004.

II. Enhancement and/or creation of enabling environment (paras. 10 and 11)

3. There are still inadequate enabling environments in most developing countries. The available assessments has shown that there is no need for further assessment on the requirements to strengthen national institutions and develop human resources for creation of enabling environments for parties participate effectively in the UNFCCC and Kyoto Protocol processes. Developed countries should assist in strengthening the systematic and institutional levels of capacity-building. Various assessments that have been undertaken and the ongoing assessments such NCSA do provide enough information in this regard.
4. Many developing countries have undertaken a number of institutional restructuring in order to accommodate global issues. Financial and technical support is important in order to create enabling environment to accommodate climate change in the national development processes.

III. Greenhouse gas inventories, emissions database management, and systems for collecting, managing, and utilizing activity data and emissions factors

5. Much as many developing countries have started to build capacity through processes of national communications there is a lot of capacity gaps existing in terms of data base management and managing and utilizing available data and emissions factors.

IV. Clean Development Mechanism

6. Tanzania believes that most developing countries still need capacity-building in order to participate actively in CDM. Many countries do not have Designated National Authority (DNA) and where they exist they are still very weak. A special initiative or programme for strengthening of DNA in developing countries, should be undertaken in respond to 2/CP 7 and should focus both the public and private sectors.

CONCLUSION

It is clear from the available submissions and document that Capacity-Building Framework as per 2/CP7 has not enjoyed the attraction as envisaged when the decision was made at Marrakech.

Many of the reported activities are testimonial dating as far back as the 1990s and do not necessary respond to 2/CP7. Activities undertaken in developing countries in order to respond to capacity-building must be country-driven, comprehensive, with the agreed scope, consistent, and must respond to the immediate and urgent needs of a particular developing country party.

Developed countries still need to do more if climate change has to be addressed comprehensively with the adequate involvement of all countries rather reporting for the sake of fulfilling the reporting agreements under the Convention.

Submission from Group of 77 and China

Package Proposal by Group of 77 and China on the Paragraphs Addressing Timing of Submission*

The three paragraphs below are to replace paragraphs 3, 4, 5, 6, and 7 of document FCCC/SBI/2004/L.10.

Invites those parties not included in Annex I to the Convention that have not prepared project proposals for the financing of second and, where appropriate, third national communications to do so, even in advance of substantially completing previously funded activities, in order to avoid a lack of continuity in project financing.

Decides that parties not included in Annex I to the Convention that have submitted their national communications may apply for the financing of their subsequent national communication at any time between 3 and 5 years of the initial disbursement of financial resources for the actual preparation of their previous national communications. This applies to the financing of second, and where appropriate third, national communications.

Decides that parties not included in Annex I to the Convention shall submit their second, and where appropriate, third national communications within five years of the initial disbursement of financial resources for the actual preparation of the national communications, in accordance with article 4, paragraph 3, of the Convention, under the expedited procedures or standard procedures, on agreed full cost basis. Parties that are least developed countries may submit their second national communications at their discretion.

Financial Mechanism (Kyoto Protocol): Adaptation Fund

Draft Decision Proposed by Jamaica on behalf of the Group of 77 and China*

The Conference of the Parties, serving as the Meeting of the Parties to the Kyoto Protocol,

Being guided by article 12.8 of the Kyoto Protocol,

* Contained in document FCCC/SBI/2004/MISC.3 of 25 June 2004.
* Contained in document FCCC/SBI/2005/CRP.1 of 3 December 2005.

Recalling decision 10/CP.7, by which an Adaptation Fund was established by the Conference of the Parties to the Convention,

Recognizing the need to operationalize the Adaptation Fund as soon as possible,

Recognizing that developing countries, least developed countries, low-lying and other Small Island countries, countries with low-lying coastal, arid, and semi-arid areas or areas liable to floods, drought, and desertification and developing countries with fragile mountain ecosystems are particularly vulnerable to the adverse effects of climate change,

Taking note of the proposed arrangements for the Adaptation Fund presented by the Global

Environment Facility as an operating entity entrusted with the operation of the financial mechanism of the Convention, as contained in paragraph 31 of the Global Environment Facility's report to the Conference of the Parties (FCCC/CP/2005/3),

1. *Decides* to adopt the following guidance to an operating entity of the financial mechanism of the Convention when making arrangements for the operation of the Adaptation Fund:
   (a) That the Adaptation Fund shall finance concrete adaptation projects and programmes in developing country parties that are parties to the Kyoto Protocol, as well as activities identified in paragraph 8 of decision 5/CP.7;
   (b) That the Conference of the Parties serving as the Meeting of the Parties to the Kyoto Protocol shall ensure that a share of the proceeds from certified project activities under the clean development mechanism is used to assist developing country parties, especially those parties that are particularly vulnerable to the adverse effects of climate change to meet the costs of adaptation;
   (c) That, as this Adaptation Fund has been established under the Kyoto Protocol for the benefit of developing country parties, to establish guidelines and adopt decisions on the operation of the Adaptation Fund that fully reflect these elements, and that disbursements should be made in the most expeditious way possible, without onerous operational policies on eligibility criteria, project cycle and approval, the application of the concept of incremental costs, and guidelines which impose considerable administrative and financial costs on these developing country parties;
   (d) That the Adaptation Fund shall be subject to the authority and guidance of the Conference of the Parties serving as Meeting of the Parties;
   (e) That other sources of funding shall be mobilized to finance activities under the Adaptation Fund;

(f) That a regular report shall be given to the Conference of the Parties serving as the Meeting of the Parties to the Kyoto Protocol on how this guidance has been followed in the financing of activities; and
(g) That a review of the entity operating the financial mechanism for the Adaptation Fund shall be conducted on a regular basis.

2. *Also decides* to adopt specific policies, programme priorities, and eligibility criteria to guide an operating entity to the financial mechanism at its second session on the operation of the Adaptation Fund;
3. *Decides further* to develop arrangements, in the form of a memorandum of understanding to be made with an operating entity of the financial mechanism of the Convention on the operation of the Adaptation Fund that would, *inter alia*, incorporate all the elements given in the above guidance;
4. *Requests* the Secretariat to prepare a document incorporating all the above guidance for the consideration of the Conference of the Parties serving as the Meeting of the Parties to the Kyoto Protocol at its next session.

Financial Mechanism (Convention):

Additional Guidance to the Global Environment Facility

Draft Decision Proposed by Jamaica on behalf of the Group of 77 and China*

The Conference of the Parties,

Recalling article 4, paragraph 3, and article 11, paragraph 4, of the Convention,

Further recalling its decision 5/CP.8 on the review of the financial mechanism,

Aiming at the conduct of a comprehensive review process on the effectiveness of the financial mechanism of the Convention,

Taking note with grave concern of the information given on the Global Environment Facility Resource Allocation Framework contained in paragraphs 80 to 85 of the report of the Global Environment Facility to the Conference of the Parties (FCCC/CP/2005/3),

1. Requests the Global Environment Facility, as an operating entity of the financial mechanism, to submit information on the Resource Allocation Framework adopted by the Global Environment Council to the Conference of the Parties, and examine its potential implications for funding of developing countries in the implementation of their commitments under the Convention

* Contained in document FCCC/SBI/2005/CRP.3 of 5 December 2005.

and to report on this evaluation to the Conference of the Parties through the UNFCCC Secretariat for its consideration during its next session;

2. Also requests the Executive Secretary to invite the Global Environment Facility Chief Executive Officer to include in its regular report to the Conference of the Parties details on the initial application of the Resource Allocation Framework to resources allocated in the fourth replenishment of the Global Environment Facility, beginning in July 2006, under the climate change focal area, and its implications and potential impacts on the funding of developing countries in the implementation of the Convention;
3. Further requests the UNFCCC Secretariat to examine whether the Resource Allocation Framework conforms with the provisions of the memorandum of understanding between the Conference of the Parties to the UNFCCC and the Council of the Global Environment Facility, as contained in the annex to decision 12/CP.2, and the decisions adopted by the Conference of the Parties on guidance to an operating entity of the financial mechanism in succeeding Conference of the Parties session;
4. Requests the Executive Secretary to invite the Global Environment Facility Chief Executive Officer to take fully into account the guidance provided in the annex to the memorandum of understanding between the Conference of the Parties and the Global Environment Facility on the determination of funding necessary and available for the implementation of the Convention, in particular information relating to paragraphs 1 to 4 of the said annex, and to include this information in the Global Environment Facility's regular report to the Conference of the Parties at its next session;
5. Requests the Executive Secretary to report its finding to the next sessions of the Subsidiary Body for Implementation, with a view to making a recommendation to the twelfth session of the Conference of the Parties.

Capacity-Building under the Convention

Capacity-Building under the Kyoto Protocol

Submission from the United Republic of Tanzania on behalf of the Group of 77 and China*

Submission by the Group of 77 (G-77) and China

In accordance with decision 2/CP.10, and after consultations in Dar es Salaam, Tanzania on 20–22 March 2006 generously supported by South Africa, the G-77 and China welcome the opportunity to submit its views on steps to be taken by the SBI to monitor regularly the implementation of capacity-building activities undertaken pursuant to decisions 2/CP.7 and 29/CMP.1.

* Contained in document FCCC/SBI/2006/MISC.4/Add.1 of 31 March 2006.

The G-77 and China reaffirm the critical importance of capacity-building as a foundation for the effective implementation of the Convention and the Protocol by developing countries. Monitoring and evaluation is important in planning and guiding the effective implementation of the capacity-building framework and making sure that the limited resources available for capacity-building are optimized. In particular, monitoring and evaluation can be used to address gaps in capacity-building, promote best practices, and encourage more efficient use of resources.

Since the adoption of the Capacity-Building Framework, some of the needs and areas for capacity-building in decision 2/CP.7 are being addressed. Most of these are being addressed indirectly through support for national communications, national adaptation programmes of action (NAPA), technology needs assessments (TNAs), national capacity self-assessments (NCSAs), and other multilateral and bilateral programs. In addition, developing countries have begun to address their own capacity needs, including through South-South cooperation. Nonetheless, many needs and areas for capacity-building are not addressed even as climate change impacts in developing countries become more discernible. Moreover, because these activities address capacity-building only indirectly, they often fail to address the institutional and systemic support needed for sustained capacity development.

Decision 2/CP.7 provides that all parties should support the implementation of the framework and promote conditions conducive to the sustainability and effectiveness of capacity-building activities. Developing and developed countries as well as the GEF have different and specific responsibilities in implementing the framework. Multilateral, bilateral, and private sector have also been invited to contribute to the implementation of the framework. Therefore, monitoring should be undertaken taking into account the varied responsibilities of these key players.

Decision 2/CP.7 also provides for a time frame for the implementation of the framework, which should be taken into account by the SBI in regularly monitoring and reviewing the implementation of the framework.

This submission provides inputs for the steps that SBI should take to regularly monitor the implementation of the capacity-building framework in order to improve the effectiveness of capacity-building activities.

Following decision 2/CP.7, SBI can consider the following sources of information:

- National communication, and other reports and submissions from parties;
- Reports from the GEF, including on relevant activities from the national capacity self-assessments, country programs for LDCs and SIDs, global support program for capacity-building, work on indicators, and small grants programme and capacity enhancements (see GEF report at COP 11);
- Inputs from bilateral and multilateral agencies, and other intergovernmental organizations and institutions.

Parties are invited to submit timely additional information on the implementation of their commitments and activities under decision 2/CP.7. Information on progress in each of the areas for capacity-building should be submitted. Information on performance indicators, benchmarks, best practices, as well as unmet requests for assistance, should also be provided as appropriate. In this regard, the SBI should provide a structured format by SBI 24 for parties to submit this additional information including data on sources and amount of funding, number of projects, programs, outcomes/outputs, number of institutions strengthened and/or established, trained individuals, and such other data at each COP.

The GEF, as the operating entity of the financial mechanism should also provide reports on steps it has taken to implement the CB framework to the COP to help the SBI in its task. The GEF report should include information on geographical coverage, gaps in capacity-building, as well as unmet requests for assistance. In order to help the SBI to consider these sources of information, the Secretariat is requested under decision 2/CP.7 to collect, compile, and synthesize the inputs above. The Secretariat should process this information to cover each of the areas identified under the scope for capacity-building. The information should be processed to show, among others, geographical coverage, gaps in capacity-building, as well as unmet requests for assistance.

The SBI should convene an expert workshop to consider the reports from the Secretariat to make recommendations to the SBI on possible ways and means to monitor and improve the implementation of the capacity-building framework on a regular basis. This expert workshop should be convened before SBI 26.

The SBI should request the Secretariat to facilitate the exchange of information on capacity-building activities being implemented, including best practices, performance indicators, benchmarks, lessons learned, and other tools and resources that can help improve capacity-building in developing countries through workshops, a web site, regular publications, and list serves.

Monitoring will require technical and financial resources. The GEF, as the financial mechanism, should allocate financial resources for the monitoring. The SBI should invite bilateral and multilateral organizations to allocate financial resources towards this. In undertaking this monitoring, the Secretariat should cooperate with the GEF and other ongoing bilateral and multilateral programmes, e.g., the Global Support Project of the GEF/UNDP).

Financial Mechanism (Kyoto Protocol): Adaptation Fund

Submission from the Group of 77 and China

(Wednesday May 24, 15:00 hrs)

Questions proposed by the Group of 77 and China to Potential Entities Interested in the Operation/Management of the Adaptation Fund*

In view of the guidance previously agreed by the COP and COP/MOP in decisions 28/CMP.1, 5/CP.7, 10/CP.7, and 17/CP.7 for the Adaptation Fund, and to assist the

* Contained in document FCCC/SBI/2006/MISC.11 of 24 May 2006.

Group in its evaluation of this matter, institutions are invited to respond to the following questions:

1. How would you work under the authority of and follow the guidance of the COP/MOP?
2. How would you propose to address access to the Adaptation Fund in view of the guidance already agreed?
3. How would you operate/manage the fund in the context of a country-driven approach? In the context of a learning by doing approach?
4. Would your institution establish its own set of eligibility criteria for access to the Fund? How would this be undertaken and how would this relate to decisions from the COP/MOP?
5. Would you propose conditions such as co-financing as a criteria for accessing the Adaptation Fund?
6. How would you propose to address the issue of complementarity with respect to the other funds established to address adaptation under the Convention?
7. What administrative and management expenses would you apply to the Adaptation Fund, on what basis and for what activities?
8. How would you propose to maintain the autonomy of the Adaptation Fund?
9. Would you be able to keep a separate account/budget line for these funds?
10. How would you keep these funds independent of your guidelines and procedures meant for other funds that you may be managing?
11. What decision-making structure would you apply to the operation/management of the Adaptation Fund?
12. What decision-making structure would you apply to the implementation of guidance from the COP/MOP?
13. What decision-making structure would you propose to apply to any questions arising in connection with the application of guidance from the COP/MOP?
14. What approach would you take to facilitate sound financial management and transparency in your management of the Adaptation Fund?
15. How would you propose to handle the Adaptation Fund in the context of a possible management committee established by the COP/MOP?
16. What independent auditing systems would you apply to the management of the Adaptation Fund?
17. How would you propose to handle separate accounts for funds other than those funds coming from the share of the proceeds of CDM projects that come into the Adaptation Fund?
18. Would you propose to mobilise additional funds and how?

National Communications from Parties Not Included in Annex I to the Convention: Provision of Financial and Technical Support

Additional Guidance to the Global Environment Facility Related to National Communications from non–Annex I Parties

Draft Decision Proposed by the Group of 77 and China*

The Conference of the Parties,

Taking into account article 4.3 of the Convention,

Taking into account paragraph 1 (a) (i) of decision 6/CP. 8 (Additional guidance to an operating entity of the financial mechanism) on matters related to national communications,

Taking into account paragraph 1 (a) and (c) of decision 17/CP. 8 (Guidelines for the preparation of national communications from parties not included in Annex I to the Convention),

Taking into account relevant provisions of decision 8/CP. 11 (Submission of second and, where appropriate, third national communications from parties not included in Annex I to the Convention),

1. The GEF is requested to:
   (a) Together with its implementing agencies, further simplify its procedures and improve the efficiency of the process by which non–Annex I parties receive funding to meet their obligations under article 12, paragraph 1, of the Convention, with the aim of ensuring the timely disbursement of funds to meet the agreed full costs incurred by developing country parties in complying with these obligations;
   (b) Ensure that the financial resources under article 4, paragraph 3 of the Convention to meet the agreed full costs incurred by developing country parties in complying with their obligations under article 12, paragraph 1 are not deducted from national or group allocations under its Resource Allocation Framework;
   (c) Establish operational procedures to ensure the timely disbursement of funds to meet the agreed full costs incurred by those non–Annex I parties that are in the process of preparation of their third and, where appropriate, fourth national communications, in the light of the paragraphs (a) and (b) above and in accordance with paragraphs 1 and 2 of decision 8/CP. 11, taking fully into consideration article 4.3 of the Convention;

* Contained in document FCCC/SBI/2007/CRP.1 of 8 December 2007.

(d) Ensure that any expedited process to be established under the operational procedures mentioned in paragraph (c) does not determine a ceiling of financial resources, given that the full costs incurred by developing country parties in complying with their obligations under article 12, paragraph 1 shall be agreed upon in individual basis, taking into account the common but differentiated responsibilities and respective capabilities of the country parties;

(e) Assist non–Annex I parties in formulating and developing project proposals identified in their national communications in accordance with article 12, paragraph 4, of the Convention and paragraph 2 of decision 5/CP.11;

(f) Establish a modality of funding to finance project proposals identified in the national communications of non–Annex I parties (decision 5/CP. 11, para. 2) in accordance with article 12, paragraph 4, of the Convention;

(g) Together with its implementing agencies, ensure that the analysis of project proposals for the financing of second and subsequent national communications is limited to the guidelines for the preparation of national communications from parties not included in Annex I to the Convention approved by a COP decision (the current ones are contained in decision 17/CP.8), and, therefore, any criteria of analysis must not be applied beyond what has been agreed in these guidelines.

Capacity-Building under the Convention:
Capacity-Building for Developing Countries

Draft Decision Proposed by the Group of 77 and China*

The Conference of the Parties,

Recalling decision 4/CP.12 on capacity-building under the Convention,

Reaffirming the capacity-building framework contained in decision 2/CP.7,

Reaffirming also that capacity-building is a pre-requisite for any serious engagement by

developing countries and will continue playing a critical role in the implementation of the Convention,

Reaffirming also that capacity-building must be part of the Bali Road Map in order to ensure that developing country parties have the necessary capacity for the future engagement in the implementation of the Climate Change Convention,

* Contained in document FCCC/SBI/2007/CRP.3 of 8 December 2007.

Noting with concern from the synthesis report the lack of a comprehensive support for the implementation of the scopes identified in the annex of decision 2/CP.7,

Noting also with concern the lack of a comprehensive reporting from Global Environment

Facility (GEF) as the operating entity of the financial mechanism on the activities they are undertaking consistent with the requirement for the implementation of decision 2/CP.7,

Noting also the submissions by the parties that have been made available to the UNFCCC website by the Secretariat as important fore information sharing,

Being aware of the ongoing work by GEF in developing capacity-building indicators,

Welcomes the synthesis report prepared by the Secretariat on the implementation of the capacity-building activities in developing countries,

Welcomes also the report of the expert workshop on monitoring and evaluating capacity-building in developing countries consistent with decision 4/CP.12.

1. *Decides* that a process for the development of capacity-building output monitoring indicators should start immediately as a matter of priority;
2. *Requests* the Subsidiary Body for Implementation (SBI) in collaboration with the GEF, based on the synthesis report, submissions from parties, and the report of the expert workshop on monitoring and evaluating capacity-building in developing countries to develop a technical paper identifying measurable output indicators for monitoring capacity-building consistent with the framework in decision 2/CP.7 for review and further elaboration at SBI at its twenty-eighth session;
3. *Decides also* that specific concrete institutional strengthening activities consistent with decision 2/CP.7 need to be undertaken as a matter of priority in the context of the Bali Road Map so as to enable proper engagement of developing countries particularly those in Africa, least developed countries, and Small Island Developing States to participate fully in the negotiations and implementation of the building blocks for the future engagement in climate change adaptation and mitigation activities;
4. *Decides also* that the development of a work plan for the implementation of decision 2/CP.7 with clear, programmable, and verifiable objectives, steps, time frames, and resources should be initiated by SBI at its twenty-eighth session as an input to the comprehensive review of the Capacity-Building Framework consistent with decision 2/CP.10;

5. *Requests* the Secretariat to organize a workshop to verify and agree on the capacity-building output indicators that will be developed through a technical paper for adoption at the Conference of the Parties (COP) at its fourteenth session;
6. *Requests* the GEF to provide the financial support for the SBI to be able to undertake and conclude the development and adoption of the said indicators;
7. *Requests* the GEF, and urges the multilateral and bilateral organizations, to provide financial and technical support, as appropriate, to support the capacity-building activities in developing countries consistent with decision 2/CP.7;
8. *Requests also* GEF to take into account the requirement of for a comprehensive reporting on all scopes of the framework consistent with decision 2/CP.7 in the future annual reports to the COP;
9. *Requests* the Secretariat to prepare the terms of reference of the comprehensive review, taking into account the synthesis reports from the submissions from parties, national communications, national adaptation plan of action, the expert works, and the annual GEF report on the implementation of decisions 2/CP.7, for consideration and approval by the SBI at its twenty-eighth session.

Paper No. 2:

United Republic of Tanzania on behalf of the Group of 77 and China

On Inputs of the Completion of the Second Comprehensive Review of the Capacity-Building Framework under the Convention and the Kyoto Protocol*

In accordance with decision 2.CP 10 paragraph 7 and paragraph 9(d), which calls for the completion of the second comprehensive review by COP-15, the United Republic of Tanzania submits the following views:

1. The second comprehensive review should be completed at COP-15 consistent to decision 2.CP 10;
2. In order to enhance the implementation of the Capacity-Building Framework, the next and subsequent comprehensive reviews should be undertaken using the performance indicator related to monitoring and evaluation of the Capacity-Building Framework, in particular with regards to the financial and technical support as agreed in 2/CP.7;
3. Furthermore, in order to support the implementation of the Capacity-Building Framework and subsequent comprehensive reviews, a plan of action with a clear time frame, financial resources, and sources of funds should be prepared and adopted by the COP;

* Contained in document FCCC/SBI/2009/MISC.12/Rev.1 of 18 May 2010.

4. Expert Groups have been useful in advancing the work programme/action in other areas of the Convention. In view of this, the G-77 and China proposes establishment an expert group on capacity-building that will, *inter alia*, support the Secretariat in developing simple and effective performance indicators for future reviews; and develop and monitor the implementation of the plan of action, taking into account new and emerging needs, particularly those arising from the AWG-LCA process. The SBI will undertake a review of the progress of work of the established expert group on capacity-building at its thirty-third session with a view to adopting the plan of action and related performance indicators at COP-16;
5. Provision of financial and technical supports which is an essential component of the capacity-building to support implementation of the Convention Consistent to articles 4.3, 4.4, and 4.7 is still lagging behind. The G-77 and China calls a new financial and technical support to be availed by Annex II parties and the GEF as well as relevant multilateral and bilateral organizations to enhance the implementation of the Convention. Such support should be consistent with the needs expressed by developing countries in various documents and submissions; and
6. In order to further enhance implementation of the Convention and the Protocol, the G-77 and China requests the Secretariat to prepare a comparative table showing the capacity needs within a given time frame for the review against the previous needs, with a view to identifying gaps and additional needs using the agreed performance indicators.
7. Furthermore, in order to expedite the process and allow the COP to complete its second comprehensive review of the Capacity-Building Framework consistent to decision 2.CP 10, we have prepared a draft decision for the COP (attached) for consideration by SBI at its thirty-first session.

Draft Decision -/CP.15 on Capacity-Building under Convention and Protocol: Proposal by the G-77 and China

Draft Decision -/CP.15
Building under the Convention

The Conference of the Parties,

Being guided by articles 4.1, 4.3, 4.4, 4.5, and 4.7, in the context of article 3 and articles 5 and 6 of the Convention,

Recalling decisions 2/CP.7, 2/CP.10, 4/CP12, and 6/CP.14,

Further recalling decision 2/CP.10 to initiate a second comprehensive review of the implementation of the framework for capacity-building in developing countries at the twenty-eighth session of the Subsidiary Body for Implementation with a view to completing this review at the fifteenth session of the Conference of the Parties,

Reaffirming that decision 2/CP.7 should continue to be the basis for and guide the

Implementation of capacity-building activities in developing countries, and that it remains effective,

Reaffirming also that capacity-building for developing countries is essential to enable them to participate fully in, and implement effectively their commitments under, the Convention,

Recognising that the scope of capacity-building needs identified in the framework for capacity-building in developing countries and the key factors identified in decision 2/CP.10 are still relevant,

Noting that although a range of the priority issues identified in the framework for capacity-building in developing countries is being addressed by developed country parties and the GEF huge gaps still remain and the availability of and access to financial resources is still an issue to be addressed,

Acknowledging that activities, projects, and programmes implemented should continue to put emphasis on defining realistic results, identifying programme beneficiaries, monitoring the progress made towards expected results, identifying and managing risks, and providing information on results achieved,

Recognising also that new capacity-building needs and priorities in developing countries emerging from the processes and initiatives launched after the completion of the first comprehensive review as well as from the negotiations under the Ad Hoc Working Group on Long-term Cooperative Action under the Convention require the necessary attention and support,

Acknowledging that capacity-building is a country-driven and a learning-by-doing process that responds to the specific needs and priorities of the countries concerned,

Acknowledging further the synthesis report on the experiences and lessons learnt in the use of performance indicators for monitoring and evaluating implementation of capacity-building activities

Recognizing further that the purpose of regular monitoring should be to facilitate assessment of progress made, identification of gaps, and effectiveness of the implementation of the Capacity-Building Framework and to support the comprehensive review;

The COP

Decides that the next and subsequent comprehensive reviews will be undertaken using the performance indicator related to monitoring and evaluation of the capacity-building framework, in particular with regards to the financial and technical support as agreed in 2/CP.7;

Decides that, in order to support the implementation of the Capacity-Building Framework and subsequent comprehensive reviews, a plan of action shall be prepared with a clear time frame, financial resources, and sources of funds;

Decides to establish an expert group that will, *inter alia*, support the Secretariat in developing simple and effective performance indicators for future reviews; and develop and monitor the implementation of the plan of action, taking into account new and emerging needs, particularly those arising from the AWG-LCA process;

Decides that the SBI will undertake a review of the progress of work of the expert group at its thirty-third session with a view to adopting the plan of action and related performance indicators at COP 16;

Decides that new financial and technical support will be availed by Annex II parties and the GEF as well as relevant multilateral and bilateral organizations. Such support should be consistent with the needs expressed by developing countries in various documents and submissions;

Requests the Secretariat to prepare a comparative table showing the capacity needs within a given time frame for the review against the previous needs, with a view to identifying gaps and additional needs using the agreed performance indicators.

G-77 and China Presentation: Forum on the Impact of the Implementation of Response Measures Views of the G-77 and China on Area A

Doha, 37th Session of the Subsidiary Bodies
November 2012

Introduction

Decision 8.CP.17: Area A: Sharing of information and expertise, including reporting and promoting understanding of positive and negative impacts of response measures.

This workshop will help us to give full consideration to what actions are necessary to meet the specific needs and concerns of developing country parties arising from the impact of the implementation of response measures, in a context in which:

- all developing countries face economic and social consequences of response measures (actual and potential) in different ways
- research on the impact of response measures is a new field

Why is area a) important?

- Promote understanding about the nature and magnitude of economic and social consequences for developing country parties of different response measures taken by developed country parties
- Assist developing country parties in identifying and addressing the impact of response measures taken by developed country parties, sharing information, promoting and cooperating on issues relating to response strategies and exploring ways to minimize negative consequences, in particular in developing country parties
- Discuss the negative economic and social consequences of response measures on developing country parties
- Facilitate technical collaboration among parties and experts on tools, including studies, modelling, and methodologies, to assist developing country parties in addressing economic and social consequences of response measures
- Discuss the consequences of trade-related response measures:

  "The Parties should cooperate to promote a supportive and open international economic system that would lead to sustainable economic growth and development in all Parties, particularly developing country Parties, thus enabling them better to address the problems of climate change. Measures taken to combat climate change, including unilateral ones, should not constitute a means of arbitrary or unjustifiable discrimination or a disguised restriction on international trade" (article 3.5 of the UNFCCC)
- Discussing climate policies in a manner that avoids and minimizes negative impacts and enhances positive impacts on developing countries, taking into account national circumstances
- Identifying, quantifying, and considering means to address the adverse impacts of measures taken to mitigate climate change on developing country parties
- Providing support for the integration of economic diversification into sustainable development strategies and for facilitating efforts to achieve economic diversification in developing countries

Lack of clear reporting guidelines

- In their national communications, 11 out of 25 Annex I parties effectively reported nothing (NC Survey 2006, Cosbey. A., 2011)
- Of those that reported, some reported purely domestic efforts as technology cooperation, and others only described their measures

There is a lack of reporting guidelines for Annex I parties on how they ". . . shall strive to implement policies and measures in such a way as to minimize adverse effects on developing country Parties . . . ", for example, in terms of including the following:

- Consideration if the special economic and social conditions of developing countries were taken into account in the design and implementation
- Information about consultation to potentially affected developing country parties
- Inclusion of scientific basis of the measure, and an assessment if it is the most effective means to achieve the objective of combating climate change
- Information about specific support to developing countries in relation to the measure, in terms of transfer of technology, financial resources, and capacity-building

Final considerations (1)
As a general framework, when dealing with social and economic consequences of response measures, there is a need to:

- observe the guiding principles and provisions of the Convention, in particular the principle of common but differentiated responsibilities
- observe relevant Convention articles 3.5, 4.8, and 4.9 and articles 2.3 and 3.14 of the KP
- bear in mind that the UNFCCC discusses the economic and social impacts of response measures, including unilateral ones
- take duly into consideration the specific needs and concerns of developing country parties

Final considerations (2)
This area of work is an opportunity to enhance the understanding on negative economic and social consequences of response measures on developing countries and in order to address both the economic and social dimensions of the issue.

Thank you very much for your attention!

G-77 and China Presentation: Forum on the Impact of the Implementation of Response Measures G-77 and China Views on Area (h)

Doha, 37th Session of the Subsidiary Bodies
November 2012

Introduction

Decision 8.CP.17: Area h: Building collective and individual learning towards a transition to a low greenhouse gas emitting society

- Transition to a low greenhouse gas emitting society is not defined in the Convention, but any transition needs to be understood under the UNFCCC principles and provisions, in particular CBDR and parties' different socio-economic contexts and specific conditions, and in the broader context of the TRANSITION TOWARDS SUSTAINABLE DEVELOPMENT
- The Convention relates to the achievement of sustainable development.

TRANSITION TOWARDS SUSTAINABLE DEVELOPMENT

- In the context of the Convention, all provisions are important, and the following provisions, among others, are relevant:
  - PP 21: "*Affirming* that responses to climate change should be coordinated with social and economic development in an integrated manner with a view to avoiding adverse impacts on the latter, taking into full account the legitimate priority needs of developing countries for the achievement of sustained economic growth and the eradication of poverty"
  - PP 3: "*Noting* that the largest share of historical and current global emissions of greenhouse gases has originated in developed countries, that per capita emissions in developing countries are still relatively low and that the share of global emissions originating in developing countries will grow to meet their social and development needs"
  - PP. 22: "*Recognizing* that all countries, especially developing countries, need access to resources required to achieve sustainable social and economic development and that, in order for developing countries to progress towards that goal, their energy consumption will need to grow taking into account the possibilities for achieving greater energy efficiency and for controlling greenhouse gas emissions in general, including through the application of new technologies on terms which make such an application economically and socially beneficial"
  - Article 4.7: "The extent to which developing country Parties will effectively implement their commitments under the Convention will depend on the effective implementation by developed country Parties of their commitments

under the Convention related to financial resources and transfer of technology and economic and social development and poverty eradication are the first and overriding priorities of the developing country Parties"

- Article 4.8: "In the implementation of the commitments in this Article, the Parties shall give full consideration to what actions are necessary under the Convention, including actions related to funding, insurance and the transfer of technology, to meet the specific needs and concerns of developing country Parties arising from the adverse effects of climate change and/or the impact of the implementation of response measures, especially on:
  (a) Small Island countries;
  (b) Countries with low-lying coastal areas;
  (c) Countries with arid and semi-arid areas, forested areas and areas liable to forest decay;
  (d) Countries with areas prone to natural disasters;
  (e) Countries with areas liable to drought and desertification;
  (f) Countries with areas of high urban atmospheric pollution;
  (g) Countries with areas with fragile ecosystems, including mountainous ecosystems;
  (h) Countries whose economies are highly dependent on income generated from the production, processing and export, and/or on consumption of fossil fuels and associated Energy-intensive products; and
  (i) Landlocked and transit countries.

Further, the Conference of the Parties may take actions, as appropriate, with respect to this paragraph:

- Article 4.9. "The Parties shall take full account of the specific needs and special situations of the least developed countries in their actions with regard to funding and transfer of technology."
- Other relevant articles of the Convention, including article 3.5: "The Parties should cooperate to promote a supportive and open international economic system that would lead to sustainable economic growth and development in all Parties, particularly developing country Parties, thus enabling them better to address the problems of climate change. Measures taken to combat climate change, including unilateral ones, should not constitute a means of arbitrary or unjustifiable discrimination or a disguised restriction on international trade."
- There are different approaches, visions, models, and tools available to each country to achieve the transition, in accordance with its national circumstances and priorities
- Need to avoid and minimize in the transition negative economic and social consequences of response measures and enhance the positive impacts
- Importance to give full consideration to what actions are necessary under the Convention, including actions related to funding, insurance, and the transfer

of technology, to meet the specific needs and concerns of developing country parties arising from the adverse effects of climate change and/or the impact of the implementation of response measures

Transition will entail adjustment and incremental costs:

- Policies and measures taken by developed countries to combat climate change shall not undermine the development nor constitute a means of transferring the burden of climate change mitigation to developing country parties
- Importance of ensuring a just transition of the workforce, the creation of decent work and quality jobs, in accordance with nationally defined development priorities and strategies

Building collective and individual learning

- Need for capacity-building, transfer of technologies, and financial resources for learning and for development of endogenous capacities in developing countries, in order for them to meet the agreed full incremental costs of implementing measures (relation to articles 4.3, 4.5, and 4.7 of the Convention)
- Importance of exchange of experiences, information, knowledge-sharing, and know-how, and of ensuring access to affordable technologies for developing countries for implementation of NAMAs and NAPAs. Need to assess the role of the protection of IPR in terms of transfer of technology

Final considerations
This area of work is an opportunity to enhance the understanding on the need to build individual and collective learning for an effective and appropriate response to climate change, in accordance with the principles and provisions of Convention and towards the achievement of sustainable development, in its social, economic, and environmental dimensions in a balanced manner. This area serves to exchange views on positive and negative impacts of response measures on developing countries.

Thank you very much for your attention!

G-77 and China Presentation: Forum on the Impact of the Implementation of Response Measures

Views of the G-77 and China on Area (g):

Just Transition of the Workforce and the Creation of Decent Work and Quality Jobs Bonn, 38th Session of the Subsidiary Bodies

5 June 2013

Dec. 8. CP/17 – Area (g)
General context

- This matter has to be seen in the broader context of the achievement of sustainable development, in accordance with nationally defined priorities.
- The results of Rio+20 should be taken into account, in particular the affirmation that poverty eradication is the greatest global challenge facing the world today (para. 2 of the Rio+20 outcome document). Also, that outcome document recognised "the importance of a just transition, including programmes to help workers to adjust to changing labour market conditions" (para. 152).

General context: Some relevant UNFCCC provisions and principles

- Preambular paragraph 21: ". . . responses to climate change should be coordinated with social and economic development in an integrated manner with a view to avoiding adverse impacts on the latter, taking into full account the legitimate priority needs of developing countries for the achievement of sustained economic growth and the eradication of poverty"
- Article 3.4: "The Parties have a right to, and should, promote sustainable development. Policies and measures to protect the climate system . . . should be appropriate for the specific conditions of each Party and should be integrated with national development programmes, taking into account that economic development is essential for adopting measures to address climate change"
- Article 3.5: "Parties should cooperate to promote a supportive and open international economic system that would lead to sustainable economic growth and development in all Parties, particularly developing country Parties . . . Measures taken to combat climate change, including unilateral ones, should not constitute a means of arbitrary or unjustifiable discrimination or a disguised restriction on international trade"
- Article 4.7: ". . . economic and social development and poverty eradication are the first and overriding priorities of the developing country Parties"
- Article 4.8: ". . . give full consideration to what actions are necessary . . . to meet the specific needs and concerns of developing country Parties arising from . . . the impact of the implementation of response measures . . ."
- Articles 2. 3 of KP: "The Parties included in Annex I shall strive to implement policies and measures . . . in such a way as to minimize adverse effects, including the . . . effects on international trade, and social, environmental and economic impacts on other Parties, especially developing country Parties and in particular those identified in Article 4, paragraphs 8 and 9, of the Convention, taking into account Article 3 of the Convention . . ."
- Article 3.14 of KP: "The COP serving as the Meeting of the Parties to this Protocol shall consider what actions are necessary to minimize the adverse impacts of response measures on developing country Parties. Among the

issues to be considered shall be the establishment of funding, insurance and transfer of technology."

Previous COP decisions: From Cancun onwards, the just transition has been included, as follows:

- Decision 1.CP/16 (just transition included both in shared vision and response measures): "Recognizing the importance of avoiding or minimizing negative impacts of response measures on social and economic sectors, promoting a just transition of the workforce, the creation of decent work and quality jobs in accordance with nationally defined development priorities and strategies . . ."
- Decision 2. CP/17 (response measures): "Urges Parties in implementing their policies and measures to promote a just transition of the workforce and the creation of decent work and quality jobs in accordance with nationally defined development priorities and strategies"
- Decision 1. CP/18: Reaffirms same content of decision 1.CP/16

Workforce as a vulnerable sector to response measures due to the following challenges:

- Adverse effects of climate change will impact employment (e.g., agriculture productivity will be diminished and jobs affected; infrastructure and industry will also be impacted)
- The transition towards sustainable development will imply social consequences for the workforce that will lose jobs in the context of economic transformation in developing countries.
- There are risks of job losses and impacts, related to specific vulnerabilities of the workforce to the economic transformation and to the negative economic and social consequences of response measures.
- Barriers implemented by developed countries—such as agriculture subsidies, standards and tariffs—could hinder economic and social development and poverty eradication in developing countries and, therefore, affect the workforce in those countries.
- The workforce in developing countries is among the most vulnerable social groups due to the rapid growth of a young population in those countries, and the need to ensure that population decent work.
- This will require education programs to enable young population to enter the labour market.

What actions are needed?

- There is a need to minimize hardships for workers ensuring them the continuation of their employment and building capacities for their integration in the context of structural transformation derived from action related to climate change.
- Public policies are instrumental in addressing the needs of workers, in accordance with nationally defined development priorities, circumstances, and conditions.
    - It is important to consider developing mechanisms for a just transition and creation of decent work through a consultation process involving the relevant stakeholders (public and private sector, trade unions, and other civil society actors, among others).
    - There will be "no one-size fits all solution." It should be country-led process, Rio+20: "We affirm that there are different approaches, visions, models and tools available to each country, in accordance with its national circumstances and priorities to achieve sustainable development in its three dimensions which is our overarching goal . . ." (para. 56).
    - In addition, there is a need for developed countries to undertake an assessment in the design and implementation of their response measures, including unilateral ones, of the economic and social consequences of those measures on developing countries.
    - This assessment should be done in terms of the impact of the response measures taken by developed countries on, *inter alia*, employment, income, economic growth rates, and living standards in developing countries.
    - This assessment needs to be undertaken both in quantitative and qualitative terms and must take into account the specific national conditions of developing countries and their priorities needs and circumstances.
    - This would be done in the context of the obligations of developed countries to striving to avoid and minimize the negative economic and social consequences of their response measures on developing countries.

Moreover, the fulfilment of the obligations of developed countries of provision of financial resources, including for transfer of technologies and capacity-building for developing countries, is also important to ensuring support for workers that may be affected by social and economic consequences of response measures.

Thank you very much for your attention!

G-77 and China Presentation: Forum on the Impact of the Implementation of Response Measures

Views of the G-77 and China on Area (c): Assessment and Analysis of Impacts

Bonn, 38th Session of the Subsidiary Bodies
6 June 2013

Area (c)
General context

- The assessment and analysis of impacts has to be seen in the broader context of the achievement of sustainable development, in accordance with nationally defined priorities.
- The results of Rio+20 should be taken into account as an overarching framework: twenty years after the landmark 1992 Earth Summit in Rio, the international community reaffirmed sustainable development as the central paradigm in its three pillars (environmental, social and economical), as well as the Rio principles, in particular CBDR. Rio outcome document agreed by UN Members leaders.
- Need to avoid and minimize negative economic and social consequences of response measures taken by developed country parties on developing country parties, in a context in which:
- all developing countries face economic and social consequences of response measures (actual and potential) in different ways
- research and assessment on those impacts of response measures is a new field
- the UNFCCC is the mandated fora to discuss the economic and social impacts of response measures, including unilateral ones
- Importance to give full consideration to what actions are necessary under the Convention, including actions related to funding, insurance and the transfer of technology, to meet the specific needs and concerns of developing country parties arising from the adverse effects of climate change and/or the impact of the implementation of response measures
- This is related to relevant provisions and principles of the Convention (such as articles 4.8, 4.9, 3.1, 3.4, 3.5) and of its Kyoto Protocol (such as articles 2.3 and 3.14).

Need for assessment and analysis of economic and social impacts of response measures taken by developed country Parties on developing country Parties as:

Policies and measures taken by developed countries to combat climate change, including unilateral ones, shall not undermine the development nor constitute a means of transferring the burden of climate change mitigation obligations of developed country parties to developing country parties

Need for assessment and analysis of impacts

- There is a need for developed countries to undertake an assessment in the design and implementation of their response measures, including unilateral ones, of the economic and social consequences of those measures on developing countries.
- This would be done in the context of the obligations of developed countries to striving to avoid and minimize the negative economic and social consequences of their response measures on developing countries.
- This assessment should be done in terms of the impact of the response measures taken by developed countries on, *inter alia*, employment, income, economic growth rates, and living standards in developing countries.
- The assessment needs to:
  - be undertaken both in quantitative and qualitative terms and *ex ante* and *ex post*
  - take into account the specific national conditions of developing countries and their priorities, needs, and circumstances

This assessment during the design and implementation of response measures taken by developed country parties will help to:

- Promote understanding about the nature and magnitude of economic and social consequences for developing country parties of different response measures taken by developed country parties
- Assist developing country parties in identifying and addressing the impact of response measures taken by developed country parties and exploring ways to avoid and minimize negative consequences in developing country parties (Annex I parties "... shall strive to implement policies and measures in such a way as to minimize adverse effects on developing country Parties ...")

The assessment should include, *inter alia*, the following:

- Consistency with the principles and provisions of the Convention, in particular the principle of common but differentiated responsibilities, articles 3.5, 4.8, and 4.9 of the UNFCCC and articles 2.3 and 3.14 of the KP
- Consideration if the special economic and social conditions of developing countries (and their first and overriding priorities in terms of economic and social development and poverty eradication) were taken into account in the design and implementation
- Information about consultation to potentially affected developing country parties
- Inclusion of scientific basis of the measure
- Analysis if the measure is the most effective means to achieve the objective of combating climate change

- Fulfilment of developed countries' obligations related to the provision of specific support to developing countries, in terms of transfer of technology, financial resources, and capacity-building

This could assist in the development of endogenous capacities in developing countries, in order for them to meet the agreed full incremental costs of implementing measures (relation to, e.g., arts. 4.3, 4.5, and 4.7 of Convention).

Summary: Assessment and analysis of impacts

- Broader context of transition to sustainable development, in accordance with nationally defined priorities
- Need for developed countries to undertake an assessment of their response measures, including unilateral ones, in terms of their economic and social consequences on developing countries
- *Ex ante*, *ex post*, quantitative and qualitative assessment on, *inter alia*, employment, income, economic growth rates, and living standards in developing countries
- Assessment of issues such as consistency with UNFCCC, scientific basis, effectiveness, consultation to affected parties, consideration of special conditions of developing countries; support to those countries, etc.

Thank you very much for your attention!

G-77 and China Presentation: Forum on the Impact of the Implementation of Response Measures

Views of the G-77 and China on Area (b): Cooperation on Response Strategies

Bonn, 39th Session of the Subsidiary Bodies
12 November 2013

General context

- *The issue of economic and social consequences of response measures, and in particular, of cooperation strategies, has to be seen in the broader context of the achievement of sustainable development (in its economic, social and environmental dimensions) and poverty eradication, in accordance with nationally defined priorities.*
- *Cooperation on response strategies needs to be done in accordance with the principles and provisions of the UNFCCC, in particular preambular paragraphs 3, 17, 21, 22, and articles 3.1, 3.4, 3.5, 4.1. (g and h), 4.3, 4.5, 4.7, 4.8 of the Convention, and articles 2.3 and 3.14 of KP.*

- *There is a need to reaffirm decisions 1.CP/16, 2.CP/17, 1.CP/18, in relation to economic and social consequences of response measures*

All of this, in a general context in which the first and overriding priorities of developing countries are economic and social development and poverty eradication.

Cooperation on response strategies in the context of the forum means:

- how developed countries are cooperating to assist developing country parties in avoiding and minimizing the economic and social consequences of response measures on developing countries, in accordance with the principles and provisions of the Convention.
- to give full consideration to what actions are necessary under the Convention, including actions related to funding, insurance and the transfer of technology, to meet the specific needs and concerns of developing country parties arising from the impact of the implementation of response measures.

What actions could help to foster this cooperation on response strategies?

- Exchange of views, sharing information and expertise to inform policy choices of response measures taken by developed country parties (and which ones would avoid and minimize economic and social consequences of response measures on developing countries).
- Facilitation of technical collaboration among parties and experts on tools, including studies, modelling and methodologies, to assist developing country parties in addressing economic and social consequences of response measures.
- Cooperation of modelling teams among parties, to seek consensus on methodology development and scenarios setting and for models to take into account the specific national economic and social conditions of developing countries.
- Partnership with organizations in the research and assessment of developing countries' concerns and needs raising from the impacts of the implementation of response measures.
- Cooperation under the Convention to enhance the reporting of Annex I countries of the impacts of their response measures on developing countries, and how they are minimizing the adverse effects on developing countries.
- Strengthening of multilateral approaches to respond to climate change, in opposition to unilateral measures that would contravene UNFCCC principles and provisions (for example, the inclusion of civil aviation in the EU ETS).

Cooperation in terms of the implementation of article 3.5 of the UNFCCC:

> "The Parties should cooperate to promote a supportive and open international economic system that would lead to sustainable economic growth and development in all Parties, particularly developing country Parties, thus enabling them

better to address the problems of climate change. Measures taken to combat climate change, including unilateral ones, should not constitute a means of arbitrary or unjustifiable discrimination or a disguised restriction on international trade" (article 3.5 of the UNFCCC)

Cooperation also means that:

- policies and measures taken by developed countries to combat climate change, including unilateral ones, shall not undermine the development nor constitute a means of transferring the burden of climate change mitigation obligations of developed countries to developing country parties
- there is a need for social negative consequences to be avoided and minimized, ensuring a just transition of the workforce, the creation of decent work and quality jobs, in accordance with nationally defined development priorities and strategies
- ensure capacity-building, transfer of technologies and financial resources for developing countries, in order for these countries to meet the agreed full incremental costs of implementing measures (relation to arts. 4.3, 4.5, and 4.7 of the Convention)
- collaboration on identification of developing countries' needs to deal with the negative impacts of response measures in the context of their unique national circumstances and priorities Cooperation means that developed countries assess the design and implementation of their response measures in terms of:
  - *Ex ante* assessment of proposed response measures by developed countries, including unilateral ones, and their expected economic and social consequences on developing countries.
  - *Ex post* assessment of current response measures of developed countries, including unilateral ones, in order to analyze economic and social consequences of those response measures on developing countries.

The assessment should include, *inter alia*, analysis of the following:

- if the measure is consistent with UNFCCC principles and provisions
- if there has been consultation to potentially affected developing country parties and if their special conditions have been duly taken into account
- if the measure is based on scientific evidence
- if the measures has a legitimate objective, like combating climate change
- if the measure is the most effective means to achieve the objective of combating climate change and the less trade restrictive
- if there is a fulfilment of developed countries' obligations related to the provision of specific support to developing countries (transfer of technology, financial resources, and capacity-building)

Final considerations

- Cooperation on response strategies: Broader context of transition to sustainable development, in accordance with nationally defined priorities
- Need for developed countries to undertake an *ex ante* and *ex post* assessment of their response measures, including unilateral ones, in terms of their economic and social consequences on developing countries
- Continuation of the forum is important for fostering cooperation on response strategies, as the forum provides a platform for the exchange of views and for dialogue to enhance cooperation in terms of exploring ways to avoid and minimize negative economic and social consequences of response measures taken by developed countries on developing countries
- Importance of strengthening multilateralism, in opposition to unilateral measures that undermine the spirit of cooperation and dialogue

Thank you very much for your attention!

Approaches to address loss and damage associated with climate change impacts in developing countries that are particularly vulnerable to the adverse effects of climate change to enhance adaptive capacity

Submission from the Group of 77 and China*

Decision x/CP.19 – International Mechanism on Loss and Damage

Recalling that the ultimate objective of this Convention is to achieve stabilization of greenhouse gas concentrations in the atmosphere at a level that would prevent dangerous anthropogenic interference with the climate system;

Also recalling that parties should protect the climate system for the benefit of present and future generations of humankind, on the basis of equity and in accordance with their common but differentiated responsibilities and respective capabilities, and should take precautionary measures to anticipate, prevent, or minimize the causes of climate change and mitigate its adverse effects;

Reaffirming that, in their actions to achieve the objective of the Convention and to implement its provisions, the parties shall be guided by the specific needs and special circumstances of developing country parties, especially those that are particularly vulnerable to the adverse effects of climate change, and of those parties, especially developing country parties, that would have to bear a disproportionate or abnormal burden under the Convention, should be given full consideration;

* Contained in document FCCC/SBI/2013/CRP.1 of 12 November 2013.

Taking into account recent findings from the IPCC that indicate that, from 1750 to 2011, cumulative anthropogenic CO_2 emissions to the atmosphere have reached 545 [460 to 630] GtC;

Noting with grave concern the significant gap between the aggregate effect of parties' mitigation pledges in terms of global annual emissions of greenhouse gases by 2020 and aggregate emission pathways consistent with having a likely chance of holding the increase in global average temperature below 2°C or 1.5°C above pre-industrial levels;

Recognizing the need to strengthen international cooperation and expertise in order to understand and reduce loss and damage associated with the adverse effects of climate change, including impacts related to extreme weather events and slow onset events;

Recognizing also the need to strengthen capacity and awareness of regional, national, sub-national, and local governments to address the threat of loss and damage;

Affirming the important role of the Convention in promoting leadership, collaboration, and cooperation, at the national, regional, and international levels, in order to enable coherent and synergistic approaches to address such loss and damage;

Recalling the decision by the Conference of the Parties, in decision 3/CP.18, to establish institutional arrangements, such as an international mechanism, to address loss and damage associated with the impacts of climate in developing countries that are particularly vulnerable to the adverse effects of climate change;

Affirming that, consistent with decision 3/CP.18 paragraphs 5, 6, and 7 an international mechanism will strengthen coherence, coordination, synergies, linkages, and cooperation on loss and damage to the adverse effects of climate change, both within and external to the Convention;

1. Decides to establish the international mechanism to address loss and damage associated with the impacts of climate change (International Mechanism on Loss and Damage, hereinafter referred to as "the international mechanism" or IMLD), in accordance with decision 3/CP.18;
2. Agrees that the international mechanism is established to address loss and damage associated with the adverse effects of climate change from extreme and slow onset events in developing country parties, especially the least developed countries and Small Island Developing States and other developing countries particularly vulnerable to the adverse effects of climate change;
3. Also agrees that the IMLD should complement existing institutions within the UNFCCC, as well as external institutions, with a view to strengthening

coherence, coordination, synergies, linkages, and cooperation on loss and damage to the adverse effects of climate change, both within and external to the Convention;

4. Further decides that the mechanism will have a Technical Facility to, *inter alia*, implement those functions of the IMLD requiring technical knowledge and expertise through activities, including, but not limited to, long-term impact assessments; knowledge and data management; the development of new approaches and tools and the building of capacity to address loss and damage from the adverse effects of climate change and a Financial Facility to, *inter alia*, implement those functions of the IMLD requiring financial knowledge and expertise, in particular by assisting with financial support required to comprehensively address loss and damage to the adverse effects of climate change in the short, medium, and long term;.
5. Decides that the international mechanism on loss and damage shall be subject to the authority and guidance of the Conference of the Parties;
6. Decides to establish an Executive Board of the Mechanism to supervise and lead the work of the IMLD;
7. Decides that the IMLD shall be funded through a dedicated trust fund established through financial support from developed country parties;
8. Further agrees that the functions of the IMLD, in accordance with paragraph 5 of 3/CP.18, are to include, *inter alia*:
   a. provide global oversight and coordination on the assessment and implementation of actions related to loss and damage associated with the adverse effects of climate change;
   b. promote synergies, enhance collaboration, cooperation, and linkages, and strengthen engagement between national, regional, and international organizations, centres, and networks involved in assessing and addressing loss and damage;
   c. develop and, as appropriate, strengthen the knowledge base at multiple levels on loss and damage to the adverse effects of climate change, including on slow onset events, non-economic losses, migration, and displacement;
   d. consolidate and enhance the coherence and sharing of relevant data, information, knowledge, experience, and good practices related to the characterization, quantification, and development of appropriate responses to loss and damage at the local, national, regional, and international levels;
   e. develop innovative measures, approaches, and modalities to assess and address permanent losses and irreversible damage, including non-economic losses, with particular attention to loss and damage associated with slow onset events and means of rehabilitation and/or compensation;

f. enhance action to address loss and damage associated with the adverse effects of climate change through provision of technical support and guidance to national governments on comprehensive approaches to risk assessment and risk management for extreme and slow onset events, including socioeconomic and non-economic impacts, with a view to building capacity at national and regional levels to increase adaptive capacity, coping capacity, and resilience;
g. facilitate and catalyse support for the efficient development and operationalization of approaches, at all levels, to address loss and damage from extreme weather events and slow onset events, including support for actions listed in decision 3/CP.18, paragraph 6, and including approaches for rehabilitation;
h. ensure enhanced action on addressing loss and damage associated with the adverse effects of climate change through the provision of new, predictable, and reliable financial support for the assessment of, and responses to, the impacts of loss and damage through an appropriate financial mechanism;
i. support the establishment of social safety net and social protection programmes to address damage to or loss of livelihoods associated with the adverse effects of climate change, including, *inter alia*, for migration and displacement.
j. support the development and ensure that a spectrum of risk transfer tools is available to parties and regional bodies, including insurance, to address loss and damage associated with the adverse effects of climate change.

8. Adopts the modalities of the International Mechanism on Loss and Damage as contained in annex I to this decision.
9. Notes that the modalities of the International Mechanism on Loss and Damage, which are based on the functions outlined in paragraph 4 of this decision, include the following six key elements:
   (a) Global oversight, coherence, and coordination;
   (b) Enhancing cooperation, collaboration, and linkages with other institutional arrangements under and outside the Convention;
   (c) Knowledge development and exchange;
   (d) Technology and capacity-building support for implementation of actions;
   (e) Financial support for implementation of actions;
   (f) Support for and coordination with risk-transfer mechanisms;
10. Requests the Executive Board of the Mechanism to further elaborate on linkages with other relevant institutional arrangements under and outside the Convention;
11. Invites all parties to strengthen and, where necessary, establish and/or designate national-level institutional arrangements, with a view to enhancing

work on loss and damage, with the adequate means of implementation for developing countries parties provided by developed country parties;

12. Invites parties to strengthen and, where necessary establish, regional centres and networks, in particular in developing countries, with support from developed country parties and relevant organizations, as appropriate, and to facilitate and enhance national and regional action to address loss and damage, in a manner that is country-driven, encourages cooperation and coordination between regional stakeholders and improves the flow of information between the Convention process and national and regional activities.

Annex I: Modalities of the International Mechanism on Loss and Damage

1. For performing the functions as contained in paragraph 4(a) of this decision, with regard to global oversight, coherence, and coordination, the modalities will include:
   i. Facilitating regional and international dialogue to strengthen coherence and cooperation on the planning and implementation of comprehensive climate risk management of extreme and slow onset events, and to ensure global reach of efforts;
   ii. Coordinating with relevant organizations on financial, technical, and associated matters;
   iii. Coordinating with global and regional institutions to address displacement, migration, and planned relocation efforts;
   iv. Providing leadership in guiding relevant stakeholders involved;
2. For performing the functions as contained in paragraph 4(b) of this decision, with regard to enhancing cooperation, collaboration, and linkages with other institutional arrangements under and outside the Convention, the modalities will include:
   ii. Supporting and facilitating international and regional centres and networks of climate risk platforms;
   iii. Promoting and strengthening coordination and collaboration between various stakeholder groups and the international community;
   iv. Encouraging the involvement of vulnerable communities and populations, and civil society, the private sector, and other relevant stakeholders, in the assessment of and response to loss and damage;
   v. Linking the level and types of expertise required to address loss and damage, including from extreme events and slow onset events;
3. For performing the functions as contained in paragraphs 4(c), (d), and (e) of this decision, with regard to knowledge development and exchange, the modalities will include:
   i. Providing guidance on data collection standards, tools, and methodologies for characterizing loss and damage, including likely biophysical and socio-economic impacts;

ii. Fostering partnerships for the application of data collection tools and methodologies at regional, national, and sub-national levels;
iii. Facilitating the establishment and use of open source models and information, including to establish baselines and long-term projections of climate change risks and impacts, including slow onset events;
iv. Coordinating data repositories and encouraging coherence across information frameworks;
v. Establishing guidelines for systematic observation, data collection and analysis, scenario development, and loss accounting for use by national, regional, and international centres;
vi. Supporting and facilitating the development of new or existing regional climate change centres and databases and associated networks to facilitate data and information transfer, use and dissemination;
vii. Facilitating research and systematic observation to understand the scope, magnitude, and character of climate change risks and impacts, and to assess the type and extent of losses, including economic and non-economic losses;
viii. Promoting research to define the thresholds and tipping points in both biophysical and socio-economic systems where adaptation is no longer feasible;
ix. Developing means to assess and address less directly measurable economic losses such as lost sustainable development opportunities and impacts on economic growth;
x. Developing means to assess and address non-economic losses;
xi. For performing the functions as contained in paragraph 4 (f) of this decision, with regard to technology and capacity-building support for implementation, the modalities will include:
xii. Channeling commitments of Annex II parties for the provision of means of implementation, including expertise, capacity-building, and transfer of technology;
xiii. Providing scientific and technological advice and guidance on socio-economic assessments;
xiv. Facilitating the development and dissemination of country-specific and appropriate risk assessment and risk management methodologies, including for slow onset disasters;
xv. Planning and implementing packages of tools for comprehensive climate risk management of extreme and slow onset events;
xvi. Supporting the development of appropriate data, risk management capability including appropriate regulatory frameworks at appropriate levels, and financial back-up;

xvii. Building awareness, understanding, and capacity to access and use climate change data and information across all levels of government;
xviii. Building capacity and awareness of regional, national, sub-national, and local governments to address the threat of loss and damage;
xix. Enabling a better understanding of principles, benefits, costs, and scalability of packages of tools available;

5. For performing the functions as contained in paragraphs 4(g), (h), and (i) of this decision, with regard to financial support for implementation, the modalities will include:
   i. Channeling commitments of Annex II parties for the provision of financial support;
   ii. Mobilizing sufficient new and additional resources in a timely manner;
   iii. Establishing a liquidity pool for swift relief in cases of episodic events and/or catastrophic shocks;
   iv. Providing funds for actions to reduce risk, and where it cannot be avoided, providing for rehabilitation or compensation of permanent loss; including undertaking fast action and investment in preventing the loss of social assets and natural resources under imminent risk of permanent loss or irreversible damage, especially those assessed with a high-cost benefit ratio and short-term results.
   v. Evaluating different roles for finance in addressing loss and damage;
   vi. Developing a suite of options for financial measures, including social protection programmes and debt relief;
   vii. Establishing a financial mechanism for redress, including for compensation and rehabilitation.

6. For performing the functions as contained in paragraph 4(j) of this decision, with regard to support for and coordination with risk transfer mechanisms, the modalities will include:
   i. Ensuring and supporting the development of regional and/or global catastrophe risk transfer facilities;
   ii. Providing support for new facilities, including through providing for initial capitalization of national and regional insurance and alternative risk transfer schemes, as well as national and regional saving schemes to address slow onset disasters;
   iii. Creating a hub for regional and national level insurance facilities, as appropriate;
   iv. Developing a portfolio of actions to reduce and transfer risk;
   v. Promoting an enabling environment that would encourage investment and the involvement of relevant stakeholders in climate risk management.

Impact of the Implementation of Response Measures: Forum and Work Programme

Proposal by the Group of 77 and China*

The Conference of the Parties,

Recalling decisions 5/CP.7, 1/CP.10, 1/CP.13, 1/CP.16, 2/CP.17, 8/CP. 17, 1/ CP. 18, and 31/CMP.1,

Reaffirming the principles and provisions of the Convention, in particular preambular paragraphs 3, 17, 21, 22, and articles 3.1, 3.4, 3.5, 4.1. g) and h), 4.3, 4.5, 4.7, 4.8, 4.9, 4.10 of the Convention, and articles 2.3 and 3.14 of the Kyoto Protocol.

Recognizing that developing country parties are affected by adverse economic and social consequences of response measures taken by developed country parties,

Reaffirming that economic and social development and poverty eradication are the overriding priorities of developing country parties,

Welcoming the establishment of the forum on the impact of the implementation of response measures and its work programme and the constructive discussions that took place at the related workshops and meetings in 2012 and 2013, under the Subsidiary Body for Implementation and the Subsidiary Body for Scientific and Technological Advice,

Acknowledging repeated calls for a continued and structured exchange of information on negative economic and social consequences of response measures taken by developed country parties on developing country parties and to implement specific actions to avoid and minimize those consequences,

Recognizing the need to give full consideration to what actions are necessary under the Convention, including actions related to funding, insurance, and the transfer of technology, to meet the specific needs and concerns of developing country parties arising from the impact of the implementation of response measures,

Reaffirming the need to consider policy issues of concern, such as unilateral measures, in accordance with decision 1/CP.18,

Affirming that there are still gaps of implementation to address the negative social and economic consequences of response measures taken by developed countries on developing countries and recognizing the need for further work in this regard,

* Contained in document FCCC/SB/2013/L.4 of 16 November 2013.

1. *Decides* to hereby continue the forum on the impact of the implementation of response measures under the Subsidiary Bodies to share, in an interactive manner, information, experiences, case studies, practices, and views on how to meet the specific needs and concerns of developing country parties in terms of social and economic consequences of response measures;
2. *Decides* to establish a mechanism under the COP to address the negative social and economic consequences of response measures taken by developed country parties on developing country parties and to recommend specific actions to avoid and minimize those consequences;
3. *Decides* that the forum will report to the mechanism;
4. *Further decides* that the mechanism will make recommendations and report to the COP with a view to adopt decisions;
5. *Decides* that the mechanism will meet for its first time in conjunction with the fortieth sessions of the subsidiary bodies;
6. *Requests* parties to undertake the necessary arrangements to develop the terms of reference and modalities of operationalization of the mechanism before the fortieth sessions of the subsidiary bodies;
7. *Agrees* that parties shall undertake a biennial evaluation of the progress made to address the specific needs and concerns of developing country parties arising from the impact of the implementation of response measures;
8. *Agrees* that some of the areas that need further dialogue in the forum and work in the mechanism would be, *inter alia*, the following below:
   - Assessment and analysis of impacts of response measures taken by developed country parties on developing country parties, including unilateral ones, in terms of their consequences on, *inter alia*, employment, income, economic growth rates, and living standards in developing countries;
   - Ways to strengthen multilateral cooperation, in opposition to unilateral measures;
   - Economic diversification and building resilience in developing country parties to deal with the adverse impacts of response measures;
   - Just transition and creation of decent work, in accordance with nationally defined priorities, and minimizing hardships for workers ensuring them the continuation of their employment and building capacities;
   - Economic modelling, studies, methodology development, and scenarios setting to assist developing country parties in addressing negative economic and social consequences of response measures. Modelling could be applied to assess consequences of response measures of developed country parties, *inter alia*, on trade, investment, income, employment, economic growth rates of developing country parties;
   - Development of specific reporting guidelines for Annex I parties on how those parties are implementing policies and measures in such a way as to minimize adverse effects on developing country parties;

- Provision of specific support by developed country parties to developing country parties in terms of transfer of technology, financial resources, and capacity-building, in order for the latter to be able to deal with the adverse economic and social effects of response measures;

Review of the Work of the Forum in the Impact of the Implementation of Response Measures

Submission by the G-77 and China[*]

The G-77 and China reaffirms the need to explore ways to avoid and minimize negative economic and social consequences of response measures taken by developed countries on developing countries. This should be done in accordance with the principles and provisions of the Convention, in particular its articles 3.1, 3.4, 3.5, 4.1. g) and h), 4.3, 4.5, 4.7, 4.8, 4.9, and 4.10 of the Convention, and articles 2.3 and 3.14 of the Kyoto Protocol and in the broader context of the achievement of sustainable development in its economic, social, and environmental dimensions, as well as well poverty eradication.

Based on the review of the work of the forum, the G-77 and China notes the progress made in the forum, while recognizing that there are still implementation gaps to give full consideration to what actions are necessary under the Convention, including actions related to funding, insurance, and the transfer of technology, to meet the specific needs and concerns of developing countries arising from the impact of the implementation of response measures. Moreover, developed countries are not fulfilling their obligations under the Convention and Kyoto Protocol in terms of minimizing the adverse effects of response measures on developing countries, particularly those under articles 4.8 and 4.9 under the Convention, and in line with relevant COP decisions. During the work programme of the forum, we had the opportunity to have a first exchange of general views, and the G-77 and China made a lot of proposals in this regard that still merit attention and further discussion. Even if the forum has proved useful for exchange of experiences, it has been incapable of taking specific actions to address implementation gaps to avoid and minimize negative economic and social consequences of response measures.

The importance of this issue was proven by the great number of parties that submitted their views, such as the G-77 and China. The group engaged constructively in all the sessions of the forum, including through G-77 and China presentations and statements in all the areas of the work program, supported by different G-77 and China regional groupings and individual delegations. In addition to those presentations and statements, the reports of the workshops and expert meetings and discussions held during the forum[6] are also useful as a summary

[*] Contained in UNFCCC document FCCC/SB/2014/L.2 of 14 June 2014.

[6] FCCC/SB/2013/INF.2, FCCC/SB/2013/INF.3, FCCC/SB/2013/INF.4, FCCC/SB/2013/INF.8, FCCC/SB/2013/INF.9, FCCC/SB/2013/INF.10, FCCC/SB/2013/INF.11, FCCC/SB/2013/MISC.2, and FCCC/SB/2013/MISC.4.

of the rich views and experiences presented by developing countries and were considered as part of the review.

Although there was participation from experts, civil society, and international organizations, many of them were not focused sufficiently on specific needs of developing countries. Therefore, for future work there needs to be clear guidance and terms of reference in terms of invitation to organizations and experts whose work is related to the issue of economic and social consequences of response measures, in particular to the avoidance and minimization of adverse effects of response measures on developing countries.

In addition, considering the importance of the issue for all developing countries, there needs to be dedicated time to address the negative economic and social consequences of response measures on developing countries. Thus, the work streams on the issue should continue to meet at least twice a year, in conjunction with Subsidiary Bodies and the COP.

Finally, we would like to share our main proposals we made in each of the areas of the work programme, as part of the review of the work of the forum mandated by decision 8/CP.17, review that was completed in Warsaw during the many sessions that were dedicated to the matter. In this way, the gaps of implementation identified on the basis of the review of the work of the forum by G-77 and China are the following:

RESULTS OF THE REVIEW OF THE WORK OF THE AREAS OF THE WORK PROGRAM OF THE FORUM

AREA A: Sharing of information and expertise, including reporting and promoting understanding of positive and negative impacts of response measures

The G-77 and China expressed that there is a lack of clear reporting guidelines. We showed that in the national communications of Annex I (AI) parties, few of those parties reported, and of those that reported, some reported purely domestic efforts as technology cooperation, and others only described their measures. Particularly, there is a lack of reporting guidelines for Annex I parties on how they "... shall strive to implement policies and measures in such a way as to minimize adverse effects on developing country Parties..." (arts. 2.3 and 3.14 of the Kyoto Protocol (KP)).

Therefore, it is crucial to elaborate specific reporting guidelines for AI parties on this issue.

AREA B: Cooperation on response strategies

The issue of economic and social consequences of response measures, and in particular, of cooperation strategies, has to be seen in the broader context of the achievement of sustainable development (in its economic, social, and environmental dimensions) and poverty eradication, in accordance with nationally defined priorities

Cooperation on response strategies needs to be done in accordance with the principles and provisions of the UNFCCC, in particular preambular paragraphs 3, 17, 21, 22, and articles 3.1, 3.4, 3.5, 4.1. g) and h), 4.3, 4.5, 4.7, 4.8 of the Convention, and articles 2.3 and 3.14 of KP.

What actions could help to foster this cooperation on response strategies?

- Exchange of views, sharing information and expertise to inform policy choices of response measures taken by developed country parties (and which ones would avoid and minimize economic and social consequences of response measures on developing countries)
- Facilitation of technical collaboration among parties and experts on tools, including studies, modelling, and methodologies, to assist developing country parties in addressing economic and social consequences of response measures
- Cooperation of modelling teams among parties, to seek consensus on methodology development and scenarios setting and for models to take into account the specific national economic and social conditions of developing countries
- Partnership with organizations in the research and assessment of developing countries' concerns and needs rising from the impacts of the implementation of response measures
- Cooperation under the Convention to enhance the reporting of Annex I countries of the impacts of their response measures on developing countries, and how they are minimizing the adverse effects on developing countries.

Finally, it is important to ensure capacity-building for developing countries as well as to strengthen multilateralism, in opposition to unilateral measures that undermine the spirit of cooperation and dialogue.

AREA C: Assessment and analysis of impacts

There is a need to research and assess the economic and social impacts of response measures, including unilateral ones. In this context, there is a need for developed countries to undertake an assessment in the design and implementation of their response measures, including unilateral ones, on the economic and social consequences of those measures on developing countries, in order to strive to minimize these impacts on, *inter alia*, employment, income, economic growth rates, and living standards in developing countries.

The assessment should include

- if the measure is consistent with UNFCCC principles and provisions
- if there has been consultation to potentially affected developing country parties and if their special conditions have been duly taken into account

- if the measure is based on scientific evidence
- if the measures has a legitimate objective, like combating climate change
- if the measure is the most effective means to achieve the objective of combating climate change and the less trade restrictive
- if there is a fulfilment of developed countries' obligations related to the provision of specific support to developing countries (transfer of technology, financial resources, and capacity-building)
- the assessment should be undertaken both in quantitative and qualitative terms and *ex ante* and *ex post* and take into account the specific national conditions of developing countries and their priorities, needs, and circumstances

AREA D: Exchanging experience and discussion of opportunities for economic diversification and transformation

Economic transformation and diversification entail high adjustment costs for developing countries, as their economies are generally characterized by a low economic diversification. They have traditionally relied heavily on the production and exports of commodities whose production is particularly vulnerable to climate change.

Also, the costs of clean technologies remain prohibitive for those countries.

In consequence, this area is an opportunity to exchange views, experiences, lessons learned on national cases and for specific action for economic transformation and diversification in the context of nationally defined priorities, circumstances and needs.

Moreover, developed countries obligations' in terms of support of financial resources, transfer of technology and capacity-building to developing countries need to be fulfilled in order to assist developing countries in that economic diversification.

AREA E: Economic Modelling and Socio-economic Trends

Economic modelling can provide accurate and objective assessment of the observed and potential economic and social consequences of response measures taken by developed country parties on developing country parties and it can produce quantitative assessment which will be complemented by qualitative assessment.

Modelling is useful to produce specific assessment on different sectors of the economy such as tourism, industry, agriculture, etc., and on consequences of response measures of developed country parties' on, *inter alia*, trade, investment, income, employment, economic growth rates of developing countries.

Therefore, it is essential to elaborate models that reflect the circumstances and contexts of developing countries, by accommodating variables that capture the uniqueness of national characteristics, taking into account their social and socio-economic factors and specific national priorities, conditions and needs.

Activities that could be carried out:

- Dissemination of modelling tools
- Ensuring increased collaboration on modelling developments on an ongoing basis
- Identify vulnerable sectors and needs in terms of technology transfer and funding (related to for example, articles 4.3, 4.5, 4.7, and 4.8 of UNFCCC)

AREA F: The relevant aspects relating to the implementation of decisions 1/CP.10, 1/CP.13, and 1/CP.16 and article 2, paragraph 3, and article 3, paragraph 14, of the Kyoto Protocol

There are implementation gaps in relation to these articles and decisions, in order to address the specific needs and concerns of developing countries related to the impact of the implementation of response measures.

There is a need to focus on these gaps in the implementation in order to give full consideration to what actions are necessary under the Convention, including action related to funding, insurance, and transfer of technology, to meet the specific needs and concerns of developing countries arising from the impact of the implementation of response measures.

Therefore, there is a need for a structured follow-up of the implementation gaps and concrete actions to ensure full implementation of, *inter alia*, the decisions mentioned in area F, that is, 1/CP.10, 1/CP.13, and 1/CP.16 and article 2, paragraph 3, and article 3, paragraph 14, of the Kyoto Protocol. In addition, there is a need to ensure the implementation of decisions 5/CP.7, 2/CP.17, 1/CP.18, and 31/CMP.1, and the relevant principles and provisions of the Convention, in particular its article 3, paragraphs 1 and 5, and article 4, paragraphs 1(g) and (h), 8, 9, and 10,

AREA G: Just Transition of the workforce and the creation of decent work and quality jobs

What actions are needed?

- Minimize hardships for workers ensuring them the continuation of their employment and building capacities for their integration in the context of the structural transformation derived from action related to climate change.
- Development of mechanisms for a just transition and creation of decent work through a consultation process involving the relevant stakeholders.

AREA H: Building collective and individual learning towards a transition to a low greenhouse gas–emitting society

Any transition needs to be understood in the broader context of the transition towards sustainable development and parties' different national socio-economic contexts, specific conditions and unique circumstances. It has also to be consistent with the principles and provisions of the Convention, in particular the principle of common but differentiated responsibilities.

Moreover, any transition should take into account the overriding priorities of developing countries in terms of the achievement of economic and social development and poverty eradication.

What actions are needed?

- Capacity-building, transfer of technologies, and financial resources for learning and for development of endogenous capacities in developing countries, in order for them to meet the agreed full incremental costs of implementing measures (relation to articles 4.3, 4.5, and 4.7 of the Convention)
- Exchange of experiences, information, knowledge-sharing, and know-how, and of ensuring access to affordable technologies for developing countries for implementation of NAMAs and NAPAs.
- Assessment of the role of the protection of intellectual property rights (IPR) in terms of transfer of technology.

Based on the review of the work of the forum completed in Warsaw, we clearly note there is much work still to be done to meet the needs and concerns of developing countries in terms of negative economic and social consequences of response measures taken by developed countries on developing countries.

To sum up, on the basis of the review, it is clear there are gaps of implementation in terms of, *inter alia*, reporting by AI parties on response measures; technical collaboration on modelling and methodologies; ways to strengthen multilateralism, in opposition to unilateral measures; assessment in the design and implementation of the response measures of developed countries of the economic and social consequences of those measures on developing countries, in order to strive to minimize adverse impacts; support to developing countries for economic diversification and in terms of transfer of technology, funding, and capacity-building; and the development of mechanisms for a just transition and creation of decent work .

Therefore, we propose the continuation of the forum, in terms of sharing experiences, information and lessons learned on areas to address the needs of developing countries, at the same time that there is a need for specific action through the establishment of a Mechanism for Enhanced Action on Response Measures under the COP. This Mechanism will facilitate implementation of enhanced action to address the negative social and economic consequences of response measures taken by developed country parties on developing country parties and to recommend specific actions, including in terms of support to developing countries, to avoid and minimize those consequences, and to deliver the functions as contained in the G-77 and China submission.

Paper No. 1: Bolivia (Plurinational State of) on behalf of the Group of 77 and China

Submission by Plurinational State of Bolivia on behalf of the Group of 77 and China:

On Second Review of the Adaptation Fund*

Annex

Proposals by parties on possible options for consideration by the second review of the Adaptation Fund.

1. Building on the views submitted and expressed before and during the fortieth session of the SBI, this note by the co-facilitators contains possible options for consideration by the SBI at its forty-first session in accordance with the terms of reference for the second review of the Adaptation Fund contained in the annex to decision 2/CMP.9.
   A. The provision of sustainable, predictable and adequate financial resources, including the potential diversification of revenue streams

Preamble

Underlining the crucial importance of the Adaptation Fund, and its status as the only fund dedicated to financing concrete adaptation projects and programmes,

Expressing deep concern about continued instability of carbon markets as a source of funds for the AF, gravely affecting the sustainability of the Fund,

Welcoming with appreciation the high ranking of the Adaptation Fund,

1. *Decides* that:
   (a) The implementation of the fundraising strategy of the Fund should be considered;
   (b) The Board should determine the scale of resources that needs to be mobilized on an annual basis, and future projected periods, and including the setting an annual resource target;
   (c) The establishment of a regular replenishment process should be considered;

* Contained in document FCCC/SBI/2014/MISC.4 of 10 November 2014.

(d) The Board could consider the development of an ongoing fundraising strategy to ensure that resources under the Adaptation Fund meet the needs according to projects already in the pipeline, as well as expected projects;
(e) The pipeline of projects expected from the different categories of implementing entities and the implication of the expected pipeline for resources available or required should be considered;
(f) The Board should consider the establishment of a mechanism that continuously reviews the status of projects in the pipeline against the availability of finance to ensure sustainability of implementation as one avenue to address the need for annual or bi-annual resource flows.

In terms of the diversification of revenue streams,

(a) In the light of the need to diversify sources of financing, further action is necessary to enhance and secure new revenue streams for the AF;
(b) Options for additional funding sources and alternative means of diversifying its funding sources should be explored as a matter of priority;
(c) The implementation on the operationalization of decision 1/CMP.8 on a 2 per cent share of proceeds levied on the first international transfers of AAUs and ERUs for article 6 projects needs to be considered;
(d) Generating resources from the carbon markets should be considered including:
   i. The allocation of 10 per cent of the carry-over units;
   ii. The consideration of a set of measures to stabilize the price of CERs including through dealing with the level of ambition through the ratification of the second commitment period of the Kyoto Protocol, and higher emission limitation commitments for developed country parties under any new agreement under the Convention;
   iii. The application of voluntary levies on developed country parties being to national and regional emission trading schemes such as the European Union Emissions Trading Scheme (EU-ETS).

2. Based on the annual revenue projections, a clear burden-sharing process through assessed scale of contribution from Annex B countries of the Kyoto Protocol, should be considered.
3. *Decides also* that the review should include an examination of funding sources for adaptation under the Financial Mechanism of the Convention.
4. *Recommends* that the Board should consider applying for accreditation to the Green Climate Fund, as a first step towards the channelling of financing for adaptation to developing countries as a medium- to long-term measure under the Adaptation Window of the Green Climate Fund.

B. Lessons learned from the application of the access modalities of the Adaptation Fund

5. *Notes* that the application of the country-ownership principle, the operationalization of direct access modalities, delivery of concrete results, the establishment of national implementing entities which allowed for promoting environmental and social safeguards, a focus on the most vulnerable, and exemplary transparency make the AF a good role model. Further notes that it would be useful to share these lessons with other adaptation financing channels.
6. In terms of access modalities, decides that:
   (a) Targeted institutional strengthening strategies are needed to assist developing countries to accredit more national or regional implementing entities to the Adaptation Fund, to carry out adaptation projects;
   (b) Challenges and obstacles facing the accreditation of national implementing entities should be addressed;
   (c) Limiting access by the Multilateral Implementing Entities (MIEs) while ensuring that accredited NIEs have increased and facilitated access, underlining the cost difference and time frame for implementation between national implementing entities and multilateral implementing entities;
   (d) Access by SIDS though Regional Implementing Entities (RIEs) is important, while countries are in the process of obtaining accreditation for their NIEs;
   (e) The accreditation process and procedures for NIEs remain challenging and should be assessed. The harmonization and rationalization of procedures, requirements, accreditation procedures and capacity-building of Implementing Entities is needed, in particular at national and regional levels;
   (f) The readiness programme to assist NIEs to become accredited is appreciated, and the further enhancement of the readiness of developing countries to access direct funding from the Adaptation Fund should is needed;
   (g) Progress made in the accreditation of different categories of implementing entities should be considered;
   (h) How access to Fund is facilitated for LDCs/SIDS should be considered.
7. With regard to the implementation of projects and programmes, the following were raised:
   (a) The geographical and regional coverage of projects, including projects in the pipeline should be considered;
   (b) Results achieved should be looked at, in terms of building institutional capacity in implementing projects;
   (c) Social and environmental standards should be considered, in terms of how securing environmental and social standards in the implementation

of projects has been taken into consideration in the arrangements with the implementing entities;

(d) A pipeline of priority projects in vulnerable sectors need to be developed, given the importance for getting projects funded in priority sectors with high vulnerability to climate change (such as health, water, agriculture, and ecosystems) with plans to eventually upscale these into national, transboundary, and regional programmes;

(e) A targeted financing window for small-size projects and programmes, which are invaluable for building adaptive capacity at the local level, needs to be considered by the Board.

C. The institutional linkages and relations, as appropriate, between the Adaptation Fund and other institutions

8. In general, parties noted that it is important to enhance coherence and coordination between the AF and other sources of adaptation finance including in terms of:

(a) The relationship between the Adaptation Fund and other financial institutions under the UNFCCC and the Kyoto Protocol;

(b) Possible options for developing the role of the AF in the broader architecture for adaptation funding;

(c) Streamlining and consistency of accreditation procedures and requirements for direct access;

(d) Operational linkages between the AF and constituted bodies under the Convention including the SCF and Adaptation Committee and the TEC and CTCN Advisory Board. It was also mentioned that such bodies could support the AF Board with fund-raising strategies and the SCF could be tasked with leading an assessment on enhancing complementarity and coherence between the LDCF, SCCF, AF and the GCF and GEF.

D. The institutional arrangements for the Adaptation Fund

9. Parties noted that permanent arrangements for the trustee and Secretariat should be considered. Some parties noted that:

(a) The interim arrangements for the trustee and Secretariat should be smoothly transformed into permanent institutional arrangements;

(b) Permanent institutional arrangements should be determined on the basis of an open and competitive bidding process;

(c) The cost and time frame for each option and its legal and financial implication should be examined;

(d) A group of parties noted that the two options presented in the Report of the Interim Arrangements (2011), for the establishment of an independent Secretariat, should also be considered.

10. A group of parties called for exploring the options for placing the AF under the Convention and/or designating it as an operating entity of the financial mechanism of the Convention.
11. A group also noted that further possible operational improvements should be considered, as should how to ensure that current institutional arrangements, if extended, would not limit the growth and efficiency of the AF. It was mentioned that the extension of the interim institutional arrangements of the AFB Secretariat and the trustee until the third review of the Adaptation Fund should also be considered.

Submission from China on behalf of the Group of 77 and China*

Submission from the G-77 and China on Elements for a Draft Decision – Capacity-Building

Recalling decisions 2/CP.7, 1/CP.16, 2/CP.17, 13/CP.17, 1/CP.18, and 4/CP.12,

Acknowledging that capacity-building unlike other constituted bodies of the Convention is not coordinated and has no mechanism to aggregate impacts in the overall implementation of the Convention and the Kyoto Protocol,

Recognizing the success of the second and third meetings of the Durban Forum for in-depth discussion on capacity-building, held during the thirty-eighth and fortieth sessions of the Subsidiary Body for Implementation,

Expressing its appreciation to parties and representatives of intergovernmental and non-governmental organizations and the private sector for their active participation in the meetings of the Durban Forum for the sharing of experiences and exchanging ideas, best practices, and lessons learned regarding the implementation of capacity-building activities,

Expressing the need to further enhance the implementation of capacity-building, including through strengthening relevant institutions, networks, and support to meet the capacity requirements of developing countries,

Recognizing the cross-cutting nature of capacity-building,

Acknowledging that capacity-building is important and is a challenge for all countries, and that the sharing of experiences and best practices is essential to continued progress worldwide in addressing climate change,

* Contained in document FCCC/SBI/2015/CRP.1 of 2 June 2015.

Emphasizes the need for a coordinated approach to address capacity-building needs for mitigation, adaptation, technology development and transfer, and access to financial resources,

Having considered the information contained in the documents1 prepared by the Secretariat to facilitate deliberations at the Durban Forum and the summary report on the second meeting of the Durban Forum,[7]

1. *Reaffirms* that the Durban Forum is a platform to share experiences and exchange ideas, best practices, and lessons learned regarding the implementation of capacity-building activities with the participation of parties, representatives of the relevant bodies established under the Convention and relevant experts and practitioners;
2. *Encourages* representatives of the constituted bodies under the Convention, operating entities of the financial mechanism of the Convention, intergovernmental and non-governmental organizations, and relevant experts and practitioners, to integrate in their work programmes and activities lessons learned at, and main outcomes of, the Durban Forum;
3. *Decides* that the fourth meeting of the Durban Forum, to be held during the forty-second session of the Subsidiary Body for Implementation (June 2015), should consider, *inter alia*, capacity-building needs and best practices emerging in the work of the bodies in paragraph 2, the effectiveness of capacity-building interventions;
4. *Decides* to establish a Capacity-Building Committee under the Convention to utilize the Durban Forum and the Capacity-Building Portal and facilitate effective capacity-building implementation at the international, regional and national levels in accordance with the framework for capacity-building in developing countries contained in the annex to decision 2/CP.7, *inter alia*, by:
   (a) Collating capacity-building related information presented during meetings of the Durban Forum and contained in national communications;
   (b) Commissioning a report analysing the information referred to in paragraph 4(a) above and any other relevant national information;
   (c) Carrying out, on the basis of the information referred to above, the following actions:
      i. Recommend nationally appropriate actions in line with identified capacity-building needs;
      ii. Coordinate the provision of capacity-building support across and between the national, regional, and international levels;
      iii. Conduct continuous monitoring and reviewing of capacity-building interventions and support;

[7] FCCC/SBI/2014/2 and Add.1, FCCC/SBI/2014/7 and FCCC/SBI/2014/MISC.2 and Add.1 and 2 and FCCC/SBI/2013/12.

iv. Identify measures which would address capacity-building needs across several countries in order to increase efficiencies;
v. Compile recommendations for enhanced interactions with other existing bodies established under the Convention;
vi. Conduct a comprehensive review of the framework for capacity-building in developing countries;
vii. Further explore potential ways to enhance the implementation of capacity-building;

5. *Decides* that the Capacity-Building Committee shall consist of two representatives from each of the existing bodies established under the Convention and regional groups, ensuring that there is a balanced representation between developed and developing country parties;
6. *Further decides* that the Capacity-Building Committee will report to the Conference of the parties on its work, including functions and further actions required;
7. *Invites* parties to submit to the Secretariat, by XX 2015, their views on the terms of reference and modalities of operation of the Capacity-Building Committee;
8. *Requests* the Subsidiary Body for Implementation to consider the submissions referred to in paragraph 13 above at its XXX session with a view to making recommendations on the matter to the Conference of the Parties at its XXX session;
9. *Decides* that the Capacity-Building Committee should start its work on XXX 2015;
10. *Invites* parties to make sufficient resources available for the operationalization of the Capacity-Building Committee;
11. *Requests* operating entities of the financial mechanism of the Convention to provide support for capacity-building needs as identified by countries.

Paper No. 9: Thailand on behalf of the Group of 77 and China[8]

Elements and Guiding Principles for the Advancement of the Lima Work Program on Gender and Climate Change

1.1. Preamble

Noting that the social consequences of climate change are not gender neutral, due to social inequalities, women and men are affected differently by climate change impacts. Persons in vulnerable situations, such as youth, children, persons with disabilities, and indigenous peoples are also affected in a differentiated manner. The Group of 77 and China welcomes the opportunity to submit its views on possible

[8] Contained in document FCCC/SBI/2016/MISC.2 of 26 October 2016.

elements for the extension of the Lima Work Program on Gender. The Group of 77 and China believes that gender is one of the key crosscutting issues that affects response to climate change and sustainable development. Therefore, gender responsiveness is very critical with regards to the global quest for sustainable and inclusive development in the context of climate change, hence, the need to mainstream gender in all the processes of climate change.

1.2. Vulnerability

Climate change and current economic growth trajectories deepen and widen existing gender inequalities. Women, particularly in developing countries, and especially poor women, face
higher risks of inequality as they tend to live in vulnerable environments. On the other hand, the impacts of climate change affect the ability to provide for livelihoods in the most vulnerable areas were they inhabit.

Limited access to capacity-enhancement programs, social services, and support further exacerbate their risks and vulnerabilities. Consequently, the effects of climate change are felt most acutely by those segments of the population that are already in vulnerable situations. For women living in rural areas and belonging to indigenous peoples, the disadvantages derived from the impacts and effects of climate change, on account of natural disasters, are greater, as they are more dependent on the natural and environmental goods and services, which is important to know about when generating knowledge through ancestral knowledge in women.

Noting that the drivers and consequences of climate change are not gender neutral, defining the roles of women and men as distinct carriers, providers, and users of climate information is important. Socially based roles and responsibilities of men and women often influence the extent of vulnerability as well as how the communities will cope with the impact of a hazard or disaster.

Women play a unique role in the management of natural resources and support to households and communities. With their knowledge that can shape adaptive mechanisms in vulnerable areas, women can play a fundamental role as agents of change. It is therefore vital that considerations of gender equality, as well as men and women's different needs, perspectives, and knowledge should be considered in planning activities community-based adaptation.

The importance of gender mainstreaming in environment, poverty eradication, and

sustainable development has been recognized in the CEDAW, Agenda 21, the MDGs, the UNCBD, and the UNCCD and recently, in the 2030 SDGs. SDG number 5 emphasizes that empowering women and promoting gender equality is crucial to accelerating sustainable development.

Recently, the UNFCCC has seen recognition of gender in a number of standalone gender decisions including the Lima Work Program on Gender. The Lima Work Program on Gender aims to advance implementation of gender-responsive climate policies, strategies, and plans across all areas under the Convention and the Paris Agreement. The Paris Agreement, which, *inter alia* acknowledges that adaptation action should follow a country-driven, gender-responsive, participatory, and fully transparent approach, taking into consideration vulnerable groups, communities, and ecosystems. As such, means of implementation that takes into account gender-based budgeting should be provided to developing countries as the global community operationalises the Paris Agreement.

The Lima Work Program on Gender has provided parties and observer organizations an opportunity for understanding the role of gender integration in the UNFCCC process. Continued engagement on gender and climate change in the UNFCCC is still required as well as putting in place mechanisms to ensure monitoring and evaluation of gender mainstreaming in climate change are put in place.

1.3. Possible elements for the decision on gender and climate change in Marrakech

The Group of 77 and China recommends that the longer-term work program on gender to enhance the work that is ongoing should include the following, where appropriate:

1. Continue to support women participation to achieve the global goal of gender balance and increase their representation at all levels including negotiating groups, delegations, bodies, and institutional arrangements. 23/CP.18 (para. 5);
2. In coordination with UN Women, discuss and agree on a glossary of gender-related terms and guiding principles in order to use the terms in a more meaningful way (gender sensitive vs. gender responsive);
3. In coordination with UN Women, commission a gender action plan with the goal of focussed strategic guidance for ensuring gender balance, gender integration, gender responsive climate policies, and women empowerment in all programs and actions of the Convention and associated work by the UNFCCC Secretariat, parties, and Observer Organizations;
4. Scale up financing to support the development and implementation of gender responsive climate policy, planning, and implementation at all levels (subnational, national, regional, international);
5. Scale up and decentralize capacity-building on training and awareness-raising for women and men negotiators, gender climate champions, women leaders, and policymakers at national and regional levels;
6. Promote gender responsive technologies; and ensure gender mainstreaming in adaptation and mitigation activities and programmes and appoint a Gender Focal Point in the UNFCCC that will ensure the conscious application of critical gender analysis by all units in the UNFCCC at all levels; and
7. Promote gender disaggregated data and integration of gender indicators in the MRV systems for effective mainstreaming of gender in climate change.

B. SUBSIDIARY BODY FOR SCIENTIFIC AND TECHNOLOGICAL ADVICE (SBSTA)

(a) Statements made on behalf of the Group of 77 at the sessions of the Subsidiary Body for Scientific and Technological Advice (SBSTA):

- Opening session, Bali, Indonesia, 3 December 2007
- Opening plenary of the twenty-eighth session, Bonn, Germany, 4 June 2008
- Opening plenary of the twenty-ninth session, Poznan, Poland, 1 December 2008
- Opening plenary of the thirty-third session, Cancun, Mexico, 30 November 2010
- Opening plenary of the thirty-fourth session, Bonn, Germany, 6 June 2011
- Closing plenary of the thirty-fifth session, Durban, South Africa, 3 December 2011
- Closing plenary of the thirty-sixth session, Bonn, Germany, 25 May 2012
- Opening plenary of the thirty-eighth session, Bonn, Germany, 3 June 2013
- Closing plenary of the thirty-eighth session, Bonn, Germany, 14 June 2013
- Opening plenary of the thirty-ninth session, Poland, Warsaw, 11 November 2013.
- Closing plenary of the thirty-ninth session, Warsaw, Poland, 16 November 2013
- Opening plenary of the fortieth session, Bonn, Germany, 4 June 2014
- Closing plenary of the fortieth session, Bonn, Germany, 15 June 2014
- Opening plenary of the forty-first session, Lima, Peru, 1 December 2014
- Closing plenary of the forty-first session, Lima, Peru, 6 December 2014
- Opening plenary of the forty-third session, Paris, France, 1 December 2015
- Closing plenary of the forty-fourth session, Bonn, Germany, 26 May 2016
- Opening plenary of the forty-fifth session, Marrakech, Morocco, 7 November 2016
- Closing plenary of forty-fifth session, Marrakech, Morocco, 14 November 2016
- Remarks during SBSTA-46, SBI-46 and APA 1.3, at the Meeting with the Deputy Secretary-General of the United Nations, (Bonn, Germany, 13 May 2017)
- Joint Opening Plenary of the forty-seventh session of SBSTA-47 and SBI-47 (Bonn, Germany, 6 November 2017)
- Joint Closing Plenary of the forty-seventh session of the SBSTA-47 and SBI-47, (Bonn, Germany, 15 November 2017)

- Statement at the opening plenary, Bonn, 30 April 2018
- Statement at the SBSTA/SBI/APA Chairs/Co-Chairs Meeting with Heads of Delegations (4 May 2018)

(b) Draft decisions and positions submitted by the Group of 77 to the Subsidiary Body for Scientific and Technological Advice (SBSTA):
- FCCC/SBSTA/1996/MISC.3 of 14 May 1996: Position on the "Establishment of Intergovernmental Technical Advisory Panels"
- FCCC/SBSTA/1997/INF.5 of 2 September 1997: Decision on "Transfer of Technology"
- FCCC/SBSTA/1997/MISC.5 of 27 July 1997: Paper No.1: The Group of 77 and China on Submission on "Activities Implemented Jointly
- FCCC/SBSTA/1998/CRP.1 of 10 June 1998: Draft decision on "Technology development and transfer"
- FCCC/SBSTA/1998/MISC.5 of 12 June 1998: Paper No.1: Development and transfer of technologies
- FCCC/SBSTA/2000/MISC.1/Add.2 of 17 July 2000: Position on "Proposed elements of draft guidelines under Article 8 of the Kyoto Protocol (Informal paper No. 8 (2000) dated June, 11th 2000)"
- FCCC/SBSTA/2000/MISC.4 of 14 July 2000: Paper No.3: Development and transfer of technologies pursuant to Article 4.5 of the Convention
- FCCC/SBSTA/2000/MISC.9 of 18 September 2000: Paper No.1: Draft decision on Development and transfer of technologies
- FCCC/SBSTA/2002/MISC.3/Add.2 of 12 June 2002: Submission on "Position on the Canadian Proposal for Environmental Credits to its Energy Export to the US (Annex-B country non-Party to the Protocol) and its impact"
- FCCC/SBSTA/2003/MISC.8 of 12 June 2003: Position on "Implementation of Article 2.3 of the Kyoto Protocol"
- FCCC/SBSTA/2006/MISC.9 of 18 September 2006: Submission on "Five Year
  programme of work on impacts: Vulnerability and adaptation to climate change"
- G-77 and China presentation on Agenda Item 7 of SBSTA and Agenda Item 11 of SBI
  Durban, 35th Session of the Subsidiary Bodies, 1 December 2011
- FCCC/SBSTA/2013/MISC.7/Add.1 of 12 June 2013: Submission on "General guidelines for domestic measurement, reporting, and verification of domestically-supported nationally appropriate mitigation actions by developing country Parties"
- Submission by G-77 and China on "the impact of the implementation of response measures (Agenda item SBSTA 10. a and SBI 15 a.)-SBs 40 Sessions, 11 June 2014"

- G-77 and China statement for the SBSTA workshops on early warning systems,
  June 2015
- G7-7 and China draft intervention for SBSTA "Issues relating to agriculture"
  May 2016
- FCCC/SBSTA/2017/CRP.1 of 10 May 2017: Submission on "Decision x/CP.23: Issues relating to Agriculture"

B. Subsidiary Body for Scientific and Technological Advice (SBSTA)

(a) Statements Made on Behalf of the Group of 77 at the Sessions of the Subsidiary Body for Scientific and Technological Advice (SBSTA)

Statement by Mr. Jamil Ahmad of Pakistan on behalf of the Group of 77 and China at the Opening Session of SBSTA (Bali, Indonesia, 3 December 2007)
Mr. Chairman,

1. It is my pleasure to make this contribution on behalf of the Group of 77 and China. I would like to assure you as well as our negotiating partners of the Group of 77 and China's resolve to engage constructively so as to ensure a substantive outcome of this important meeting.
2. The IPCC reports and the recent scientific findings demonstrate, irrefutably, that climate change is posing a very serious and immediate challenge to the efforts of developing countries.
3. The adverse effects of climate change and the associated phenomena threaten the sustainable development, livelihoods, and the very existence of many developing countries and in particular Africa, the LDCs, the LLDCs, SIDS, and disaster-prone developing countries.
4. According to the Fourth Assessment Report of IPCC:
   - In Africa, climate change is projected to expose between 75 and 250 million people to increased water stress and reduced yields from rain-fed agriculture by up to 50%.
   - In Asia, freshwater availability is projected to decrease, coastal areas will be at greater risk due to increased flooding, and climate change is projected to compound pressures on natural resources and public health.
   - In Latin America, climate change threatens significant loss of biodiversity through species extinction. Reduction in productivity of important crops will pose risks to food security.
   - Small Islands are expected to face inundation, storm surges, erosion, and other coastal hazards, threatening vital infrastructure, settlements, and livelihoods of island communities.

5. In all developing countries, water available for human consumption, agriculture, and energy generation is likely to be significantly affected.

Mr. Chairman,

6. New institutional and financial mechanisms would significantly enhance technology co-operation, development, transfer and meet the incremental costs. Enhancing action in pursuit of this objective is fundamental to the overall climate change agenda. Notwithstanding the lack of progress, the elements and key issues have now been raised and the stage is now set for real and meaningful progress on this agenda item.
7. Transfer of technology remains an enormous challenge to efforts for adaptation and mitigation keeping in view the issue of incremental costs and capacity-building. Addressing current and future changes in the climate system depends on early and effective development, deployment, transfer, and diffusion of environmentally friendly technologies to developing countries. A key question is also the treatment of intellectual property rights (IPRs) over climate-friendly technologies. Developing countries must also be helped, on affordable preferential and concessional terms, through technology transfer, directed R&D and other assistance, to acquire and build capacity for the application of technologies to meet sustainable development targets and goals. The G-77 and China would like to express its disappointment about the progress made on this agenda item. Development of performance indicators to monitor if commitments have been honoured in this area will be a useful tool.
8. As reflected in the recent IPCC Reports, reducing emissions from deforestation deserves serious global attention. Further, during this process, it has become clear that implementation of relevant policy approaches and positive incentives will require new and additional financial resources that are predictable, sustainable, and at sufficient scale. The G-77 and China recognizes the interests of the parties to consider policy approaches and positive incentives that address compensated forest conservation and also forest degradation.

Opening Statement on behalf of the Group of 77 and China by Ms. Ruleta Camacho, Delegate of Antigua and Barbuda, at the Opening Plenary of the Twenty-Eighth Session of the Subsidiary Body for Scientific and Technological Advice of the UN Framework Convention on Climate Change
(Bonn, Germany, 4 June 2008)

Madam Chair,

It is my pleasure to make this contribution on behalf of the Group of 77 and China.

Madam Chair,

The Group of 77 and China would like to express its appreciation to the Government and the people of the Federal Republic of Germany for their warm hospitality and excellent arrangements for our meeting. I would like to assure you as well as our negotiating partners of the Group of 77 and China's determination to engage constructively so as to ensure a substantive outcome of this important meeting.

Climate Change poses serious risks and challenges, especially to developing countries, and it is therefore imperative to have urgent global action and response. The Group is very concerned about the fact that the adverse effects of climate change and the associated phenomena threaten the sustainable development, livelihoods, and the very existence of many developing countries.

Madam Chair,

Technology development and transfer of technology is key to the achievement of the ultimate objectives of the Convention. It constitutes one of the major means through which developing countries can meet their commitments under the Convention. We look forward at this session to reaching agreement on the terms of reference for the development of performance indicators forwarded to the SBSTA for its approval by the EGTT, to facilitate the work of the EGTT. The Group of 77 and China looks forward to the early approval of the 2008–2009 work programme presented by the EGTT. In this light, the Group wishes to express its gratitude to the Chair and members of the EGTT for the good work done thus far and hopes that the EGTT works assiduously in order to achieve the objectives of its renewed mandate.

Madam Chair,

With regard to SBSTA agenda item 9, scientific, technical, and socio-economic aspects of mitigation of climate change, a series of workshops have been held and proved to be very useful. We believe the goal of this item has been successfully achieved. Since mitigation is also a key element of AWG-KP, LCA, and the fourth assessment report of the IPCC, to avoid duplication and proliferation of negotiations, this agenda item should be concluded within this session.

In conclusion, Madam Chair, the success and effectiveness of the process going forward will depend to a significant degree on the extent to which we use openness, transparency, and inclusiveness as our guiding principles. We should endeavour to afford equal opportunity for participation of all parties

Statement on behalf of the Group of 77 and China by Ruleta Camacho, Antigua and Barbuda, at the Opening Plenary of the Subsidiary Body for Scientific and Technological Advice (SBSTA), Twenty-Ninth Session
(Poznan, Poland, 1 December 2008)

Madam Chair,

The Group of 77 and China would like to express its appreciation to the Government and the people of the Republic of Poland for their hospitality and to the Secretariat and the Executive Secretary of the UNFCCC for all their hard work. Although the agenda is very full, I would like to assure you of the Group's support and cooperation to make this meeting successful. We are looking forward to working in the spirit of openness, transparency, and cooperation to make this meeting successful.

Madam Chair,

The IPCC reports and the recent scientific findings demonstrate, irrefutably, that climate change is posing a very serious and immediate challenge to the efforts of developing countries. The adverse effects of climate change and the associated phenomena threaten the sustainable development, livelihoods, and the very existence of many developing countries and in particular Africa, the LDCs, the LLDCs, SIDS, and disaster-prone developing countries.

The Group of 77 and China is anxious to advance work on approaches to stimulate action, in areas such as capacity-building and demonstration projects. In this regard, the Group will actively participate in the consideration of the EGTT interim reports on new financing sources to support the development diffusion and transfer of technology. The Group also attaches utmost importance to assessing the gaps and barriers in the financing of the development and transfer of environmentally sound technologies and to the implementation of suitable recommendations on future financing options.

Madam Chair,

Technology development and transfer is key to the achievement of the ultimate objectives of the Convention. It constitutes one of the major means through which developing countries can meet their commitments under the Convention. In this regard, the Group of 77 and China has called for the establishment of a technology mechanism under the UNFCCC. The Group looks forward to advancing its proposal and would hope that it can contribute to the work of the SBSTA.

The role of the Nairobi Work Program in providing information to the SBI on the scientific, technical, and socio-economic aspects of impacts, vulnerability and adaptation to climate change cannot be understated. In this regard, we look forward to discussions around the need for and role of a group of expects to support the work of the NWP.

The Group of 77 also notes the information contained in the technical paper on Disaster Risk Reduction strategies, yet another grim reminder of the challenges we face.

The Group of 77 and China also stresses the need for SBSTA to open an agenda item initiate work related to common metrics to calculate the CO_2 equivalence of GHGs as noted in the AWG-KP report from the Accra meeting.

In conclusion, Madam Chair, the success and effectiveness of the process going forward will depend to a significant degree on the extent to which we use openness, transparency, and inclusiveness as our guiding principles. We should endeavour to afford equal opportunity for participation of all parties.

Statement on behalf of the Group of 77 and China by H.E. Ambassador Abdullah M. Alsaidi, Head of Delegation of the Republic of Yemen, at the Opening Plenary of the 33rd Session of the Subsidiary Body for Scientific and Technological Advice (SBSTA 33)
(Cancun, Mexico, 30 November 2010)

Mr. Chairman,

1. I have the honour to deliver this statement on behalf of the Group of 77 and China.
2. The Group of 77 and China notes the limited progress made in implementing activities under the Nairobi Work Programme on impacts, vulnerability, and adaptation to climate change. The Group, in a party-driven manner, will like to consider action-oriented outcomes of the Nairobi Work Programme that contribute to improving the developing countries' ability to undertake practical adaptation actions.
3. We believe that the objective and scope of this work program must be evaluated in light of the objective set in decision 2/CP.11. We need to go beyond workshops, for it is important to have a timely support for an effective implementation of adaptation actions.
4. The Group also urges SBSTA to determine actions on technology from the report prepared by the Secretariat in order to enrich the discussion under AWG-LCA and to strengthen the linkages with technology issues under AWG-LCA.
5. With regard to SABSTA agenda item No 6, Research and Systematic Observation, we demand a specific decision to build and/or enhance national and regional climate centres, as well as a decision to strengthen systematic observation network of climate change on the different regions of developing countries.

Mr. Chairman,

6. The Group urges international organizations to enhance the coordination of actions to avoid duplication of efforts and resources. Furthermore, we look forward for more country-driven interaction between parties and those organizations. We would also like to highlight the importance of the programme as one source of relevant knowledge that should feed the ongoing work on adaptation under the AWG-LCA.

Mr. Chairman,

7. We are fully aware of the time limitations and that this SBSTA session will be quite short; however, we expect more efficient allocation of time and constructive engagement in discussion with our partners to achieve real progress on all issues under the SBSTA. In this context, Mr. Chairman, the Group of 77 and China reiterates its commitment to continue to be engaged in all discussions under the SBSTA during this session as well as future sessions.

Statement on behalf of the Group of 77 and China by Ambassador Jorge Arguello, Permanent Representative of Argentina to the United Nations and Chairman of the Group of 77, at the Opening Plenary of the 34th Session of the Subsidiary Body for Scientific and Technological Advice (SBSTA 34)
(Bonn, Germany, 6 June 2011)

Mr. Chairman,

1. I have the honour to deliver this statement on behalf of the Group of 77 and China. Allow me at the outset to assure you of the support and cooperation of the Group to your work. We are certain that, under your leadership, we will be able to make progress in this important subsidiary body.
2. The Group of 77 and China is still concerned about the limited progress made in implementing activities under the Nairobi Work Programme on impacts, vulnerability, and adaptation to climate change, and supports the improvement of the objectives, scope of work, and modalities focused on the Nairobi Work Programme that contribute to enhancing the developing countries' ability to undertake practical adaptation actions, in a party-driven manner.
3. We are convinced that in order to make the necessary progress, we need to have a timely support for an effective implementation of adaptation actions, and for the work that is being undertaken in the Climate Change negotiations at large.

Mr. Chairman,

4. We are aware that Cancun outcomes introduced new issues under the Subsidiary Body on Scientific and Technical Advice, as per decision 1CP/16, and, consequently, the SBSTA agenda has been enlarged. Some assignments to the SBSTA agenda following Cancun are clear enough, yet the new processes needing further political development therefore must be kept under the AWG-LCA sphere. In this sense, we believe that discussions on unresolved issues should continue in the AWG-LCA track, and not be transferred to other bodies, since that would not be in line with the Convention nor with the mandate given by parties to the AWG-LCA, which was extended in Cancun. We further emphasize that the AWG-LCA must maintain an overview of the specific issues that were mandated to SBI through decision 1CP/16, and that the progress made under SBI must feed into the comprehensive and balanced outcome of the AWG-LCA.

Mr. Chairman,

5. The Group urges international organizations to enhance the coordination of actions to avoid duplication of efforts and resources. Furthermore, we look forward for more country-driven interaction between parties and those organizations.

Mr. Chairman,

6. We are fully aware of the time limitations and are ready, again, to engage constructively in discussions as soon as possible in order to make real substantive progress in this session. On the other hand, the Group of 77 and China is convinced that even with the best use of the time available to us, these sessions cannot be the last ones before convening in Durban, and there is a clear necessity for an additional session to be held in the fall. In this regard, we expect to receive further clarity on the preparations under way and definitions of such meeting at the earliest possible time, and before we adjourn our work this session.

Statement on behalf of the Group of 77 and China by H.E. Ambassador Silvia Merega, Head of Delegation of the Argentine Republic, at the Closing Plenary of the 35th Session of the Subsidiary Body for Scientific and Technological Advice (SBSTA 35)
(Durban, South Africa, 3 December 2011)

Mr. Chairman,

1. I have the distinct honor to deliver this statement on behalf of the Group of 77 and China.

2. At the outset, allow me to say that under your guidance we were able to find ways of convergence that helped us to interchange ideas in a constructive and productive way in order to move forward the items under the SBSTA agenda.

Mr. Chairman,

3. The G-77 and China welcomes the progress made since the thirty-fourth session of SBSTA, in particular the technical paper on water and climate change and the compilation of information on ecosystem-based approaches to adaptation.
4. Furthermore, the Group welcomes the joint SBSTA-SBI in-session workshop to consider the outcomes of the Nairobi Work Programme most relevant to the SBI and its report prepared by the Chairs of the SBSTA and SBI. The participation of the Members of the Groups and the views expressed in the above-mentioned workshop should help us advance towards a more action-oriented implementation of the Programme. We would like to highlight the importance of the process leading to the review of the Nairobi Work Programme's objectives, action-oriented sub-themes and working areas, and the need for the Programme to further enhance its work with a view to support the Adaptation Framework and its provisions.
5. We look forward to engage in the activities agreed at this session for the next three sessions of the SBSTA with a focus on the working areas under the Nairobi Work Programme which will help developing countries further understand the implications of the impacts of climate change.

Mr. Chairman,

6. The G-77 and China recognizes the activities done by the Technology Executive Committee (TEC) during 2011 and urge parties to ensure the adequate financial resources for the implementation of the TEC's program of work for 2012. We expect the TEC can consider, as part of this program of work, the interaction with other institutional arrangements under the Convention, including the Climate Technology Center Network, the Financial Mechanism, and the Adaptation Committee.
7. The Group of 77 and China welcomes the draft conclusions and COP decisions on agenda item 6 on Research and Systematic Observations. We recognize the important contribution of the research dialogue in informing discussions under the Convention and in enhancing communication between the science communities and policymakers. In this regard, the Group thanks the participation of the research organizations and would like the research dialogue and workshops to continue.
8. Mr. Chairman, these workshops and dialogues are also important to discuss the needs for climate change related research and research related

capacity-building, particularly those of developing countries to support the work of the Convention. They can be used by developing countries as a forum to communicate research findings, successes, and lessons learnt from climate change research related activities.

9. G-77 and China recognizes the importance of research and communication between the scientific community, policymakers, and users. We support the views of others that the UNFCCC website can be used as a channel to further enhance the availability and visibility of scientific information produced by the international and regional research programmes and organizations under the Convention. The web-casting of the proceedings of any workshops under the research dialogue would enhance communication of scientific information for those who are unable to attend.
10. We look forward to discuss systematic observation in SBSTA 36.

Mr. Chairman,

11. The G-77 and China engaged constructively in the forum on the impact of the implementation of response measures at the Subsidiary Bodies, with the objective of developing a work programme under the SBSTA and the SBI to address these impacts, and to adopt at this seventeenth COP modalities for the operationalization of the Work Programme and a forum on response measures, as mandated by paragraph 93 of 1.CP/16.
12. However, the G-77 and China expresses its disappointment to the lack of agreement for a draft decision on the development of the Work Programme, modalities for its operationalization and a forum on the impact of implementation of response measures. We look forward to the full implementation of paragraph 93 of 1.CP/16.
13. The Group of 77 and China welcomes the draft conclusion and COP decision on agenda item 9(b) on the Updated Annex I Inventory Guidelines after two years of intense and rather technical work. The new Guidelines will allow Annex I parties to report their anthropogenic emissions by sources and removals by sinks in a more complete, transparent, and accurate way and implementing the use of the IPCC 2006 Guidelines, including for reporting in the second commitment period of the Kyoto Protocol.
14. The Group regrets, however, that parties could not reach agreement in all issues. The G-77 and China is ready to engage in further discussions with a view to conclude this work still at this session.

Finally, Mr. Chairman,

15. I would like to reiterate the full commitment of the G-77 and China to continue working to achieve concrete results during this session of the COP and CMP.

Statement on behalf of the Group of 77 and China by H.E. Ambassador Latifa Benazza, Head of Delegation of Algeria, at the Closing Plenary of the 36th Session of the Subsidiary Body for Scientific and Technological Advice (SBSTA 36) (Bonn, Germany, 25 May 2012)

Mr. Chairman,

1. I have the honor to deliver this statement on behalf of the Group of 77 and China.
2. Allow me first to underline that under your guidance, this session helped us to have a constructive exchange of ideas in a productive way to move forward our work under the SBSTA agenda.

Mr. Chairman,

3. The G-77 and China noted with great interest the exchange of views on issues related to agriculture done in accordance with decision 2.CP/17 and called for the need to ensure that work on agriculture is related to the SBSTA mandate of the article 9 of the Convention, and is done on the basis of the principles and provisions of the Convention, in particular the principle of common but differentiated responsibilities. We need to assess existing scientific and technological knowledge on adaptation of agriculture to the adverse effects of climate change, and increase capacity-building in developing countries, what could contribute to improve agricultural productivity. The Group believes that adaptation shall be the scope of the work undertaken in the SBSTA on agriculture, in order to safeguard food security, particularly in developing countries.

Mr. Chairman,

4. The G-77 and China welcomes the discussion at the first meeting of the forum to implement the work program on the impact of the implementation of response measures that took place at the thirty-sixth session of Subsidiary Bodies, with the objective to set a clear set of modalities for the operationalization of the forum and work programme including, *inter alia*, assigning specific tasks and activities for the rest of the year and creating an outline schedule for 2013 to address specific needs and concerns of developing countries arising from the impact of the implementation of response measures. In this respect, we welcome the conclusion in this session of an agreement on the activities to implement the work programme, and we look forward to engaging constructively in the forum workshops and discussions at the forum planned for the thirty-seventh, thirty-eighth, and thirty-ninth session of the Subsidiary Bodies.

5. Furthermore, the G-77 and China welcomes the progress made in the implementation of the Nairobi Work Programme since its thirty-fifth session as it was reported prepared by the Chair of the SBSTA. We would like to highlight the importance of the process leading to the review of the Nairobi Work Programme's objectives, action-oriented sub-themes and working areas, and the need for the Programme to further enhance its work with a view to support the Adaptation Framework and its provisions.
6. We look forward to engage in the activities scheduled for the next two sessions of the SBSTA with a focus on the working areas under the Nairobi Work Programme which will help developing countries further understand the implications of the impacts of climate change and how best to support the objectives of the Nairobi Work Programme.

Mr. Chairman,

7. The G-77 and China recognizes the activities done by the Technology Executive Committee (TEC) during 2012 and welcomed its rolling work plan for 2012– 2013. The group emphasized the necessity for the TEC to structure its work plan in short and medium term, including the organisation of a thematic dialogue on enabling environment and on barriers to technology development and transfer.
8. We recommend the TEC can consider, as part of this Programme of Work, the interaction with other institutional arrangements under the Convention, including the Climate Technology Center Network, the Financial Mechanism, and the Adaptation Committee.
9. The G-77 and China welcomes the exchange of views on the item relating to carbon dioxide capture and storage in geological formations under the clean development mechanism projects activities with the aim to provide clarification on certain technical and legal issues at the thirty-seventh session of SBSTA, while requesting that the necessary resources are allocated for the technical paper to be prepared by the Secretariat for this purpose.
10. On the methodological issues under the Convention, the G-77 and China welcomes the discussions on the general guidelines for domestic measurement, reporting, and verification of domestically supported nationally appropriate mitigation actions by developing countries with the aim to continue the interactive exchange of views on the guidelines at the thirty-seventh session of SBSTA.
11. The G-77 and China considers appropriate the discussion on methodological guidance for activities relating to reducing emissions from deforestation and forest degradation and the role of conservation, sustainable management of forests, and enhancement of forest carbon stocks in developing countries, considering both market and non-market approaches. In this regard, the group calls for further discussions to ensure transparency,

consistency, comprehensiveness, and effectiveness in the presentation of the summary of information on how the safeguards referred to decision 1/CP.16 are being addressed and respected.

12. The G-77 and China supports the dialogue on this issue taking into account the results of discussions on finances under the LCA and the need for adaptation in each country.

Mr. Chairman,

13. On the methodological discussions related to the completion of the Guidelines for the Biennial Reports from Annex I parties, developing a common tabular format for reporting part of the information required, the group acknowledges the progress of the work. However, it expresses its concern with the delay of the work on the review guidelines for biennial reports, national communications and annual inventories from Annex I parties. While recognizing that the completion of this work is due only at COP-19, the amount of work required and its importance requires immediate engagement of the parties in order to ensure a comprehensive outcome.
14. On the common metrics to compare emissions of different GHGs, the G-77 and China welcomes the workshop held last April here in Bonn that confirmed the importance of the exchange between science and policy. The group reiterates the relevance of the choice of the common metric in the context of future policy considerations under the Convention and its Kyoto Protocol.

Mr. Chairman,

15. We express deep concern that no conclusion was reached in agenda item 6 on research and systematic observation. Progress and support on this item are of critical importance, in particularly for developing countries with high mountain ecosystems.
16. On items 10 (a) and (b), we emphasize that the ability of developing countries to undertake MRV issues depends on the extend of support they receive from developed country parties, methodological guidance for biennial reports to enable MRV requires financial support by developed countries to develop infrastructure, effective technology transfer, and capacity-building.

Finally, Mr. Chairman,

17. I would like to reiterate the full commitment of the G-77 and China to continue working to achieve concrete results during the next session of SBSTA in Doha.

Statement on behalf of the Group of 77 and China by Ambassador Amena Yauvoli, Permanent Secretary of Foreign Affairs and International Cooperation of the Republic of Fiji, Chair of the Group of 77, at the Opening Plenary of the 38th Session of the Subsidiary Body for Scientific and Technological Advice (SBSTA 38) of the United Nations Framework Convention on Climate Change (UNFCCC) (Bonn, Germany, 3 June 2013)

Thank you, Mr. Chairman,

Excellencies,
Distinguished representatives
Ladies and gentlemen,

1. I have the honour to deliver this statement on behalf of the Group of 77 and China in the Opening Plenary of the Thirty-eighth Session of the Subsidiary Body on Scientific and Technological Advice.
2. The Group is ready to engage meaningfully with all members, you are assured of our support

Mr. Chairman.

3. These are the views of the Group in relation to following agenda items under SBSTA.
4. On agenda item 3, the Group of 77 and China underscore the need that the Nairobi Work Programme should promote concrete adaptation actions on the ground across different communities and eco-systems. It should move beyond just partnership and help facilitate enhanced implementation of adaptation activities.
5. In relation to agenda items 4 and 5, about reducing emissions from deforestation and forest degradation the Group is of the view that we have before us a quite comprehensive and heavy agenda. Besides the methodological discussions under SBSTA [agenda item 4], our work this year includes a joint SBSTA-SBI process on coordination of support and institutional arrangements [agenda item 5], as well as a work programme under the COP on financing and results-based payments.
6. The Group would like to highlight that all these items are closely interlinked and should advance together. Their consideration requires therefore a balanced approach negotiating agenda items 4 and 5 in a contact group setting. We are confident that this approach will allow us to move forward in pending issues, in particular financing of all phases of the activities referred to in paragraph 70 of decision 1/CP.16. Also, we must ensure that all policy approaches regarding deforestation and forest degradation must be considered, including joint mitigation and adaptation approaches that are attempted to address climate change in an integrated and holistic manner.

Mr. Chairman,

7. On agenda item 6, the G-77 and China took note of the first meeting of the Advisory Board of the Climate Technology Center and Network and the ongoing efforts to set the modalities and procedures of CTCN and its Advisory Board. In order to fully implement the technology mechanism to enhance the action of technology development and transfer, we believe it is of crucial importance to ensure coordination between the two bodies of technology mechanism, the Technology Executive Committee and the CTCN. We look forward to the tangible development and transfer of technologies to developing countries for climate change.

Mr. Chairman,

8. On agenda item 7, Research and Systematic observation, the G-77 and China would like to express its support for the research dialogue and its Objectives. This forum continues to provide an opportunity for the scientific community to communicate up-to-date scientific knowledge on climate change to policymakers, and the policymakers in turn provide feedback to the research community on areas that may require further research.
9. However, the forum alone however is far from fulfilling the obligations under article 5 of the Convention and subsequent COP decisions. Financing for the conducting the necessary research and assessment, and data collection, is sadly inadequate. Facilitated access, including through financing of the technology, is not forthcoming. More than just an exchange of information, what is necessary is to meet the needs of developing countries and to cooperate in the improvement of their endogenous capacities and capabilities for them to participate in international efforts to strengthen systematic observation and national and scientific and technical research. Concrete action and effective financing are now necessary in the light of the increasing intensity of extreme weather events.
10. The Group of 77 and China also recognizes the important role of the Intergovernmental Panel on Climate Change in undertaking regular assessments of published scientific information on climate change and of preparing special reports, and in communicating this information to the Convention. We look forward to hearing from the IPCC on its progress and plans pertaining to the Fifth Assessment Report. The SBSTA provides the link between the findings of the IPCC and the policy recommendations for the necessary measures to be undertaken to address climate change, through an assessment of the IPCC findings. There must be balance of views reflected in the IPCC reports so as to make these relevant to the needs of the Convention.

11. The IPCC fourth assessment report informed us that climate change is interlinked with sustainable development in a wide variety of ways. It is well established that climate responses require both mitigation and adaptation. For a long time, emphasis has been on mitigation and all aspects of mitigation implementation have been widely explored. In contrast, adaptation has received less attention and support. Adaptation is the priority for many developing countries and is more and more necessary for them in the light of recent climate-related extreme weather events. The SBSTA must therefore request the IPCC to undertake an integrated and comprehensive approach to dealing with climate change, as fragmentation of responses have so far not proven helpful and reinforced the erroneous perception that mitigation and adaptation are separate options. The reality and concrete experience show that they are two faces of the same coin. They go hand in hand and should be approached in an integrated manner.
12. We, as policymakers, need to have a better understanding of adaptation responses and options in the face of the different levels of mitigation now being undertaken. The IPCC is in the best position to provide us with this crucial scientific and technical information.

Mr. Chairman,

13. On agenda item 8, Response Measures, the G-77 and China looks forward to continuing engaging constructively in the forum on the impact of the implementation of response measures at the Subsidiary Bodies and its work program to address these impacts. In particular, we welcome the activities that will take place in these sessions in the areas of the work program related to the assessment of impacts; the just transition of the workforce; economic diversification; and modelling. In addition, as mandated by decision 1.CP.18, we also look forward to sharing views in the forum on policy issues of concern, such as unilateral measures.
14. In this respect, we attach great importance to this issue as all developing countries will be affected by economic and social consequences of response measures taken by developed countries. Therefore, there is a need to take full consideration on the specific needs and concerns of developing countries arising from the impact of the implementation of response measures, in accordance with the provisions and principles of the Convention.

Mr. Chairman,

15. Under this agenda item 10a, Methodological issues under the Convention, reference is made to the revision of the review guidelines for inventories, biennial reports, and national communications. The main area of discussion during 2012 was when the guidelines would be reviewed. It was agreed by all

parties that biennial report and national communication review guidelines would be concluded in a work programme ending at COP-19. Work on revising the GHG inventory guidelines would however only begin in 2014 and conclude at COP-20 so as to coincide with the piloting of Annex I GHG inventory guidelines taking place in the same year.

16. As a Group, we also agreed to one workshop for each work programme with the possibility for additional workshops if required by parties. Overall, the Group's main concern is to ensure that biennial report review guidelines are in place before submission of the first biennial reports by Annex I parties in January 2014. With the current work programme, this will be concluded by COP-19, in time for the first biennial report submission. Therefore, we urge all parties to work together so that we achieve these important timelines. It is also necessary that after this scientific and technical work, the issue of the guidance is brought over to the Subsidiary of Implementation which has the main responsibility for the consideration of this information. In particular, it is necessary for the SBSTA to agree on a common tabular format for reporting information related to the implementation of the obligations of developed country parties on the details of measures taken to implement article 4, sub-paragraph 3 on the provision of new and additional financial resources, sub-paragraph 4 on meeting costs of adaptation, and subparagraph 5 on access and transfer of technology, as required by article 12.3. This information and format should be in such a form as to allow verification and measurement of this information, as well as comparability.

17. On item 10b, "General guidelines for domestic measurement, reporting, and verification of domestically-supported nationally appropriate mitigation actions by developing country Parties," the Group of 77 and China view that guidelines are voluntary and only apply for nationally appropriate mitigation actions (NAMAs) for which developing countries are provided with financial support and technology transfer to address mitigation, and not for mitigation using domestic resources.

18. Furthermore, the guidelines should not be more onerous than other general guidelines, such as those developed for international assessment and review and international consultation and analysis. The Group of 77 and China is of the view that it may be helpful to reflect on significant work already undertaken which can sharpen the focus of the work under these guidelines. The work on this item would also benefit greatly from detailed information from developed country parties on how they undertake the work of domestic MRV of their domestically financed mitigation actions in all different sectors.

19. In relation to reporting, our view is that the guidelines for biennial update reports are detailed and agreed (decision 1/CP.17, Annex III). Measurement by its nature is done domestically, there are IPCC guidelines already being

applied, and our Group is of the view that guidelines are not necessary in this respect. The international component of verification is covered by the general guidelines on international consultation and analysis (decision 1/CP.17, Annex IV). Consequently, the focus of the general guidelines is on domestic verification, which is consistent with decision 1/CP.16, paragraph 66.

20. Having considered what is already agreed, the view of the G-77 and China is that the guidelines could include elements that:
    i. Build on existing domestic systems and capacity, including domestic data, methodologies, modelling (if any), experts, and other aspects;
    ii. Assists domestic experts in applying international best practice; e.g., 2006 IPCC GHG guidelines (or 1996);
    iii. Recognize existing verification systems and applying national standards of verification, thereby enhancing cost-effectiveness;
    iv. Voluntary use of independent third-party verification at domestic level.

Mr. Chairman,

21. On item 11, LULUCF, the Group welcomes the opportunity to continue consideration here in Bonn of more comprehensive accounting of anthropogenic emissions by sources and removals by sinks from LULUCF. Discussions so far have indicated the need to achieve a common understanding of the meaning of comprehensiveness in this context.
22. The Group also finds it opportune to continue the discussion on possible additional LULUCF activities under the CDM, which are presently limited to afforestation and reforestation; and on alternative approaches to addressing the risk of non-permanence under the CDM. We are confident that this session will stimulate more focused discussions to facilitate conclusions on these items at CMP-9.

Mr. Chairman,

23. Regarding item 12, "Framework of various approaches, non-market mechanisms and new market mechanisms," the Group of 77 and China wishes to express the necessity for SBSTA to continue this discussion to help parties identify some important issues to develop and implement various approaches, including opportunities for using markets and non-markets, to enhance the cost effectiveness, and to promote mitigation actions, jointly with adaptation, bearing in mind different circumstances of developed and developing countries.
24. The three work programs that SBSTA is going to conduct in each issue should give parties the opportunity to continue clarifying the different views that are reflected in the submissions presented.

Mr. Chairman,

25. Finally, on agenda item 13, the 2013–2015 Review, the Group of 77 and China has the honour to inform you that we have endorsed the candidature of Professor ZOU Ji from China as co-facilitator of the expert dialogue of the 2013–2015 Review under the Convention representing non–Annex I parties.
26. The Group of 77 and China reserves its position on other agenda items.

Statement on behalf of the Group of 77 and China by Mr. Luke Daunivalu, Counsellor, Deputy Permanent Representative of Fiji to the United Nations, at the Closing Plenary of the 38th Session of the Subsidiary Body for Scientific and Technological Advice (SBSTA 38) of the United Nations Framework Convention on Climate Change (UNFCCC)
(Bonn, Germany, 14 June 2013)

Thank you, Mr. Chairman,

Excellencies,
Distinguished Representatives,
Ladies and Gentlemen,

Mr. Chairman,

1. I have the honour to deliver this closing statement on behalf of the Group of 77 and China.
2. The Group of 77 and China appreciates that SBSTA initiated reconsideration of the work areas of the Nairobi Work Programme on Impacts, Vulnerability and Adaptation to Climate Change. We want a more relevant and effective work programme to be launched by moving beyond partnerships and taking concrete adaptation action on to the ground, so far which is missing. We expect that after receiving parties' submissions, technical papers, and recommendations of the Adaptation Committee, SBSTA at its thirty-ninth session could agree on draft decisions on Nairobi Work Programme for adoption at the COP-19 in Warsaw.

Mr. Chairman,

3. On agenda items 4 and 5, regarding policy approaches and policy incentives for the reducing emissions from deforestation and forest degradation and the role of conservation, sustainable management of forests, and enhancement of forest carbon stocks in developing countries, we are pleased to see the progress achieved on methodological issues and the identification of the

way forward on some of its most sensitive elements. Also, in the recognition that non-market-based approaches, are important to implement the activities referred to in decision 1/CP.16, paragraph 70.

4. However, the failure to open the work of the SBI meant as well that the joint process on coordination of support and institutional arrangements for reducing emissions from deforestation and forest degradation and the role of conservation, sustainable management of forests, and enhancement of forest carbon stocks in developing countries under agenda item 5 could not go further than a workshop, as we had hoped to. The direct consequence is that this session did not address properly the priorities of developing countries with regard to this matter, namely, scaling up finance and increasing the coordination of its delivery. This unbalance must be corrected in our following session, and we respectfully request this to be addressed in the organization of our work in Warsaw.
5. The Group of 77 and China welcomes the draft conclusions on agenda item 7 on Research and Systematic Observations. The Group of 77 and China reiterates its support for the research dialogue and recognizes its contribution in enhancing communication between the science communities and policymakers. In this regard, the Group of 77 and China thank the IPCC and the research organization for their participation in the recent research dialogue.

Mr. Chairman,

6. The Group of 77 and China also welcomes the workshop to consider information on the technical and scientific aspects of coastal marine ecosystems. These workshops are important to discuss updated information on emergent scientific findings.
7. The Group of 77 and China also commends the work done on the UNFCCC website in enhancing the availability and visibility of scientific information produced by the international and regions research programmes and organisations under the Convention.

Mr. Chairman,

8. The G-77 and China reaffirms the importance of the forum on the impact of the implementation of response measures at the Subsidiary Bodies and its work program to address these impacts. In particular, we welcome the activities that took place in these sessions in the areas of the work program related to the assessment of impacts; the just transition of the workforce; economic diversification; and modelling. In addition, as mandated by decision 1.CP.18, we also look forward to sharing views in the forum on policy issues of concern, such as unilateral measures.

9. In this respect, we attach great importance to this issue as all developing country parties will be affected by negative economic and social consequences of response measures taken by developed country parties. Therefore, we reaffirm the need for the forum to take full consideration of the specific needs and concerns of developing country parties arising from the impact of the implementation of response measures, in accordance with the provisions and principles of the Convention. In this regard, the focus of the next activities of the forum should address specifically how developed countries parties are minimizing the adverse economic and social effects of their response measures on developing countries parties.

Mr. Chairman,

10. As for agriculture and the related issues in agenda item 10, the G-77 and China has been so cooperative in the constructive work during this very session that led to an instrumental set of conclusions. Such conclusions reflect the particularities of agriculture, in terms of its relation to food security and the fundamental importance of agriculture for social and economic development and rural development, in particular for developing countries, where a large proportion of the population depends on agriculture for its livelihood.
11. In a context of the need to feed a world growing population in the coming decades, there will be a need to produce food in different climate conditions. To this end, it will be necessary to increase the adaptive capacity of agriculture. Hence, the need to work on adaptation and agriculture is crucial, a fact that needs to be reflected in the forthcoming submissions and a workshop to explore the needs of survival and sustainable development for all related activities and all involved farmers in our developing countries.
12. On the issues relating to agriculture, we stress that the focus of discussions must remain on adaptation, which is the key priority in developing countries in light of the linkages of agricultural sector with livelihood of millions, food security, and poverty alleviation. Needless to add, these should be done under the principles of the Convention, including CBDR.

Mr. Chairman,

13. The G-77 and China reiterates the importance of supporting multilateral solutions when addressing the issue of emissions from the international maritime and civil aviation sectors working through the International Maritime Organization (IMO) and International Civil Aviation Organization (ICAO), respectively, while taking into account the principles and provisions of the Convention and not on the basis of unilateral measures.

Mr. Chairman,

14. Regarding item 12, the Group considers that the questions agreed will enrich further discussions for SBSTA 39.
15. On the framework for various approaches, the Group agreed that it is important that the work programme define and clarify the purpose of the framework and the scope of approaches to be included under it. The Group is of the view that the framework should be elaborated under the authority and guidance of the COP.

Mr. Chairman,

16. The Group of 77 and China looks forward to continuing engaging constructively in the design of the FVA, new-market mechanism, and non-market-based approaches. Also, the Group recognizes that non-market-based approaches are means of crucial importance to ensure the implementation of the ultimate objective of the Convention, according to its principles and provisions.
17. We stress that the discussions on new market mechanism and non-market mechanisms must be framed in the context of framework of various approaches These mechanisms should focus on climate change and not become a mere source of revenue.

Mr. Chairman,

18. In agenda items under SBSTA where conclusions have mandated further workshops, we must ensure to the extent possible, balanced representation to ensure effective participation of developing country parties in such workshops. These workshops must be open to all parties and scheduled to avoid undue overlaps, particularly with, respect to country group meetings. The organization of such workshops must provide the necessary support to ensure effective participation of developing country parties.
19. The workshops should allow for expression of a range of views to ensure that developing countries' perspectives are reflected.
20. Parties should be informed ahead of time of the themes to be dealt with in these workshops to ensure transparency, openness, and inclusiveness.

Mr. Chairman,

21. The Group of 77 and China appreciates the efforts by all parties during this session to achieve progress on the clarification of developed country parties' emission reduction targets as mandated in Doha, although the progress is not as significant as desired. We have high expectation of fulfilment of the

mandate with a view to ensuring the comparability of efforts among developed country parties, and look forward to working constructively with all.

Mr. Chairman,

22. Recognizing the importance of the work of other subsidiary bodies for progress in this working group, the Group of 77 and China wishes to express its disappointment and deep concern at the inability of the Subsidiary Body for Implementation to begin the work of its thirty-eighth session. This delay has the potential to profoundly impact the progress of the work under the SBSTA. The Group of 77 and China calls on the Chair of the SBI, relevant bodies under the Convention, and parties to resolve this impasse prior to the start of the thirty-ninth session of the SBI.
23. We need to be conscious of the fact that progress of work in SBSTA is important for our progress in the post-2020 period and for the work in the ADP.

Statement on behalf of the Group of 77 and China by Mr. Amena Yauvoli, Ambassador, UNFCCC Chair of the G-77 and China, at the Opening Plenary of the 39th Session of the Subsidiary Body for Scientific and Technological Advice (SBSTA 39)
(Poland, Warsaw, 11 November 2013)

Thank you, Mr. Chairman,

Excellencies,
Distinguished Representatives,
Ladies and Gentlemen,

Mr. Chairman,

1. I have the honour to deliver this statement on behalf of the Group of 77 and China.
2. The Group appreciates that this Subsidiary Body has initiated reconsideration of the work areas of the Nairobi Work Programme on Impacts, Vulnerability and Adaptation to Climate Change. We want a more relevant and effective work programme to be launched by moving beyond partnerships and taking concrete adaptation action on to the ground, so far which is missing. We want this Group desire to form part of the decision to be adopted in this Conference.

Mr. Chairman,

3. The Group will make appropriate recommendations for decisions to be considered and adopted at this Session on the work of the Adaptation

Committee. We express our serious concern over the shortfalls in resources available to the Committee and will be working with others to consider ways to address it.

4. On agenda items 5 and 6, regarding policy approaches and policy incentives for reducing emissions from deforestation and forest degradation and the role of conservation, sustainable management of forests and enhancement of forest carbon stocks in developing countries, we are pleased with the progress achieved thus far on methodological issues and on the identification of the way forward on some of the most sensitive elements. Also, in the recognition that non-market-based approaches are important to implement the activities referred to in decision 1/CP.16, paragraph 70. Also, in the recognition that non-market-based approaches are important to implement the activities referred to in decision 1/CP.16, paragraph 70, taking into account decision 2/CP.17, paragraphs 65 to 67.
5. However, the failure of SBI to conduct its business in June has meant that the joint process on coordination of support and institutional arrangements for reducing emissions from deforestation and forest degradation and the role of conservation, sustainable management of forests, and enhancement of forest carbon stocks in developing countries under agenda item 6 was unable to progress. Therefore, the priorities of developing countries with regard to this matter, namely, scaling up finance and increasing the coordination of its delivery was not considered properly. This imbalance must be corrected during this session.
6. The Group of 77 and China supports the draft conclusions on agenda item 8 on Research and Systematic Observations. The Group of 77 and China reiterates its support for the research dialogue and recognizes its contribution in enhancing communication between the science communities and policymakers. In this regard, the Group of 77 and China thanks the IPCC and the research organization for their participation this year's research dialogue.

Mr. Chairman,

7. The G-77 and China reaffirms the importance of the forum on the impact of the implementation of response measures at the Subsidiary Bodies and its work program to address these impacts. In particular, we welcome the organization for this session of the workshop on area b of the work programme (cooperation on response strategies) and, as mandated by decision 1/CP.18, we also look forward to sharing views in the forum on policy issues of concern, such as unilateral measures.
8. In this respect, all developing country parties will be affected in different ways by negative economic and social consequences of response measures taken by developed country parties. Therefore, we affirm the importance of the continuation of the forum, as there is a need to take full consideration of what actions

are necessary to meet the specific needs and concerns of developing country parties arising from the impact of the implementation of response measures, in accordance with the provisions and principles of the Convention. In this regard, we look forward to continuing working in the forum, in COP-19 and beyond, in order to address specifically how developed countries parties are minimizing the adverse economic and social effects of their response measures on developing countries parties.

Mr. Chairman,

9. As for agriculture and the related issues in agenda item 10, the G-77 and China has worked cooperatively and constructively during the previous session that lead to an instrumental set of conclusions. Such conclusions reflect the particularities of agriculture, in terms of its relation to food security and the fundamental importance of agriculture for social and economic development and rural development, in particular for developing countries, where a large proportion of the population depends on agriculture for its livelihood.
10. In a context of the need to feed a growing world population in the coming decades, there will be a need to produce food under different climatic conditions. To this end, it will be necessary to increase the adaptive capacity of agriculture. Given that the need to work on adaptation and agriculture is crucial, the Group looks forward to the workshop on the current state of scientific knowledge on how to enhance the adaptation of Agriculture to Climate Change impact while promoting rural and sustainable development and productivity of Agricultural Systems and Food Security in all Countries, particularly Developing Countries, scheduled to be held on Tuesday, 12 November, 2013.
11. Further, on agriculture, we stress that the focus of discussions must remain primarily on adaptation, which is the key priority in developing countries in light of the linkages of agricultural sector with livelihood of millions, food security, and poverty alleviation. Needless to add, these should be done under the principles of the Convention, including CBDR and RC.

Mr. Chairman,

12. The G-77 and China reiterates the importance of supporting multilateral solutions when addressing the issue of emissions from the international maritime and civil aviation sectors working through the International Maritime Organization (IMO) and International Civil Aviation Organization (ICAO), respectively, while taking into account the principles and provisions of the Convention and not on the basis of unilateral measures.

Mr. Chairman,

13. The Group of 77 and China looks forward to continuing engaging constructively this session in the design of the FVA, new-market mechanism, and non-market-based approaches. Also, the Group recognizes that non-market-bases approaches are means of crucial importance to ensure the implementation of the ultimate objective of the Convention, according to its principles and provisions.
14. We stress that the discussions on new market mechanism and non-market mechanisms must be framed in the context of framework of various approaches. These mechanisms should focus on climate change and not become a mere source of revenue.

Mr. Chairman,

15. The Group of 77 and China appreciates the efforts by all parties this year to achieve progress on the clarification of developed country parties' emission reduction targets as mandated in Doha, although the progress is not as significant as desired. We have high expectation of the complete fulfilment of the mandate with a view to ensuring the comparability of efforts among developed country parties, and look forward to working constructively with all.

Mr. Chairman,

16. In conclusion, the Group is conscious of the fact that progress of work in SBSTA is important for our progress in the post-2020 period and for the work in the ADP.

Statement on behalf of the Group of 77 and China by Mr. Amena Yauvoli, Ambassador, for the UNFCCC Chair of the G-77 and China, at the Closing Plenary of the 39th Session of the Subsidiary Body for Scientific and Technological Advice (SBSTA-39)
(Warsaw, Poland, 16 November 2013)

Mr. Chairman,

1. I have the honor to deliver this statement on behalf of the Group of 77 and China.
2. As we draw to a close the thirty-ninth session of this Subsidiary Body, I wish to first express the sincere appreciation of the Group to all parties for the hard work that they have exerted into the work on the various agenda item of this Body.

Mr. Chairman,

3. I just wish to make a comment on a number of issues.
4. On Agriculture, the Group G-77 and China welcomes the rich exchange of views by parties during the in-session workshop on the current state of scientific knowledge on how to enhance the adaptation of agriculture to climate change impacts while promoting rural development, sustainable development and productivity of agricultural systems, and food security in all countries, particularly in developing countries, taking into account the diversity of the agricultural systems and the differences in scale as well as possible adaptation co-benefits

   The Group is looking forward to consider the report of the in-session workshop of the SBSTA 39, the submissions and the views expressed by the parties at the workshop, on the elements agreed at SBSTA 38, and to discuss them at the SBSTA 40 (June 2014), and to determine the way forward. In saying this, let me categorically state that when you Chair called for a decision on this particular item, there was no confusion by my Group in the matter in which the decision was made and concluded.
5. On Response Measures, the G-77 and China welcomes the forum on the impact of the implementation of response measures and its work programme to address these impacts. In particular, we welcome the organization for this session of the workshop on area b of the work programme (cooperation on response strategies) and, as mandated by decision 1/CP.18, we look forward to continuing sharing views in the forum on policy issues of concern, such as unilateral measures.
6. Given the importance of this issue to all developing countries, the G-77 and China tabled a text proposal for a decision here in Warsaw for the continuation of the forum and the establishment of a mechanism, with substantive proposals for specific areas of work. We want to express our disappointment at the lack of progress made on the review of the work of the forum and its continuation. This is due to the fact that the proposals made by developed country parties did not address adequately the negative economic and social consequences of their response measures on developing country parties.
7. We look forward to a favourable consideration of this issue under COP-19, for the adoption of a decision for the continuation of the forum and the establishment of a mechanism to give full consideration on what actions are necessary to meet the specific needs and concerns of developing country parties on this matter
8. On the Nairobi Programme of Work, the G-77 and China welcomes the progress made in the implementation of the Nairobi Work Programme and would like to highlight the importance of the process leading to the review of its objectives, action-oriented sub-themes and working areas, and the need for

the Programme to further enhance its work and the visibility of its products with a view to support the Adaptation Framework and its provisions.

9. The G-77 and China welcomed the progress made at this session towards the 2013–2015 review. We underscored the importance of continuing the work under this agenda item in an inclusive, transparent, and balanced manner.

Mr. Chairman,

10. On technology, the G-77 and China recognizes the activities done by the Technology Executive Committee (TEC) during 2012 and welcomes its rolling work plan for 2012–2013. The group emphasizes the necessity for the TEC to structure its work plan in short and medium term, including the organisation of a thematic dialogue on enabling environment for technology development and transfer including the mechanisms needed to remove all barriers.
11. On the CDM, the Group takes note of the exchange of views on the item relating to the agenda of carbon dioxide capture and storage under the clean development mechanism projects activities.
12. On REDD+, the G-77 and China looks forward to continuing the discussion on methodological guidance for activities relating to reducing emissions from deforestation and forest degradation and the role of conservation, sustainable management of forests, and enhancement of forest carbon stocks in developing countries.
13. On Research and Systematic Observations. The Group of 77 and China welcomes the draft conclusions on this agenda item. We welcome the information provided by the WMO on the developments regarding the implementation of the Global Framework for Climate Services and the outcome of the first session of the Intergovernmental Board on Climate Services. We also welcome the contribution of Working Group 1 to the Fifth Assessment Report (AR5) of the IPCC noting the importance of research and systematic observation for such assessments. We look forward to the release of Working Group II and Working Group III and the Synthesis Report of the AR5.

Mr. Chairman,

14. The G-77 and China continue to emphasize the importance of systematic observation for the UNFCCC Process. We affirm that systematic observation is critical to advance scientific knowledge on climate change and for decision-making on adaptation. However, there are still gaps in key observational data in developing countries particularly in the ocean domain.
15. The G-77 and China also recognize the importance of historical data records, and the need to enhance data rescue and digitization efforts and climate monitoring. We believe that a workshop on systematic observation could

help to identify ways to strengthen systematic observation and to enhance capacity in support of adaptation planning.

16. On the methodological discussions related to the completion of the Guidelines for the Biennial Reports from Annex I parties, with the view to developing a common tabular format for reporting part of the information required, the Group acknowledges the progress of the work.
17. The G-77 and China reiterates the importance of supporting multilateral solutions when addressing the issue of emissions from the international maritime and civil aviation sectors working through the International Maritime Organization (IMO) and International Civil Aviation Organization (ICAO), respectively, while taking into account the principles and provisions of the Convention and not on the basis of unilateral measures.
18. The Group of 77 and China reiterates its disappointment in relation to the opposition by Annex I countries to consider the Group's proposal, as originally presented by Brazil's submission to the SBSTA, on the development of a reference methodology on historical responsibilities by the IPCC to guide domestic consultations for the ADP 2015 Agreement. Refusal from Annex I countries to discuss in an open, transparent and inclusive manner objective and scientific-based information on historical responsibilities to climate change is a clear indication of their lack of political willingness to stand up to their responsibilities, as required by the principles and provisions of the Convention, in particular the principle of common but differentiated responsibilities. This is a very negative signal for the regime at this critical juncture. We would have hoped that the Warsaw COP had sent a positive signal regarding parties' willingness to openly discuss issues we know are complex and sensitive, but nonetheless essential to the ambition we all wish to see in 2015.

Finally, Mr. Chairman,

19. I would like to reiterate the full commitment of the G-77 and China to continue working to achieve concrete results during the next session of SBSTA next year.

Statement on behalf of the Group of 77 and China by Ambassador Rene Orellana, Chair of the Group of 77 and China at the Opening of Plenary of the 40th Session of the Subsidiary Body for Scientific and Technological Advice (SBSTA40) (Bonn, Germany, 4 June 2014)

Thank you, Mr. Chairman,

Excellencies,
Distinguished representatives,
Ladies and gentlemen,

1. I have the honour to deliver this statement on behalf of the Group of 77 and China during the Opening Plenary of the Fortieth Session of this Subsidiary Body.
2. Let me congratulate you on your appointment as Chair of the SBSTA. You can count on the full support of our Group to secure the successful work of this Subsidiary Body. I wish to assure you that the Group is willing and ready to engage meaningfully with all parties. Our support and assistance to you is reaffirmed.

Mr. Chairman,

3. At your request we held our statement to the end. However, please consider the content of this statement in each applicable agenda item as well.
   Mr. Chairman, allow me to express the views of the Group in relation to the following items on the agenda:
4. Agriculture is a very sensitive economic sector that touches a wide range of population in many of our countries, where economies of scale are absent and need to be enhanced by increasing the adaptive capacity to deal with the adverse effects of climate change. In this regard the group is open to discuss the results of the in-session workshop in formal consultation mode and in the context of the importance of agriculture for social and economic development and rural development, sustainable development, and poverty eradication.
5. The Group of 77 and China also welcomes the rich exchange of views by parties during the in-session workshop which, we had on the side line of SBSTA 39 on the current state of scientific knowledge on how to enhance the adaptation of agriculture to climate change impacts while promoting rural development, sustainable development, and productivity of agricultural systems and food security in all countries, particularly in developing countries, taking into account the diversity of the agricultural systems and the differences in scale as well as possible adaptation co-benefits.
6. In a context of the need to feed a growing world population in the coming decades, there will be a need to produce food under different climatic conditions. To this end, it will be necessary to increase the adaptive capacity of agriculture. Furthermore, we stress that the focus of discussions must remain on adaptation, which is the key priority in developing countries in light of the linkages of agricultural sector with the livelihood of millions, food security, and poverty eradication. Needless to add, these should be done under the principles and provisions of the Convention, including the principle of CBDR.
7. On Response Measures, the G-77 and China reaffirms the importance to give full consideration to what actions are necessary to meet the specific needs and concerns of developing country parties arising from the impacts of the

implementation of response measures, in accordance with the principles and provisions of the Convention. In this regard, we regret the lack of progress made in Warsaw on the matter, but we still look forward to the favourable consideration of the issue in these Subsidiary Bodies sessions, towards the adoption of a decision at COP-20 for the continuation of the forum and the establishment of a mechanism to address the negative economic and social consequences of response measures taken by developed country parties on developing country parties.

8. In this regard, we recall the contents of the submission that the G-77 and China tabled in Warsaw on the matter, and we believe our proposal has key substantive elements towards the achievement of progress in these sessions.
9. The G-77 and China welcomes the report of the joint meeting of the AC and NWP on available tools for the use of indigenous and traditional knowledge and practices for adaptation, needs of local and indigenous communities, and the application of gender-sensitive approaches and tools for adaptation. We also welcome the recently released report on the progress of the NWP and highlight that the progress report reflects only activities that are related to meetings, workshop, and knowledge management, which has very less impacts on the ground. We want a more relevant and effective work programme to be launched by moving beyond partnerships and taking concrete adaptation action on to the ground, which is missing so far.
10. The G-77 and China looks forward to the progress to be made at this session towards the 2013–2015 review. We underscore the importance of continuing the work under this agenda item in an inclusive, transparent, and balanced manner.
11. With respect to agenda item 12(a) and 12(b), relating to the rule set for the Kyoto Protocol's second commitment period, it was unfortunate that this agenda item could not be concluded in Warsaw, due to last-minute issues raised by parties. It is the view of the G-77 that the Doha Amendment and its important article 3.7 must not be rewritten or undermined through creative interpretation.
12. On technology, the Group emphasizes the necessity for the TEC to structure its work plan in short and medium term, including the organisation of a thematic dialogue on enabling environment for technology development and transfer including the mechanisms needed to address all barriers, such as IPR.
13. The G-77 and China reiterates the importance of supporting multilateral solutions when addressing the issue of emissions from the international maritime and civil aviation sectors working through the International Maritime Organization (IMO) and International Civil Aviation Organization (ICAO), respectively and not on the basis of unilateral measures, while taking into account the principles and provisions of the Convention.

14. The Group welcomes the outcome of the COP-19 decision of the Warsaw international mechanism for loss and damage associated with climate change impacts, and the need to make this mechanism functional is paramount. This mechanism must address the needs of developing countries emerging from extreme and slow-onset events, and the urgency for this mechanism has only increased. This mechanism cannot be an empty shell, and it is therefore the great concern that the Group finds itself isolated from the development of the work plan of the Mechanism being undertaken by the interim Executive Committee of the Mechanism. We call to immediately find a solution to address this unprecedented lack of transparency on this, a matter of survival and development for the group. We also call for the operationalization of the Mechanism established by this decision, taking into account the principles of the Convention and the national development processes. Carrying out such actions requires the provision of adequate support and creating the appropriate arrangements and for meaningful activities.
15. For this session, we look forward to being engage in discussions on the composition and procedures. We call for a composition that is equitable with membership of this Convention, with a majority from developing countries with a similar membership structure as the Adaptation Committee. On procedures, it is important to think of proper procedures of a mechanism, for example, on integration of outside experts on key issues like migration, humanitarian issues, recovery and rehabilitation, and insurance to complement the work of the Mechanism.
16. The Group of 77 and China reiterates its support for the research dialogue and recognizes its contribution in enhancing communication between the science communities and policymakers. This is the first opportunity we have to meet since the release of the Fifth Assessment Report of the IPCC Working Groups II and III on Impacts, Adaptation and Vulnerability of Climate Change and on Mitigation. We hope that the Dialogue will provide us with an opportunity to interact with the research community on what the latest report tells us about the vulnerability of developing countries to the impacts of climate change, the adaptation opportunities, and the mitigation pathways available to reduce global emissions and therefore our vulnerabilities.
17. The Group of 77 and China looks forward to continuing to engage constructively at this session in the discussions related to the framework for various approaches, new-market mechanism and non-market-based approaches in a balanced manner. Also, the Group recognizes that non-market-based approaches are means of crucial importance to ensure the implementation of the ultimate objective of the Convention, according to its principles and provisions.
18. In conclusion, Mr. Chairman, the Group of 77 and China reserves its position on the remaining agenda items not articulated in this statement and wishes to reiterate our commitment for a fruitful session.

Statement on behalf of the Group of 77 and China by Ambassador Rene Orellana, Chair of the Group of 77 and China at the Closing Plenary of the 40th Session of the Subsidiary Body for Scientific and Technological Advice (SBSTA 40 (Bonn, Germany, 15 June 2014)

Thank you, Mr. Chairman,

Excellencies,
Distinguished representatives,
Ladies and gentlemen,

1. I have the honour to deliver this statement on behalf of the Group of 77 and China during the Closing Plenary of the fortieth session of this Subsidiary Body.

Mr. Chairman, allow me to express the views of the Group in relation to the following items on the agenda:

2. On issues related to agriculture, the Group considers the conclusions that were reached by parties are a concrete step forward on the issue, and we welcome the four in-sessions workshops that we will have up till SBSTA 44, and consider the output in SBSTA 45. It is clear that those workshops and the technical and scientific SBSTA work will be conducted under SBSTA 38 mandate on the current state of scientific knowledge on how to enhance the adaptation of agriculture to climate change impacts while promoting rural development, sustainable development and productivity of agricultural systems and food security in all countries, particularly in developing countries, taking into account the diversity of the agricultural systems and the differences in scale as well as possible adaptation co-benefits.
3. All this, on the basis of the objective, principles and the provisions of the Convention, and to ensure that food production is not threatened and to enable economic development to proceed in a sustainable manner, even more taking into account the importance of the agricultural sector for the achievement of economic and social development and poverty eradication in developing countries.
4. On Response Measures, the G-77 and China reaffirms the importance to give full consideration on what actions are necessary to meet the specific needs and concerns of developing country parties arising from the impacts of the implementation of response measures, in accordance with the principles and provisions of the Convention. In this regard, even if we regret the initial procedural discussions held in these sessions on the review that was already completed in Warsaw, we welcome the final progress we achieved in terms of the request for a technical paper and synthesis report; the recognition of the

formal conclusion of the review of the work of the forum; and the definition of the way forward for the adoption of a decision at COP-20.

5. In this regard, we reaffirm the contents of the submissions that the G-77 and China tabled in Warsaw and here in Bonn for the continuation of the forum and the establishment of a mechanism to address the negative economic and social consequences of response measures taken by developed country parties on developing country parties. We believe our proposal has key substantive elements towards the achievement of progress and we trust parties will continue the constructive engagement we had in these sessions in Lima towards the adoption of a decision on the issue.
6. On technology, the Group emphasizes the necessity for the TEC to structure its work plan in short and medium term, including the organisation of a thematic dialogue on enabling environment for technology development and transfer including the mechanisms needed to address all barriers, such as IPR.
7. On the matters of the Warsaw international mechanism for loss and damage associated with climate change impacts, the Group stressed the need to make this mechanism functional is paramount. The Group welcomes exchanges held during this session while stressing that a long road remains towards making the mechanism meaningful. This mechanism must address the needs of developing countries emerging from extreme and slow-onset events, and the urgency for this mechanism has only increased. This mechanism cannot be an empty shell, and it is therefore the great concern that the Group finds itself isolated from the development of the work plan of the Mechanism being undertaken by the interim Executive Committee of the Mechanism. We call for finalizing the organization and governance of the executive committee and the necessary arrangements that respond to the expectations of particularly vulnerable developing countries.

Mr. Chairman,

8. The Group of 77 and China stands committed to continue working together on all three work programs on the Framework for Various Approaches, Non-Market Based Approaches and New Market Mechanism in a balanced way. We firmly believe that information should be shared amongst parties based on experience and good practice relevant to the design and operation of both market and non-market-based approaches, including proposals on approaches developed or being developed by parties individually or jointly, so that the SBSTA may consider the design and operation of the Framework for Various Approaches.

Mr. Chairman,

9. The Group of 77 and China welcomes the draft conclusions on agenda item 6 on Research and Systematic Observations. The G-77 and China

also acknowledges the important contribution of the research dialogue in communicating scientific findings, research-planning activities, research priorities and gaps, and research-related capacity-building activities. We express our appreciation to the Intergovernmental Panel on Climate Change and to the research programmes and organizations for their active participation and contribution to the research dialogue.

10. The G-77 and China is concerned that capacity is still limited in climate research in regions. In addition, geographic disparities continue in available evidence for assessing climate change impacts. The G-77 and China is of the view that we need to enhance scientific and technical capacity in those regions to fill these gaps.

Mr. Chairman,

11. Under the SBSTA's agenda items 12(a) and 12(b), that relate to articles 578 and 3.7 ter, the Group of 77 and China had worked constructively to generate the necessary clarification on the rules to achieve a sustained and effective implementation of the second commitment period of the Kyoto Protocol in manner that maintains the environmental integrity of the commitments agreed in Doha.
12. Unfortunately, flexibility and constructiveness were not always presented by our Partners. We hope this is not being taken by parties as an excuse for not ratifying the second commitment period of the Kyoto Protocol, as, in our view, any ambiguity in our understanding of 3.7 ter has been raised by parties with commitments under Annex B to the KP.
13. We recognize that important work is needed on the in-session discussion document, which the parties were close to finishing in Warsaw. However, here in Bonn, we have not advanced in removing the problematic text within those brackets. Our hope is that we close this document in Lima and have a chance to move onwards with consideration of other issues related to this agenda item.
14. In regard to 3.7 ter, we must all strive to protect the environmental integrity of the Kyoto Protocol.

Mr. Chairman,

15. The G-77 and China recognizes the importance of research and communication between the scientific community, policymakers, and users. Therefore, we support the views of parties that the UNFCCC website continues to be used as a channel to further enhance the availability and visibility of scientific information, including through social media, the UNFCCC e-newsletter, and other tools. We look forward to the discussion on systematic observation in SBSTA 41 and to recommence discussions in a frank and focused manner on this matter in Lima, Peru.

Statement on behalf of the Group of 77 and China by Ambassador Rene Orellana, Chair of the Group of 77 and China, at the Opening Plenary of the 41st Session of the Subsidiary Body for Scientific and Technological Advice (SBSTA 41) (Lima, Peru, 1 December 2014)

Excellencies,
Distinguished representatives,
Ladies and gentlemen,

1. I have the honour to deliver this statement on behalf of the Group of 77 and China during the Opening Plenary of the fortieth session of this Subsidiary Body.
2. On the matters of the Warsaw international mechanism for loss and damage associated with climate change impacts, the Group stresses the paramount need to make this mechanism functional. This mechanism must address the needs of developing countries suffering from extreme and slow-onset climate change induced events, and the urgency for this mechanism has only increased. We call for finalizing the organization and governance of the executive committee, the necessary arrangements including the financial mechanism, and the approval of a two-year work plan that responds to the expectations of particularly vulnerable developing countries.
3. On Response Measures, the G-77 and China reaffirms the importance to give full consideration on what actions are necessary to meet the specific needs and concerns of developing country parties arising from the impact of the implementation of response measures, in accordance with the principles and provisions of the Convention. In this regard, we welcome the process agreed in the fortieth session of the Subsidiary Bodies for submissions and the preparation of the technical paper and synthesis report by the Secretariat, with the aim for the SBs to providing recommendations to COP-20.
4. In this regard, we reaffirm the contents of the recent G-77 and China submissions for the continuation of the forum and the establishment of a mechanism to avoid and minimize the negative economic and social consequences of response measures taken by developed country parties on developing country parties, and in particular to address policy issues of concern, such as unilateral measures. We believe our proposal has key substantive elements towards the achievement of progress in these sessions and we trust parties will continue to engage constructively towards the adoption of a decision on the issue in Lima.
5. The Group would like to highlight the Warsaw Framework for REDD+, as the methodological guidance for the activities referred to in decision 1/CP.16, paragraph 70 seeking to obtain and receive results-based payments for results-based actions, expressed in tons of carbon dioxide equivalent per year (9/CP.19).

6. The Group would also like to recognize that alternative policy approaches, such as joint mitigation and adaptation approaches, need differentiated methodological guidance, in accordance to national circumstances and national policies, in the context of sustainable development supported by financial, technical, capacity-building within the context of the Convention.
7. The Group is eager to move this issue further into implementation, in the context of adequate and predictable support from developed countries.
8. On Development and Transfer of Technologies, the Group of 77 and China believes that in order to fully implement the technology mechanism to enhance the action of technology development and transfer, it is crucial to ensure coordination between the two bodies of technology mechanism, the Technology Executive Committee and the CTCN. We look forward to the tangible development and transfer of technologies to developing countries for climate change. The Group emphasizes the necessity for the TEC to structure its work plan for the short and medium term, including the organisation of a thematic dialogue for technology development and transfer, including the mechanisms needed to address all barriers.
9. The Group of 77 and China looks forward to continuing to engage constructively at this session in the discussions related to the framework for various approaches, new-market mechanism and non-market-based approaches in a balanced manner thereafter, noting the importance of this discussion for the 2015 Agreement. Also, the Group recognizes that non-market-based approaches are important to ensure the implementation of the objective of the Convention, according to its principles and provisions.

Mr. Chairman,

10. Setting the date for completion of the expert review process in time for an informed process in Paris will entail understanding the historical difficulties in completing the review process, as well as understanding the importance to the G-77 and China of knowing the compliance status of the KP parties in the first Commitment Period. Setting also the modalities and procedures for the operationalization of the second period of the Kyoto Protocol will allow to start to work under these new procedures in 2015 and facilitate the process of ratification of the Doha Amendment. We should not allow technical excuses to delay these very important and politically sensitive issues. The Group highlights that this matter is paramount to trust building among parties to the ADP negotiations.

Mr. Chairman,

11. The G-77 and China welcome the progress made under item 13 on the work programme on clarification of quantified economy-wide emission reduction

targets of developed country parties. The Group noticed the mandate from decision 1/CP.18 requesting the SBSTA to report to the COP-21 on the outcome of the programme, and the SBSTA-40 agreed to prepare conclusions at SBSTA-41, including activities conducted, and information on issues addressed and shared understandings during the work programme. However, the Group expresses its concern on the lack of progress on ensuring the comparability of efforts among developed country parties, and would like to address these issues during this session. The Group assures you to work actively on the unfinished work under this mandate.

12. The G-77 and China reiterates the importance of supporting multilateral solutions when addressing the issue of emissions from the International Maritime Organization and International Civil Aviation Organization, sectors working through the IOM and ICAO, respectively, while taking into account the principles and provisions of the Convention and not on the basis of unilateral measures.
13. In conclusion, Mr. Chairman, the Group of 77 and China reserves its position on the remaining agenda items not articulated in this statement and wishes to reiterate our commitment for a fruitful session.

Statement on behalf of the Group of 77 and China by Ambassador Rene Orellana, Chair of the Group of 77 and China, at the Closing Plenary of the 41st Session of the Subsidiary Body for Scientific and Technological Advice (SBSTA 41)
(Lima, Peru, 6 December 2014)

Mr. Chairman,

1. I have the honour to deliver this statement on behalf of the Group of 77 and China during the Closing Plenary of the forty-first session of this Subsidiary Body.
2. We welcome the work of the Adaptation Committee and their recommendations that have been taken up at this session. We value the work of the AC since promoting coherence on adaptation activities globally is vital to our Group. We underscore the importance of collaboration between the AC and other constituted Bodies under the Convention. In particular, we strongly emphasise the need for the operating entities of the financial mechanisms to work together with the AC in fulfilling our adaptation priorities. We trust that the decision adopted today allows these bodies to take into account the activities recommended by the Adaptation Committee.
3. Significant and substantial impacts of Nairobi Work Programme (NWP) are absent at the field level of the vulnerable countries. The G-77 and China are strongly in favour of an action-oriented approach of NWP, particularly to address the needs of the vulnerable developing countries. The Cancun

Adaptation Framework and SBI might be the useful vehicle for successful implementation of Nairobi Work Programme.

4. The G-77 and China is strongly in favour of an action-oriented approach of NWP, to especially address the needs of the particularly vulnerable developing countries. We hope to see the NWP make contributions to the Cancun Adaptation Framework. We hope to see the Programme evolve in that direction.

Mr. Chairman,

5. On Development and Transfer of Technologies, the Group of 77 and China welcome the operation of the technology mechanism, but there are big gaps for the technology mechanism to delivery tangible and meaningful development and transfer of technologies to developing countries for climate change. It is crucial to establish clear linkages between financial mechanism and technology mechanism.
6. The Group emphasizes the necessity for the TEC to continue its work plan on enabling environment and removing barriers, with a view to come up with policy recommendations to the COP for consideration.

Mr. Chairman,

7. Regarding REDD+, the G-77 is frustrated that SBSTA was not able to conclude the consideration of the matters under this agenda item, in spite of our great flexibility and constructive efforts. The G-77 and China reiterates that it is time to move towards implementing the Warsaw Framework for REDD+.
8. The G-77 and China stresses that there is no need for further guidance on safeguards and moves to concluding the consideration of this agenda item. The need for further guidance is to be determined by those parties who are to implement such guidance, not on the basis of expectations from donor countries. We attempted a compromise with developed countries by taking the issue to the meeting set by decision 10/CP.19 but this was not successful.
9. The G-77 and China further emphasizes the Warsaw Framework for REDD+ has concluded the methodological guidance on non-market-based approaches to results-based finance. The G-77 and China finally underlined that consensus was close to be achieved on alternative policy approaches, such as joint mitigation and adaptation and that there is the opportunity to reach conclusions on this matter at next SBSTA session.
10. The Group would also like to recognize that alternative policy approaches, such as joint mitigation and adaptation approaches, need differentiated methodological guidance, in accordance to national circumstances and national policies, in the context of sustainable development supported by financial, technical, and capacity-building within the context of the Convention.

Mr. Chairman,

11. On Response Measures, the G-77 and China reaffirms the importance to give full consideration on what actions are necessary to meet the specific needs and concerns of developing country parties arising from the impact of the implementation of response measures, in accordance with the principles and provisions of the Convention. In this regard, we still believe that there is space to continue the consideration of the issue under COP-20 towards the adoption of a decision on this agenda item in Lima, and we are prepared to continue to engage constructively towards a resolution of the matter.
12. In this sense, we reaffirm the contents of the recent G-77 and China submissions for the continuation of the forum and the establishment of a mechanism to avoid and minimize the negative economic and social consequences of response measures taken by developed country parties on developing country parties, and in particular to address policy issues of concern, such as unilateral measures, and strengthen multilateral cooperation.

Statement by Ambassador Nozipho Mxakato-Diseko from South Africa on behalf of the Group of 77 and China, at the Opening Plenary of 43rd Session of the Subsidiary Body for Scientific and Technological Advice (SBSTA-43)
(Paris, France, 1 December 2015)

Madam Chair,
Excellencies,
Distinguished representatives,
Ladies and gentlemen,

1. I have the honour to deliver this statement on behalf of the Group of 77 and China. The Group wishes to express its full support towards a successful outcome to these negotiations.
2. The importance of SBSTA as the subsidiary body that provides scientific and technical advice to the COP cannot be emphasised enough. The work of SBSTA plays an important role in our understanding of the science of climate change, and in strengthening the implementation of the Convention and, therefore, has a direct bearing on the negotiations under the ADP.

Madam Chair,

3. The Group of 77 and China appreciates the progress made in SBSTA42 on a number of important areas, and with the same spirit we believe we can achieve more here in Paris.

4. The Group regards all issues on the SBSTA agenda as having the same priority and not only those draft texts that will be tabled by the Facilitators. All the agenda items are important and need to be concluded as soon as possible.
5. In this regard, the Group would like to reiterate the importance of the achievement reached at COP-19 with the Warsaw Framework for REDD+, which has concluded most of the negotiations under this agenda item. Also, we appreciate the conclusion of the development of alternative policy approaches to results-based payments, such as joint mitigation and adaptation approaches for the integral and sustainable management of forests. We look forward to closing this agenda item at this session with the adoption of the three draft decisions agreed upon in Bonn last June. The G-77 and China is ready and willing to move REDD+ and alternative policy approaches further into implementation, provided that adequate and predictable support is made available from developed countries.
6. The G-77 and China welcomes the Report of the Adaptation Committee and the effort to make balanced progress in all its work areas. We take note of the future work plan of the Adaptation Committee, and look forward to discussing it in the Contact Group. The Group also welcomes the work completed related to means of implementation for adaptation and hopes that its outcome translates into something that can expedite support for developing countries. We are prepared to engage with partners in reviewing the recommendations to the COP contained in the report.
7. Regarding the important issues related to agriculture, which is the backbone of the socio-economic development of developing countries and has a special role for the livelihood of millions, food security, and poverty eradication, the Group welcomes the reports on the workshops that took place in SBSTA42 and their findings on the importance of continuing to improve the understanding of the adverse effects of climate change on agriculture and exploring effective ways to increase its adaptive capacity to these effects, including through sharing of knowledge, experience, and good practices. Adaptation continues to be the key priority for developing countries in light of the particular vulnerabilities of the agricultural sector and its relationship with the livelihood of millions, food security, and poverty eradication. The Group looks forward to discussing the reports and to have a procedural conclusion, consistent with the mandated work agreed upon in SBSTA40.
8. The G-77 and China welcomes the Report of the Executive Committee of the Warsaw International Mechanism for Loss and Damage associated with Climate Change Impacts. The work of the WIM on loss and damage under this Convention is of critical importance to the Group, and we take note of the adjustments relating to the terms of office of the members and Co-Chairs of the Executive Committee. In line with urgency of this matter, the G-77 also notes the need for resources for the successful and timely implementation of the initial two-year work plan of the Executive Committee and urges

developed country parties to make available resources for this purpose in view of the ambitious nature of the work plan.

9. The G-77 and China notes the importance of global observation of the earth's atmosphere, ocean, and land is essential for identifying climate variability and climate change, and for understanding their causes. We recognise that these observations serve other purposes, including weather and air quality forecasting, disaster risk reduction, water and food security, protection of biodiversity and ecosystems, and sustainable development. We look forward to progress here on this agenda item.
10. The Group appreciates the work of the Structured Expert Dialogue (SED) on the 2013–2015 Review of the adequacy of the long-term global goal. The Group expects that a thorough consideration will be made of the report in order for COP-21 to take forward the work of the SED, as well as on linkages with work under the ADP. This work is important as it relates to ambition as well as requisite support, particularly to developing countries towards the realisation of the ultimate objective of the Convention.
11. On Response Measures, the G-77 and China reaffirms the importance of giving full consideration to what actions are necessary to meet the specific needs and concerns of developing country parties arising from the impact of the implementation of response measures, in accordance with the principles and provisions of the Convention. In this regard, we look forward to engaging constructively on the text of the draft decision forwarded from the forty-second session of the SBs in order to adopt a decision at COP-21. The G-77 and China position remains firm that the negative economic and social consequences of response measures taken by developed country parties on developing country parties must be avoided and minimised. Policy issues, such as unilateral measures, must also be addressed.
12. As for agenda item 10(a) on methodologies for reporting of financial information by parties included in Annex I to the Convention, the actions taken to comply with obligations on the provision of financial resources, access and transfer of technology—and particularly on meeting the costs of adaptation—have to be reported by developed country parties in a manner that is comparable and verifiable. This has not been the case in the twenty years since the entry into force of the Convention. Such lack of reporting is one of the most serious gaps in our implementation of the Convention. It is of utmost importance that progress be made on this item to ensure that the SBSTA fulfils its mandate as set out in decision 2/CP.17 and that COP-21 takes a decision in this regard.
13. Regarding the issue of emissions from fuel used for international aviation and maritime transport, the G-77 and China thanks the presentations and submissions made by ICAO and IMO on this agenda item. In this regard, the Group reiterates the importance of supporting multilateral solutions when addressing the issue of emissions from the international maritime and civil

aviation sectors working through the International Maritime Organization (IMO) and International Civil Aviation Organization (ICAO), respectively, while taking into account the principles and provisions of the Convention and not on the basis of unilateral measures.

14. In this sense, the Group is of the view that the Secretariats of ICAO and IMO should continue to report, at future sessions of the SBSTA, on relevant work on this issue, and parties presenting their views in this regard. Thus, the G-77 and China supports to keep this matter under this agenda item under SBSTA, avoiding any attempts to include it in the ADP.
15. The Group has been working very hard to bring the item on methodological issues under the Kyoto Protocol to a conclusion. Any further obstacles to finalising the Kyoto Protocol's second commitment period must be dealt with during this session. This sub-item needs to be finalised so that parties included Annex I can submit their initial and annual reports and that the review for 2015–2016 can start. This would allow the second commitment period under the Kyoto Protocol to become effective. If progress is not made on this agenda item, it would not bode well for the 2015 Agreement in Paris.

In conclusion, Madam Chair,

16. We are looking forward to participating meaningfully in all mandated workshops that have been organised at this session and to a constructive engagement on all issues here in Paris.

Statement by H.E. Mr. Manasvi Srisodapol, Special Representative of the Chair of the Group of 77 and China for Climate Change on behalf of the Group of 77 and China, at the Closing Plenary of 44th Session of the Subsidiary Body for Scientific and Technological Advice (SBSTA-44)
(Bonn, Germany, 26 May 2016)

Mr. Chairman,
Excellencies,
Distinguished representatives,
Ladies and gentlemen,

1. I have the honour to deliver this statement on behalf of the Group of 77 and China. First of all, allow me to express our appreciation to the Chair and the facilitators for the efforts you have made during this session in Bonn.

Mr. Chairman,

2. The Group reiterates that the work of SBSTA must proceed in a comprehensive, coherent, balanced, and party-driven manner.

3. We would like to re-emphasize the urgent need to enhance pre-2020 action and support, which will lay solid foundation for post-2020 implementation. In this regard, the Group has engaged constructively in the Technical Expert Meetings on mitigation and adaptation held during this session. On the path to Marrakech, we look forward to an early engagement in the facilitative dialogue, in order to assess the progress in implementing decision 1/CP.19, paragraphs 3 and 4, and identify relevant opportunities to enhance the provision of financial resources, including for technology development and transfer, and capacity-building support.

   Mr. Chairman, allow me to express the views of the Group in relation to the following items on the agenda:
4. On the elaboration of the Technology Framework under article 10, paragraph 4, of the Paris Agreement, the Group notes the progress made during this session, highlighting that the Technology Framework should play a strategic role in the implementation of the Paris Agreement. The guidance to the technology mechanism should be flexible, balanced, systematic, and comprehensive in order to respond the evolving needs of climate technology development and dissemination in developing countries.
5. On agriculture, the Group has engaged constructively in the informal consultations to continue the consideration of the reports of the first two workshops held at SBSTA 42, as well as in its participation in the two workshops mandated at SBSTA 44. The Group regrets that despite our constructive approach, and rich exchanges of views during the informal consultations, we were unable to reach conclusions, due to the objection of some partners to make reference to the Convention, including its objective, principles and provisions, despite that it is agreed language from the previous SBSTA conclusions.
6. The Group would like to express its concern in this regard, as it does not send the right signal for future work. The Group would like to reaffirm in this regard its position, as outlined in the opening of this session, that Paris Agreement represents an important step in our efforts on climate change, through enhancing the implementation of the Convention, including its provisions and principles, in particular equity and common but differentiated responsibilities and respective capabilities, and that the delicate balance of all issues which we have achieved in Paris as well as the principles and provisions of the Convention must be preserved.
7. The G-77 and China considers that adaptation of agriculture to the adverse effects of climate change continues to be the key priority for developing countries for SBSTA work, in light of the particular vulnerabilities of the agricultural sector and its relationship with the livelihood of millions, food security, and poverty eradication. This is in line with the Paris Agreement, which recognizes the fundamental priority of safeguarding food security and ending hunger, and the particular vulnerabilities of food production

systems to the adverse effects of climate change. As well, it is important to recall that the Agreement states in its objective that food production is not to be threatened.

8. Regarding matters related to science and review, the Group welcomes the draft conclusions on Research and Systematic Observations and commends the cooperative spirit demonstrated by parties which enabled the SBSTA to successfully conclude its discussions on this sub-agenda item. We emphasize the importance of addressing regional climate research and data needs and request our partners to continue to provide the necessary resources to support these initiatives.
9. We are also pleased that we were able to conclude on "advice of how the assessments of the IPCC can inform the global stocktake" and look forward to the continued discussion at SBSTA 45. At the same time, we also look forward to continuing the discussion to further consider the scope of the next periodic review at SBSTA-46 and refining it.
10. On Response Measures, the Group reaffirms the importance of giving full consideration to identify necessary actions to meet the specific needs and concerns of developing country parties arising from the impact of the implementation of response measures and avoid the negative economic and social consequences of response measures on developing countries. The Group welcomes the progress made to operationalize the work programme of the improved forum on the impact of implementation of response measures, and the terms of reference developed for ad hoc technical expert groups that will support the work of the improved Forum. We look forward to continue engaging constructively in COP-22 and beyond, to recommend specific actions.
11. The Group reiterates the importance of supporting multilateral solutions when addressing emissions from fuel used for international aviation and maritime transport, while taking into account the principles and provisions of the Convention and not on the basis of unilateral measures. We take note of the report by the Secretariats of ICAO and IMO.
12. On matters relating to article 6 of Paris Agreement, the Group welcomes the call for submissions and reiterates the need to ensure a party-driven process in the way forward as well as the balance of all three sub-items, namely the guidance on cooperative approaches; the rules, modalities, and procedures for the mechanism established by article 6, paragraph 4 of the Paris Agreement; and the work programme under the framework for non-market approaches.
13. On accounting of financial resources, the Group reaffirms that the modalities for accounting of financial resources by developed country parties to developing country parties, mobilized through public interventions, in accordance with article 9, paragraph 7, of the Paris Agreement, must aim to provide transparency and consistency. The reported information must also be comparable and verifiable.

Mr. Chairman,

14. In conclusion, the Group conveys its appreciation to you for your leadership and looks forward to engage further with all parties during the next session.

Statement by H.E. Mr. Manasvi Srisodapol, Special Representative of the Chair of the Group of 77 and China for Climate Change, on behalf of the Group of 77 and China, at the Opening Plenary of 45th Session of the Subsidiary Body for Scientific and Technological Advice (SBSTA-45)
(Marrakech, Morocco, 7 November 2016)

Mr. Chairman,

1. I have the honour to deliver this statement on behalf of the Group of 77 and China. We wish to express our full support and readiness to engage constructively with all parties towards the successful work of this Subsidiary Body.
2. The important work carried out by SBSTA has always played a fundamental role in strengthening the implementation of the Convention. As we are now preparing the groundwork for the Paris Agreement, that applies only to the parties that have ratified it, the tasks mandated to this Subsidiary Body will therefore contribute tremendously to enhancing the implementation of the Convention.

Mr. Chairman,

3. The Group reiterates that the work of SBSTA must proceed in a comprehensive, coherent, balanced, and party-driven manner. We emphasize the need to ensure comprehensive and balanced progress in all issues, with respect to the mandates given under the Paris Agreement.
4. We re-emphasize the urgent need to enhance pre-2020 action and support and to focus on delivering major tasks on pre-2020 implementation. In this regard, we welcome and look forward to constructive engagement in the Facilitative Dialogue on enhancing ambition and support as well as the Global Climate Action events during this session. We emphasize that the work on pre-2020 must lead to enabling concrete actions on the ground, as well as making the most progress on all issues that we have agreed in the decisions of the COP.

Mr. Chairman, allow me to express the views of the Group in relation to the following items on the agenda:

5. The Group recognizes the progress made under the Nairobi Work Programme on impacts, vulnerability and adaptation to climate change. We

expect concrete implementation of activities and undertakings by AC, LEG, and NWP which lead to implementation on the ground.

6. The Group welcomes the report of the Adaptation Committee (AC) and takes note of the progress made by the AC in all areas of its work. We reiterate that developing countries require enhanced support as they advance in the process to formulate and implement NAPs. The Group notes with concern, however, that the current financial availability for the AC is inadequate for supporting the implementation of NAPs relating activities.
7. Regarding the work of the executive committee of the Warsaw International Mechanism for Loss and Damage associated with Climate Change Impacts, the Group takes note of its key achievements in the implementation of initial two-year work plan and looks forward to a constructive discussion on the draft five-year rolling work plan and its adoption at COP-22.
8. On Technology, the Group believes that the Technology Framework can provide the much-needed guidance to the work of the technology mechanism in promoting and facilitating actions on technology development and transfer in order to support the implementation of the Convention and the Paris Agreement, in particular its article 10. The Group expects the Technology Framework to facilitate the four working areas identified in decision 1/CP.21, paragraph 67, as well as other areas beyond them, including establishing linkage with financial mechanism and supporting the implementation of NDCs, among others.
9. The Group considers that adaptation, including co-benefits, of agriculture to the adverse effects of climate change continues to be the key priority for developing countries for SBSTA work, in light of the particular vulnerabilities of the agricultural sector and its relationship with the livelihood of millions, food security, and poverty eradication. This is in line with the Paris Agreement, which recognizes the fundamental priority of safeguarding food security and ending hunger, and the particular vulnerabilities of food production systems to the adverse effects of climate change and that food production is not to be threatened. The Group looks forward to engaging in the constructive discussion in this session based on the outcome from previous workshops and submissions.
10. Regarding matters related to science and review, the Group welcomes the report on the status of the observing system for climate prepared by GCOS and looks forward to considering the information contained in this report.
11. On "advice of how the assessments of the IPCC can inform the global stocktake," the Group looks forward to continued discussion at this session, recognizing that the IPCC can play an important role in providing scientific inputs in a comprehensive manner for the Global Stocktake.
12. On Response Measures, the Group reaffirms the importance of giving full consideration to identify necessary actions to meet the specific needs and concerns of developing country parties arising from the impact of the

implementation of response measures and avoid the negative economic and social consequences of response measures on developing countries. The Group takes note of the report from the workshop, welcomes the technical paper on a just transition of the workforce and the creation of decent work and quality job, and looks forward to engage in the in-forum discussion on priority area, including constituting and ad hoc technical experts and to advance work on developing the modalities, work program, and function of forum. We look forward to a meaningful outcome of the high-level event on sustainable economic transition and economic diversification.

13. The Group reiterates the importance of supporting multilateral solutions when addressing emissions from fuel used for international aviation and maritime transport, while taking into account the principles and provisions of the Convention and not on the basis of unilateral measures. We take note of the developments made under the ICAO and IMO in addressing these matters.
14. On matters relating to article 6 of Paris Agreement, the Group reiterates the need to ensure a party-driven process as well as the balance of all three sub-items, namely, the guidance on cooperative approaches; the rules, modalities, and procedures for the mechanism established by article 6, paragraph 4 of the Paris Agreement; and the work programme under the framework for non-market approaches.
15. On accounting of financial resources, the Group reaffirms that the modalities for accounting of financial resources by developed country parties to developing country parties, mobilized through public interventions, in accordance with article 9, paragraph 7, of the Paris Agreement, must aim to provide transparency and consistency. The reported information must also be comparable and verifiable. No developing countries are to be excluded from receiving financial support for their enhanced climate change actions whether they have or have not ratified the Paris Agreement.
16. Last but not least, Mr. Chairman, the Group looks forward to participating meaningfully and engaging constructively with all parties to fulfil all the mandates of this session here in Marrakech.

Statement by H.E. Mr. Manasvi Srisodapol, Special Representative of the Chair of the Group of 77 and China for Climate Change, on behalf of the Group of 77 and China, at the Closing Plenary of 45th Session of the Subsidiary Body for Scientific and Technological Advice (SBSTA-45)
(Marrakech, Morocco, 14 November 2016)

Mr. Chair,

1. I have the honour to deliver this statement on behalf of the Group of 77 and China. I would like to express our appreciation to the Chair and the facilitators for the efforts you have made during this session.

Mr. Chair,

2. The Group reiterates that the work of SBSTA must proceed in a comprehensive, coherent, balanced, and party-driven manner. We would like to re-emphasize the urgent need to enhance pre-2020 action and support, which will lay a solid foundation for post-2020 implementation.
3. The Group welcomes the work undertaken by the Nairobi work programme on impacts, vulnerability, and adaptation to climate change under the SBSTA agenda item 3 here at COP-22. We will further engage productively with the NWP in the near future.
4. On Technology, the Group believes that the Technology Framework can provide the much-needed guidance to the work of the technology mechanism, especially in providing support for actions on technology development and transfer in developing countries in order to implement the Convention and the Paris Agreement. We look forward to the further elaboration of the technology framework.
5. The Group considers that adaptation, including adaptation co-benefits, of agriculture to the adverse effects of climate change continues to be the key priority for developing countries for SBSTA work, in light of the particular vulnerabilities of the agricultural sector and its relationship with the livelihood of millions, food security, and poverty eradication. We take note of the progress achieved on this agenda item during this session and look forward to continuing discussion on this item during the next session in Bonn.
6. On Science and Review, the Group welcomes the GCOS Implementation Plan 2016 and emphasizes the need for capacity-building of parties to be able to undertake the planned activities. We acknowledge the contribution of IPCC to the Global Stocktake through its assessment cycles. In particular, the outcome of the sixth Assessment Report will be valuable inputs to the initial stocktake in 2023.
7. On Response Measures, the Group emphasizes the importance of giving full consideration to identifying necessary actions to meet the specific needs and concerns of developing country parties arising from the impact of the implementation of response measures and avoid its negative economic and social consequences. In this regard, we look forward to enhanced actions through strengthening institutional arrangements and the establishment of a cooperative mechanism to address the adverse impacts of the implementation of response measures on developing countries. Moreover, following decision 11/CP.21 it is important to move towards the implementation of an enhanced forum and technical group of experts to allow for an institutional arrangement post-2020 in the context of the Paris Agreement.
8. The Group takes note of the reports by the Secretariats of ICAO and IMO. We reiterate the importance of supporting multilateral solutions when addressing emissions from fuel used for international aviation and maritime

transport, while taking into account the principles and provisions of the UNFCCC.

9. On matters relating to article 6 of the Paris Agreement, the Group welcomes the productive exchange of views and focused discussion on the matters related to the guidance on cooperative approaches referred to in article 6 paragraph 2, the rules, modalities, and procedures for the mechanism established in article 6 paragraph 4, and the work programme under the framework for non-market approaches to sustainable development referred to in article 6, paragraph 8. We hope to continue to engage constructively in these discussions, including by responding to the invitation to submit our views on, *inter alia*, the operationalization of the above-mentioned mandates included in article 6 of the Paris Agreement and in the roundtable discussion to be held in conjunction with SBSTA 46.
10. On Modalities for the accounting of financial resources provided and mobilized through public interventions in accordance with article 9, paragraph 7, of the Paris Agreement, the Group welcomes the decision agreed upon on this agenda item. We hope that it will assist in providing clarity through transparent and consistent information by developed country parties on support for developing country parties as an essential input to the work on modalities, principles, and guidelines on the transparency framework of the Paris Agreement.
11. In conclusion, the Group conveys its appreciation to you for your leadership and looks forward to engage further with all parties during the next session.

Remarks on behalf of the Group of 77 and China by Mr. Walter Schuldt, Chair of the Group of for Climate Change during SBSTA-46, SBI-46 and APA 1.3, at the Meeting with the Deputy Secretary-General of the United Nations, Amina Mohamed
(Bonn, Germany, 13 May 2017)

Distinguished Chair,

Ecuador has the honour to deliver these remarks on behalf of the Group of 77 and China:

1. First of all, allow me to convey the warm welcome of the Group of 77 and China to Mrs. Amina Mohamed, Deputy Secretary-General of the United Nations, and our appreciation for the leadership in the process towards the adoption of the 2030 Agenda for Sustainable Development, which is already a fundamental asset for the role that she can play in her new position, in the implementation of the SDGs at all levels.
2. SDG 13, by which all our Heads of State and Governments re-committed to take urgent action to combat climate change and its impacts, is an integral and

indivisible part of sustainable development, and a crosscutting requirement for the achievement of all 17 Sustainable Development Goals.

3. We recall that the 2030 Agenda describes climate change as one of the greatest challenges of our time and its impacts, while acknowledging that the UNFCCC is the primary international intergovernmental forum for negotiating the global response to climate change. Therefore, all other activities on climate change in the UN system should be consistent with the objective, purpose and principles of the Convention, the Kyoto Protocol, and the Paris Agreement.
4. The year 2015 was truly historic, as the world adopted four landmark documents: the Sendai Framework for Disaster Risk Reduction, the 2030 Agenda for Sustainable Development, the Addis Ababa Action Agenda on Financing for Development, and the Paris Agreement. The four are closely interlinked and represent a global architecture for a better future for all, where no one is left behind.
5. On Agenda 2030, we emphasize the importance of building a culture of thematic integration, in order to avoid the "silos approach," which could prevent the fulfilment of Agenda 2030 in its entirety. We support an integrated approach to the SDGs implementation.
6. The UNFCCC is a legally binding Convention with related legal Instruments. The Paris Agreement adopted under the UNFCCC is the collective achievement of all parties, which seeks to enhance the implementation of the UNFCCC, in accordance with its principles and provisions, in particular equity and common but differentiated responsibilities and respective capabilities, in the light of different national circumstances, and the right to development, in the context of sustainable development and efforts to eradicate poverty. The global effort to fight climate change is an irreversible process that cannot be postponed.
7. In effectively implementing their commitments under the Convention and the Paris Agreement, developing country parties will require support from developed country parties, including through the fulfilment of their commitments and obligations under the Convention related to the provision of financial resources, based on their responsibilities for historical emissions. Economic and social development and poverty eradication are the first and overriding priorities of the developing country parties.
8. We have reiterated the importance of preserving the delicate balance of all the issues that was achieved in Paris at COP-21 and in Marrakech at COP-22. These outcomes are not to be renegotiated nor reinterpreted, as the process under the Paris Agreement is irreversible. We have stressed the importance of moving from conceptual discussions to textual negotiations by COP-23 while maintaining the balance struck in the Paris Agreement between mitigation, adaptation, and means of implementation.

9. Effective implementation of the Paris Agreement and the attainment of pre-2020 commitments will significantly contribute to the achievement of the SDGs. Urgent action is required since our countries are currently experiencing the adverse impacts of climate change, that seriously affect our natural environment, the survival of many societies, the biological support systems of the planet, and undermine the ability of our countries to achieve sustainable development.
10. In spite of that, developing countries are already making a significant contribution to the fight against climate change, even if constraint by limited financial and technological support. The challenge of implementing the Paris Agreement for this group of countries is therefore means of implementation: the provision of financial and technological resources in a scale that meets the ambition of the commitments made in the Paris Agreements through NDC.
11. We underline that both the 2030 Agenda and the Paris Agreement stress the importance of means of implementation, which should be simplified and granted to ensure proper implementation of climate action plans and the achievement of the objectives of the Convention and of SDGs. We also recall that the SDGs has set the target to implement the commitment undertaken by developed country parties to the UNFCCC to a goal of mobilizing jointly US$100 billion annually by 2020 from all sources to address the needs of developing countries. We thus call on a strengthened and genuine global partnership to achieve this.
12. This mobilization of resources must be accompanied by even more ambitious and urgent measures by developed countries, which have the greatest responsibility for the problem, have a greater capacity to cope with it, and should continue taking the lead by undertaking economy-wide absolute emission reduction targets.
13. The G-77 and China reaffirms its determination to take concrete and urgent actions to continue engaging the fight against climate change, a common threat that is directly linked to economic growth, reduction of inequalities, protection of the environment, and sustainable development for all.

Statement of the Group of 77 and China, delivered by Mr. Walter Schuldt, Deputy Special Representative of the Chair of the Group of 77 and China fo Climate Change, at the Joint Opening Plenary of the 47th Session of the Subsidiary Body for Scientific and Technological Advice (SBSTA-47), and the 47th Session of the Subsidiary Body for Implementation (SBI-47)
(Bonn, Germany, 6 November 2017)

Mr. Chair,

I have the honor to deliver this statement on behalf of the Group of 77 and China.

At the outset allow me to express the Group's full support and readiness to engage meaningfully with all the parties to work constructively throughout this session, and to continue to move forward with the implementation of the Convention, its Kyoto Protocol, and its Paris Agreement towards the achievement of its objective, purpose and goals, in accordance with the principles of equity, common but differentiated responsibilities and respective capabilities, and in the context of sustainable development and efforts to eradicate poverty.

The Group trusts that under the guidance of the two Chairs and the leadership of the Republic of Fiji, we will achieve concrete progress in all the different agenda items of both the SBI and SBSTA agendas, through a comprehensive, coherent, balanced, and party-driven process. Furthermore, we call for a balanced and comprehensive treatment of all additional matters related to the implementation of the Paris Agreement, as mandated by the Paris Outcome.

The work under SBSTA has a direct impact for both the post-2020 implementation and for the enhancement of the pre-2020 action, and in that regard, we would like to re-emphasize the urgent need to enhance pre-2020 action and support in finance, technology, and capacity-building from developed countries to developing countries, as a solid foundation for post-2020 implementation. The Group looks forward for the assessment of the progress of implementation of decision 1 C.P/19 paragraphs 3 and 4 on what parties agreed to in Warsaw 2013 to accelerate the full implementation of the decision as agreed under the Bali Action Plan and in relation to the provision of means of implementation, including technology, finance, and capacity-building support for developing country parties, recognizing that such implementation will enhance pre-2020 action, and will help to identify relevant opportunities to enhance the provision of financial resources, including technology development and transfer and capacity-building support. The engagement of the SBI in this subject is needed.

On agenda item 3, we recognize the progress under the Nairobi Work Programme on impacts, vulnerability, and adaptation to climate change, and the reports prepared by the Secretariat, while noting that these collaborative activities have enhanced the role of the NWP as a knowledge hub for enhanced action on adaptation and a knowledge-for-action network for climate resilience.

With regard to the report of the Adaptation Committee we welcome the progress in the implementation of the flexible work plan of the Committee for the years 2016–2018 in the areas of: promotion of overarching coherence; mandates arising from decision 1/CP.21, including the technical examination process on adaptation; the provision of technical support and guidance on adaptation actions and means of implementation to developing countries before and during the presentation of projects; and the increase of awareness, outreach, and information-sharing.

We stress the need to fully implement article 8 of the Paris Agreement as a matter of urgency, in order to allow a better integration of loss and damage issues into the broader ongoing work of the UNFCCC, to identify and implement concrete alternatives of support and cooperation for developing country parties that are increasingly experiencing losses and damages resulting from extreme weather events and slow-onset events to facilitate this fully implementation. The G-77 and China calls for loss and damages to be included as a permanent item on the agendas of the subsidiary bodies, with a broader and more inclusive scope of inputs from all parties that will be available at regular meetings of the subsidiary bodies, including the Warsaw International Mechanism on Loss and Damage and its five-year work program. In this regard we stress further our need for special financial resources from developed country parties to cover activities and further actions in countries.

The Technology Executive Committee (TEC) is fundamental to identifying policies that accelerate the development and transfer of resilient technologies. Its join work with the CTCN is vital to strengthen the technology mechanism, especially for the provision of support for action in developing countries in order to implement the Convention and the Paris Agreement. Both, the TEC and CTCN should strengthen the linkages between both the Technology and the Financial Mechanism on matters related to technology and collaborative research and development, particularly with regard to the technology needs assessment (TNA) to formulate and implement national climate action plans.

Also, the development of the Technology Framework should take into account the challenges presented by the Agreement's long-term goals, to accelerate innovation, development, transfer, diffusion, and implementation of technologies, in order to operationalize the vision of technology described in paragraph 1 of article 10 of the Agreement.

The Group considers that adaptation, including associated health and socio-economic co-benefits, of agriculture and food production systems to the adverse effects of climate change, continue to be a key priority for developing countries, in light of the particular vulnerabilities of the agriculture sector and its relationship with ending hunger and achieving food security and nutrition.

On response measures, the Group reaffirms the importance of giving full consideration to identify necessary actions to meet the specific needs and concerns of developing country parties arising from the impact of the implementation of response measures and to avoid the negative economic and social consequences of response measures on developing countries. The Group welcomes the invitation to the pre-sessional workshop on modalities, work programme and functions under the Paris Agreement of the forum on the impact of the implementation of response measures and looks forward to the report, inputs and recommendations from the roundtable to support the work of the improved forum. The group also emphasizes the importance of fulfilling the mandate of decision 11/CP21 and advancing the work on the pre-2020 and post-2020 tracks on the modalities, functions, and work programmes for the forum under the Paris Agreement.

In relation to the methodological issues under the Convention, we encourage all parties to strengthen their efforts with regard to the common metrics to calculate the carbon dioxide equivalence of greenhouse gases in a manner that takes into account its linkage with the agenda item 3 of the APA on accounting for Nationally

Determined Contributions, and the different capacities and needs of developing countries in this regard.

On matters relating to article 6 of the Paris Agreement, we reiterate our continued engagement to achieve progress in the guidance on cooperative approaches; the rules, modalities, and procedures for the sustainable development mechanism; and on the work programme under the framework for non-market approaches to sustainable development, in order to ensure their operationalization and effectiveness.

On the issue of modalities for accounting of financial resources provided and mobilized by developed countries, we would like to stress the importance of the interlinkages with articles 3, 4, and 13 of the Paris Agreement, particularly to provide a clear outline of the climate finance flows that are being channelled to developing countries, which are crucial to the implementation of climate action from the members of our group. Appropriate considerations need to be agreed upon in order to guarantee that financial resources are new, additional, predictable, appropriate and address the needs and priorities of developing countries.

On agenda item 13, the Group welcomes the report by the Secretariat about the proposal on the operationalization of the Indigenous Peoples and Local Communities Platform established in the Paris decision. Nevertheless, the Group believes that much more still needs to be done, including with regard to the enhancement of the participation of indigenous peoples and local communities in climate action, the protected share of their traditional knowledge and best practices on mitigation and adaptation in a holistic and integrated manner. In this sense the Group will engage constructively in this discussion with the view to achieve a concrete result at this COP in the design of an effective platform within the UNFCCC that benefits our local communities and indigenous peoples.

Mr. Chair, in relation to the agenda of the SBI,

The Group believes that the organization of the workshop of the facilitative sharing of views (FSV) under the international consultation and analysis (ICA) that will take place on 10 November, is crucial to reinforce MRV under the Convention and should lead to identify the capacity-building needs of developing countries in order to facilitate reporting of information in preparing future BURs.

On the provision on financial and technical support, the Group regrets to bring to your attention the increasing difficulties and conditionalities faced by several developing countries in accessing financial resources from the GEF, including through the establishment of program priorities and eligibility criteria that have not been agreed at the intergovernmental level. The Group is deeply concerned about the no response from GEF to continued communication of these parties.

The Group expresses its deepest concern that some developed countries are unilaterally applying into the decision-making processes eligibility criteria that are not agreed to and that limit the access of funding to developing countries under the GCF; such criteria is not compatible with guidance from the COP and is a clear departure from the letter and spirit of the Convention and the Paris Agreement. We also feel that the process and procedures of these institutions are creating continuous additional barriers to access financial resources for climate action, which severely undermine the level of ambition of developing countries in the global effort against climate change. Also, we expect this issue to be clearly addressed in the guidance of the COP to the financial mechanism.

On development of modalities and procedures for the operation and use of a public registry referred to in article 4.12 of the Paris Agreement (NDC), the group recalls that Nationally Determined Contributions communicated by parties shall be recorded in a public registry maintained by the Secretariat and that article 7.12 establishes the same provision for the adaptation communications. We also believe that the registration needs to be made only by the focal point, and that the registry must be clear and transparent, ensure security, and avoid any possible manipulation.

With regard to National Adaptation Plans, the Group reaffirms the important role of adaptation planning in reducing climate vulnerabilities of local communities and looks forward to address the interlinkages between national adaptation plans and means of implementation, with a view to enhance access to finance and technology support and capacity-building for the formulation and implementation of the NAPs.

On item 10, we think that the work must continue on the approach and modalities for the periodic assessment of the technology mechanism in relation to supporting developing country parties in the implementation of the Paris Agreement; the evaluation should be coherent, cross-functional, and participatory. We believe that it should take into account sustainable development, gender, global action, and the special needs and circumstances of the developing countries.

On capacity-building, we welcome the sharing of experiences and lessons learned in the sixth meeting of the Durban Forum on "Enhancing capacities for adaptation in the context of NAPs and NDCs," but much more needs to be done in this regard, including in relation to the annual monitoring and evaluation of the Capacity-Building Framework in Developing Countries. We hope that we can make concrete progress in relation to the development of capacities for developing countries, taking into account their need of resources, planning, and monitoring of capacity development activities. We also welcome the launch of the work of the Paris Committee on capacity-building, and we expect that through its first report and work programme, a transformation of capabilities on a global scale for the achievement of the Agreement long-term goals is pursued.

On the Standing Committee on Finance, we note that there is a lack of funding for the Executive Committee of the Warsaw International Mechanism for Loss and Damage associated with Climate Change Impacts. It also needs to look into the issue of linkages and overall coherence among the mechanisms under the Convention, specially the relation between the financial mechanism and the technology mechanism, as well as in the light of the ongoing work on the transparency regime under the Paris Agreement and the related upcoming APA round table. We stress the need for the SCF to stay engaged in these ongoing processes.

On agenda item 10, we call for additional contributions from developed countries for the LDCF of the GEF for the LEG. We also recognize the technical guidance and advice provided by the LEG to LDCs on the process to formulate and implement National Adaptation Plans, and on accessing funding from the Green Climate Fund, for the formulation of NAPs. We encourage the active engagement and collaboration of the LEG with the Adaptation Committee, the Paris Committee on Capacity-Building, the Nairobi Work Programme, among others.

On budget, we look forward to engaging with Secretariat on the 2018–2019 Biennium Budget Programme and we look forward for the Technical Workshop that will take place during this session.

The Group of 77 and China highlights the importance of Action for Climate Empowerment (ACE) to enhance actions in the implementation of the Paris Agreement, and the National Determined Contributions (NDCs), in accordance with article 12 of the Paris Agreement.

We look forward to engage on the issue of common time frames for Nationally Determined Contributions, as mandated by article 4, paragraph 10 of the Paris Agreement.

The Group expresses its support to the ongoing negotiations to adopt the Gender Action Plan, which will be an important deliverable of COP-23, as mandated in decision 21/CP.22, under the Lima Work Programme. In this regard, we highlight that gender-responsive climate policy still requires further strengthening in all activities concerning adaptation, mitigation, and related means of implementation, finance, technology development and transfer, and capacity-building, as well as decision-making on the implementation of climate policies. We look forward to engaging with partners and advance this important agenda.

We also express our concern on negative implications resulting out of unilateral coercive economic measures for climate action in developing countries, to avoid undermining developing countries capacities to fight climate change and the rights to live of our peoples.

Finally, the G-77 and China conveys its appreciation to both of you, Chairs, and reaffirm its commitment to continue engaging in the process during this COP.

Statement on behalf of the Group of 77 and China at the Closing Plenary of the 47th Session of the Subsidiary Body for Scientific and Technological Advice and the 47th Session of the Subsidiary Body of Implementation (Bonn, Germany, 15 November 2017)

Mr. Chair,

The Group recognizes the work undertaken by you and the facilitators under SBSTA and SBI during these almost three weeks, in which our Group has been engaging constructively to make progress in all agenda items under each of the bodies.

At the closing of the work under this bodies, we realize that unfortunately much work needs still to be done to achieve a balanced treatment of mitigation, adaptation, and means of implementation throughout the different agenda items; ensuring that there will be no reinterpretation or renegotiation of the Convention and of the Paris Agreement; and the need to respect and operationalize the differentiation between developed and developing country parties as clearly reflected in the Convention and in the Paris Agreement.

The Group would like to reemphasize the urgent need to enhance the pre-2020 action and support, as a solid foundation for post-2020 implementation. We believe that the provision of financial resources, including for technology development and transfer, as well as capacity-building support need to be enhanced.

The Group thanks you for all your reports, and we reaffirm our full support to you, while reiterating our will to continue engaging constructively in the textual work that is needed for the operationalization of the Paris Agreement and the enhancement of the full implementation of the Convention and its Kyoto Protocol.

However, we regret to transmit our concern about certain procedural and substantial issues. On process, unequal treatment of certain elements remained during the sessions within the agenda items, unequal modalities and guidance followed by parties in the discussions, and also different levels of engagement and preference in terms of how and when to capture the outcomes of the discussions.

Nevertheless, our Group wishes to acknowledge the progress achieve in some specific agenda items, including *inter alia*, in the negotiations related to Loss and Damage, where we were able to adopt an initial positive step towards the operationalization of the WIM. The mandate to the ExCom to strengthen its five-year rolling work plan, together with the meeting of the task force on displacement in May 2018, and the request to the Secretariat. Under the guidance of the ExCom and the Chair of SBI, to organize in conjunction with SBI48, the Suva Expert Dialogue constitutes a step in the right direction towards a permanent agenda item under both SBs that will ensure discussions on the WIM inter-sessionally. We also hope that the dialogue will help the future establishment of an ExCom expert group on action and support, the establishment of the dates for activities related to the 2019 review of the WIM, and the call for mobilization of resources for averting, minimizing, and addressing loss and damage. However, there is still a serious gap in the effective support that the WIM can provide to developing countries that have been impacted by climate change, and therefore we stress the need for the full implementation of article 8 of the Paris Agreement.

On agenda item 3, we recognize the progress under the Nairobi Work Programme on impacts, vulnerability, and adaptation to climate change, and the reports prepared by the Secretariat, while noting that these collaborative activities have enhanced the role of the NWP as a knowledge hub for enhanced action on adaptation and a knowledge-for-action network for climate resilience.

We reaffirm our view that the Technology Executive Committee (TEC) is fundamental to identifying policies that accelerate the development and transfer of resilient technologies. Its join work with the CTCN is vital to strengthen the technology mechanism, especially for the provision of support for action in developing countries in order to implement the Convention and the Paris Agreement. Both the TEC and CTCN should strengthen the linkages between both the Technology and the Financial Mechanism on matters related to technology and collaborative research and development, particularly with regard to the technology needs assessment (TNA) to formulate and implement national climate action plans.

Likewise, as mentioned in our opening statement, our Group believes that the development of the Technology Framework should take into account the challenges presented by the Agreement's long-term goals, to accelerate innovation, development, transfer, diffusion, and implementation of technologies, in order to operationalize the vision of technology described in paragraph 1 of article 10 of the Agreement.

The Group recalls that adaptation continue to be the key priority for developing countries, including adaptation co-benefits, of agriculture and food production systems, in light of the particular vulnerabilities of the agriculture sector and its relationship with the livelihood of millions and the fundamental priority of ensuring food security and ending hunger. Therefore we stress the importance of having reached an outcome after several years, and we look forward to receive all the proposed elements on this issue, including modalities for the implementation of the outcomes of the five in-session workshops, the methods and approaches for assessing adaptation, adaptation co-benefits and resilience, etc., with a view to begin a more comprehensive understanding and treatment of this issue by both SBSTA and SBI, especially in relation to adaptation and agriculture.

On the Adaptation Committee report, our Group agreed on the draft decision that welcomes the recommendations made by the Committee on paragraph 42 of decision 1/CP.21, while recognizing that the AC-LEG provided a good technical input with the collaboration of the SCF. However, our Group has identified some gaps, since these mandates are an integral part of the implementation of the adaptation section of the Paris Agreement. The draft conclusions provide more time to deliberate on those gaps during the SBs48 and COP-24 and we are willing to engage constructively in that discussion with our partners.

On response measures, we need to identify and establish actions to meet the specific needs and concerns of developing country parties arising from the impact of the implementation of response measures and the avoidance of its negative economic and social consequences, including with regard to equitable access to sustainable development and poverty eradication. We look forward for the strengthening of the institutional arrangements and the establishment of a cooperative mechanism to address the adverse impacts of the implementation of response measures on developing countries. The Group considers important the creation of an institutional arrangement post-2020 in the context of the Paris Agreement.

On the Adaptation Fund serving the Paris Agreement, we regret to see the continued lack of will to move forward with a decision that ensures that the Fund shall serve the Agreement, without prejudice to the discussions on the strategic role of the Fund within the broader climate finance panorama, or on the detailed definition of the governance, arrangements and sources of the Fund, particularly when we know that these arrangements can be developed until 2020. We urge developed country parties to demonstrate their political will for a decision at this COP, particularly taking into account the importance of this Fund to developing countries and SIDS in particular.

On adaptation, we reiterate the high priority that our countries assign to adaptation, particularly in the current context of the increasing occurrence and severity of extreme weather and slow onset events and the increasingly high costs involved. Therefore, our Group has worked hard in this session to continue having a common position on adaptation and especially with regard to adaptation communication. We have reached a document that attempts to advance aspects of the guidance of adaptation communication in the understanding that this is the time to generate substantive progress. One of the key points of this guidance is the support needed from developed to developing country parties in order to implement article 7.13 of the Paris Agreement, considering the need for public and grant-based resources for adaptation under article 9.4. We hope that after this session we can begin a more substantive work on the basis of the skeleton, headings, subheadings, and textual inputs submitted or proposed so far from different parties.

On the Local Communities and Indigenous Peoples Platform, the Group expresses its appreciation and thankfulness to both the Chair of the SBSTA and the Fijian Presidency for their clear support for the operationalization of the Platform and we are proud to have contributed decisively to adopt a decision that will allow us to ensure that objective. We consider this as one of the concrete achievements of this COP and we look forward for the establishment of the Facilitative Working Group, including the development of its work plan for the full implementation of the functions of the Platform. The G-77 and China encourages a balanced representation of local communities and indigenous peoples as well as parties in the multi-stakeholder workshop, as the first activity of the Platform's work plan.

In relation to the agenda of the SBI, our Group notes the successful organization of the workshop of the facilitative sharing of views (FSV) under the international consultation and analysis (ICA) that took place on 10 November and welcomes the progress report and technical reports of the Consultative Group of Experts on National Communications from parties not included in Annex I to the Convention (CGE) related to the implementation of its work plan for 2017. On this subject we need to reiterate the crucial role of these processes that serve to reinforce MRV under the Convention and should lead to identify the capacity-building needs of developing countries in order to facilitate reporting of information in preparing future BURs.

On the provision on financial and technical support, the Group regrets to reiterate once again the increasing difficulties and conditionalities faced by several developing countries in accessing financial resources from the GEF, including through the establishment of program priorities and eligibility criteria that have not been agreed at the intergovernmental level.

Likewise, with regard to the GCF, the Group reiterates its deepest concern that some developed countries are unilaterally applying into the decision-making processes, eligibility criteria that are not agreed upon and that limit the access of funding to developing countries under the GCF. Such criteria are not compatible with the guidance from the COP and a clear departure from the letter and spirit of the Convention and the Paris Agreement. We also feel that the process and procedures of these institutions are creating continuous additional barriers to access financial resources for climate action, which severely undermine the level of ambition of developing countries in the global effort against climate change, and therefore, we expect this issue to be clearly addressed in the guidance of the COP to the financial mechanism.

The Group looks forward on the discussions that will take place in May next year on development of modalities and procedures for the operation and use of a public registry referred to in article 4.12 of the Paris Agreement. In this regard, we recall that NDCs communicated by parties shall be recorded in a public registry maintained by the Secretariat and that article 7.12 establishes the same provision for the adaptation communications. We reiterate that in our view, the registration needs to be made only by the focal point and that the registry must be clear and transparent, ensure security, and avoid any possible manipulation.

With regard to NAPs, the Group stress the important role of adaptation planning in reducing climate vulnerabilities of local communities and looks forward to address the interlinkages between national adaptation plans and means of implementation, with a view to enhance access to finance and technology support and capacity-building for the formulation and implementation of NAPs.

On item 10, we think that the work must continue on the approach and modalities for the periodic assessment of the technology mechanism in relation to supporting developing country parties in the implementation of the Paris Agreement; the evaluation should be coherent, cross-functional, and participatory. Also, we believe that it should take into account sustainable development, gender, global action, and the special needs and circumstances of the developing countries.

On capacity-building, we welcome the progress reflected on the synthesis report prepared to facilitate the annual monitoring of progress in the implementation of the framework for capacity-building in developing countries, and the summary report on the sixth Durban Forum on Capacity-Building, however there are still gaps in terms of capacity-building provided with regards to the obligation under the Convention and the Paris Agreement. On the adoption of the report of the first meeting of the Paris Committee on Capacity-Building, in Paris we agreed the PCCB to collaborate and coordinate capacity-building activities in developing countries. However, the PCCB was not given the resources to carry out its mandate.

We reiterate our concern on the lack of funding for the Executive Committee of the Warsaw International Mechanism for Loss and Damage associated with Climate Change Impacts. Also, we reaffirm the need to look into the issue of linkages and overall coherence among the mechanisms under the Convention, specially the relation between the financial mechanism and the technology mechanism, as well as in the light of the ongoing work on the transparency regime under the Paris Agreement. We stress the need for the SCF to stay engaged in these ongoing processes.

The Group expresses its support to the issue of Gender and Climate Change, including through the development of a Gender Action Plan, in order to support the implementation of gender-related decisions and mandates in the UNFCCC process and to complete the mandates of decision 21/CP.22, under the Lima Work Program, and decision 21/CP22. Our Group highlights that gender-responsive climate policy still requires further strengthening in all activities concerning adaptation, mitigation, and related means of implementation, finance, technology development and transfer, and capacity-building, as well as decision-making on the implementation of climate policies. In this regard, we are also proud to have contributed to the decision on the adoption of the Gender Action Plan at this COP and we look forward to engaging with partners in all the activities of the priority areas of the Plan, the future annual in-session workshops, and the future review of its implementation, as well as short- and long-term impacts.

Finally, we express our concern about the negative implications resulting out of unilateral coercive economic measures for climate action in developing countries, and the need to avoid undermining developing countries capacities to fight climate change and the rights to live of our peoples.

In conclusion, the Group conveys its appreciation to both of you for your work and leadership and we look forward to engage further with all parties during the next session in May 2018.

Statement of the Group of 77 and China, delivered by Ambassador Wael Aboulmagd, Chair of the G-77 and China for the Climate Change Process, at the Opening Plenary of the Subsidiary Body for Scientific and Technological Advice (Bonn, 30 April 2018)

Distinguished Chair,

It is my honor to deliver this statement on behalf of the Group of 77 and China.

The work under SBSTA has a direct impact for both the post-2020 implementation and the enhancement of the pre-2020 action, and in that regard, we would like to reemphasize the urgent need to enhance pre-2020 action and support in terms of finance, technology, and capacity-building from developed countries to developing countries, as a solid foundation for post-2020 implementation.

We assure you of the G-77's commitment to achieving significant progress and reaching outcomes on the various agenda items. We highlight the importance of ensuring balance between the different agenda items whilst assuring sufficient attention is paid to elements related to the Convention and to operationalization of its Paris Agreement. In this regard, we would like to highlight the G-77 and China's views on the different agenda items.

on agenda item 3, the group highlights the importance of the Nairobi Work Program as one of the main platforms within the Secretariat dealing with adaptation issues, and we look forward to an outcome that will enhance its role under the UNFCCC as a platform to provide answers related to knowledge needs of parties. We also note its key role in continuing to enhance action on adaptation in the context of collaboration and knowledge sharing on climate resilience best practices.

On agenda item 4, we take note of the report of the adaptation committee and welcome further work on the implementation of the flexible work plan of the committee for the years 2016–2018.

On agenda item 5, the Group welcomes the great efforts made by the SBSTA Chair in preparing an initial draft for the technology framework. We believe this summarizes the views of all the previous elaborations by parties and it is a good starting point to work on. We also stress that the technology framework should provide a clear guidance on how to improve the current technology mechanism. The guidance should be workable and easy to implement, in order to enhance the technology development and transfer to developing country parties. The technology framework should also strengthen the linkages between both the technology and the financial mechanism on matters related to technology and collaborative research and development, particularly with regard to the technology needs assessment (TNA) to formulate and implement national climate action plans. We underline that developed country parties shall continue their obligations under the Convention to provide technological development and transfer support to developing countries. The framework should make necessary arrangements to enhance such support in this regard.

On agenda item 7, we look forward to the workshop being organized as the first activity of the local communities and indigenous people's platform. However, our Group recognizes the need to achieve meaningful progress on the additional work required to the full operationalization of the platform during this session and we expect that in accordance with decision 2/CP.23, the Facilitative Working Group is formally established, as part of the further operationalization of the platform, as well as the modalities for the development of a work plan for the full implementation of the platform's function agreed at COP-23.

On agenda item 8 relating to agriculture, the Group welcomes the breakthrough on the negotiations related to agriculture in COP-23 and is expecting significant progress under the Koronivia joint work program. We welcome the opportunity to cooperate with SBSTA and the SBI and the Koronivia joint work on agriculture. The Group stresses that adaptation including associated health and socio-economic co-benefits of agriculture and food production systems to the adverse effects of climate change continue to be a key priority for developing countries, in light of particular vulnerabilities of the agriculture sector and its relation to ending hunger and achieving food security and nutrition. We hope the joint work could provide an opportunity to debate methods and approaches for assessing adaptation needs, adaptation co-benefits, and resilience, as well as for evaluating the socio-economic dimension of the impacts of climate change in the agriculture sector.

On agenda item 9, the Group reaffirms the importance of giving full consideration to identifying necessary actions to meet the specific needs and concerns of developing country parties arising from the impact of the implementation of response measures and to avoid the negative economic and social consequences of response measures on developing countries. The Group welcomes the in-forum training workshop on the use of economic modelling tools related to economic diversification and just transition of workforce. The Group also emphasizes the importance of fulfilling the mandate of decision 11/CP21 and advancing the work on the pre-2020 and post-2020 on the modalities, functions, and work programs for the permanent forum under the Paris Agreement.

On agenda item 10, the G-77 and China would like to see progress on the recommendations for further development of guidelines for the technical review on technical information provided by Annex I countries. Furthermore, the Group expresses concerns regarding the work, with no mandate from the UNFCCC, under the ICAO and IMO, and highlights the importance of reflecting the principles of the Convention and its Paris Agreement and securing adequate means of implementation for developing countries to implement the policies in the international civil aviation and maritime sectors.

On agenda item 12 relating to Article 6 of the Paris Agreement, the Group welcomes the efforts made by the SBSTA Chair in preparing an informal document containing draft elements and highlights that progress needs to be achieved on the three elements of this agenda item as part of the expected comprehensive outcome at Katowice.

On agenda item 13, which relates to article 9.7 of the Paris Agreement, the G-77 and China would like to highlight that the work should aim at enhancing reporting on financial resources provided and mobilized, as reflected in the common tabular formats, including information on new and additional financial resources and how they effectively address the needs of developing countries. This information should be dealt with on the same basis as our approach in relation to transparency of action to ensure that new and additional resources are made available to developing country parties in a predictable manner. The Group further stresses that we expect the outcome of this agenda item to reflect the required balance between the support and the action component of the Transparency Framework.

On agenda item 14, relating to cooperation with international organizations, the G-77 and China stresses that the engagement of the Secretariat with other international organizations should be in line with the relevant COP decisions adopted by the parties.

Statement on behalf of the G-77 and China at the SBSTA/SBI/APA Chairs/Co-Chairs Meeting with HoDs, 4 May 2018

- *What are the critical milestones on our road to Katowice and what is needed for each milestone?*

Starting from the end objective of seeking a successful outcome at Katowice in the form of a comprehensive, balanced, fair, and implementable package for the operationalization of the Paris Agreement, we agree that there is need to best utilize the various opportunities that are being provided to us between now and the conclusion of COP-24. Some of these opportunities are at the technical negotiating level, while others are at the ministerial level. We certainly believe that every effort must be made to resolve the outstanding issues at the technical level, and this obviously requires affording as much time as possible. Indeed, as much time as needed to address these issues and find reasonable compromises on them. Many of us may recall that prior to Paris in 2015 the negotiating needs dictated a large number of technical negotiating sessions. COP-24 might seem to warrant the same treatment particularly since it is essentially about implementation which means that what is needed most is technical work. To this end, we think that based on the level of progress made thus far at this session, there will be little disagreement on the need to hold at least one additional negotiating session as proposed to be held in Bangkok.

As for the optimal utilization of ministerial opportunities, such as the MoCA and the pre-COP and others, we certainly see value in these forums but we also insist that for them to represent a real contribution towards the ultimate objective, the agenda for such meetings needs to be carefully drafted and the guiding questions prepared with the utmost simplification and precision. Ministers, in our view, should not be expected to resolve the minutiae of the various negotiating tracks, nor make determinations on the details of these tracks. Rather, they should be presented with broader conceptual problems with the negotiations which they would be encouraged to discuss and then perhaps provide guidance to the technical negotiators.

- *What would help us to get from the initial basis for negotiations to draft decision text?*

We believe that the starting point in this regard is acknowledging that everyone has to have a clear picture regarding the process before we actually embark on it. This means that it is about time to take a holistic approach and move away from the fragmented process of dealing with each individual track or issue as a stand-alone exercise. The key word is that we are ultimately negotiating a package, and all of its components must be there as we transition to text (NDCs, Support, Transparency, GST, Compliance, Homeless issues), and those issues which have reached the requisite level of maturity can start transitioning to text, and those which have not might have to settle for bullets at this time until ready to move to text. We will not pronounce ourselves at this time as to the question of who will be entrusted with actually coming up with text, and will leave that for a later stage, but suffice it to say that we believe that the overall process would most certainly be best served by a transition to text as soon as possible.

On a related note, Madame Co-Chairs and distinguished Chairs, I think we owe it to you to bring to your attention, at this early stage, of our process towards COP-24 that there are some concerns as to the working methods within some of the negotiating tracks. This has been, and always should be, a party-driven process. Procedural impediments or otherwise inhibiting the ability of parties to advance work may succeed on the short term, but we sincerely believe that absent a true sense of equality and balance in progress on all negotiating tracks the overall shared objective of reaching an acceptable package by the end of COP-24 will not be well served.

- *And what do we need to achieve here, by the end of this session?*

As for the last question regarding our expectations for this session, I believe that our comments on the previous two points represent an integral part of the answer to this third question. I would only add that by the end of this session, we need a solid basis for negotiation. Everyone should feel equally treated throughout this package. Options on structure and details should be balanced and reflective of the various perspectives. And as we have insisted on the past, and will continue to do so, now and in the future. There should be comparable progress reflected in whatever comes out of this session.

(b) Draft Decisions and Positions Submitted by the Group of 77 to the Subsidiary Body for Scientific and Technological Advice (SBSTA)

Summary of the Statement of the Philippines and the Position of the Group of 77 and China at the Second Session of the Subsidiary Body for Scientific and Technological Advice on the Establishment of Intergovernmental Technical Advisory Panels (Geneva, 27 February to 4 March 1996)*

The representative of the Philippines, as Coordinator of the G-77 and China on this item, explained that the Group of 77 and China had spent long hours of discussion, examined all possibilities, made all possible concessions without prejudicing

* Contained in document FCCC/SBSTA/1996/MISC.3 of 14 May 1996.

basic interests of the developing countries in the issue of global climate change. The Group was fighting for survival, physical and economic, in the context of the Convention. Climate was global, with varying specificities. A technical advisory panel must reflect all these.

The Group was deeply disappointed that the ITAPs had not been set up despite the Group's willingness to make all possible compromises, short of endangering basic interests.

The Group felt that the ITAPs had an important role to play in the implementation of this Convention, and in advancing the interests of developing countries. It therefore suggested that the Secretariat should undertake the setting-up of a roster of experts, nominated by parties, with full curriculum vitae for each. This would allow members time to get their nominations together, a task which is not an easy one for a number of developing countries.

The position of the Group of 77 and China is as follows:

Position of the Group of 77 and China on the establishment of intergovernmental technical advisory panels (ITAPS)

The Subsidiary Body for Scientific and Technological Advice,

Recalling the relevant provisions of the United Nations Framework Convention on Climate Change, in particular articles 9 and 4.1(c) and (e),

Pursuant to the relevant decisions of the Conference of the Parties at its first session, in particular decisions 3, 4, 5, 6, and 13, and to the relevant conclusions of the Ad Hoc Group on the Berlin Mandate (FCCC/AGBM/1995/2, conclusions (j), (k), and (l)),

1. *Decides* that:
   (a) An intergovernmental technical advisory panel on methodologies and technologies is hereby established on a provisional basis, functioning under the terms of reference of the Subsidiary Body for Scientific and Technological Advice, decision 6/CP.1. It will implement the initial programme of work, on the basis of the list of tasks attached hereto. The future operations of the panel will be reviewed by the SBSTA in 1997. The members of the panel will serve for the period leading up to the third session of the Conference of the Parties; they will be technical and scientific experts nominated by the Government of the Parties;
   (b) The panel shall be composed of twenty experts: four from each of the five UN regional groups. The panel shall be Co-Chaired by two of its members;
   (c) Each regional group shall nominate four experts for the panel within their group, taking into account the initial work programme. The list of these experts would be sent to the Bureau of the SBSTA, which would present

it to the SBSTA for adoption. A full curriculum vitae of each proposed expert shall be provided. In finalizing the names of experts, each group may take into account the need for representation of the different areas of expertise bearing in mind the initial work programme;

(d) The terms of the panel members may be extended, taking into account the need for stability, the need to rotate members, and the review by the SBSTA in 1997;

(e) A roster of experts, nominated by parties, shall be maintained for specialized tasks that cannot be undertaken by panel members. Each party may nominate up to ten experts for the roster and will provide a full curriculum vitae of each nominee. Whenever such specialized tasks that cannot be undertaken by panel members are entrusted, on an *ad hoc* basis, to experts from the roster, equitable representation should be ensured;

(f) The panel shall organize its own work in accordance with the priorities of the initial work programme. The panel may seek cooperation and advice from other competent international bodies to complement and facilitate its work. Reports from the panel shall be advisory; they will be circulated to all parties prior to their consideration by the SBSTA. The panel shall operate in a cost-effective manner, taking advantage of all possible means to communicate among members and to facilitate its work.

2. *Authorizes* its Bureau to convene an initial panel meeting as early as practicable after all the UN regional Groups have sent in their nominations, and further authorizes two meetings of the panel to be held in both 1996 and 1997.
3. *Notes* that funding the participation in the panel meetings shall be ensured to experts' participants from eligible parties in accordance with normal practice and subject to the availability of resources.

Decision on Transfer of Technology Submitted by Tanzania on behalf of the Group 77 and China*

The Conference of the Parties,

Reaffirming the relevant provisions of chapter 34 of Agenda 21 on the transfer of environmentally-sound technology, cooperation, and capacity-building,

Underlining the commitments renewed at the United Nations General Assembly Special Session on transfer of environmentally sound technologies that access to and transfer of environmentally-sound technologies are essential requirements for sustainable development and that this calls for the urgent fulfilment of all the United Nations Conference on Environment and Development commitments concerning concrete measures for the transfer of environmentally sound technologies to developing countries,

* Contained in document FCCC/SBSTA/1997/INF.5 of 2 September 1997.

Recalling its decisions 13/CP.1 and 7/CP.2 on the development and transfer of technologies,

Taking note with concern of the slow progress reported by the Convention Secretariat as shown in documents FCCC/SBI/1997/1, FCCC/SBI/1997/3, FCCC/SBI/1997/4, and in particular, FCCC/TP/1997/1,

Stressing the vital role of transfer of technology to developing countries in addressing climate change and its adverse impacts in order to achieve sustainable development,

1. *Decides* to undertake in the Subsidiary Body for Scientific and Technological Advice:
   (a) The full implementation of article 9, paragraph 2(c) for the Subsidiary Body for Scientific and Technological Advice to identify innovative, efficient, and state-of-the-art technologies and know-how and to advise on the ways and means of promoting development and/or transferring such technologies, through the establishment of the necessary panels to do so, as authorised in decision 6/CP.1, paragraph 3 on the establishment of the intergovernmental technical advisory panels;
   (b) A methodological study on the possibility of using supplemental activities for transfer of technology, taking into account the following criteria:
      (i) Universal availability to all developing country parties;
      (ii) Transparency and equitability in its operation; and that
      (iii) The operation is managed by a broadly-based and representative body of countries; and
   (c) To accelerate the development of methodologies for adaption technologies appropriate to the impacts of climate change, coastal zone management, water resources, agriculture, flood, and drought and desertification.
2. *Decides also*, in the Subsidiary Body for Implementation,
   (a) To undertake in accordance with paragraph 1 of article 10 of the Convention to access and review the effective implementation of article 9, paragraph 2(c);
   (b) To formulate pilot projects on technology transfer in every developing region to demonstrate the practical application of technology for mitigation and adaptation of climate-related technology.
3. *Calls upon* the Convention Secretariat to implement paragraph 2(e) of decision 7/CP.2 to organize a round table on transfer of technologies and know-how in conjunction with the third session of the Conference of the Parties;
4. *Requests* the operating entity of the financial mechanism to consider the full implementation of article 11, paragraph 1, which states that the financial mechanism shall "provide financial resources on a grant and concessional

basis, including for the transfer of technology," taking into account the relevant provisions of chapter 34 of Agenda 21, and to include the activities taken in such implementation in its annual report to the Conference of the Parties; and

5. *Requests* the Secretariat to continue to include in its regular report on transfer of technology, a review of progress made by Annex II parties implementing article 4.5 of the Convention.

Paper No. 1: Group of 77 and China*

The G-77 and China on Activities Implemented Jointly

1. Article 4.2 a) of the Convention allows developed country parties to implement policies and measures jointly with other parties and to assist other parties in the achievement of the objective of the Convention, in particular the objective of paragraph 4.2 a), namely, to take measure to mitigate climate change by limiting their anthropogenic emissions of greenhouse gases.
2. As the G-77 and China has consistently stated, this clearly means that the concept of Joint Implementation under the Convention only applies to activities undertaken by parties which are bound by article 4.2 a), in other words Annex I parties. It does not apply to activities undertaken between Annex I and non–Annex I parties.
3. Through decision 5/CP.1 the First Conference of the parties agreed to initiate a pilot phase of Activities Implemented Jointly, which is an entirely different notion from that of Joint Implementation. AIJ applies to all those parties who wish to undertake these activities on a voluntary basis. As we all know, the main difference between AIJ and JI is that in the former there is no crediting, during the pilot phase, for emission reductions with respect to Annex I parties' commitments. The G-77 and China wish to underscore this fundamental principle and the fact that decision 5/CP.1 and the conditions which it incorporates for carrying out AIJ must be adhered to strictly.
4. The object of the pilot phase is to gain experience on potential advantages and disadvantages of activities and projects undertaken by Annex I parties in cooperation with non–Annex I parties, again with the specific proviso that no credits would accrue to any Annex I party for any emission reductions obtained, during this pilot phase, through the activity or project in question. It was agreed that the pilot phase would be reviewed in the year 1999. We see no reason to modify this date as there is a need to allow sufficient time for experiences to be collected in order to make a final decision on this matter, especially in view of the fact that so far there is a limited number of projects which are mainly concentrated in certain sectors and regions.

* Contained in document FCCC/SBSTA/1997/MISC.5 of 27 July 1997.

5. The G-77 and China wishes to emphasize that AIJ, and its pilot phase, is a mechanism for parties—particularly developing country parties—to carry out, on a strictly voluntary basis, activities which contribute to the abatement of global climate change. However, we consider AIJ as supplemental and as a subsidiary means of achieving the objectives of the Convention. While it could contribute to the fulfilment of commitments of Annex II parties under article 4.5, it should never be made a conditionality for the transfer of technology. Whether there are AIJ projects or not, developed country parties have the commitments of technology transfer to developing countries as provided in the Convention.
6. We would like to express our concern at attempts being made to confuse the nature of AIJ in the pilot phase with JI and to link it—implicitly or explicitly—with existing obligations such as the transfer of technology, the provision of new and additional financial assistance, and particularly to issues relating to the protocol or other legal instrument to the Convention.

Development and Transfer of Technologies

Draft Decisions for the Fourth Session of the Conference of the Parties Proposed by the Group of 77 and China*

Technology development and transfer

The Conference of the Parties,

Recalling the relevant provisions of chapter 34 of Agenda 21 and the relevant provisions of the programme for the further implementation of Agenda 21, which was adopted by the, United Nations General Assembly at its nineteenth special session, on the transfer of environmentally sound technologies,

Pursuant to articles 4.1, 4.5, 4.7, 4.8, 4.9, 9.2, and 11.1 of the United Nations Framework Convention on Climate Change,

Recalling its decisions 13/CP.1, 7/CP.2, and 9/CP.3 on development and transfer of technology,

Noting the slow progress of practical activities with regard to the transfer of technology,

Bearing in mind article 10, paragraph (c) of the Kyoto Protocol, which states that all parties shall "cooperate in the promotion of effective modalities for the

* Contained in document FCCC/SBSTA/1998/CRP.1 of 10 June 1998.

development, application and diffusion of, and take all practicable steps to promote, facilitate and finance, as appropriate, the transfer of, or access to, environmentally sound technologies, know-how, practices and processes pertinent to climate change, in particular to developing countries, including the formulation of policies and programmes for the effective transfer of environmentally sound technologies that are publicly owned or in the private domain and the creation of an enabling environment for the private sector, to promote and enhance the transfer of, and access to environmentally sound technologies,"

1. *Reaffirms* its decisions 13/CP.1, 7/CP.2, and 9/CP.3 on transfer of technology;
2. *Urges:*
   (a) Parties listed in Annex II, as the first step, to provide a list of environmentally sound and economically viable technologies and know-how related to adaptation to and mitigation of climate change that are publicly owned or in the private domain for reference by developing country parties;
   (b) Non–Annex I parties, in the light of their social and economic conditions and taking into account the state-of-the-art environmentally sound technologies, to submit their prioritized technology needs, especially as concerns some key technologies needed in particular sectors of their national economy conducive to addressing climate change; and
   (c) Both developed and developing country parties to create an enabling environment to stimulate private sector investment in and transfer of environmentally sound technologies and know-how to developing countries, taking into full account article 10(c) of the Kyoto Protocol.
3. *Requests the Convention Secretariat:*
   (a) To prepare an inventory of environmentally sound and economically viable technologies and know-how conducive to adapting to and mitigating climate change, taking into account submissions made, under subparagraphs 2 (a) and (b) above;
   (b) To submit the documents on the elaboration of the terms under which transfers of technologies and know-how could take place, through the SBSTA, to the Conference of the Parties for consideration;
4. *Decides* to define hereby a technology transfer mechanism (TTM) to address climate change. The purpose of TTM shall be to assist developing country parties to obtain their needed environmentally sound technologies and know-how conducive to addressing climate change on non-commercial, preferential terms and thus contribute to the ultimate objective of the Convention. The functions of the TTM shall be elaborated by the Conference of the Parties, taking into account recommendations of the subsidiary bodies of the Convention. Such further elaboration may include, *inter alia*, the following:
   (a) The developed country parties shall take all practicable steps, including regulatory, legal, and economic instruments or incentives, to promote, facilitate, and finance the transfer of technologies and know-how to

developing country parties on non-commercial, preferential terms as provided for in chapter 34 of Agenda 21;

(b) The developed country parties shall also take the necessary steps to promote capacity-building in non–Annex I country parties; and

(c) The developing country parties shall create an enabling environment for those environmentally sound technologies and know-how to be transferred to them on preferential terms related to adaptation to and mitigation of climate change.

5. *Further decides* to establish an Intergovernmental Technical Advisory Panel (ITAP) in accordance with 6/CP.1, Annex II. The functions of the ITAP will include, *inter alia*, assessing environmentally sound technologies and making recommendations to SBSTA, advising on methodological issues, and developing guidelines on the development and transfer of environmentally sound technologies;
6. *Decides* to, at the fifth session of the Conference of the Parties, and at the sessions of the Conference of the Parties thereafter, elaborate modalities and procedures for reviewing the implementation of the Annex II parties' commitments under article 4.5 of the Convention regarding technology transfer with the objective of ensuring effective transfer of environmentally sound technologies and know-how to developing country parties.

Capacity-Building

The Conference of the Parties,

Recalling its decisions 13/CP.1, 7/CP.2, and 9/CP.3 on development and transfer of technologies,

Reaffirming the ultimate objective of the United Nations Framework Convention on Climate Change as contained in its article 2,

Acknowledging that human activities since the industrial revolution have been substantially increasing the atmospheric concentrations of greenhouse gases,

Noting that the largest share of historical and current global emissions of greenhouse gases has originated from developed countries, that per capita emissions in developing countries are still low and that the share of global emissions originating from developing countries will grow to meet their social and developmental needs,

Taking note of the Kyoto Protocol to the Convention,

Recognizing that the global nature of climate change calls for the widest possible cooperation and participation by all countries in accordance with their common but differentiated responsibilities, respective capabilities, and their social and economic conditions,

Recognizing the right of all countries to promote sustainable development and the legitimate needs of the developing countries for achievement of sustained economic growth and the eradication of poverty,

Recalling the relevant provisions of the programme for the further implementation of Agenda 21 on transfer of environmentally sound technology, cooperation, and capacity-building, as adopted by the United Nations General Assembly at its nineteenth special session in 1997, and as reaffirmed by decision 9/CP.3,

Reaffirming the provisions of article 4.7 of the Convention,

7. *Agrees* that strengthening the capacities and capabilities of developing country parties to address climate change will help these parties to make their contributions to modifying the long-term trends of climate change, address climate change, achieve sustainable development, and contribute to the ultimate objective of the Convention;
8. *Decides* to mobilize efforts of all relevant international organizations, particularly those of the financial institutions, to provide financial resources needed by developing country parties to meet their incremental costs, including transfer and development of technology, enhancement of endogenous capacities, implementation of such measures as improving energy efficiency, exploiting renewable energies, enhancing sinks, and preparing for adaptation to adverse effects of climate change;
9. *Requests* Annex I parties to the Convention to take all practical steps to promote, facilitate, and finance the transfer and development of environmentally sound technologies, or access to environmentally sound technologies, know-how, and practices, to developing country parties. Annex I parties are also requested to support capacity-building and strengthening of national institutions to enable transfer of environmentally sound technologies;
10. *Further requests* Annex I parties to the Convention:
    (a) To assist the developing country parties in their efforts to build capacity and institutional framework to improve energy efficiency and utilization of renewable energies through multilateral and bilateral cooperative efforts;
    (b) To provide assistance to developing country parties for sustainable management, conservation, and enhancement, as appropriate, of sinks and reservoirs of all greenhouse gases not controlled by the Montreal Protocol, including forests, biomass, and seas;
    (c) To assist developing country parties to build capacity to adapt to adverse effects of climate change;

(d) To assist developing country parties to strengthen their endogenous capacities and capabilities in the areas of technological, technical, and socio-economic research and systematic observation relevant to climate change and its associated adverse effects; and
(e) Taking into account article 6 of the Convention, to cooperate in and promote capacity-building of developing country parties at the international, regional, sub-regional, and national levels through cooperation programmes supported by multilateral, bilateral, and United Nations agencies;

Requests the Secretariat to further strengthen its activities related to technical and financial support to developing country parties with regard to strengthening of their capacity-building.

Development and Transfer of Technologies

Paper No. 1: Indonesia
(On behalf of the Group of 77 and China)*

The SBSTA having noted the result of the consultations of the Secretariat with the GEF and other relevant international organizations in accordance with decision 9/CP.3, paragraph 2 (b) agreed to request the SBI to take the steps to provide necessary financial resources for establishing/ enhancing support for national, regional centers.

The SBSTA recommends that COP-4 give guidance to GEF to respond to the need for improving existing, and setting up technology information centers as stated in paragraph 2 (b) of decision 9/CP.3, through the establishment of dedicated/specialized information systems, comprising of enhanced national and regional centers, that would, *inter alia*, facilitate national/regional access to the information provided by international centers, and strengthen national/regional capacities to work with these centers for the dissemination of information, information services, and transfer of environmentally sound technologies and know-how in support of the Convention.

G-77 and China Position on Elements to Be Included in the Preparation of Proposed Elements of Draft Guidelines under Article 8 of the Kyoto Protocol (Informal Paper No. 8 (2000) dated 11 June 2000)*

The following note will outline the G-77 and China views to assist the Secretariat in preparing the above-mentioned document for discussions in the upcoming SB-13. The views draw upon the above document and key questions given during the session by the Secretariat.

* Contained in document FCCC/SBSTA/1998/MISC.5 of 12 June 1998.
* Contained in document FCCC/SBSTA/2000/MISC.1/Add.2 of 17 July 2000.

GENERAL COMMENTS

The G-77 and China believes that the decision by COP-6 on reporting and guidelines (articles 7 and 8) must take into account the following provisions of the protocol: articles 2, 3.2, 3.14, 10, and 11.

All sections of the guideline mentioned in the above referenced document must be fully developed. The guideline should elaborate on all the commitments in the Kyoto Protocol including the above-mentioned provisions. Further elaboration may be required following further requirements resulting from COP-6 decisions on the elements included in the Buenos Aires Plan of Action.

As for what part of the guidelines need distinction between FCCC and KP commitments? We believe that all parts of the guidelines should show distinct clarification between the FCCC and KP review of commitments. Article 7 of the Protocol requires supplemental information for the commitments under the protocol. Therefore article 8 review is a supplemental review of the information under the protocol.

SPECIFIC COMMENTS:

The following comments are specific elements to be added to the element paper mentioned above (Informal paper No. 8 (2000) dated 11 June 2000).

- The document and the guideline to be elaborated by the Secretariat for the SB-13 session must clearly show that the review is intended for parties included in Annex I as mandated by article 8 of the Protocol. Therefore, all references must be made to Annex I parties through out this and future documents.
- Page 1, Part I (general Approach to review), section A (objective), add the following element: "To ensure that the [compliance body] has the information necessary to carry out the functions assigned to it."
- Page 1, Part I (general Approach to review), section B (General Approach), amend, the second sentence of the third bullet point: "Review teams will not determine whether or not a party included in Annex I is in compliance with its commitments."
- Page 2, Part I (general Approach to review), section D (Timing and procedures to be undertaken), paragraph 1 (review prior to the commitment period) add the following elements:
- Under (1.a), the bullet related to National Communications add the following elements:
  - Information related to article 3.2
  - Information related to article 3.14
- Under (1.a) as a new bullet add the following element: "Any eligibility criteria as determined by COP-6."

- Page 4, Part I (general Approach to review), section D (Timing and procedures to be undertaken), paragraph 4 (Periodic review) add the following new elements:
  - Information regarding article 2
  - Information regarding article 3.2
  - Information regarding article 3.14
  - Information regarding articles 10 and 11.
- Page 4, Part I (general Approach to review), section E (Composition and institutional arrangement), bullet 1, line 3, after Geographic balance add: "in a manner that ensures the participation of nonAnnex I experts."
- Page 12, Part VI, Section A (purpose), add the following bullet:
  - "To ensure the implementation of Articles 2, 3.2, 3.14, 10 and 11."

Further comments may be elaborated.

Paper No. 3: Group of 77 and China*
Development and Transfer of Technologies Pursuant to Article 4.5
of the Convention

The presentation of this position paper does not preclude further submissions to be made by the group as negotiations proceeds. The G-77 and China will like to have separate decisions made on article 4.5 of the Convention and article 12 of the Kyoto Protocol.

Basic Position and important issues:

1. CDM shall not be seen as a mechanism to implement article 4.5 of the Convention.
2. Technology transfer should be put on a fast track in the same way as is being done for the other Convention/Protocol operational entities
3. A prioritized set of technology needs to be identified for each region or sub-region respectively with inputs from each country within the region/sub-region.
4. Inventories of ESTs, which have been tried and tested or are being developed, should be compiled with sufficient information to allow developing countries to make informed decisions on what is best for their peoples.
5. A technology transfer clearinghouse with national, sub-regional, and regional linkages should be established to facilitate an access to information on technology, projects on technologies transferred, and on financial sources.
6. Financial assistance should be provided to developing countries in order for them to create the enabling environment for private sector investment

* Contained in document FCCC/SBSTA/2000/MISC.4 of 14 July 2000.

and to set up the internal mechanisms to prevent "dumping" of inefficient technologies and to ensure transfer of state-of-the-art ESTs.

7. Capacity-building should be emphasised as a major need to allow for the development and transfer of technologies under article 4.5.
8. An evaluation and monitoring mechanism should be put in place to assess the effectiveness of actions to be carried out to implement article 4.5.
9. A fund should be established within the Convention financial mechanism to support capacity-building, information transfer, needs assessment, and research and development in developing endogenous capacities to screen mitigation and adaptation projects for environmental friendliness and enhancement of commitments under the Convention.
10. South-South transfer of technology to be supported by developed country parties.
11. Some developing countries will have a priority for adaptation technology transfer while others will have a priority for mitigation technology transfer.
12. All parties shall be involved in the creation of the enabling environment for technology transfer.
13. The critical role of the private sector in the Annex I and non–Annex I countries must be taken into consideration.
14. Research, development, and demonstration projects are effective means for technology transfer.
15. Technology transfer should be approached in an integrated, country-driven, and coordinated manner.
16. The industrial sector (including SMEs) should be afforded access to information on available technologies and financial resources.
17. Monitoring, reporting, evaluating and assessing transferred technologies must be done on a continuous basis.
18. Education, training, public awareness, and stakeholders' involvement are essential.

Possible Elements of a Framework for Meaningful and Effective Actions to Enhance the Implementation of Article 4.5 of the Convention (The main sources are documents FCCC/SBSTA/2000/4, FCCC/SBSTA/1999/11, FCCC/SBSTA/2000/INF.2, INF.6, and MISC.2.)

1. Financial Commitment for Technology Transfer

It is recognized that there must be a commitment by the Developed Countries to fund the programmes identified under article 4.5. Also, all parties must work towards a COP-6 decision on a clear timetable to start the process of technology transfer such that, by the time of COP-7, the following milestones will have been achieved:

- Needs assessment
- Creation of necessary enabling environment
- Clearinghouse set up
- Capacity-building needs identified and capacity-building initiated
- Initiation of Pilot Projects

2. Technology needs and technology needs assessments

- Countries should be assisted to carry out their technology needs and needs assessment.
- Developing cooperative programmes through which financial and technical assistance could be provided to developing countries to conduct technology needs assessments.
- Technology needs assessments should include technology impact analyses, identifying and prioritizing technology needs, and building appropriate institutional and human capacity for sustainable technology transfer.
- Such programmes should coordinate the activities of stakeholders from both donors and developing countries in the technology transfer process.
- The programmes should evaluate local EST needs and barriers to technology transfer by providing for processes that include all stakeholders, for example, government, business, technical institutions, and NGOs.
- The outcome of these needs assessments could be a prioritized set of technology needs and a portfolio of climate technology activities for both mitigation and adaptation.

3. Creating the enabling environment

Both developed and developing countries shall take actions to create an enabling environment for technology transfer.

Developed Countries

- Provide financial and technical assistance for developing countries to carry out needs assessments, including technology impact analysis, to identify and prioritize technology needs and develop a portfolio of climate technology actions for mitigation and adaptation;
- Develop and implement domestic programmes which discourage industries in Annex II countries from utilizing restrictive business practices. These efforts could also include reassessment of national development assistance programmes which promote tied aid;
- Remove restriction of transfer of advanced technologies proven climate sound;
- Enhance export credits and other instruments which provide incentives for the private sector to participate in the transfer of ESTs;

- Develop and implement domestic actions and incentives, e.g., ear-marked subsidies linked with development and transfer of EST, government purchase contracts, tax preferences, as well as appropriate regulations to promote the transfer of ESTs by the private sector;
- Enhance or develop linkages between the climate technology related research and development communities and the official development assistance communities within donor countries with a view to delivering support more efficiently to developing countries;
- Examine options to boost the effectiveness of the private sector as an important and successful delivery vehicle for transferring technology for mitigation and adaptation technologies;

Developing Countries

Developing countries may also make efforts to improve the enabling environment for transfer of technology. Some of the targeted efforts may be as follows:

- Identify and establish "focal points" to coordinate domestic technology transfer activities and actions related to the transfer of ESTs and develop a portfolio of climate technology actions (strategies) for mitigation and adaptation;
- Build public awareness and support for development and adoption of ESTs through development of effective standards and labelling programmes, consumer education, as well as documentation of the social, environmental, and human health related benefits of ESTs;
- Develop regional and South-South technology transfer initiatives with an integration of appropriate assistance from developed countries;
- Enhance, develop, and strengthen research and development programmes for ESTs and promote complementary policies for their diffusion;

International Bodies

The GEF must initiate programmes to implement COP decisions under article 4.5. Some of the above actions may be conducted by developed and developing countries respectively, or jointly by both developed and developing countries and related intergovernmental organizations.

4. Capacity-building for technology transfer

- Capacity-building activities which can most successfully help to achieve and sustain effective technology transfer are those which measurably utilize and enhance existing endogenous capacities and technologies.
- Technology transfer concerns not only so-called "hard technologies," but also so-called "soft technologies" (e.g., know-how and practices)

- Transferring experiences, knowledge, skills, know-how, and practices is of a great importance in capacity-building;
- The assessment of existing capacities and the identification of gaps where capacity-building activities can be targeted is a critical step.
- Existing projects incorporating country-driven, multi-stakeholder assessments of technology needs provide a useful model in relation to the assessment of capacity-building needs, especially those closely linked to technology transfer;
- Capacity-building through international bilateral or multilateral activities is usually a two-way process resulting in the building of capacities on both sides, i.e., the host country as well as the donor countries or organizations themselves
- In practical terms, often the best way to build capacity is through demonstration or pilot projects.
- Strengthen existing regional institutions, taking into consideration country and sector-specific peculiarities.
- Capacity-building elements related to technology transfer that could be considered include assisting developing countries to:
  - Identify technology needs;
  - Improve organizations and institutions;
  - Strengthen human resources;
  - Overcome technological barriers; and
  - Access to technology information.

5. Transfer of technology mechanisms

- Existing mechanisms are inadequate for the implementation of article 4.5 of UNFCCC and innovative mechanism in the context of UNFCCC shall be established without delay.
- The purpose of the Technology Transfer Mechanism in the context of the Convention is to assist developing country parties to obtain environmentally sound technologies and know-how helpful to address climate change in non-commercial and preferential terms, thus contributing to the ultimate objective of the Convention.
- Technology Transfer Mechanism is an umbrella conception, through which the technology needs of developing countries can be identified, capacity and capability-building can be enhanced, and the needed technologies and know-how can be transferred, operated disseminated, and maintained.
- The most fundamental components for this mechanism are as follows:
  - Institutional mechanism, under which national focal points specific for technology transfer, an intergovernmental technical advisory body, and a unit in the UNFCCC Secretariat shall be established, with their TORs to be addressed in detail.

- Funding mechanism, under which a trust fund specifically for technology transfer shall be established. Funding sources can be from the Annex II parties, international organizations, and multilateral development banks, etc.

6. Technology information

- Information should be specific, case-study/project-based, and target real-world problems with lessons learned.
- Establish, in each developed country, a one-stop technology transfer "shop" to coordinate and implement technology transfer programmes. These "shops" could assist with the preparation of projects and programmes to respond to prioritised needs for mitigation and adaptation.
- Develop inventories of available environmentally sound technologies including those in the public domain as well as technology transfer activities in the past or at present.

7. Monitoring, Reporting, Evaluation, and Assessment

Technologies which have been transferred must be assessed on a continuous basis in order to verify its environmental soundness and to bring, to the attention of the COP, any information which will allow it to make informed decisions on future use of the technology or on modifications which will be necessary for making them ESTs.

Paper No. 1: Group of 77 and China

G-77 and China Draft Decision on the Development and Transfer of Technologies*

The Conference of the Parties,

Recalling Chapter 34 of Agenda 21 of the UN Conference on Environment and Development (UNCED), and paragraphs 88 to 97 of the Programme for the Further Implementation of Agenda 21, on the transfer of environmentally sound technologies adopted by the United Nations General Assembly at its nineteenth special session in 1997,

Basing itself on articles 4.1, 4.3, 4.5, 4.7, 4.8, and 4.9, as well as articles 9.2 (c),

11.1, 11.5, 12.3, and 12.4 of the Convention,

* Contained in document FCCC/SBSTA/2000/MISC.9 of 18 September 2000.

Keeping in mind articles 10 (c) and 11.2 (b) of the Kyoto Protocol to the UN Framework Convention on Climate Change,

Taking fully into account its decisions 11/CP.1, 13/CP.1; 9/CP.3, 2/CP.4, 4/CP.4, and 9/CP.5,

Reaffirming its decision 1/CP.4 on the Buenos Aires Plan of Action, which in its paragraph 2 resolves to demonstrate substantial progress on the implementation of the Convention, including on the development and transfer of technologies,

1. *Agrees* that the promotion of the implementation of the commitment of developed country parties and other developed parties included in Annex II for the transfer of, or access to, environmental sound technologies and know-how, as stated in article 4.5, together with the provision of new and additional financial resources as stated in article 4.3, are essential conditions for the effective implementation of developing country parties of their commitments under the Convention, taking fully into account that economic and social development and poverty eradication are the first and overriding priorities of the developing country parties;
2. *Agrees also* that issues relating to the implementation of article 4.5 on transfer of and access to technology is a continuing process, and that, *inter alia*, the assessment of technologies, terms of access, and technological needs of parties will continue to be undertaken in the Convention, to ensure that real progress is achieved promptly.
3. *Decides*, for this purpose, to establish an intergovernmental panel of experts, nominated by governments and based on equitable geographical representation, to provide scientific and technical advice on the implementation of the commitment on article 4.5, including assessments of technologies and technology needs under the Convention.
4. *Decides also* to establish a separate funding mechanism for technology transfer through which technical and financial assistance from Annex II parties shall be made available to achieve meaningful and effective actions to enhance implementation of article 4.5 of the Convention, in accordance with the modalities contained in the Annex.
5. *Decides further* that the funding mechanism will provide the necessary resources, including for the following purposes:
   a) enhance capacity-building for developing countries, including through demonstration projects, as shown in the annexed initial framework;
   b) promote joint research and development programmes between Annex I and non–Annex I parties, and also non–Annex I parties among themselves;
   c) develop and implement concrete programmes to conduct technology needs identification and needs assessment, taking into account the different levels of readiness among developing countries;

d) develop specialised information centers relating to the state-of-the-art, environmentally sound and economically feasible technologies and know-how that are accessible and available to developing countries, their accessibility and conditions for accessibility; and
e) leverage other funding sources to initiate concrete transfer of technology projects for energy-efficient technologies, new and renewable energies, enhancing sinks, and preparing for adaptation to adverse impacts of climate change.

6. *Requests* the Chairman of the SBSTA, building upon the progress done so far in the consultative process, as contained in the initial framework for the implementation of article 4.5 of the Convention, and in order to move forward in the implementation of 4.5, to continue the consultations on this item, focused at addressing the remaining questions contained in the Annex to decision 4/CP.4, in particular on practical steps to promote, facilitate, and finance, as appropriate, transfer of, and access to, environmentally sound technologies and know-how, and to identify concrete actions for the implementation of the commitment in article 4.5.
7. *Agrees*, in this regard, to take fully into account the recommendations contained in IPCC special report on technology transfer; paragraphs 34.18 to 34.21 of chapter 34 of Agenda 21, and the Secretariat technical papers on terms of transfer and adaptation technologies; the information contained in national communications of Annex I parties on details of measures taken to implement article 4.5, in accordance with article 12.3, and any other information provided by interested international organizations and other institutions on the availability and conditions of transfer of and access to climate-related environmentally sound technologies, especially adaptation technologies;
8. *Requests also* the Chairman of the SBSTA to include in its work programme, the establishment of the intergovernmental panel of experts on transfer of technology, in order to assist in the implementation of the commitments under article 4.5 of the Convention,
9. *Requests* the Global Environment Facility, as an operating entity of the financial mechanism of the Convention and acting in accordance with article 11.1, which calls for new and additional financial resources to be provided on a grant and concessional basis including for transfer of technology, to ensure that their programmes for facilitating transfer of, and access to, environmentally sound technologies follow closely the guidance and the timetables contained in the relevant COP decisions, in particular decision 2/CP.4, and to report on the progress of this implementation in their report to the COP;
10. *Requests* the Secretariat to provide the necessary assistance for the discussions on this item, including making available the documentation referred to in paragraph 7 above, both in printed and electronic form, and to focus its subsequent work on transfer of technology transfer on the

availability of technologies, conditions of access, means of facilitating access to these technologies, in particular adaptation technologies.

11. *Decides* to continue the consideration of this item at each session under the agenda item "matters relating to commitments," as provided for in decision 13/CP.1.

Annex

Modalities of a Funding Mechanism for Technology Transfer

1. There hereby is established the Developing Countries' Technology Transfer Fund (hereinafter called "the Fund");
2. The annual funding level of the Fund shall be at the rate of ___billion US dollars beginning with the year 2001 and continuing at that level each year thereafter during the period ending 31 December 2005 unless the funding level is changed by decision of the Conference of the Parties;
3. Each year on the 15th day of April, during the period beginning in 2001 and ending in 2025, each developed country party and other developed parties included in Annex II of the Convention (hereinafter called "Annex II Party") shall contribute to the Fund its share of the annual funding level of the Fund in accordance with the formula set forth in Annex I to this Decision; and
4. "Failure of an Annex II Party to make its annual contribution to the Fund, as provided for in Paragraph 2(c), automatically be the subject of a proceeding by the Enforcement Branch in accordance with Decision___."

Executive Body

5. The Fund shall be administered by the Developing Countries' Technology Transfer Fund Executive Body (hereinafter called the "Executive Body");
   (a) The Executive Body shall consist of __members, reflecting equal representation of each of the five United Nations regional groups, who have been elected by the Conference of the Parties upon the nomination of the regional groups to serve for a term of two years;
   (b) The first election of members of the Executive Body shall be held at the sixth session of the Conference of the Parties;
   (c) The Executive Body shall invest and reinvest the monies held by the Fund, pending distributions from the Fund and its income to developing country parties, in accordance with guidelines for investments to be adopted by the Conference of the Parties no later that at its seventh session and, until such guidelines are adopted, in accordance with the highest standards of care to be exercised by bodies or persons entrusted with managing Funds of comparable size for the benefit of others; and
   (d) The Executive Body shall make distributions from the Fund and its income to developing country parties on an equitable basis, by way of

grants, loans and loan guarantees, in accordance with guidelines adopted from time to time by the Conference of the Parties for the acquisition of technologies, including know-how, by developing country parties to facilitate their implementation of their commitments under the Convention.

Submission from Venezuela

(On behalf of the Group of 77 and China)*

The G-77/C Position on the Canadian Proposal for Environmental Credits to its Energy Export to the US (Annex-B country non-Party to the Protocol) and its impact.

The Canadian proposal is outlined in FCCC/SBSTA/2002/MISC.3/ADD.1 document.

The Group of 77 and China has strong reservation on the Canadian proposal. In the workshop on cleaner or less greenhouse gas emitting energy, 7–8 May 2002, Whistler, Canada, the Canadian government indicated that it will submit a proposal in the June Subsidiary Body meeting to be granted a 70 Mt CO_2-equivalent per year as an environmental credit for its energy export (electricity and natural gas) to the US. They argued that such an action would result in a "global environmental benefit" because it replaces US coal. The Canadian view had very little support by the workshop participants.

There are several reasons why many countries did not support the Canadian proposal for additional reduction (about 30% of their reduction commitment) in their agreed 1990 assigned amounts by granting the so-called "environmental credit." Some of these are:

- It will not result in any real reduction in GHG emission in neither Canada nor the US. Giving Canada environmental credit for its energy export to the US will negatively impact the Clean Development Mechanism (CDM) and Joint Implementation projects and will not result in global environmental benefit. CDM projects result in real emission reductions and transfer of technology. The negative impact on CDM projects as a result of giving environmental credit to Annex-I electricity and natural gas export must be fully assessed before any action on the Canadian request. There are many methodical concerns, which will take several years for a body such as the Intergovernmental Panel for Climate Change (IPCC) to address. The literature does not have detailed scientific research to evaluate the merit of this new approach.
- The proposed environmental credit will distort the critical balance achieved in the Kyoto

* Contained in document FCCC/SBSTA/2002/MISC.3/Add.2 of 12 June 2002.

Protocol under articles 3.14 and 2.3 where mitigation actions and response measures taken by Annex I parties, including Canada, shall be done in a way to minimize their impact on developing countries included in articles 4.8 and 4.9 of the Convention.

- There is no legal basis to the Canadian request. Revisions to the Kyoto Protocol requires full consensus of the parties after entry into force. The Kyoto Protocol counts emission based on assigned amount baseline for each Annex B country where it is produced and not to the consuming country. All parties agreed to this concept in 1997 when they adopted the Kyoto Protocol. Also, emission credit based on energy trade is not addressed in the Kyoto protocol. Any change will require an amendment to the Protocol after its entry into force. This may open the door for many additional amendments from other parties and will result in further dilution of the already weakened Kyoto Protocol. The environmental integrity of the process is in jeopardy. We are cognizant that the Bonn Agreement and the Marrakech Accord have already severely weakened the Protocol.
- The value of carbon in emission trading will be further diminished if Canada and other Annex B countries are allowed to have environmental credit for their energy export to the US (Annex B country non-party to the Protocol). This will also reduce incentives for domestic mitigation throughout Annex I countries. The US pullout of the Kyoto Protocol and the Bonn Agreement on sinks had greatly reduced the carbon trading value. Any additional environmental credit will severely affect the future of CDM and international emission trading. In effect, giving environmental emission credit to Canada and other Annex I countries may result in greater environmental harm.
- Canada is expanding its energy export to the US to gain economic benefit. Some countries may see the "Global Environmental Benefit" concept as a sugar-coating to maintain export market share and gain competitive advantage in large energy markets such as the USA. The Canadian proposal, in effect, is asking the parties to guarantee their natural gas market-share in the US. This is not part of Climate Change Convention objectives and granting environmental credit may be considered as subsidies under the WTO rules.
- The argument that Canadian energy export to the US results in GHG emission avoidance from US coal power plants is not valid when Canada continues to use its coal and plans to expand coal power production. Annual GHG emissions from Canadian coal are around 95 Mt CO_2 equivalent which is much higher that 70 Mt CO_2 equivalent claimed for energy export to the USA. In addition, the Canadian natural gas export to the US replaces mostly cleaner and less GHG gas emitting energy not coal. The Canadian submission at the Cleaner Energy Workshop at Whistler, indicates that Canadian gas replaces

only 30% of higher coal consumption while the rest is distributed amongst US natural gas (26%), LNG (6%), oil (30%), and higher energy efficiency (8%). However, the report of Cheminfo (survey of energy experts) indicated that Canadian gas exports replaces only 9% of coal, 35% alternate natural gas supply, 33% oil, and 23% lower demand or non-fossil fuels.

- Canada should use its gas and hydro energy production to reduce its CO_2 emissions associated with the Canadian use of coal and production of unconventional oil.
- Expanding the energy production, including its export, will discourage conservation measures in Canada and the US. And thus reduces global environmental benefit.
- It is more environmentally beneficial to collect flared gas in developing countries for use in Annex I, including USA. This will not only greatly serve the same purpose stated by Canada as "Global Environmental Benefit," but it will also contribute to the sustainable development of oil and gas producers in developing countries. It can also be considered as part of implementing Marrakech decision 9/CP7 on article 3.14. It also can be considered as part of minimizing the impact of Annex I response measures and article 2.3 of Kyoto "minimize the impact on international trade."
- Environmental additionally: The proposal refers to present and future exports to the US in the framework of pre-exiting agreements (commercial). Therefore, this amounts to obtaining credit for business-as-usual scenario.
- The proposal modifies the concept of baseline for Annex-I countries from the current reference year, 1990, to a reference scenario that is difficult to control and measure.
- The Canadian proposal is circumventing the Protocol system based on GHG mitigation relative to assigned amounts. The "assigned amount" is with reference to emissions. The commitments of an Annex I party in the Protocol are prescribed in terms of its emissions and limitation and reduction of emissions. The Protocol seeks the requisite mitigation by a party either on its own or together with other Annex I parties which have accepted commitments under the Protocol. The Canadian proposal does not subscribe to this.

In the event of a country seeking to achieve its target together with other Annex I parties through mechanisms in articles 6, 12, and 17, the principles and rules have been settled. These subscribe to a definition of "assigned amounts" based on emissions. Under this, the requisite transactions of assigned amounts and credits can take place only under the systems derived under articles 6, 12, and 17 of the Protocol, which contribute to real and measurable reduction. The Protocol system does not recognise the Canadian Proposal.

Group of 77 and China

Group of 77 and China Position on Issues Relating to the Implementation of Article 2.3 of the Kyoto Protocol*

Reference: SBSTA Agenda Item, 9 (b), Document FCCC/SBSTA/2003/1

Saudi Arabia on behalf of the Group of 77 and China welcomes the opportunity to discuss the issues relating to the implementation of article 2.3 of the Kyoto Protocol and considers that such discussion is very important. In Marrakech, a year and a half ago, it was concluded that this article consideration should take place during the SBSTA seventeenth session.

As we all know, the consideration of this issue started since SBSTA 16. However, the consideration of the issue did not complete whereby at SBSTA 17 it was agreed to continue the consideration of this item in SBSTA 18.

The Group of 77 and China position in this regarded is four-fold:

1. This agenda item should be moved to be a regular SBSTA agenda item starting this session;
2. The Secretariat should carry out SBSTA mandate in its conclusion 66. (c) of document FCCC/SBSTA/2002/6 to revise document FCCC/SBSTA/2002/INF.13 by assessing the impact of these policies and measures on developing countries as outlined in article 2.3 of the Kyoto Protocol;
3. Consider an initial workshop before the SBSTA nineteenth session;
4. Consider a draft decision to The COP at its ninth session to outline the required recommended initial actions for consideration by the first meeting of the COP/MOP.

In order to implement the provisions of this article, the Group of 77 and China requests SBSTA to consider number of elements including:

1. What can developed countries do to minimize the impacts of their policies and measures on developing countries?
2. How can developed countries assist developing countries to adapt to such impacts?
3. What are the spillover effects of these policies and measures and what can be done to minimize their adverse effects, including the adverse effects of Climate Change, social, environmental, and economic impacts with specific emphasis of effects on international trade on developing countries?

* Contained in document FCCC/SBSTA/2003/MISC.8 of 12 June 2003.

Finally, the Group of 77 and China believes that the way forward to tackle this issue is by deliberations via informal consultations and workshops with the view to prepare a decision by COP-9 to recommend initial actions for consideration by the first meeting of the COP/MOP.

Submission from the Group of 77 and China* G-77 and China Position – 25 May 2006, 2pm: SBSTA Agenda Item 3
Five-Year Programme of Work on Impacts:
Vulnerability and Adaptation to Climate Change

<table>
<tr><td colspan="3">A (i). Promoting development and dissemination of methodologies and tools for impact and vulnerability assessments, such as rapid assessments and bottom-up approaches, including as they apply to sustainable development
B (i). Promoting the development and dissemination of methods and tools for assessment and improvement of adaptation planning, measures and actions, and integration with sustainable development</td></tr>
<tr><td colspan="3">Activities</td></tr>
<tr><td colspan="3">• Application and development of methodologies and tools for impact, vulnerability and adaptation assessments
• Development of methodologies and tools for adaptation planning, measures and actions, and integration with sustainable development and strengthen their use.
• Dissemination of existing and new methods and tools and facilitation of the sharing of experiences and lessons
• Methods and tools for the assessment of costs and benefits of adaptation options (including those contained in the UNFCCC Compendium on methods and tools to evaluate impacts of, vulnerability and adaptation to, climate change)[9]</td></tr>
<tr><td>Modalities</td><td>Deliverables</td><td>Timing</td></tr>
<tr><td>• Invite submissions from Parties on availability, accessibility and ways to promote development, application and dissemination of existing and emerging methods and tools with a view to identifying:
- Lessons learned
- Gaps and needs
- Possible ways to better disseminate information, including a possible update and enhancement of the compendium on tools and methods
- Methods and tools for the assessment of costs and benefits of adaptation options</td><td></td><td>SBSTA 26</td></tr>
</table>

* Contained in document FCCC/SBSTA/2006/MISC.9 of 18 September 2006.
9 <http://unfccc.int/adaptation/methodologies_for/vulnerability_and_adaptation/items/2674.php>.

Request the secretariat to prepare a synthesis report based on Parties' submissions and on relevant input from the Least Developed Countries Expert Group (LEG), the Consultative Group of Experts on National Communication from Parties not included in Annex I to the Convention (CGE) and the Expert Group on Technology Transfer (EGTT)	• Report on availability and accessibility of methods and tools, on gaps and needs, and on lessons learned, and recommendations for follow-up activities	SBSTA 27
• Invite relevant organizations to inform the SBSTA on their work relating to this activity including the identification of training opportunities.		SBSTA 25
Request the Secretariat to compile the information in a miscellaneous document	• Miscellaneous document on information from organizations	SBSTA 26
• Request the Secretariat, under the guidance of the Chair of the SBSTA, to organize an expert meeting with participation of Parties, users of methods and tools, relevant organizations, and representatives from sectoral and other communities addressing thematic areas or sectors and specific regional characteristic	• Summary Report of the expert meeting taking into consideration the synthesis report	Before SBSTA 28
• Request the Secretariat to prepare a summary report on the main results of this activity	• Input into summary progress report referred to in paragraph 6 of the conclusions	SBSTA 28

A (ii). Improving collection, management, exchange, access to and use of observational data and other relevant information on current and historical climate and its impacts, and promoting improvement of observations, including the monitoring of climate variability
Activities
• Promote the implementation of systematic observation (including Global Climate Observing System (GCOS) Implementation Plan and regional • workshops programme), focusing on issues relating to impacts, vulnerability and adaptation taking into account stakeholder data needs and needs to enhance capacity to supply and use the data especially at the regional and national level • Improve capacity for collecting, managing and use of observation data, and identify practical ways of enhancing technical capacity • Exchange of information on observed climate change impacts, including those observed through traditional knowledge

Modalities	Deliverables	Timing
• Include consideration of relevant aspects of this activity, in particular stakeholder data and observation needs, at the expert meeting referred to under the modalities of activity 1	• Inclusion of relevant information in the report from the expert meeting referred to under the modalities of activity 1	Before SBSTA 27
• Invite the GCOS secretariat to focus specifically on relevant issues under this activity in its reports on the implementation of the GCOS Implementation Plan and taking into account relevant information in the implementation plan and the regional action plans from the regional workshop programme	• GCOS progress report	SBSTA 25
• Invite WMO and its associated national weather service, the GEOS, the GCOS and its partner organizations to explore how their work could contribute more to the work on impacts, vulnerability and adaptation, including the identification of gaps and deficiencies, including those to improve technical infrastructure, focusing on regions which were identified as not providing observational data, taking into account stakeholder data needs and needs to enhance capacity to supply and use the data especially at the regional and national levels	• Synthesis Report by the WMO, GEOS and GCOS secretariats on needs, and gaps and ways to address them	SBSTA 27
• Encourage Parties to share information including that observed through traditional knowledge, on observed impacts of climate change, including through national communications and participation in relevant scientific activities such as those of the Intergovernmental Panel on Climate Change (IPCC)	• Information on observed impacts of climate change included in the compilation and synthesis of national communications	SBSTA 25
• Request the Secretariat to prepare a summary report on the main results of this activity	• Input into summary progress report referred to in paragraph 7 of the conclusions	SBSTA 28

A (iii). Promoting the development of, access to, and use of information and data on projected climate change		
Activities		
• Identify gaps in the development or regional and subregional climate scenarios, including the need for, availability and applicability of climate models, and options to fill them • Identify of practical opportunities to improve access to, and use of different models' outputs, including assessment of their applicability and training opportunities • Analyse means to improve the availability and applicability of climate change modelling and downscaling data to policy makers at all levels		
Modalities	Deliverables	Timing
• Invite inputs from relevant organizations on matters identified in this activity including work undertaken on reducing uncertainties in model projections	Inclusion of relevant information in the report from the expert meeting, referred to under the modalities of activity 1.	SBSTA 26
• Invite the IPCC and its task group on scenarios for climate impact assessment (TGICA), other international organizations, modelling centres, and regional and national agencies with relevant experience, to provide information on their products and services on matters identified in this activity	Technical report on scenarios for climate impact assessment	SBSTA 26
• Request the Secretariat to organize an expert meeting on this activity with participation of experts and representatives from relevant organizations	• Summary Report of the Expert Meeting	Before SBSTA 27
• Request the Secretariat to prepare a summary report on the main results of this activity	• Input into summary progress report referred to in paragraph 7 of the conclusions	SBSTA 28

<table>
<tr><td colspan="3">A (iv). Promoting understanding of impacts of, and vulnerability to, climate change, current and future climate variability and extreme events, and the implications for sustainable development</td></tr>
<tr><td colspan="3">Activities</td></tr>
<tr><td colspan="3">• Enhance capacity and ability to predict extreme events and analyse their impacts.
• Enhance capacity to use information on extreme events and their impacts, including use this information to analyse their impacts, including assessment of climate related risks, impact thresholds, trends and implications for sustainable development
• Share and use of information on, and analysis of, experiences in climate risks assessment and management
• Promote the analysis, interpretation and prediction of the occurrence of extreme events, analysis of their impacts and the further development of tools and systems for these purposes</td></tr>
<tr><td>Modalities</td><td>Deliverables</td><td>Timing</td></tr>
<tr><td>• Request the Secretariat, under the guidance of the Chair of the SBSTA, to organize a workshop with participation of Parties, experts and relevant organizations to consider current climate variability, extreme events, existing predictive capacities across regions and hazards as well as relating changes in extreme events under climate change and implications for sustainable development</td><td>• Summary Report of the workshop</td><td>SBSTA 26</td></tr>
<tr><td>• Request the Secretariat to prepare a summary report on the main results of this activity</td><td>• Input into summary progress report referred to in paragraph 7 of the conclusions</td><td>SBSTA 28</td></tr>
<tr><td colspan="3">A (v). Promoting the availability of information on the socio-economic aspects of climate change and improving the integration of socio-economic information into impact and vulnerability assessments</td></tr>
<tr><td colspan="3">Activities</td></tr>
<tr><td colspan="3">• A stock-take on what socio-economic information and approaches are available (and being used), and what needs to be done to ensure for better integration of socio-economic information, into:
• developing socio-economic scenarios
• vulnerability and adaptive capacity assessment
• adaptation costing and planning</td></tr>
</table>

Modalities	Deliverables	Timing
• Invite structured submissions from Parties and relevant organizations on matters relating to the availability and use of socio-economic information for scenarios, vulnerability and adaptive capacity assessment, adaptation costing and planning with a view to identifying: - Existing approaches and available data - Needs and gaps - Ways and means to improve availability and access to relevant information as well as the integration	• Miscellaneous document on information from parties	SBSTA 25
Request the Secretariat to prepare a synthesis report based on the above information	• Technical report, based on the information provided by submissions with recommendations	SBSTA 26
• Request the secretariat to organize an expert meeting on means and ways to improve the integration of socio-economic information into impact and vulnerability assessments and adaptation planning, taking the above synthesis report into account	• Summary Report on the expert meeting	Before SBSTA 27
• Request the Secretariat to prepare a summary report on the main results of this activity	• Input into summary progress report referred to in paragraph 7 of the conclusions	SBSTA 28
B (ii). Collecting, analysing and disseminating information on past and current practical adaptation actions and measures, including adaptation projects, short- and long-term adaptation strategies, and local and indigenous knowledge *B (iv). Facilitating communication and cooperation among and between Parties and relevant organizations, business, civil society, and decision makers, and other stakeholders*		

<table>
<tr><th colspan="3">Activities</th></tr>
<tr><td colspan="3">• Exchange of information on experiences, lessons learned, constraints and barriers of past and current adaptation measures and actions, and the implications for sustainable development, and derive recommendations for enhancing adaptation measures and actions
• Establishment of a web-based interface for dissemination of information on existing experiences and case studies on adaptation planning, measures and actions, taking into account existing sectoral, national and other relevant databases and information sources
• Promotion of different ways and means for information sharing and for the enhancement of cooperation among Parties and relevant institutions and communities, including the provision of a forum to exchange information between Parties and relevant communities, in particular sectoral, disaster risk reduction and management communities.
• Promotion of understanding of response strategies, including early warning systems, local coping strategies and lessons learned that can be applied elsewhere
• Assessment of available resources to support adaptation and address barriers and constraints to its implementation</td></tr>
<tr><th>Modalities</th><th>Deliverables</th><th>Timing</th></tr>
<tr><td>• Invite inputs from Parties and relevant organizations through structured submissions on adaptation approaches, practices and technologies at the regional, national and local levels in different sectors, as well as on needs and concerns</td><td></td><td>SBSTA 25</td></tr>
<tr><td>Request the Secretariat to make the inputs available on the UNFCCC website</td><td>• Information on website</td><td>SBSTA 26</td></tr>
<tr><td>Request the Secretariat to prepare a synthesis report based on submissions from Parties</td><td>• Synthesis report on submissions from Parities</td><td>SBSTA 27</td></tr>
<tr><td>• Invite inputs from the LEG, CGE and EGTT on matters identified in this activity</td><td>• Synthesis report on inputs from the LEG, CGE and EGTT</td><td>SBSTA 26</td></tr>
</table>

• Provide a forum for the exchange of information on the contribution of existing adaptation practices and traditional knowledge to the work on impacts and vulnerability assessment and adaptation	Summary report on information provided at the forum	As of SBSTA 26
• Considering the synthesis report and inputs from the LEG, CGE and EGTT, the SBSTA to decide upon possible follow-up activities, including workshop(s), publications and a web-based information interface	Synthesis report with recommendations for follow-up activities	SBSTA 28
• Request the Secretariat to prepare a summary report on the main results of this activity	• Input into summary progress report referred to in paragraph 7 of the conclusions	SBSTA 28

B (iii). Promoting research on adaptation options and the development and diffusion of technologies, know-how and practices for adaptation, particularly addressing identified adaptation priorities and building on lessons learned from current adaptation projects and strategies		
Activities		
• Analysis of opportunities and ways to promote research and development of adaptive capacities and adaptation practices that increase resilience		
Modalities	Deliverables	Timing
• Consider research relevant to this activity in future work under the agenda item on the research and systematic observation	Synthesis report on relevant research	SBSTA 26
• Request the Secretariat to extract and synthesize information on ongoing and planned adaptation research as well as research needs identified in submissions from Parties and relevant organizations under this activity	• Synthesis report on adaptation and research needs	
• Request the Secretariat to prepare a summary report on the main results of this activity	• Input into summary progress report referred to in paragraph 7 of the conclusions	SBSTA 28

B (iii). Promoting research on adaptation options and the development and diffusion of technologies, know-how and practices for adaptation, particularly addressing identified adaptation priorities and building on lessons learned from current adaptation projects and strategies		
Activities		
• Enhancement of work on different aspects of technologies and know-how for adaptation, as well as on opportunities for their transfer and diffusion, taking into account local and indigenous knowledge and experience as well as ongoing activities and projects		
Modalities	Deliverables	Timing
• Request the Secretariat to extract and synthesize examples of adaptation technologies identified in submissions from Parties and relevant organizations under activity 6	Technical report on adaptation technologies identified in submissions from Parties and relevant organizations under activity 6	Before SBSTA 26
• The SBSTA to consider the recommendations of the EGTT on the technical paper on technology for adaptation and the outcome of the SBSTA 25 EGTT side event, the synthesis of technology needs assessments for adaptation, and previous work relating to adaptation technologies in the national adaptation programme of actions, and to decide upon possible follow-up activities under the programme of work on adaptation	Technical report on recommendations from the EGTT with recommendations for follow-up activities	SBSTA 26
• Request the Secretariat to prepare a summary report on the main results of this activity	Input into summary progress report referred to in paragraph 7 of the conclusions	SBSTA 28

B (v). Promoting understanding and the development and dissemination of measures, methodologies and tools, including for economic diversification, aimed at increasing economic resilience and reducing reliance on vulnerable economic sectors, especially for the relevant categories of countries listed in Article 4, paragraph 8, of the Convention
Activities
• Exchange of experiences and opportunities on the development and dissemination of measures, methodologies and tools aimed at increasing economic resilience

Modalities	Deliverables	Timing
• Invite Parties and relevant organizations to provide information on examples of measures to increase economic resilience of vulnerable sectors		SBSTA 26
Request the secretariat to prepare a synthesis report	• Synthesis report	Before SBSTA 27
• Request the Secretariat to prepare a summary report on the main results of this activity	• Input into summary progress report referred to in paragraph 7 of the conclusions	SBSTA 28

1. The SBSTA Chair, in consultation with representative experts from parties should ensure that the deliverables of the Programme of Work, as set out above, pursues its objectives and outcomes as contained in the Annex to decision 2/CP 11 and provide a solid basis for the implementation of the Five-Year Programme of Work. These deliverables, as described above, should contain concrete information that will inform users at different levels on:
   (a) Analysis of the issues as addressed by the activity, including current status and lessons learned;
   (b) Identifications of gaps, needs (including any capacity needs), barriers, and constraints;
   (c) Options on ways and means on how to practically address identified needs and gaps;
   (d) Practical recommendations on how to implement the options identified in paragraph c, by parties and users, at all levels.
2. The SBSTA should request the Secretariat, subject to the availability of resources, to widely disseminate by effective means, the deliverables resulting from the specific activities, to the appropriate target audiences.
3. The SBSTA should request the Secretariat, under the guidance of the Chair of the SBSTA, to prepare progress reports on the results of the activities undertaken, to be presented to SBSTA, at each meeting from SBSTA 25 through to SBSTA 27, in order that the SBSTA may begin to consider further activities as well as appropriate timing and modalities for their inclusion in the programme of work at SBSTA 28.
4. The SBSTA should the Secretariat, under the guidance of the Chair of the SBSTA, to prepare a summary progress report on the activities undertaken, with recommendations for further activities as well as appropriate timing and modalities, for consideration by SBSTA at its twenty-eighth session (June 2008) as provided in decision 2/CP11, paragraph 6 (d).

5. The SBSTA should request parties, before SBSTA 25, to submit to the Secretariat, suggested draft terms of reference for a group or groups of experts to provide technical advice and support in the implementation of the programme of work.
6. The SBSTA should request the Secretariat to synthesise these submissions for consideration by SBSTA 25 with a view to preparing a recommendation inviting the COP at its twelfth session, to adopt a decision on the formulation of the work of this group or groups of experts.

G-77 and China Presentation on Agenda Item 7 of SBSTA and Agenda Item 11 of SBI Durban, 35th Session of the Subsidiary Bodies
1 December 2011

Introduction

Agenda item 7 of the SBSTA and agenda item 11 of the SBI: "Forum on the impact of the implementation of response measures at the thirty-fourth and thirty-fifth sessions of the subsidiary bodies, with the objective of developing a work programme under the Subsidiary Body for Scientific and Technological Advice and the Subsidiary Body for Implementation to address these impacts, with a view to adopting, at the seventeenth session of the Conference of the Parties, modalities for the operationalization of the work programme and a possible forum on response measures"
(footnote: Decision 1. CP/16, para. 93)

Introduction

- Economic and social consequences of response measures is an important issue for all developing countries, as adverse impacts of response measures constitute an additional burden that developing countries should not have to bear.
- All developing countries face economic and social consequences of response measures actual and potential).
- Response measures impact on developing countries in different ways.
- Responses to climate change should be coordinated with social and economic development in an integrated manner, with a view to avoiding adverse impacts on the latter, taking into full account the legitimate priority needs of developing countries for the achievement of sustained economic growth and the eradication of poverty.

Framework

When dealing with social and economic consequences of response measures, there is a need to:

- respect the principles and provisions of the Convention, in particular articles relevant to this issue
- respect the Bali Action Plan
- implement decision 1.CP/16, paragraph 93
- take duly into consideration the specific needs and concerns of developing country parties

Content and modalities for the work programme to address the impact of the implementation of response measures

Mandate for development of WP: "*Further decides to provide a forum on the impact of the implementation of response measures, and to that end requests the Chairs of the Subsidiary Body for Scientific and Technological Advice and the Subsidiary Body for Implementation to convene such a forum at the thirty-fourth and thirty-fifth sessions of these bodies, with the objective of* developing a work programme under the subsidiary bodies to address these impacts, *with a view to adopting, at the seventeenth session of the Conference of the Parties, modalities for the operationalization of the work programme and a possible forum on response* measures" [1]

- [1] 1. CP/16, paragraph 93

a) Objective and scope of the work programme

- There is a need for a work programme to address the economic and social consequences of response measures taken by developed country parties on developing country parties.
- This work programme would:

  Give full consideration to what actions are necessary to meet the specific needs and concerns of developing country parties arising from the impact of the implementation of response measures

- Promote understanding about the nature and magnitude of economic and social consequences for developing country parties of different response measures taken by developed country parties
- Gather and share information on what the potential magnitude of problem will be for planning purposes

- Assist developing country parties in identifying and addressing the impact of response measures taken by developed country parties, and share information on this specific matter
- Promote and cooperate on issues relating to response strategies and explore ways to minimize negative consequences for developing country parties

(b) Activities and milestones of the work programme

- Discuss the negative economic and social consequences of response measures on developing country parties, to assess the specific impacts of already implemented and planned RM on developing countries, taking into account their special circumstances and constraints.
- Identify ways and means to minimize those negative economic and social consequences
- Discuss the consequences of trade-related response measures

  "The Parties should cooperate to promote a supportive and open international economic system that would lead to sustainable economic growth and development in all Parties, particularly developing country Parties, thus enabling them better to address the problems of climate change. Measures taken to combat climate change, including unilateral ones, should not constitute a means of arbitrary or unjustifiable discrimination or a disguised restriction on international trade" (article 3.5 of the UNFCCC)

- Facilitate technical collaboration among parties and experts on tools, including studies, modelling, and methodologies, to assist developing country parties in addressing economic and social consequences of response measures
- Explore activities related to the following: *"Also urges developed country Parties to strive to implement policies and measures to respond to climate change in such a way as to avoid negative social and economic consequences for developing country Parties, taking into account Article 3 of the Convention, and to assist these Parties to address such consequences by providing support, including financial resources, transfer of technology and capacity-building, in accordance with Article 4 of the Convention, to build up the resilience of societies and economies negatively affected by response measures"* [1] (activities to facilitate assistance, through technologies and capacity-building to strengthen resilience and foster economic diversification in developing countries).

- [1] 1. CP/16, paragraph 89

(c) Management of WP Stakeholder engagement

- Invite inputs for the activities of the work programme from, *inter alia*,
  - Parties
  - regional and international organizations

- civil society
- private sector
- academia, and
- experts

(d) Review and possible further activities

- Review of ongoing and new WP activities, as appropriate.

(e) Links to the existing processes (e.g., national communications, a possible forum)

- The information presented in national communications on negative consequences of response measures (actual and potential) on developing country parties could serve as a valuable input to the WP.
- The forum will implement the activities of the WP.

Content of and modalities for a possible forum on response measures

- Mandate: *"Further decides to provide a forum on the impact of the implementation of response measures, and to that end requests the Chairs of the Subsidiary Body for Scientific and Technological Advice and the Subsidiary Body for Implementation to convene such a forum at the thirty-fourth and thirty-fifth sessions of these bodies, with the objective of developing a work programme under the subsidiary bodies to address these impacts, with a view to adopting, at the seventeenth session of the Conference of the Parties, modalities for the operationalization of the work programme and* a possible forum on response measures" [1].

- [1] 1. CP/16, paragraph 93

a) Role, form, scope, and functions of a possible forum

- The role of the possible forum would be:
- To give full consideration to what actions are necessary to meet the specific needs and concerns of developing country parties arising from the impact of the implementation of response measures.
- To provide a platform for interactive and constructive discussion and direct exchange among parties on consequences of response measures taken by developed country parties on developing country parties
- To implement the activities and objectives of the work programme described above.

(b) Organization of a possible forum

- Participation: Open to all parties and international organizations, civil society, private sector, academia, and experts in accordance with the UNFCCC practices and guidelines
- Duration: ongoing until completion of its work programme
- Frequency: Meetings twice a year, in conjunction with the Subsidiary Bodies

(c) Relationship with COP/SBs

- Report annually to the COP on its activities and progress
- Give recommendations to the COP on future work

(d) Links to existing processes

- The information presented in national communications on negative consequences of response measures (actual and potential) on developing country parties could serve as a valuable input to the WP undertaken under the forum
- There would also be links to IPCC

Thank you very much for your attention!

Submission from the Group of 77 and China* General Guidelines for Domestic Measurement, Reporting, and Verification of Domestically Supported Nationally Appropriate Mitigation Actions by Developing Country Parties

Principles of Guidelines

The guidelines are to be general, voluntary, pragmatic, non-prescriptive, non-intrusive, and country-driven, take into account national circumstances and national priorities, respect the diversity of nationally appropriate mitigation actions, build on existing domestic systems and capacities, recognize existing domestic measurement, reporting and verification systems and promote a cost-effective approach (FCCC/SBSTA/2012/5, paragraph 89).

Purpose

The purpose is to provide general guidelines, for the voluntary use by developing countries, based on the agreed principles above to describe the domestic MRV of domestically supported NAMAs.

* Contained in document FCCC/SBSTA/2013/MISC.7/Add.1 of 12 June 2013.

Recognising, using and reporting on domestic verification of NAMAs
Developing countries are encouraged to utilise existing domestic systems, including domestically available information, methodologies, experts, and other aspects;

Where they exist, recognise existing domestic verification systems, if appropriate, and encourage domestic verification processes, thereby enhancing cost-effectiveness including adverse impacts and costs of mitigation. Otherwise, developing country parties may wish to put in place domestic verification processes, as necessary, for their domestically supported nationally appropriate mitigation actions.

Support
Decides that in accordance with article 4.3 of the Convention developed country parties shall provide enhanced support to interested developing countries, including financial, technical, and capacity-building, and addressing specific capacity-building needs as determined nationally, including the training of domestic experts and local practitioners in applying best available approaches.

Chair of G-77 and China

Submission by G-77 and China on the Impact of the Implementation of Response Measures (Agenda Item SBSTA 10. a and SBI 15 a.)-SBS 40 Sessions, 11 June 2014

I) RESULTS OF THE REVIEW OF THE WORK OF THE FORUM:

The G-77 and China reaffirms the need to explore ways to avoid and minimize negative economic and social consequences of response measures taken by developed countries on developing countries. This should be done in accordance with the principles and provisions of the Convention, in particular its articles 3.1, 3.4, 3.5, 4.1. g) and h), 4.3, 4.5, 4.7, 4.8, 4.9, and 4.10 of the Convention, and articles 2.3 and 3.14 of the Kyoto Protocol and in the broader context of the achievement of sustainable development in its economic, social, and environmental dimensions, as well as well poverty eradication.

Based on the review of the work of the forum, the G-77 and China notes the progress made in the forum, while recognizing that there are still implementation gaps to give full consideration to what actions are necessary under the Convention, including actions related to funding, insurance, and the transfer of technology, to meet the specific needs and concerns of developing countries arising from the impact of the implementation of response measures. Moreover, developed countries are not fulfilling their obligations under the Convention and Kyoto Protocol in terms of minimizing the adverse effects of response measures on developing countries, particularly those under articles 4.8 and 4.9 under the Convention, and in line with relevant COP decisions. During the work programme of the forum, we had the opportunity to have a first exchange of general views, and the G-77 and China made a lot of proposals in this regard that still merit attention and further discussion. Even if the forum has proved useful for exchange of experiences, it has been incapable of taking specific actions to address implementation gaps to avoid and minimize negative economic and social consequences of response measures.

The importance of this issue was proven by the great number of parties that submitted their views, such as the G-77 and China. The Group engaged constructively in all the sessions of the forum, including through G-77 and China presentations and statements in all the areas of the work program, supported by different G-77 and China regional groupings and individual delegations. In addition to those presentations and statements, the reports of the workshops and expert meetings and discussions held during the forum[10] are also useful as a summary of the rich views and experiences presented by developing countries and were considered as part of the review.

Although there was participation from experts, civil society and international organizations, many of them were not focused sufficiently on specific needs of developing countries. Therefore, for future work there needs to be clear guidance and terms of reference in terms of invitation to organizations and experts whose work is related to the issue of economic and social consequences of response measures, in particular to the avoidance and minimization of adverse effects of response measures on developing countries.

In addition, considering the importance of the issue for all developing countries, there needs to be dedicated time to address the negative economic and social consequences of response measures on developing countries. Thus, the workstreams on the issue should continue to meet at least twice a year, in conjunction with Subsidiary Bodies and the COP.

Finally, we would like to share our main proposals we made in each of the areas of the work programme, as part of the review of the work of the forum mandated by decision 8/CP.17, review that was completed in Warsaw during the many sessions that were dedicated to the matter. In this way, the gaps of implementation identified on the basis of the review of the work of the forum by the G-77 and China are the following:

[10] FCCC/SB/2013/INF.2, FCCC/SB/2013/INF.3, FCCC/SB/2013/INF.4, FCCC/SB/2013/INF.8, FCCC/SB/2013/INF.9, FCCC/SB/2013/INF.10, FCCC/SB/2013/INF.11, FCCC/SB/2013/MISC.2, and FCCC/SB/2013/MISC.4.

RESULTS OF THE REVIEW OF THE WORK OF THE AREAS OF THE WORK PROGRAM OF THE FORUM

AREA A: Sharing of information and expertise, including reporting and promoting understanding of positive and negative impacts of response measures

The G-77 and China expressed that there is a lack of clear reporting guidelines. We showed that in the national communications of Annex I (AI) parties, few of those parties reported, and of those that reported, some reported purely domestic efforts as technology cooperation, and others only described their measures. Particularly, there is a lack of reporting guidelines for Annex I parties on how they ". . . shall strive to implement policies and measures in such a way as to minimize adverse effects on developing country Parties . . ." (arts. 2.3 and 3.14 of the Kyoto Protocol (KP)).

Therefore, it is crucial to elaborate specific reporting guidelines for AI parties on this issue.

AREA B: Cooperation on response strategies

The issue of economic and social consequences of response measures, and in particular, of cooperation strategies, has to be seen in the broader context of the achievement of sustainable development (in its economic, social and environmental dimensions) and poverty eradication, in accordance with nationally defined priorities.

Cooperation on response strategies needs to be done in accordance with the principles and provisions of the UNFCCC, in particular preambular paragraphs 3, 17, 21, 22, and articles 3.1, 3.4, 3.5, 4.1. g) and h), 4.3, 4.5, 4.7, 4.8 of the Convention, and articles 2.3 and 3.14 of KP.

What actions could help to foster this cooperation on response strategies?

- Exchange of views, sharing information and expertise to inform policy choices of response measures taken by developed country parties (and which ones would avoid and minimize economic and social consequences of response measures on developing countries)
- Facilitation of technical collaboration among parties and experts on tools, including studies, modelling and methodologies, to assist developing country parties in addressing economic and social consequences of response measures
- Cooperation of modelling teams among parties, to seek consensus on methodology development and scenarios setting and for models to take into account the specific national economic and social conditions of developing countries

- Partnership with organizations in the research and assessment of developing countries' concerns and needs rising from the impacts of the implementation of response measures
- Cooperation under the Convention to enhance the reporting of Annex I countries of the impacts of their response measures on developing countries, and how they are minimizing the adverse effects on developing countries.

Finally, it is important to ensure capacity-building for developing countries as well as to strengthen multilateralism, in opposition to unilateral measures that undermine the spirit of cooperation and dialogue.

AREA C: Assessment and analysis of impacts

There is a need to research and assess the economic and social impacts of response measures, including unilateral ones. In this context, there is a need for developed countries to undertake an assessment in the design and implementation of their response measures, including unilateral ones, on the economic and social consequences of those measures on developing countries, in order to strive to minimize these impacts on, *inter alia*, employment, income, economic growth rates, and living standards in developing countries.

The assessment should include:

- if the measure is consistent with UNFCCC principles and provisions
- if there has been consultation to potentially affected developing country parties and if their special conditions have been duly taken into account
- if the measure is based on scientific evidence
- if the measures has a legitimate objective, like combating climate change
- if the measure is the most effective means to achieve the objective of combating climate change and the less trade restrictive
  if there is a fulfilment of developed countries' obligations related to the provision of specific support to developing countries (transfer of technology, financial resources, and capacity-building)
- the assessment should be undertaken both in quantitative and qualitative terms and *ex ante* and *ex post* and take into account the specific national conditions of developing countries and their priorities, needs and circumstances

AREA D: Exchanging experience and discussion of opportunities for economic diversification and transformation

Economic transformation and diversification entail high adjustment costs for developing countries, as their economies are generally characterized by a low economic diversification. They have traditionally relied heavily on the production and exports of commodities whose production is particularly vulnerable to climate change.

Also, the costs of clean technologies remain prohibitive for those countries.

In consequence, this area is an opportunity to exchange views, experiences, lessons learned on national cases and for specific action for economic transformation and diversification in the context of nationally defined priorities, circumstances, and needs.

Moreover, developed countries obligations' in terms of support of financial resources, transfer of technology and capacity-building to developing countries need to be fulfilled in order to assist developing countries in that economic diversification.

AREA E: Economic Modelling and Socio-economic Trends

Economic modelling can provide accurate and objective assessment of the observed and potential economic and social consequences of response measures taken by developed country parties on developing country parties and it can produce quantitative assessment which will be complemented by qualitative assessment.

Modelling is useful to produce specific assessment on different sectors of the economy such as tourism, industry, agriculture, etc., and on consequences of response measures of developed country parties' on, *inter alia*, trade, investment, income, employment, economic growth rates of developing countries.

Therefore, it is essential to elaborate models that reflect the circumstances and contexts of developing countries, by accommodating variables that capture the uniqueness of national characteristics, taking into account their social and socioeconomic factors and specific national priorities, conditions and needs.

Activities that could be carried out:

- Dissemination of modelling tools
- Ensuring increased collaboration on modelling developments on an ongoing basis
- Identify vulnerable sectors and needs in terms of technology transfer and funding (related to for example, articles 4.3, 4.5, 4.7, and 4.8 of UNFCCC)

AREA F: The relevant aspects relating to the implementation of decisions 1/CP.10, 1/CP.13, and 1/CP.16 and article 2, paragraph 3, and article 3, paragraph 14, of the Kyoto Protocol

There are implementation gaps in relation to these articles and decisions, in order to address the specific needs and concerns of developing countries related to the impact of the implementation of response measures.

There is a need to focus on these gaps in the implementation in order to give full consideration to what actions are necessary under the Convention, including action related to funding, insurance, and transfer of technology, to meet the specific needs and concerns of developing countries arising from the impact of the implementation of response measures.

Therefore, there is a need for a structured follow-up of the implementation gaps and concrete actions to ensure full implementation of, *inter alia*, the decisions mentioned in area F, that is, 1/CP.10, 1/CP.13, and 1/CP.16 and article 2, paragraph 3, and article 3, paragraph 14, of the Kyoto Protocol. In addition, there is a need to ensure the implementation of decisions 5/CP.7, 2/CP.17, 1/CP.18, and 31/CMP.1, and the relevant principles and provisions of the Convention, in particular its article 3, paragraphs 1 and 5, and article 4, paragraphs 1(g) and (h), 8, 9, and 10.

AREA G: Just transition of the workforce and the creation of decent work and quality jobs

What actions are needed?

- Minimize hardships for workers ensuring them the continuation of their employment and building capacities for their integration in the context of the structural transformation derived from action related to climate change.
- Development of mechanisms for a just transition and creation of decent work through a consultation process involving the relevant stakeholders.

AREA H: Building collective and individual learning towards a transition to a low greenhouse gas emitting society

Any transition needs to be understood in the broader context of the transition towards sustainable development and parties' different national socio-economic contexts, specific conditions, and unique circumstances. It has also to be consistent with the principles and provisions of the Convention, in particular the principle of common but differentiated responsibilities.

Moreover, any transition should take into account the overriding priorities of developing countries in terms of the achievement of economic and social development and poverty eradication.

What actions are needed?

- Capacity-building, transfer of technologies, and financial resources for learning and for development of endogenous capacities in developing countries, in order for them to meet the agreed full incremental costs of implementing measures (relation to articles 4.3, 4.5, and 4.7 of the Convention).
- Exchange of experiences, information, knowledge-sharing, and know-how, and of ensuring access to affordable technologies for developing countries for implementation of NAMAs and NAPAs.

- Assessment of the role of the protection of intellectual property rights (IPR) in terms of transfer of technology.

Based on the review of the work of the forum completed in Warsaw, we clearly note there is much work still to be done to meet the needs and concerns of developing countries in terms of negative economic and social consequences of response measures taken by developed countries on developing countries.

To sum up, on the basis of the review, it is clear there are gaps of implementation in terms of, *inter alia*, reporting by AI parties on response measures; technical collaboration on modelling and methodologies; ways to strengthen multilateralism, in opposition to unilateral measures; assessment in the design and implementation of the response measures of developed countries of the economic and social consequences of those measures on developing countries, in order to strive to minimize adverse impacts; support to developing countries for economic diversification and in terms of transfer of technology, funding, and capacity-building; and the development of mechanisms for a just transition and creation of decent work.

Therefore, we propose the continuation of the forum, in terms of sharing experiences, information, and lessons learned on areas to address the needs of developing countries, at the same time that there is a need for specific action through the establishment of a Mechanism for Enhanced Action on Response Measures under the COP. This Mechanism will facilitate implementation of enhanced action to address the negative social and economic consequences of response measures taken by developed country parties on developing country parties and to recommend specific actions, including in terms of support to developing countries, to avoid and minimize those consequences, and to deliver the functions as contained in the G-77 and China submission.

II) SUBMISSION BY THE G-77 AND CHINA ON A DRAFT DECISION ON THE IMPACT OF THE IMPLEMENTATION OF RESPONSE MEASURES (AGENDA ITEM SBSTA 10.a AND SBI 15.a.) FOR ITS ADOPTION AT COP-20

The Conference of the Parties,

Recalling decisions 5/CP.7, 1/CP.10, 1/CP.13, 1/CP.16, 2/CP.17, 8/CP.17, 1/CP.18, and 31/CMP.1, the objective, principles, and provisions of the Convention, in particular article 3, paragraphs 1 and 5, and article 4, paragraphs 1(g) and (h), 8, 9, and 10, of the Convention, and article 2, paragraph 3, and article 3, paragraph 14, of the Kyoto Protocol,

Reaffirming that economic and social development and poverty eradication are the first and overriding priorities of developing countries, and that developing country parties face economic and social consequences of response measures to climate change,

Stressing the need for an effective mechanism for enhanced action to address the social and economic consequences of the implementation of response measures,

Acknowledging that the objective of enhanced action to deal with the social and economic consequences of the implementation of response measures is to address the negative social and economic consequences of response measures taken by developed country parties on developing country parties,

Affirming that parties should cooperate fully to enhance understanding of the economic and social consequences of response measures, and further reaffirming the need to consider how existing channels, such as national communications and biennial reports by developed country parties, could be improved and built upon,

Recalling the constructive discussions that took place during the meetings under the work programme on the impact of the implementation of response measures held in conjunction with the thirty-sixth, thirty-seventh, thirty-eighth, and thirty-ninth sessions of the subsidiary bodies,

Acknowledging that the work of the forum on the impact of the implementation of response measures has provided opportunities to engage in in-forum workshops, an expert meeting and valuable initial discussions by parties, in order to improve the understanding of the impact of the implementation of response measures in the areas of the work programme referred to in decision 8/CP.17, paragraph 1,

Noting that parties concluded the review pursuant to decision 8/CP.17, paragraph 5, and that this review indicated that it is important to improve the need for a more focused consideration of the effectiveness of the process and the substantive consideration of the issues in terms of addressing the specific needs and concerns of developing countries in relation to the impact of the implementation of response measures,

Recognizing the need to focus future work under the forum on the impact of the implementation of response measures on expert input, the provision of concrete examples, case studies, and practices, in order to enhance the capacity of developing country parties to deal with the negative impacts of the implementation of response measures,

Welcoming the progress made in the work of the forum on the impact of the implementation of response measures convened under the Subsidiary Body for Implementation and the Subsidiary Body for Scientific and Technological Advice, and recognizing the need for parties to continue to participate in the forum, including the sharing of views on policy issues of concern, such as unilateral measures,

Recognizing the need to give full consideration to what actions are necessary under the Convention, including actions related to funding, insurance, and the transfer of technology, to meet the specific needs and concerns of developing country parties arising from the impact of the implementation of response measures,

Affirming that there are still gaps in implementation related to how developed country parties are implementing their policies and measures to respond to climate change in such a way as to avoid negative social and economic consequences for developing country parties and that there is a need for further work and specific action, building on the forum on the impact of the implementation of response measures and its work programme,

1. *Decides to* hereby continue the forum on the impact of the implementation of response measures in order for it to provide a platform allowing parties to share, in an interactive manner, information, experiences, case studies, best practices, and views,
2. *Decides* that the forum shall be convened by the Chairs of the subsidiary bodies to implement the work programme included in the Annex A and meet twice a year in conjunction with the sessions of the subsidiary bodies,
3. *Reiterates* that the forum will be convened under a joint agenda item of the subsidiary bodies and will operate in accordance with the procedures applicable to contact groups,
4. *Requests* the subsidiary bodies to review, at their forty-fifth sessions (December 2016), the work of the forum, with a view to providing recommendations to the Conference of the parties at its twenty-second session,
5. *Adopts* the modalities for the operationalization of the work programme on the impact of the implementation of response measures, which could include, as appropriate and subject to the availability of financial resources, convening workshops, and meetings, receiving inputs from experts, practitioners, and relevant organizations, and preparing reports and technical papers,
6. *Requests* participants in the forum to focus on enhancing understanding and building the capacity of developing countries to deal with the negative economic and social consequences of response measures on those countries through the provision of support and discussion of concrete examples, case studies, and practices,
7. *Decides* to establish a Mechanism for Enhanced Action on Response Measures under the Conference of the Parties to facilitate implementation of enhanced action to address the negative social and economic consequences of response measures taken by developed country parties on developing country parties and to recommend specific actions, including in terms of support to

developing countries, to avoid and minimize those consequences, and to deliver the functions as included in Annex B,

8. *Decides* that the forum will report to the Mechanism and that the Mechanism will make recommendations and report to the Conference of the Parties annually on its work with a view for adopting relevant decisions,
9. *Further decides* that the Mechanism will report to the Conference of the Parties on its review of its work, including functions and further actions that may be required, starting in COP-25 and every five years thereafter, with a view to provide recommendations and adopt relevant decisions,
10. *Decides* that the Mechanism will meet for the first time in the first half of 2015 and shall continue to meet at least twice a year, in conjunction with Subsidiary Bodies and the COP,
11. *Decides* that the Mechanism will engage and develop linkages and synergies with relevant work programmes, bodies, and institutions under the Convention,
12. *Further decides* that the Mechanism will collaborate with relevant intergovernmental, regional, national, and subnational level institutions, organizations, networks, and centers,
13. *Requests* parties to undertake the necessary arrangements at the forty-first session of the Subsidiary Bodies (December 2014) to finalize the development of the terms of reference of the Mechanism, including its membership and participation as contained in Annex C below, and its modalities of operationalization, with the view to providing recommendations to the Conference of the Parties.

Annex A: Elements to be included in the new work programme of the forum

- Dialogue on assessment and analysis of adverse impacts of response measures, including unilateral ones, in terms of their consequences for, *inter alia*, employment, income, economic growth rates, and living standards in developing countries; and explore ways to minimize adverse impacts of response measures
- Ways to strengthen multilateral cooperation, in opposition to unilateral measures
- Overview of progress on activities to address adverse economic and social consequences of response measures on developing countries made at various levels, including bilateral, regional, and multilateral;
- Economic diversification and resilience-building in developing country parties, to deal with the adverse impacts of response measures;
- Exchange of views on just transition and creation of decent work, in accordance with nationally defined development priorities and strategies;
- Dialogue on how developed countries report on actions and impacts related to the implementation of response measures, in such a way as to minimize adverse impacts.

Annex B: Functions of the Mechanism (to be further elaborated in TORs)

- Development of methodologies and tools for the assessment and analysis of adverse impacts of response measures, including unilateral ones, in terms of their consequences for, *inter alia*, employment, income, economic growth rates, and living standards in developing countries; and explore ways to minimize adverse impacts of response measures;
- Provision of specific support by developed country parties to developing country parties in terms of transfer of technology, financial resources, and capacity-building, in order for the latter to be able to deal with the adverse economic and social effects of response measures;
- Capacity-building and support for developing countries for economic diversification and resilience-building to deal with the adverse impacts of response measures;
- Capacity-building and assessments on ways to ensuring a just transition and creation of decent work, in accordance with nationally defined priorities;
- Capacity-building related to economic modelling, studies, methodology development, scenario-setting, and technology transfer to assist developing country parties in addressing the negative economic and social consequences of response measures;
- Development of specific guidelines for developed countries on how to report on actions and impacts related to the implementation of response measures, in such a way as to minimize adverse impacts;
- Cooperation at various levels, including at bilateral level, with regional and multilateral organizations, experts and institutions, to address adverse economic and social consequences of response measures on developing countries;
- Secretariat to develop a structured and user-friendly repository of information on response measures.

Annex C: Membership and participation

1. The Mechanism shall comprise 16 members, who shall serve in their personal capacity, as follows:
   - 2 members from each of the 5 United Nations regional groups (Africa, Asia Pacific, Latin America and Caribbean, Eastern European Group, Western European and Other Groups)
   - 1 member from a Small Island Developing State
   - 1 member from a least developed country party
   - 2 members from parties included in Annex I to the Convention
   - 2 members from parties not included in Annex I to the Convention
2. The Mechanism shall elect annually a Chair and a Vice-Chair from among its members for a term of one year each, with one being a member from an Annex I party and the other being a member from a non–Annex I party. The

positions of the Chair and Vice-Chair shall alternate annually between a member from an Annex I party and a member from a non–Annex I party.

3. Each member shall be elected by their regional groups to serve for two years.
4. Meetings shall be open to all parties in character of observers.
5. Meetings shall be open to attendance by accredited observer organizations, except where otherwise decided by the Mechanism by consensus.

G-77 and China Statement for the SBSTA Workshops on Early Warning Systems, June 2015

The G-77 and China had contributed positively during SBSTA-40 in paving the way for conducting these in-session workshops that will be held consecutively in SBSTA-42 and SBSTA-44 according to COP-20 decision. The Group will continue to engage constructively on the SBSTA-42 technical and scientific discussions, taking into account the conclusions of SBSTA-38, and towards the consideration at SBSTA-43 of the reports of both workshops. In this sense, the reports need to be comprehensive and to capture the views of developing country parties, taking into consideration that agriculture is the backbone of developing countries' and economic systems. In this context, there is an urgent need to increase the adaptive capacity of agriculture to deal with the adverse effects of climate change. This continues to be the key priority for developing countries in light of the particular vulnerabilities of the agricultural sector and its relationship with the livelihood of millions, food security, and poverty eradication.

On development of early warning systems and contingency plans:

The areas of early warning systems and risk assessments and vulnerability of agricultural systems merit specific attention, as there is enough evidence to support that climate change is increasing the frequency and intensity of adverse climatic events, such as torrential rains, long droughts, frost, and hail, among others, threatening seriously the future development of the agricultural production systems, according to conditions of each country or local area. Moreover, the increase of temperatures is generating favorable conditions for the proliferation and outbreak of pests and diseases that will make agriculture productive systems even more vulnerable.

Early warning systems coupled with contingency plans contribute immensely to Adaptation of Agriculture system in developing countries, particularly small holders. Due to diversity of agro-ecosystems, small holders and supporting institutions, taking them to the ground level needs huge investments and large-scale implementation strategies. If these plans are implemented, with supporting capacity-building at regional and sub-region level adaptive capacity of Agriculture Systems can be strongly enhanced.

Thus, extreme weather events are becoming more frequent and more severe, threatening the reliability and productivity of agriculture, exacerbating already extreme levels of poverty, and reinforcing persistent inequity and chronic undernutrition. There is scientific knowledge of climate change impacts on agriculture that have not yet been assessed, developed, and/or modelled either due to data limitations or shortcomings in conceptualizing the problem.

In this context, early warning systems are one of the major tools to reduce climate change impacts in agriculture, as they can estimate the probability of occurrence of risky climatic events, and help making decisions that prevent or reduce damages. At the same time, vulnerability assessments are necessary to identify risks and design appropriate measures to prevent or reduce the negative effects of climate change.

Due to the aforementioned, the G-77 and China considers that the SBSTA needs to address the following issues in order to assist developing countries on the areas covered by this workshop, taking into account the diversity of their agricultural systems and the differences in scale and the short, medium and long-term challenges:

- Provide access to scientific and technical information and means of implementation of early warning systems and contingency plans, including different information and communication technology (ICT) platforms and processes;
- Information, experience, tools, and technology of real-time monitoring, data visualization, data-sharing, and management;
- Assist governments and communities with expertise in developing early warning systems and contingency plans in relation to extreme weather events and their effects including models and technologies of early warning of extreme climatic events;
- Encourage the collaborative participation by farmers in any contingency plans in relation to extreme weather events and climate change that will affect them;
- Provide means of implementation to developing countries in the assessment of risk and vulnerability of agricultural systems to different climate change scenarios at regional, national, and local level, taking into consideration that developed countries should play a role in technology transfer and capacity-building for developing countries on adaptation;
- Enhancing regional systems that would remove barriers to the use and uptake of EWS messaging that would encompass; packaging of information appropriately to meet the needs of end users; timely access of EWS messages by end users;
- Downscaling of regional information to local level for actual actions; building capacity of the coordinating institutions, including technical, financial, and human; promoting and strengthening Public Private People Partnerships (PPPP) in the design and implementation of EWS;
- Support research in addressing climate change related contingency planning, risk and vulnerability assessment, and early warning systems, including in terms of potential economic impacts, for example, predictions of resulting impacts on agriculture production;

- Develop tools to analyse climate data and assess the risks and vulnerabilities of agricultural systems at regional, national, and local levels; according to different national and/or regional characteristics;
- Strengthen national systems for collecting, analysing, and disseminating risk and vulnerability data and information;
- Collect and establish accessible regional climate databases;
- Support research and development to promote better understanding of the trends as well as promote use of appropriate control and management methods for climate related pest and diseases;
- To develop more timely and accurate forecasting system for rainfall and inflow seasonally and annually.
- To support accurate forecasting of demand in agricultural products.

The G-77 and China countries believe there is a wide space for collaboration among parties in order to build better early warning systems, adapted to the local, national, and regional circumstances. There are also big opportunities to draw and share lessons from the experience of the different parties. Developed countries with high capacities can play a very positive role in the means of implementation with developing countries in addressing adaptation. Article 4.1.e. of the Convention stated clearly that parties should "Cooperate in preparing for adaptation to the impacts of climate change" among various issues including agriculture.

The G-77 remains on its position to undertake scientific and technical work on impacts of climate change impacts on agriculture consistent with SBSTA mandate in article 9 taking into account the commitments in articles 4.3, 4.4, 4.5 of the Convention.

G-77 and China Draft Intervention for SBSTA "Issues Relating to Agriculture" May 2016

The G-77 and China reaffirms its previous statements and presentations made under the SBSTA agenda item related to agriculture, recalling that the Group has contributed positively in paving the way for conducting the four in-session workshops under this agenda item, including the ones that were held in SBSTA-42. The Group will continue to engage constructively on the SBSTA-44 technical and scientific discussions, taking into account the conclusions of SBSTA 38, and towards the consideration at SBSTA 44 and 45 of the reports of the workshops.

The G-77 and China underlines that the report of the workshop need to be comprehensive and to capture the views of developing country parties, taking into consideration that agriculture is the backbone of developing countries and their economic systems. In this context, there is an urgent need to increase the adaptive capacity of agriculture to deal with the adverse effects of climate change. This continues to be the key priority for developing countries for SBSTA work, in light of the particular vulnerabilities of the agricultural sector and its relationship with the livelihood of millions, food security, and poverty eradication.

This is in line with the Paris Agreement, which recognizes the fundamental priority of safeguarding food security and ending hunger, and the particular vulnerabilities of food production systems to the adverse effects of climate change. As well, it is important to recall that the Agreement states in its objective that food production is not to be threatened.

On the issue of "identification of adaptation measures" to be addressed by this workshop, the Group believes it merits specific attention, as there is enough evidence to support that climate change is increasing the frequency and intensity of adverse climatic events, such as torrential rains, long droughts, frost, and hail, among others, threatening seriously the future development of the agricultural production systems, according to conditions of each country or local area. Moreover, the increase of temperatures is generating favorable conditions for the proliferation and outbreak of pests and diseases that will make agriculture productive systems even more vulnerable.

Extreme weather events are becoming more frequent and more severe, putting at risk the reliability and productivity of agriculture, exacerbating already extreme levels of poverty, and reinforcing persistent inequity and chronic undernutrition. The scientific knowledge of climate change impacts on agriculture have not yet been assessed, developed, and/or modelled either due to data limitations or shortcomings in conceptualizing.

The identification of adaptation measures and support to capacity-building are urgently needed in developing countries, particularly for smallholder farmers. Also, huge investments and large-scale implementation strategies are requested, taking them to the ground level, considering the diversity of agricultural systems, indigenous knowledge systems, and the differences in scale, as well as possible co-benefits.

The G-77 and China considers that the SBSTA needs to address the following issues in order to assist developing countries on the areas covered by this workshop:

- Access to scientific and technical information and means of implementation related to adaptation measures;
- Access to information, experience, tools, and technology of real-time monitoring, data visualization, data-sharing, and management related, *inter alia*, to early warning systems and contingency plans;
- Support research in addressing climate change impacts on agriculture, including in terms of potential economic impacts, for example, predictions of resulting impacts on agriculture production; promote better understanding of the trends as well as promote use of appropriate control and management methods for climate-related pest and diseases;

- Develop tools to analyse climate data and assess the risks and vulnerabilities of agricultural systems at regional, national, and local levels; according to different national and/or regional characteristics;
- Strengthen national systems for collecting, analysing, and disseminating risk and vulnerability data and information;
- Develop more timely and accurate forecasting system for rainfall and inflow seasonally and annually.
- Assist governments and communities with expertise in adaptation measures in relation to extreme weather events and their effects including models and technologies of early warning of extreme climatic events and vulnerability assessments;
- Encourage the collaborative participation by farmers in adaptation measures in relation to extreme weather events and climate change that will affect them;
- Provide means of implementation, including finance, technology transfer, and capacity-building, to developing countries in the assessment of risk and vulnerability of agricultural systems to different climate change scenarios at regional, national, and local level, taking into consideration the commitments by developed countries to provide finance, technology transfer, and capacity-building for developing countries on adaptation;
- Building capacity of the coordinating institutions, including technical, financial, and human;
- Promoting and strengthening Public Private People Partnerships (PPPP) in the design and implementation of adaptation measures.
- Support and establish accessible regional climate databases;

The G-77 and China countries believes there is a wide space for collaboration among parties in order to develop adaptation measures, in view of the local, national, and regional circumstances. There are also big opportunities to draw and share lessons from the experience of the different parties.

Developed countries can play a very positive role in providing means of implementation to developing countries in addressing adaptation. Article 4.1.e. of the Convention stated clearly that parties should "Cooperate in preparing for adaptation to the impacts of climate change" among various issues including agriculture.

Finally, the G-77 and China reaffirms its position to undertake scientific and technical work on impacts of climate change impacts on agriculture consistent with SBSTA mandate in article 9 taking into account the commitments in articles 4.3, 4.4, 4.5 of the Convention. The Group is willing to continue engaging constructively in this session to continue the consideration of the reports of the first two workshops at SBSTA 44 and, together with the reports on the two in-session workshops to be held at these sessions at SBSTA 45, in accordance with what was agreed in Paris.

Submission from Egypt on behalf of the Group of 77 and China•*

Decision x/CP.23 Issues Relating to Agriculture

The Conference of the Parties
Recalling the Principles and provisions of the Convention and its Paris Agreement,

Also recalling decision 2/CP.17,[11]

Recognizing the fundamental priority of safeguarding food security and ending hunger, and the particular vulnerabilities of agricultural systems to the adverse impacts of climate change,

Emphasizing that climate change and its adverse impacts on food security and agriculture markets have to be addressed through cooperation of all parties at all levels, with a view to enhance the implementation of the Convention

Recognizing also that a majority of the population in developing countries especially smallholder farmers rely on agriculture for securing their livelihoods and food security, while affirming the urgent need to take meaningful action as determined by each party through any of the communications under the Convention

Noting that building resilience of agricultural and food production systems to the adverse impacts of climate change requires sustainable and predictable access to adequate means of implementation including finance, technology development and transfer, and capacity-building, to developing country parties,

Noting also that adaptation builds resilience of agricultural systems while *recognizing* the relevant synergies between adaptation and adaptation co-benefits,

Noting further that resilient agricultural systems are critical to ensuring food security, eradication of poverty, and achieving sustainable development,

Recognizing that the needs of the most vulnerable groups in developing countries and particularly smallholder farmers, fishers, pastoralists, local and indigenous peoples need to be addressed, through building resilient and gender-responsive agricultural and food production systems,

* Contained in document FCCC/SBSTA/2017/CRP.1 of 10 May 2017.
[11] Decision 2/CP.17, paragraphs 75–77.

Emphasizing that measures taken to combat climate change should not constitute a means of arbitrary or unjustifiable discrimination or a disguised restriction on international trade,

Recognizing the importance of the inputs by the IPCC to the work of the Subsidiary Body for Scientific and Technological Advice on issues relating to agriculture,

Having considered the Subsidiary Body for Scientific and Technological Advice reports[12] of the four in-session workshops held in conjunction with SBSTA 42 and SBSTA 44 on the issues related to agriculture,

The Conference of the Parties hereby:

1. *Invites* parties to further support and strengthen national, regional, and international efforts, as determined by each party through any of the communications under the Convention, towards building and fostering resilience and increasing ability to adapt to the adverse impacts of climate change, harnessing relevant synergies between adaptation and adaptation co-benefits in agricultural systems, in order to safeguard food security, contribute to achieving sustainable development and poverty eradication.
2. *Requests* Subsidiary Body for Implementation to consider how to effectively support technical capacity-building, and institutional capacity of developing country parties for the implementation of the following measures for adaptation and adaptation co-benefits, taking into account national, sub-regional, and regional circumstances:
   i. Early warning and contingency planning for agricultural systems,
   ii. Risk and vulnerability assessment of agricultural systems,
   iii. Climate risk finance and insurance for agricultural systems,
   iv. Climate information services, ICT, and applications for agriculture,
   v. Improve disaster risk reduction planning and implementation,
   vi. Priority actions identified by each party through any of the communications under the Convention.
3. *Requests* the Technology Executive Committee and the Climate Technology Centre and Network, in accordance with their mandates, to accelerate and scale up support and investments to developing country parties in technology development and transfer that enhance resilience of agriculture systems, including:
   a. Crop, livestock, silviculture, fisheries, and integrated systems,
   b. Integrated soil and water management,
   c. Land management,
   d. Post-harvesting and agro-processing,
   e. Integrated pest and disease management,

[12] FCCC/SBSTA/2015/INF.6; FCCC/SBSTA/2015/INF.7; FCCC/SBSTA/2016/INF.5; FCCC/SBSTA/2016/INF.6.

f. Climate information services, ICT, and applications for agriculture.
g. Early warning and contingency planning for agricultural systems,
h. Coastal management,
i. Urban agriculture, and
j. Priority actions identified by each party through any of the communications under the Convention

4. *Requests* Subsidiary Body for Scientific and Technological Advice to provide guidance on methods and approaches for assessing adaptation and resilience in agricultural systems by:
   a. *Inviting* parties and accredited observer organizations to submit by xxx of 2018 their views on methods and approaches for assessing adaptation and resilience in agricultural systems to be compiled into a miscellaneous document for consideration by the Subsidiary Body for Scientific and Technological Advice at its forty-eighth session, and
   b. *Requesting* the Secretariat to organize an in-session workshop on issues identified in paragraph 4a above, in conjunction with its forty-eighth session and to prepare a report on the workshop for consideration by the Subsidiary Body for Scientific and Technological Advice at its forty-ninth session.
5. *Further requests* the Subsidiary Body for Scientific and Technological Advice to provide guidance on climate risk management and insurance in the context of agriculture, by:
   a. *Inviting* parties and accredited observer organizations to submit, by xxxxxx 2018, their views on climate risk management and insurance in the context of agriculture, to be compiled into a miscellaneous document for consideration by the Subsidiary Body for Scientific and Technological Advice at its forty-eighth session; and
   b. *Requesting* the Secretariat to organize an in-session workshop on issues identified in paragraph 5a above, in conjunction with its forty-eighth session and to prepare a report on the workshop for consideration by the Subsidiary Body for Scientific and Technological Advice at its forty-ninth session.
6. *Requests* the Secretariat to prepare a technical paper on tools for early warning systems, risk, and vulnerability assessments in agricultural systems, taking into account local and indigenous knowledge.
7. *Further requests* the Secretariat to establish learning and experience sharing interactive web-based platform for parties on the UNFCCC website on good practices of resilient agricultural systems.[13]
8. *Invites* developed country parties to mobilize resources and *encourages* the operating entities of the Financial Mechanisms of the Convention, within their mandates, to provide resources to support actions referred to in paragraphs 2–7 above.

[13] Develop ToRs that will be part of the decision.

Acronyms

AAU	Assigned Amount Unit
AC	Adaptation Committee
ACE	Action for Climate Environment
AC-LEG	Adaptation Committee—Least Developed Countries Expert Group
AF	Adaptation Fund
AFB	Adaptation Fund Board
AGBM	Ad Hoc Group on the Berlin Mandate
AIJ	Activities Implemented Jointly
AIP	Accelerated Implementation Process
AOSIS	Alliance of Small Island Developing States
APA	Ad Hoc Working Group on the Paris Agreement
AWG	Ad Hoc Working Group
AWG-DP	Ad Hoc Working Group on the Durban Platform
AWG-KP	Ad Hoc Working Group on Kyoto Protocol
AWG-LCA	Ad Hoc Working Group on Long-Term Cooperative Action
BAP	Bali Action Plan
BPoA	Barbados Programme of Action
BURs	Biennial Update Reports
CBD	Convention on Biological Diversity
CBDR&RC	Common but Differentiated Responsibilities and Respective Capabilities
CBIT	Capacity-Building Initiative for Transparency
CC	Climate Change
CDM	Clean Development Mechanism
CER	Certified Emission Reduction
CG	Consultative Group
CGE	Consultative Group of Experts
CH_4	Methane
CMA	Conference of the Parties Serving as the Meeting of the Parties to the Parties Agreement
CMP	Conference of the Parties Serving as the Meeting of the Parties
CMP-KP	Conference of the Parties Serving as the Meeting of the Parties to the Kyoto Protocol
CO	Carbon Monoxide

CO_2	Carbon Dioxide
COP	Conference of the Parties
COP-MOP	The Conference of the Parties serving as the meeting of the Parties
CRP	Conference Room Paper
CSD	Commission on Sustainable Development
CST	Committee on Science and Technology
CTC	Climate Technology Centre
CTCN	Climate Technology Centre and Network
DNA	Designated National Authority
ECOSOC	Economic and Social Council
EGF	Expert Group on Funding
EGTT	Expert Group on Technology Transfer
ENSO	El Niño Southern Oscillation
EOSG	Executive Office of the Secretary-General
ERU	Emission Reduction Unit
EST	Environmentally Sound Technology
ETF	Enhanced Transparency Framework for Action and Support
EU-ETS	European Union Emissions Trading Scheme 142
FCCC	Framework Convention on Climate Change
FM	Financial Mechanism
FSV	Facilitative Sharing of Views
FVA	Framework for Various Approaches
G-77	Group of Seventy-Seven
GA	General Assembly
GATT	General Agreement on Tariffs and Trade
GCF	Green Climate Fund
GCISC	Global Change Impact Studies Centre
GCOS	Global Climate Observing System
GDP	Gross Domestic Product
GEF	Global Environment Facility
GEF/PA	Global Environment Facility/Participants' Assembly
GEOS	Global Earth Observation System
GHG	Greenhouse Gases
GM	Global Mechanism
GNI	Gross National Income
GNP	Gross National Product
GST	Global Stocktake

GWP	Global Warming Potential
HFCs	Hydrofluorocarbons
IADGs	Internationally Agreed Development Goals
IAR	International Assessment and Review
IBRD	International Bank for Reconstruction and Development
ICA	International Consultation and Analysis
ICAO	International Civil Aviation Organization
IDA	International Development Association
IMLD	International Mechanism on Loss and Damage
IMO	International Maritime Organization
INC	Intergovernmental Negotiating Committee
INC-FCCC	Intergovernmental Negotiating Committee for a Framework Convention on Climate Change
INDCs	Intended Nationally Determined Contributions
IPCC	Intergovernmental Panel on Climate Change
IPM	Intergovernmental Preparatory Meeting
IPR	Intellectual Property Right
ISO	International Organization for Standardisation
ITAP	Intergovernmental Technical Advisory Panel
JCG	Joint Contact Group
JPOI	Johannesburg Plan of Implementation
KP	Kyoto Protocol
LCA	Long-Term Cooperative Action
LDCs	Least Developed Countries
LDCF	Least Developed Countries Fund
LEG	Least Developed Countries Experts Group
LLDCs	Land-Locked Developing Countries
LTF	Long-Term Climate Finance
LTGs	Long-Term Goals
LULUCF	Land-Use, Land-Use Change and Forestry
MA	Multilateral Assessment
MCTF	Multilateral Climate Technology Fund
MDGs	Millennium Development Goals
MEAs	Multilateral Environmental Agreements
MoCA	Ministerial on Climate Action
MOI	Means of Implementation
MoU	Memorandum of Understanding
MRV	Measurement, Reporting and Verification
MSI	Mauritius Strategy for Implementation

MYPA	Multi-Year Plan of Action
MYPOW	Multi-Year Programme of Work
NAMAs	Nationally Appropriate Mitigation Actions
NAP	National Action Program
NAPs	National Adaptation Plans
NAPA	National Adaptation Programme of Action
NCSA	National Capacity Self-Assessment
NDC	Nationally Determined Contributions
NGOs	Non-Governmental Organizations
NIEs	National Implementing Entities
NMVOCs	Non-Methane Volatile Organic Compounds
N_2O	Nitrous Oxide
NO_x	Nitrogen Oxide
NPA	Nairobi Plan of Action
NWP	Nairobi Work Program
OCHA	Office for Coordination and Humanitarian Assistance
ODA	Official Development Assistance
ODS	Ozone Depleting Substances
OECD	Organisation for Economic Co-operation and Development
OOF	Other Official Flows
PA	Paris Agreement
PAA	Part of Assigned Amount
PAWP	Paris Agreement Work Programme
PCCB	Paris Committee on Capacity-Building
PFCs	Perfluorocarbons
PGTF	Perez-Guerrero Trust Fund for South-South Cooperation
PoA	Programme of Action
POPs	Persistent Organic Pollutants
PPPP	Public Private People Partnerships
QA	Quality Assurance
QC	Quality Control
QELRCs	Quantified Emission Limitation and Reduction Commitments
QELROs	Quantified Emission Limitation and Reduction Objectives
R&D	Research and Development
RAF	Resource Allocation Framework
RCU	Regional Coordination Unit
RD&D	Research, Development and Dissemination/Demonstration
REDD	Reducing Emissions from Deforestation and Forest Degradation

RIEs	Regional Implementing Entities
RMU	Removal UnitsSAMOA SIDS Accelerated Modalities of Action
SB	Subsidiary Body
SBI	Subsidiary Body for Implementation
SBSTA	Subsidiary Body for Scientific and Technological Advice
SBSTTA	Subsidiary Body for Scientific, Technical and Technological Advice
SCF	Standing Committee on Finance
SCCF	Special Climate Change Fund
SCPI	Southern Climate Partnership Incubator
SDGs	Sustainable Development Goals
SED	Structured Expert Dialogue
SF_x	Sulphur Hexafluoride
SG	Secretary-General
SIDS	Small Island Developing States
SO_x	Sulphur Oxide
SREX	Special Report on Managing the Rights of Extreme Events and Disasters to Advance Climate Change Adaptation
SSC	South-South Cooperation
STAP	Scientific and Technical Advisory Panel
TAR	Third Assessment Report
TCDC	Technical Cooperation among Developing Countries
TEC	Technology Executive Committee
TEMs	Technical Expert Meetings
TEP	Technical Examination Process
TGICA	Task Group on Data Scenario Support for Impact and Climate Analysis
TNA	Technology Needs Assessment
TORs	Terms of References
TRIPS	Agreement on Trade-Related Aspects of Intellectual Property Rights
TTM	Technology Transfer Mechanism
UN	United Nations
UNCBD	United National Convention on Biological Diversity
UNCED	United Nations Conference on Environment and Development
UNCTAD	United Nations Conference on Trade and Development
UNDP	United Nations Development Programme
UNEP	United Nations Environment Programme
UNFCCC	United Nations Conference of the Parties to the Framework Convention on Climate Change
UNGASS	United Nations General Assembly Special Session

UNIDO	United Nations Industrial Development Organization
USD	United States Dollar
WIM	Warsaw International Mechanism
WMO	World Meteorological Organisation
WS	Work Stream
WSSD	World Summit on Sustainable Development
WTO	World Trade Organisation

The Member States of the Group of 77

(As of 31 October 2023)

1. Afghanistan
2. Algeria
3. Angola
4. Antigua & Barbuda
5. Argentina
6. Azerbaijan
7. Bahamas
8. Bahrain
9. Bangladesh
10. Barbados
11. Belize
12. Benin
13. Bhutan
14. Bolivia (Plurinational State of)
15. Botswana
16. Brazil
17. Brunei Darussalam
18. Burkina Faso
19. Burundi
20. Cabo Verde
21. Cambodia
22. Cameroon
23. Central African Republic
24. Chad
25. Chile
26. China
27. Colombia
28. Comoros
29. Congo
30. Costa Rica
31. Côte d'Ivoire
32. Cuba
33. Democratic People's Republic of Korea
34. Democratic Republic of the Congo
35. Djibouti
36. Dominica
37. Dominican Republic
38. Ecuador
39. Egypt
40. El Salvador
41. Equatorial Guinea
42. Eritrea
43. Eswatini

44. Ethiopia
45. Fiji
46. Gabon
47. Gambia
48. Ghana
49. Grenada
50. Guatemala
51. Guinea
52. Guinea-Bissau
53. Guyana
54. Haiti
55. Honduras
56. India
57. Indonesia
58. Iran (Islamic Republic of)
59. Iraq
60. Jamaica
61. Jordan
62. Kenya
63. Kiribati
64. Kuwait
65. Lao People's Democratic Republic
66. Lebanon
67. Lesotho
68. Liberia
69. Libya
70. Madagascar
71. Malawi
72. Malaysia
73. Maldives
74. Mali
75. Marshall Islands
76. Mauritania
77. Mauritius
78. Micronesia (Federated States of)
79. Mongolia
80. Morocco
81. Mozambique
82. Myanmar
83. Namibia
84. Nauru
85. Nepal
86. Nicaragua
87. Niger
88. Nigeria
89. Oman
90. Pakistan
91. Panama
92. Papua New Guinea
93. Paraguay
94. Peru
95. Philippines
96. Qatar
97. Rwanda

98. St. Kitts and Nevis
99. St. Lucia
100. St. Vincent & the Grenadines
101. Samoa
102. Sao Tome and Principe
103. Saudi Arabia
104. Senegal
105. Seychelles
106. Sierra Leone
107. Singapore
108. Solomon Islands
109. Somalia
110. South Africa
111. South Sudan
112. Sri Lanka
113. State of Palestine
114. Sudan
115. Suriname
116. Syrian Arab Republic
117. Tajikistan
118. Thailand
119. Timor-Leste
120. Togo
121. Tonga
122. Trinidad and Tobago
123. Tunisia
124. Turkmenistan
125. Uganda
126. United Arab Emirates
127. United Republic of Tanzania
128. Uruguay
129. Vanuatu
130. Venezuela (Bolivarian Republic of)
131. Viet Nam
132. Yemen
133. Zambia
134. Zimbabwe